The Couriers
THE COMPLETE SERIES

The Couriers
THE COMPLETE SERIES

01. THE COURIERS
02. DIRTBIKE MANIFESTO
03. THE BALLAD OF JOHNNY FUNWRECKER
04. COUSCOUS EXPRESS

writer BRIAN WOOD
artists ROB G x BRETT WELDELE
letterers RYAN YOUNT x LARRY YOUNG

Introduction

Brian Wood I Brooklyn I 07.29.12

What you're holding in your hand is probably more notable than at first glance, in terms of my career output. The Couriers "quadrilogy", a label I just now invented and now apply, is much of the comics writing I did from 2001-2003. Somewhere in there Pounded was written, and Jennie One and Fight For Tomorrow, but The Couriers came out every year in January, the lynchpin of what used to be called "Brian Wood Month". The Couriers is also, technically, the first comic I created.

I worked as a bike messenger for the first three years of college, a job that is equal parts terrifying and boring as hell. This was also around the time I decided I wanted to be a comics creator, and would let my mind wander while biking around the city and think up ideas. What ended up as The Couriers started off in my sketchbook as "1%", inspired by the 1991 Murphy's Law track (how time has changed the meaning of that title).
I knew what I wanted it to be about – lawlessness, New York, bike messengers – but that was about it at the time. I think if I had been a better artist and could have managed the task of drawing an action comic, it would have happened first. Instead, I made Channel Zero.

Skip ahead a few years and a few false starts later, I write a script for Couscous Express and steal from my Couriers bank of ideas to populate it with characters. It was my second creator-owned comic, and the first one I wrote for someone else to draw. Food culture was added to the mix, as well as a scooter girl. Brett Weldele bravely stepped up and endured a situation where I was still learning how to write a script and the mechanics of an original graphic novel, and did so with professionalism and grace. He also drew the hell out of the story.

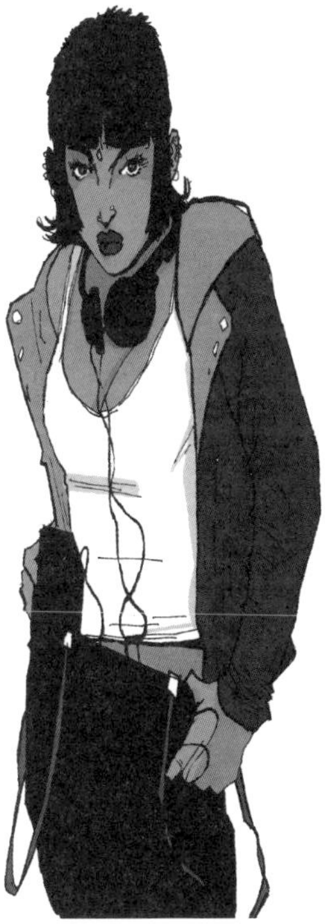

Armed with the completed Couscous Express and some newly earned confidence, I felt ready to try and figure out The Couriers. I knew what I wanted it to look like, which was very NYC-heavy, absurd action, and lots of speed lines. I was pretty heavy into Hong Kong and Luc Besson action films and that's all I wanted. I wanted to make a comic that existed for no other reason than I wanted to have a blast making it with some friends. Rob G was simpatico on all of that, and committed to the book for the long haul – I knew I wanted to write 3 of 4 of these books (the fourth, lost to history, was to be called "Hooligans For Life"). We launched the series in 2002.

Looking back on the series, I can see a series that is very much of its time and of what was important to me. I feel like in 2003 with Demo, my focus shifted significantly, but prior to that what the Couriers was all about is what I was ingesting, media-wise. I was working fulltime in the videogame industry. My head was wired that way. These days, not so much, and so while The Couriers feels a bit like a relic from a previous era, I'm also a bit jealous of those days. Comics were a hobby then, not a job. I wasn't worrying about page rates (never got 'em) or selling big numbers (that didn't happen either). It wasn't a step on the ladder of career advancement... I didn't have a plan or a goal in mind other than trying to make Rob G laugh and have some fun, and, in the end, hold a finished book in my hands. I don't know how to replicate that these days, and a part of me truly misses it.

I love Moustafa and Special and Olive. I LOVE Johnny Funwrecker. The book's been optioned for film since 2006 or so, and maybe one day they'll be a movie or a videogame. Maybe one day I'll feel compelled to write "Hooligans For Life". The days of meeting up with Rob G in some dive bar garden in the East Village on a Sunday afternoon, looking at sketches and drinking beer... those are long over. What we do that is this volume, which is as pure an expression of comics making as I've ever done. Hope you enjoy.

-brian

01

The Couriers

Brian Wood x Rob G x Ryan Yount

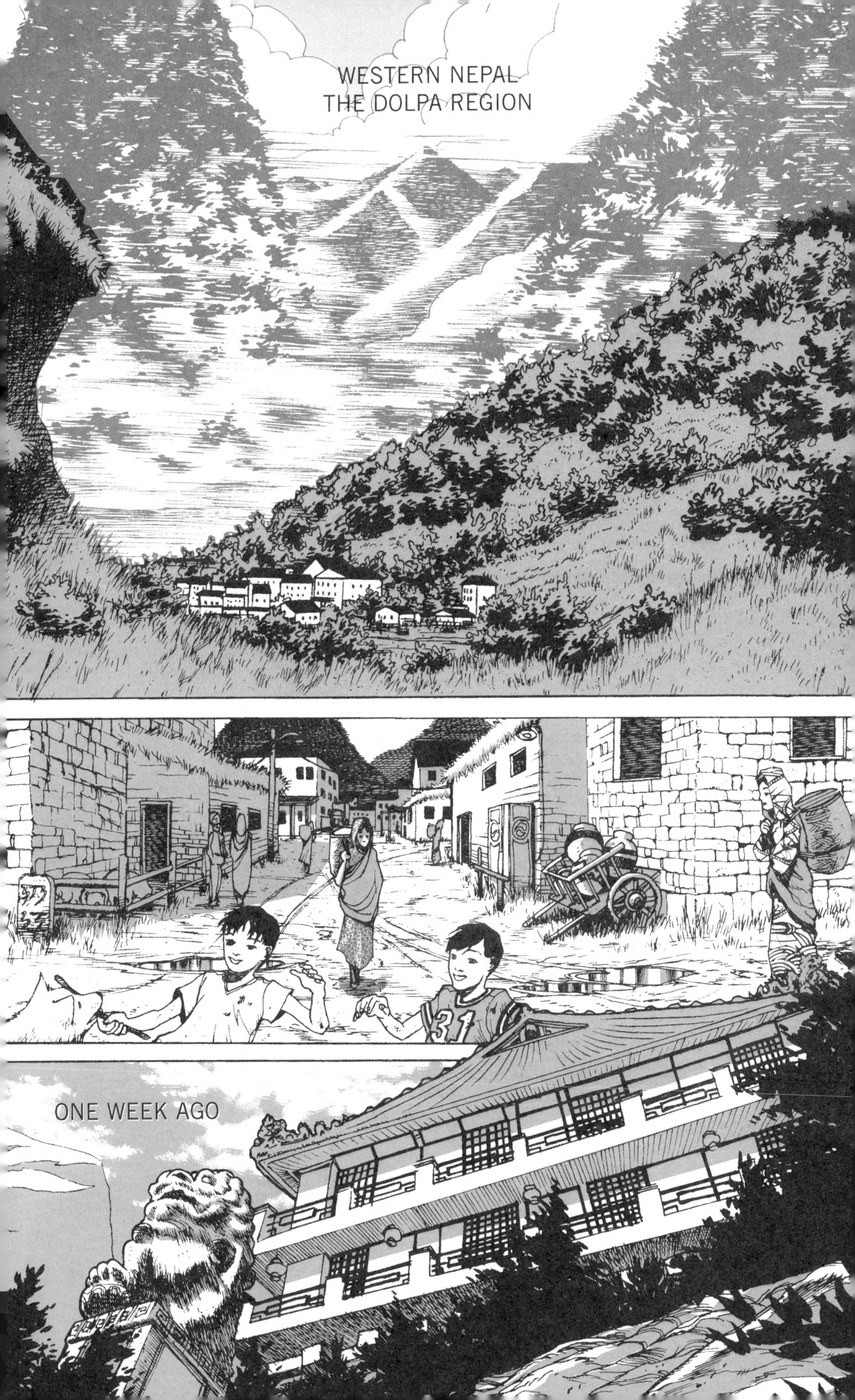
WESTERN NEPAL
THE DOLPA REGION
ONE WEEK AGO

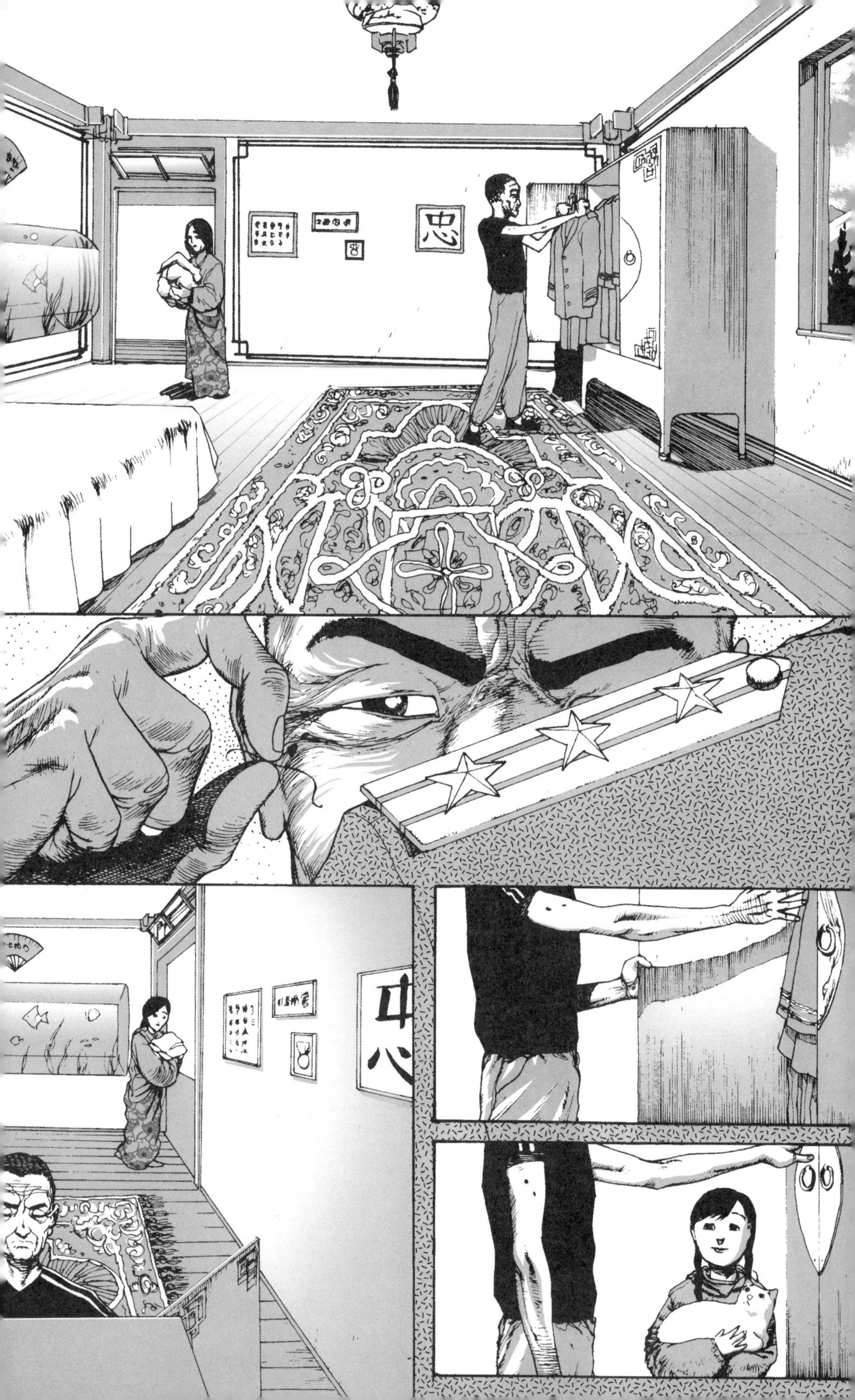
忠

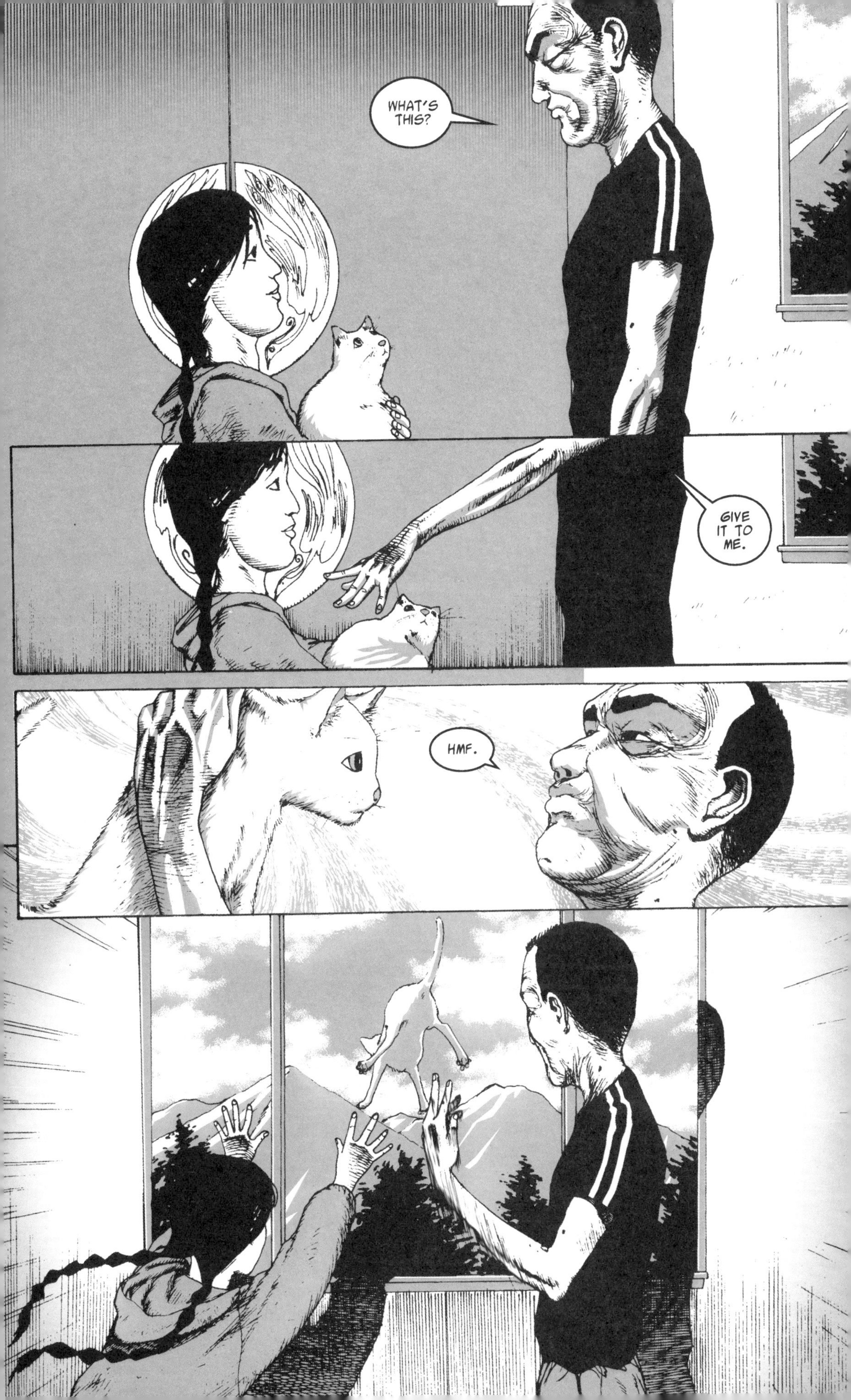
WHAT'S THIS?
GIVE IT TO ME.
HMF.

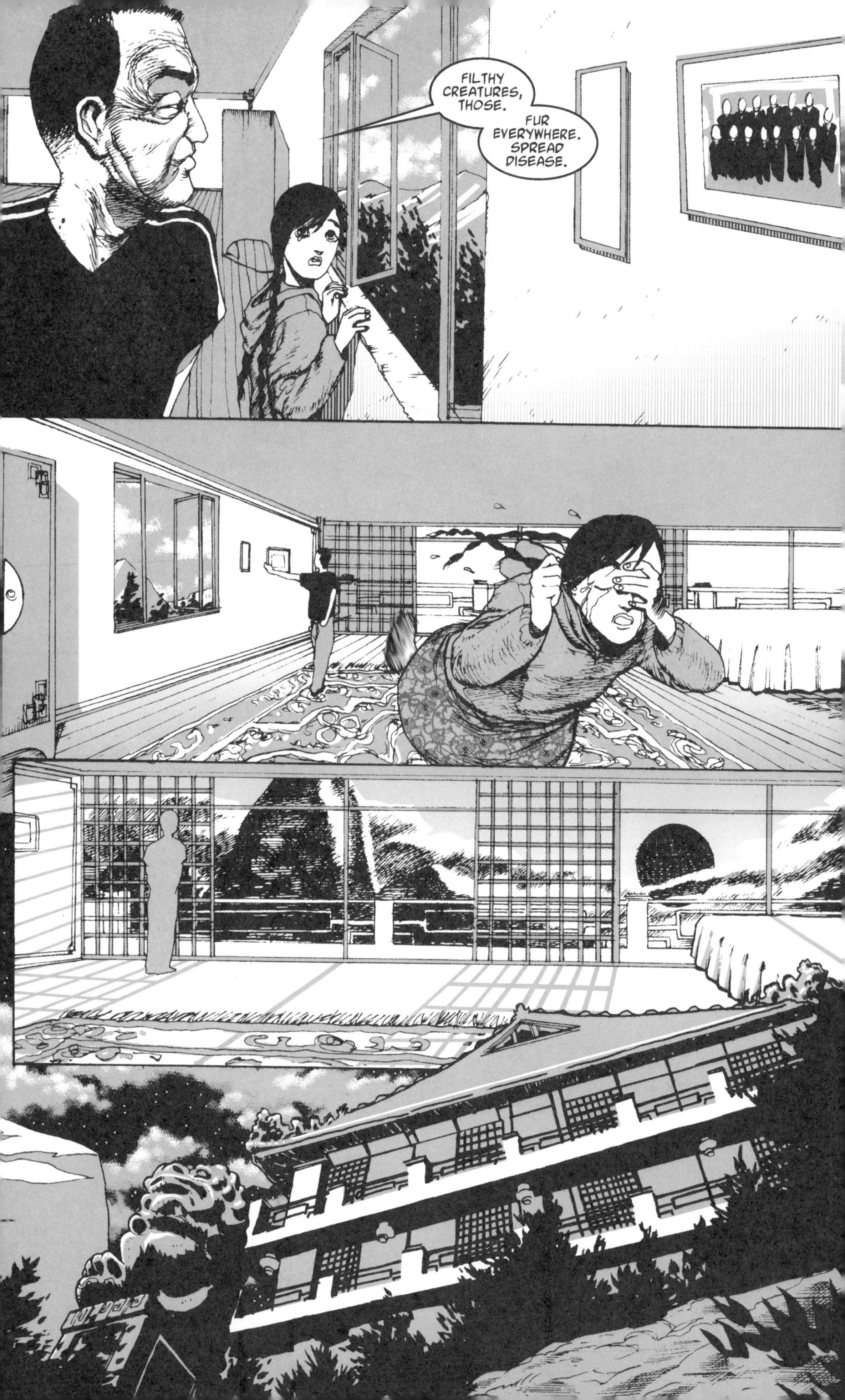
FILTHY CREATURES, THOSE.
FUR EVERYWHERE. SPREAD DISEASE.

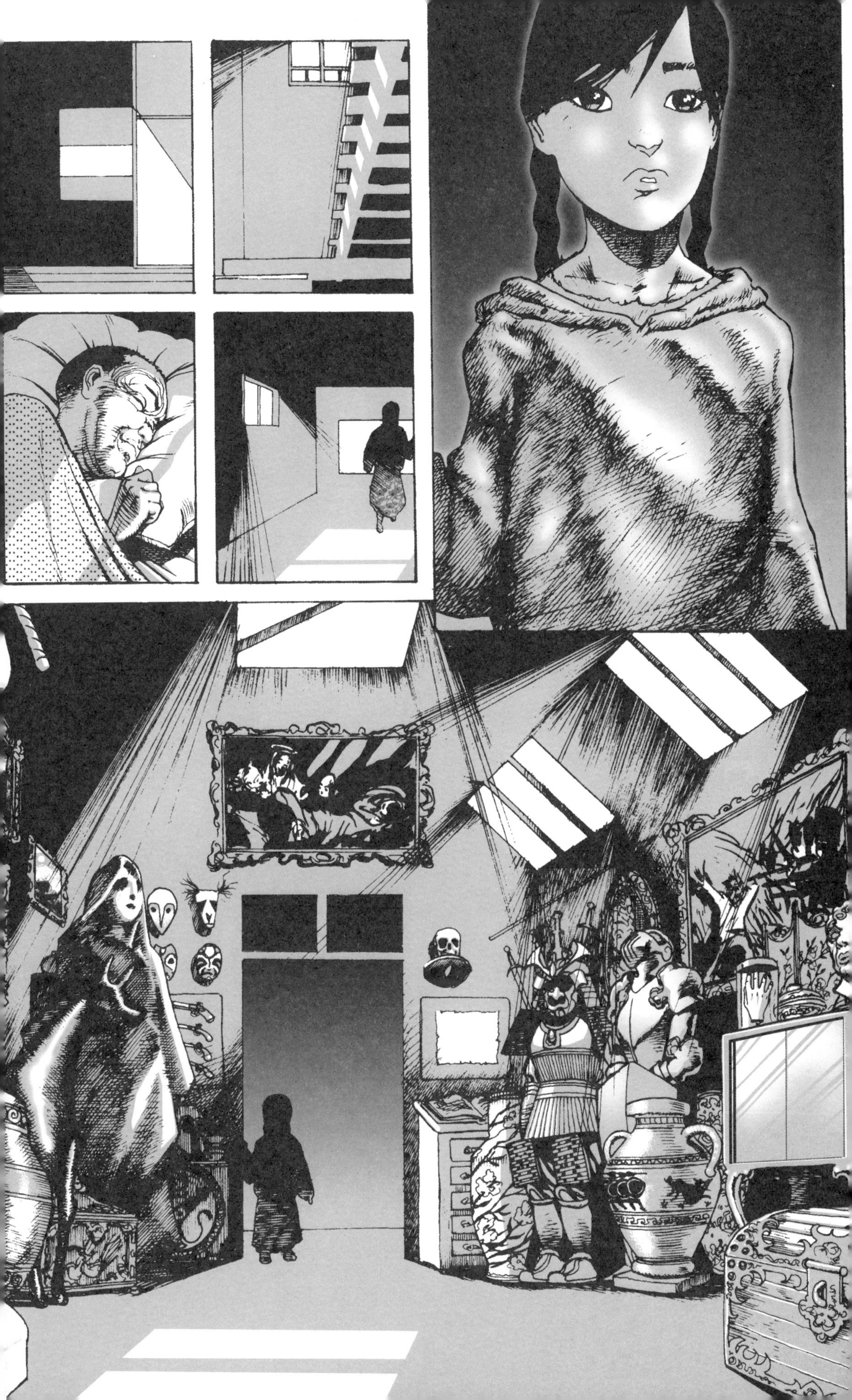

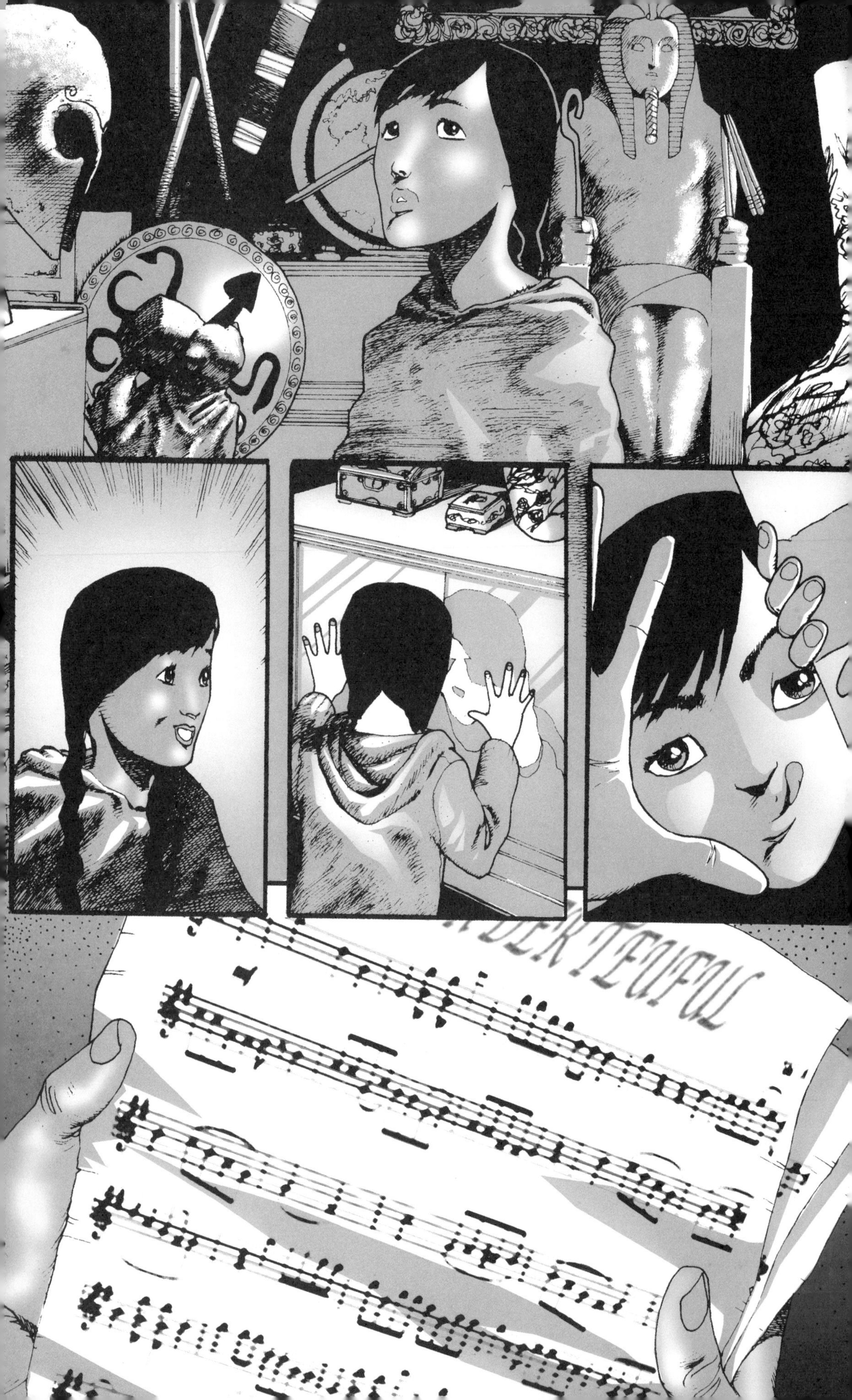

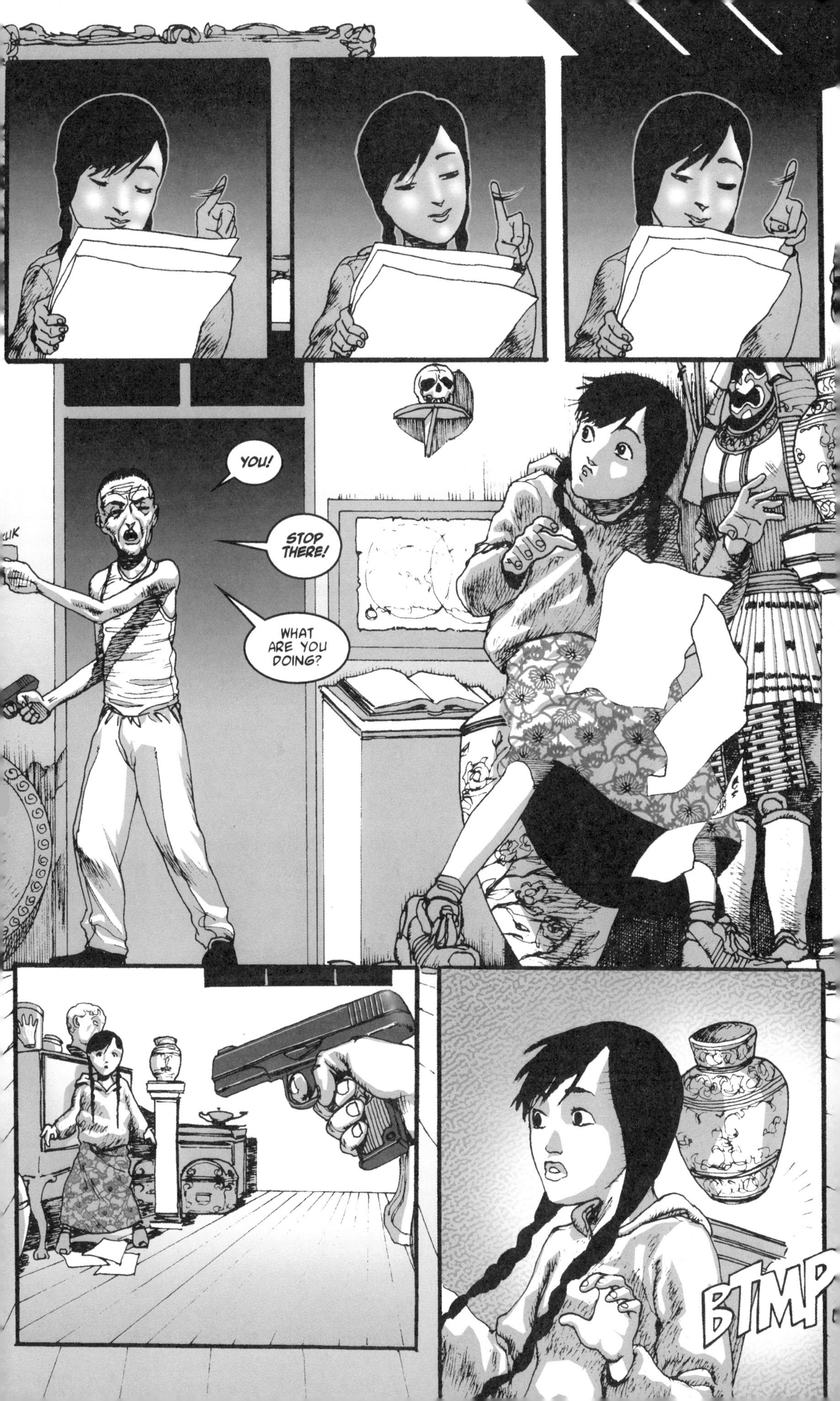

KLIK
YOU!
STOP THERE!
WHAT ARE YOU DOING?
BTMP

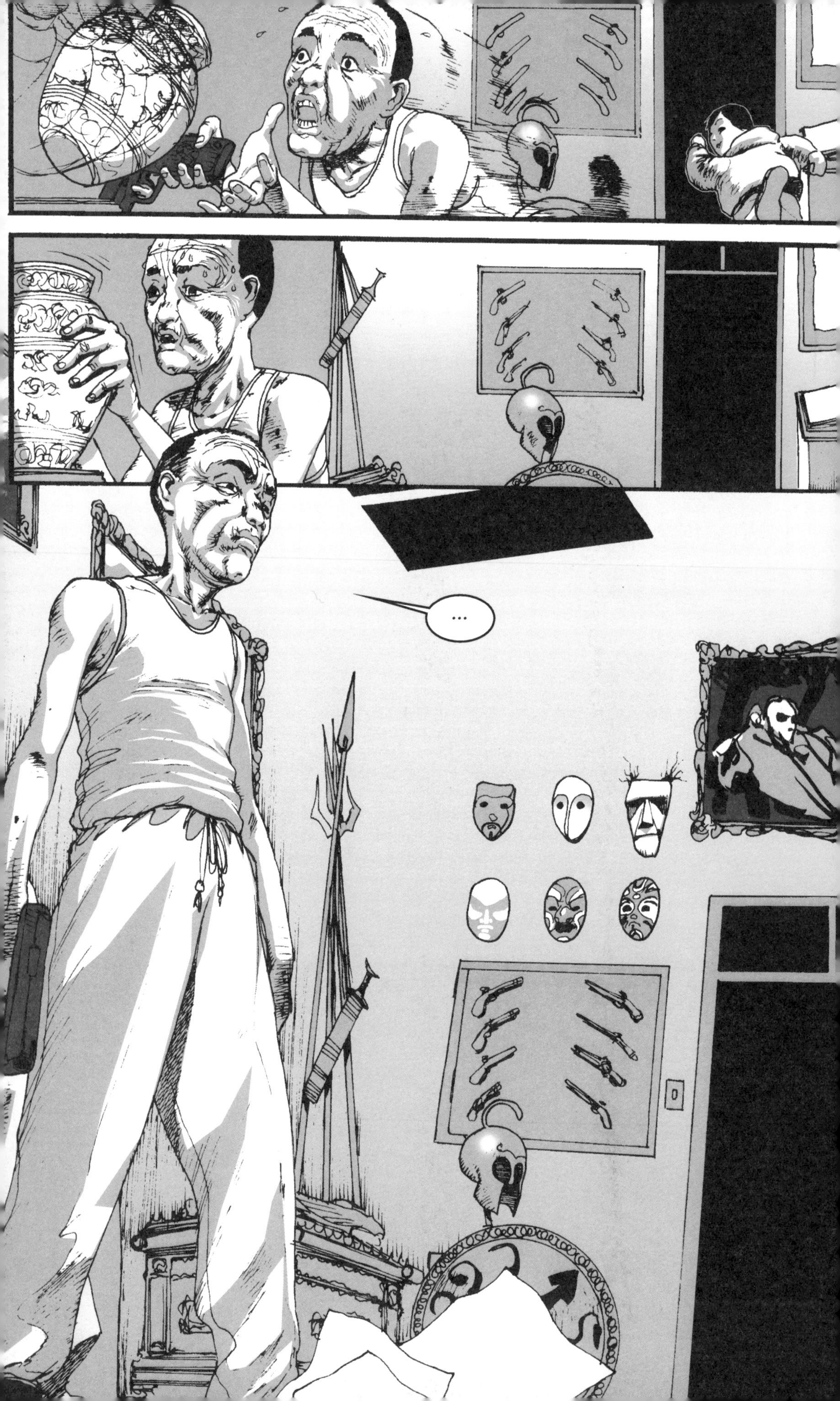
...

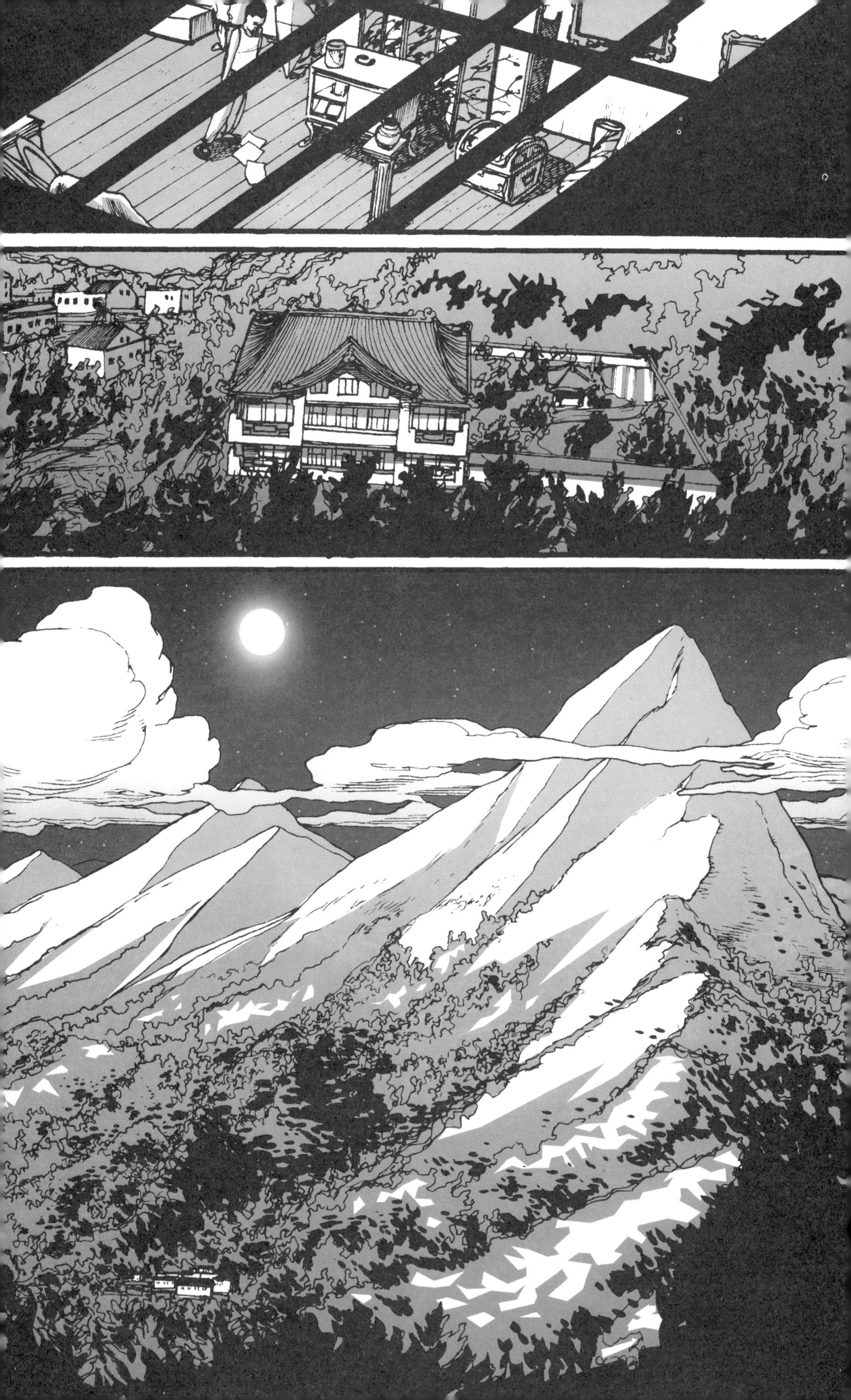

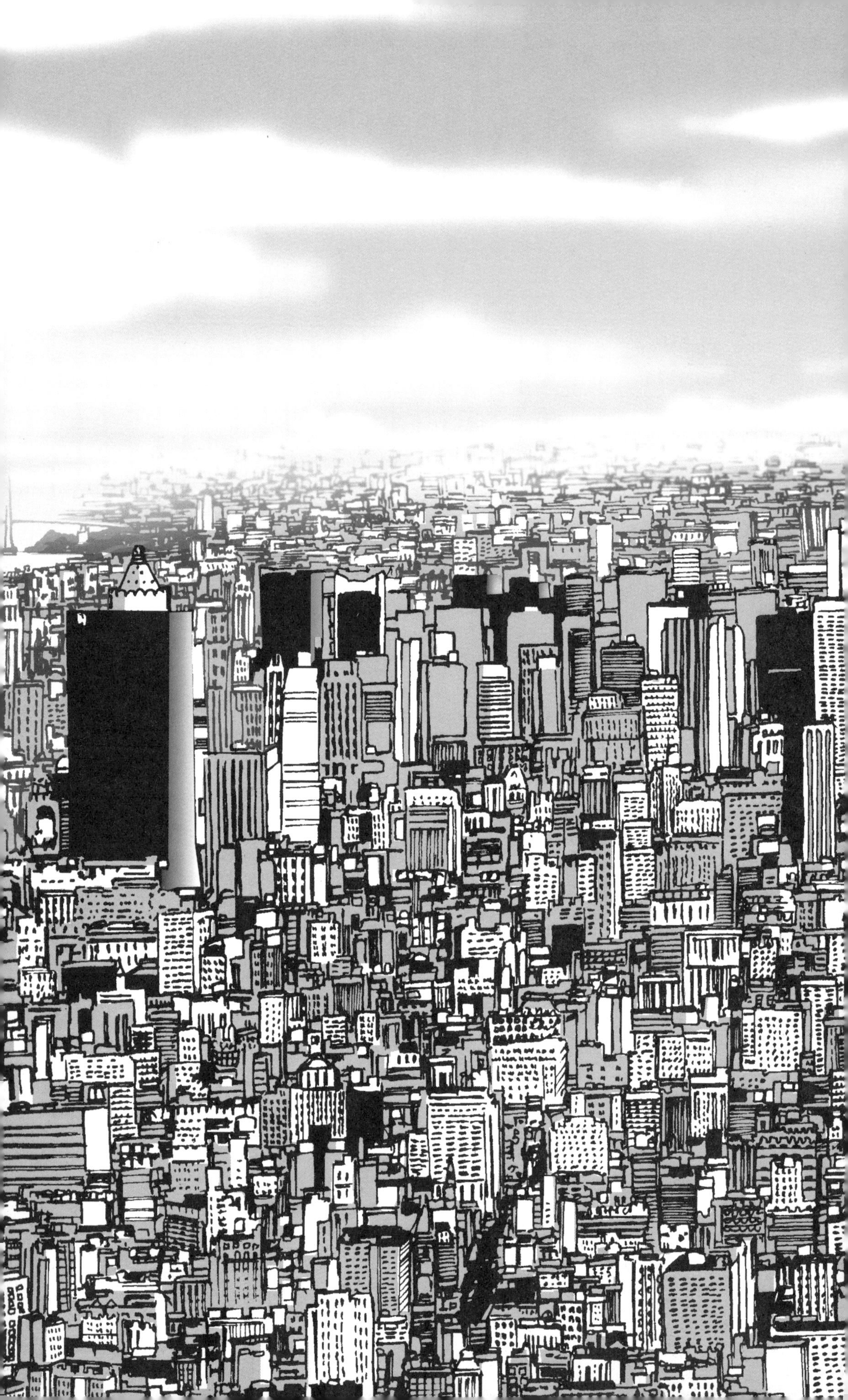

NEW YORK CITY

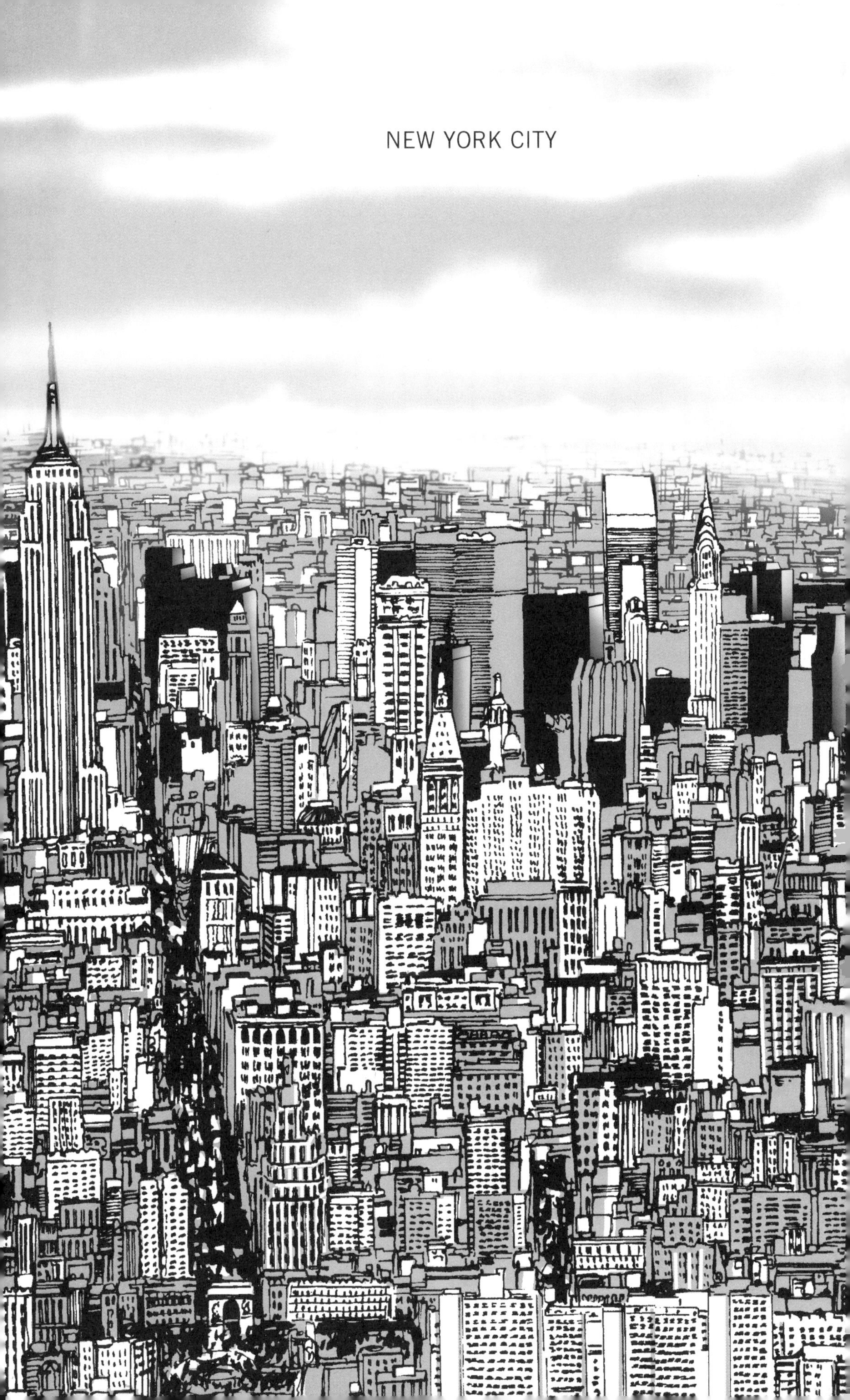

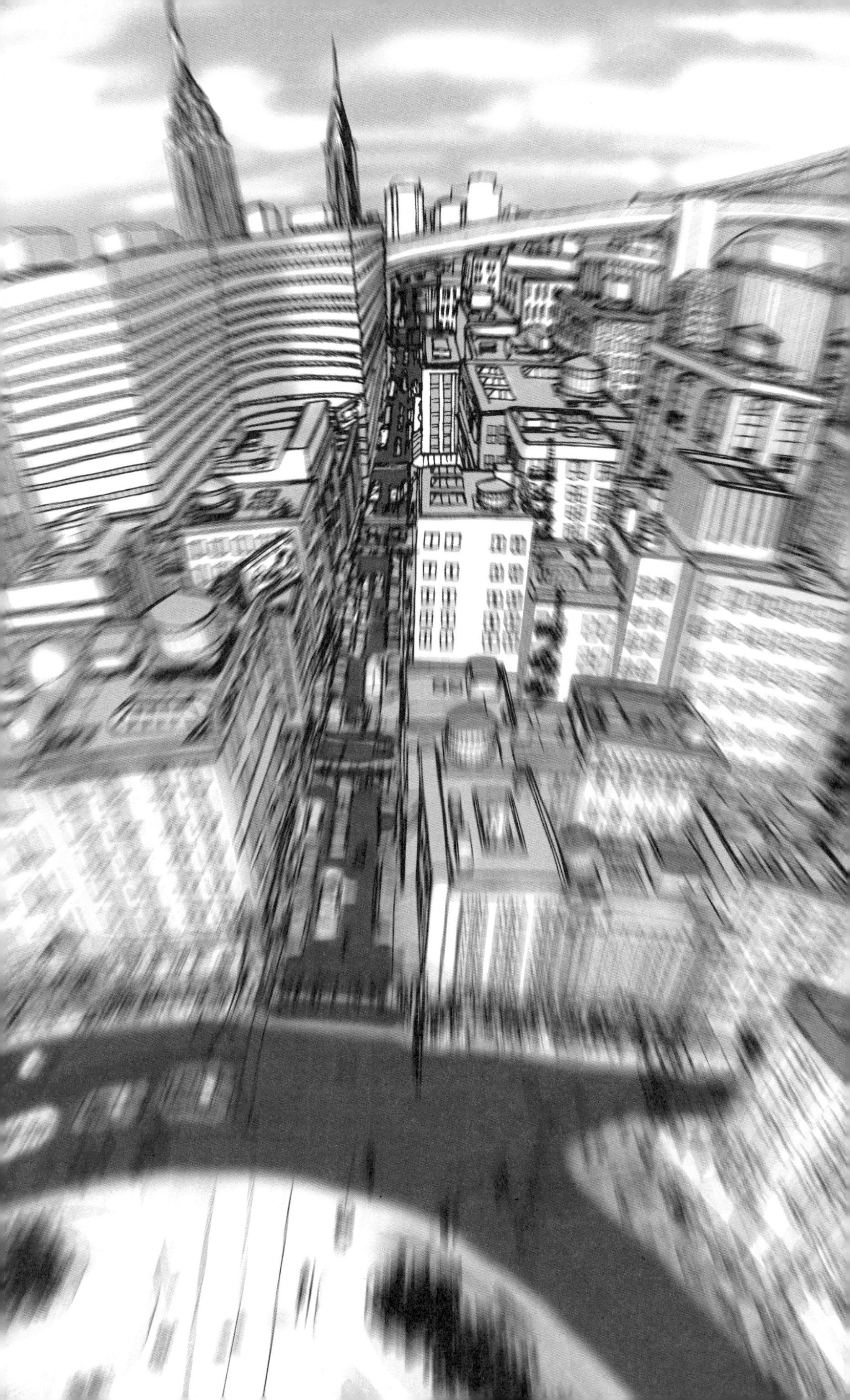

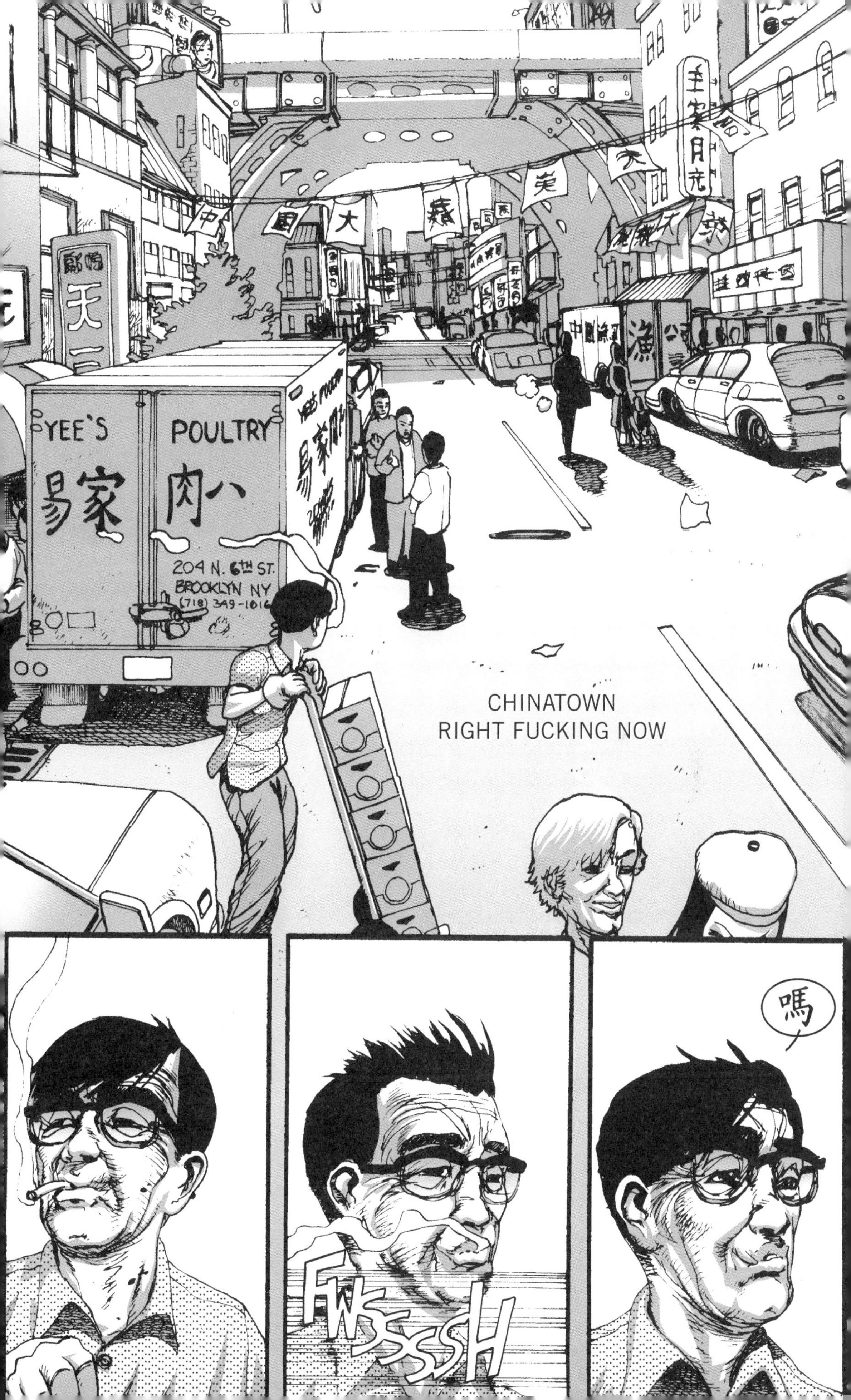
YEE`S POULTRY
204 N. 6TH ST.
BROOKLYN NY
(718) 349-1016
CHINATOWN
RIGHT FUCKING NOW
FWSSSSH
嗎

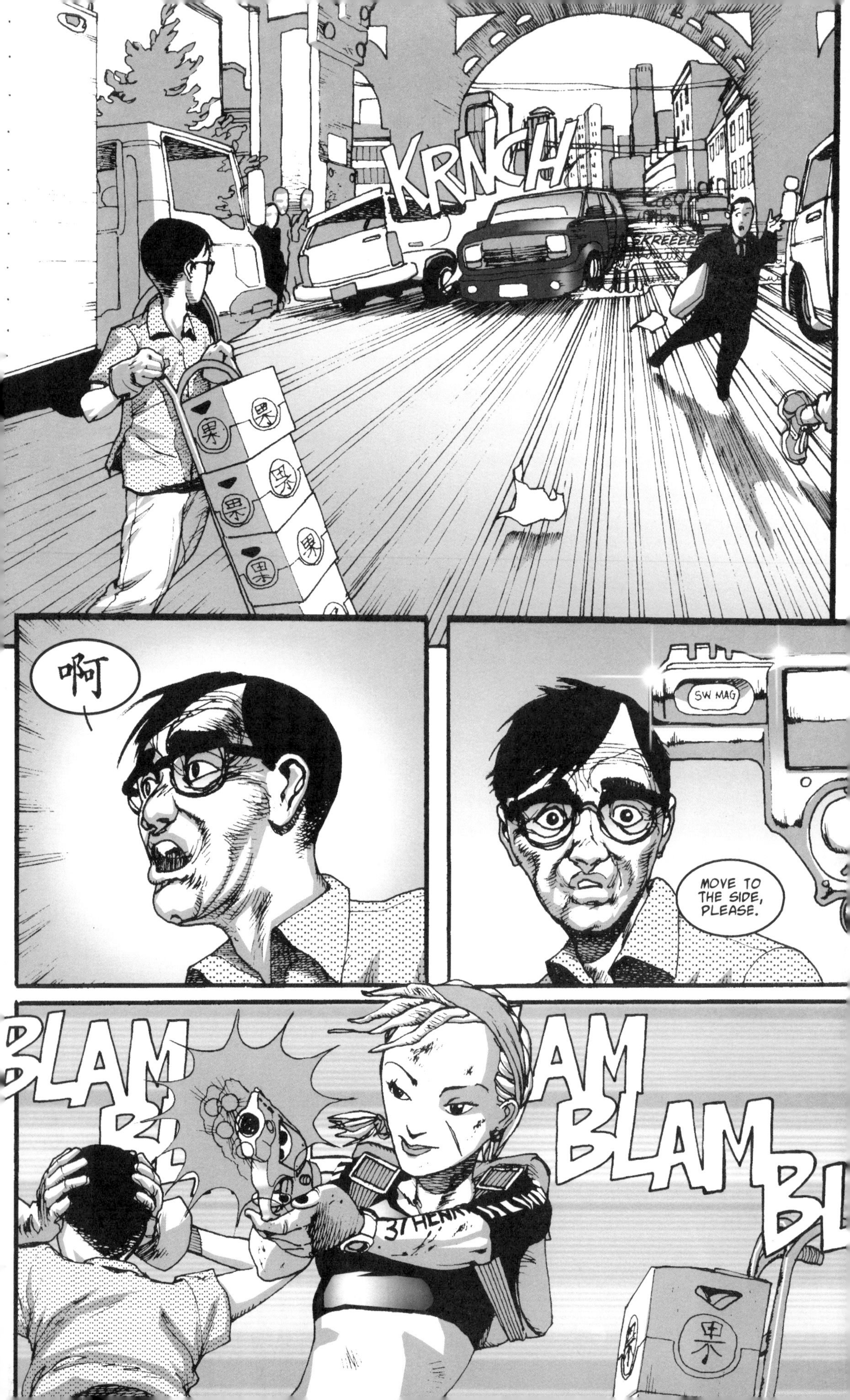
KRNCH
SKREEEEE
啊
SW MAG
MOVE TO THE SIDE, PLEASE.
BLAM
BLAM
BLAM
37 HENR

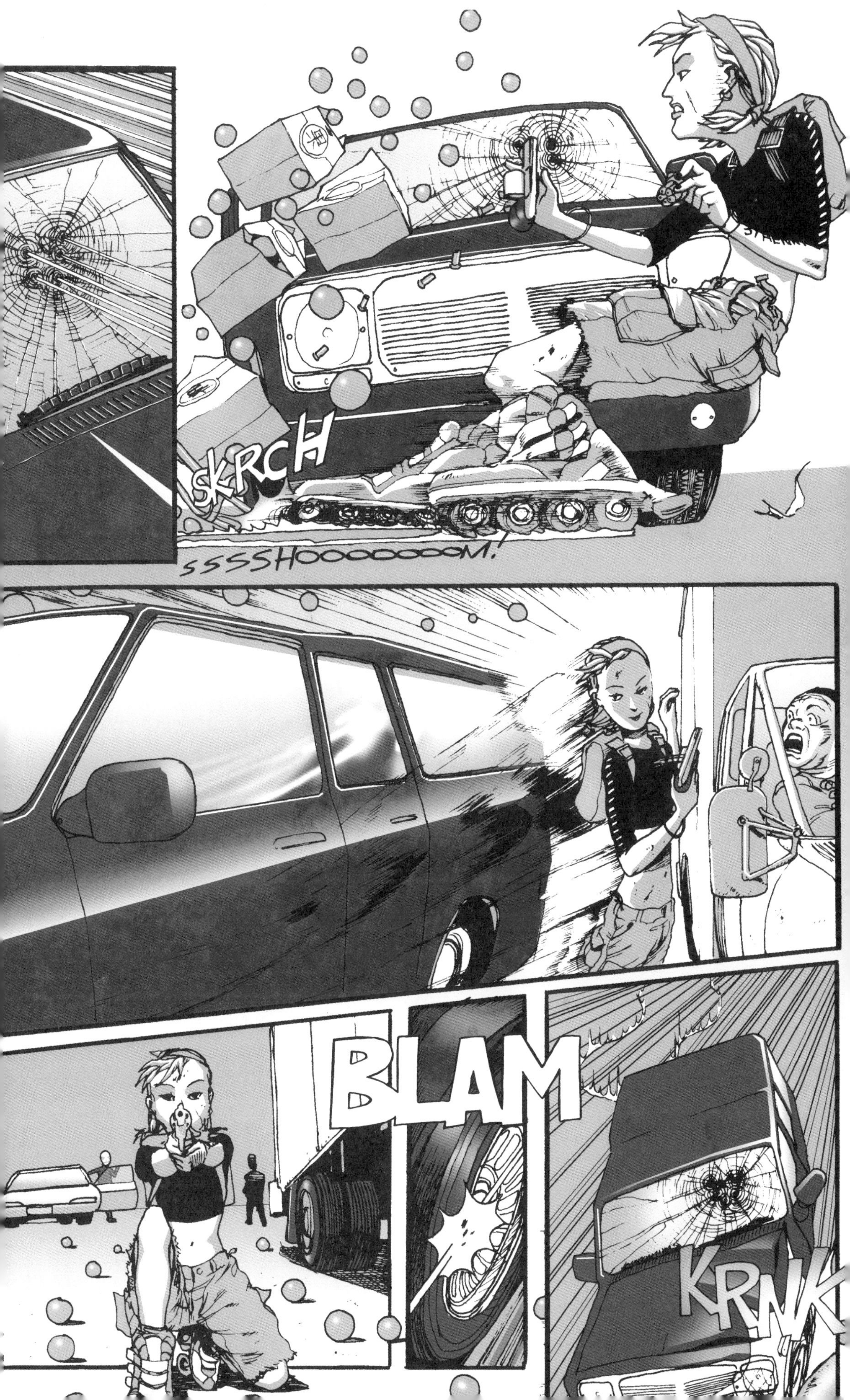
SKRCH
SSSSHOOOOOOOOM!
BLAM
KRNK

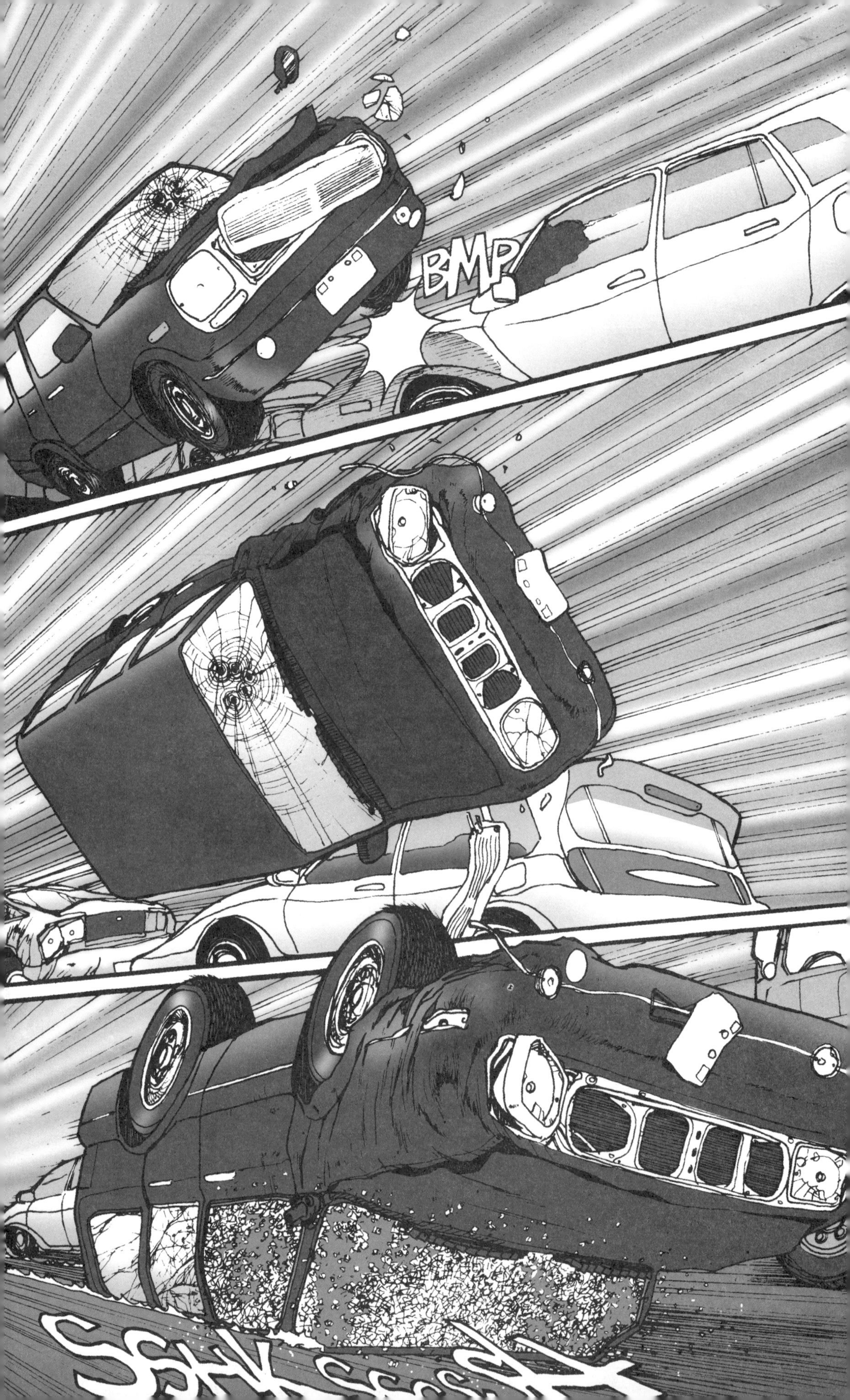
BMP

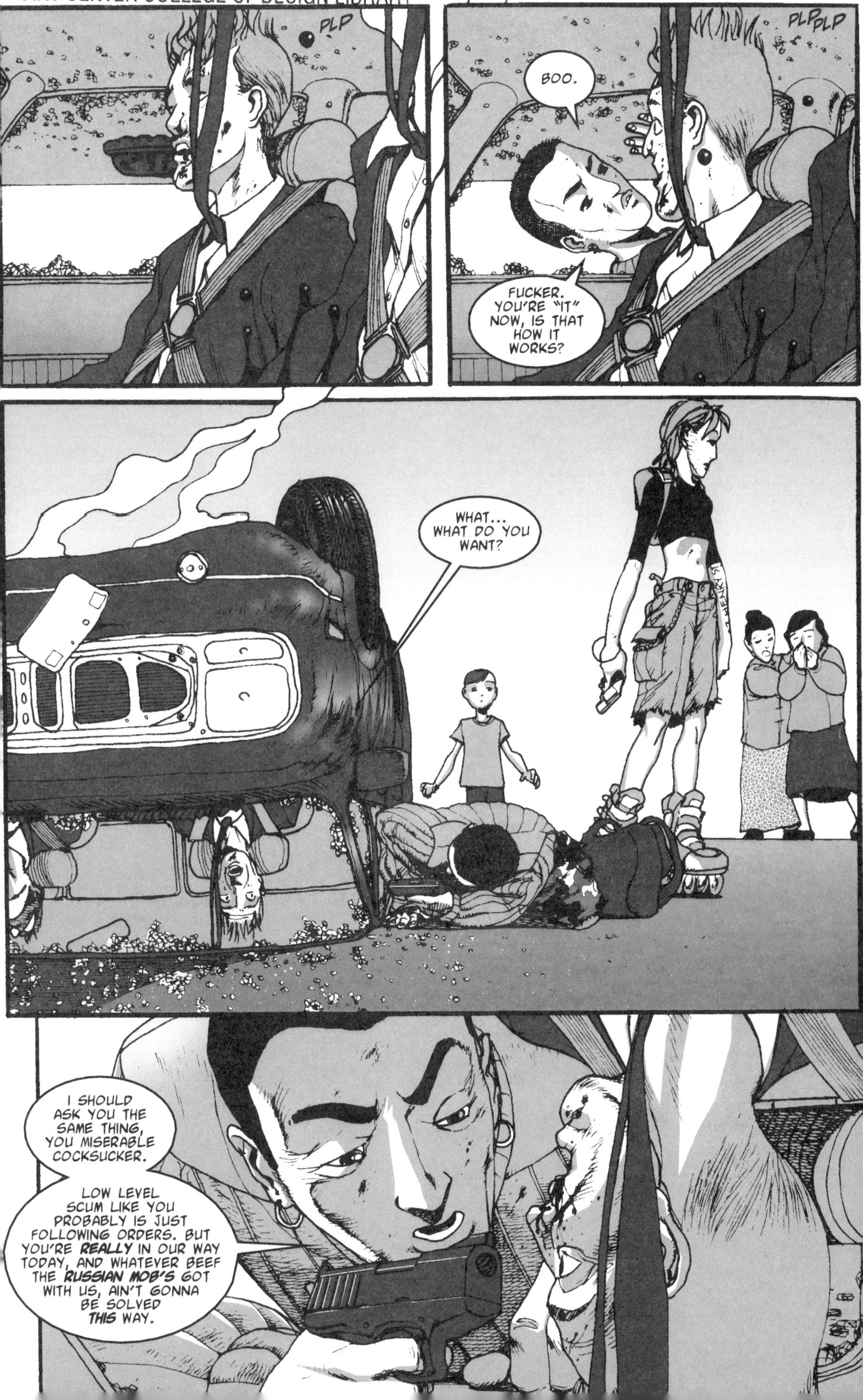
PLP
PLPPLP
BOO.
FUCKER. YOU'RE "IT" NOW, IS THAT HOW IT WORKS?
WHAT... WHAT DO YOU WANT?
I SHOULD ASK YOU THE SAME THING, YOU MISERABLE COCKSUCKER.
LOW LEVEL SCUM LIKE YOU PROBABLY IS JUST FOLLOWING ORDERS. BUT YOU'RE **REALLY** IN OUR WAY TODAY, AND WHATEVER BEEF THE **RUSSIAN MOB'S** GOT WITH US, AIN'T GONNA BE SOLVED **THIS** WAY.

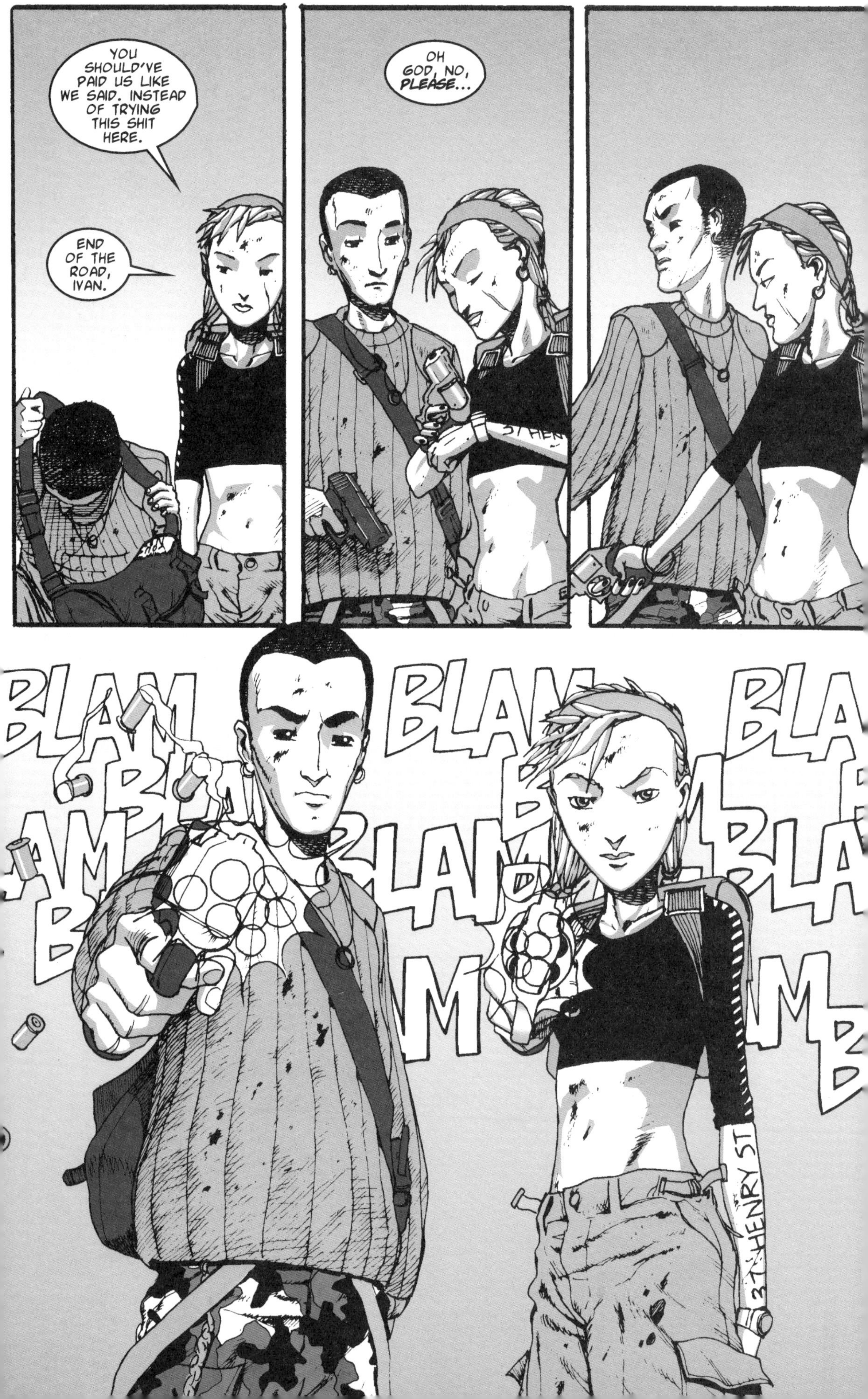
YOU SHOULD'VE PAID US LIKE WE SAID. INSTEAD OF TRYING THIS SHIT HERE.
END OF THE ROAD, IVAN.
OH GOD, NO, **PLEASE...**
BLAM
BLAM
BLAM
BLAM
BLAM
BLAM
BLAM
37 HENRY ST

A WOOD/G JOINT

The Couriers

written by BRIAN WOOD
art by ROB G
letters RYAN YOUNT

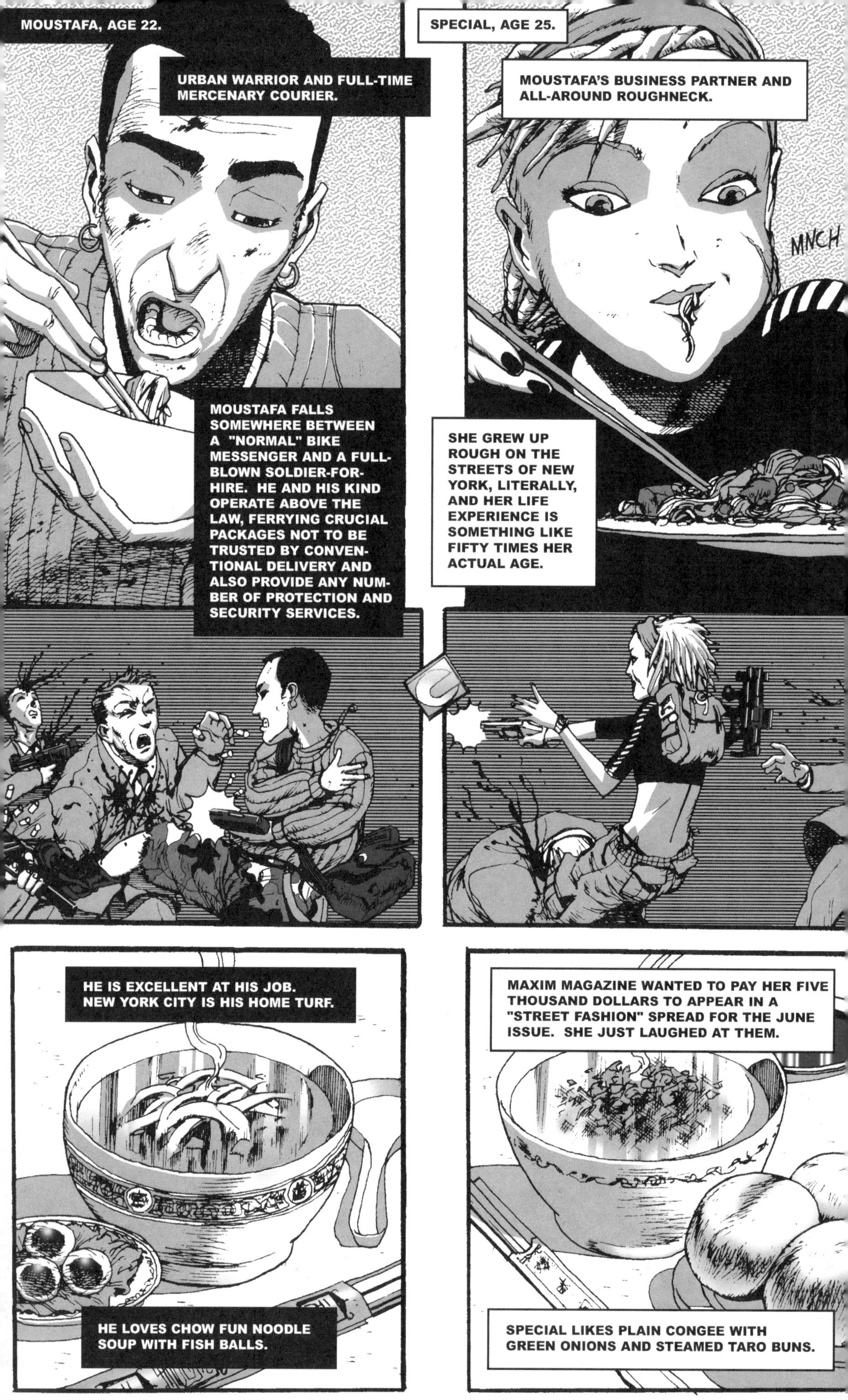
MOUSTAFA, AGE 22.
URBAN WARRIOR AND FULL-TIME MERCENARY COURIER.
MOUSTAFA FALLS SOMEWHERE BETWEEN A "NORMAL" BIKE MESSENGER AND A FULL-BLOWN SOLDIER-FOR-HIRE. HE AND HIS KIND OPERATE ABOVE THE LAW, FERRYING CRUCIAL PACKAGES NOT TO BE TRUSTED BY CONVENTIONAL DELIVERY AND ALSO PROVIDE ANY NUMBER OF PROTECTION AND SECURITY SERVICES.
SPECIAL, AGE 25.
MOUSTAFA'S BUSINESS PARTNER AND ALL-AROUND ROUGHNECK.
MNCH
SHE GREW UP ROUGH ON THE STREETS OF NEW YORK, LITERALLY, AND HER LIFE EXPERIENCE IS SOMETHING LIKE FIFTY TIMES HER ACTUAL AGE.
HE IS EXCELLENT AT HIS JOB. NEW YORK CITY IS HIS HOME TURF.
HE LOVES CHOW FUN NOODLE SOUP WITH FISH BALLS.
MAXIM MAGAZINE WANTED TO PAY HER FIVE THOUSAND DOLLARS TO APPEAR IN A "STREET FASHION" SPREAD FOR THE JUNE ISSUE. SHE JUST LAUGHED AT THEM.
SPECIAL LIKES PLAIN CONGEE WITH GREEN ONIONS AND STEAMED TARO BUNS.

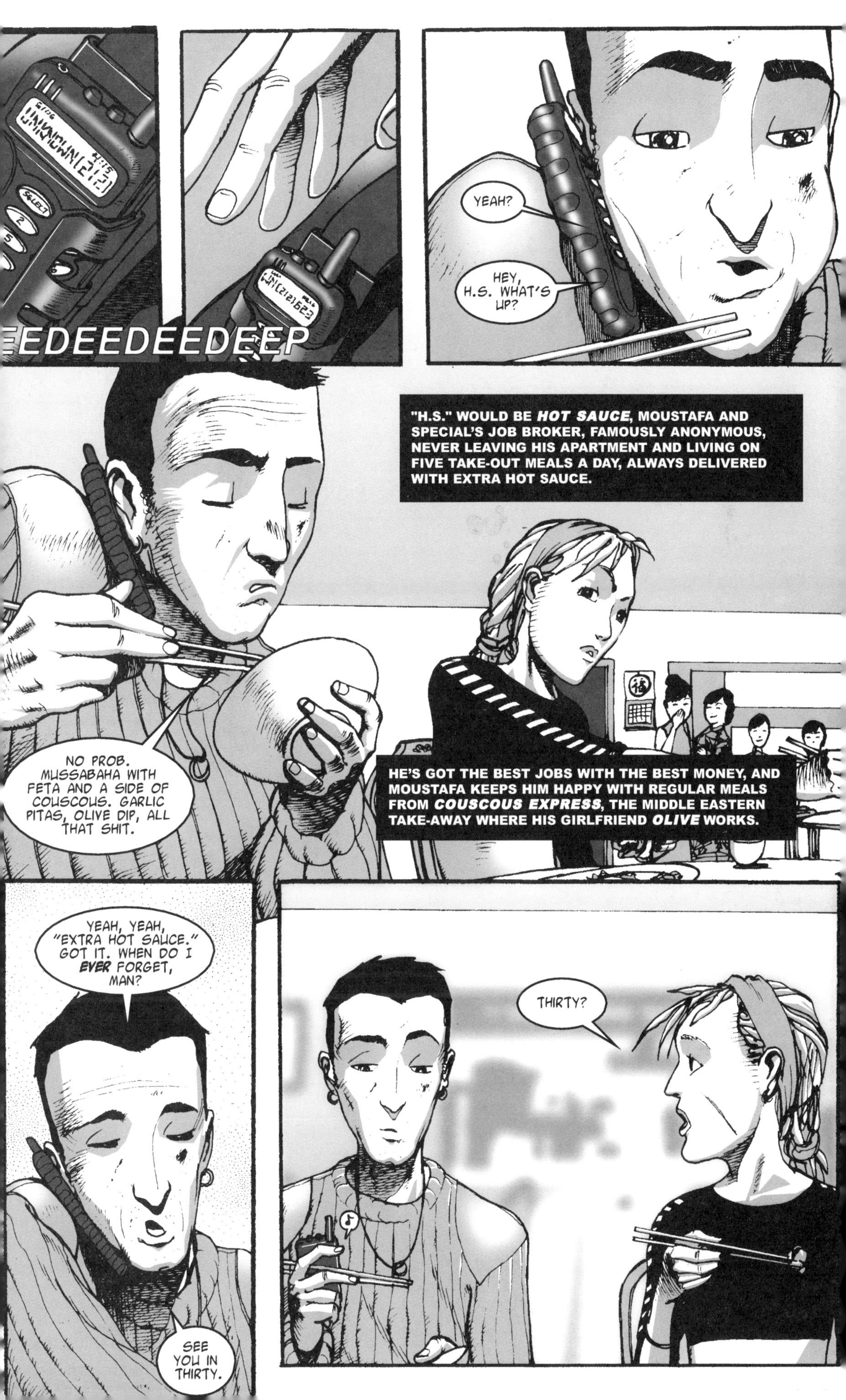
UNKNOWN (212)
EEDEEDEEDEEP
YEAH?
HEY, H.S. WHAT'S UP?
"H.S." WOULD BE HOT SAUCE, MOUSTAFA AND SPECIAL'S JOB BROKER, FAMOUSLY ANONYMOUS, NEVER LEAVING HIS APARTMENT AND LIVING ON FIVE TAKE-OUT MEALS A DAY, ALWAYS DELIVERED WITH EXTRA HOT SAUCE.
NO PROB. MUSSABAHA WITH FETA AND A SIDE OF COUSCOUS. GARLIC PITAS, OLIVE DIP, ALL THAT SHIT.
HE'S GOT THE BEST JOBS WITH THE BEST MONEY, AND MOUSTAFA KEEPS HIM HAPPY WITH REGULAR MEALS FROM COUSCOUS EXPRESS, THE MIDDLE EASTERN TAKE-AWAY WHERE HIS GIRLFRIEND OLIVE WORKS.
YEAH, YEAH, "EXTRA HOT SAUCE." GOT IT. WHEN DO I EVER FORGET, MAN?
SEE YOU IN THIRTY.
THIRTY?

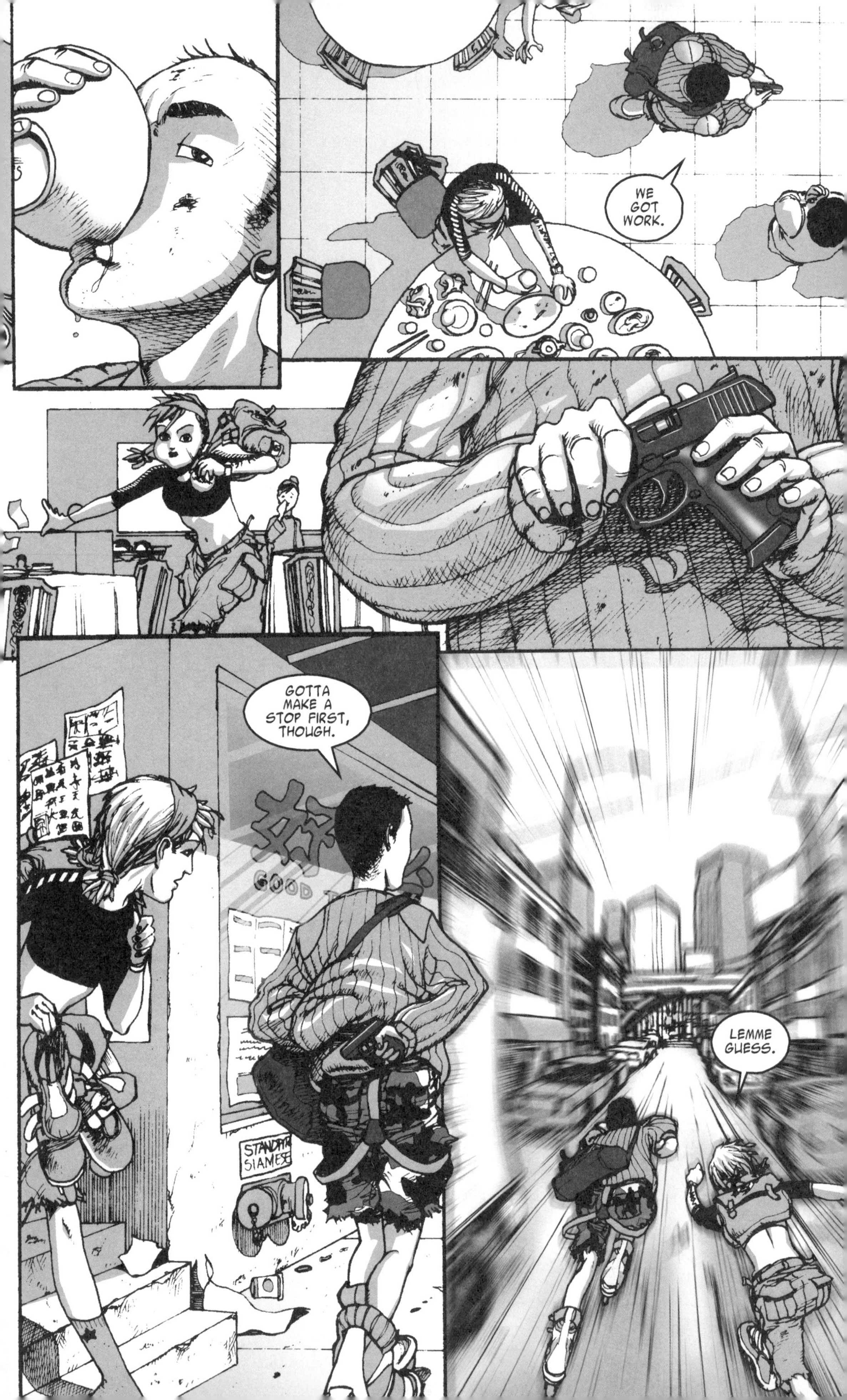
WE GOT WORK.
GOTTA MAKE A STOP FIRST, THOUGH.
GOOD
STANDPIPE SIAMESE
LEMME GUESS.

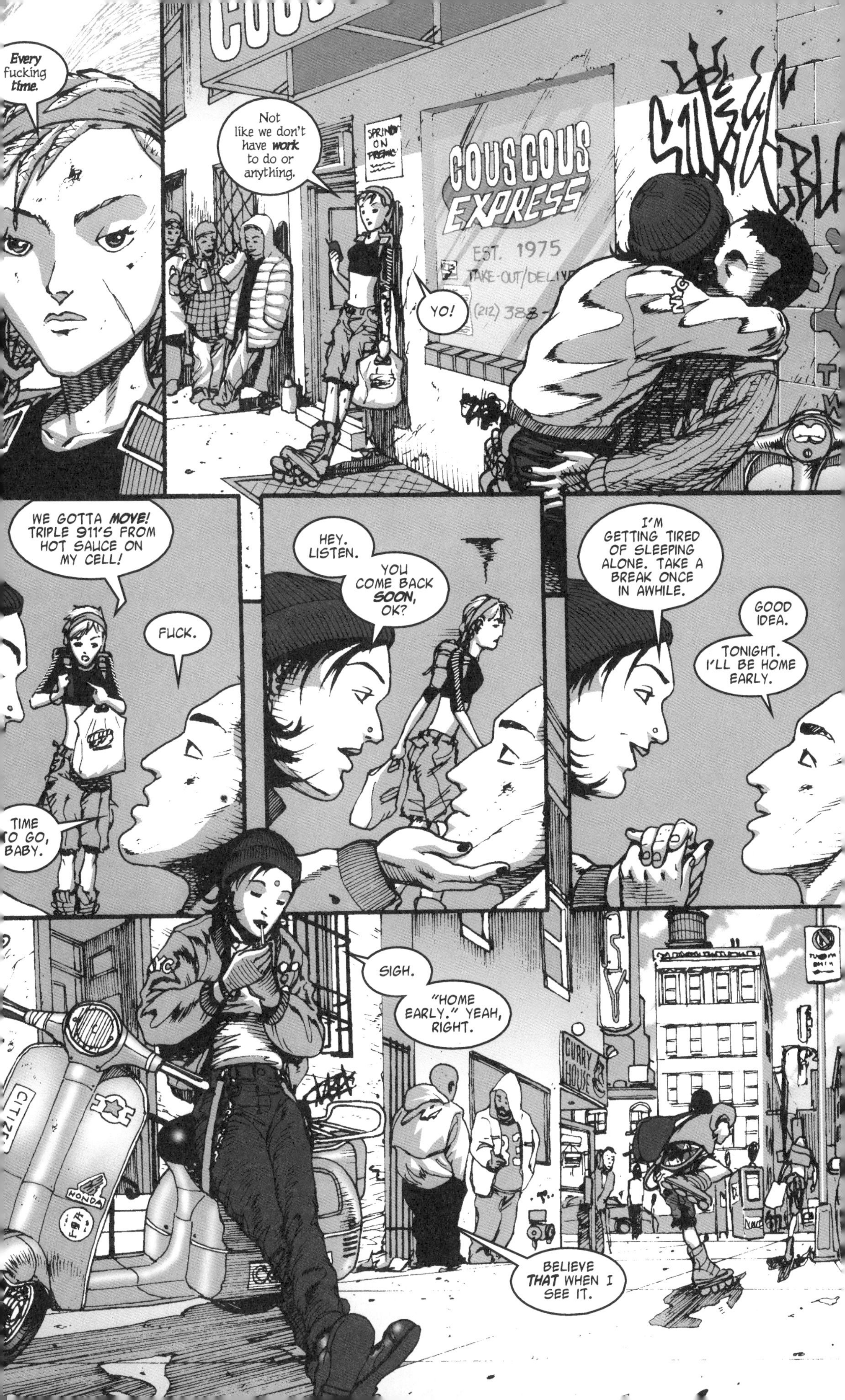

Every fucking time.
Not like we don't have work to do or anything.
COUS COUS EXPRESS
EST. 1975
TAKE-OUT/DELIVE
(212) 388-
YO!
WE GOTTA MOVE! TRIPLE 911'S FROM HOT SAUCE ON MY CELL!
FUCK.
TIME TO GO, BABY.
HEY. LISTEN.
YOU COME BACK SOON, OK?
I'M GETTING TIRED OF SLEEPING ALONE. TAKE A BREAK ONCE IN AWHILE.
GOOD IDEA.
TONIGHT. I'LL BE HOME EARLY.
SIGH.
"HOME EARLY." YEAH, RIGHT.
CURRY HOUSE
BELIEVE THAT WHEN I SEE IT.

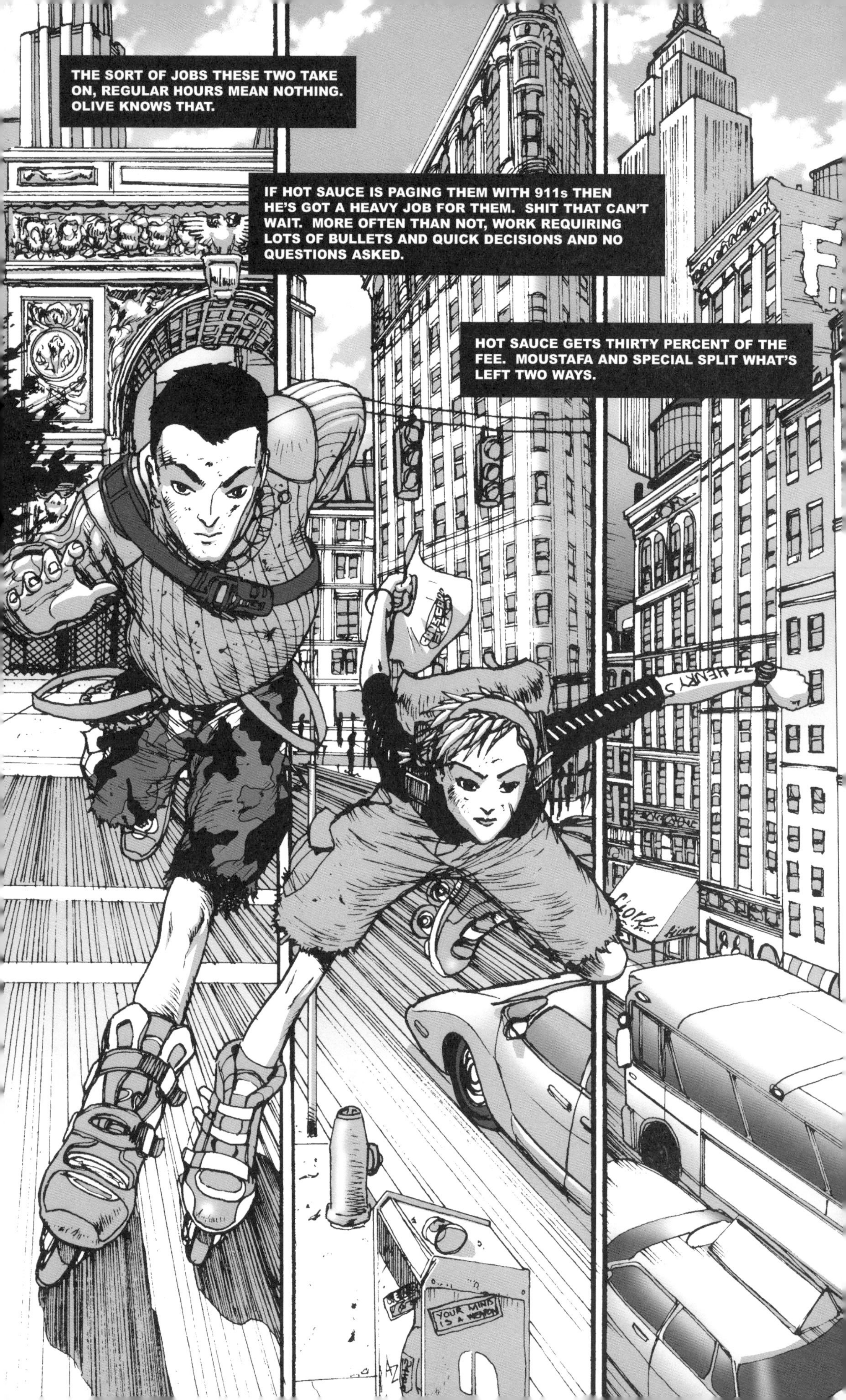
THE SORT OF JOBS THESE TWO TAKE ON, REGULAR HOURS MEAN NOTHING. OLIVE KNOWS THAT.
IF HOT SAUCE IS PAGING THEM WITH 911s THEN HE'S GOT A HEAVY JOB FOR THEM. SHIT THAT CAN'T WAIT. MORE OFTEN THAN NOT, WORK REQUIRING LOTS OF BULLETS AND QUICK DECISIONS AND NO QUESTIONS ASKED.
HOT SAUCE GETS THIRTY PERCENT OF THE FEE. MOUSTAFA AND SPECIAL SPLIT WHAT'S LEFT TWO WAYS.

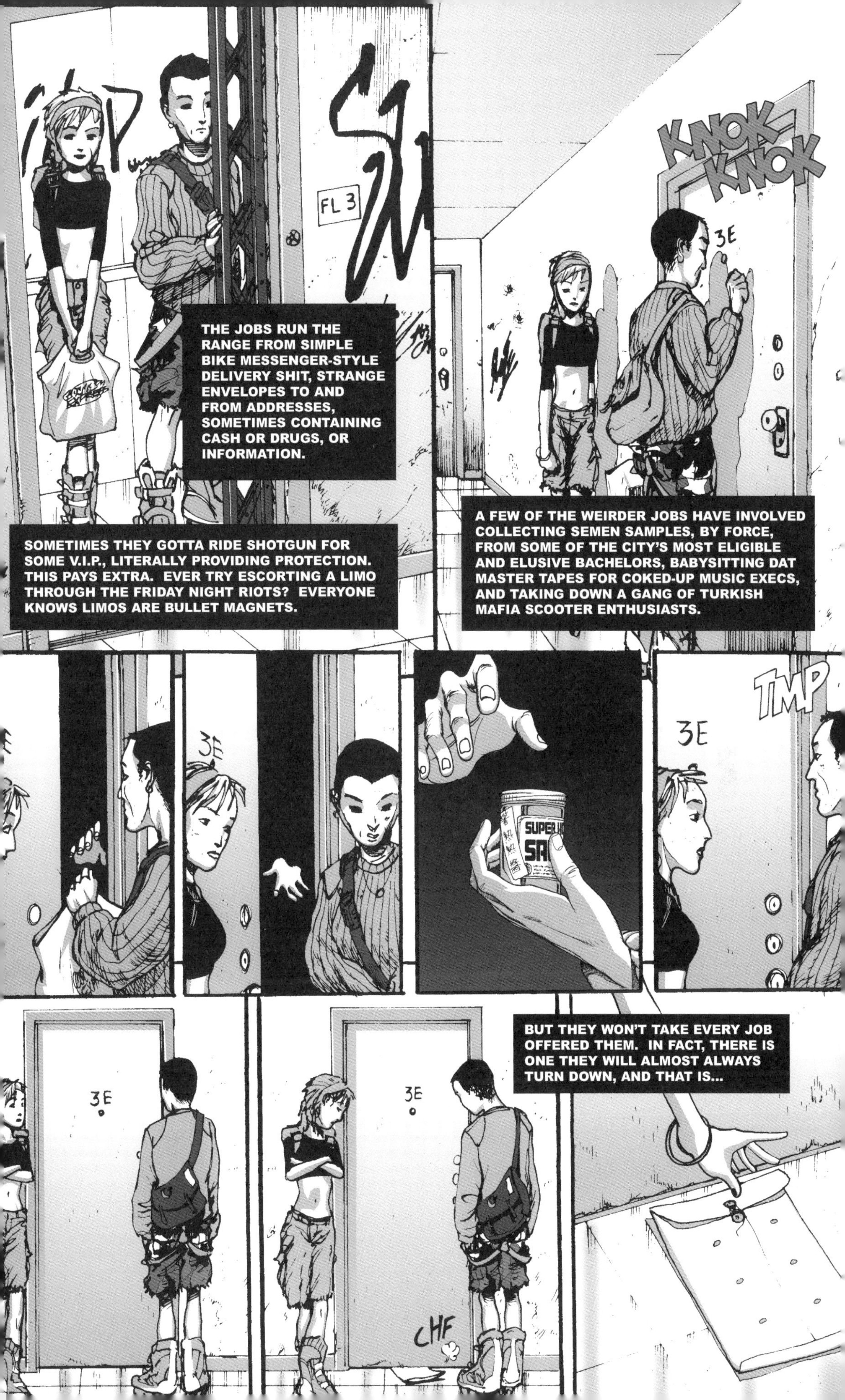

FL 3
THE JOBS RUN THE RANGE FROM SIMPLE BIKE MESSENGER-STYLE DELIVERY SHIT, STRANGE ENVELOPES TO AND FROM ADDRESSES, SOMETIMES CONTAINING CASH OR DRUGS, OR INFORMATION.
SOMETIMES THEY GOTTA RIDE SHOTGUN FOR SOME V.I.P., LITERALLY PROVIDING PROTECTION. THIS PAYS EXTRA. EVER TRY ESCORTING A LIMO THROUGH THE FRIDAY NIGHT RIOTS? EVERYONE KNOWS LIMOS ARE BULLET MAGNETS.
KNOK-KNOK
3E
A FEW OF THE WEIRDER JOBS HAVE INVOLVED COLLECTING SEMEN SAMPLES, BY FORCE, FROM SOME OF THE CITY'S MOST ELIGIBLE AND ELUSIVE BACHELORS, BABYSITTING DAT MASTER TAPES FOR COKED-UP MUSIC EXECS, AND TAKING DOWN A GANG OF TURKISH MAFIA SCOOTER ENTHUSIASTS.
3E
TMP
3E
3E
3E
BUT THEY WON'T TAKE EVERY JOB OFFERED THEM. IN FACT, THERE IS ONE THEY WILL ALMOST ALWAYS TURN DOWN, AND THAT IS...
CHF

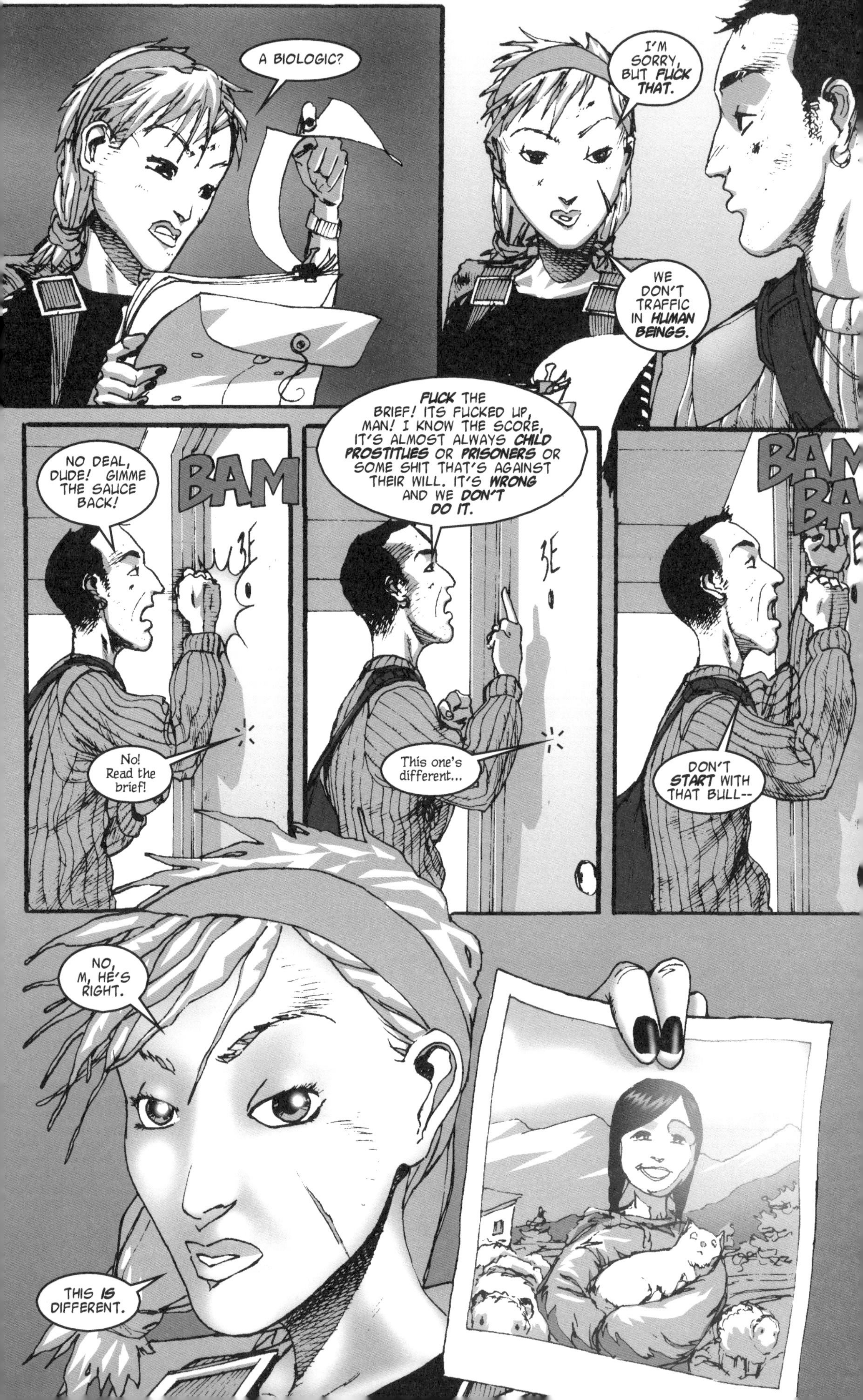

A BIOLOGIC?
I'M SORRY, BUT FUCK THAT.
WE DON'T TRAFFIC IN HUMAN BEINGS.
NO DEAL, DUDE! GIMME THE SAUCE BACK!
BAM
3E
No! Read the brief!
FUCK THE BRIEF! ITS FUCKED UP, MAN! I KNOW THE SCORE, IT'S ALMOST ALWAYS CHILD PROSTITUES OR PRISONERS OR SOME SHIT THAT'S AGAINST THEIR WILL. IT'S WRONG AND WE DON'T DO IT.
3E
This one's different...
BAM
DON'T START WITH THAT BULL--
NO, M, HE'S RIGHT.
THIS IS DIFFERENT.

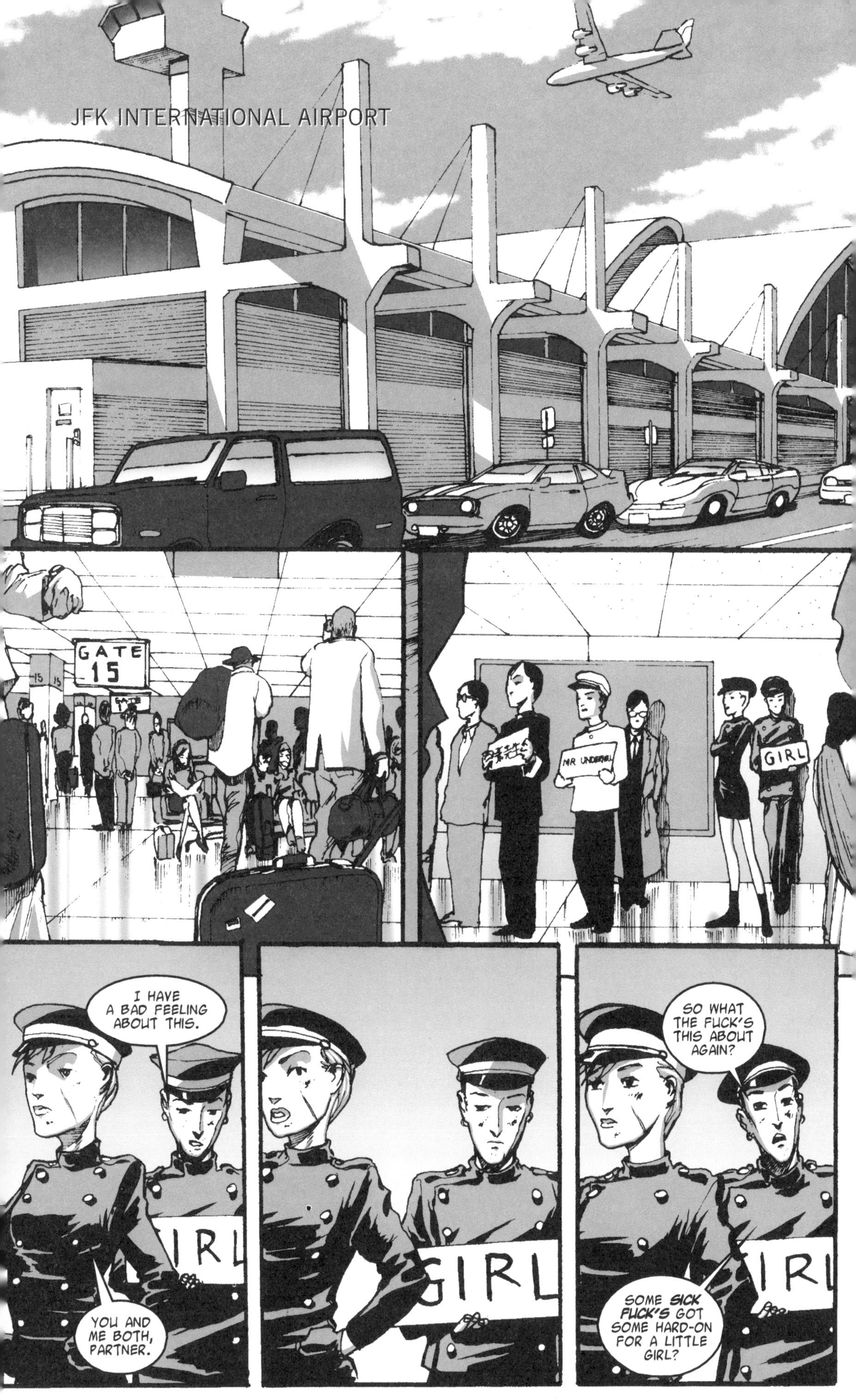
JFK INTERNATIONAL AIRPORT
GATE 15
MR UNDERHILL
GIRL
I HAVE A BAD FEELING ABOUT THIS.
YOU AND ME BOTH, PARTNER.
SO WHAT THE FUCK'S THIS ABOUT AGAIN?
SOME SICK FUCK'S GOT SOME HARD-ON FOR A LITTLE GIRL?

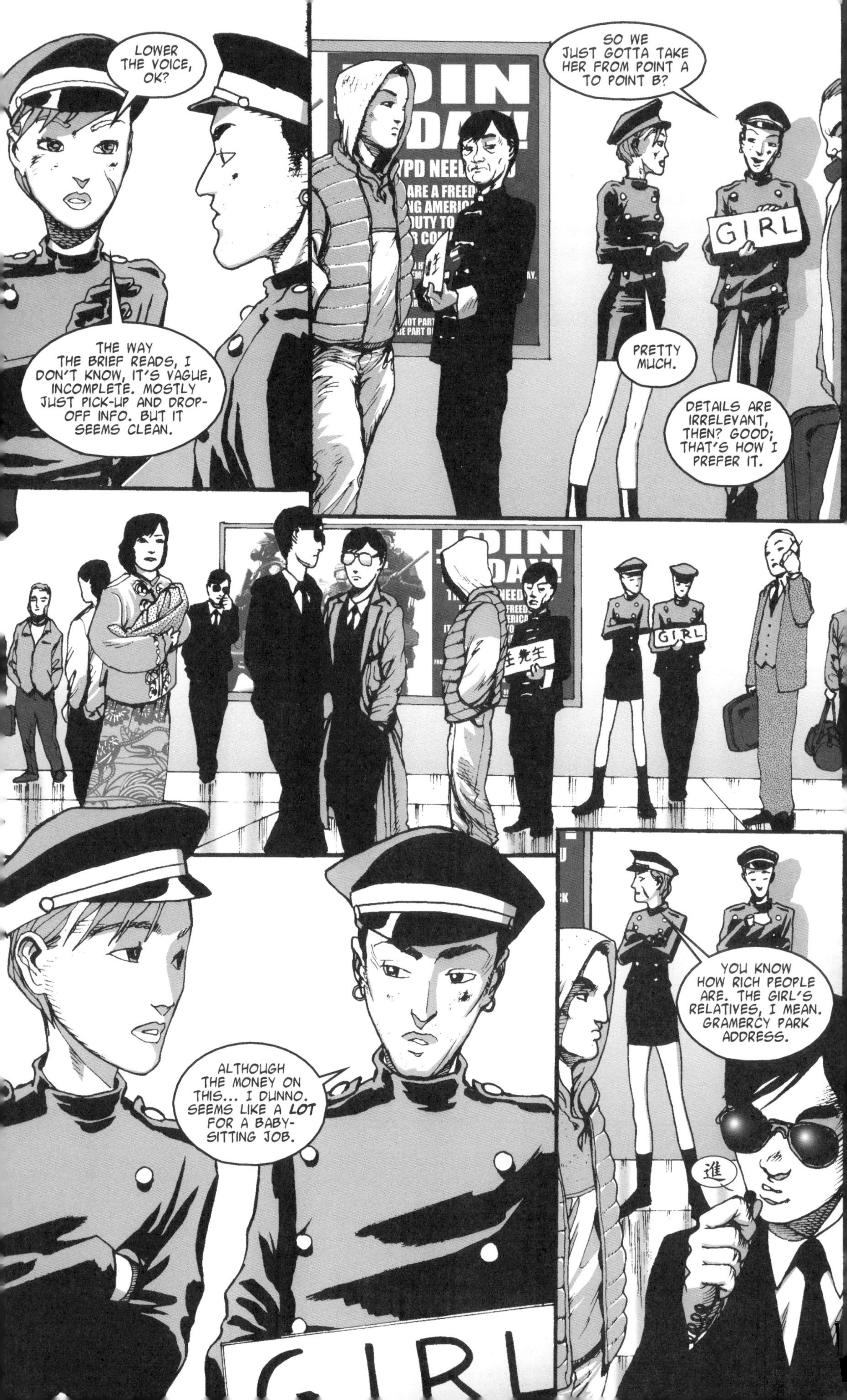
LOWER THE VOICE, OK?
THE WAY THE BRIEF READS, I DON'T KNOW, IT'S VAGUE, INCOMPLETE. MOSTLY JUST PICK-UP AND DROP-OFF INFO. BUT IT SEEMS CLEAN.
SO WE JUST GOTTA TAKE HER FROM POINT A TO POINT B?
GIRL
PRETTY MUCH.
DETAILS ARE IRRELEVANT, THEN? GOOD; THAT'S HOW I PREFER IT.
GIRL
ALTHOUGH THE MONEY ON THIS... I DUNNO. SEEMS LIKE A LOT FOR A BABY-SITTING JOB.
GIRL
YOU KNOW HOW RICH PEOPLE ARE. THE GIRL'S RELATIVES, I MEAN. GRAMERCY PARK ADDRESS.
進

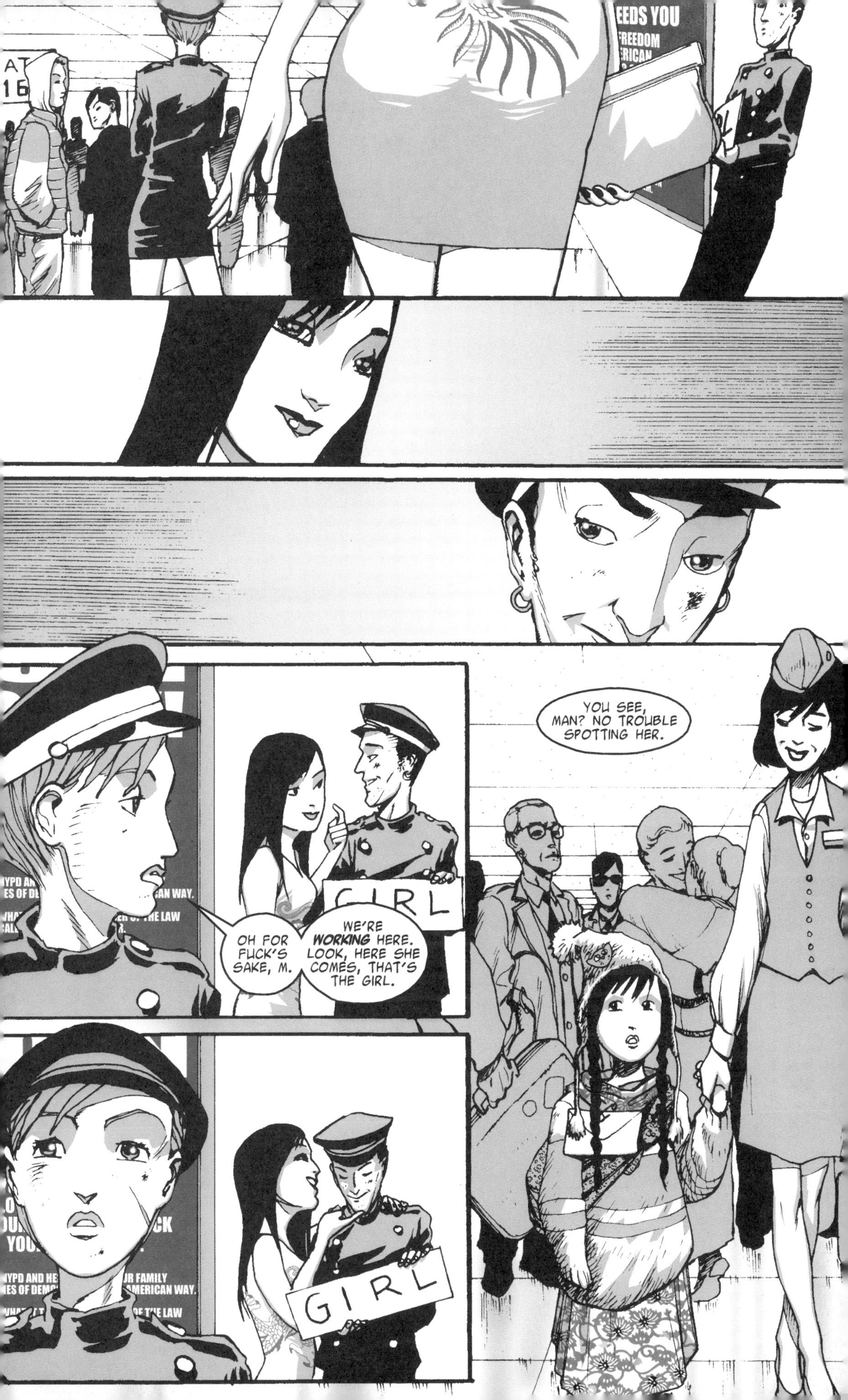
EEDS YOU
FREEDOM
ERICAN
OH FOR FUCK'S SAKE, M.
WE'RE WORKING HERE. LOOK, HERE SHE COMES, THAT'S THE GIRL.
GIRL
YOU SEE, MAN? NO TROUBLE SPOTTING HER.
GIRL

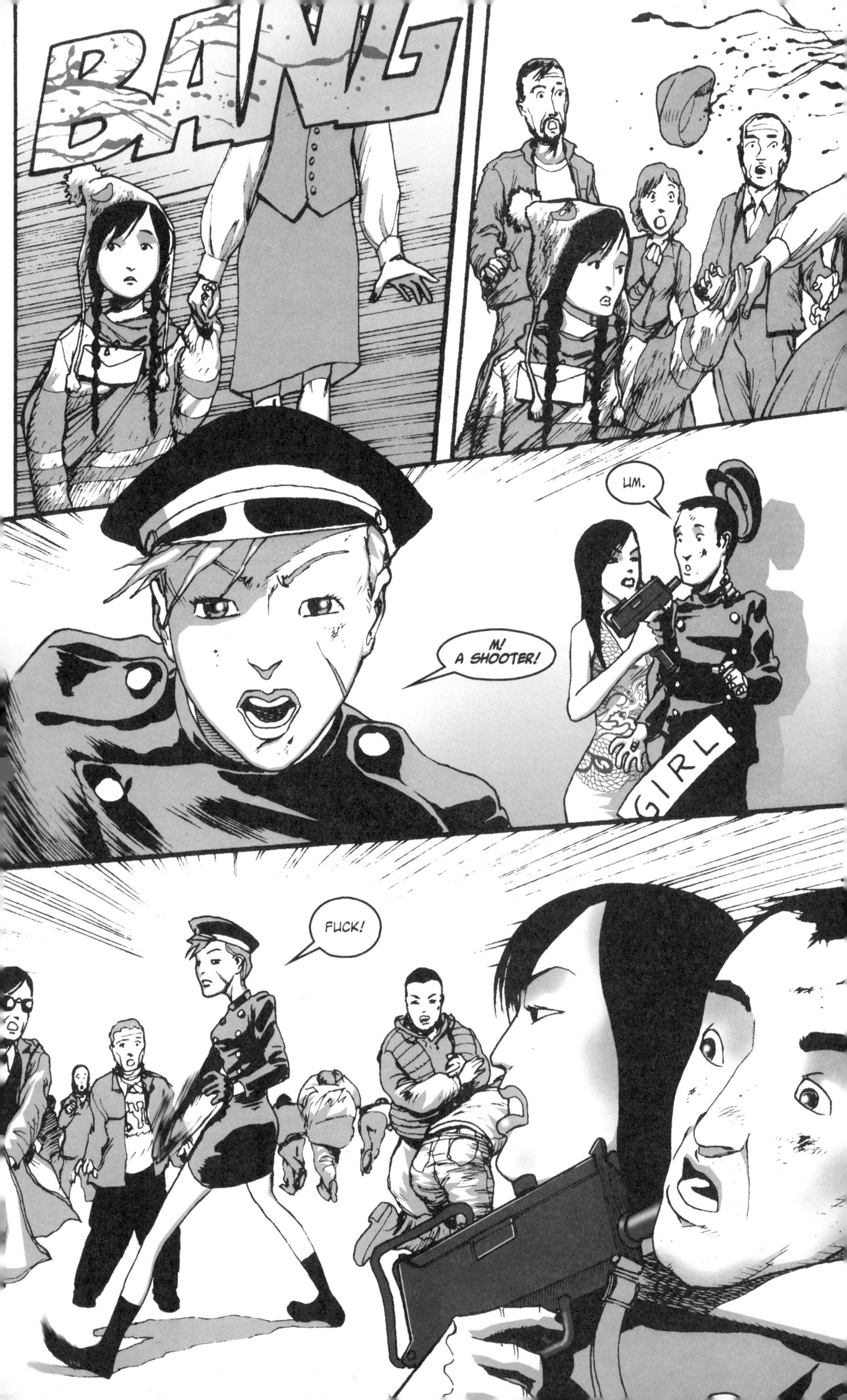
BANG
UM.
M!
A SHOOTER!
GIRL
FUCK!

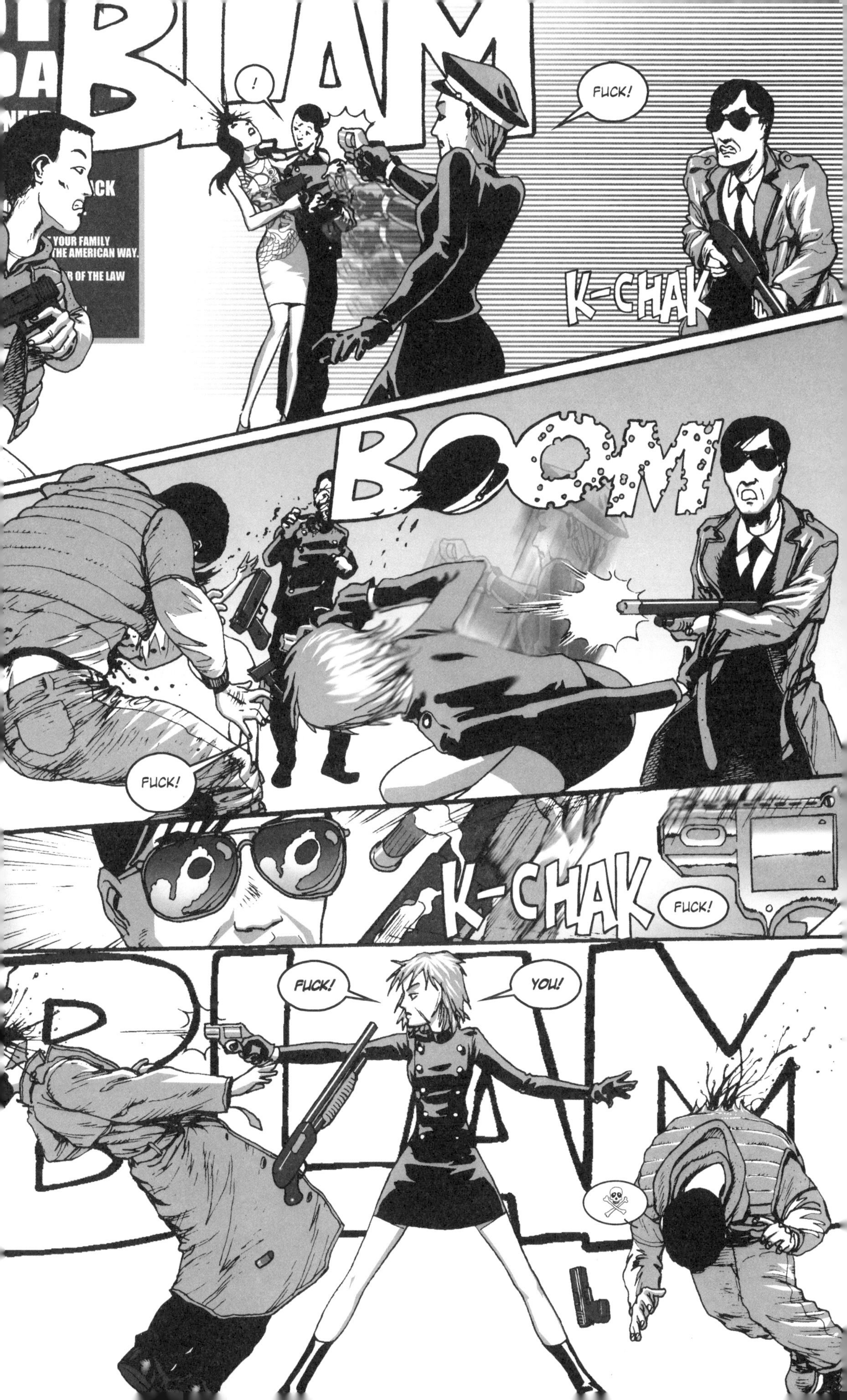
BLAM
!
YOUR FAMILY
THE AMERICAN WAY.
OF THE LAW
FUCK!
K-CHAK
BOOM
FUCK!
K-CHAK
FUCK!
FUCK!
YOU!

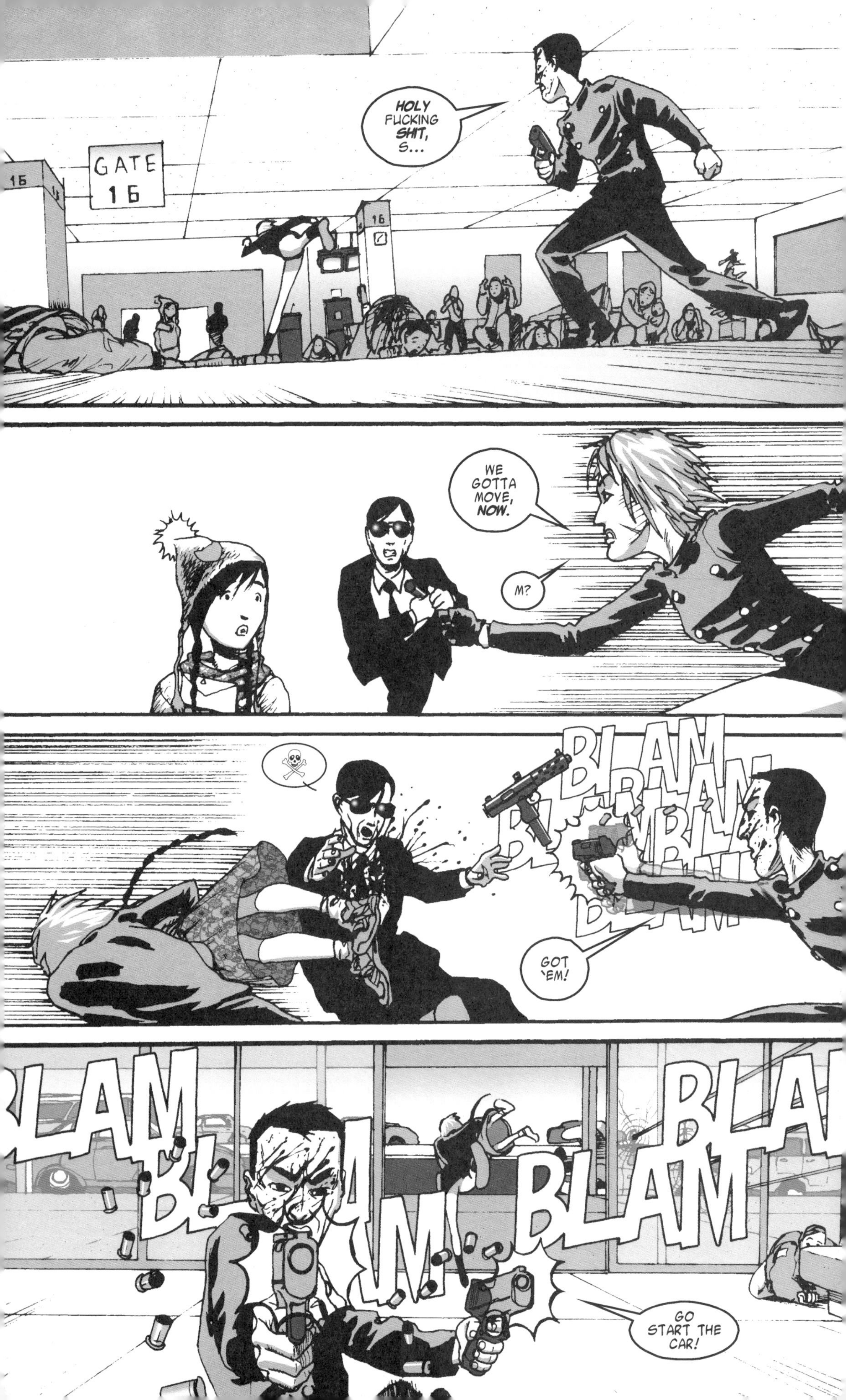
HOLY FUCKING SHIT, S...
GATE 16
WE GOTTA MOVE, NOW.
M?
BLAM BLAM BLAM
GOT 'EM!
BLAM BLAM
BLAM BLAM
GO START THE CAR!

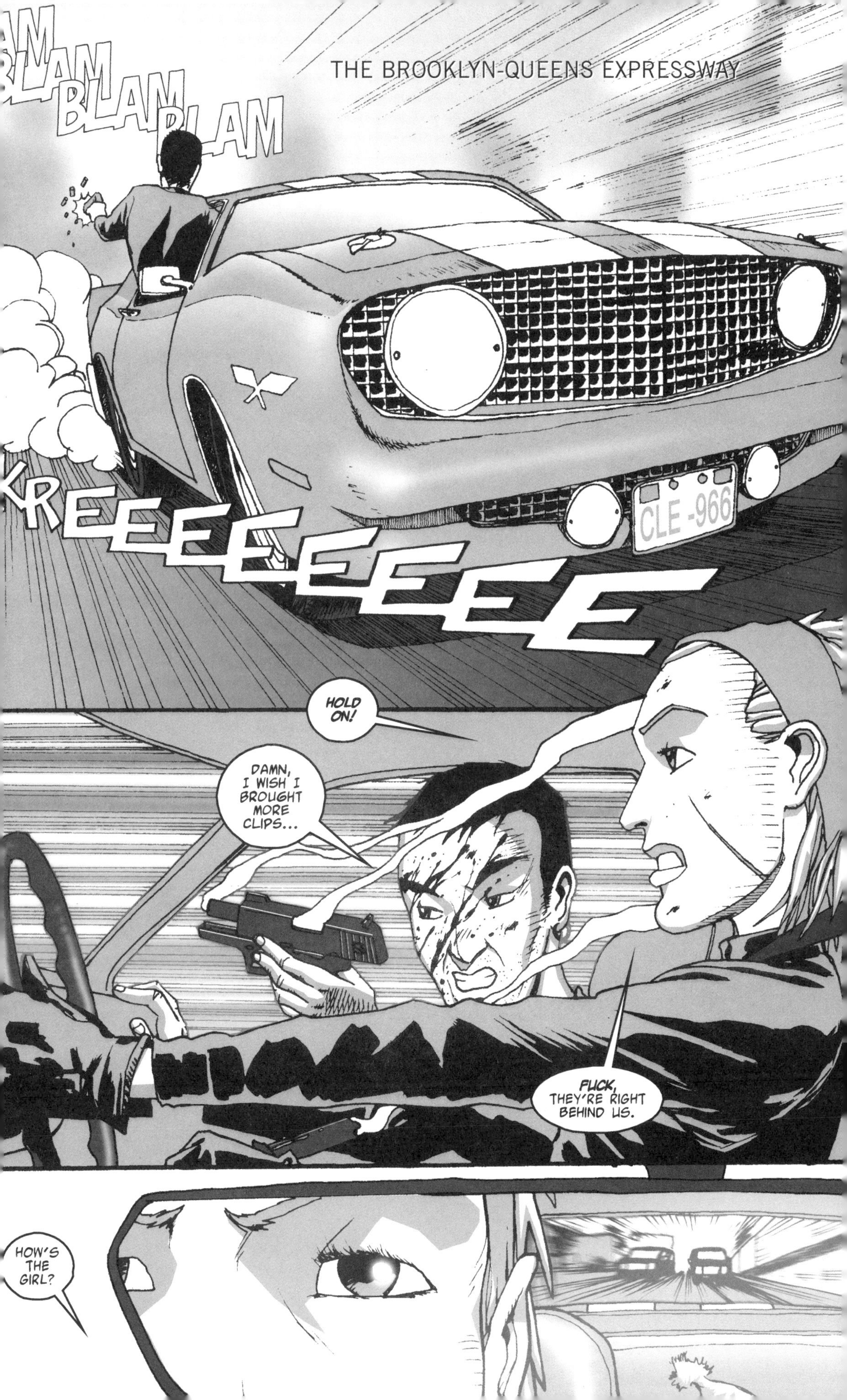

AM BLAM BLAM BLAM BLAM
THE BROOKLYN-QUEENS EXPRESSWAY
CLE -966
KREEEEEEEEE
HOLD ON!
DAMN, I WISH I BROUGHT MORE CLIPS...
FUCK, THEY'RE RIGHT BEHIND US.
HOW'S THE GIRL?

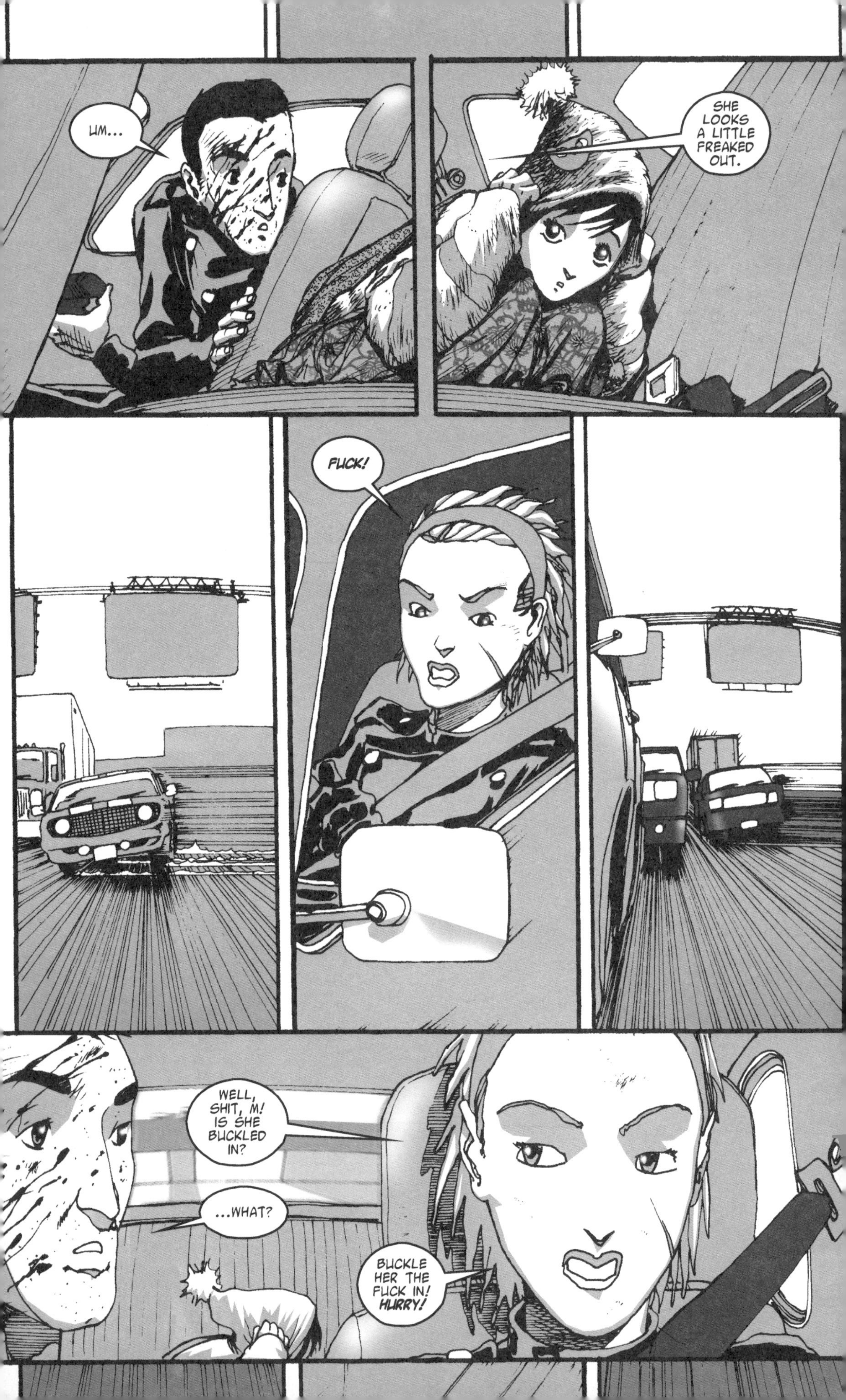
UM...
SHE LOOKS A LITTLE FREAKED OUT.
FUCK!
WELL, SHIT, M! IS SHE BUCKLED IN?
...WHAT?
BUCKLE HER THE FUCK IN! HURRY!

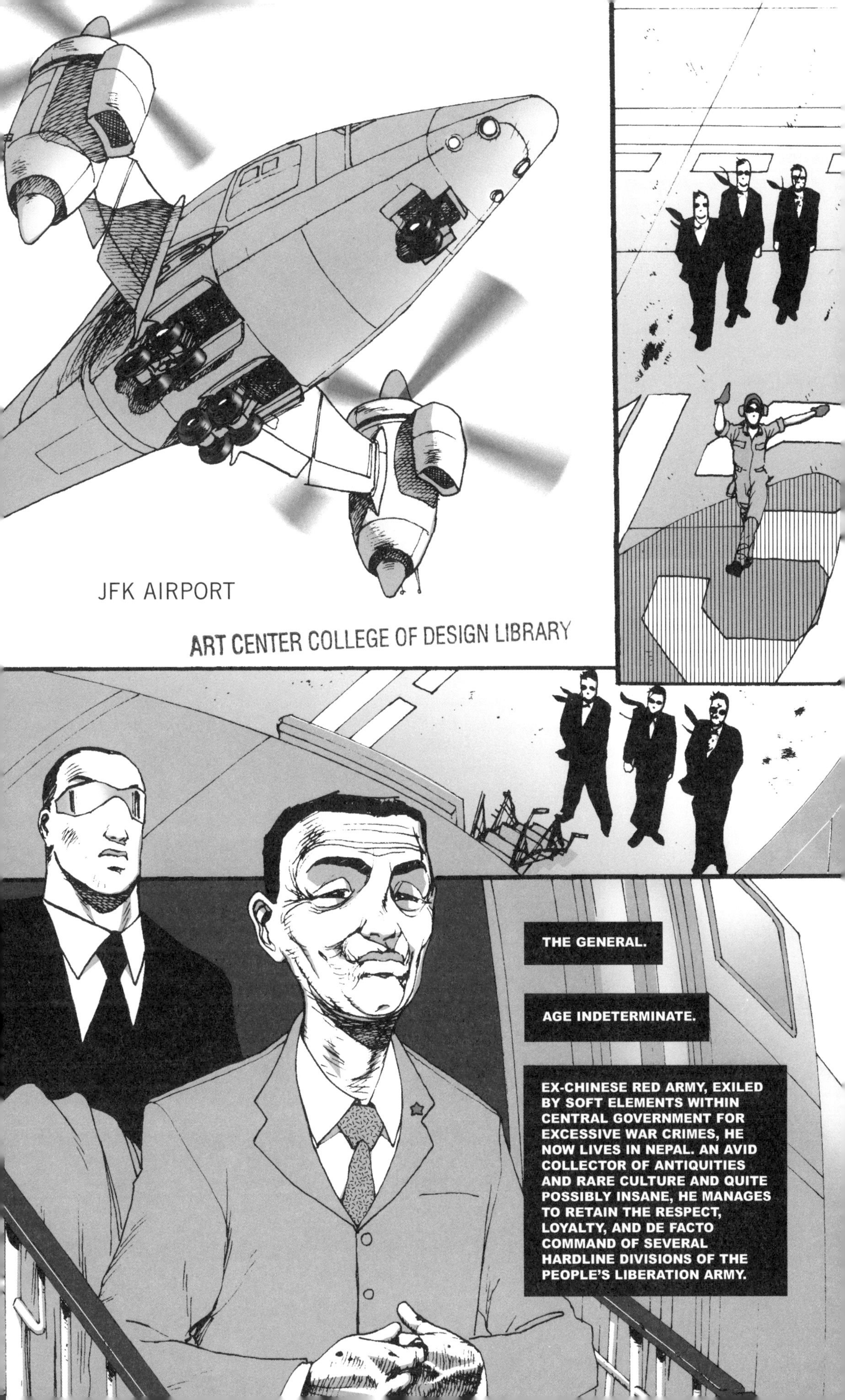
JFK AIRPORT
THE GENERAL.
AGE INDETERMINATE.
EX-CHINESE RED ARMY, EXILED BY SOFT ELEMENTS WITHIN CENTRAL GOVERNMENT FOR EXCESSIVE WAR CRIMES, HE NOW LIVES IN NEPAL. AN AVID COLLECTOR OF ANTIQUITIES AND RARE CULTURE AND QUITE POSSIBLY INSANE, HE MANAGES TO RETAIN THE RESPECT, LOYALTY, AND DE FACTO COMMAND OF SEVERAL HARDLINE DIVISIONS OF THE PEOPLE'S LIBERATION ARMY.

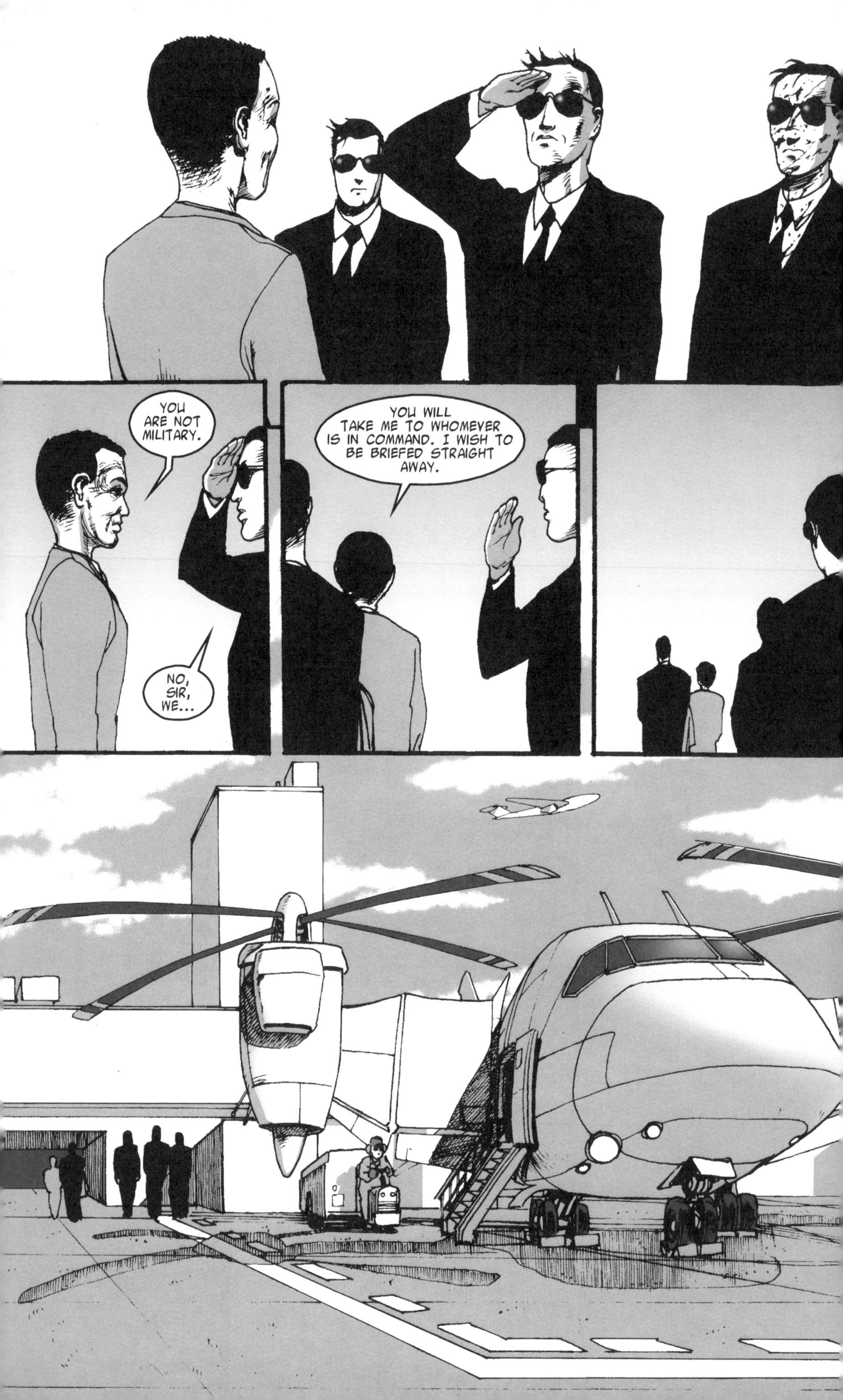
YOU ARE NOT MILITARY.
NO, SIR, WE...
YOU WILL TAKE ME TO WHOMEVER IS IN COMMAND. I WISH TO BE BRIEFED STRAIGHT AWAY.

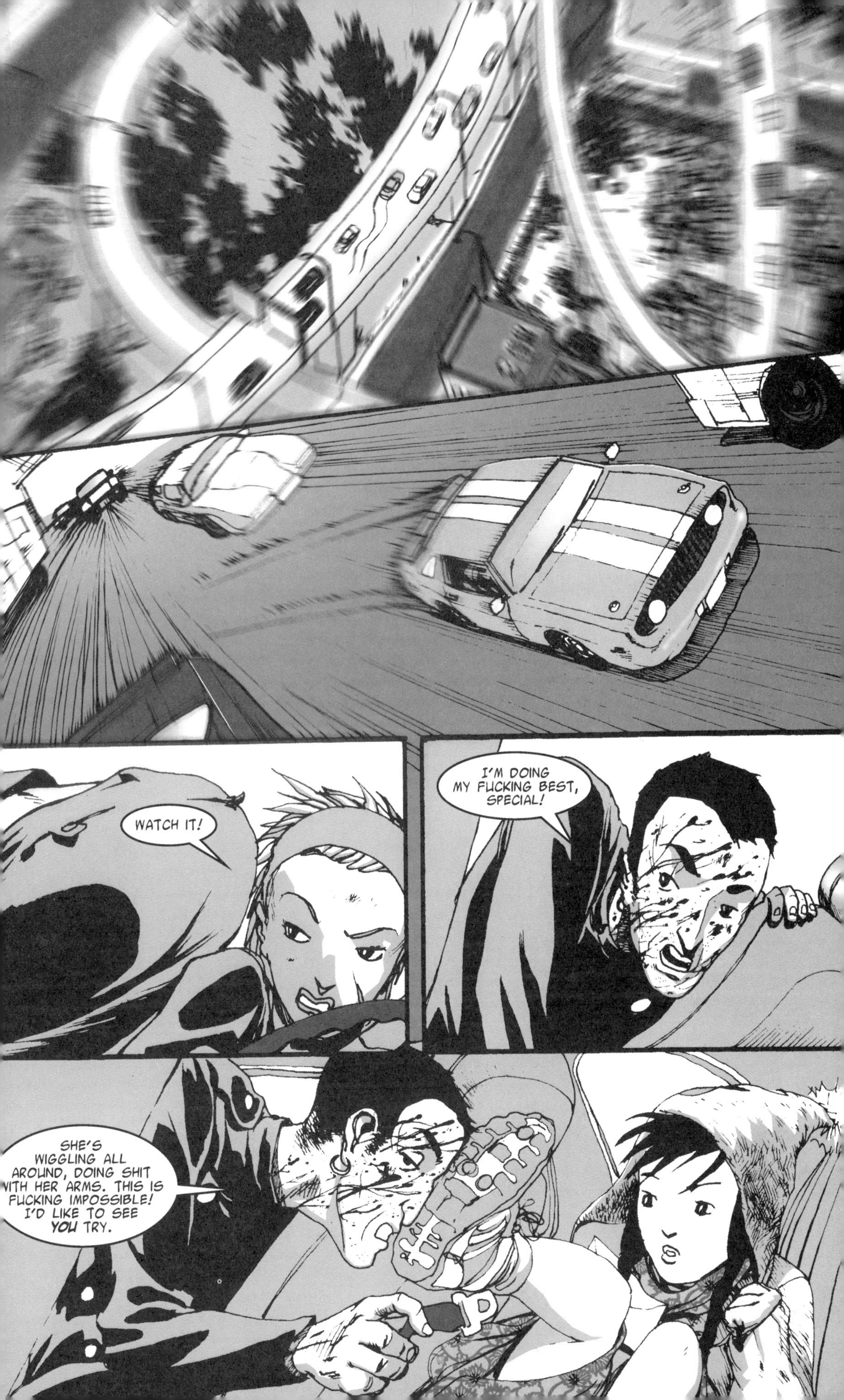
WATCH IT!
I'M DOING MY FUCKING BEST, SPECIAL!
SHE'S WIGGLING ALL AROUND, DOING SHIT WITH HER ARMS. THIS IS FUCKING IMPOSSIBLE! I'D LIKE TO SEE YOU TRY.

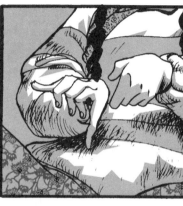

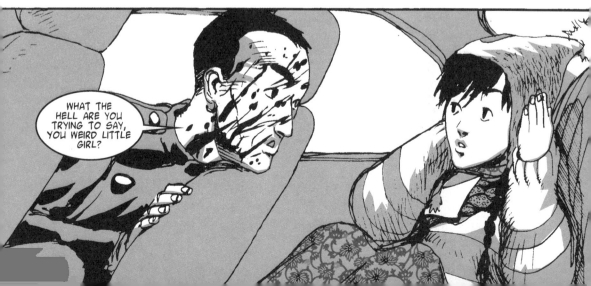

WHAT THE HELL ARE YOU TRYING TO SAY, YOU WEIRD LITTLE GIRL?

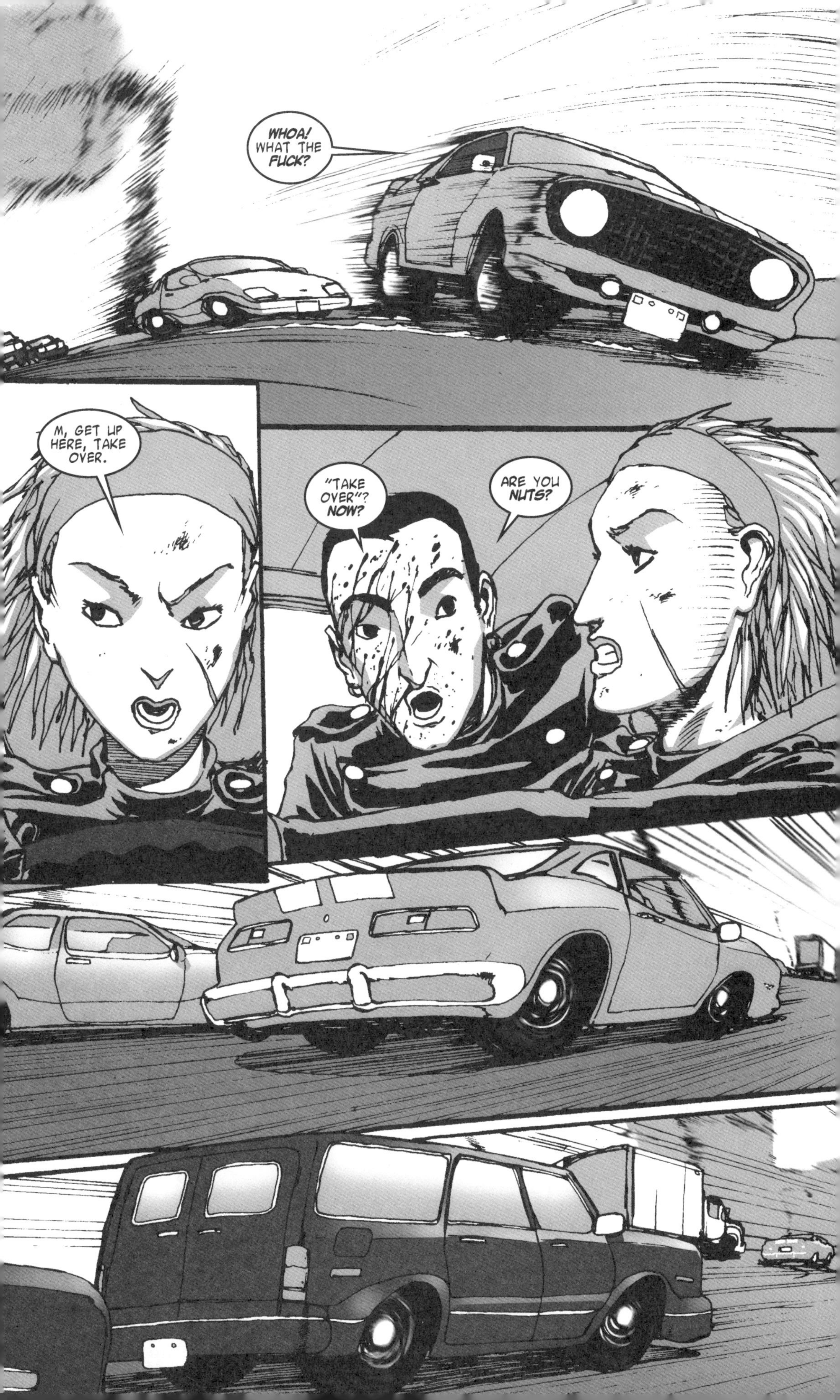

WHOA! WHAT THE FUCK?
M, GET UP HERE, TAKE OVER.
"TAKE OVER"? NOW?
ARE YOU NUTS?

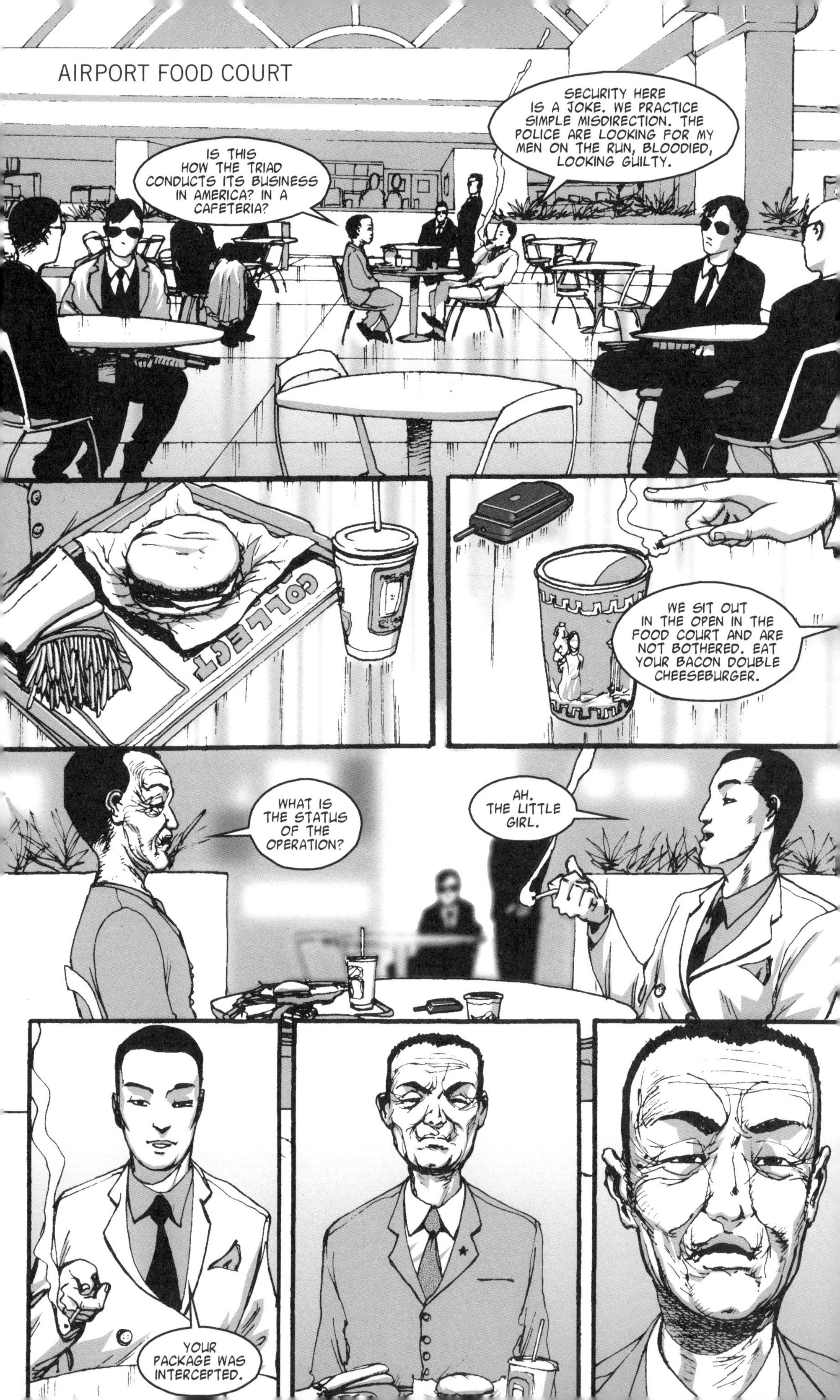
AIRPORT FOOD COURT
IS THIS HOW THE TRIAD CONDUCTS ITS BUSINESS IN AMERICA? IN A CAFETERIA?
SECURITY HERE IS A JOKE. WE PRACTICE SIMPLE MISDIRECTION. THE POLICE ARE LOOKING FOR MY MEN ON THE RUN, BLOODIED, LOOKING GUILTY.
COLLECT
WE SIT OUT IN THE OPEN IN THE FOOD COURT AND ARE NOT BOTHERED. EAT YOUR BACON DOUBLE CHEESEBURGER.
WHAT IS THE STATUS OF THE OPERATION?
AH. THE LITTLE GIRL.
YOUR PACKAGE WAS INTERCEPTED.

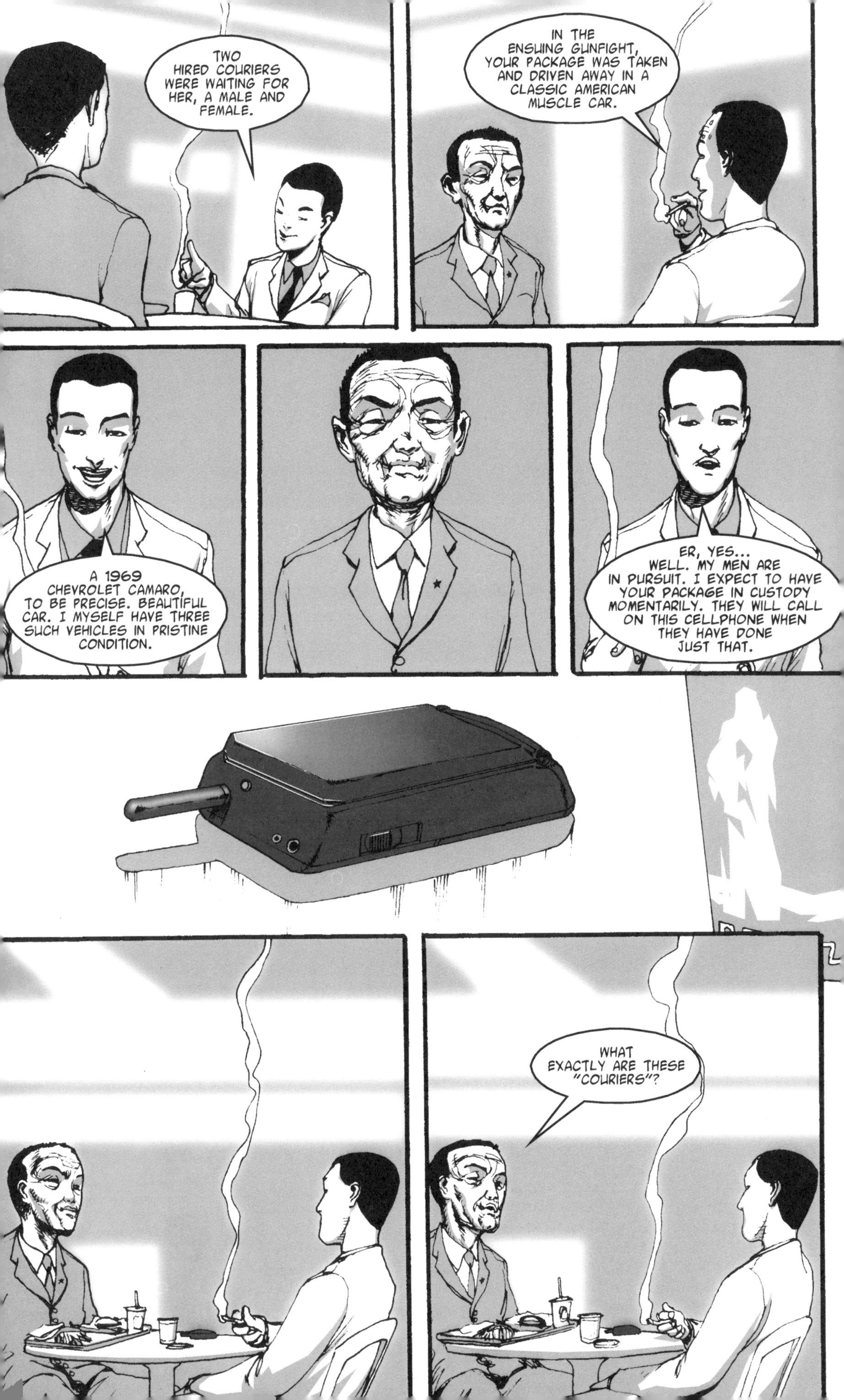
TWO HIRED COURIERS WERE WAITING FOR HER, A MALE AND FEMALE.
IN THE ENSUING GUNFIGHT, YOUR PACKAGE WAS TAKEN AND DRIVEN AWAY IN A CLASSIC AMERICAN MUSCLE CAR.
A 1969 CHEVROLET CAMARO, TO BE PRECISE. BEAUTIFUL CAR. I MYSELF HAVE THREE SUCH VEHICLES IN PRISTINE CONDITION.
ER, YES... WELL. MY MEN ARE IN PURSUIT. I EXPECT TO HAVE YOUR PACKAGE IN CUSTODY MOMENTARILY. THEY WILL CALL ON THIS CELLPHONE WHEN THEY HAVE DONE JUST THAT.
WHAT EXACTLY ARE THESE "COURIERS"?

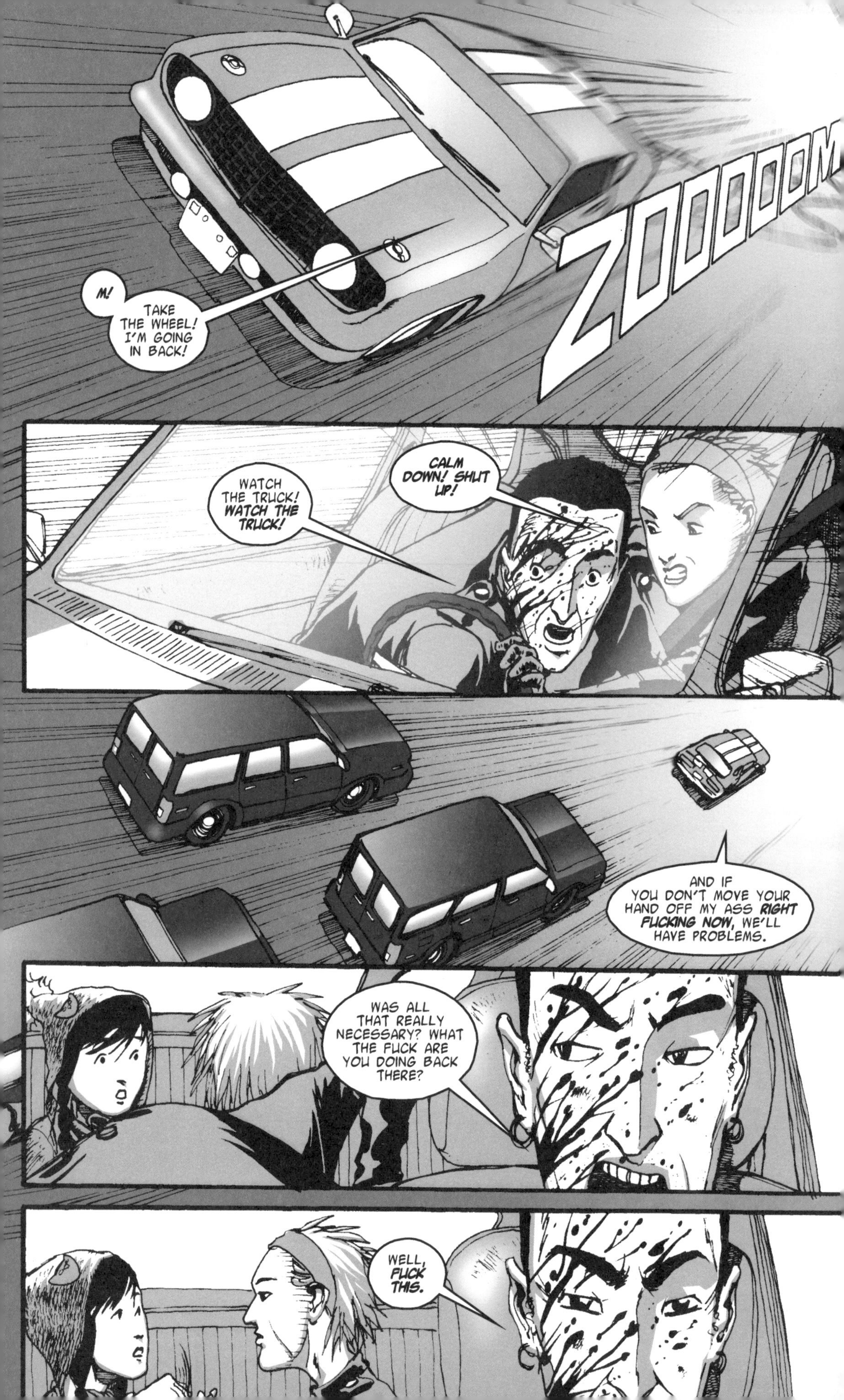
ZOOOOOM
M!
TAKE THE WHEEL! I'M GOING IN BACK!
WATCH THE TRUCK! WATCH THE TRUCK!
CALM DOWN! SHUT UP!
AND IF YOU DON'T MOVE YOUR HAND OFF MY ASS RIGHT FUCKING NOW, WE'LL HAVE PROBLEMS.
WAS ALL THAT REALLY NECESSARY? WHAT THE FUCK ARE YOU DOING BACK THERE?
WELL, FUCK THIS.

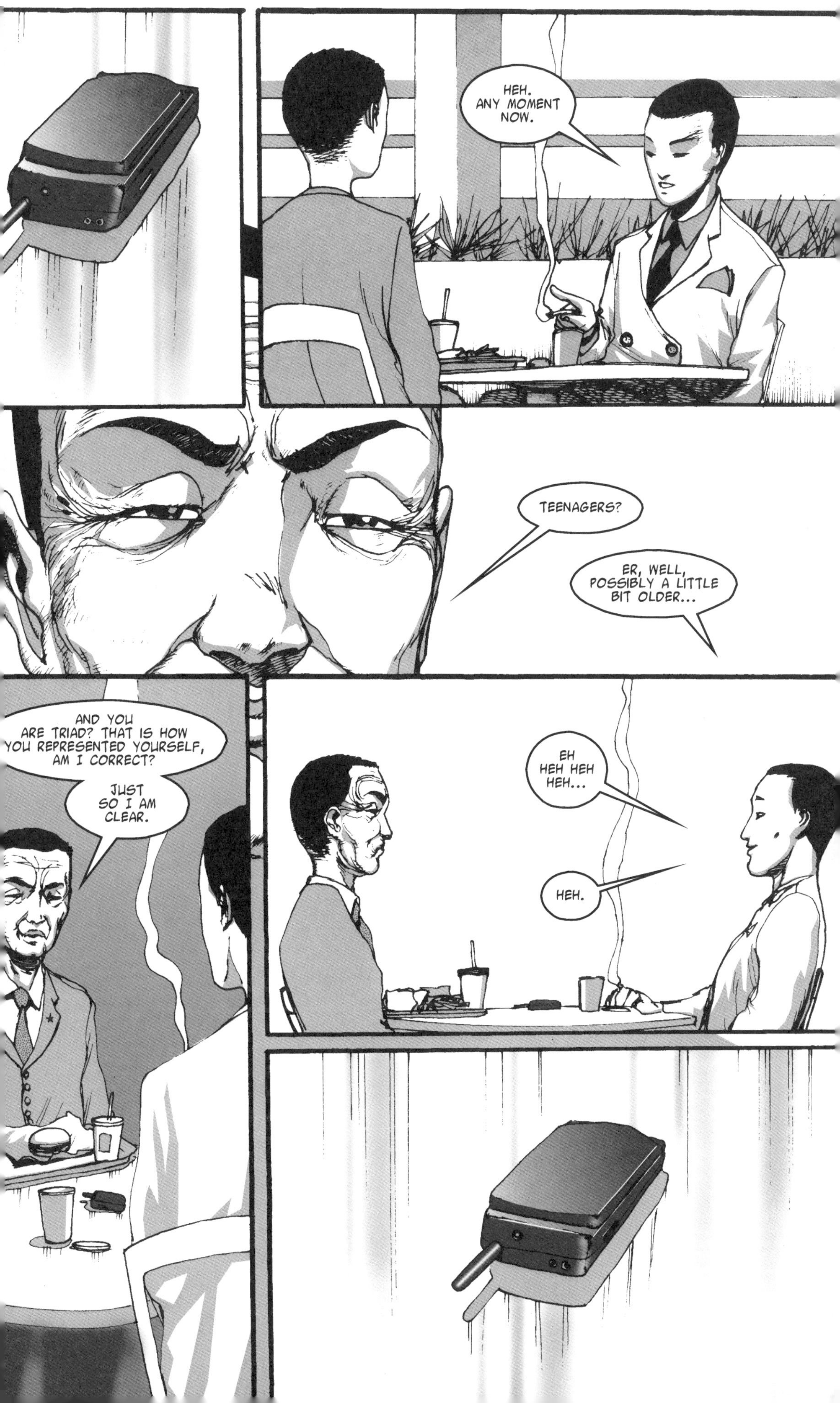
HEH. ANY MOMENT NOW.
TEENAGERS?
ER, WELL, POSSIBLY A LITTLE BIT OLDER...
AND YOU ARE TRIAD? THAT IS HOW YOU REPRESENTED YOURSELF, AM I CORRECT?
JUST SO I AM CLEAR.
EH HEH HEH HEH...
HEH.

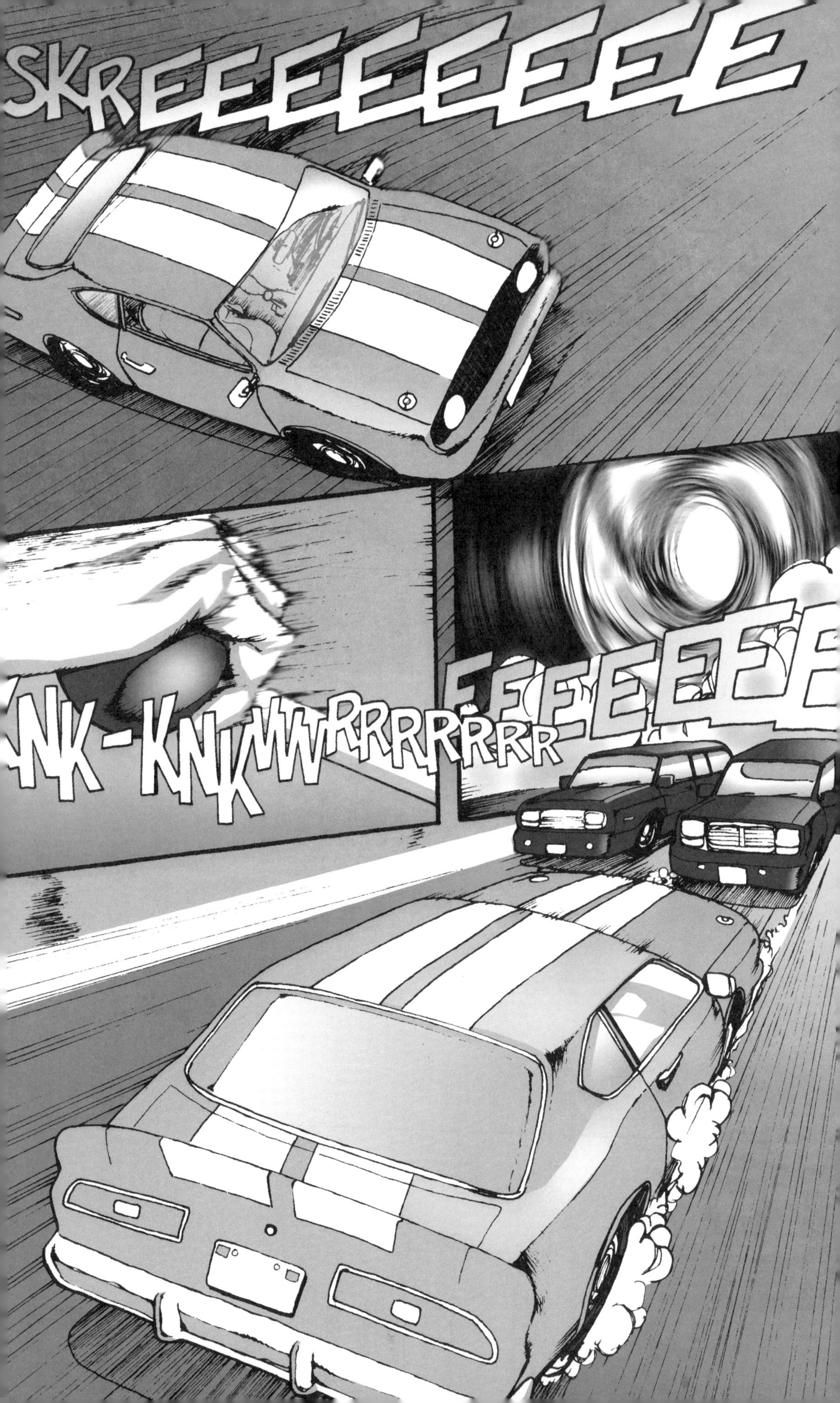
SKREEEEEEEEEE
NK-KNK
MWRRRRRRRR
EEEEEE

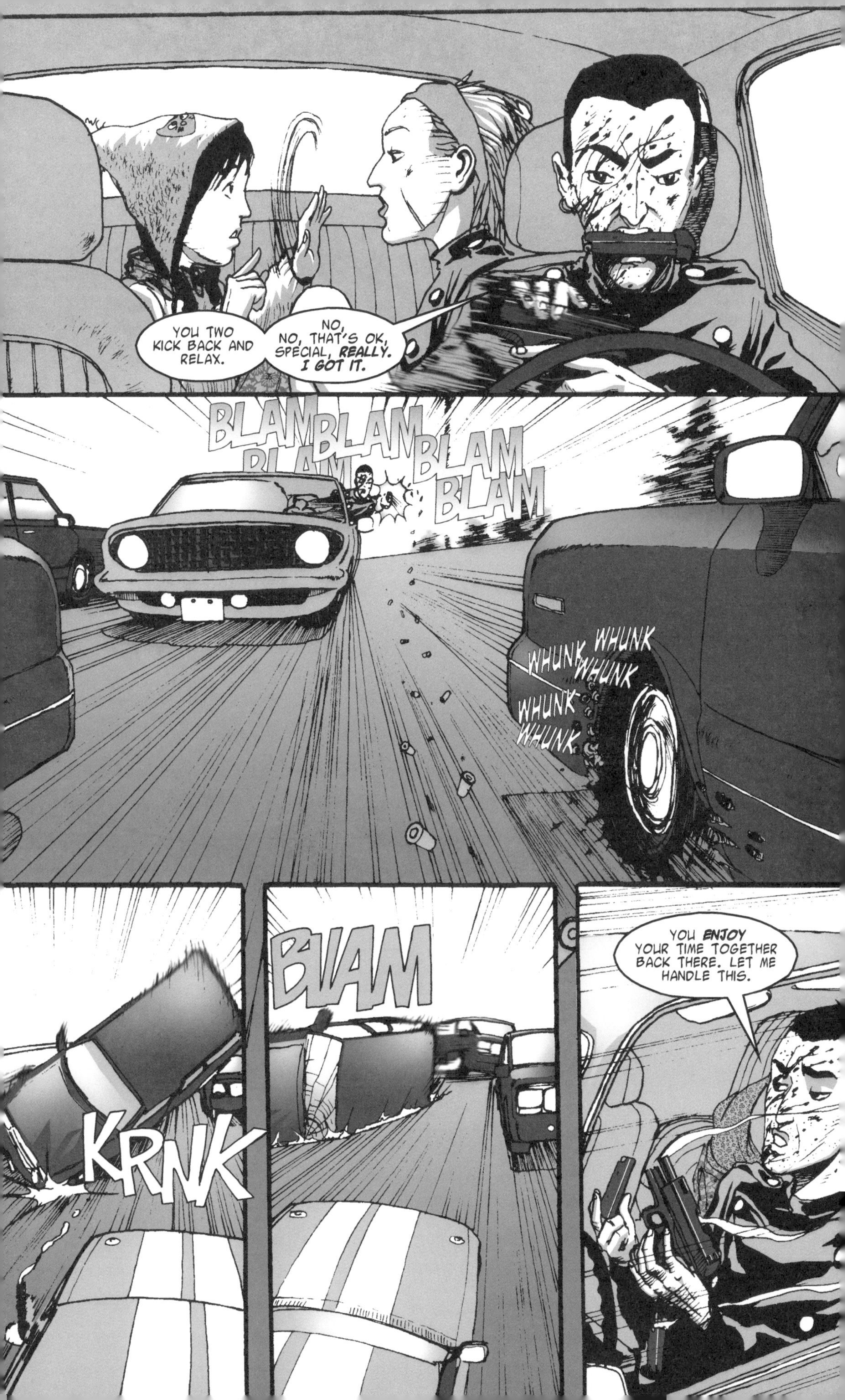
YOU TWO KICK BACK AND RELAX.
NO, NO, THAT'S OK, SPECIAL, **REALLY. I GOT IT.**
BLAM BLAM BLAM BLAM BLAM BLAM
WHUNK WHUNK WHUNK WHUNK WHUNK
KRNK
BLAM
YOU **ENJOY** YOUR TIME TOGETHER BACK THERE. LET ME HANDLE THIS.

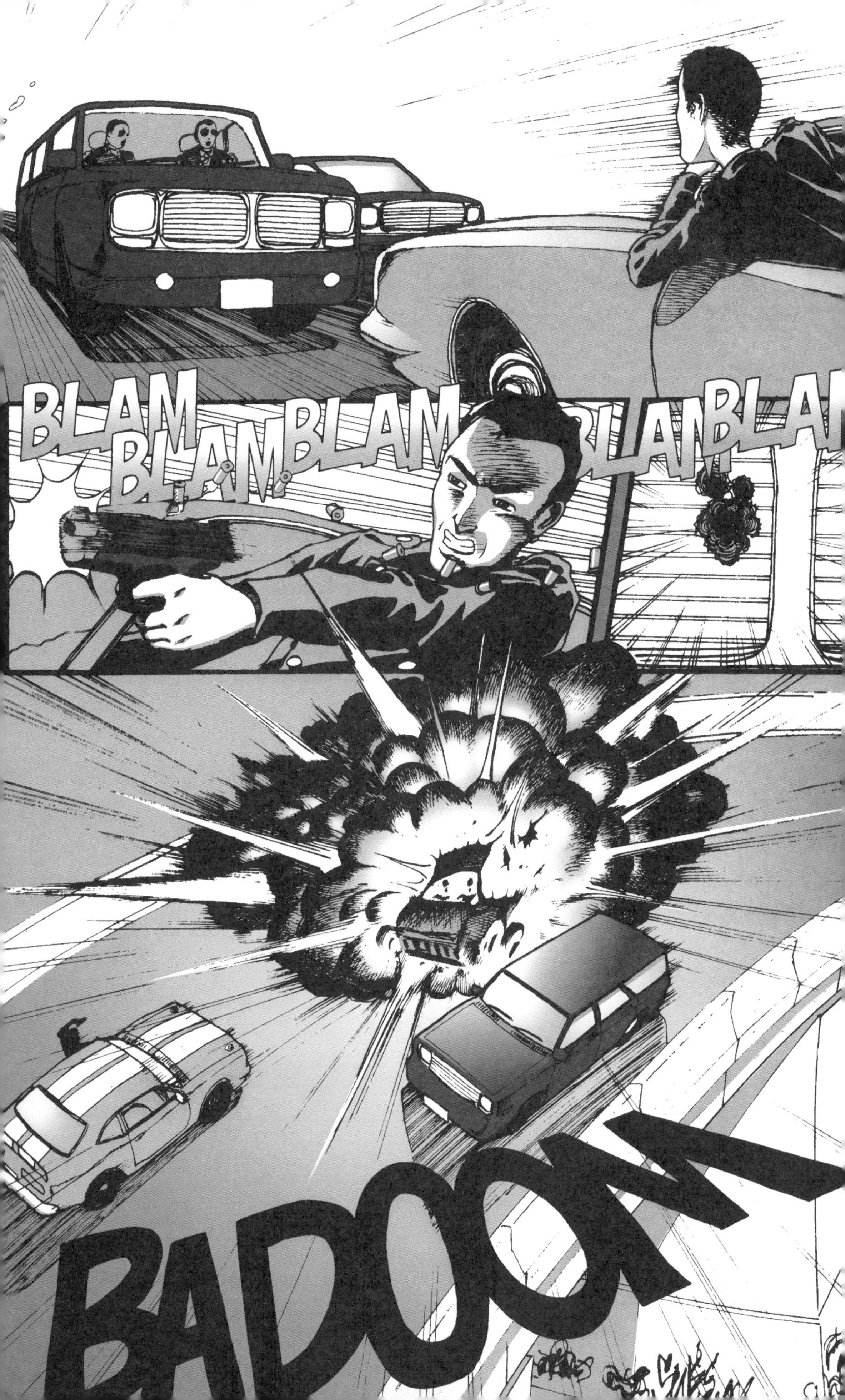
BLAM
BLAM BLAM BLAM
BLAM BLAM
BADOOM

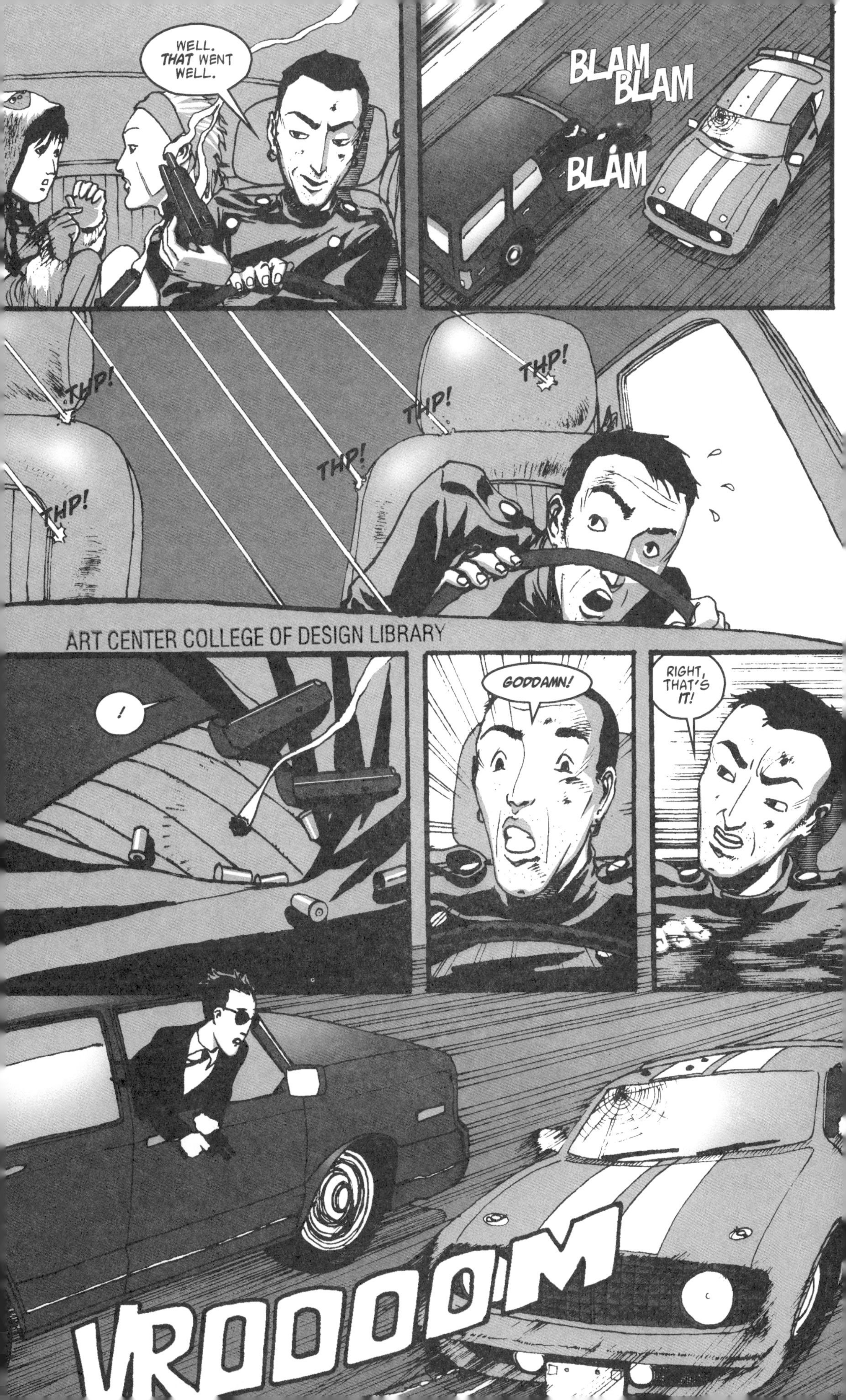
WELL. THAT WENT WELL.
BLAM
BLAM
BLAM
THP!
THP!
THP!
THP!
THP!
!
GODDAMN!
RIGHT, THAT'S IT!
VROOOOOM

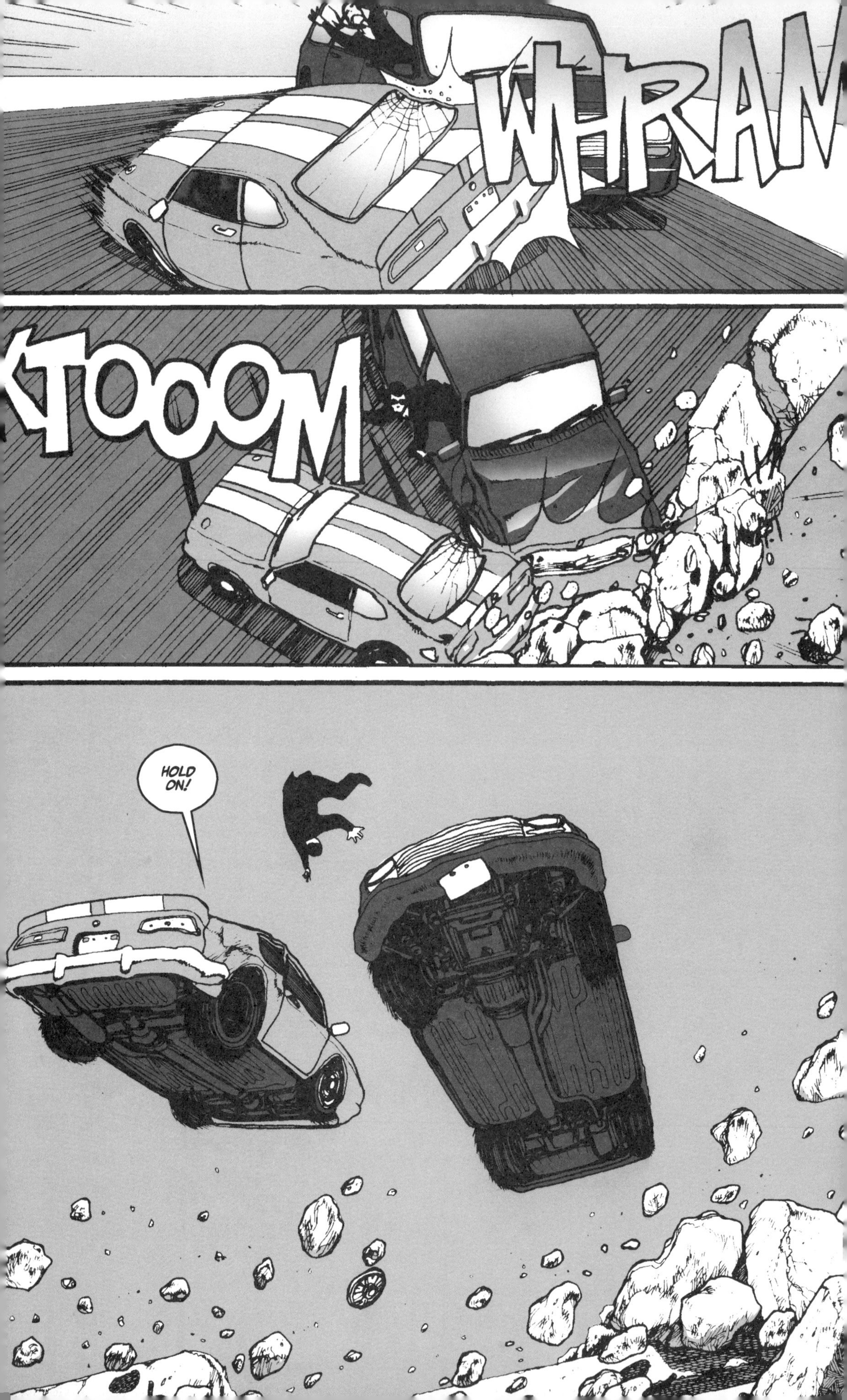
WHRAM
KTOOOM
HOLD ON!

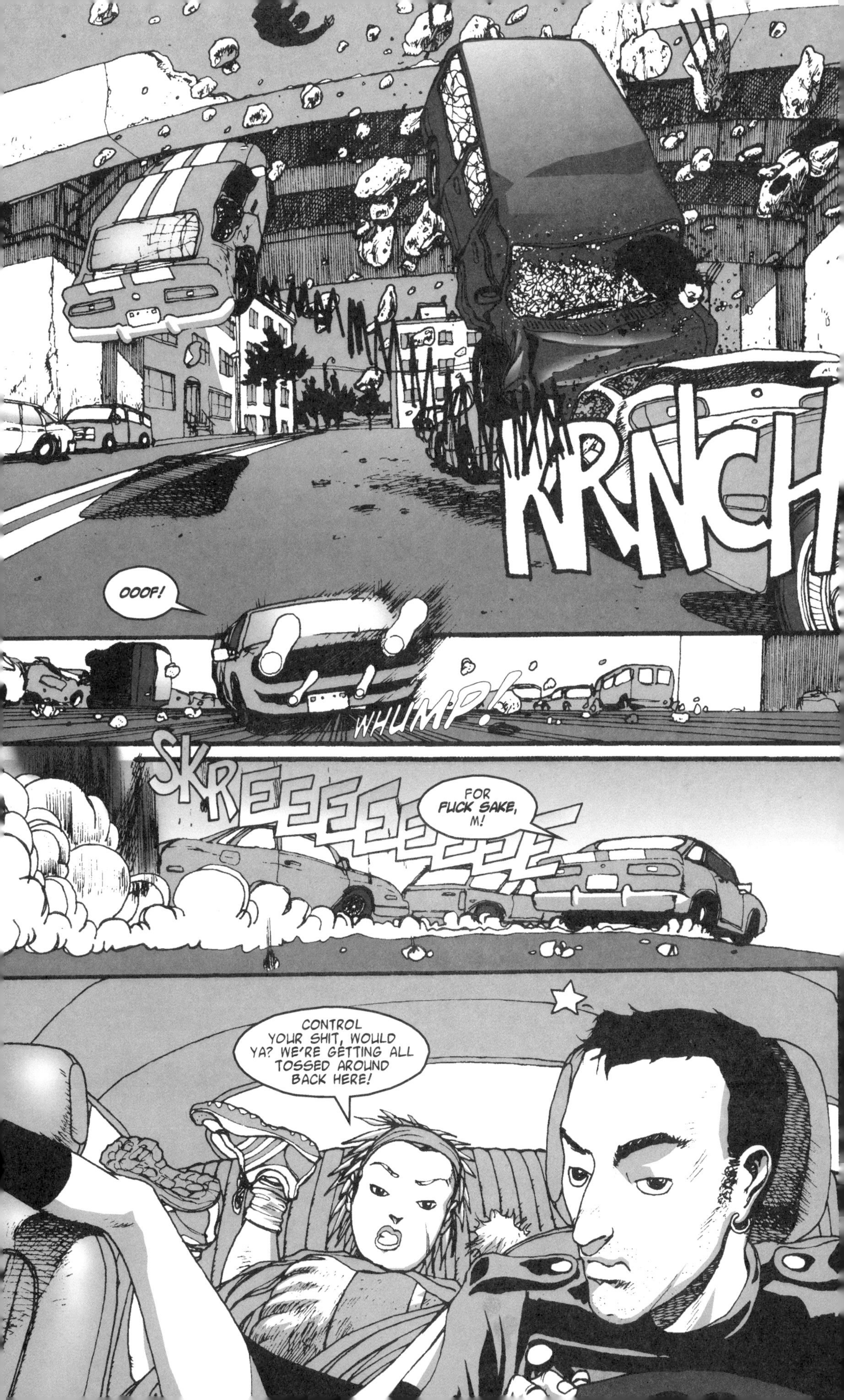
KRNCH
OOOF!
WHUMP!
SKREEEEEEEEEE
FOR FUCK SAKE, M!
CONTROL YOUR SHIT, WOULD YA? WE'RE GETTING ALL TOSSED AROUND BACK HERE!

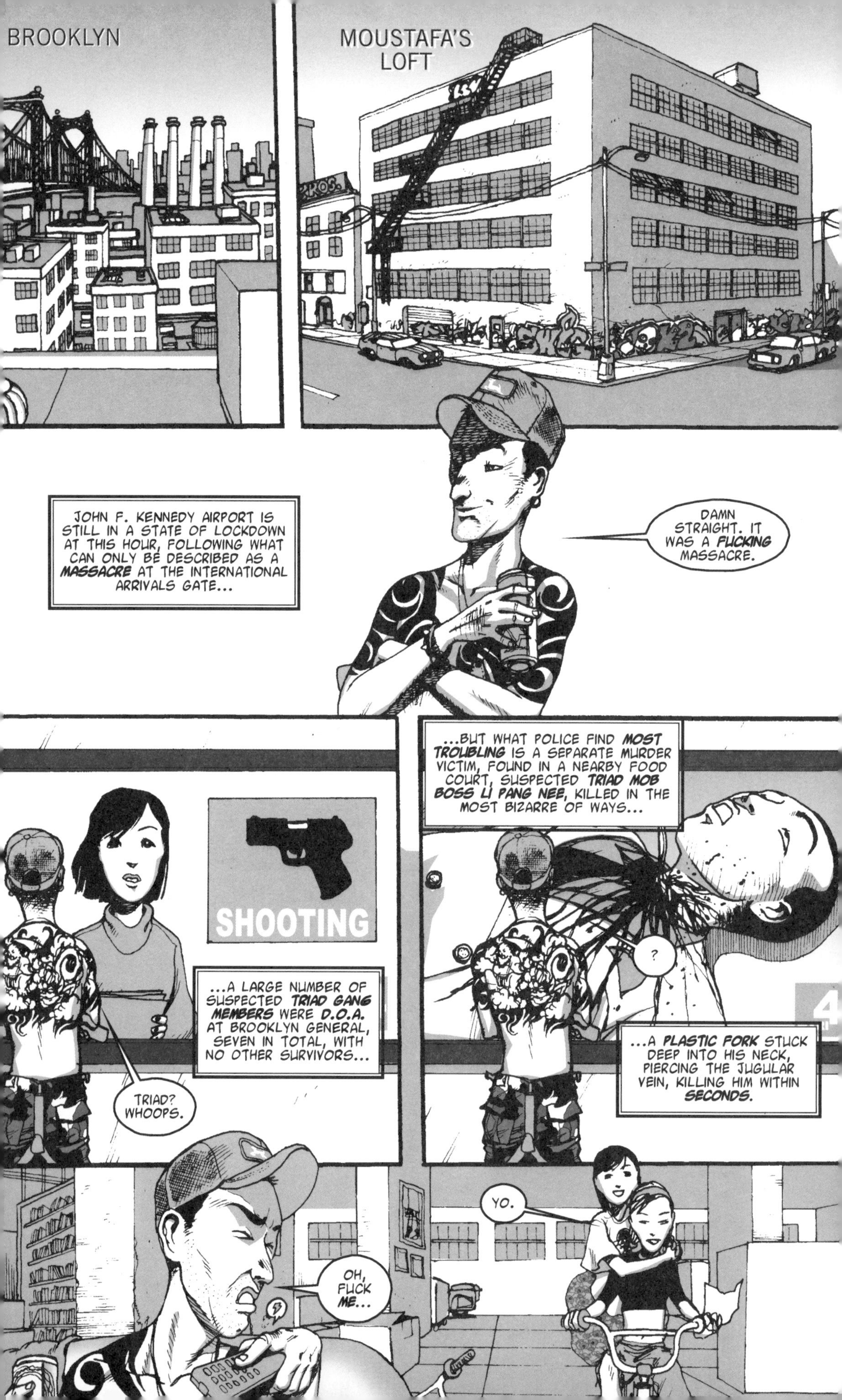

BROOKLYN
MOUSTAFA'S LOFT
JOHN F. KENNEDY AIRPORT IS STILL IN A STATE OF LOCKDOWN AT THIS HOUR, FOLLOWING WHAT CAN ONLY BE DESCRIBED AS A MASSACRE AT THE INTERNATIONAL ARRIVALS GATE...
DAMN STRAIGHT. IT WAS A FUCKING MASSACRE.
SHOOTING
...A LARGE NUMBER OF SUSPECTED TRIAD GANG MEMBERS WERE D.O.A. AT BROOKLYN GENERAL, SEVEN IN TOTAL, WITH NO OTHER SURVIVORS...
TRIAD? WHOOPS.
...BUT WHAT POLICE FIND MOST TROUBLING IS A SEPARATE MURDER VICTIM, FOUND IN A NEARBY FOOD COURT, SUSPECTED TRIAD MOB BOSS LI PANG NEE, KILLED IN THE MOST BIZARRE OF WAYS...
?
...A PLASTIC FORK STUCK DEEP INTO HIS NECK, PIERCING THE JUGULAR VEIN, KILLING HIM WITHIN SECONDS.
YO.
OH, FUCK ME...

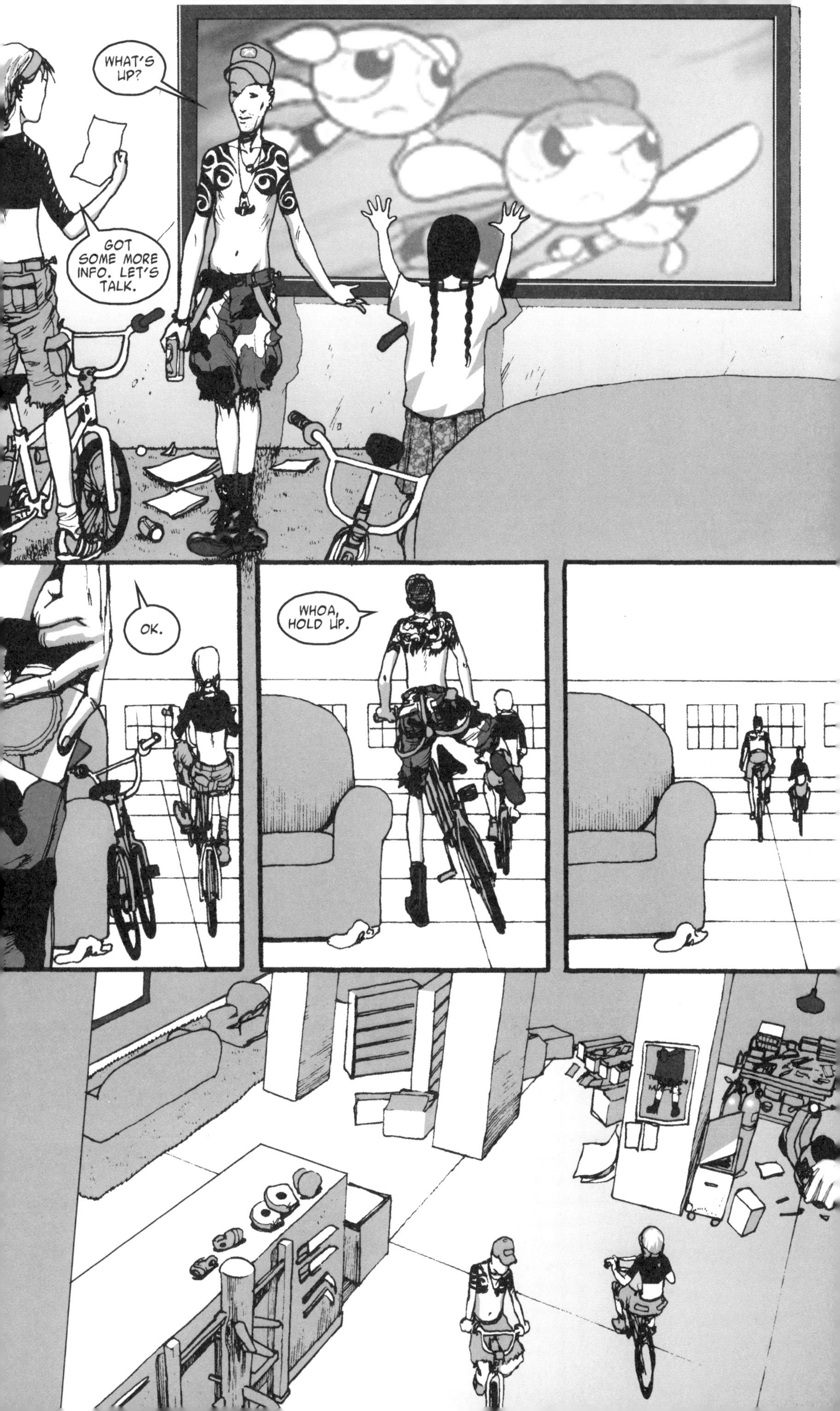
WHAT'S UP?
GOT SOME MORE INFO. LET'S TALK.
OK.
WHOA, HOLD UP.

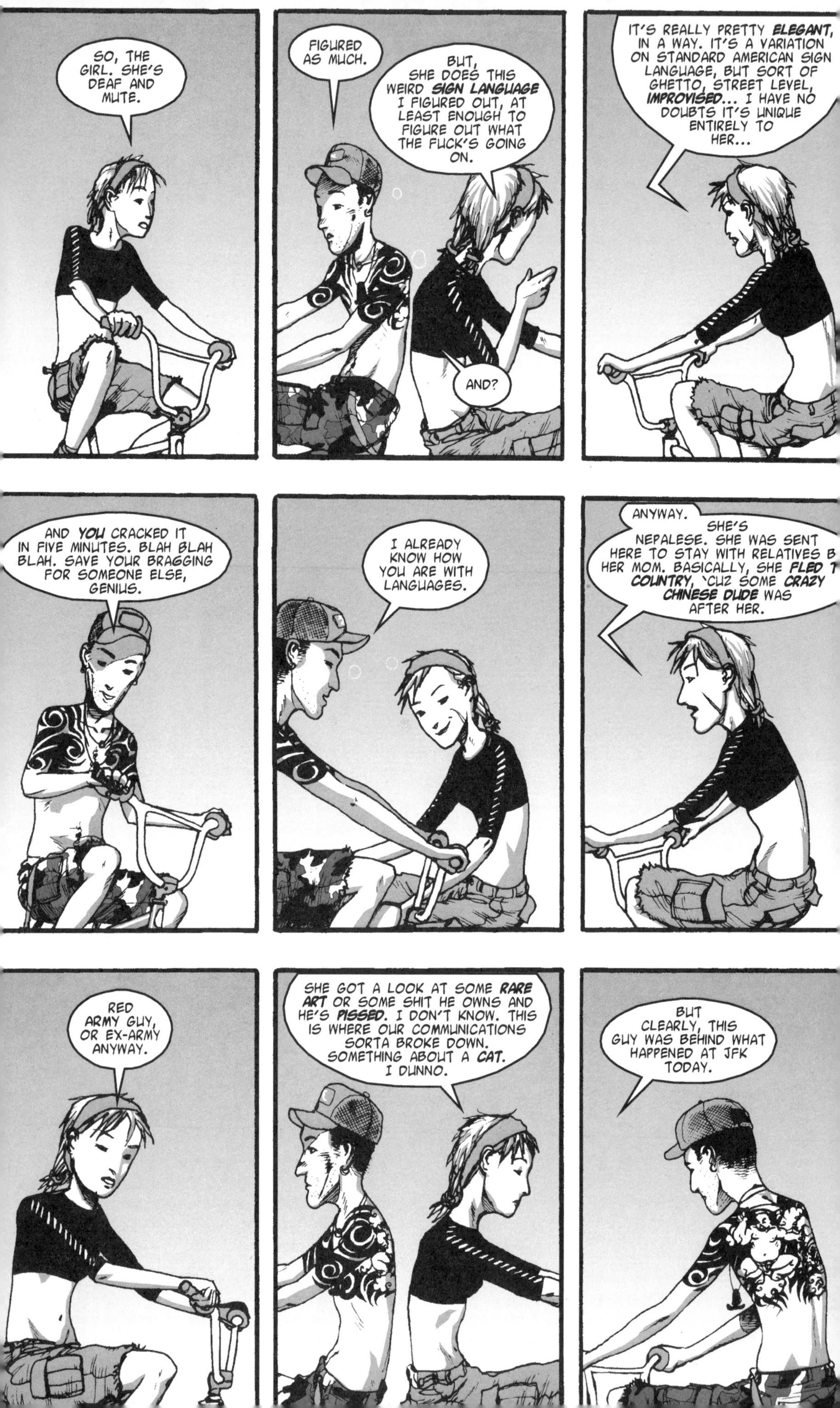
SO, THE GIRL. SHE'S DEAF AND MUTE.
FIGURED AS MUCH.
BUT, SHE DOES THIS WEIRD **SIGN LANGUAGE** I FIGURED OUT, AT LEAST ENOUGH TO FIGURE OUT WHAT THE FUCK'S GOING ON.
AND?
IT'S REALLY PRETTY **ELEGANT**, IN A WAY. IT'S A VARIATION ON STANDARD AMERICAN SIGN LANGUAGE, BUT SORT OF GHETTO, STREET LEVEL, **IMPROVISED**... I HAVE NO DOUBTS IT'S UNIQUE ENTIRELY TO HER...
AND **YOU** CRACKED IT IN FIVE MINUTES. BLAH BLAH BLAH. SAVE YOUR BRAGGING FOR SOMEONE ELSE, GENIUS.
I ALREADY KNOW HOW YOU ARE WITH LANGUAGES.
ANYWAY.
SHE'S NEPALESE. SHE WAS SENT HERE TO STAY WITH RELATIVES B HER MOM. BASICALLY, SHE **FLED T COUNTRY**, 'CUZ SOME **CRAZY CHINESE DUDE** WAS AFTER HER.
RED ARMY GUY, OR EX-ARMY ANYWAY.
SHE GOT A LOOK AT SOME **RARE ART** OR SOME SHIT HE OWNS AND HE'S **PISSED**. I DON'T KNOW. THIS IS WHERE OUR COMMUNICATIONS SORTA BROKE DOWN. SOMETHING ABOUT A **CAT**. I DUNNO.
BUT CLEARLY, THIS GUY WAS BEHIND WHAT HAPPENED AT JFK TODAY.

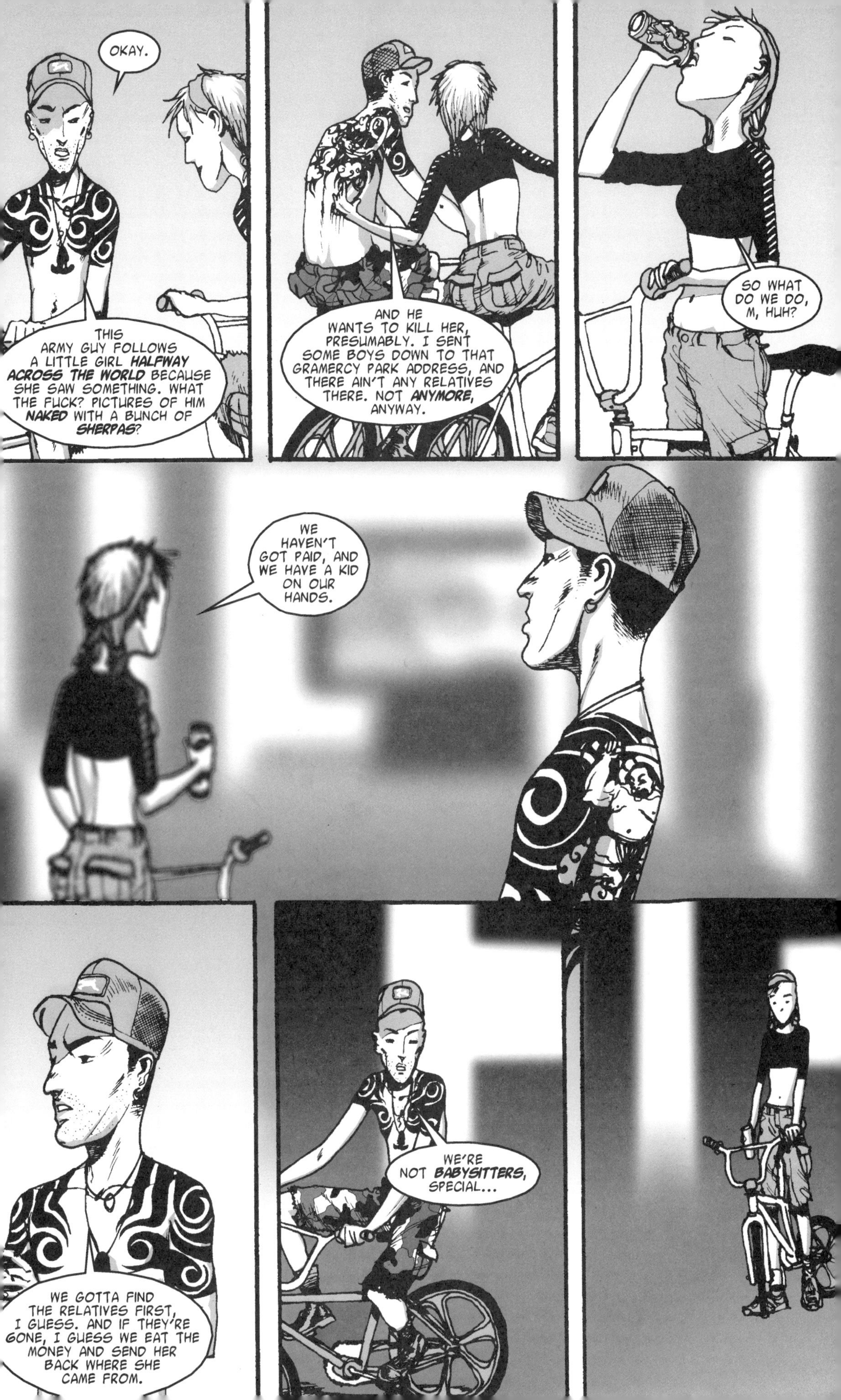

OKAY.
THIS ARMY GUY FOLLOWS A LITTLE GIRL HALFWAY ACROSS THE WORLD BECAUSE SHE SAW SOMETHING. WHAT THE FUCK? PICTURES OF HIM NAKED WITH A BUNCH OF SHERPAS?
AND HE WANTS TO KILL HER, PRESUMABLY. I SENT SOME BOYS DOWN TO THAT GRAMERCY PARK ADDRESS, AND THERE AIN'T ANY RELATIVES THERE. NOT ANYMORE, ANYWAY.
SO WHAT DO WE DO, M, HUH?
WE HAVEN'T GOT PAID, AND WE HAVE A KID ON OUR HANDS.
WE GOTTA FIND THE RELATIVES FIRST, I GUESS. AND IF THEY'RE GONE, I GUESS WE EAT THE MONEY AND SEND HER BACK WHERE SHE CAME FROM.
WE'RE NOT BABYSITTERS, SPECIAL...

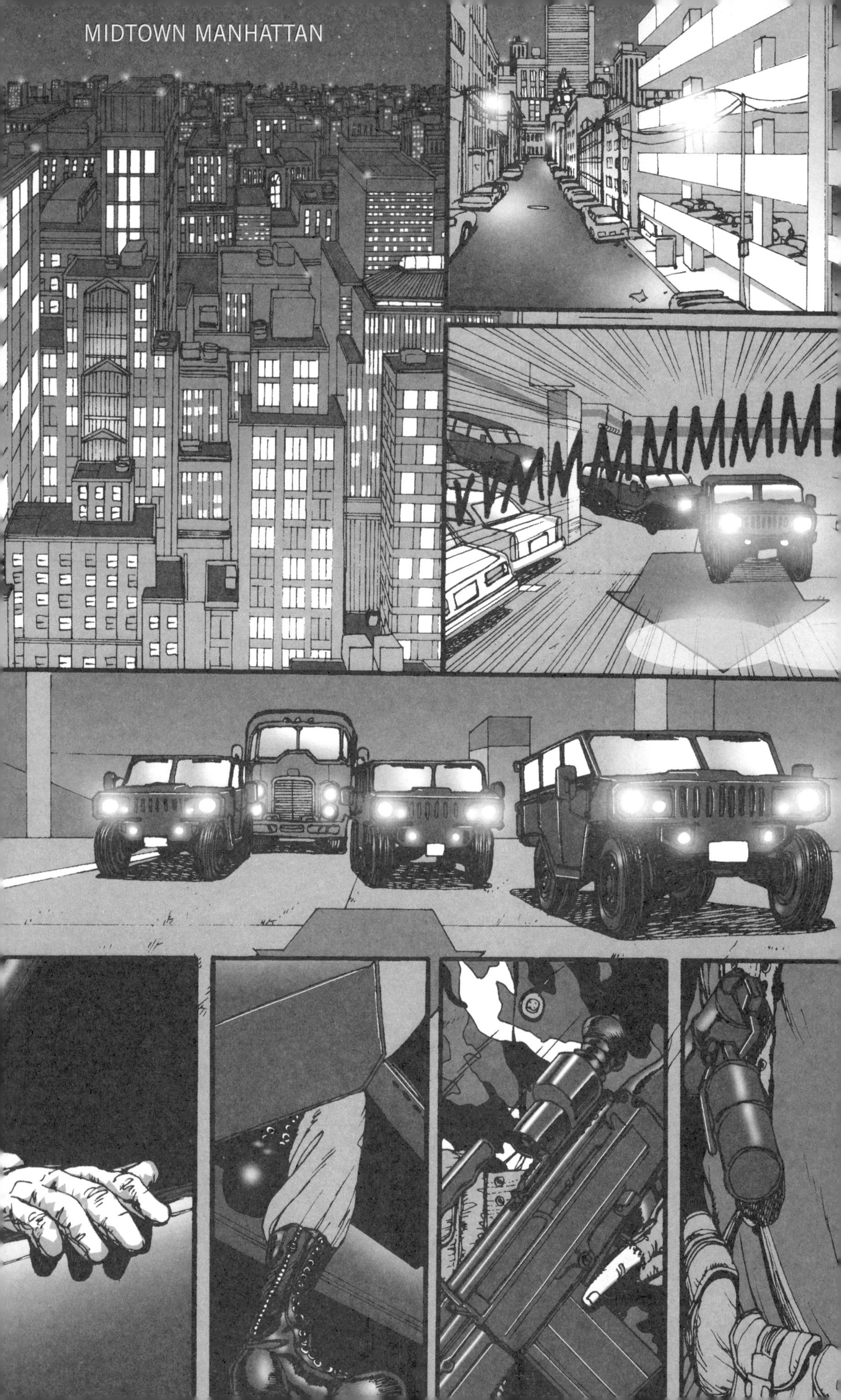
MIDTOWN MANHATTAN
VMMMMMMMMMMM

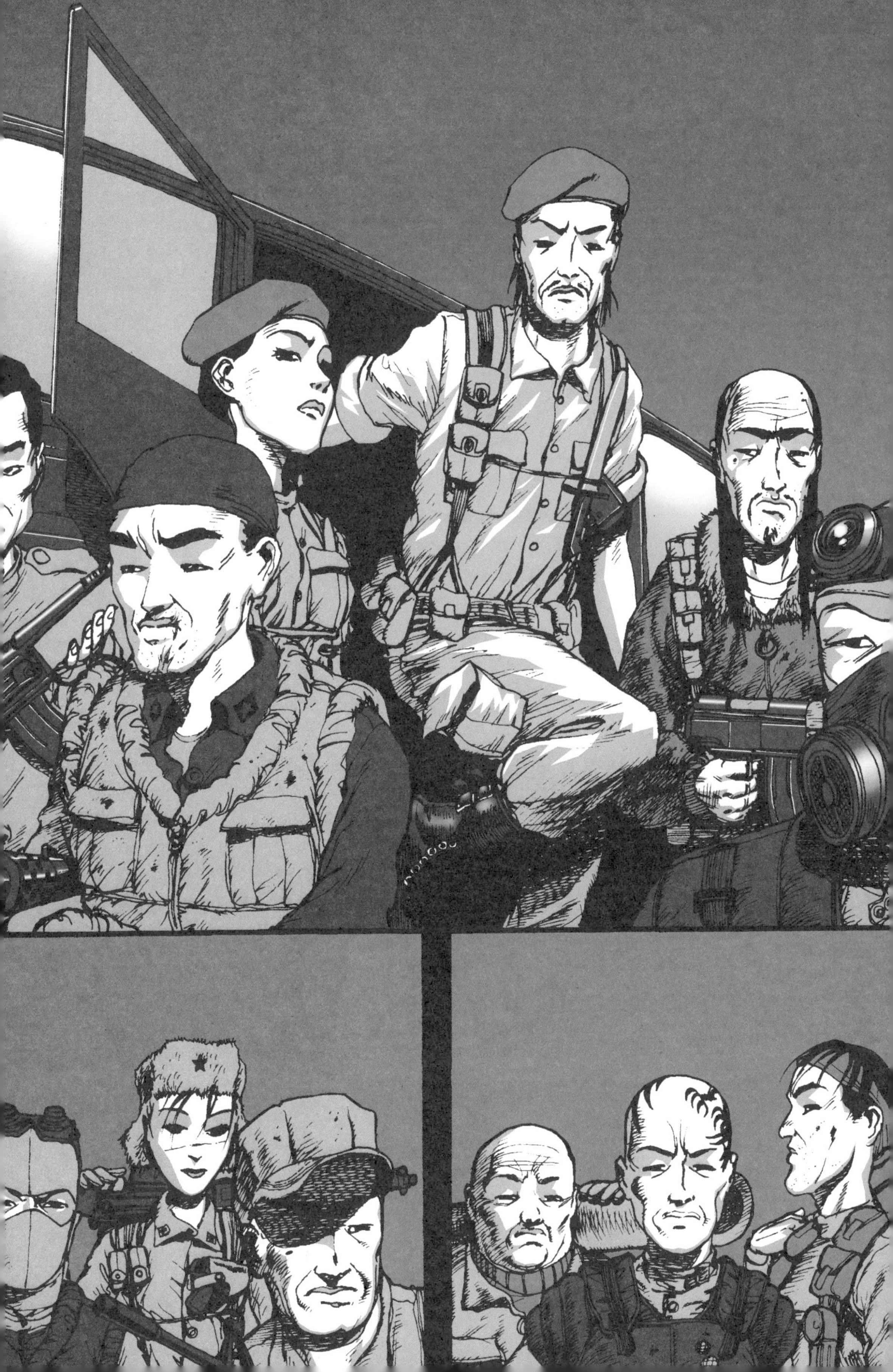

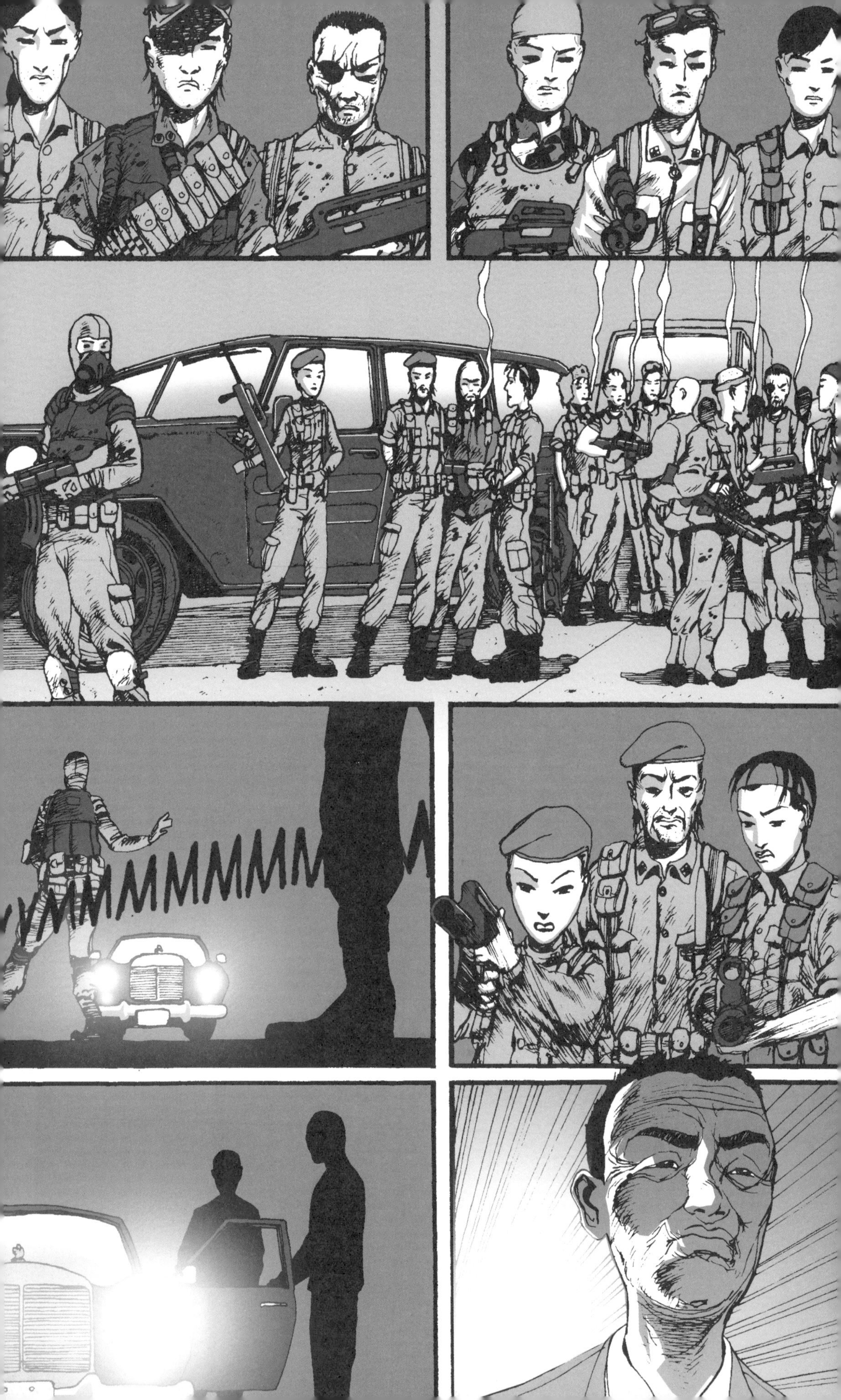
MMMMMMMMMM

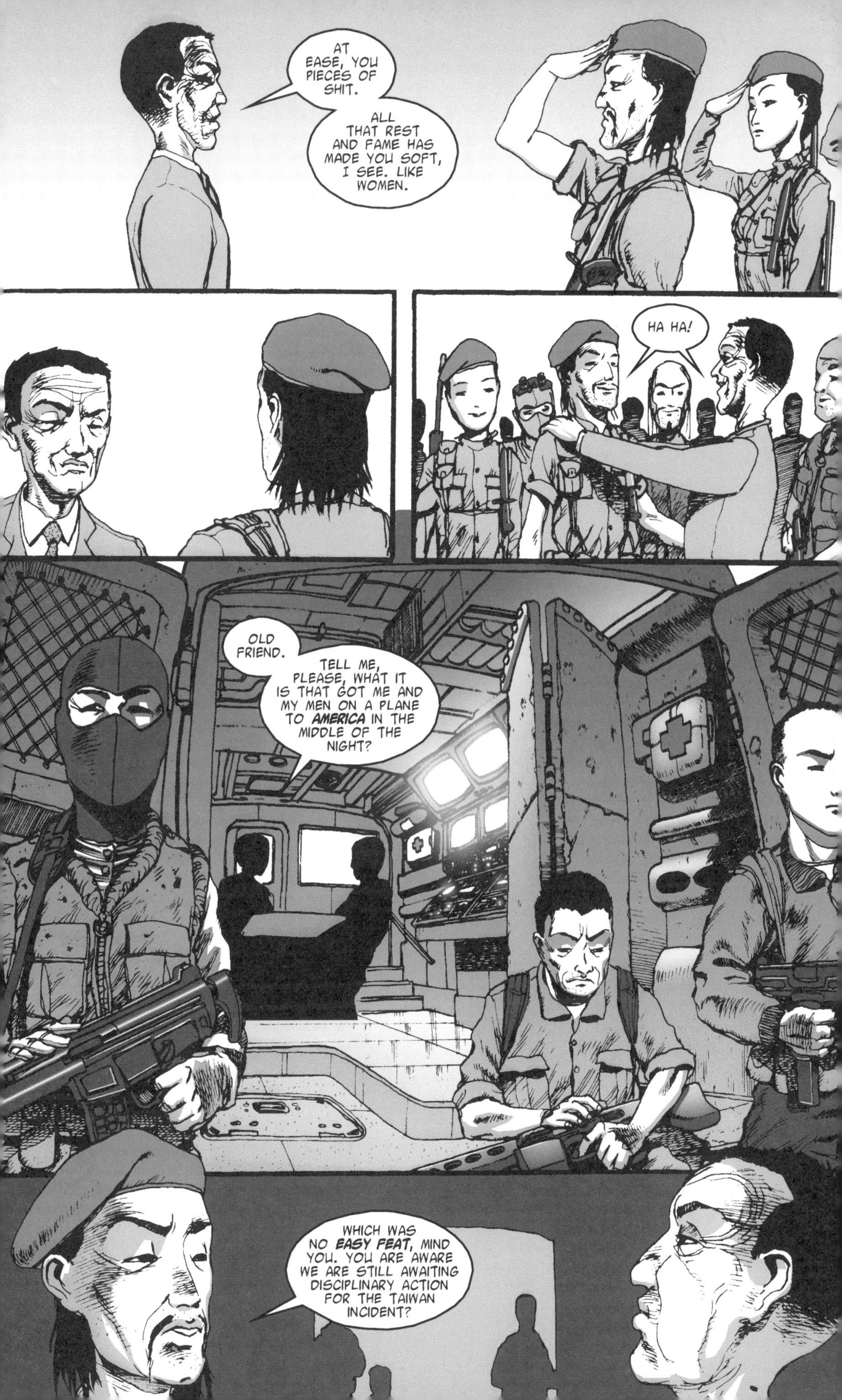
AT EASE, YOU PIECES OF SHIT.
ALL THAT REST AND FAME HAS MADE YOU SOFT, I SEE. LIKE WOMEN.
HA HA!
OLD FRIEND.
TELL ME, PLEASE, WHAT IT IS THAT GOT ME AND MY MEN ON A PLANE TO AMERICA IN THE MIDDLE OF THE NIGHT?
WHICH WAS NO EASY FEAT, MIND YOU. YOU ARE AWARE WE ARE STILL AWAITING DISCIPLINARY ACTION FOR THE TAIWAN INCIDENT?

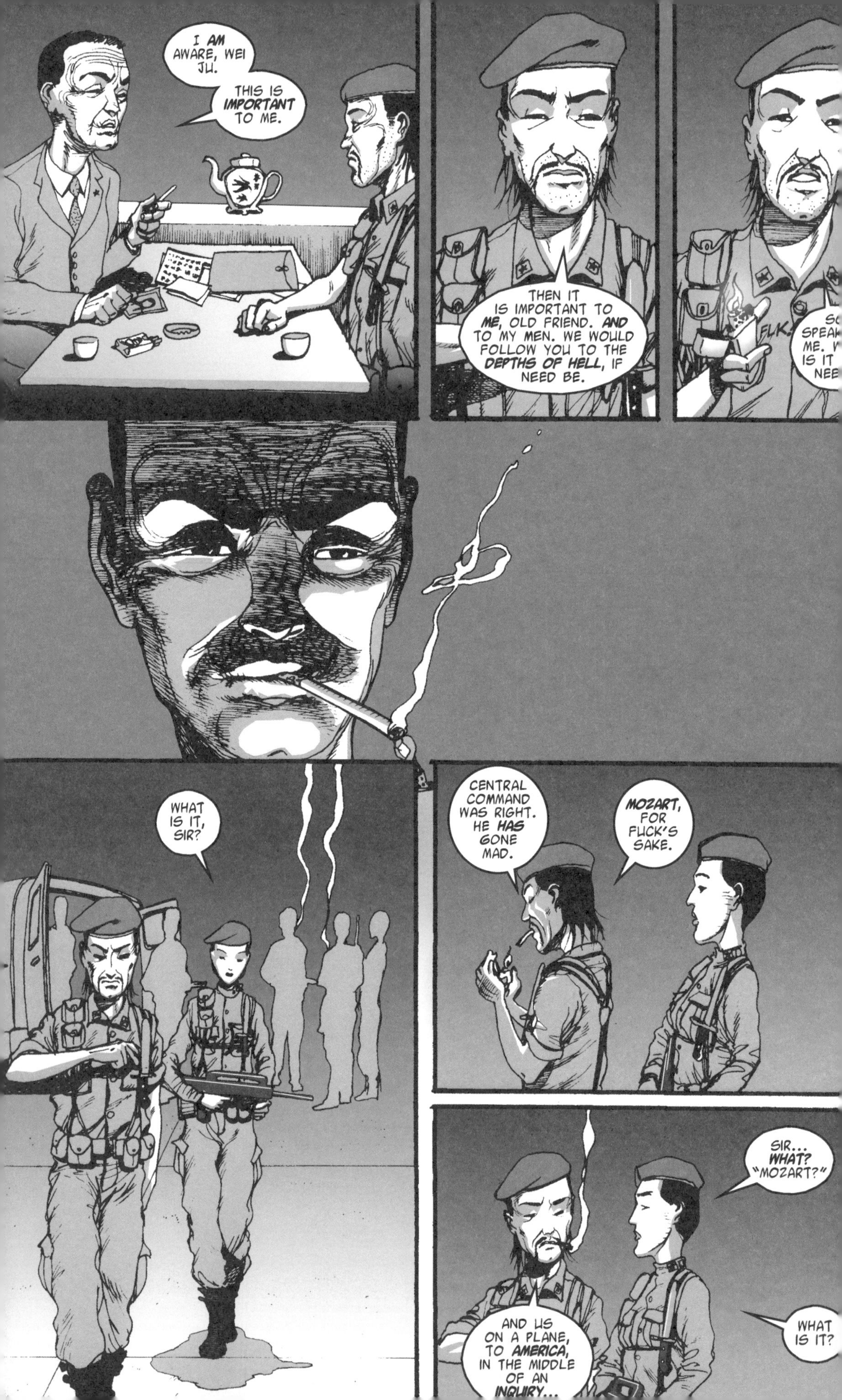
I AM AWARE, WEI JU.
THIS IS IMPORTANT TO ME.
THEN IT IS IMPORTANT TO ME, OLD FRIEND. AND TO MY MEN. WE WOULD FOLLOW YOU TO THE DEPTHS OF HELL, IF NEED BE.
FLK.
WHAT IS IT, SIR?
CENTRAL COMMAND WAS RIGHT. HE HAS GONE MAD.
MOZART, FOR FUCK'S SAKE.
SIR... WHAT? "MOZART?"
AND US ON A PLANE, TO AMERICA, IN THE MIDDLE OF AN INQUIRY...
WHAT IS IT?

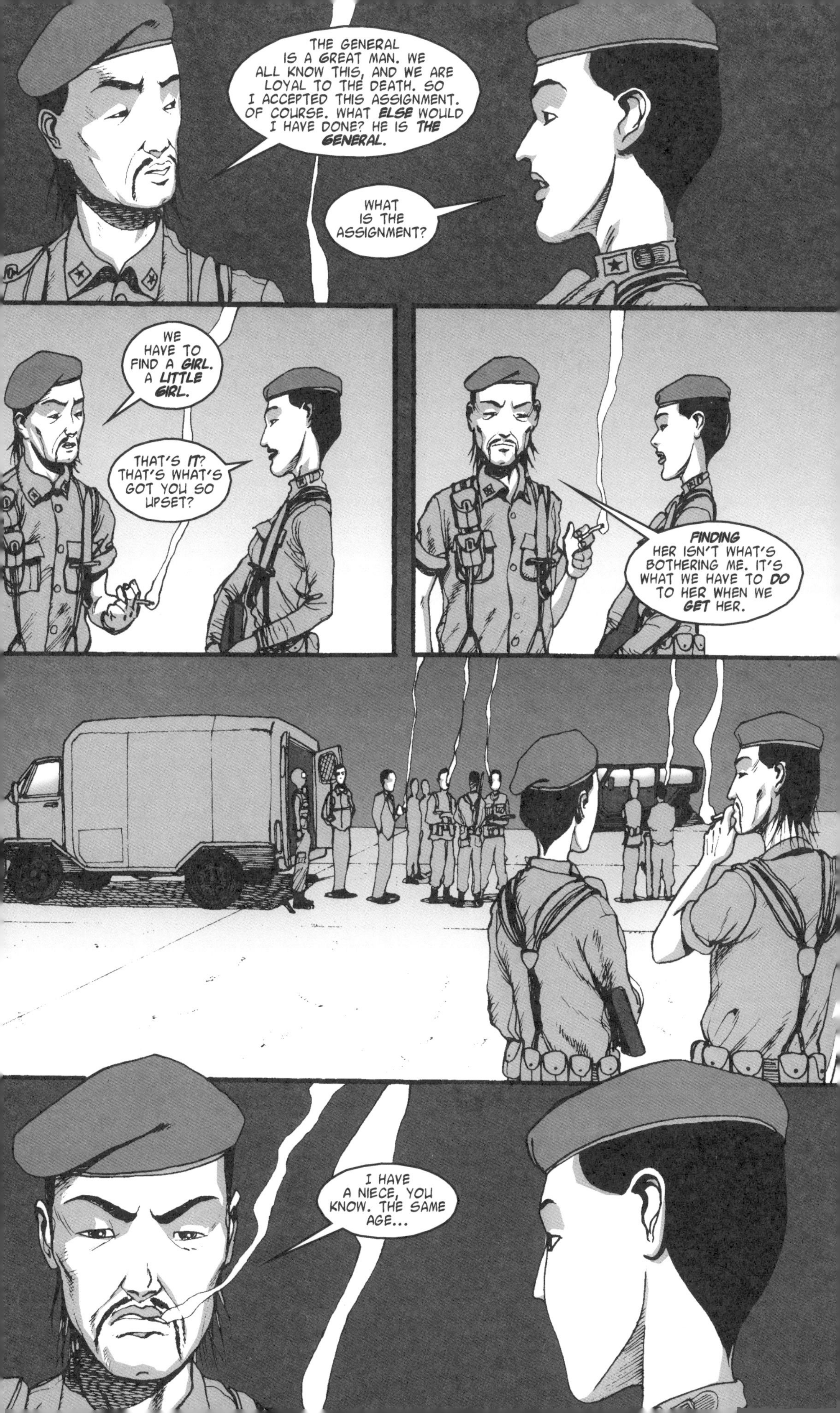
THE GENERAL IS A GREAT MAN. WE ALL KNOW THIS, AND WE ARE LOYAL TO THE DEATH. SO I ACCEPTED THIS ASSIGNMENT. OF COURSE. WHAT ELSE WOULD I HAVE DONE? HE IS THE GENERAL.
WHAT IS THE ASSIGNMENT?
WE HAVE TO FIND A GIRL. A LITTLE GIRL.
THAT'S IT? THAT'S WHAT'S GOT YOU SO UPSET?
FINDING HER ISN'T WHAT'S BOTHERING ME. IT'S WHAT WE HAVE TO DO TO HER WHEN WE GET HER.
I HAVE A NIECE, YOU KNOW. THE SAME AGE...

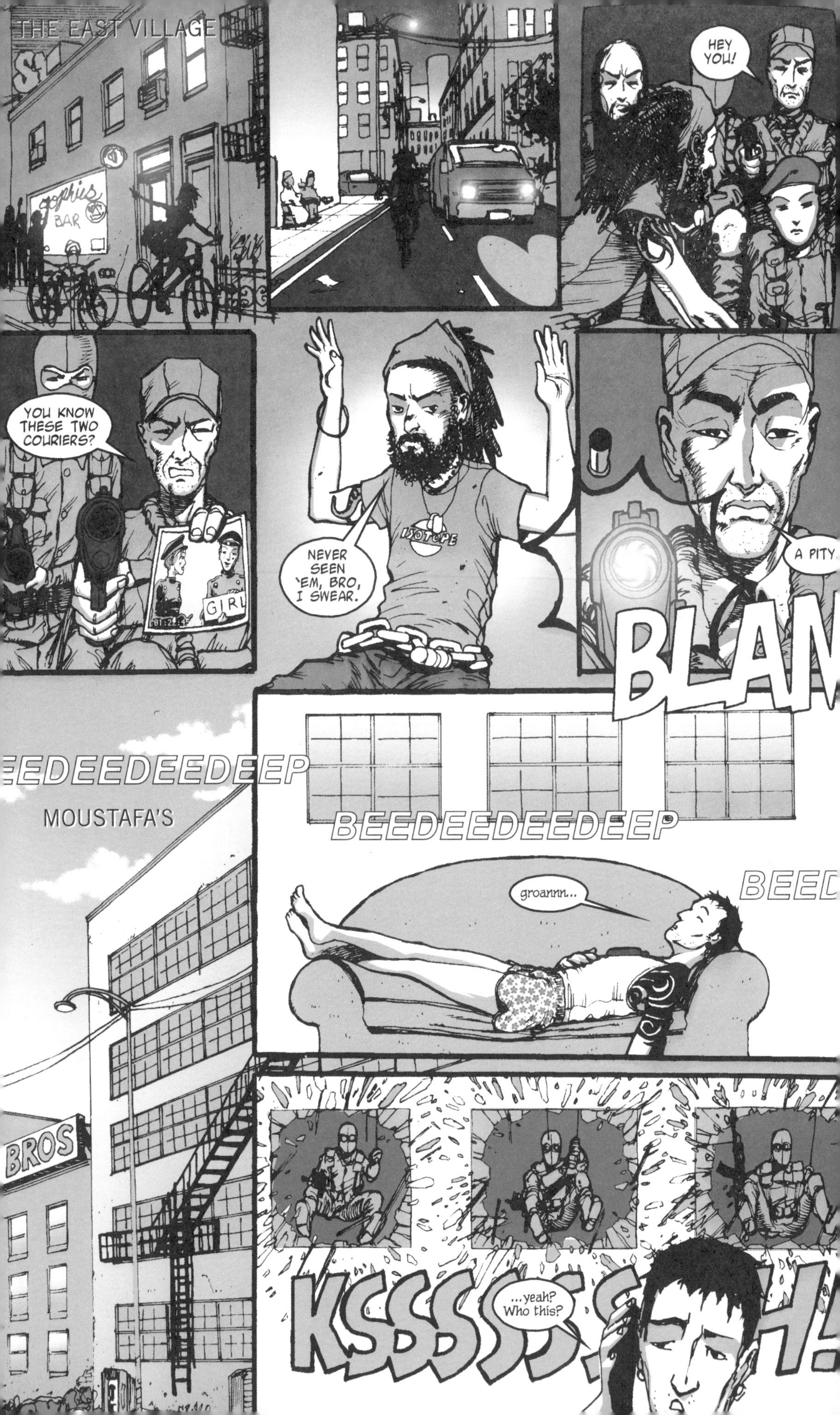

THE EAST VILLAGE
Sophie's
BAR
HEY YOU!
YOU KNOW THESE TWO COURIERS?
GIRL
NEVER SEEN 'EM, BRO, I SWEAR.
ISOTOPE
A PITY.
BLAM
EEDEEEDEEEDEEP
MOUSTAFA'S
BEEDEEEDEEEDEEP
BEED
groannn...
BROS
KSSSSSSH!
...yeah? Who this?

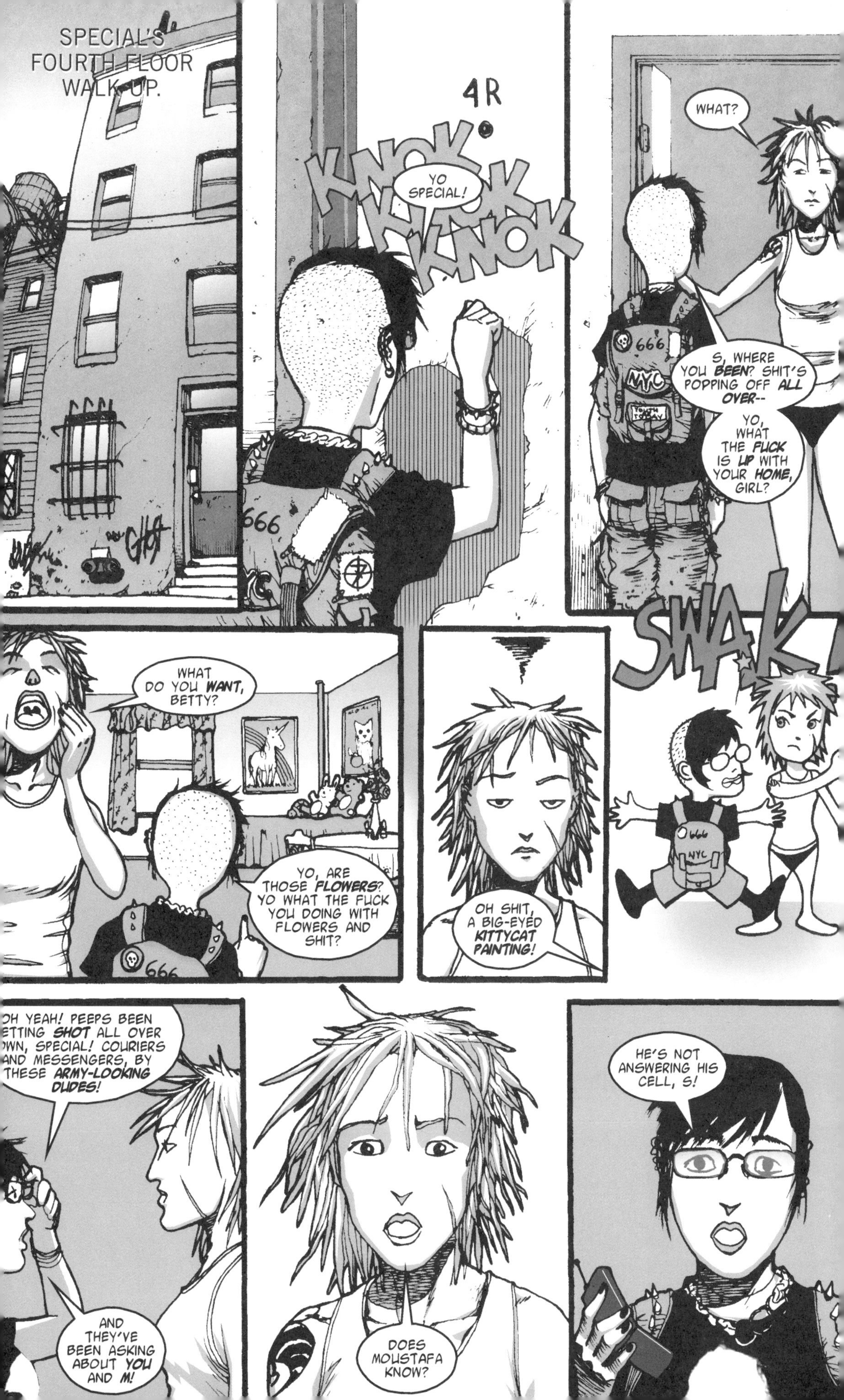
SPECIAL'S FOURTH FLOOR WALK-UP.
4R
KNOK KNOK KNOK
YO SPECIAL!
WHAT?
S, WHERE YOU BEEN? SHIT'S POPPING OFF ALL OVER--
YO, WHAT THE FUCK IS UP WITH YOUR HOME, GIRL?
WHAT DO YOU WANT, BETTY?
YO, ARE THOSE FLOWERS? YO WHAT THE FUCK YOU DOING WITH FLOWERS AND SHIT?
OH SHIT, A BIG-EYED KITTYCAT PAINTING!
SWAK
OH YEAH! PEEPS BEEN GETTING SHOT ALL OVER TOWN, SPECIAL! COURIERS AND MESSENGERS, BY THESE ARMY-LOOKING DUDES!
AND THEY'VE BEEN ASKING ABOUT YOU AND M!
DOES MOUSTAFA KNOW?
HE'S NOT ANSWERING HIS CELL, S!

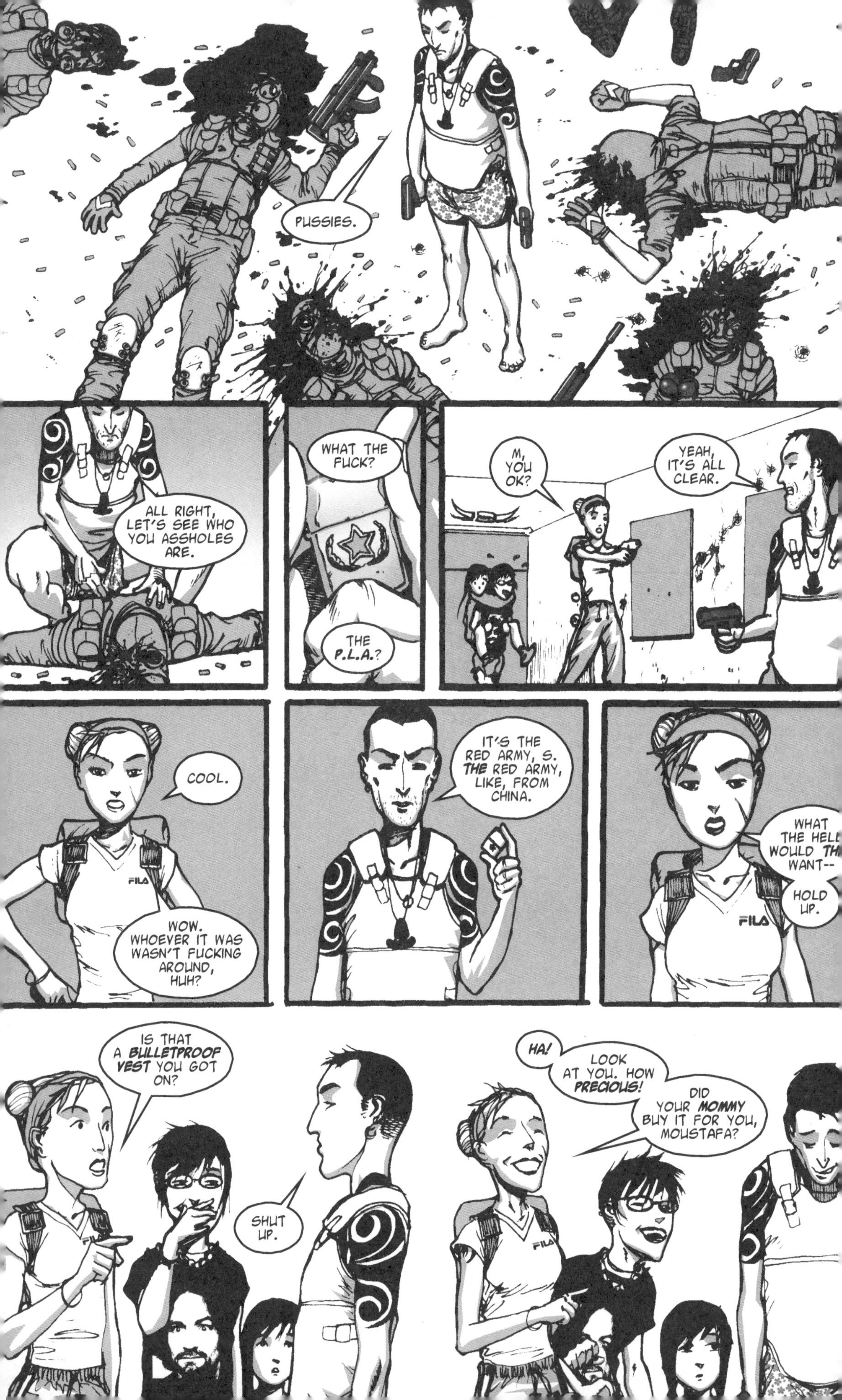
PUSSIES.
ALL RIGHT, LET'S SEE WHO YOU ASSHOLES ARE.
WHAT THE FUCK?
THE P.L.A.?
M, YOU OK?
YEAH, IT'S ALL CLEAR.
COOL.
WOW. WHOEVER IT WAS WASN'T FUCKING AROUND, HUH?
IT'S THE RED ARMY, S. THE RED ARMY, LIKE, FROM CHINA.
WHAT THE HELL WOULD TH WANT--
HOLD UP.
IS THAT A BULLETPROOF VEST YOU GOT ON?
SHUT UP.
HA!
LOOK AT YOU. HOW PRECIOUS!
DID YOUR MOMMY BUY IT FOR YOU, MOUSTAFA?

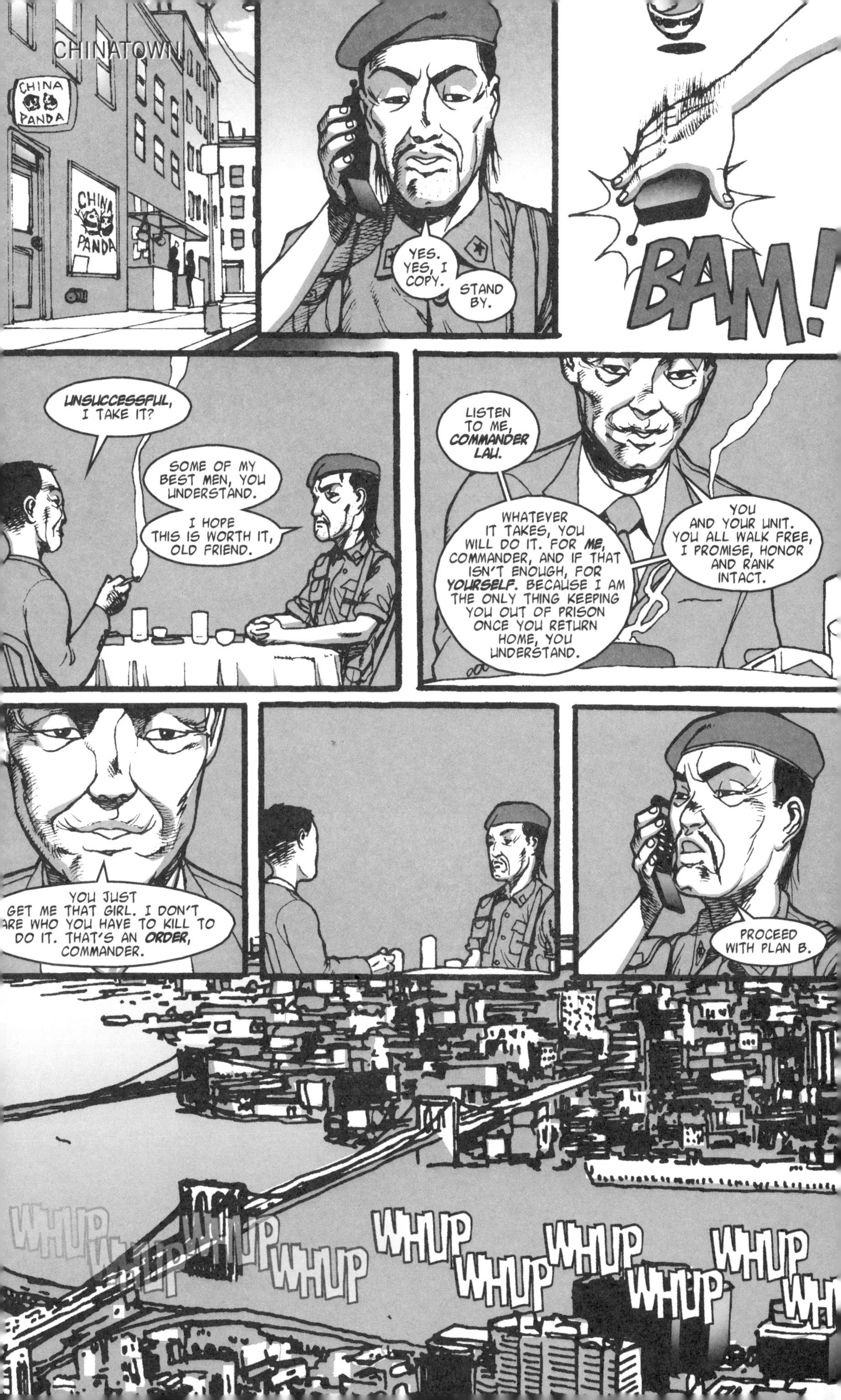
CHINATOWN
CHINA PANDA
CHINA PANDA
YES. YES, I COPY.
STAND BY.
BAM!
UNSUCCESSFUL, I TAKE IT?
SOME OF MY BEST MEN, YOU UNDERSTAND.
I HOPE THIS IS WORTH IT, OLD FRIEND.
LISTEN TO ME, COMMANDER LAU.
WHATEVER IT TAKES, YOU WILL DO IT. FOR ME, COMMANDER, AND IF THAT ISN'T ENOUGH, FOR YOURSELF. BECAUSE I AM THE ONLY THING KEEPING YOU OUT OF PRISON ONCE YOU RETURN HOME, YOU UNDERSTAND.
YOU AND YOUR UNIT. YOU ALL WALK FREE, I PROMISE, HONOR AND RANK INTACT.
YOU JUST GET ME THAT GIRL. I DON'T ARE WHO YOU HAVE TO KILL TO DO IT. THAT'S AN ORDER, COMMANDER.
PROCEED WITH PLAN B.
WHUP WHUP WHUP WHUP WHUP WHUP WHUP WHUP WHUP WHUP

THE EAST-RIVER.

WHUP WHUP WHUP WHUP

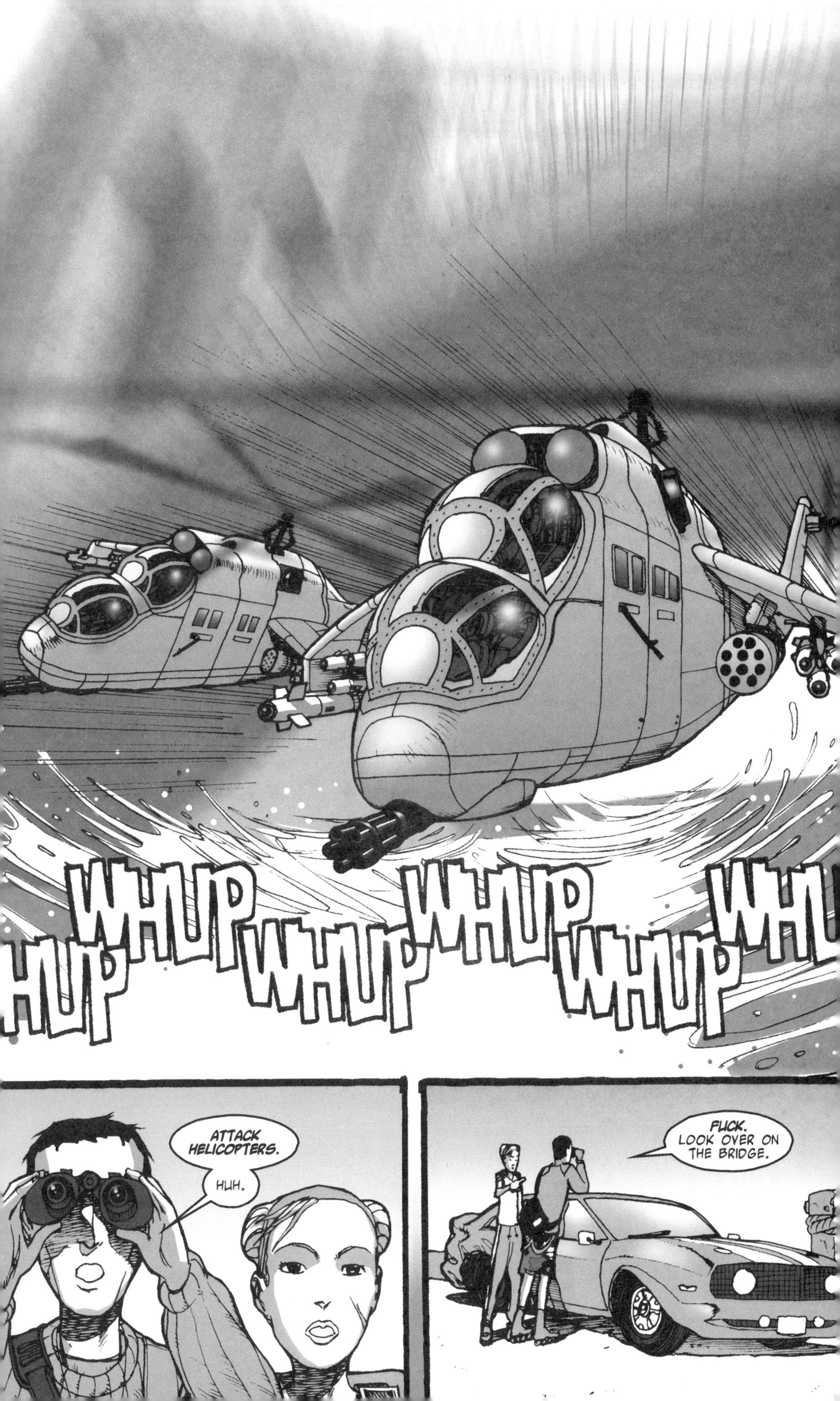
HUP WHUP WHUP WHUP WHUP WHU
ATTACK HELICOPTERS.
HUH.
FUCK. LOOK OVER ON THE BRIDGE.

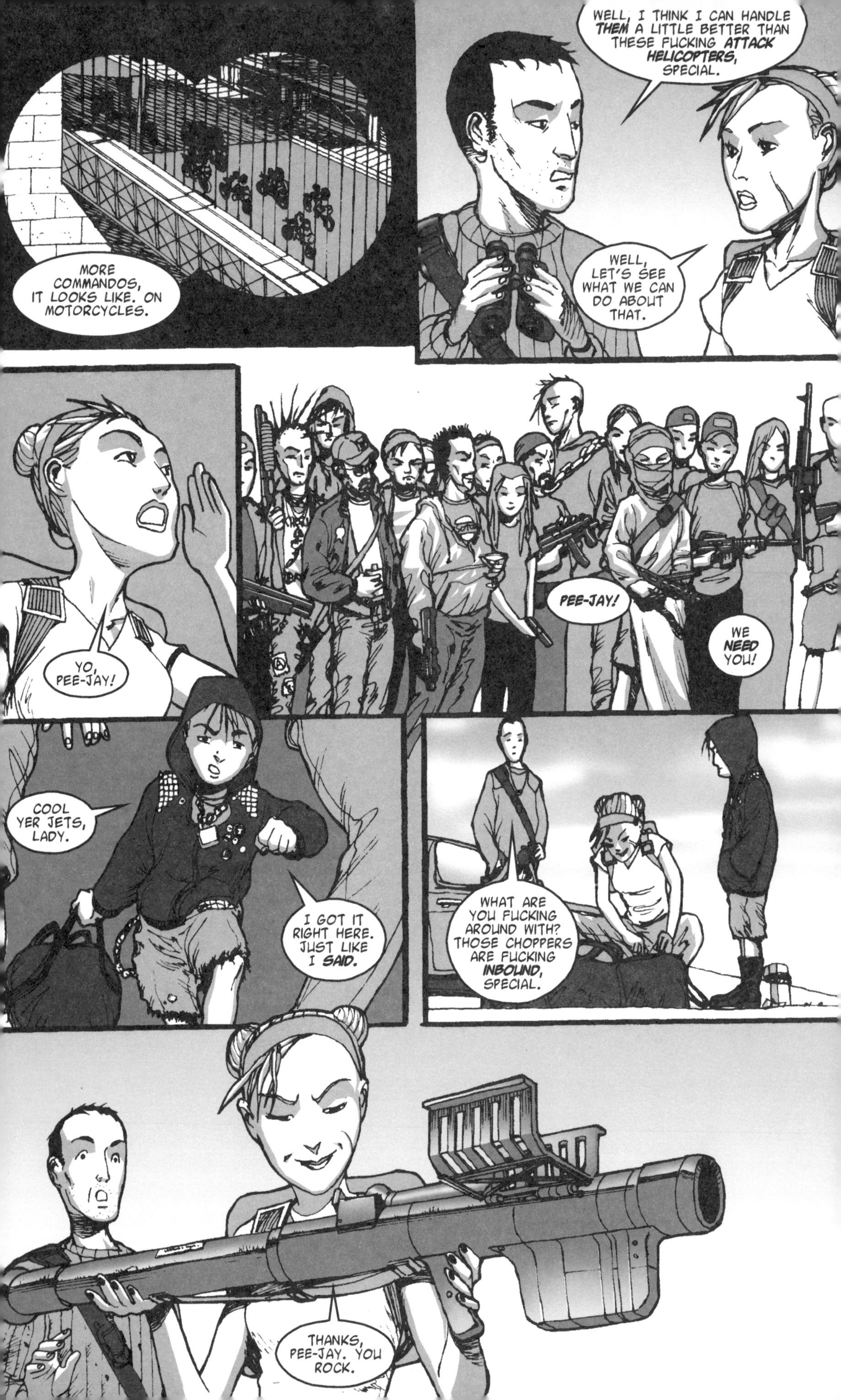
MORE COMMANDOS, IT LOOKS LIKE. ON MOTORCYCLES.
WELL, I THINK I CAN HANDLE THEM A LITTLE BETTER THAN THESE FUCKING ATTACK HELICOPTERS, SPECIAL.
WELL, LET'S SEE WHAT WE CAN DO ABOUT THAT.
YO, PEE-JAY!
PEE-JAY!
WE NEED YOU!
COOL YER JETS, LADY.
I GOT IT RIGHT HERE. JUST LIKE I SAID.
WHAT ARE YOU FUCKING AROUND WITH? THOSE CHOPPERS ARE FUCKING INBOUND, SPECIAL.
THANKS, PEE-JAY. YOU ROCK.

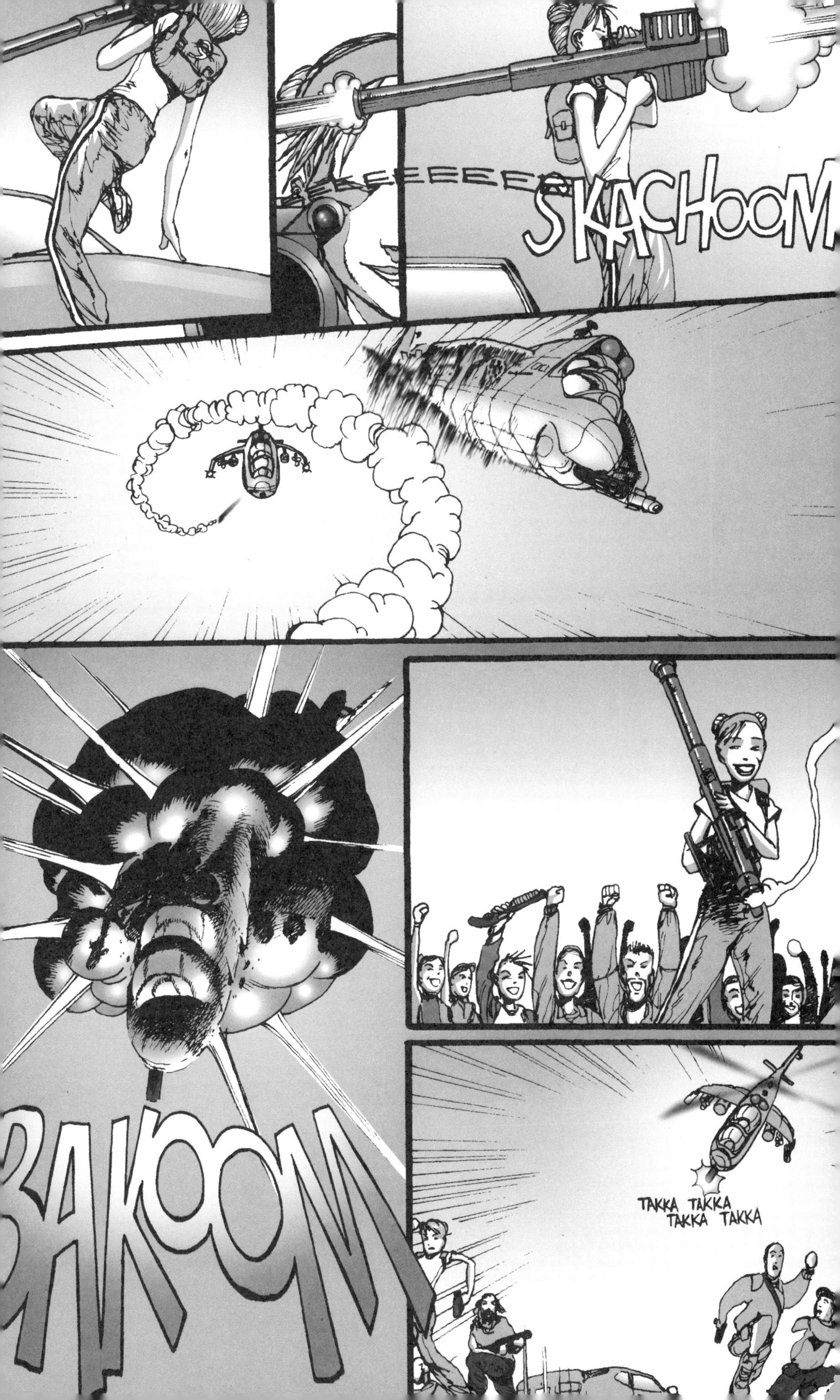

EEEEEEEEEE
SKACHOOM
BAKOOM
TAKKA TAKKA
TAKKA TAKKA

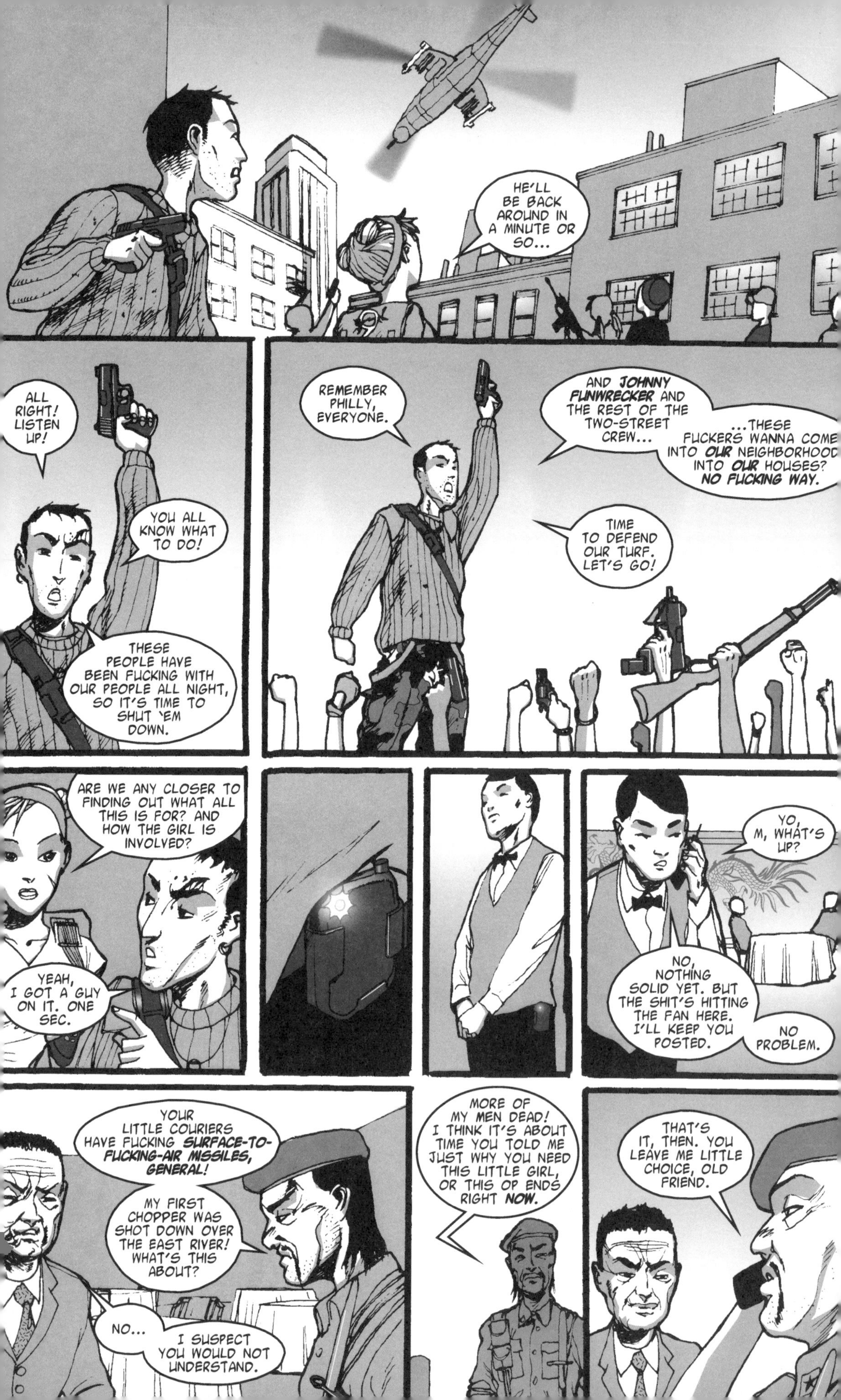
HE'LL BE BACK AROUND IN A MINUTE OR SO...
ALL RIGHT! LISTEN UP!
YOU ALL KNOW WHAT TO DO!
THESE PEOPLE HAVE BEEN FUCKING WITH OUR PEOPLE ALL NIGHT, SO IT'S TIME TO SHUT 'EM DOWN.
REMEMBER PHILLY, EVERYONE.
AND JOHNNY FUNWRECKER AND THE REST OF THE TWO-STREET CREW...
...THESE FUCKERS WANNA COME INTO OUR NEIGHBORHOOD INTO OUR HOUSES? NO FUCKING WAY.
TIME TO DEFEND OUR TURF. LET'S GO!
ARE WE ANY CLOSER TO FINDING OUT WHAT ALL THIS IS FOR? AND HOW THE GIRL IS INVOLVED?
YEAH, I GOT A GUY ON IT. ONE SEC.
YO, M, WHAT'S UP?
NO, NOTHING SOLID YET. BUT THE SHIT'S HITTING THE FAN HERE. I'LL KEEP YOU POSTED.
NO PROBLEM.
YOUR LITTLE COURIERS HAVE FUCKING SURFACE-TO-FUCKING-AIR MISSILES, GENERAL!
MY FIRST CHOPPER WAS SHOT DOWN OVER THE EAST RIVER! WHAT'S THIS ABOUT?
NO...
I SUSPECT YOU WOULD NOT UNDERSTAND.
MORE OF MY MEN DEAD! I THINK IT'S ABOUT TIME YOU TOLD ME JUST WHY YOU NEED THIS LITTLE GIRL, OR THIS OP ENDS RIGHT NOW.
THAT'S IT, THEN. YOU LEAVE ME LITTLE CHOICE, OLD FRIEND.

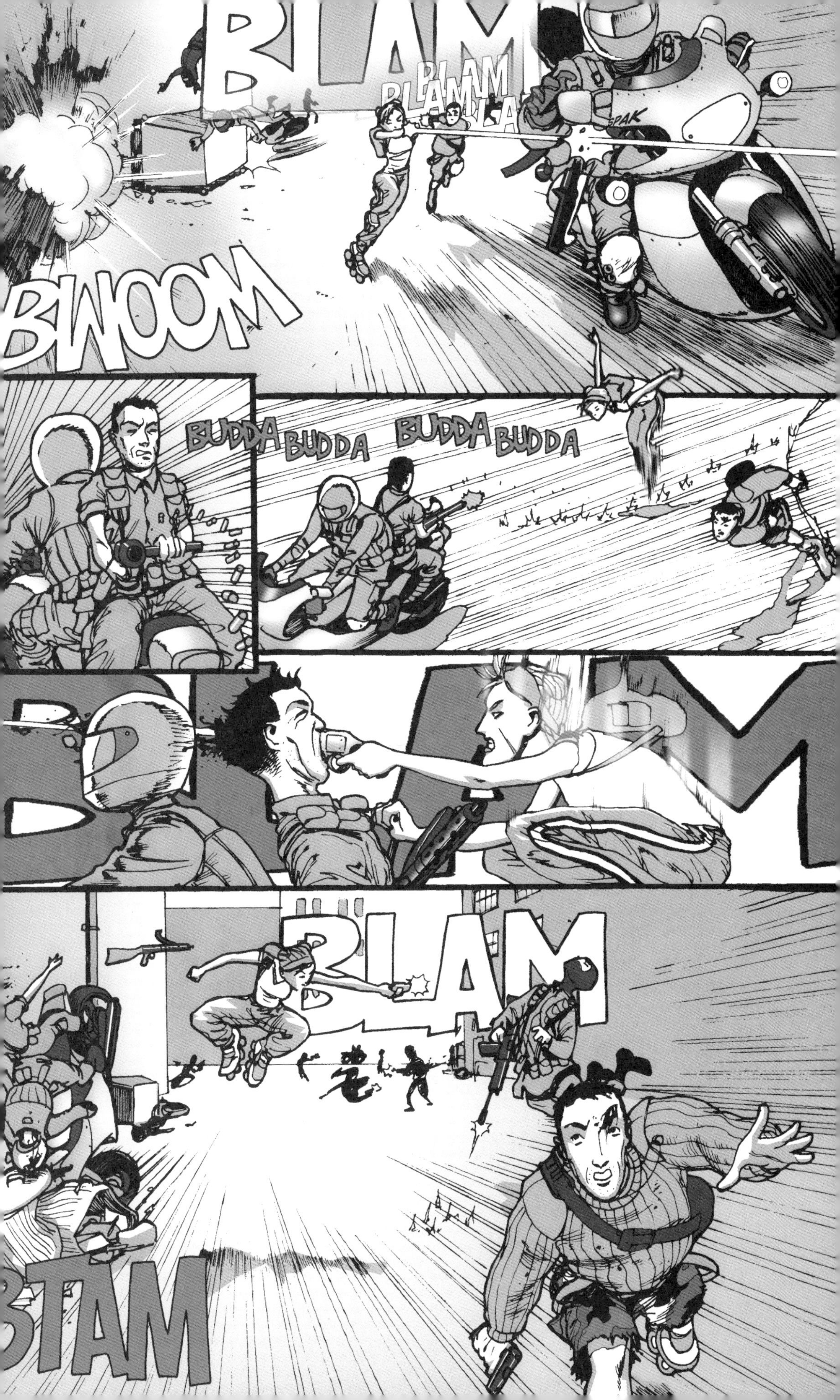
BLAM
BLAM
BLAM
BLAM
SPAK
BWOOM
BUDDA BUDDA BUDDA BUDDA
BLAM
STAM

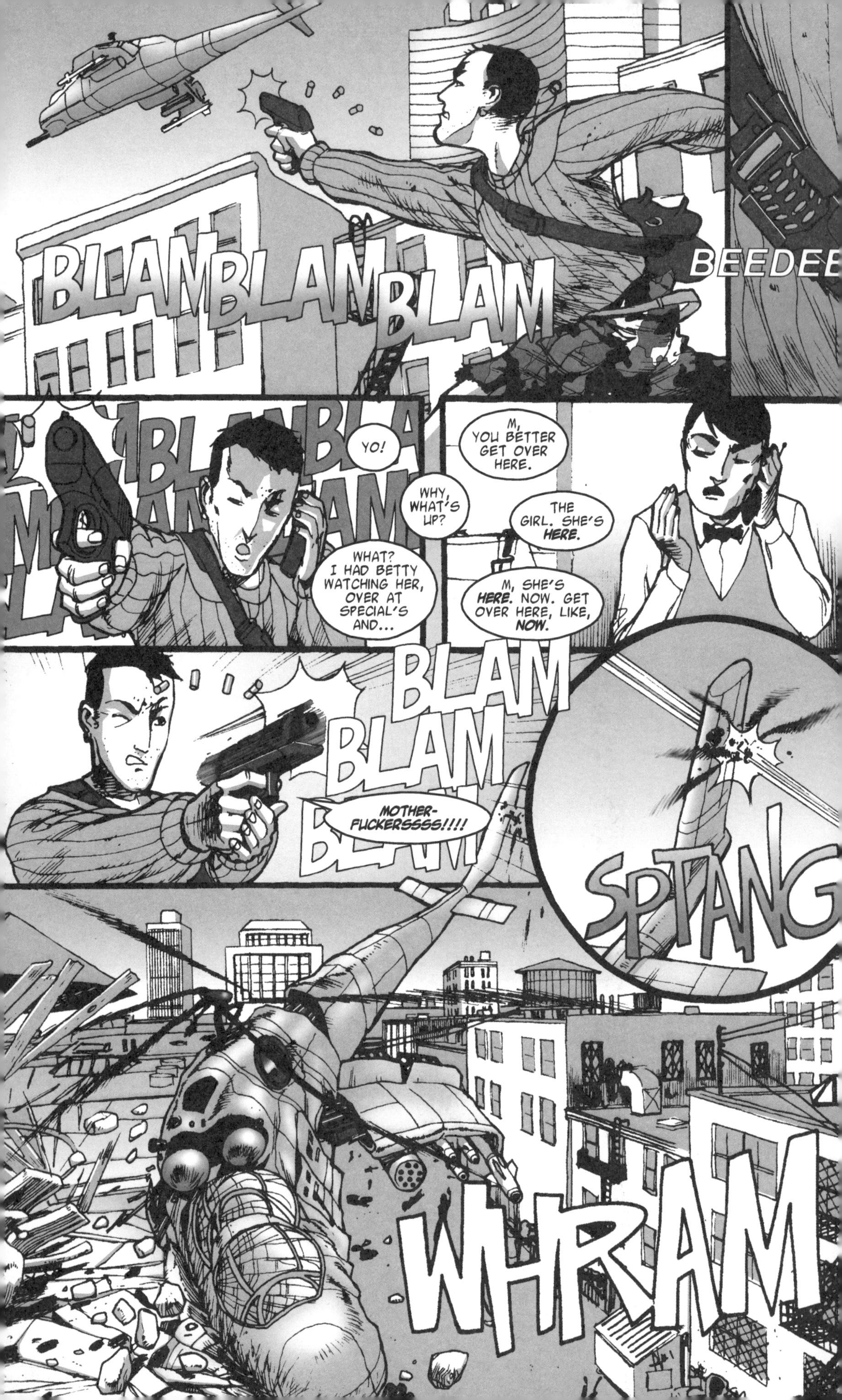

BLAM BLAM BLAM
BEEDEE
YO!
WHY, WHAT'S UP?
WHAT? I HAD BETTY WATCHING HER, OVER AT SPECIAL'S AND...
M, YOU BETTER GET OVER HERE.
THE GIRL. SHE'S HERE.
M, SHE'S HERE. NOW. GET OVER HERE, LIKE, NOW.
BLAM
BLAM
MOTHER-FUCKERSSSS!!!!
SPTANG
WHRAM

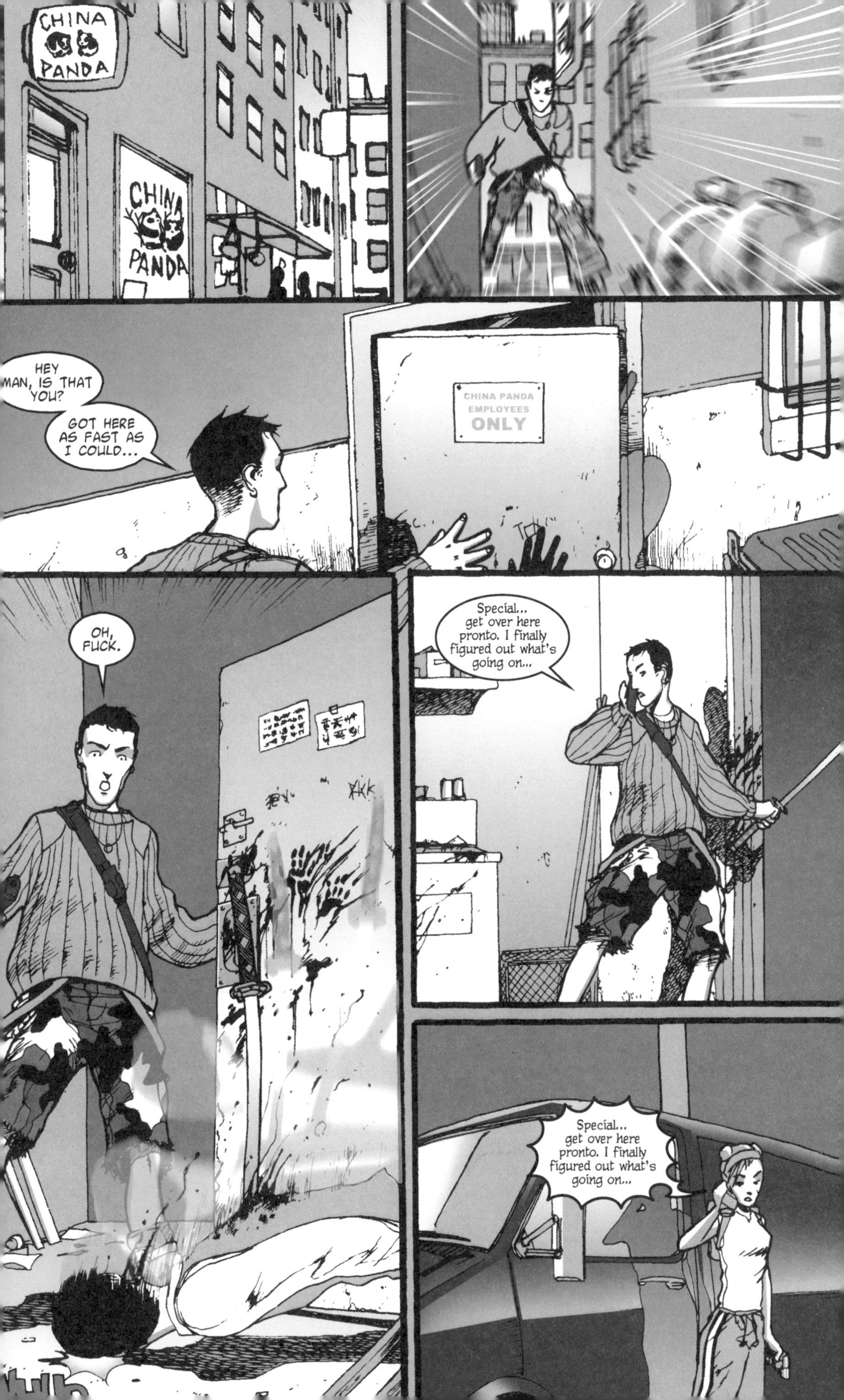
CHINA PANDA
CHINA PANDA
HEY MAN, IS THAT YOU?
GOT HERE AS FAST AS I COULD...
CHINA PANDA EMPLOYEES ONLY
OH, FUCK.
Special... get over here pronto. I finally figured out what's going on...
Special... get over here pronto. I finally figured out what's going on...

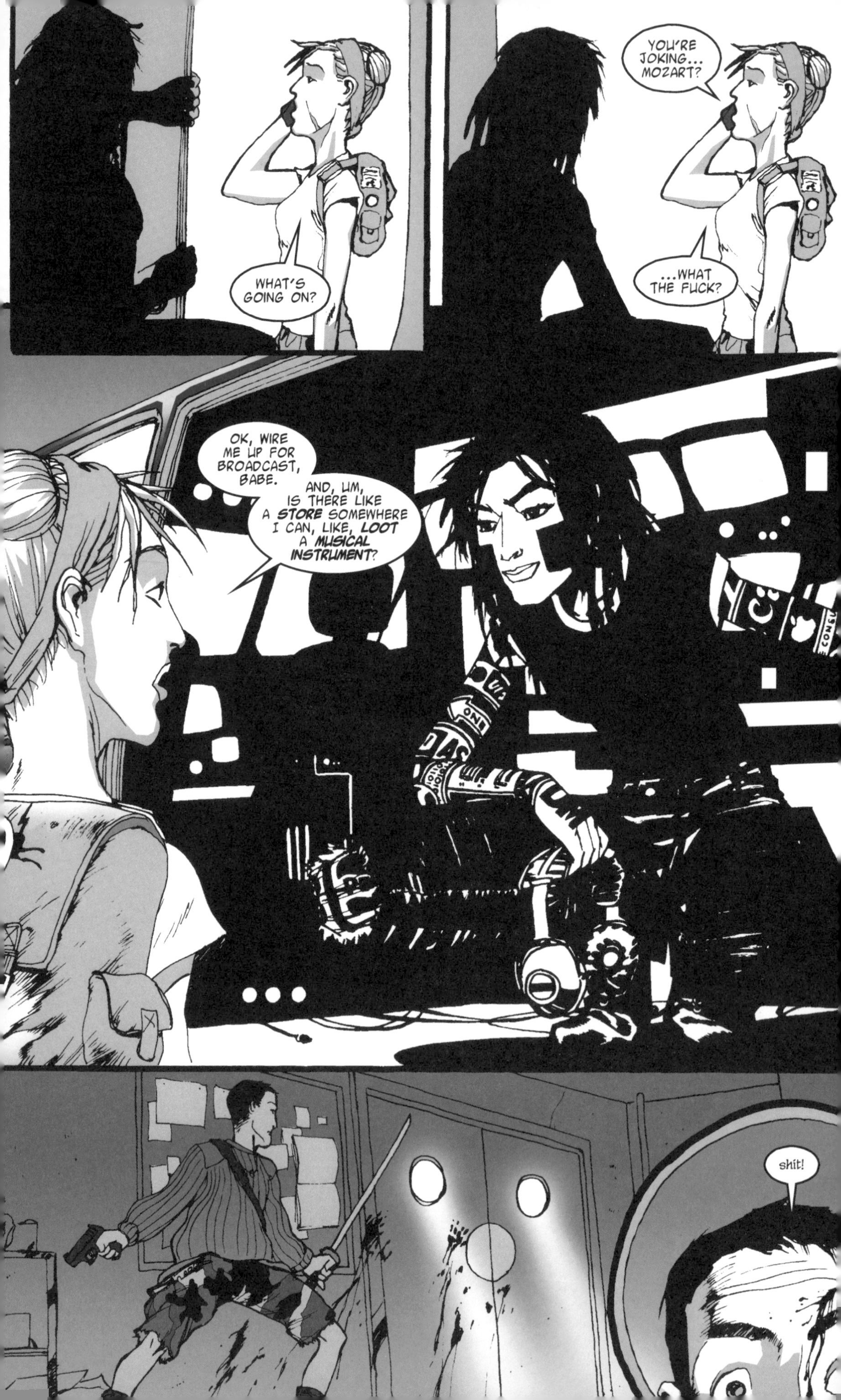
WHAT'S GOING ON?
YOU'RE JOKING... MOZART?
...WHAT THE FUCK?
OK, WIRE ME UP FOR BROADCAST, BABE.
AND, UM, IS THERE LIKE A **STORE** SOMEWHERE I CAN, LIKE, **LOOT** A **MUSICAL INSTRUMENT**?
shit!

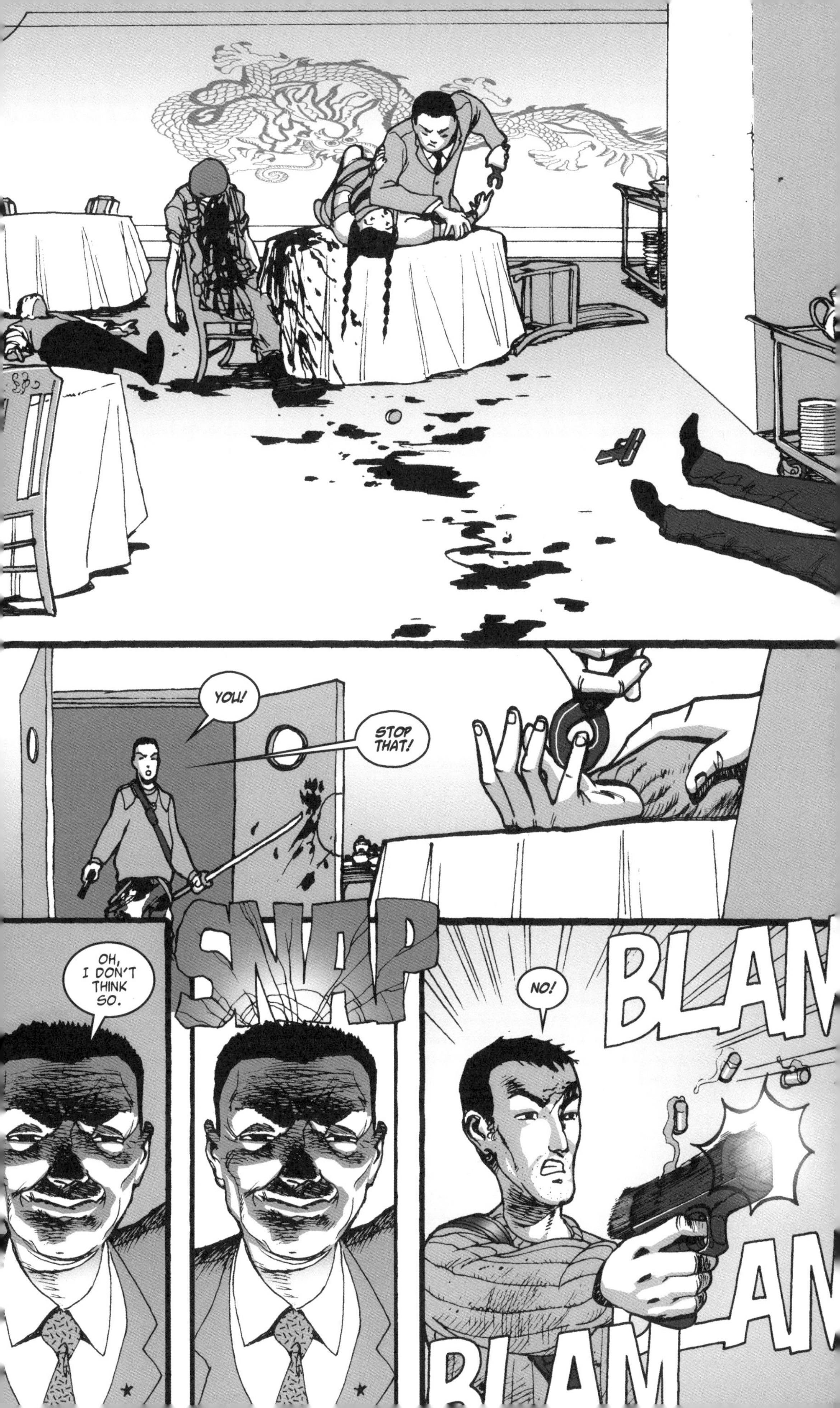
YOU!
STOP THAT!
OH, I DON'T THINK SO.
SNAP
NO!
BLAM
BLAM
BLAM

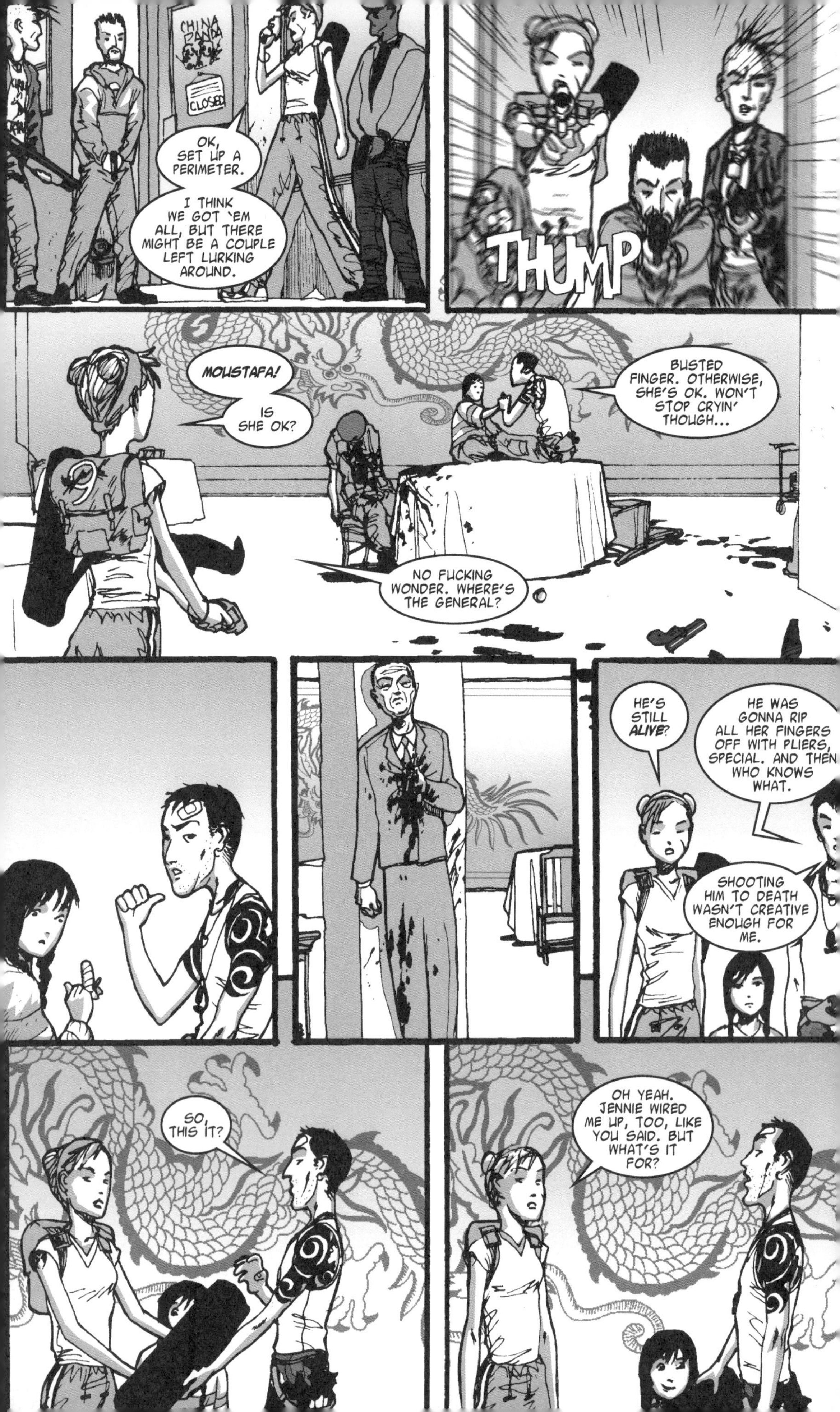
CHINA PANDA
CLOSED
OK, SET UP A PERIMETER.
I THINK WE GOT 'EM ALL, BUT THERE MIGHT BE A COUPLE LEFT LURKING AROUND.
THUMP
MOUSTAFA!
IS SHE OK?
BUSTED FINGER. OTHERWISE, SHE'S OK. WON'T STOP CRYIN' THOUGH...
NO FUCKING WONDER. WHERE'S THE GENERAL?
HE'S STILL ALIVE?
HE WAS GONNA RIP ALL HER FINGERS OFF WITH PLIERS, SPECIAL. AND THEN WHO KNOWS WHAT.
SHOOTING HIM TO DEATH WASN'T CREATIVE ENOUGH FOR ME.
SO, THIS IT?
OH YEAH. JENNIE WIRED ME UP, TOO, LIKE YOU SAID. BUT WHAT'S IT FOR?

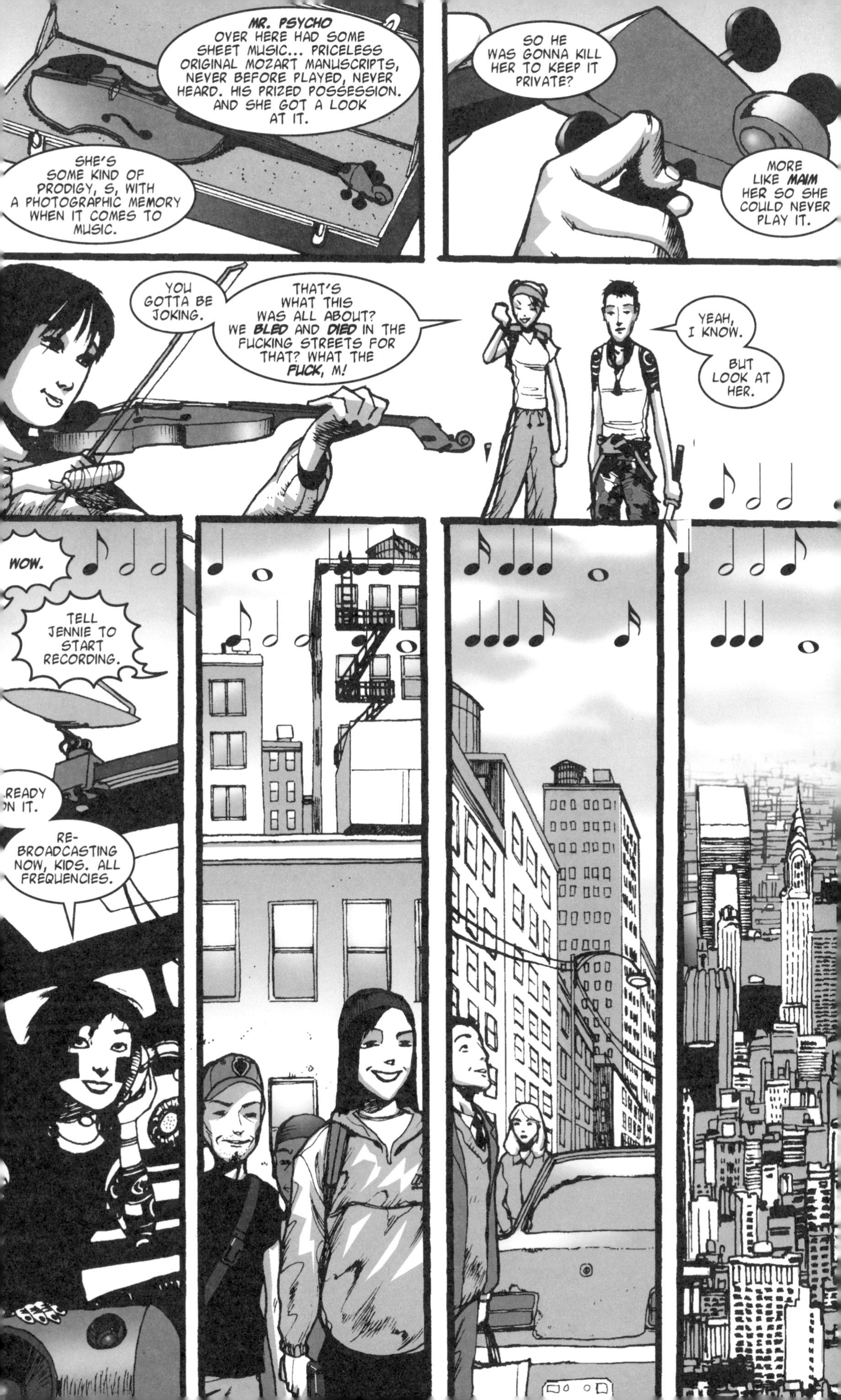
MR. PSYCHO OVER HERE HAD SOME SHEET MUSIC... PRICELESS ORIGINAL MOZART MANUSCRIPTS, NEVER BEFORE PLAYED, NEVER HEARD. HIS PRIZED POSSESSION. AND SHE GOT A LOOK AT IT.
SHE'S SOME KIND OF PRODIGY, S, WITH A PHOTOGRAPHIC MEMORY WHEN IT COMES TO MUSIC.
SO HE WAS GONNA KILL HER TO KEEP IT PRIVATE?
MORE LIKE MAIM HER SO SHE COULD NEVER PLAY IT.
YOU GOTTA BE JOKING.
THAT'S WHAT THIS WAS ALL ABOUT? WE BLED AND DIED IN THE FUCKING STREETS FOR THAT? WHAT THE FUCK, M!
YEAH, I KNOW.
BUT LOOK AT HER.
WOW.
TELL JENNIE TO START RECORDING.
READY ON IT.
RE-BROADCASTING NOW, KIDS. ALL FREQUENCIES.

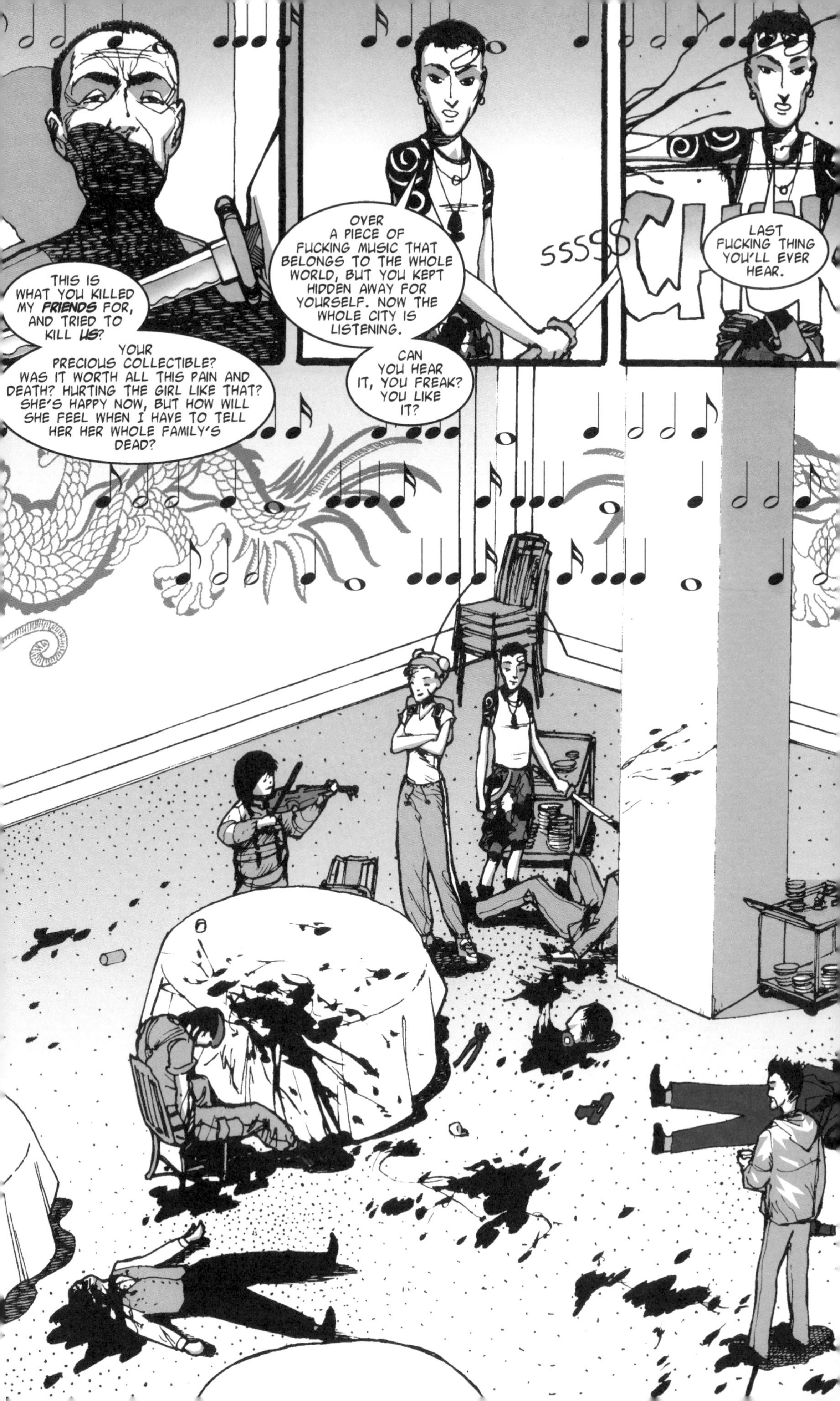

THIS IS WHAT YOU KILLED MY FRIENDS FOR, AND TRIED TO KILL US?
YOUR PRECIOUS COLLECTIBLE? WAS IT WORTH ALL THIS PAIN AND DEATH? HURTING THE GIRL LIKE THAT? SHE'S HAPPY NOW, BUT HOW WILL SHE FEEL WHEN I HAVE TO TELL HER HER WHOLE FAMILY'S DEAD?
OVER A PIECE OF FUCKING MUSIC THAT BELONGS TO THE WHOLE WORLD, BUT YOU KEPT HIDDEN AWAY FOR YOURSELF. NOW THE WHOLE CITY IS LISTENING.
CAN YOU HEAR IT, YOU FREAK? YOU LIKE IT?
SSSSS
LAST FUCKING THING YOU'LL EVER HEAR.

THE END

Production Notes

Rob G | Brooklyn | 2003

P. 6 - Chinese character is 'Jung' which means 'loyal'

♪♩♩ ♩ ₒ ♪♪♪♪ ♪♪♪♪ ₒ ♩♩♩♪

P. 9 - the two paintings are: "the Third of May" by Francisco Goya, which is supposedly on exhibit in Madrid, Spain. "Christ in the Garden" by Caravaggio. This painting was supposedly destroyed by fire in 1945. There is a hand, which belonged to Francios Babeuf, a French Communist writer, in a glass jar. The Ark of the Covenant is also in this room.

♪♩♩ ♩ ₒ ♪♪♪♪ ♪♪♪♪ ₒ ♩♩♩♪

P. 10 - the paper says "the Devil's dance" in German.

♪♩♩ ♩ ₒ ♪♪♪♪ ♪♪♪♪ ₒ ♩♩♩♪

P. 11 - The pistol is a Tokarev Type 54 Chinese Army Issue.

♪♩♩ ♩ ₒ ♪♪♪♪ ♪♪♪♪ ₒ ♩♩♩♪

P. 14 and 15 - view of Manhattan looking north from a helicopter.

P. 17 - Chinese character is 'Ma" which is a question mark (?)

♪♩♩ ♩ ₒ ♪♪♪♪ ♪♪♪♪ ₒ ♩♩♩♪

P. 18 - Chinese character means Exclamation (!) Special's gun is a Smith & Wesson hammerless M340PD that has been converted to carry .45 ACP ammunition. This reduces her maximum load to five shots, but they are really powerful shots. Plus, it means that both she and Moustafa can carry the same ammo.

♪♩♩ ♩ ₒ ♪♪♪♪ ♪♪♪♪ ₒ ♩♩♩♪

P. 21 - Moustafa's gun is a Taurus PT-145 .45 ACP. He carries two at all times. He also puts "hot loads" in the second and third shots in the magazines. Hot loads are custom-made rounds that use more than the normal amount of gunpowder in a bullet. The drawback is that it really fucks up the barrel fast, so he puts on a new one every other time he uses it. He claims that having a new barrel makes him shoot better.

P. 27 - Special's shirt by Helly Hanson.

♪♩♩ ♩ ₒ ♫♫♪ ♪♫♫ ₒ ♩♩♩♪

P. 29 - the Vespa is cherry red, and all the stickers are the same as Kaneda's motorcycle in the manga AKIRA by Katsuhiro Otomo.

♪♩♩ ♩ ₒ ♫♫♪ ♪♫♫ ₒ ♩♩♩♪

P. 30 - the backgrounds are Washington Square, the Flatiron building, and the Empire State building.

♪♩♩ ♩ ₒ ♫♫♪ ♪♫♫ ₒ ♩♩♩♪

P. 36 - the girl has an Ingram Mac-10 9mm.

♪♩♩ ♩ ₒ ♫♫♪ ♪♫♫ ₒ ♩♩♩♪

P. 37 - the pistol is a Glock 19 and the shotgun is a Remington 870 .12 gauge pump (riot version)

♪♩♩ ♩ ₒ ♫♫♪ ♪♫♫ ₒ ♩♩♩♪

P. 38 - the gun is a Goncz 9mm Machine Pistol.

♪♩♩ ♩ ₒ ♫♫♪ ♪♫♫ ₒ ♩♩♩♪

p. 39 - A blue 1969 Chevy Camaro SS (I removed the SS plates front and back).

♪♩♩ ♩ ₒ ♫♫♪ ♪♫♫ ₒ ♩♩♩♪

P. 41 - I totally made up this helicopter.

♪♩♩ ♩ ₒ ♫♫♪ ♪♫♫ ₒ ♩♩♩♪

P. 33 - The BQE is like 20 feet from my window. It really sucks.

♪♩♩ ♩ ₒ ♫♫♪ ♪♫♫ ₒ ♩♩♩♪

P. 50 - Don't try this trick at home kids, you'll drop Mommy's transmission all over the freeway.

♪♩♩ ♩ ₒ ♫♫♪ ♪♫♫ ₒ ♩♩♩♪

P. 52 - My first ever comicbook explosion. You saw it here first.

♪♩♩ ♩ ₒ ♫♫♪ ♪♫♫ ₒ ♩♩♩♪

P. 54 - He should've buckled-up.

♪♩♩ ♩ ₒ ♫♫♪ ♪♫♫ ₒ ♩♩♩♪

P. 57. *The Powerpuff Girls* is trade-marked and copyrighted 2003 by the Cartoon Network. They save the world before bedtime.

♪♩♩ ♩ ₒ ♫♫♪ ♪♫♫ ₒ ♩♩♩♪

P. 66 - The bar is Sophie's on East 5th St.

♪♩♩ ♩ ₒ ♫♫♪ ♪♫♫ ₒ ♩♩♩♪

P. 67 - The first appearance of Becky Cloonan, artist on JENNIE ONE. In reality, she could probably take down Special, easy.

♪♩♩ ♩ ₒ ♫♫♪ ♪♫♫ ₒ ♩♩♩♪

P. 68 - Special's gear by FILA

♪♩♩ ♩ ₒ ♫♫♪ ♪♫♫ ₒ ♩♩♩♪

P. 69 - China Panda is a restaurant in Richmond VA. Yum-yum. The drawing of Brooklyn is a nod to COUSCOUS EXPRESS.

♪♩♩ ♩ ₒ ♫♫♪ ♪♫♫ ₒ ♩♩♩♪

P. 70 - Two familiar faces from TEENAGERS FROM MARS, fishing for body parts in the East River.

♪♩♩ ♩ ₒ ♫♫♪ ♪♫♫ ₒ ♩♩♩♪

P. 72 - Please note James Sime, owner of San Francisco's Isotope: The Comic Book Lounge, with the Uzi and martini glass. And our esteemed publisher Larry Young, flask in hand, at his right. That, of course, is a Stinger Surface-to-Air missle. And again more guns than I can name appear here.

♪♩♩ ♩ ₒ ♫♫♪ ♪♫♫ ₒ ♩♩♩♪

P. 75 - I'm not sure sure if you could shoot through two heads like that or not.

02

The Couriers
DIRTBIKE MANIFESTO

Brian Wood x Rob G x Ryan Yount

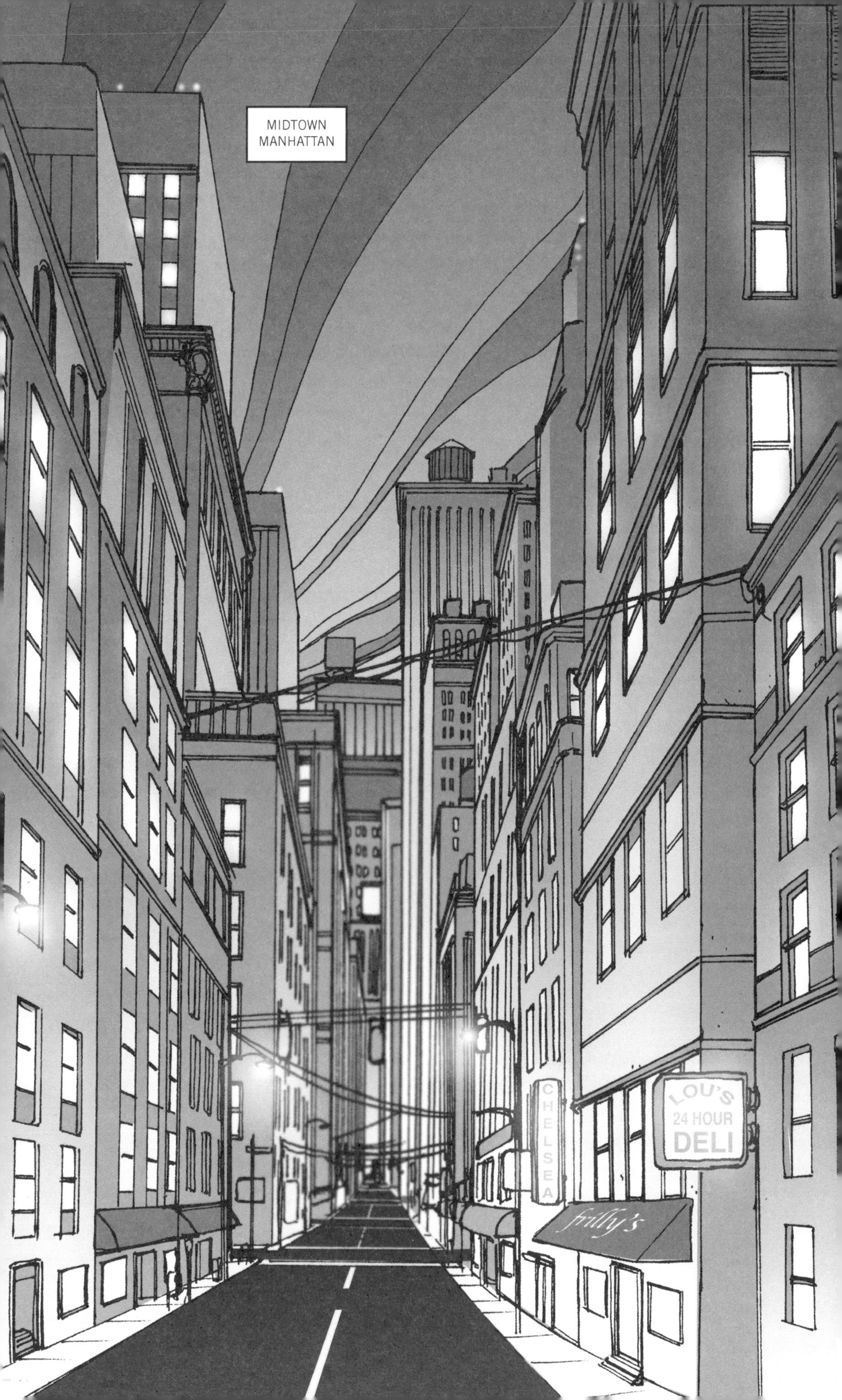
MIDTOWN
MANHATTAN
CHELSEA
LOU'S
24 HOUR
DELI
frilly's

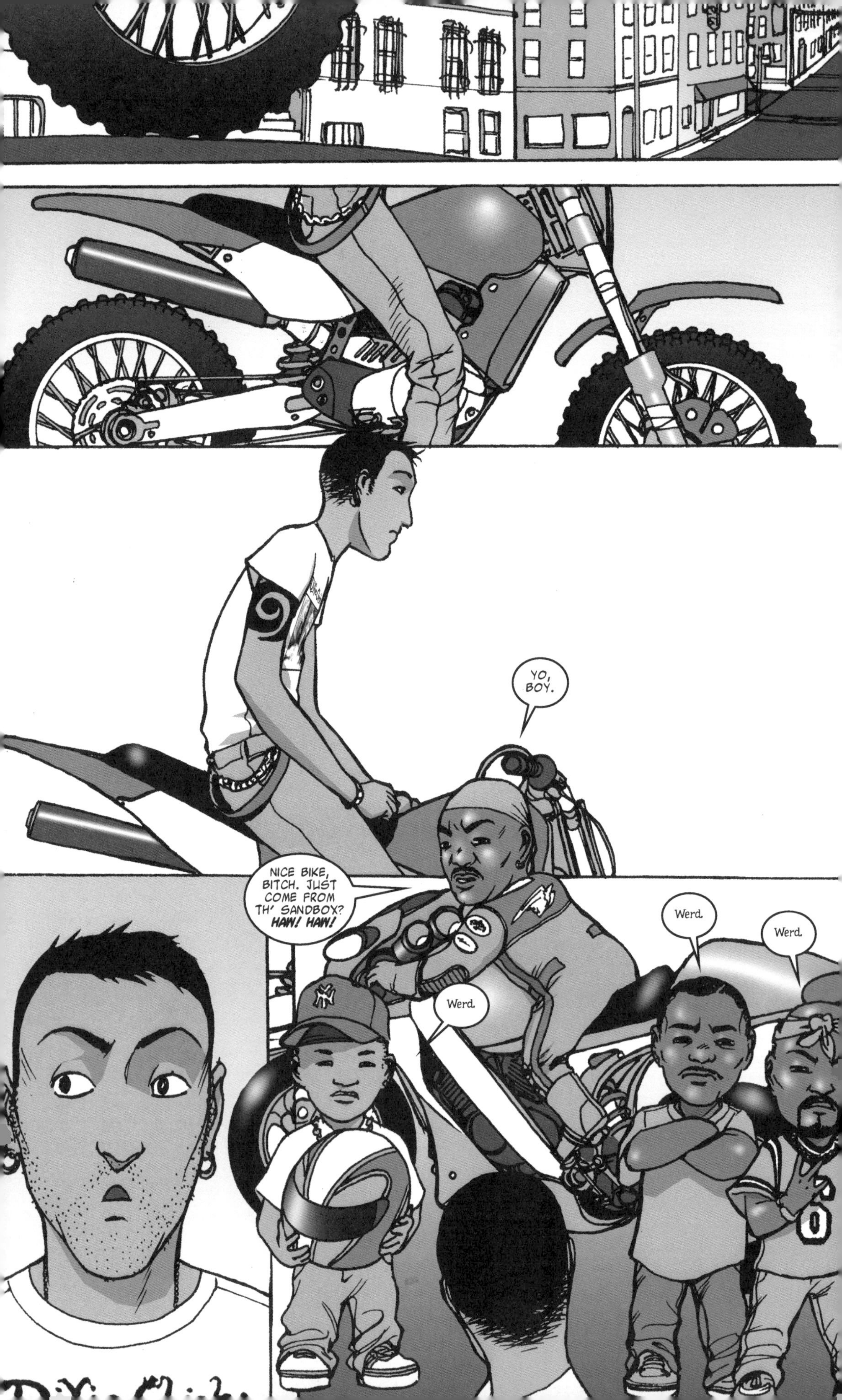
YO, BOY.
NICE BIKE, BITCH. JUST COME FROM TH' SANDBOX? **HAW! HAW!**
Werd.
Werd.
Werd.

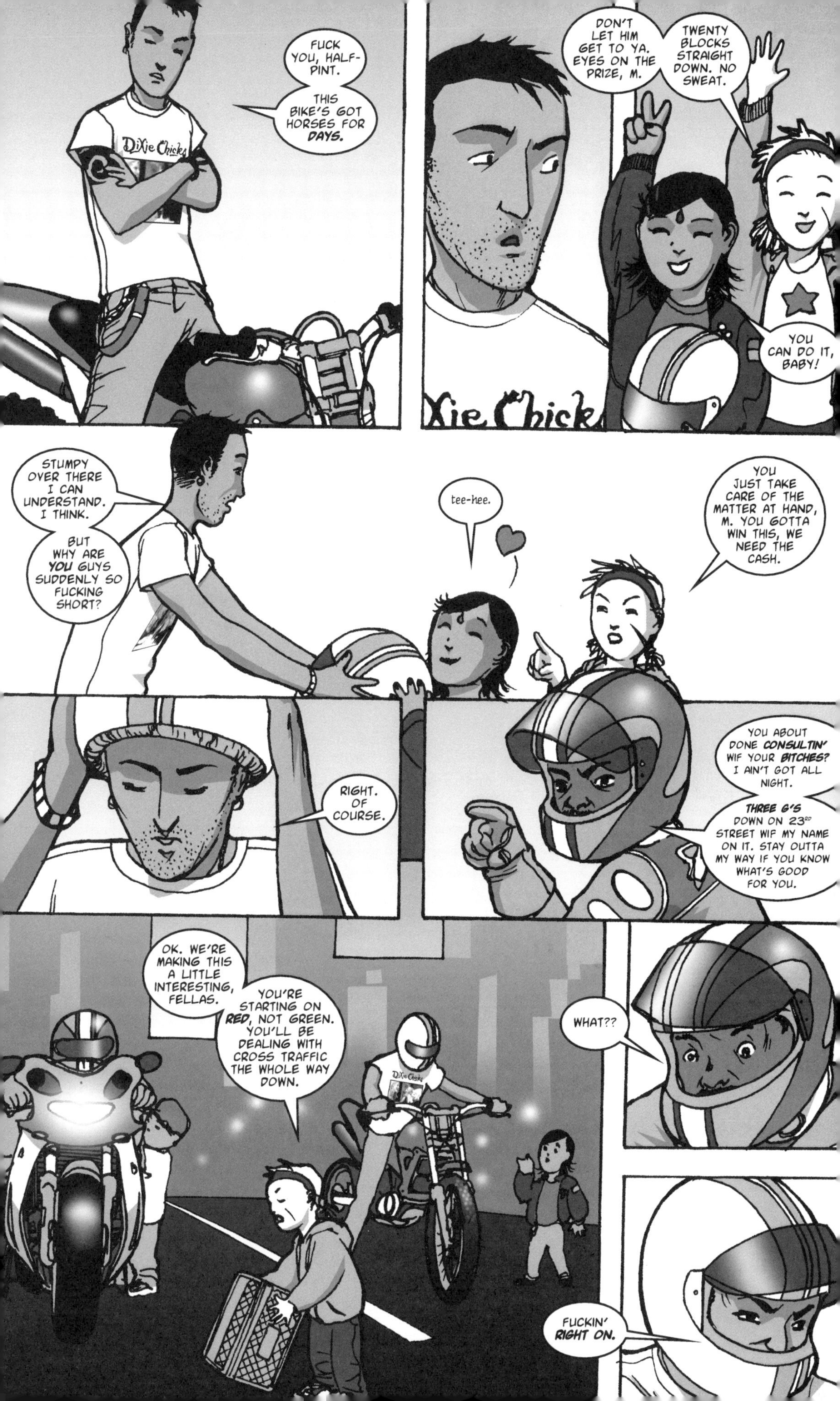
FUCK YOU, HALF-PINT.
THIS BIKE'S GOT HORSES FOR DAYS.
DiXie Chicks
DON'T LET HIM GET TO YA. EYES ON THE PRIZE, M.
TWENTY BLOCKS STRAIGHT DOWN. NO SWEAT.
YOU CAN DO IT, BABY!
STUMPY OVER THERE I CAN UNDERSTAND. I THINK.
BUT WHY ARE YOU GUYS SUDDENLY SO FUCKING SHORT?
tee-hee.
YOU JUST TAKE CARE OF THE MATTER AT HAND, M. YOU GOTTA WIN THIS, WE NEED THE CASH.
RIGHT. OF COURSE.
YOU ABOUT DONE CONSULTIN' WIF YOUR BITCHES? I AIN'T GOT ALL NIGHT.
THREE G'S DOWN ON 23RD STREET WIF MY NAME ON IT. STAY OUTTA MY WAY IF YOU KNOW WHAT'S GOOD FOR YOU.
OK. WE'RE MAKING THIS A LITTLE INTERESTING, FELLAS.
YOU'RE STARTING ON RED, NOT GREEN. YOU'LL BE DEALING WITH CROSS TRAFFIC THE WHOLE WAY DOWN.
WHAT??
FUCKIN' RIGHT ON.

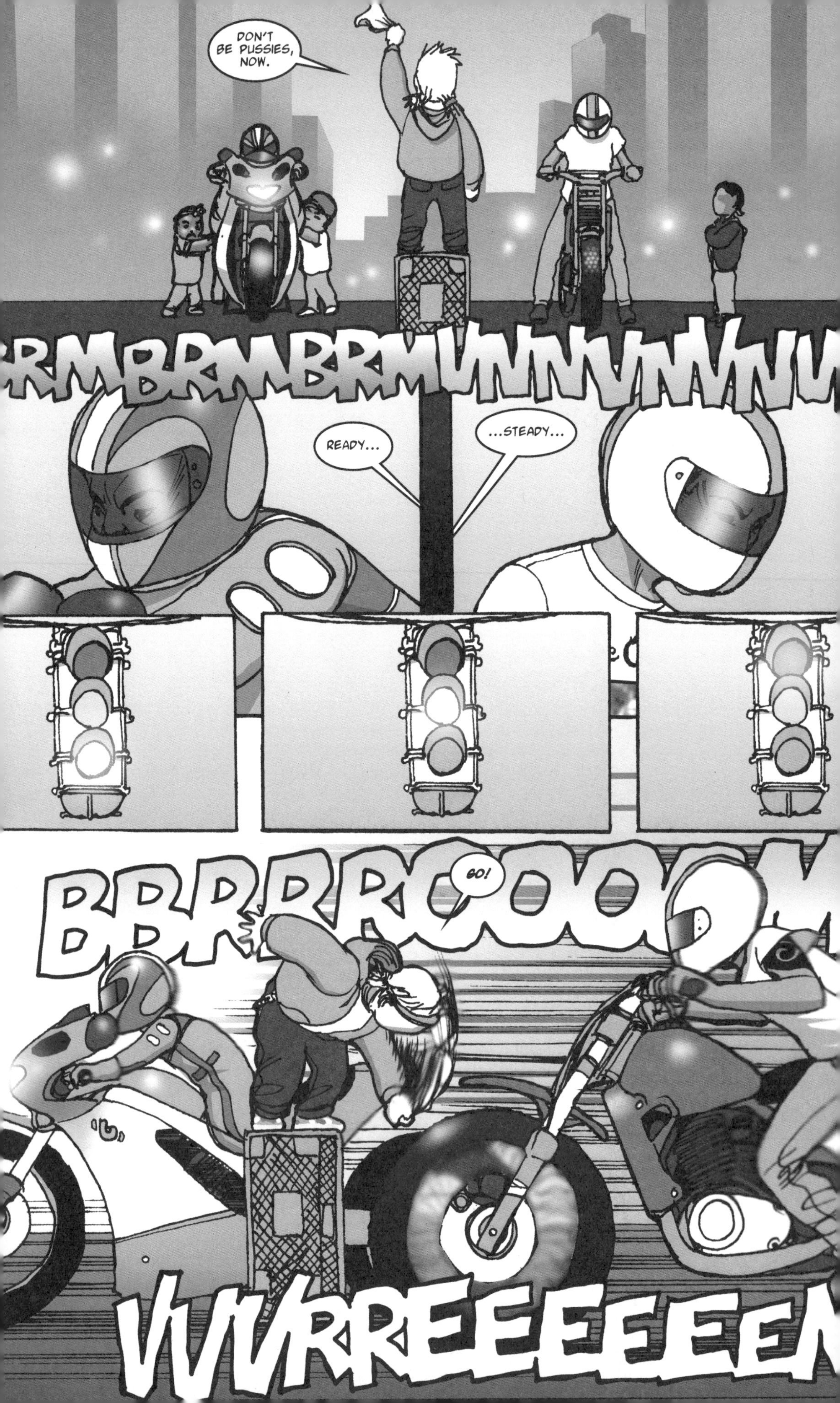

DON'T BE PUSSIES, NOW.
RMBRMBRMUNNNNNNUN
READY...
...STEADY...
BRRRROOOOOM
GO!
VVVRREEEEEEEN

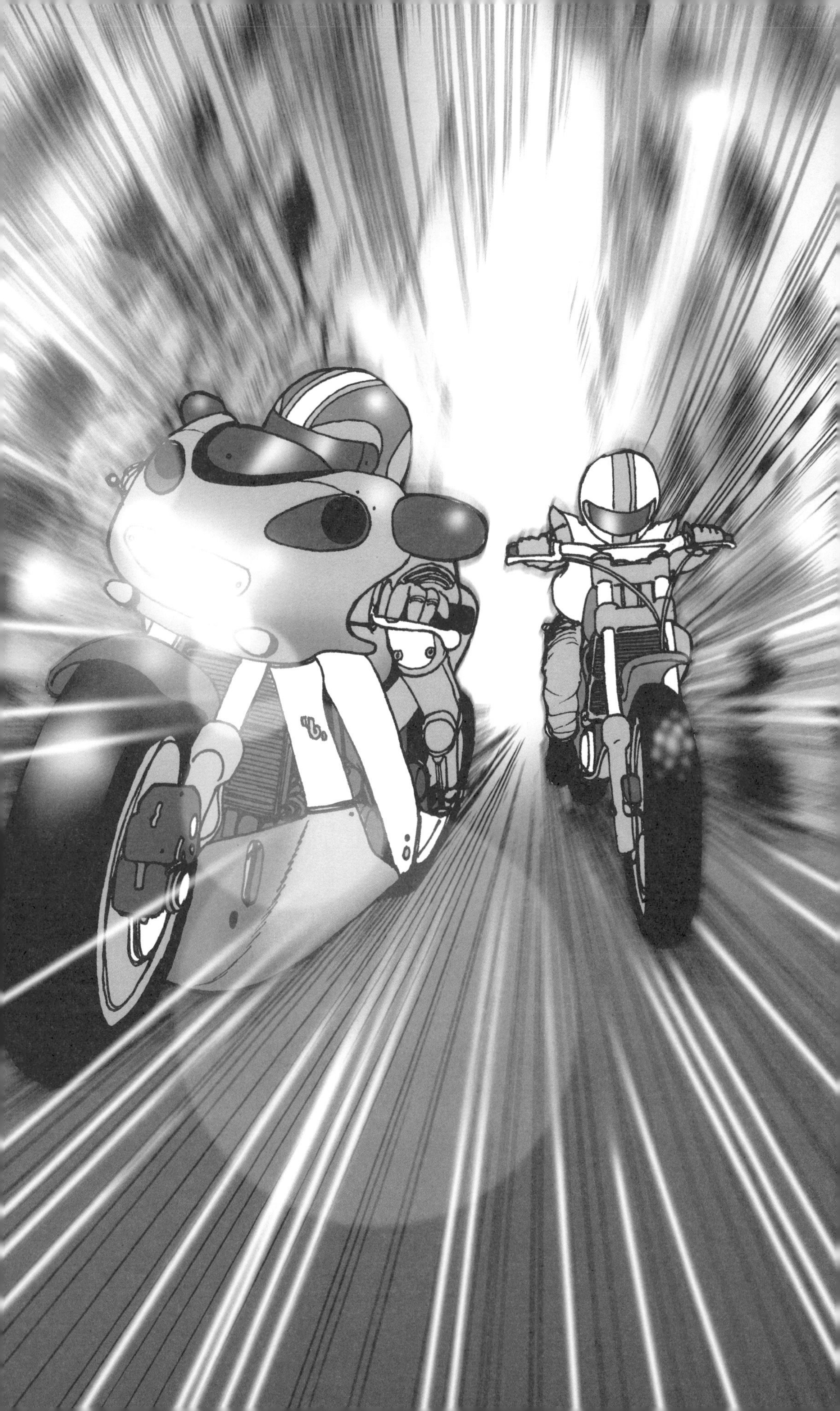

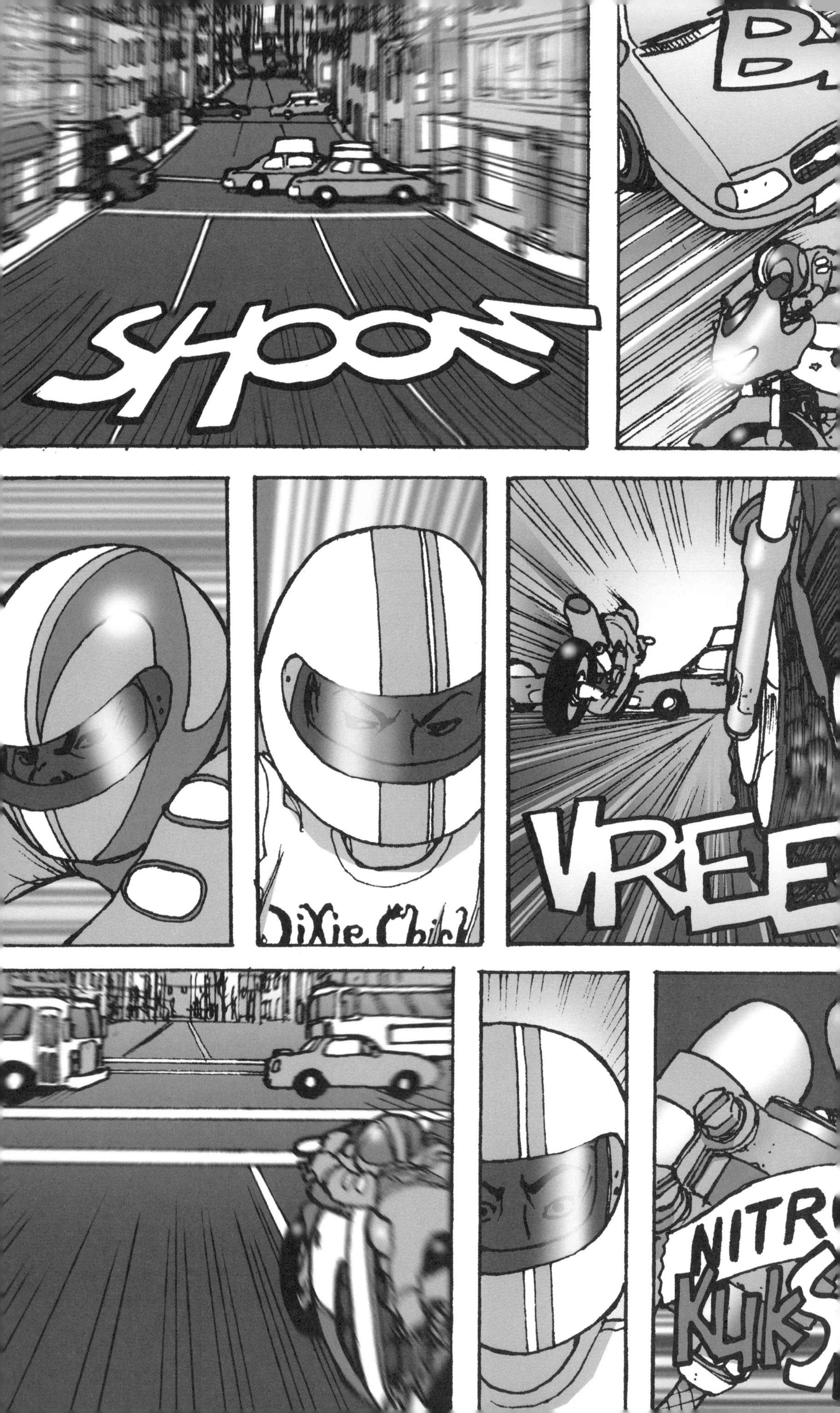
SHOOS
VREE
Dixie Chick
NITR
KLIKS

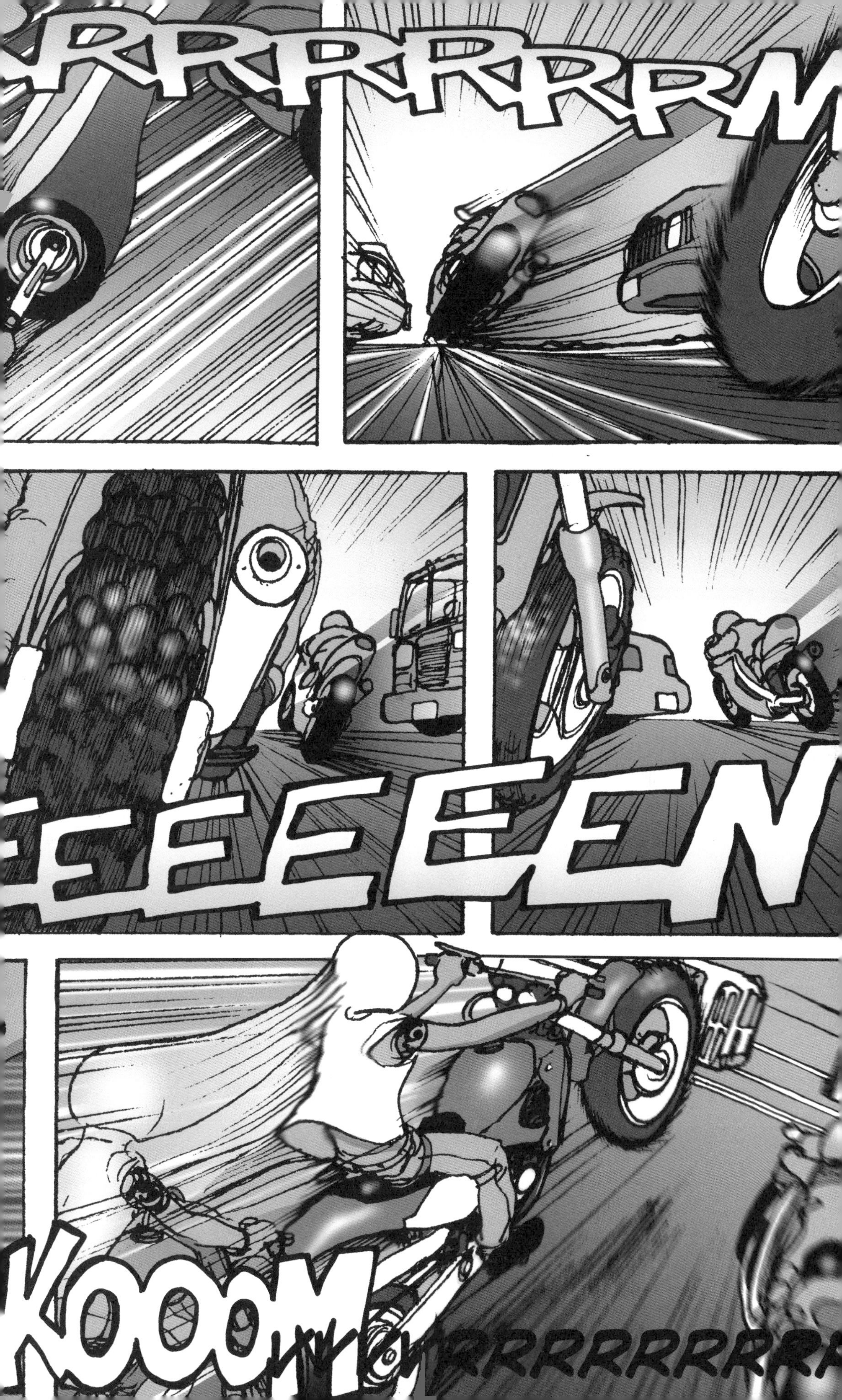
RRRRRRRRRM
EEEEEN
KOOOM
VRRRRRRRRR

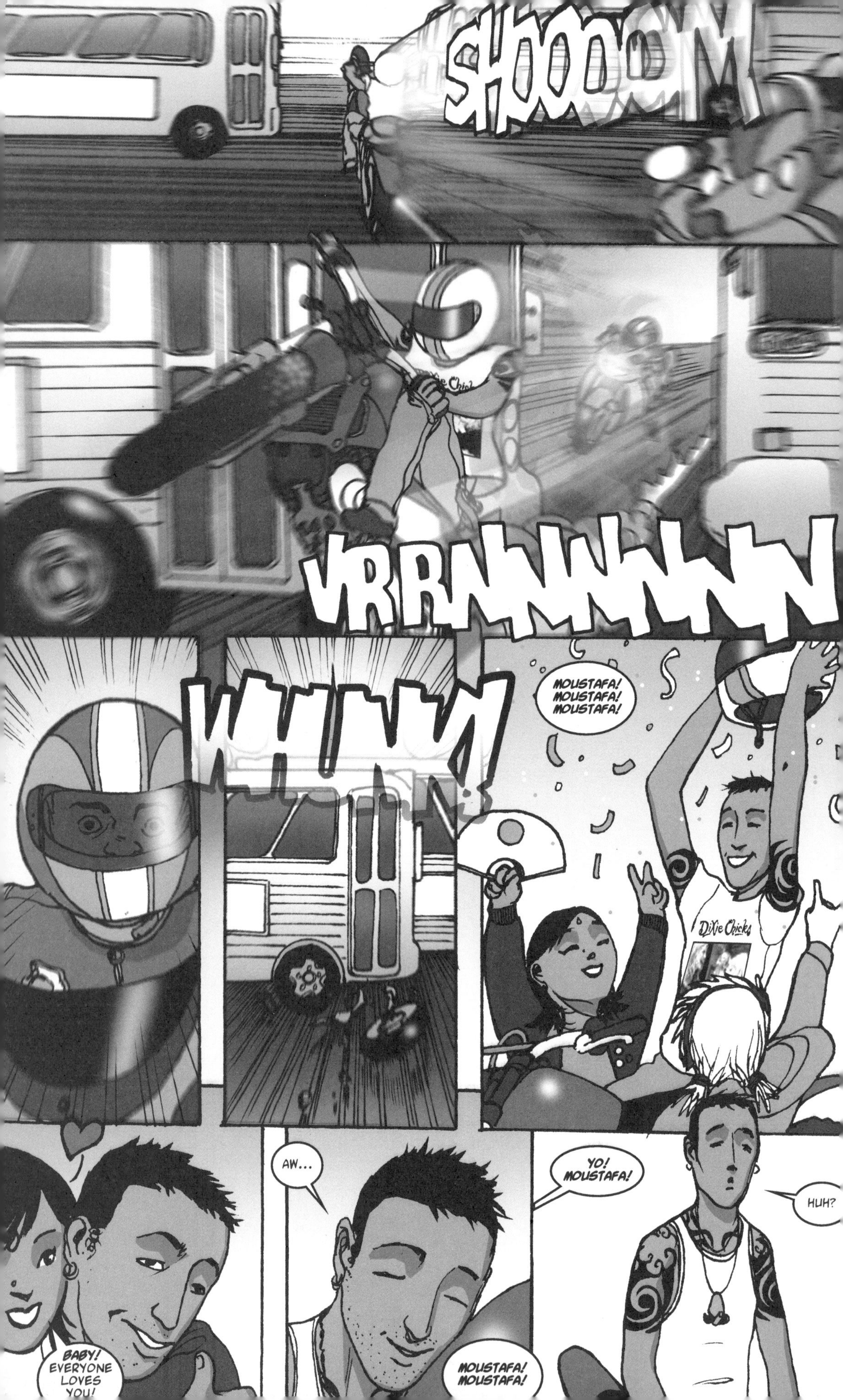
SHOOOOM!
VRRAAAAAAAAAN
WHAAM!
MOUSTAFA!
MOUSTAFA!
MOUSTAFA!
BABY!
EVERYONE
LOVES
YOU!
AW...
MOUSTAFA!
MOUSTAFA!
YO!
MOUSTAFA!
HUH?

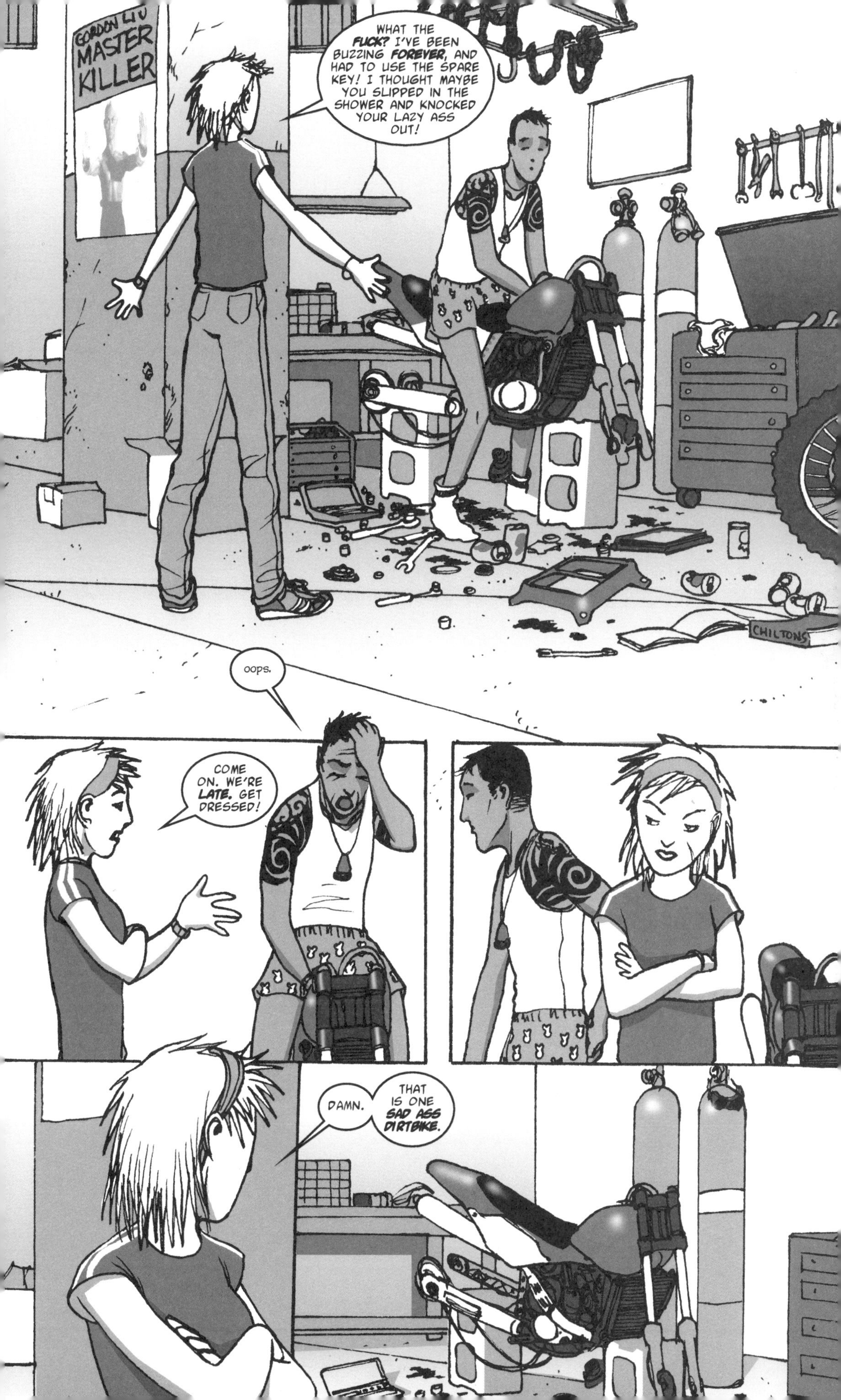
GORDON LIU
MASTER KILLER
WHAT THE FUCK? I'VE BEEN BUZZING FOREVER, AND HAD TO USE THE SPARE KEY! I THOUGHT MAYBE YOU SLIPPED IN THE SHOWER AND KNOCKED YOUR LAZY ASS OUT!
CHILTONS
oops.
COME ON. WE'RE LATE. GET DRESSED!
DAMN.
THAT IS ONE SAD ASS DIRTBIKE.

The Couriers 02
DIRTBIKE MANIFESTO

written by BRIAN WOOD
art by ROB G
letters RYAN YOUNT

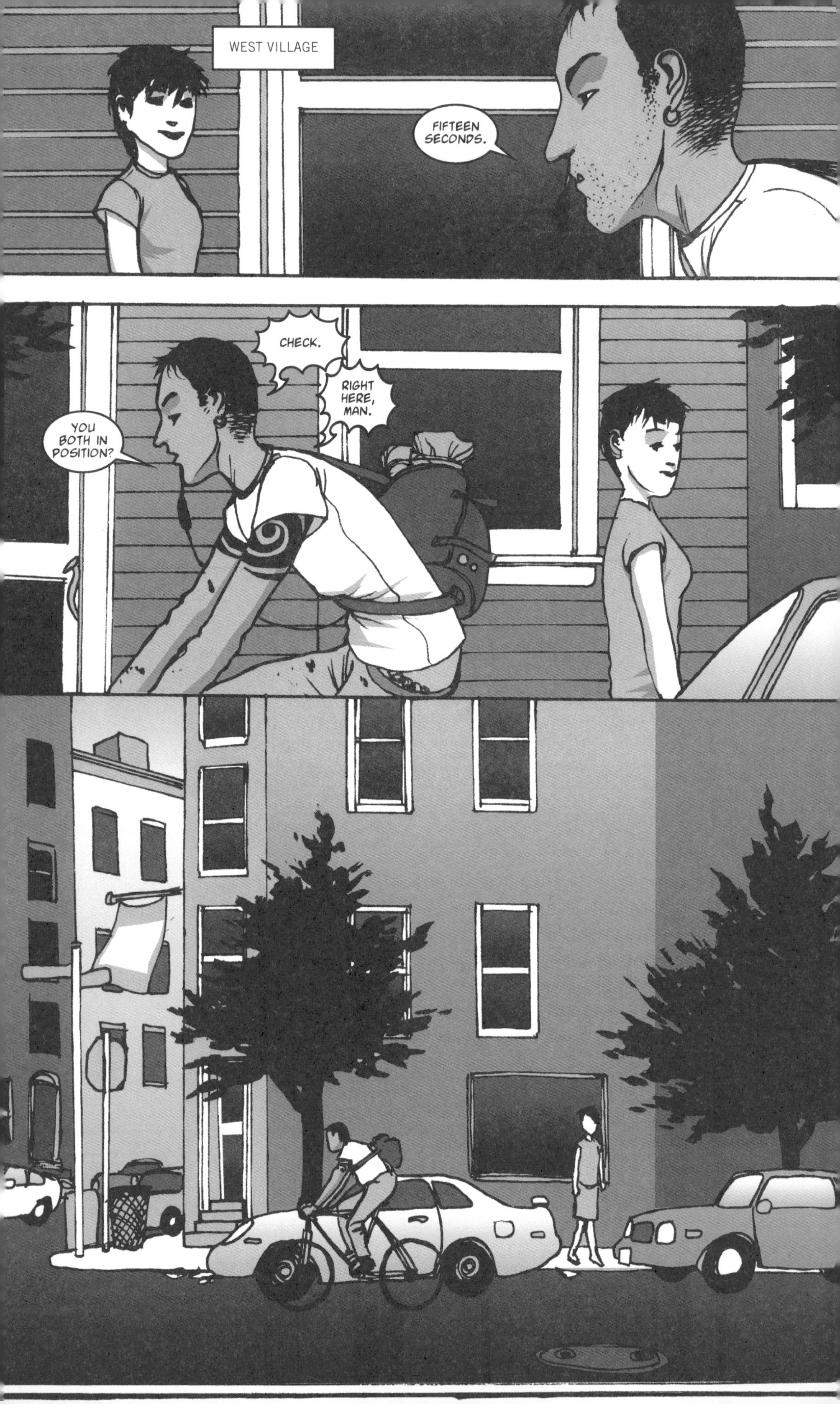
WEST VILLAGE
FIFTEEN SECONDS.
YOU BOTH IN POSITION?
CHECK.
RIGHT HERE, MAN.

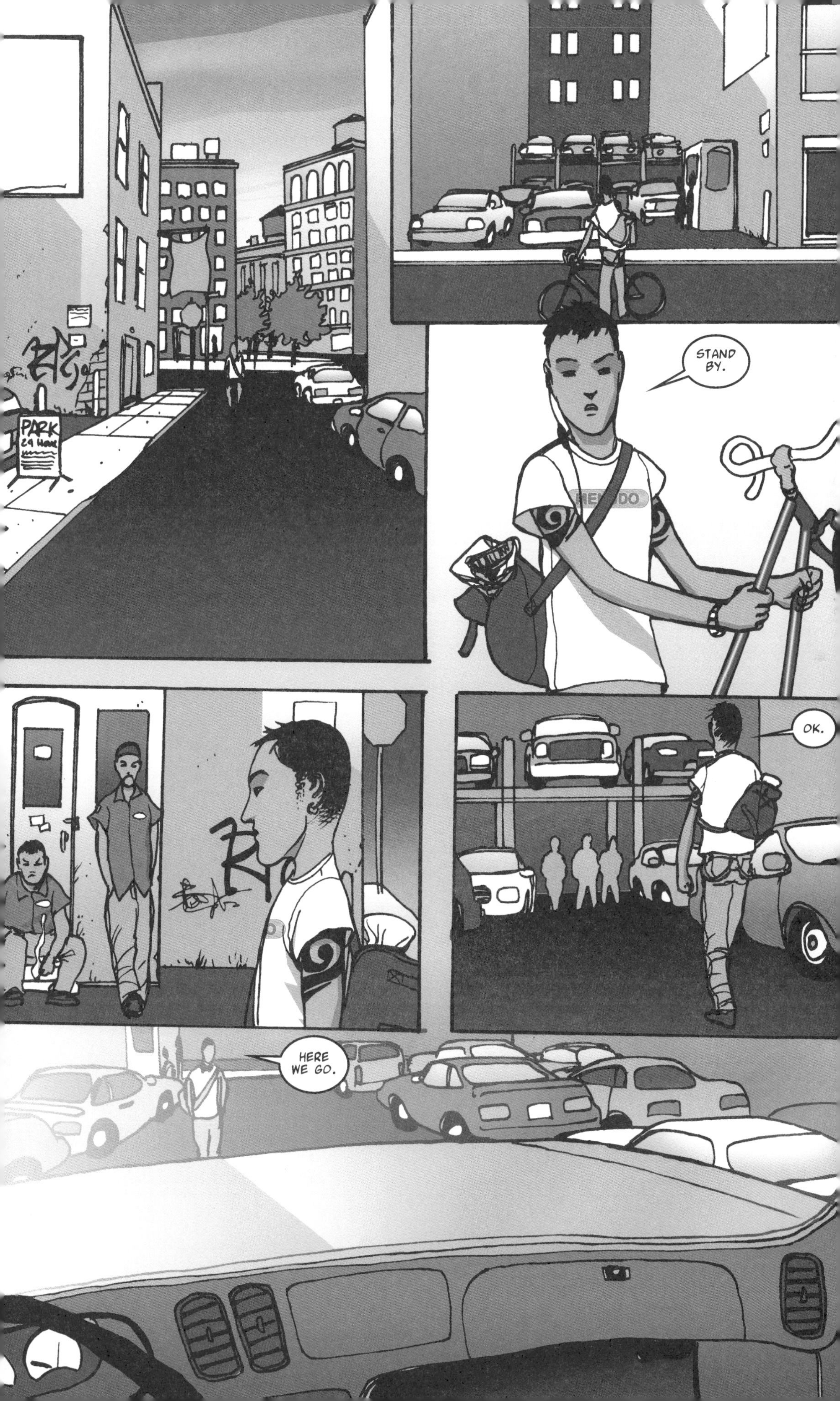
PARK
24 Hour
STAND BY.
OK.
HERE WE GO.

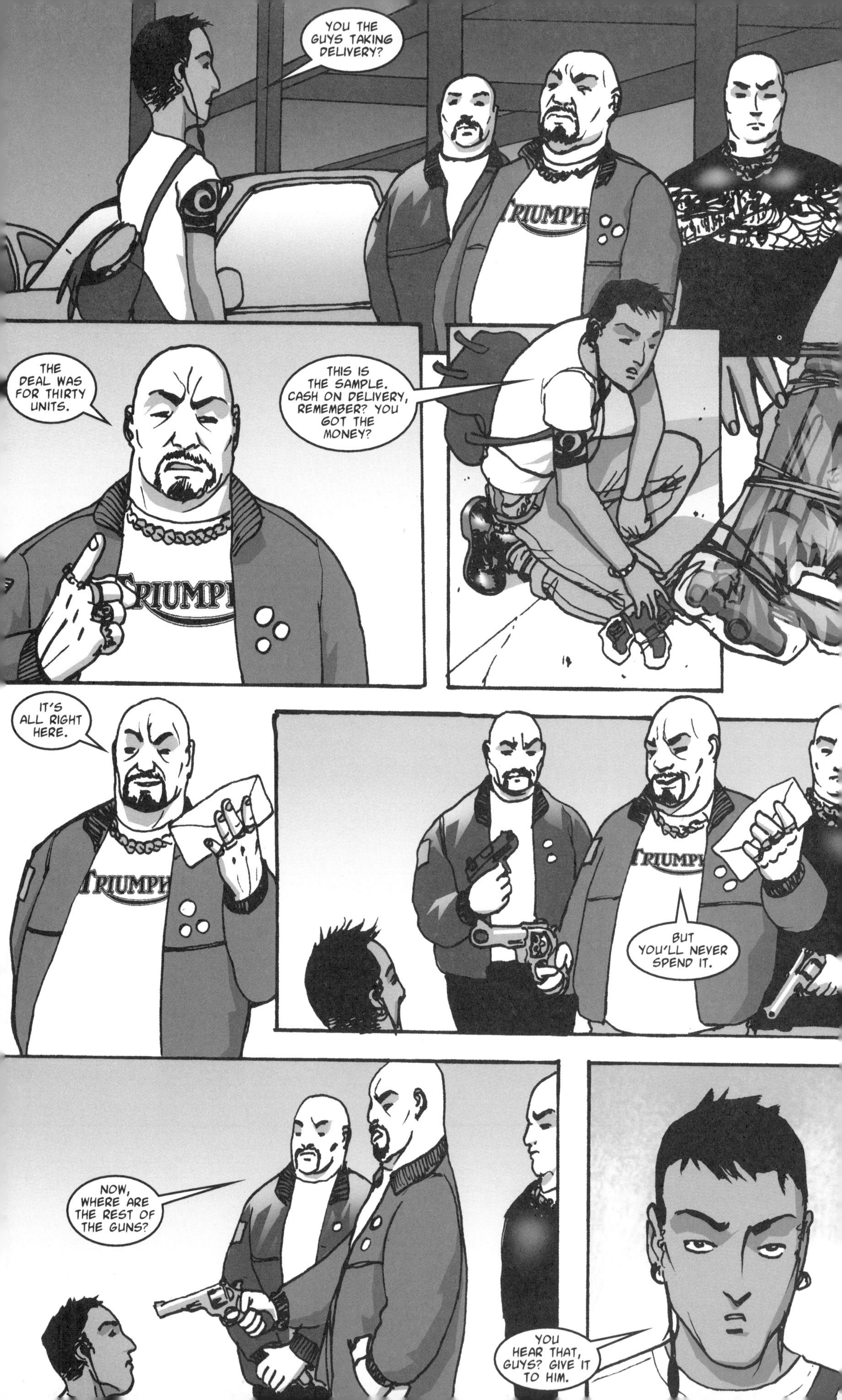
YOU THE GUYS TAKING DELIVERY?
THE DEAL WAS FOR THIRTY UNITS.
THIS IS THE SAMPLE. CASH ON DELIVERY, REMEMBER? YOU GOT THE MONEY?
TRIUMPH
IT'S ALL RIGHT HERE.
BUT YOU'LL NEVER SPEND IT.
NOW, WHERE ARE THE REST OF THE GUNS?
YOU HEAR THAT, GUYS? GIVE IT TO HIM.

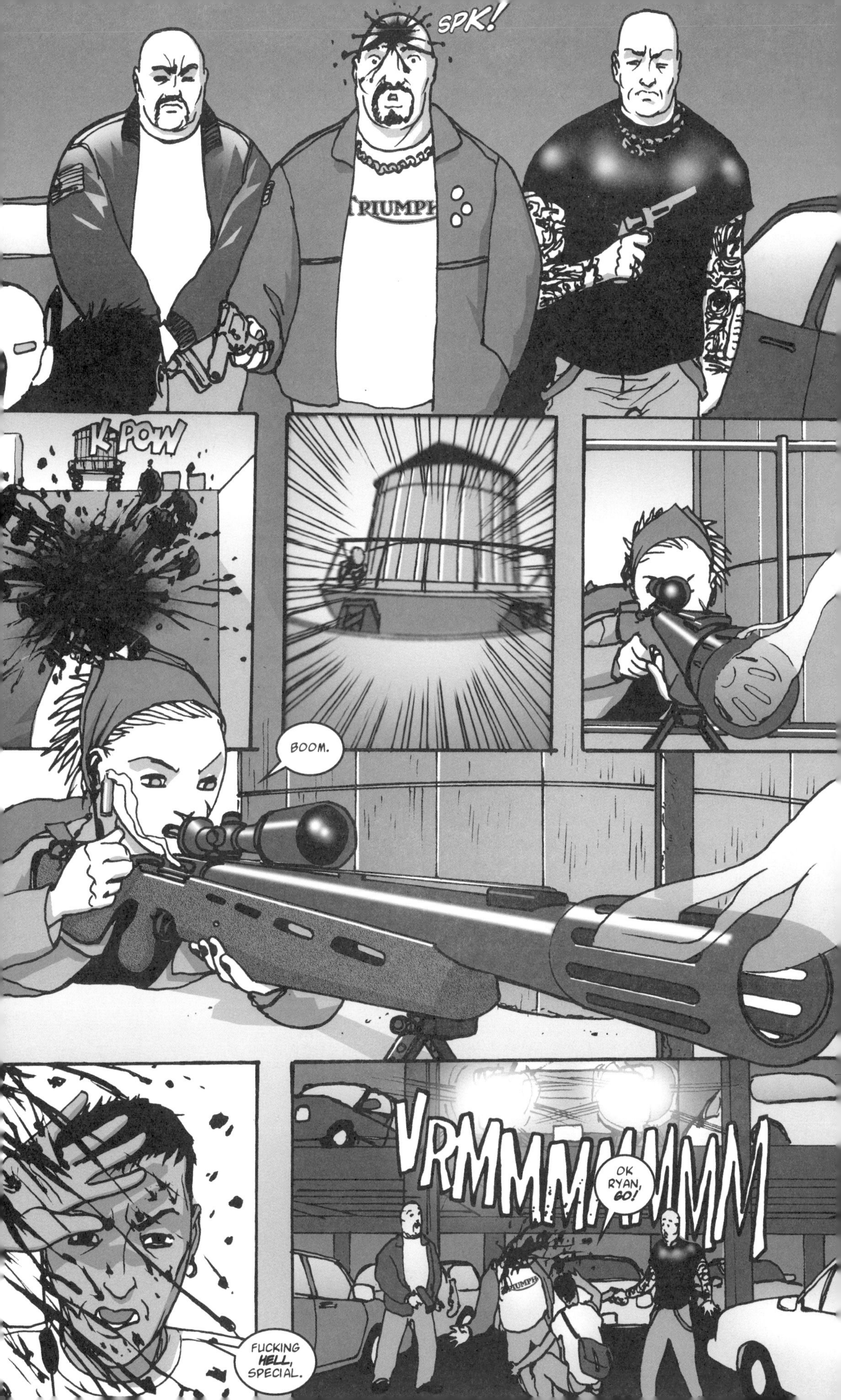
SPK!
TRIUMPH
K-POW
BOOM.
VRMMMMMMMM
OK RYAN, GO!
FUCKING HELL, SPECIAL.

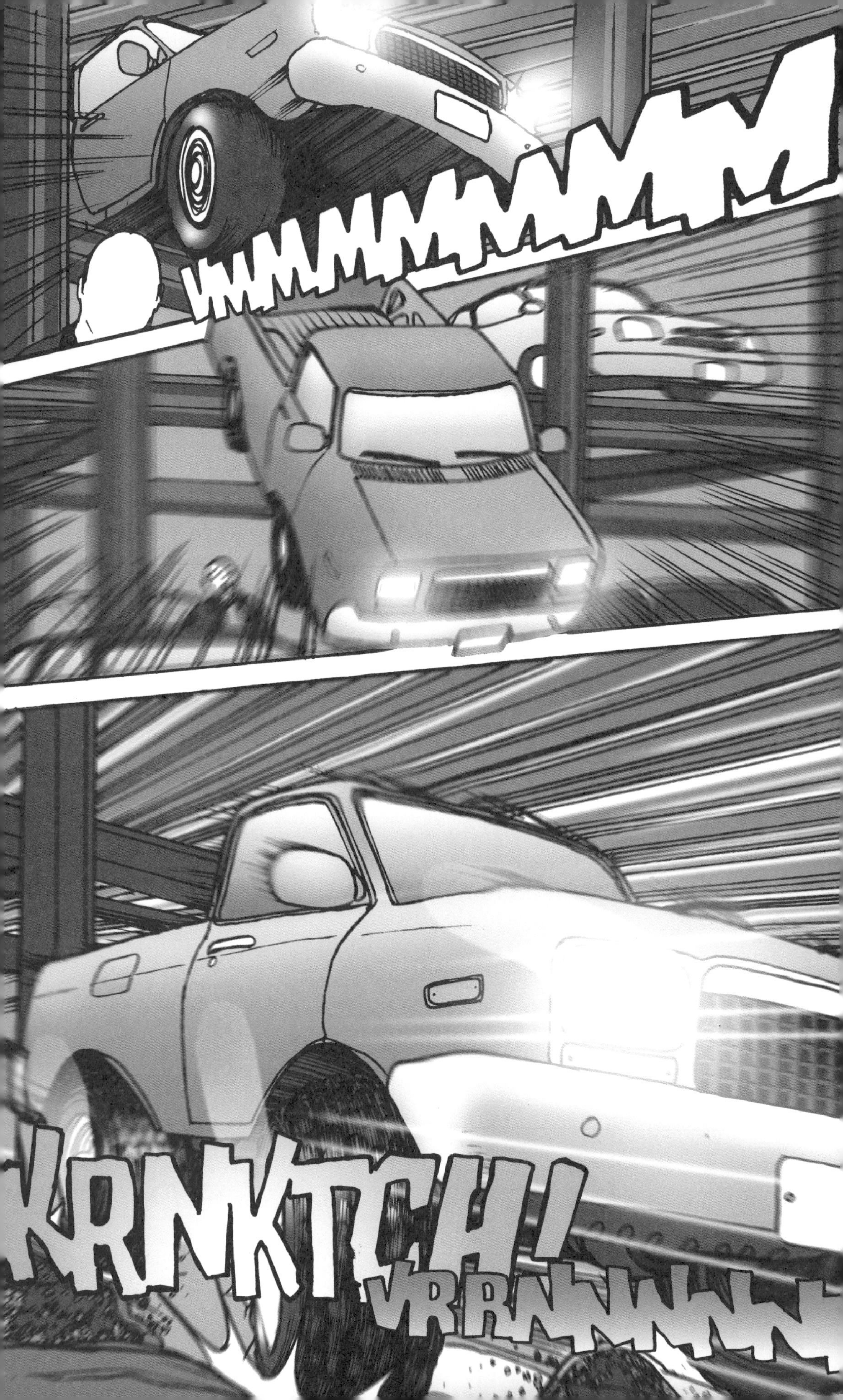
VMMMMMMMMMM
KRNKTCH!
VRRNNNNN

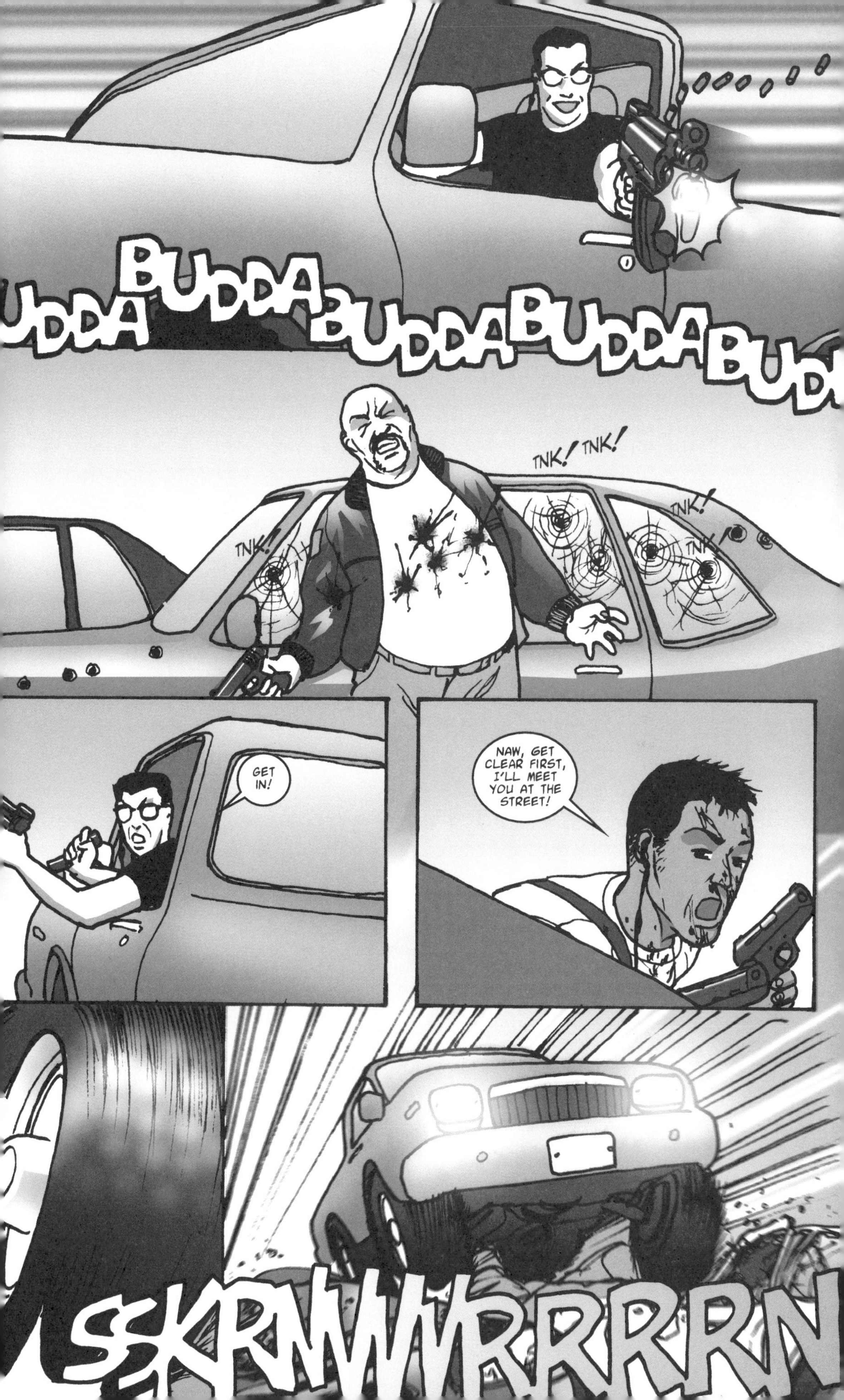

UDDA BUDDA BUDDA BUDDA BUD
TNK! TNK!
TNK!
TNK!
TNK!
GET IN!
NAW, GET CLEAR FIRST, I'LL MEET YOU AT THE STREET!
SKRNVVVRRRRN

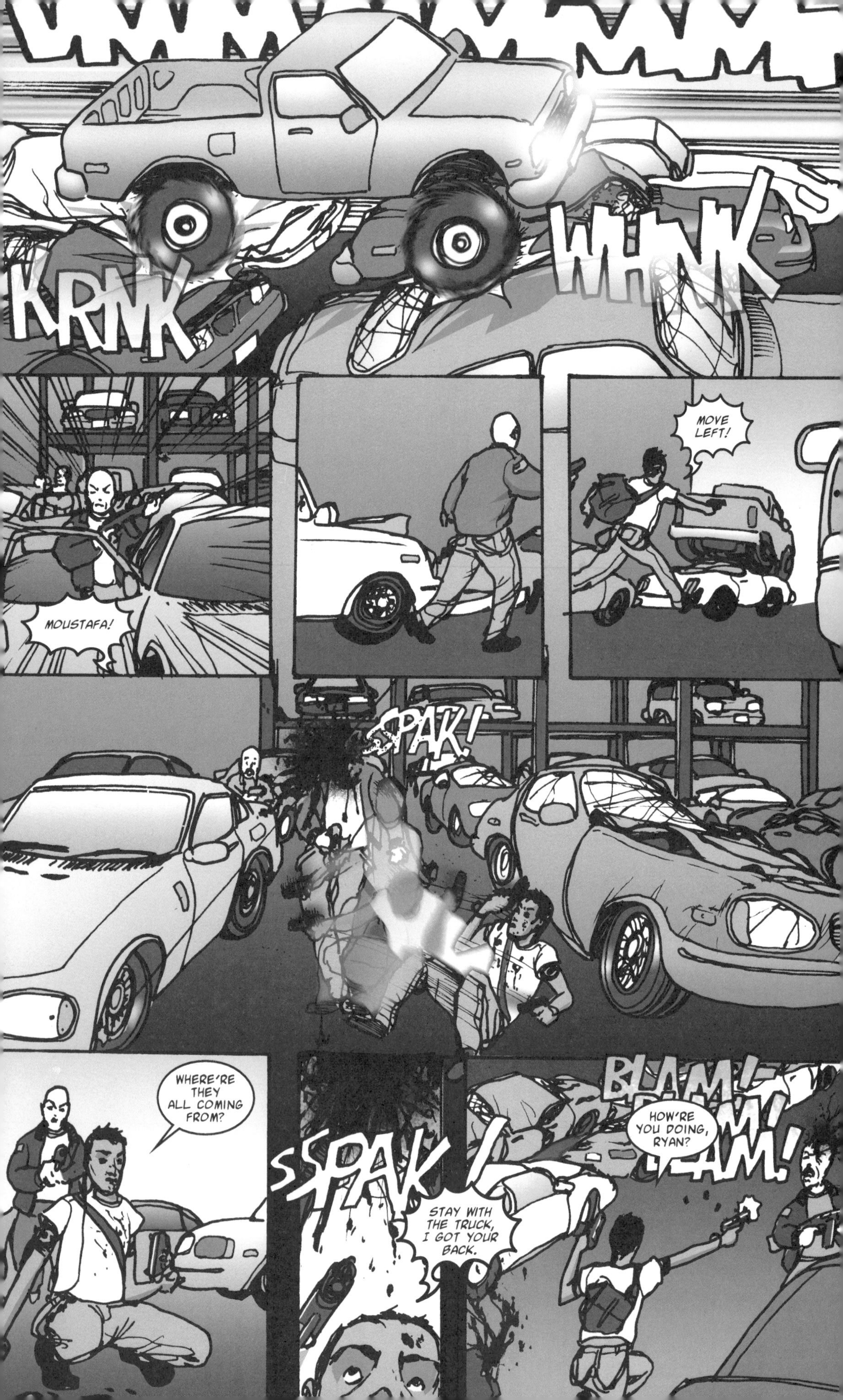
KRNK
WHNK
MOUSTAFA!
MOVE LEFT!
SPAK!
WHERE'RE THEY ALL COMING FROM?
SPAK!
STAY WITH THE TRUCK, I GOT YOUR BACK.
BLAM!
HOW'RE YOU DOING, RYAN?

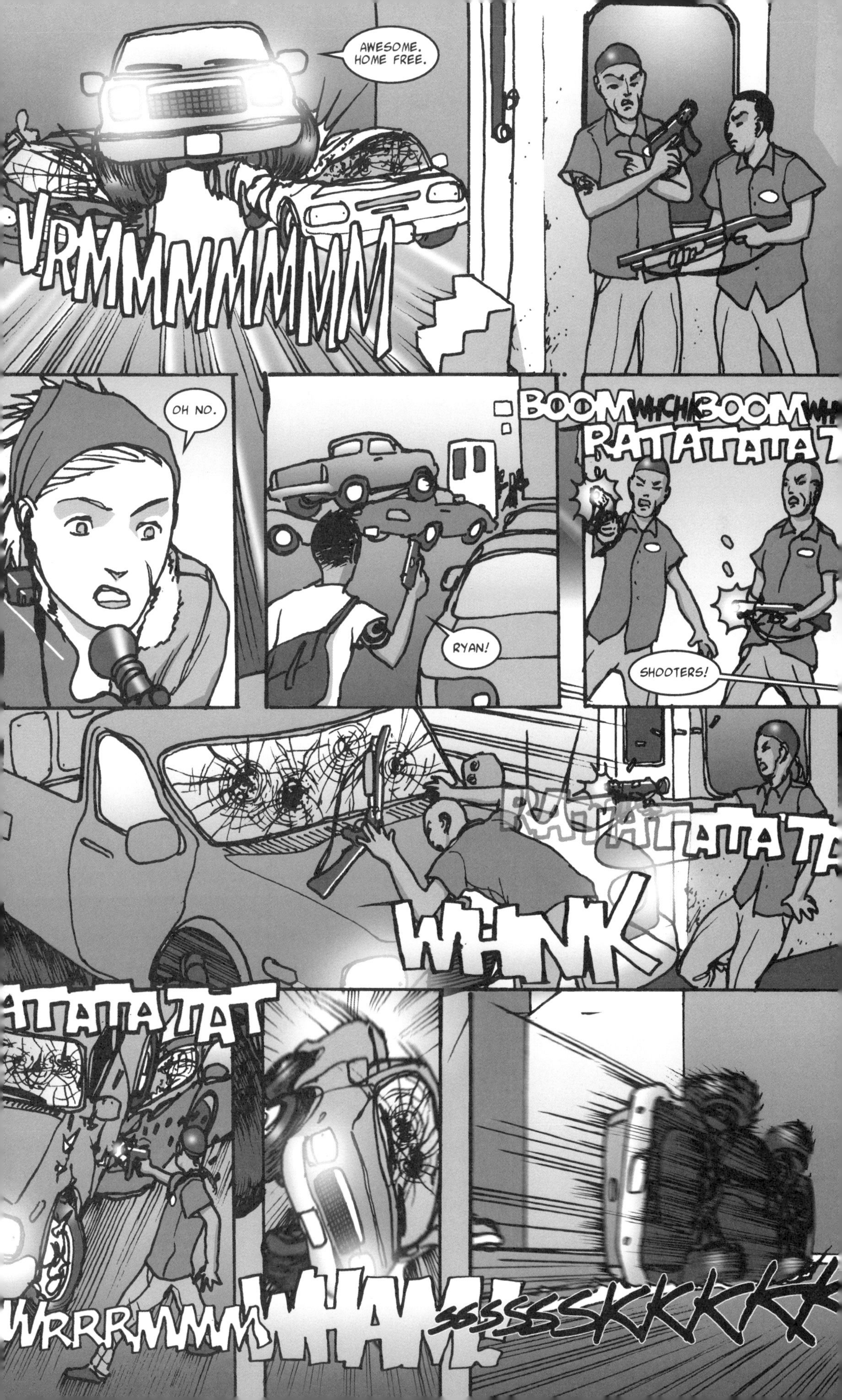
AWESOME. HOME FREE.
VRMMMMMMMM
OH NO.
RYAN!
BOOM WHCHK BOOM
RATATATATA T
SHOOTERS!
RATATATATA TA
WHNK
ATATA TAT
WRRRMMM
WHAM!
SSSSSSSKKKK

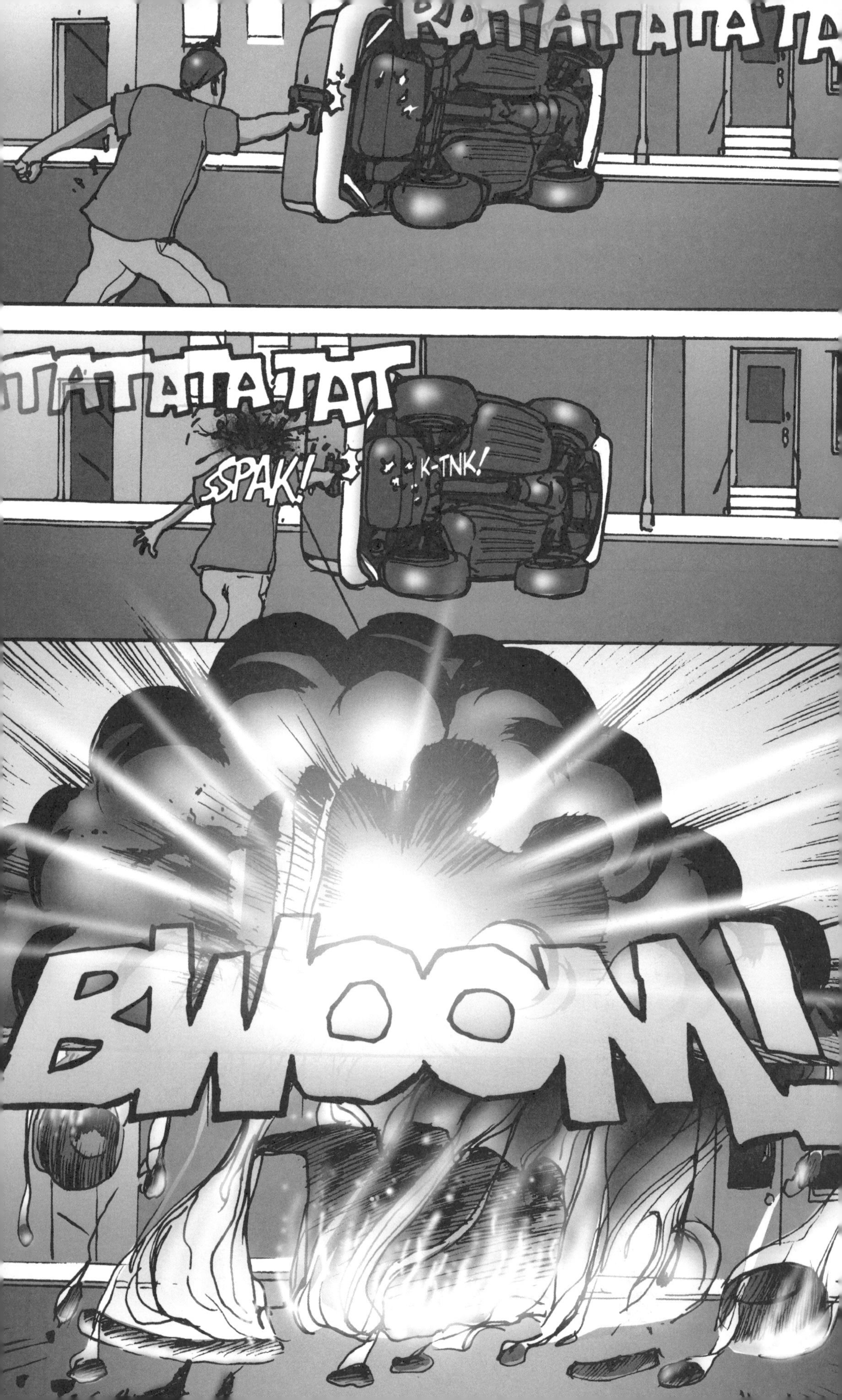
RATATATATATAT
TATATATATAT
SSPAK!
K-TNK!
BWOOM!

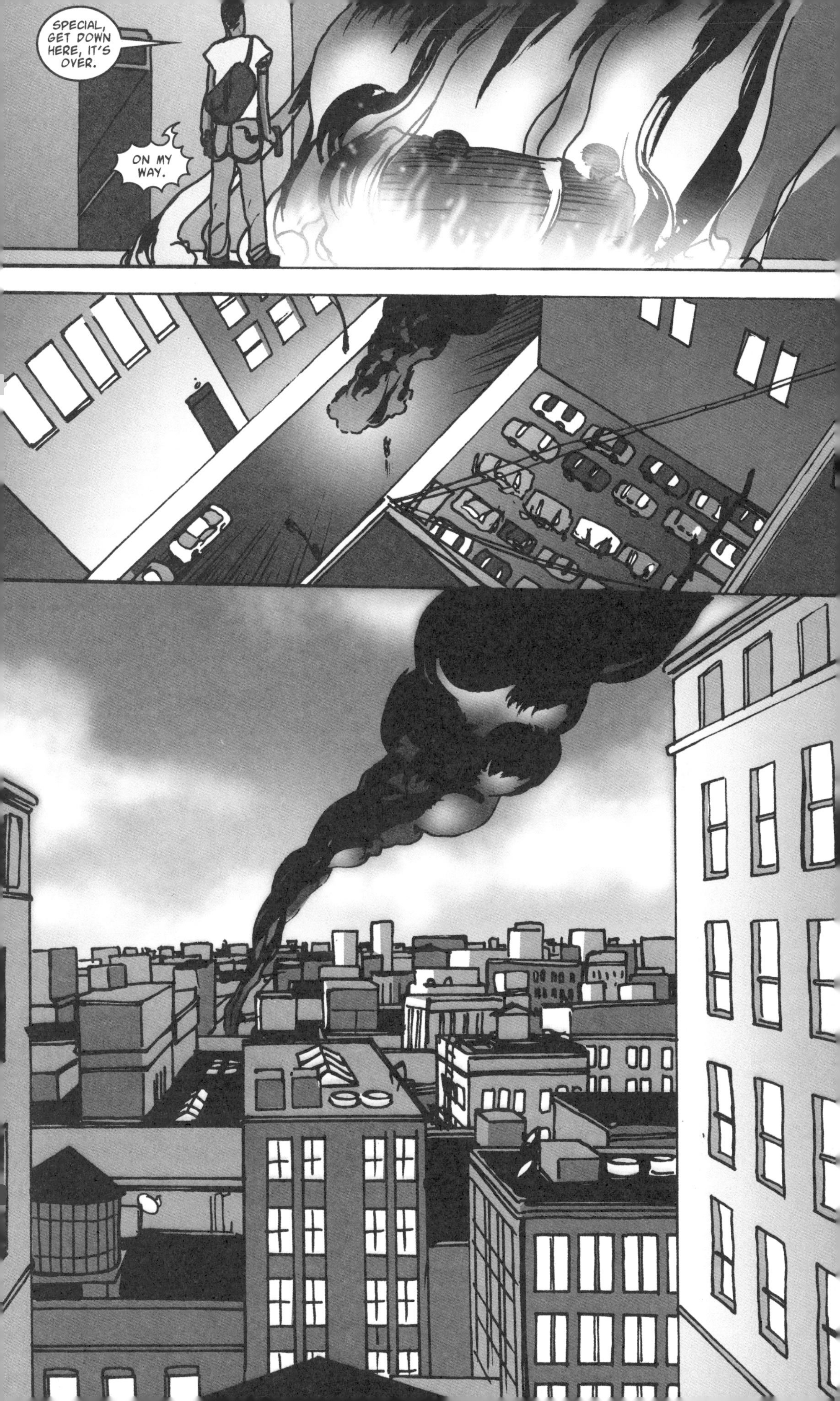
SPECIAL, GET DOWN HERE, IT'S OVER.
ON MY WAY.

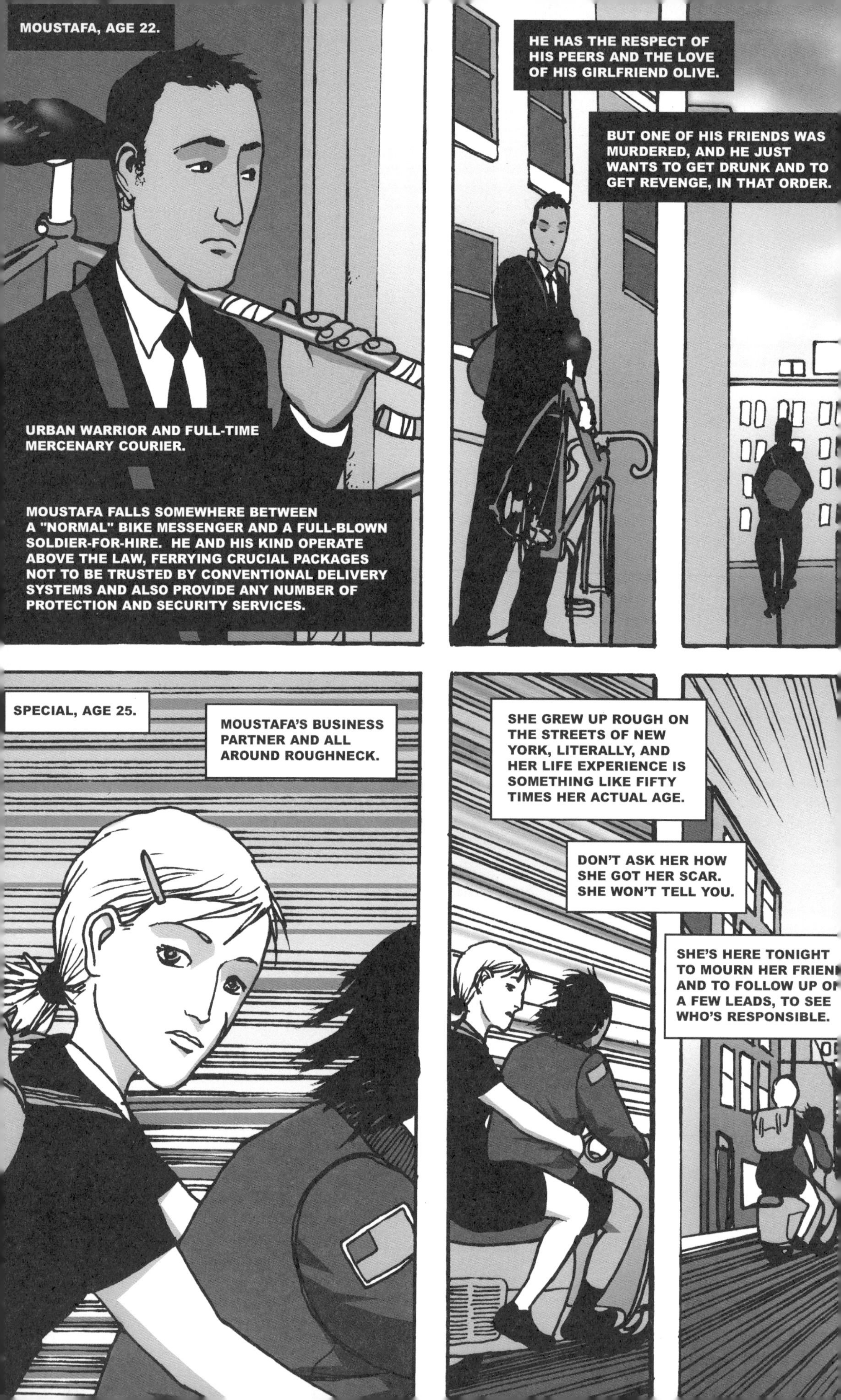
MOUSTAFA, AGE 22.
URBAN WARRIOR AND FULL-TIME MERCENARY COURIER.
MOUSTAFA FALLS SOMEWHERE BETWEEN A "NORMAL" BIKE MESSENGER AND A FULL-BLOWN SOLDIER-FOR-HIRE. HE AND HIS KIND OPERATE ABOVE THE LAW, FERRYING CRUCIAL PACKAGES NOT TO BE TRUSTED BY CONVENTIONAL DELIVERY SYSTEMS AND ALSO PROVIDE ANY NUMBER OF PROTECTION AND SECURITY SERVICES.
HE HAS THE RESPECT OF HIS PEERS AND THE LOVE OF HIS GIRLFRIEND OLIVE.
BUT ONE OF HIS FRIENDS WAS MURDERED, AND HE JUST WANTS TO GET DRUNK AND TO GET REVENGE, IN THAT ORDER.
SPECIAL, AGE 25.
MOUSTAFA'S BUSINESS PARTNER AND ALL AROUND ROUGHNECK.
SHE GREW UP ROUGH ON THE STREETS OF NEW YORK, LITERALLY, AND HER LIFE EXPERIENCE IS SOMETHING LIKE FIFTY TIMES HER ACTUAL AGE.
DON'T ASK HER HOW SHE GOT HER SCAR. SHE WON'T TELL YOU.
SHE'S HERE TONIGHT TO MOURN HER FRIEN AND TO FOLLOW UP O A FEW LEADS, TO SEE WHO'S RESPONSIBLE.

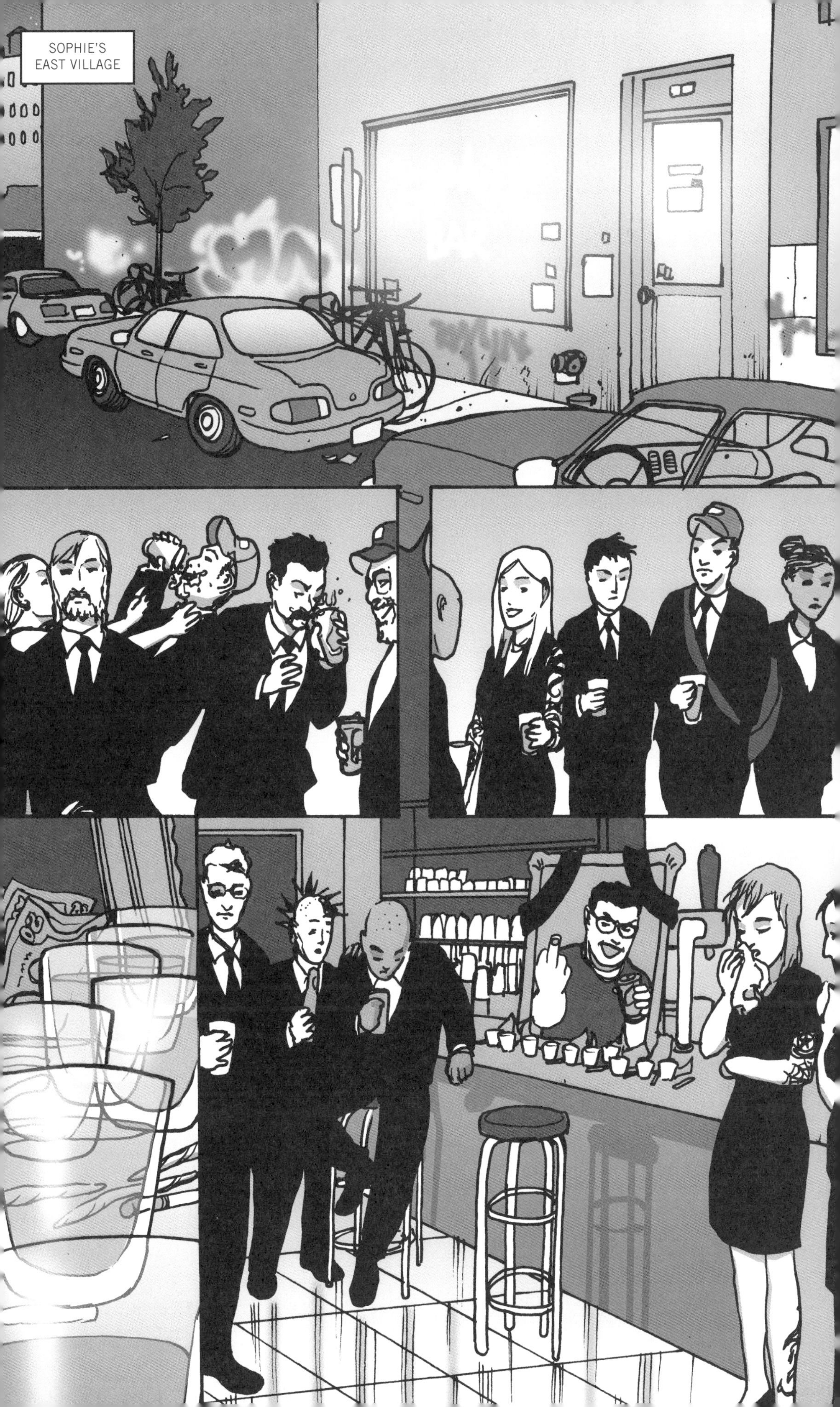
SOPHIE'S
EAST VILLAGE

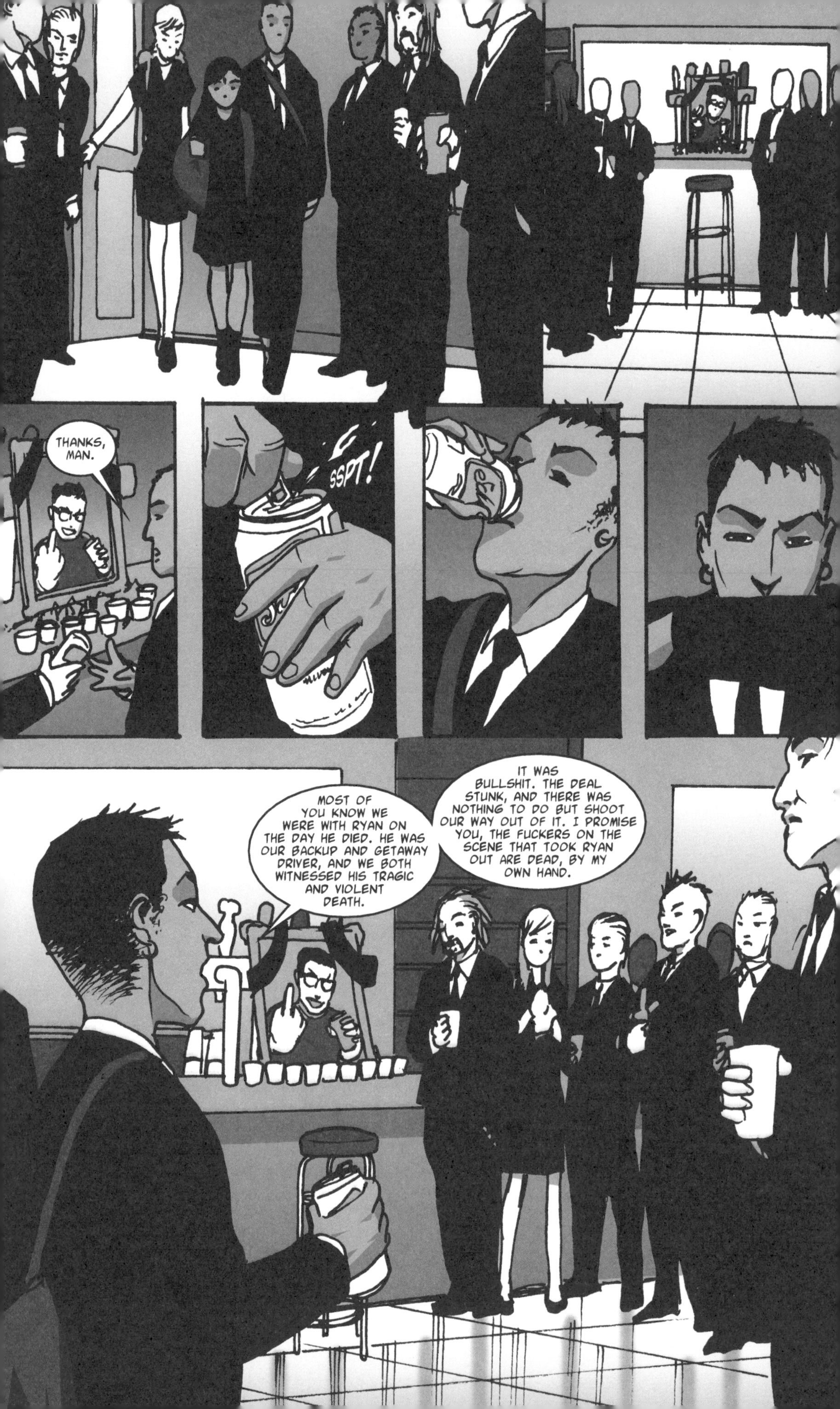

THANKS, MAN.
SSPT!
MOST OF YOU KNOW WE WERE WITH RYAN ON THE DAY HE DIED. HE WAS OUR BACKUP AND GETAWAY DRIVER, AND WE BOTH WITNESSED HIS TRAGIC AND VIOLENT DEATH.
IT WAS BULLSHIT. THE DEAL STUNK, AND THERE WAS NOTHING TO DO BUT SHOOT OUR WAY OUT OF IT. I PROMISE YOU, THE FUCKERS ON THE SCENE THAT TOOK RYAN OUT ARE DEAD, BY MY OWN HAND.

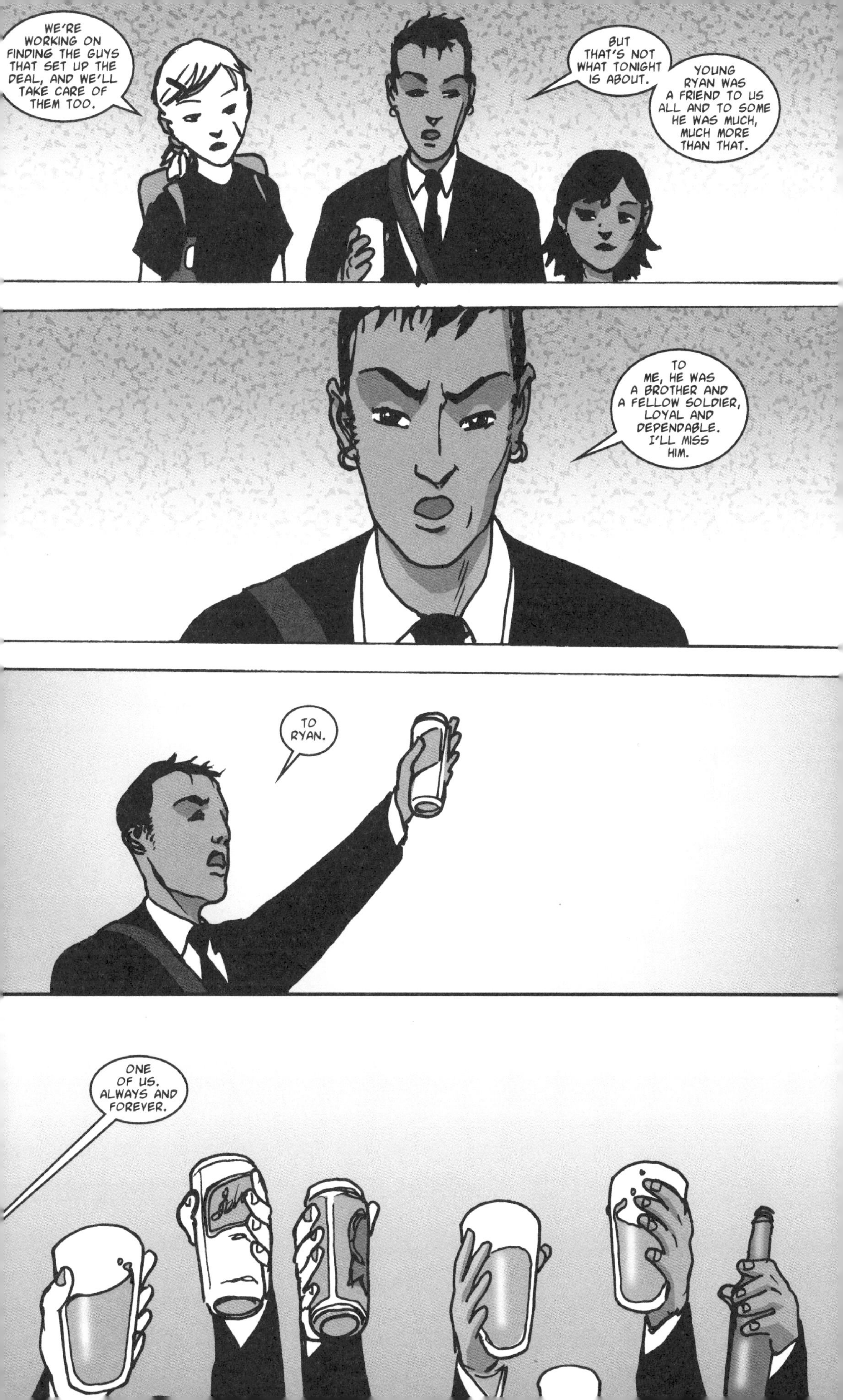
WE'RE WORKING ON FINDING THE GUYS THAT SET UP THE DEAL, AND WE'LL TAKE CARE OF THEM TOO.
BUT THAT'S NOT WHAT TONIGHT IS ABOUT.
YOUNG RYAN WAS A FRIEND TO US ALL AND TO SOME HE WAS MUCH, MUCH MORE THAN THAT.
TO ME, HE WAS A BROTHER AND A FELLOW SOLDIER, LOYAL AND DEPENDABLE. I'LL MISS HIM.
TO RYAN.
ONE OF US. ALWAYS AND FOREVER.

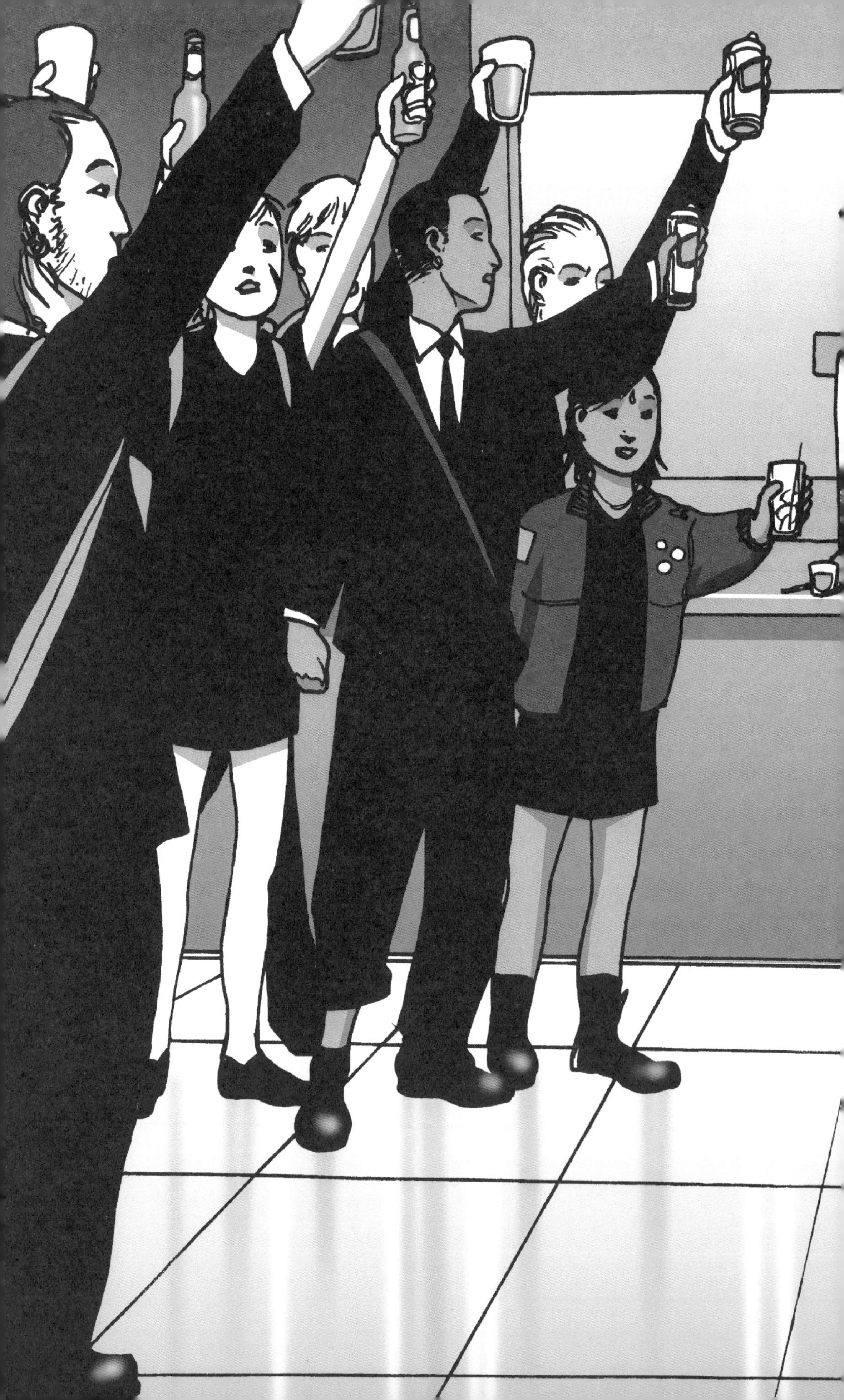

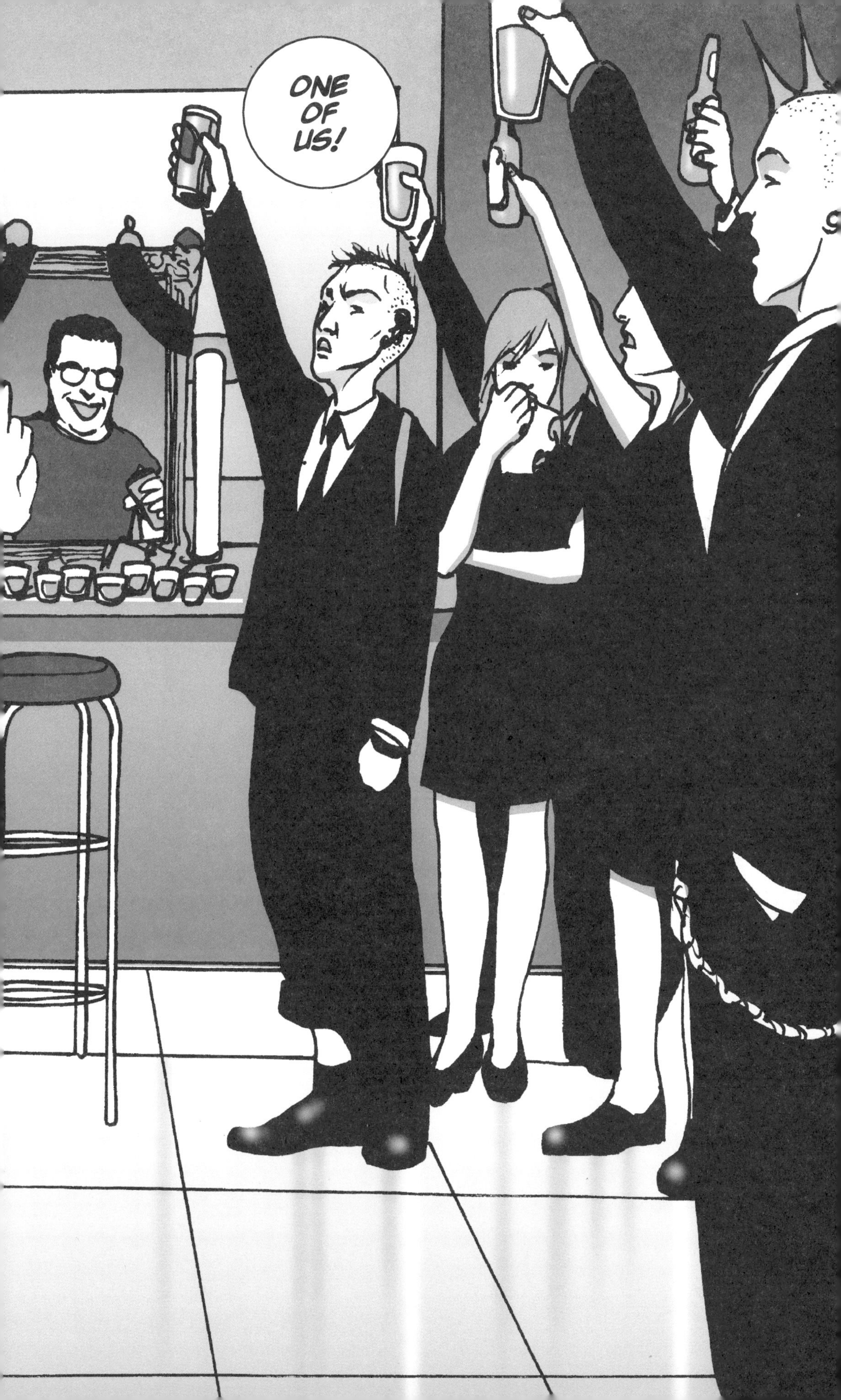
ONE OF US!

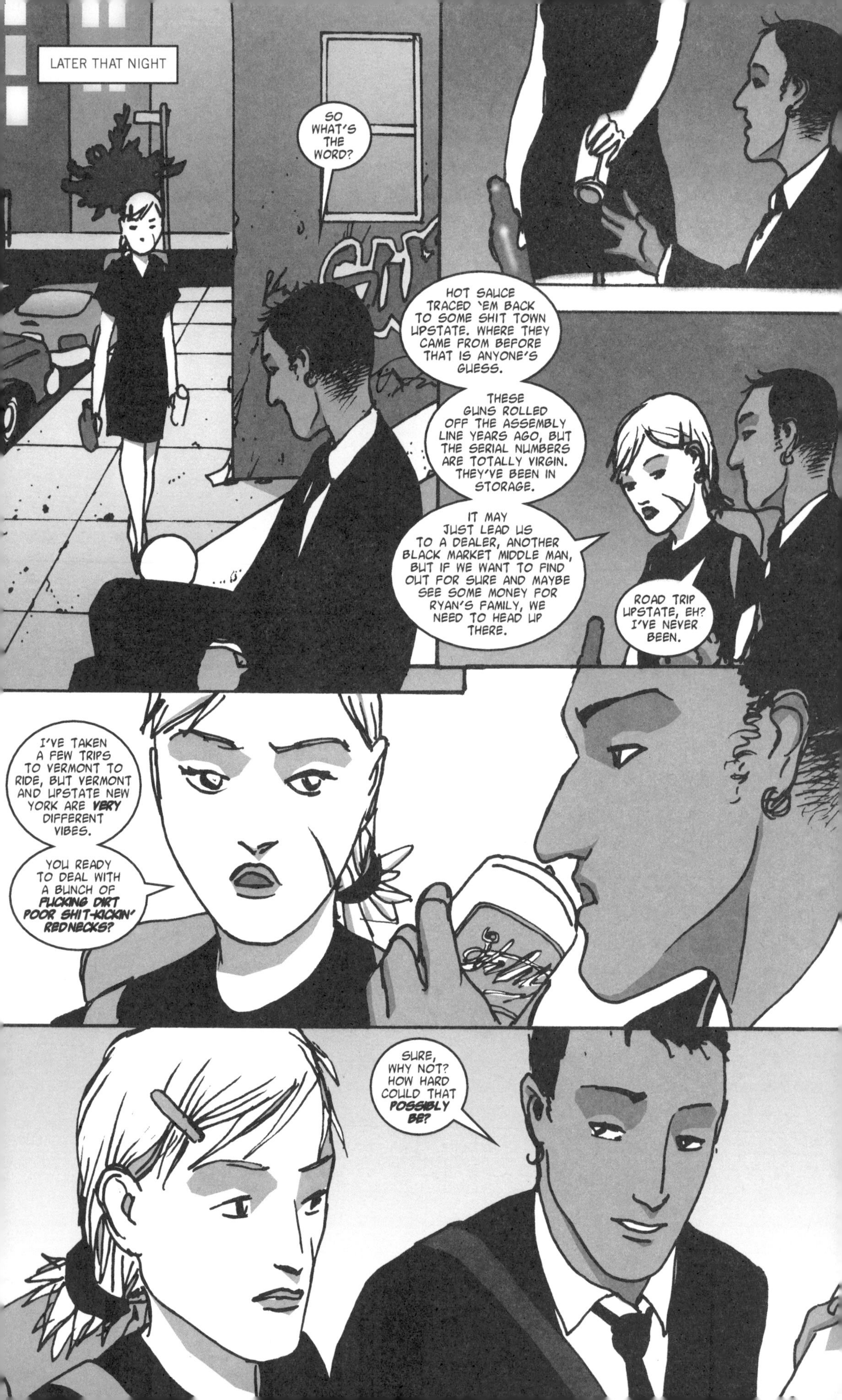

LATER THAT NIGHT
SO WHAT'S THE WORD?
HOT SAUCE TRACED 'EM BACK TO SOME SHIT TOWN UPSTATE. WHERE THEY CAME FROM BEFORE THAT IS ANYONE'S GUESS.
THESE GUNS ROLLED OFF THE ASSEMBLY LINE YEARS AGO, BUT THE SERIAL NUMBERS ARE TOTALLY VIRGIN. THEY'VE BEEN IN STORAGE.
IT MAY JUST LEAD US TO A DEALER, ANOTHER BLACK MARKET MIDDLE MAN, BUT IF WE WANT TO FIND OUT FOR SURE AND MAYBE SEE SOME MONEY FOR RYAN'S FAMILY, WE NEED TO HEAD UP THERE.
ROAD TRIP UPSTATE, EH? I'VE NEVER BEEN.
I'VE TAKEN A FEW TRIPS TO VERMONT TO RIDE, BUT VERMONT AND UPSTATE NEW YORK ARE **VERY** DIFFERENT VIBES.
YOU READY TO DEAL WITH A BUNCH OF **FUCKING DIRT POOR SHIT-KICKIN' REDNECKS?**
SURE, WHY NOT? HOW HARD COULD THAT **POSSIBLY BE?**

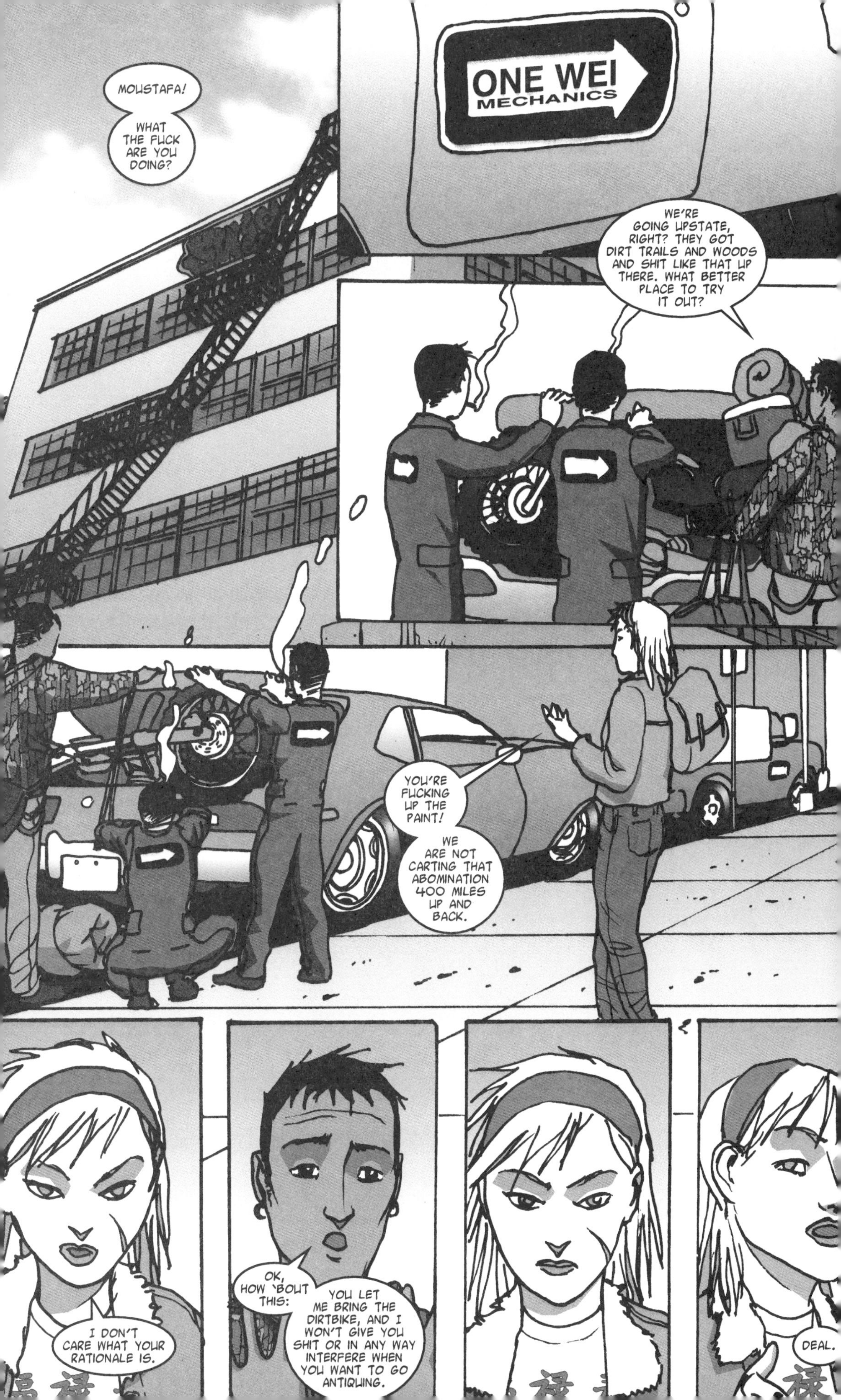
MOUSTAFA!
WHAT THE FUCK ARE YOU DOING?
ONE WEI MECHANICS
WE'RE GOING UPSTATE, RIGHT? THEY GOT DIRT TRAILS AND WOODS AND SHIT LIKE THAT UP THERE. WHAT BETTER PLACE TO TRY IT OUT?
YOU'RE FUCKING UP THE PAINT!
WE ARE NOT CARTING THAT ABOMINATION 400 MILES UP AND BACK.
I DON'T CARE WHAT YOUR RATIONALE IS.
OK, HOW 'BOUT THIS:
YOU LET ME BRING THE DIRTBIKE, AND I WON'T GIVE YOU SHIT OR IN ANY WAY INTERFERE WHEN YOU WANT TO GO ANTIQUING.
DEAL.

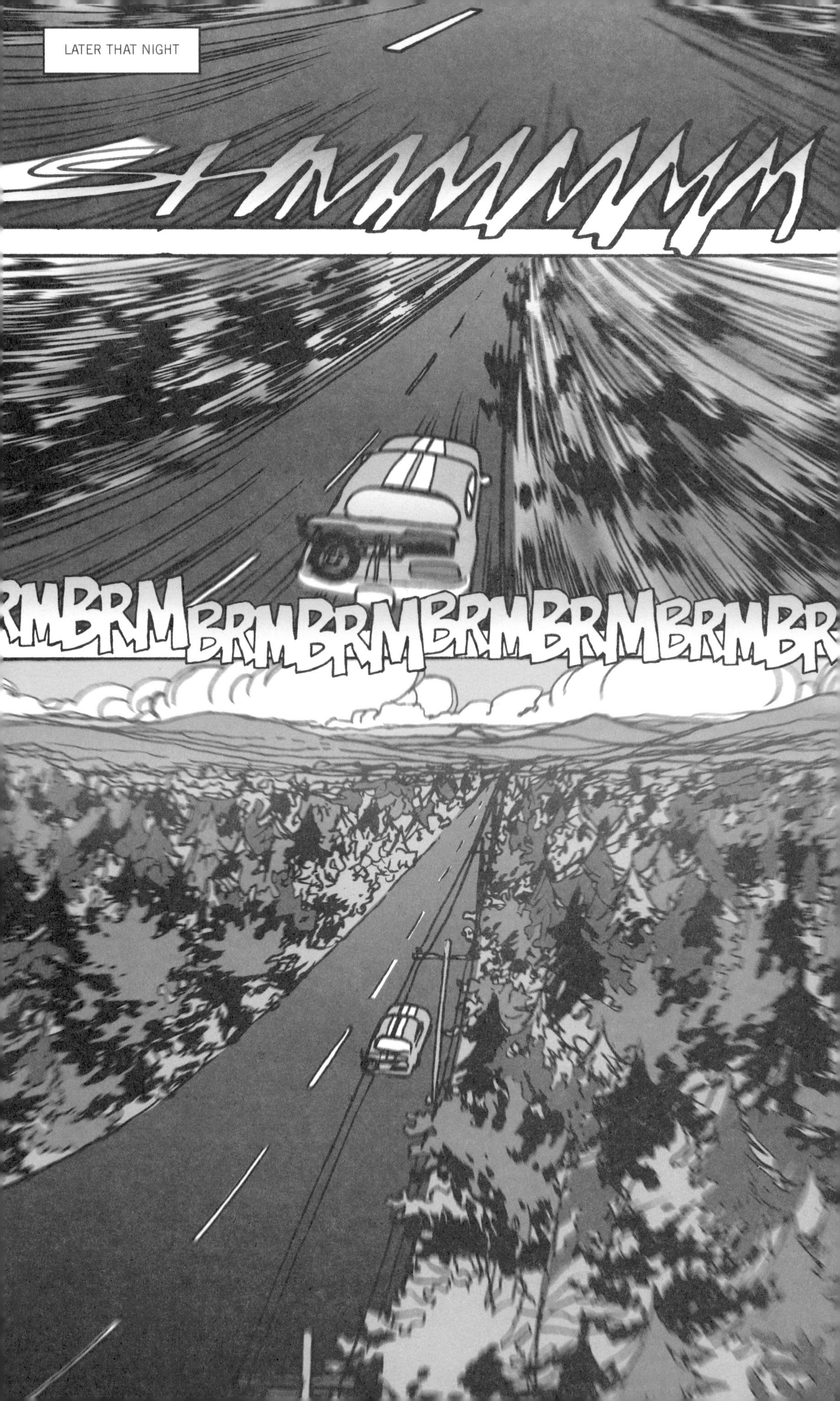

LATER THAT NIGHT
SHMMMMM
BRMBRMBRMBRMBRMBRMBR

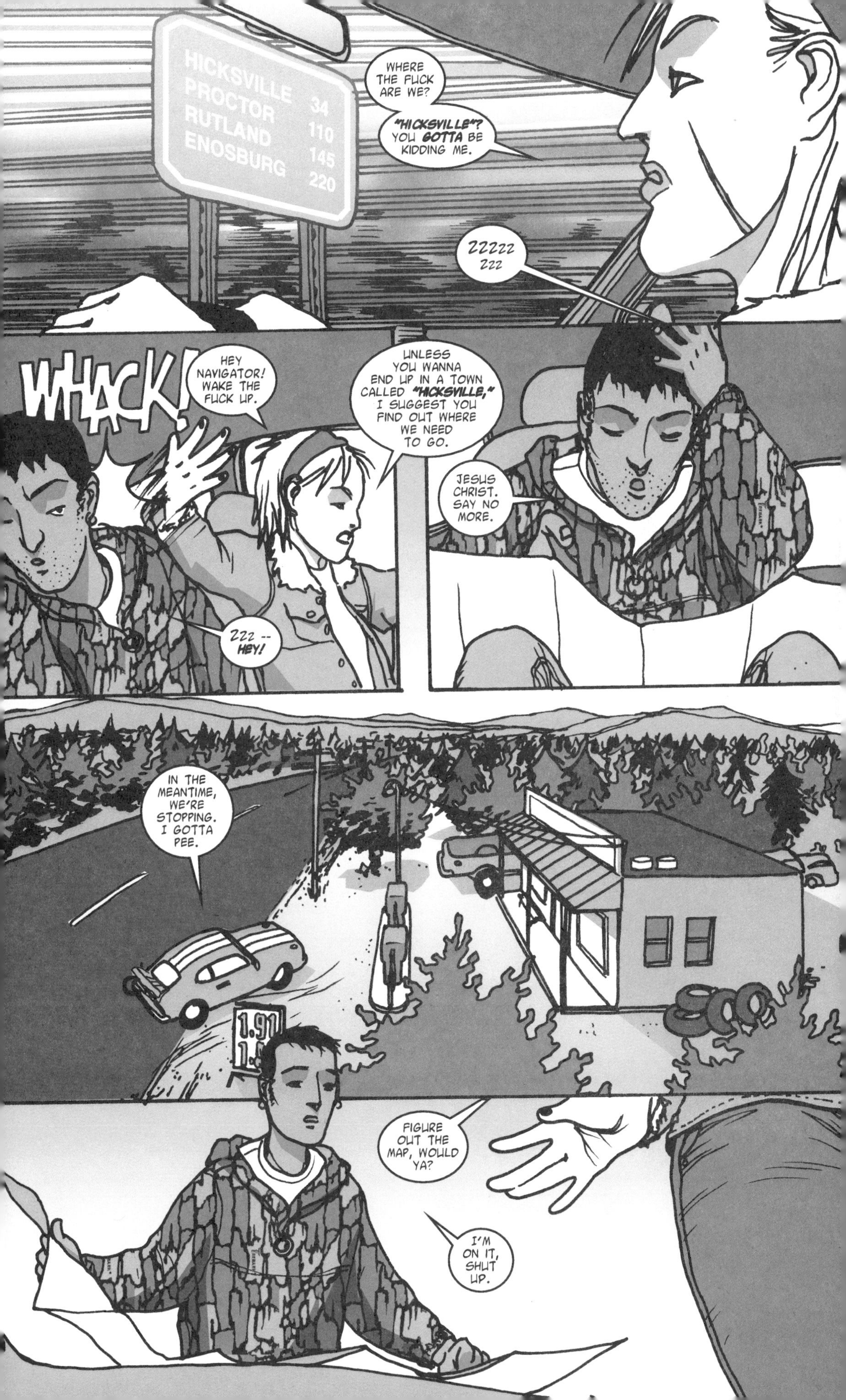
HICKSVILLE 34
PROCTOR 110
RUTLAND 145
ENOSBURG 220
WHERE THE FUCK ARE WE?
"HICKSVILLE"? YOU GOTTA BE KIDDING ME.
ZZZZZ ZZZ
WHACK!
HEY NAVIGATOR! WAKE THE FUCK UP.
ZZZ -- HEY!
UNLESS YOU WANNA END UP IN A TOWN CALLED "HICKSVILLE," I SUGGEST YOU FIND OUT WHERE WE NEED TO GO.
JESUS CHRIST. SAY NO MORE.
IN THE MEANTIME, WE'RE STOPPING. I GOTTA PEE.
FIGURE OUT THE MAP, WOULD YA?
I'M ON IT, SHUT UP.

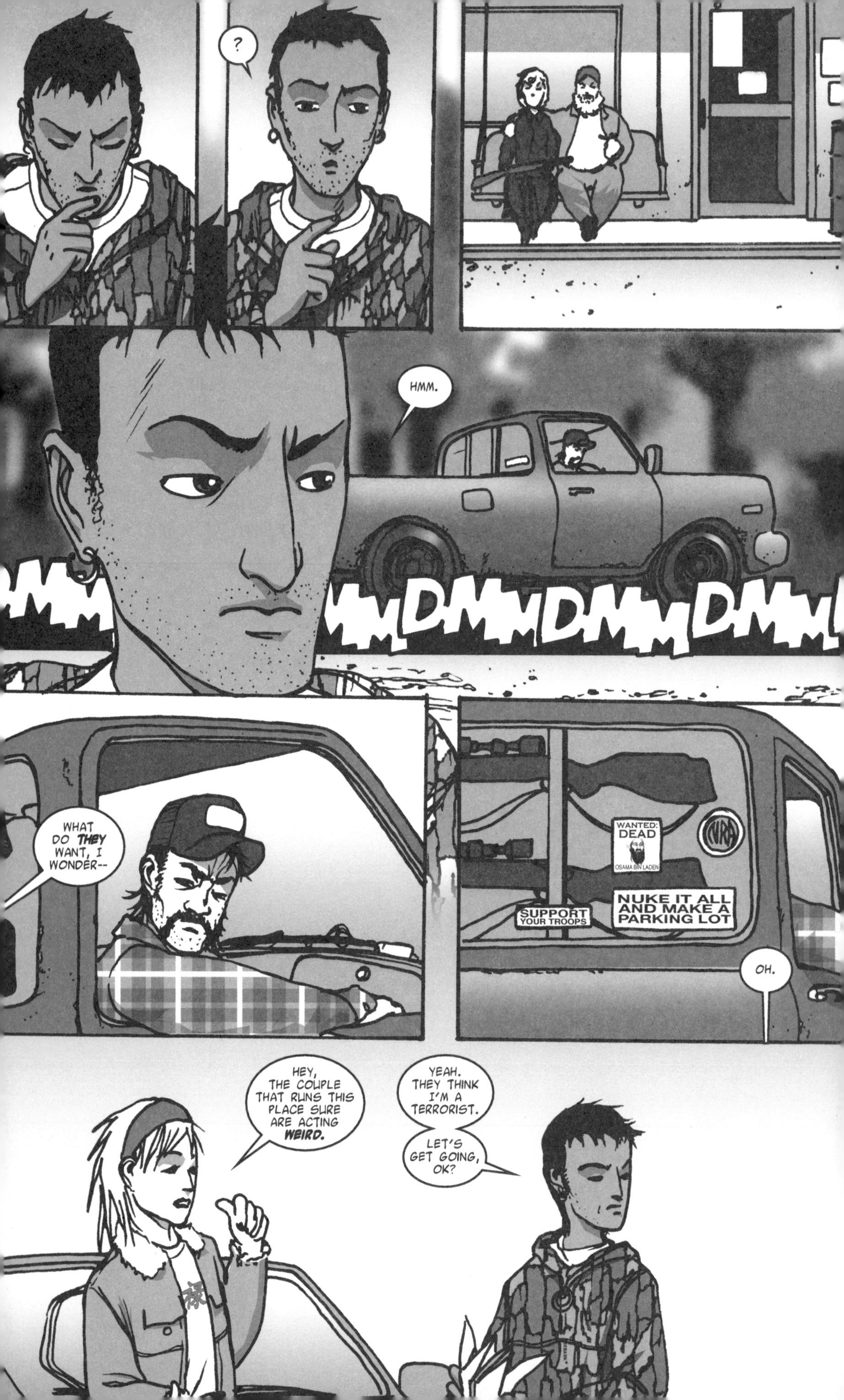
?
HMM.
MMMMDMMDMMDMM
WHAT DO THEY WANT, I WONDER--
WANTED: DEAD
OSAMA BIN LADEN
NRA
NUKE IT ALL AND MAKE A PARKING LOT
SUPPORT YOUR TROOPS
OH.
HEY, THE COUPLE THAT RUNS THIS PLACE SURE ARE ACTING WEIRD.
YEAH. THEY THINK I'M A TERRORIST.
LET'S GET GOING, OK?

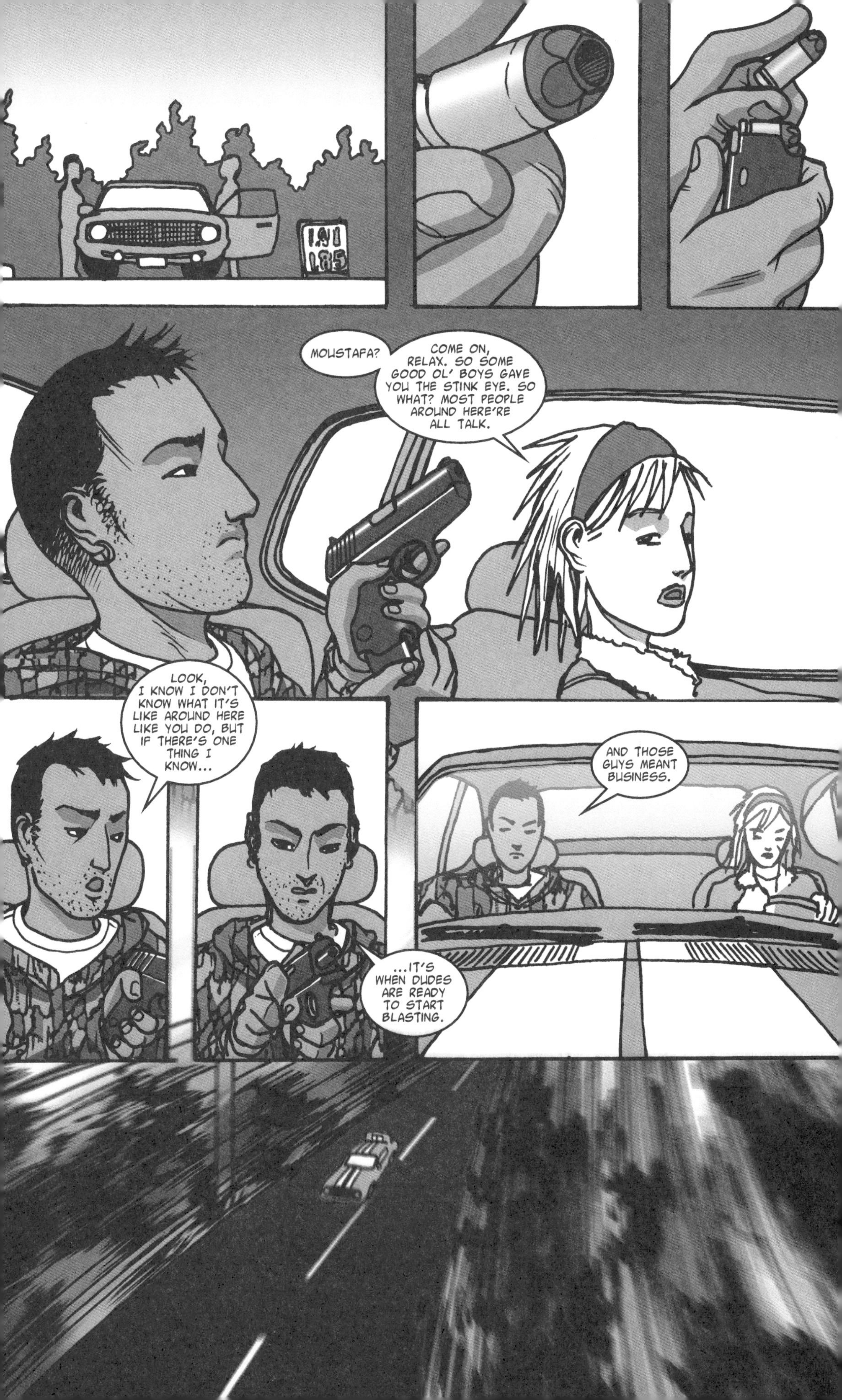
MOUSTAFA?
COME ON, RELAX. SO SOME GOOD OL' BOYS GAVE YOU THE STINK EYE. SO WHAT? MOST PEOPLE AROUND HERE'RE ALL TALK.
LOOK, I KNOW I DON'T KNOW WHAT IT'S LIKE AROUND HERE LIKE YOU DO, BUT IF THERE'S ONE THING I KNOW...
...IT'S WHEN DUDES ARE READY TO START BLASTING.
AND THOSE GUYS MEANT BUSINESS.

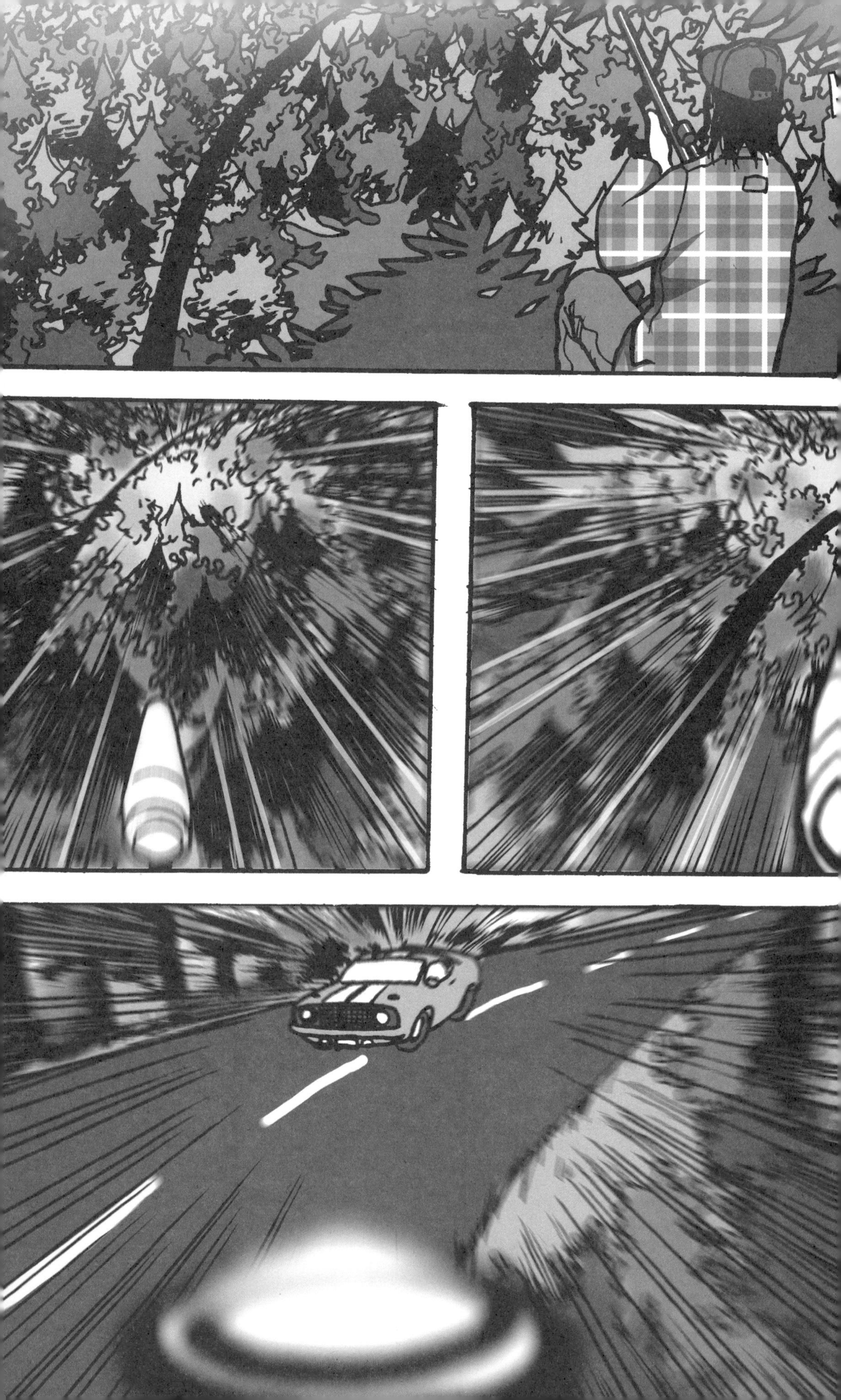

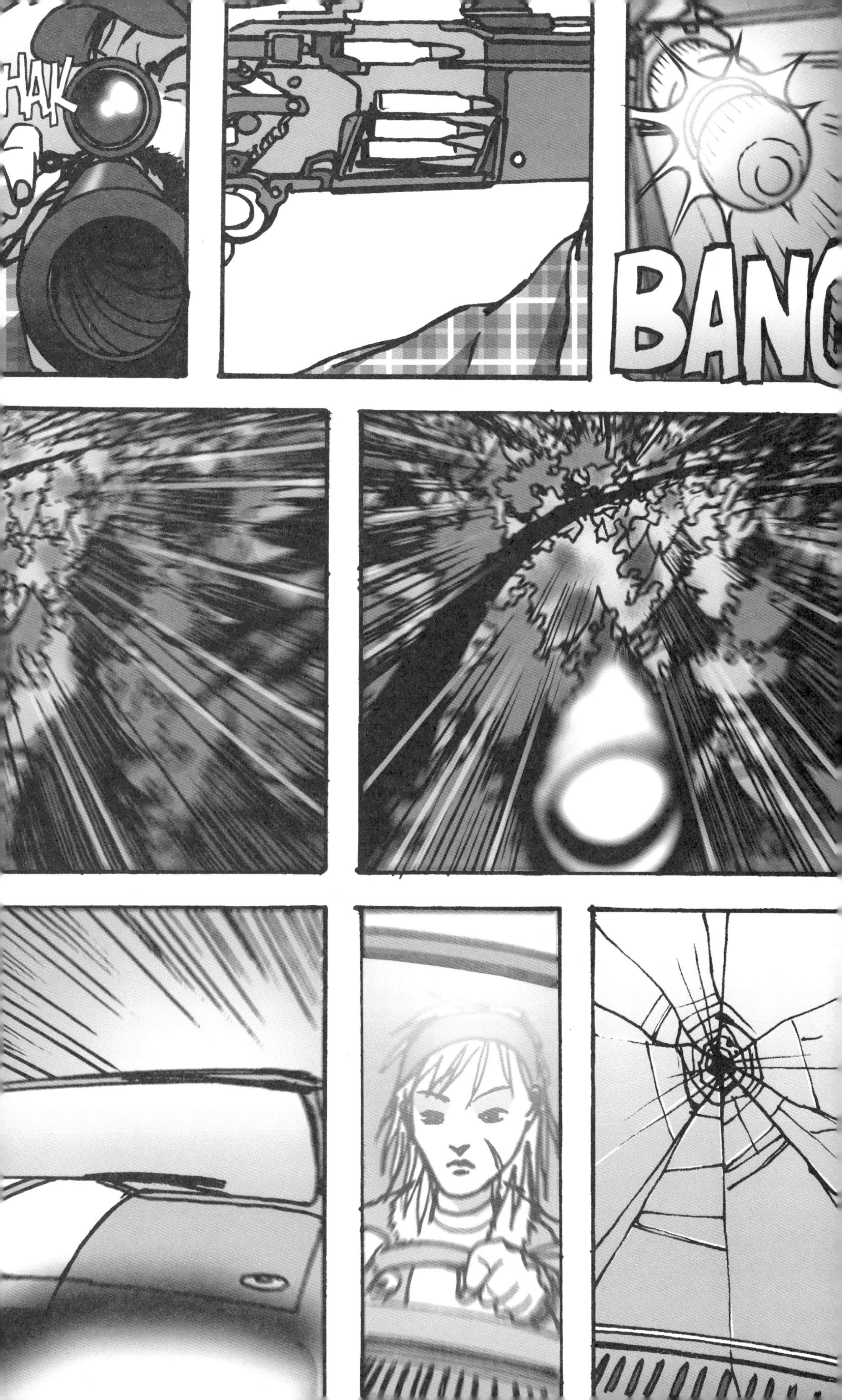

CHAK
BANG

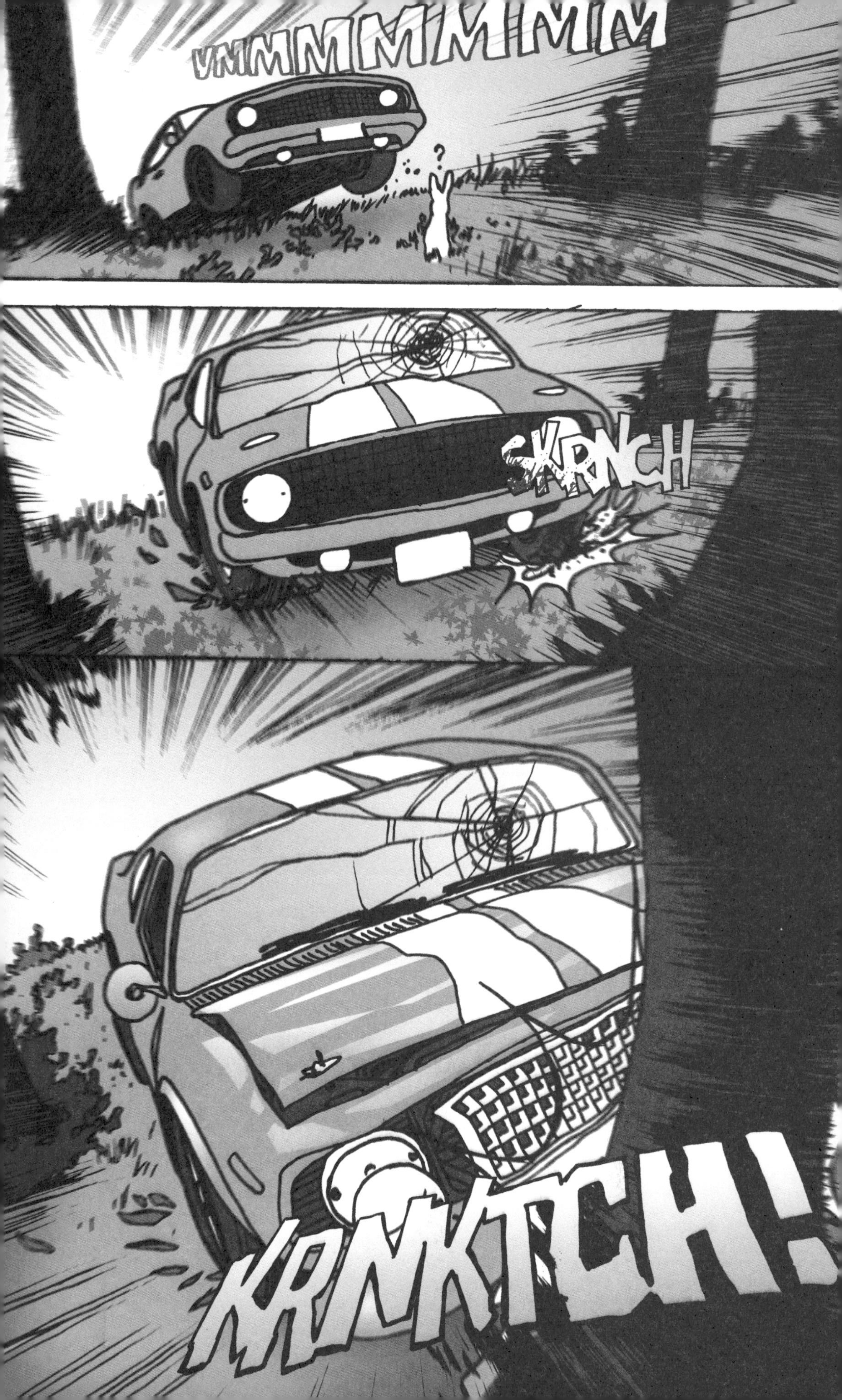
VMMMMMMMM
?
SKRNCH
KRNKTCH!

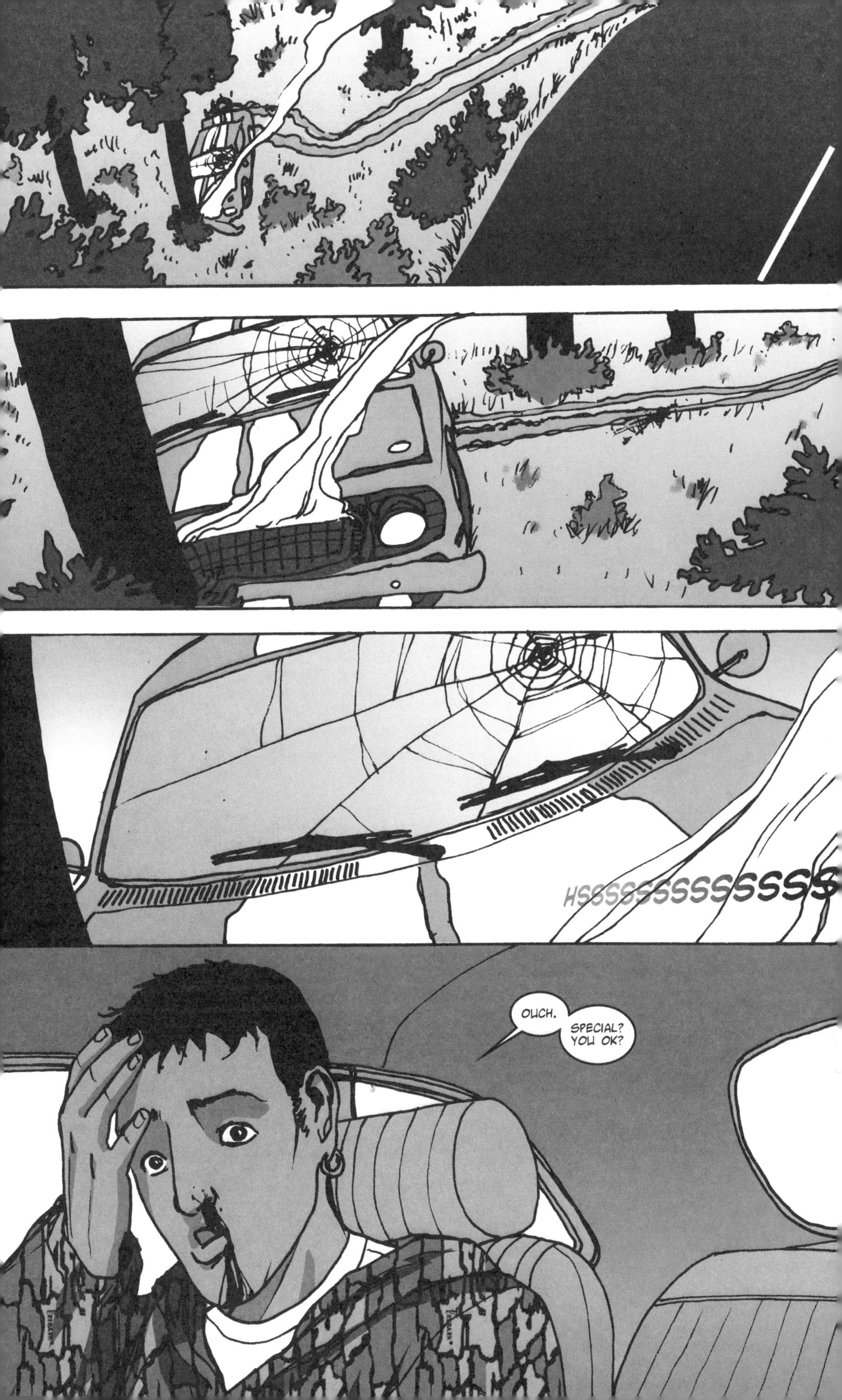
HSSSSSSSSSSSSSS
OUCH.
SPECIAL? YOU OK?

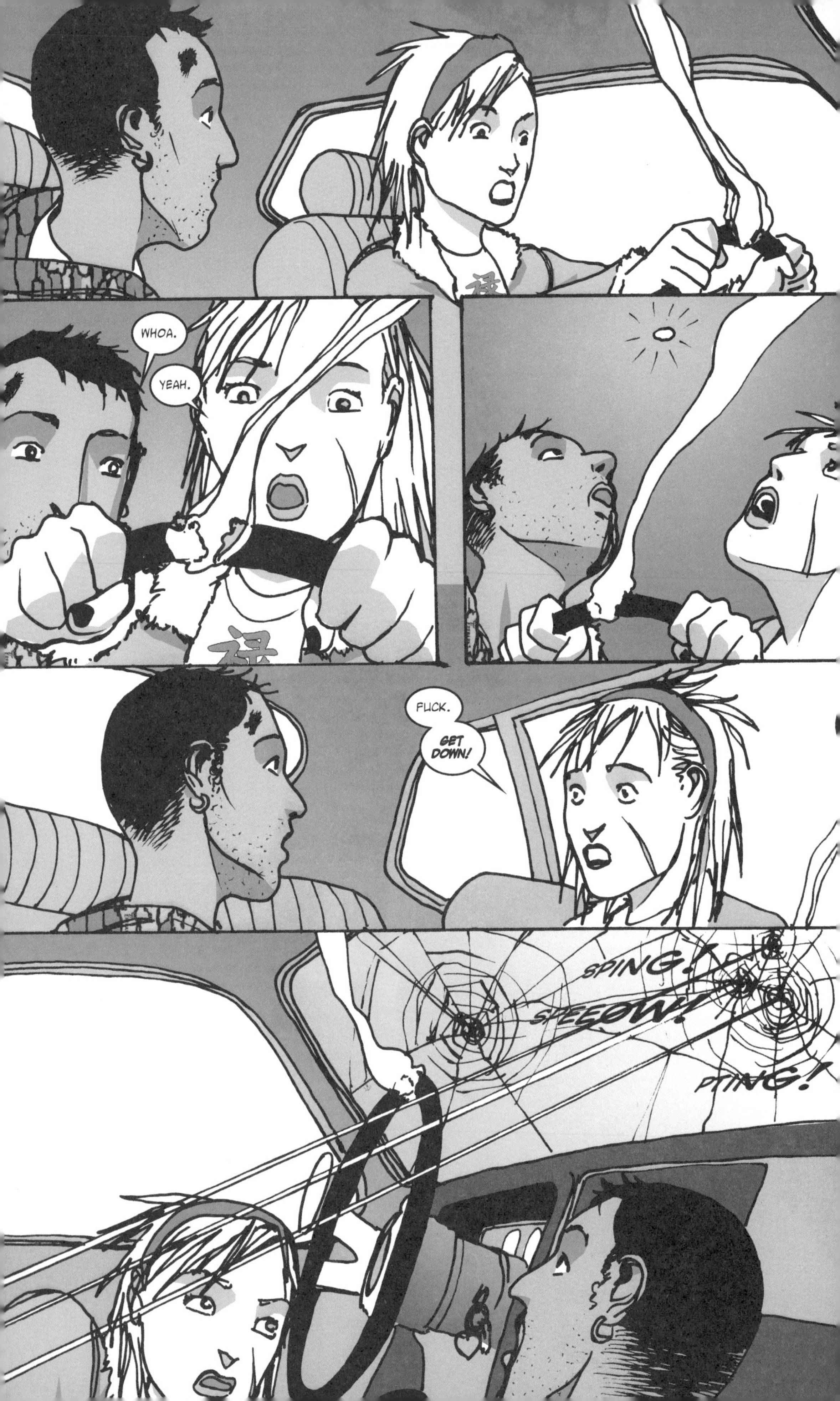
WHOA.
YEAH.
FUCK.
GET DOWN!
SPING!
SPEEOW!
DTING!

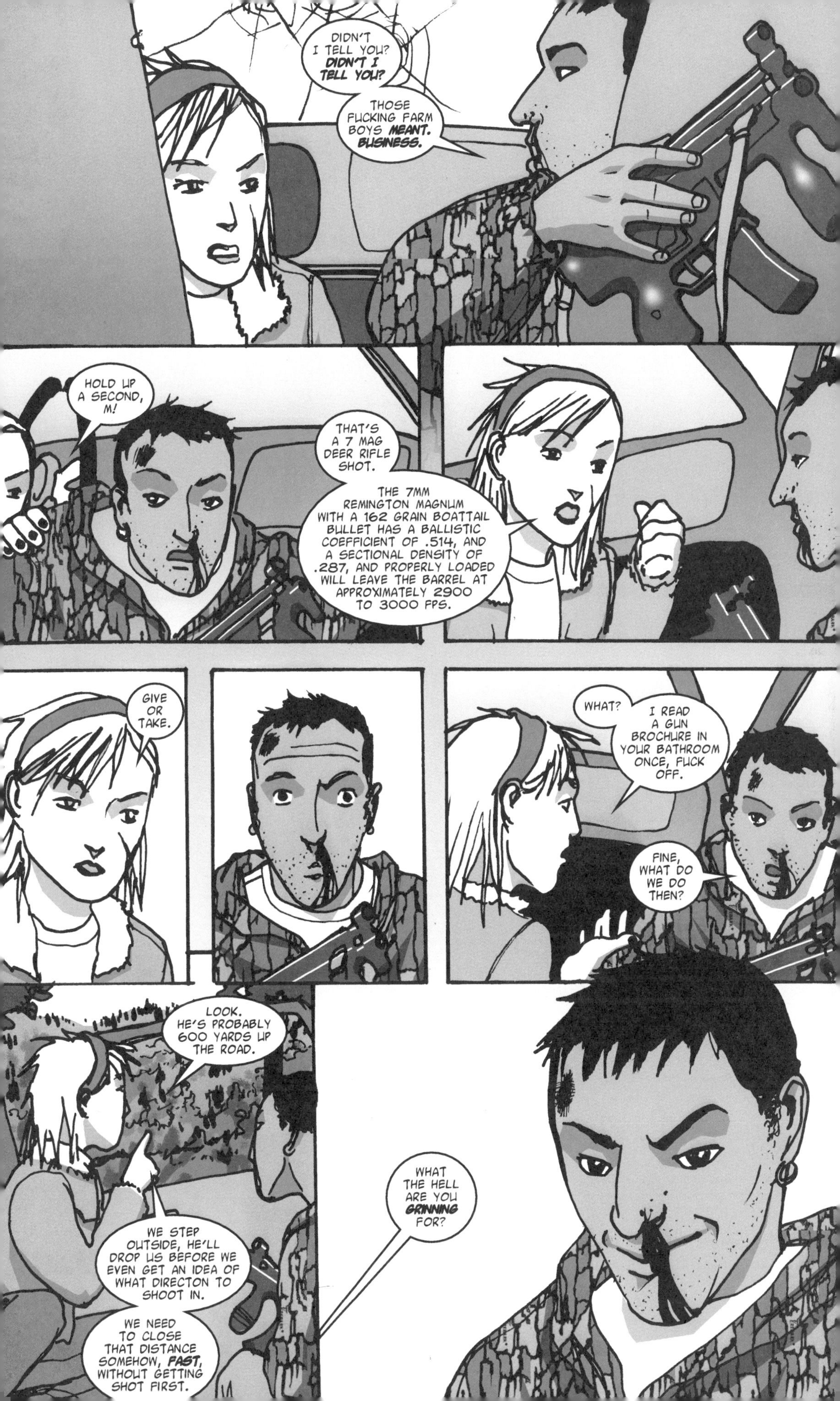
DIDN'T I TELL YOU? DIDN'T I TELL YOU?
THOSE FUCKING FARM BOYS MEANT. BUSINESS.
HOLD UP A SECOND, M!
THAT'S A 7 MAG DEER RIFLE SHOT.
THE 7MM REMINGTON MAGNUM WITH A 162 GRAIN BOATTAIL BULLET HAS A BALLISTIC COEFFICIENT OF .514, AND A SECTIONAL DENSITY OF .287, AND PROPERLY LOADED WILL LEAVE THE BARREL AT APPROXIMATELY 2900 TO 3000 FPS.
GIVE OR TAKE.
WHAT?
I READ A GUN BROCHURE IN YOUR BATHROOM ONCE, FUCK OFF.
FINE, WHAT DO WE DO THEN?
LOOK. HE'S PROBABLY 600 YARDS UP THE ROAD.
WE STEP OUTSIDE, HE'LL DROP US BEFORE WE EVEN GET AN IDEA OF WHAT DIRECTON TO SHOOT IN.
WE NEED TO CLOSE THAT DISTANCE SOMEHOW, FAST, WITHOUT GETTING SHOT FIRST.
WHAT THE HELL ARE YOU GRINNING FOR?

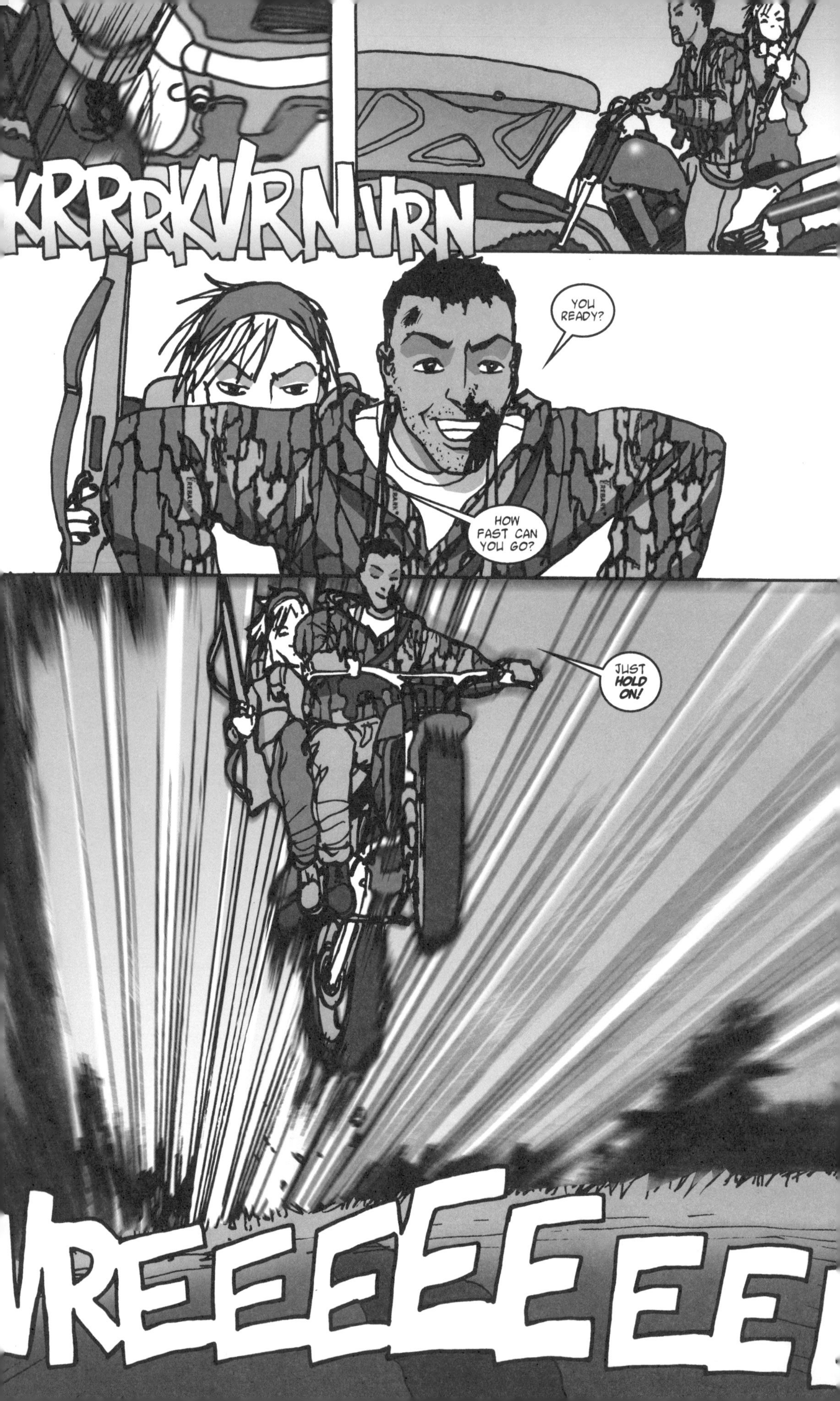
KRRRKVRN VRN
YOU READY?
HOW FAST CAN YOU GO?
JUST HOLD ON!
VREEEEEEEE

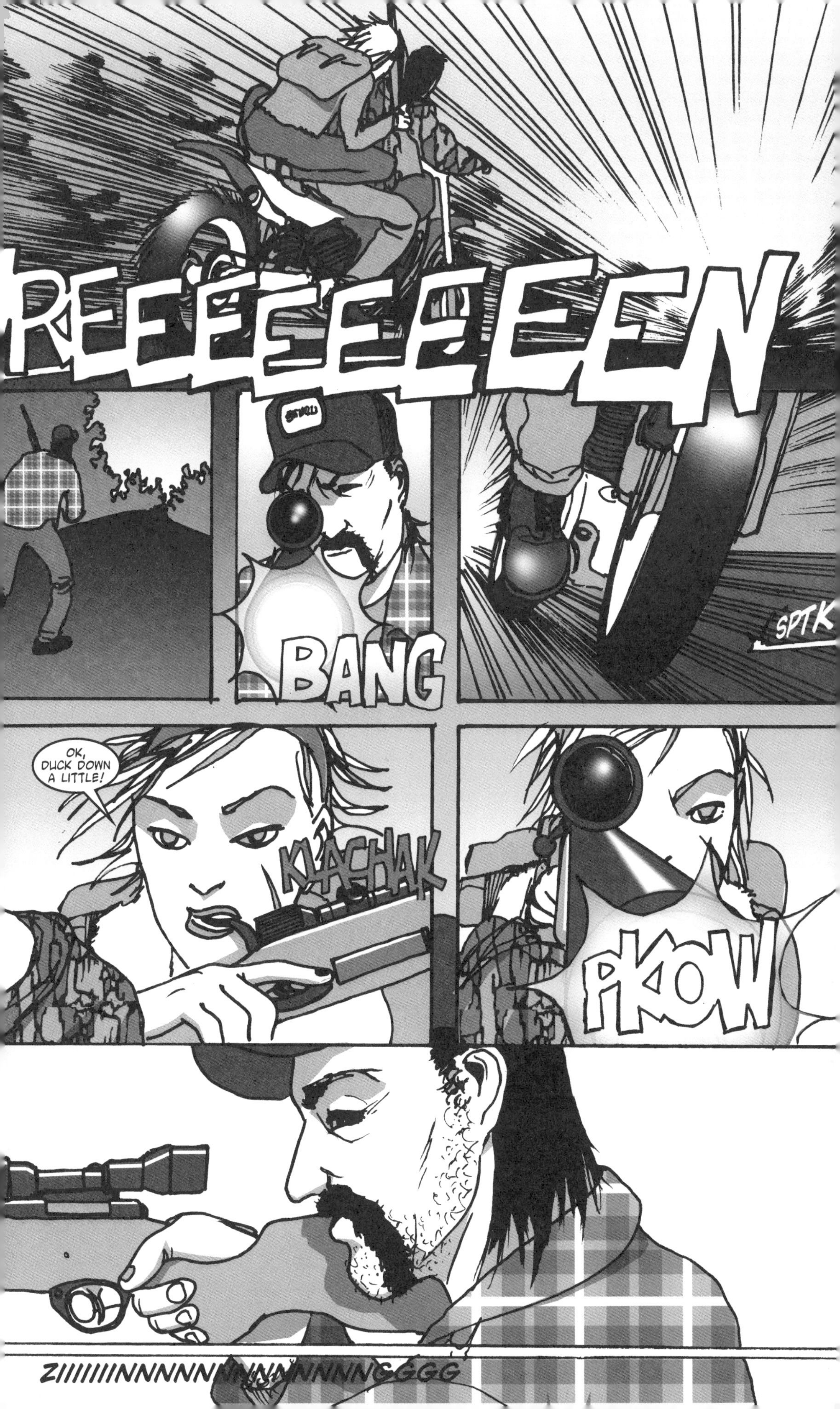
REEEEEEEEEN
BANG
SPTK
OK, DUCK DOWN A LITTLE!
KLACHAK
PKOW
ZIIIIIINNNNNNNNNNNNNNNGGGG

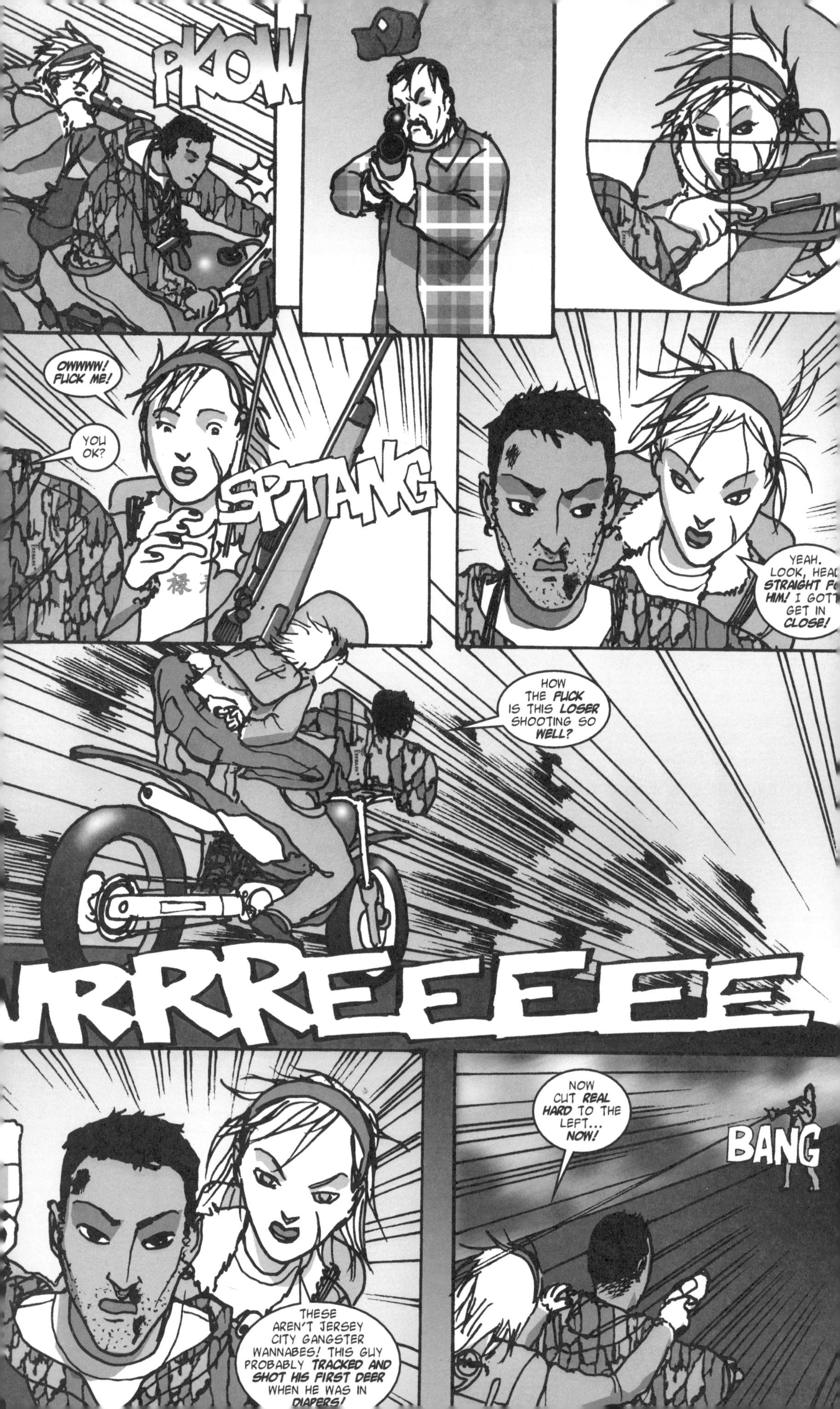

PKAOW
OWWWW! FUCK ME!
YOU OK?
SPTANG
YEAH. LOOK, HEAD STRAIGHT F HIM! I GOTT GET IN CLOSE!
HOW THE FUCK IS THIS LOSER SHOOTING SO WELL?
RRREEEEE
THESE AREN'T JERSEY CITY GANGSTER WANNABES! THIS GUY PROBABLY TRACKED AND SHOT HIS FIRST DEER WHEN HE WAS IN DIAPERS!
NOW CUT REAL HARD TO THE LEFT... NOW!
BANG

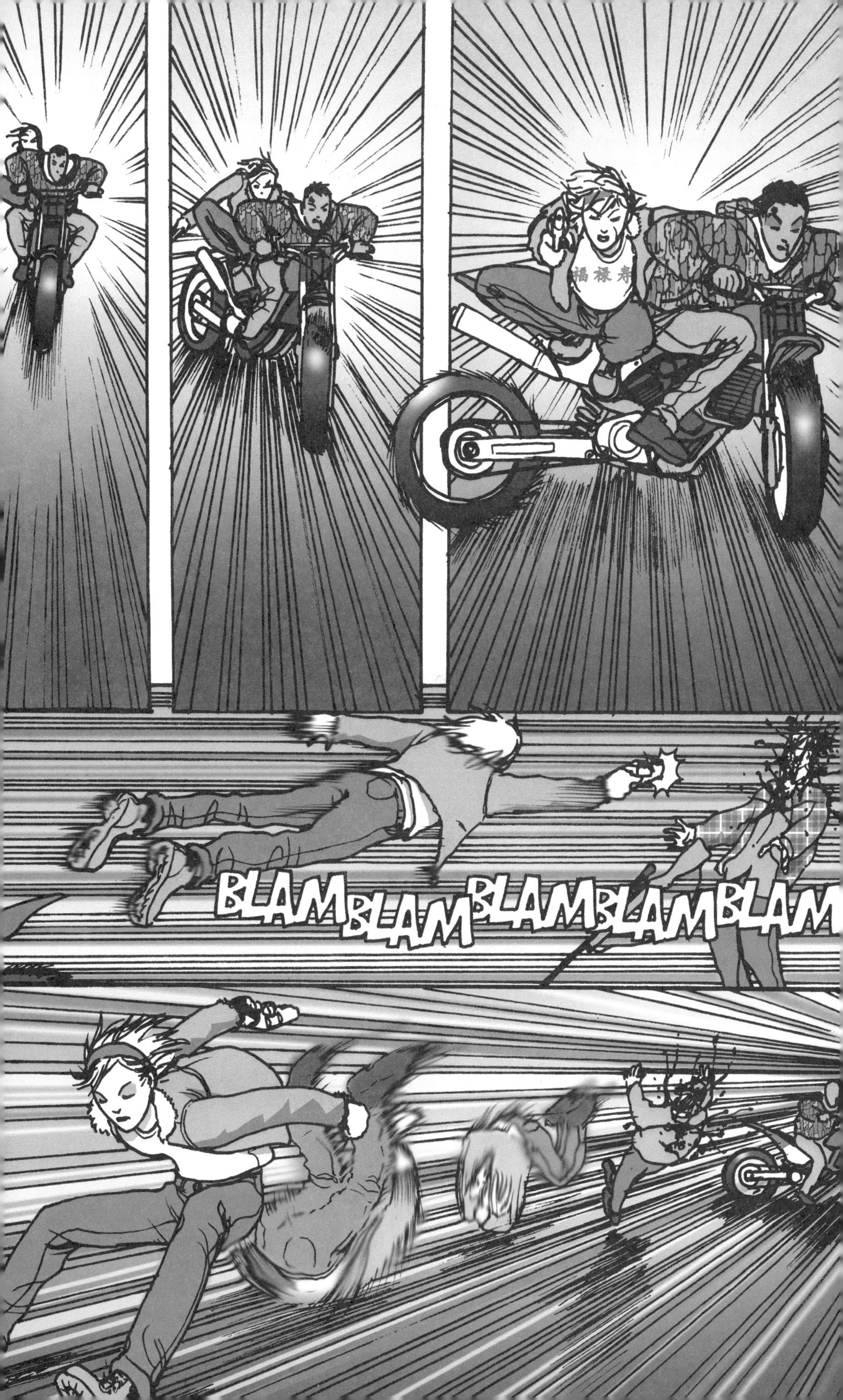
福禄寿
BLAM BLAM BLAM BLAM BLAM

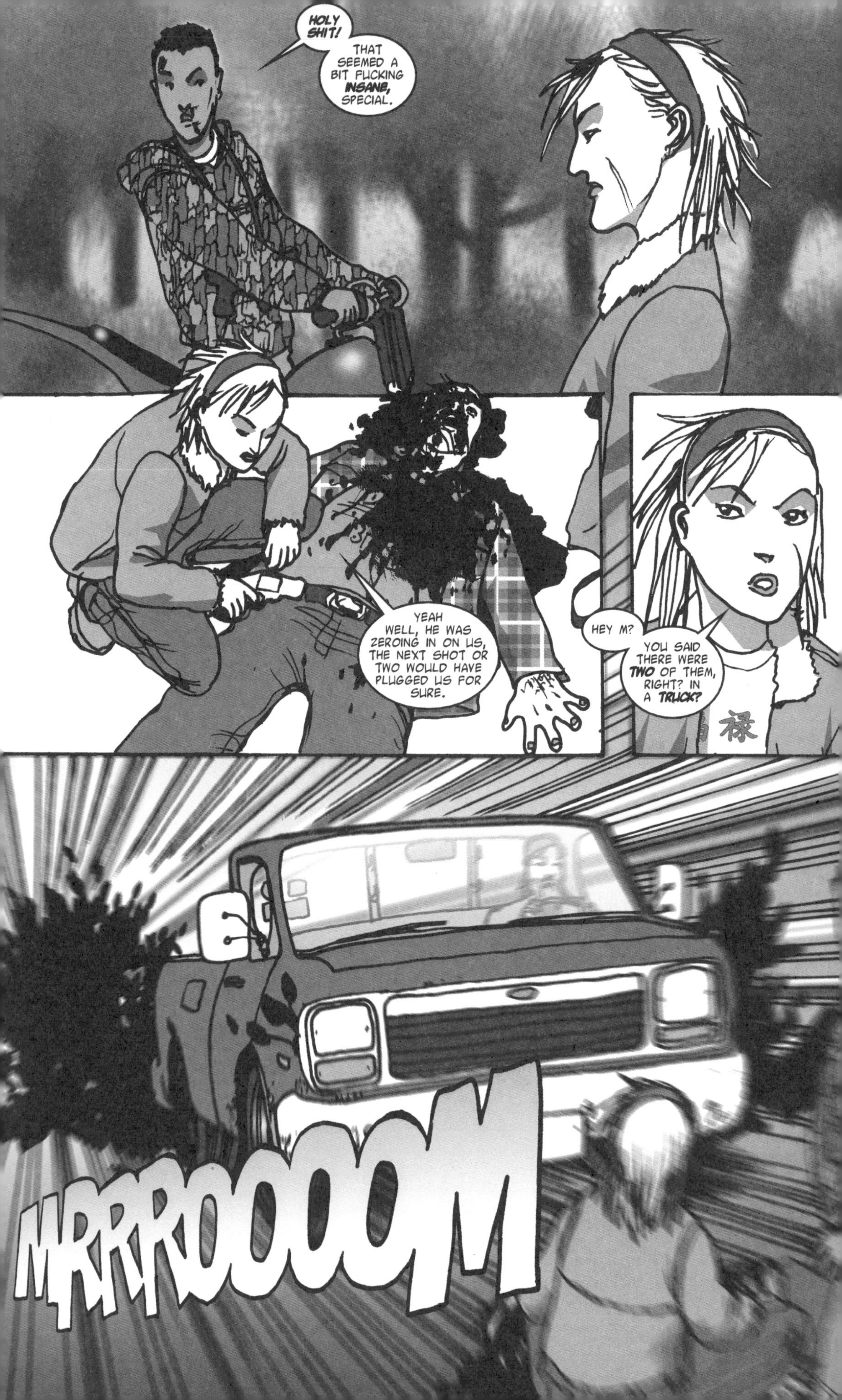
HOLY SHIT!
THAT SEEMED A BIT FUCKING INSANE, SPECIAL.
YEAH WELL, HE WAS ZEROING IN ON US, THE NEXT SHOT OR TWO WOULD HAVE PLUGGED US FOR SURE.
HEY M?
YOU SAID THERE WERE TWO OF THEM, RIGHT? IN A TRUCK?
MRRROOOOM

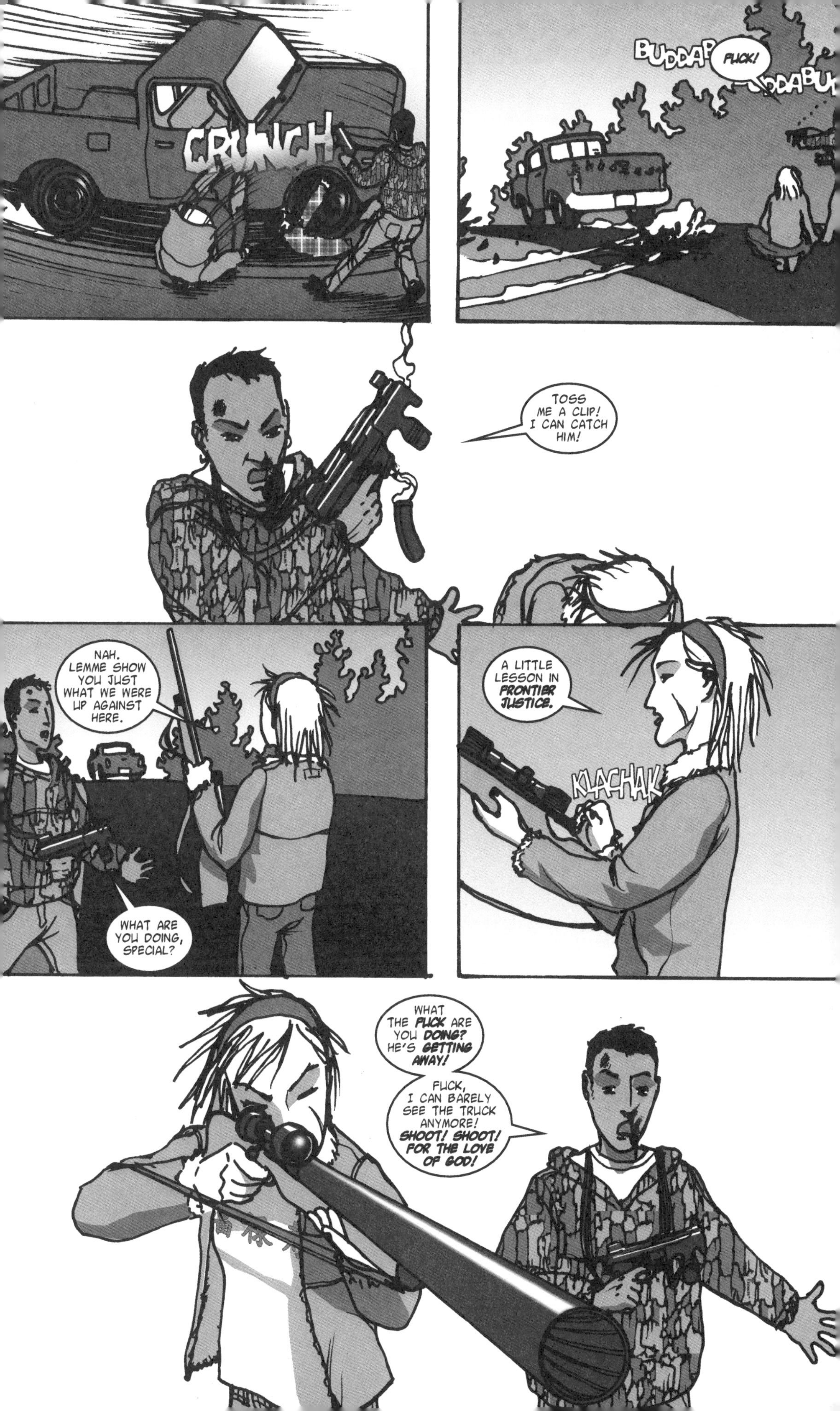
CRUNCH
BUDDAP
FUCK!
DDABU
TOSS ME A CLIP! I CAN CATCH HIM!
NAH. LEMME SHOW YOU JUST WHAT WE WERE UP AGAINST HERE.
WHAT ARE YOU DOING, SPECIAL?
A LITTLE LESSON IN FRONTIER JUSTICE.
KLACHAK
WHAT THE FUCK ARE YOU DOING? HE'S GETTING AWAY!
FUCK, I CAN BARELY SEE THE TRUCK ANYMORE! SHOOT! SHOOT! FOR THE LOVE OF GOD!

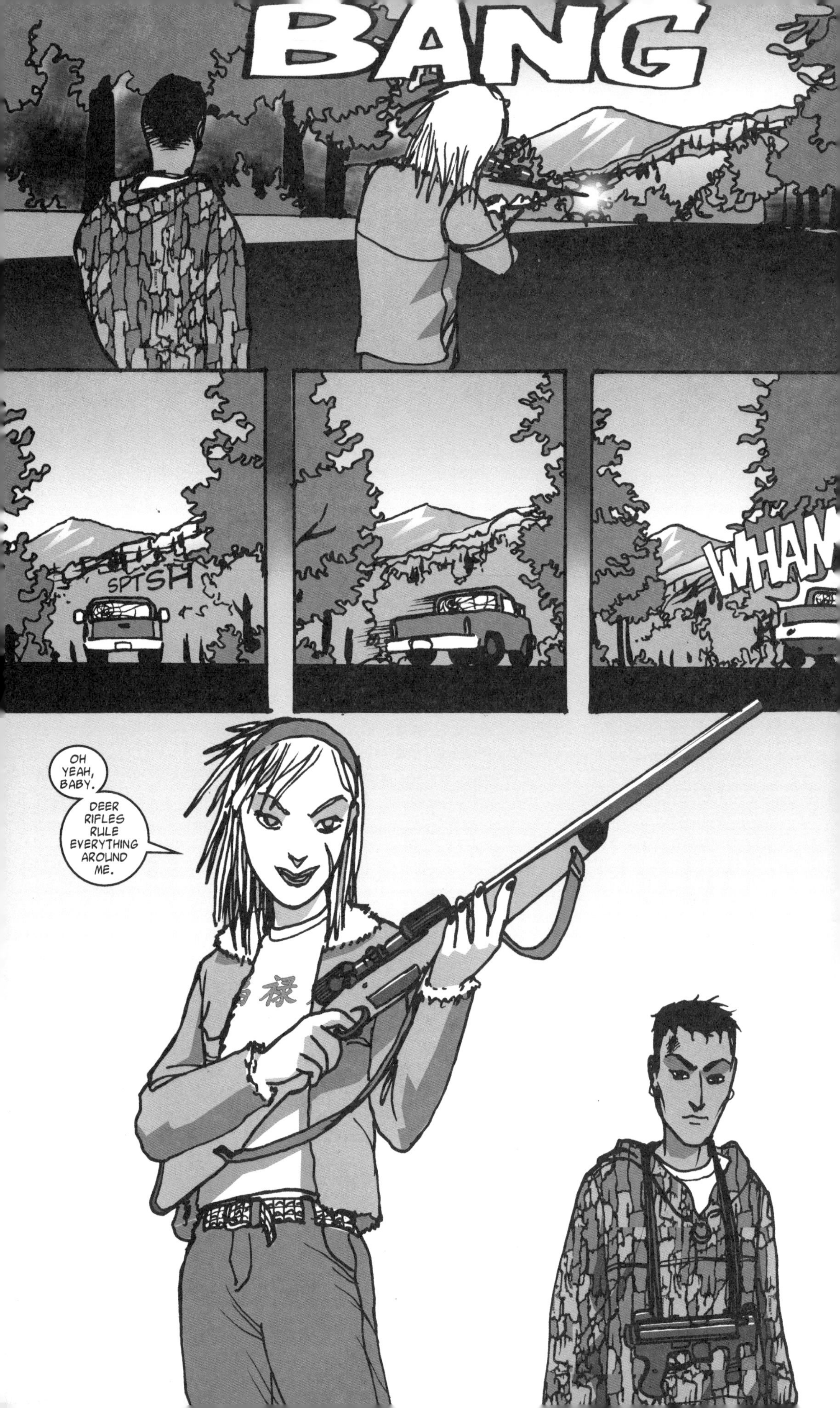
BANG
SPTSH
WHAM
OH YEAH, BABY.
DEER RIFLES RULE EVERYTHING AROUND ME.

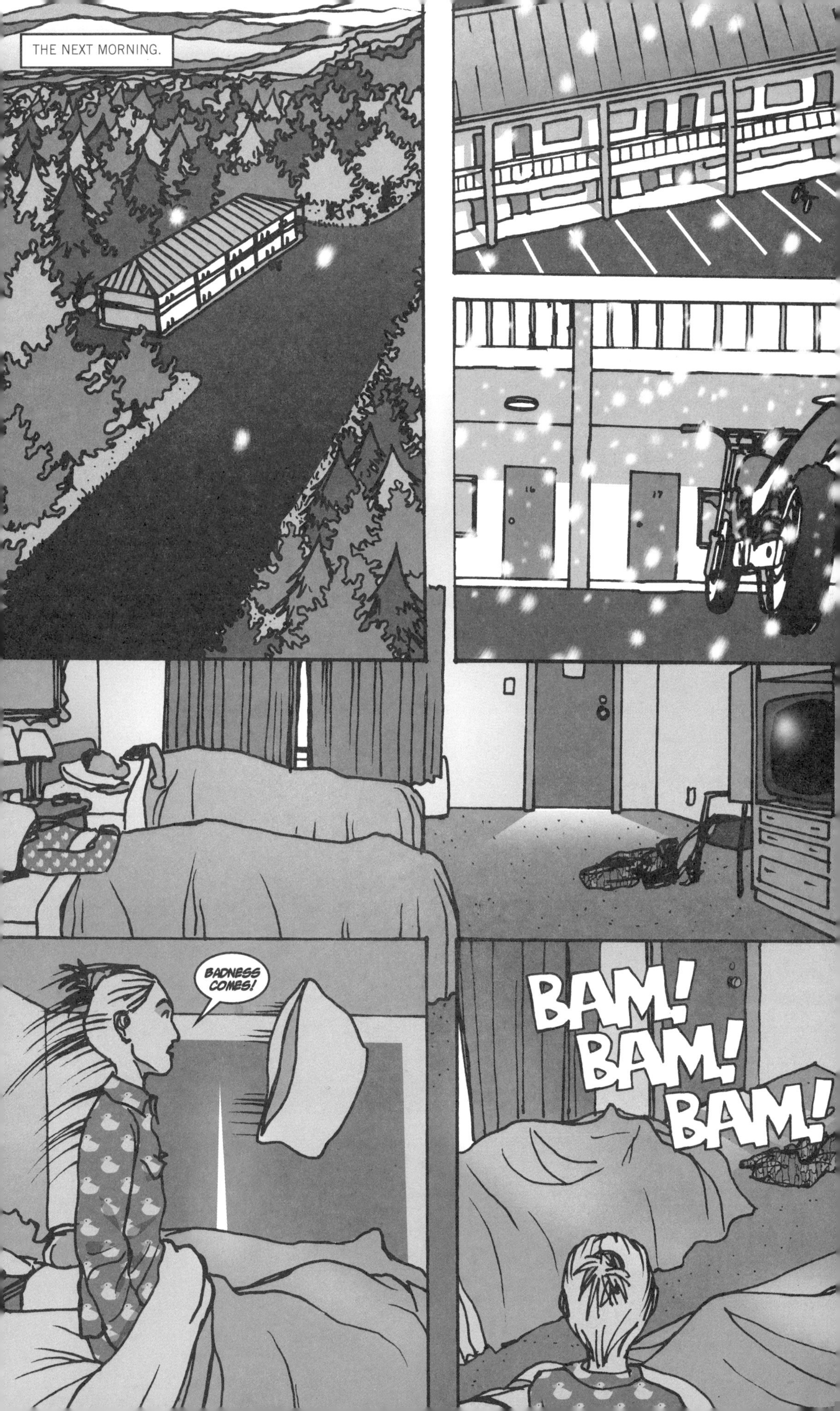
THE NEXT MORNING.
16
17
BADNESS COMES!
BAM! BAM! BAM!

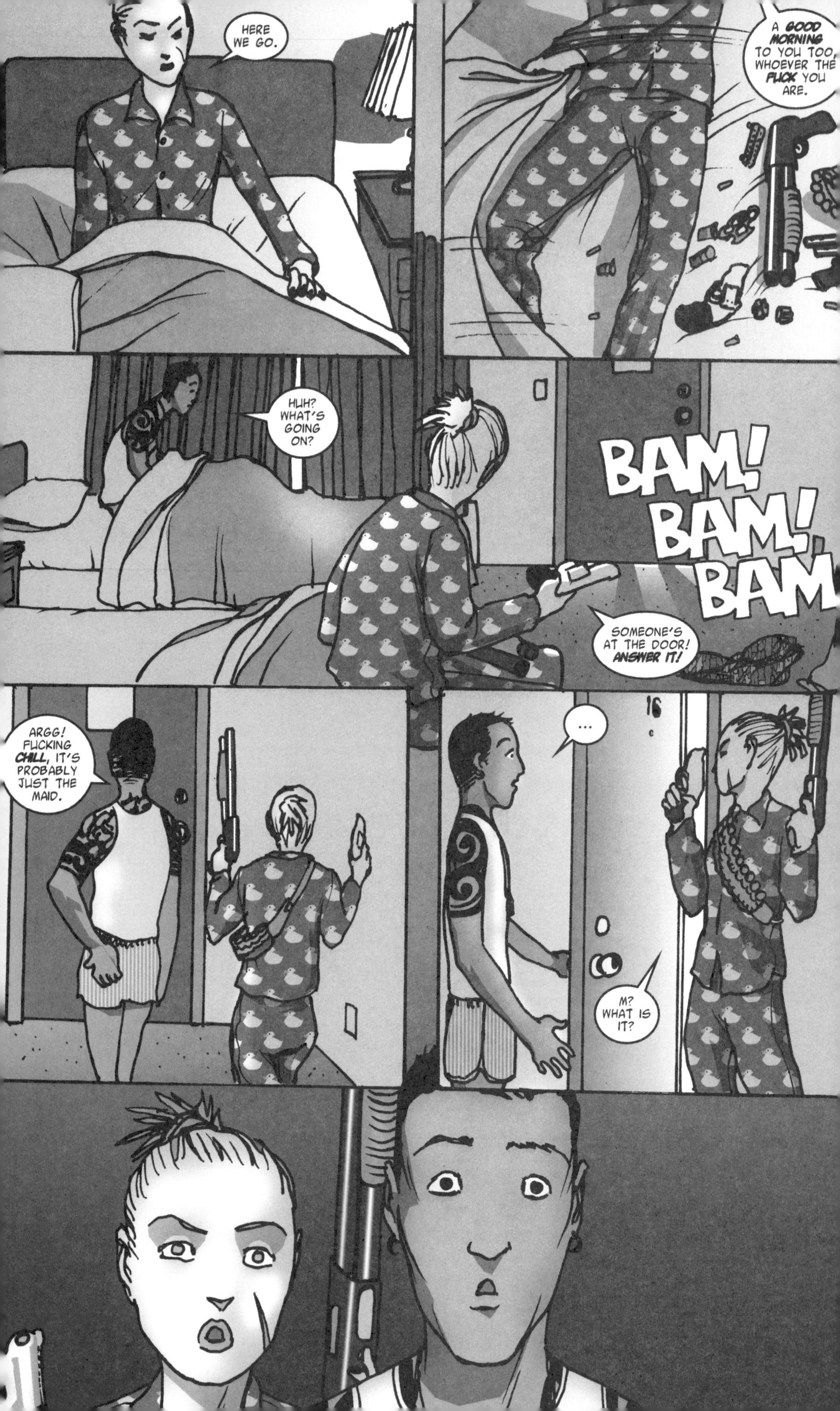

HERE WE GO.
A GOOD MORNING TO YOU TOO, WHOEVER THE FUCK YOU ARE.
HUH? WHAT'S GOING ON?
BAM! BAM! BAM
SOMEONE'S AT THE DOOR! ANSWER IT!
ARGG! FUCKING CHILL, IT'S PROBABLY JUST THE MAID.
...
M? WHAT IS IT?

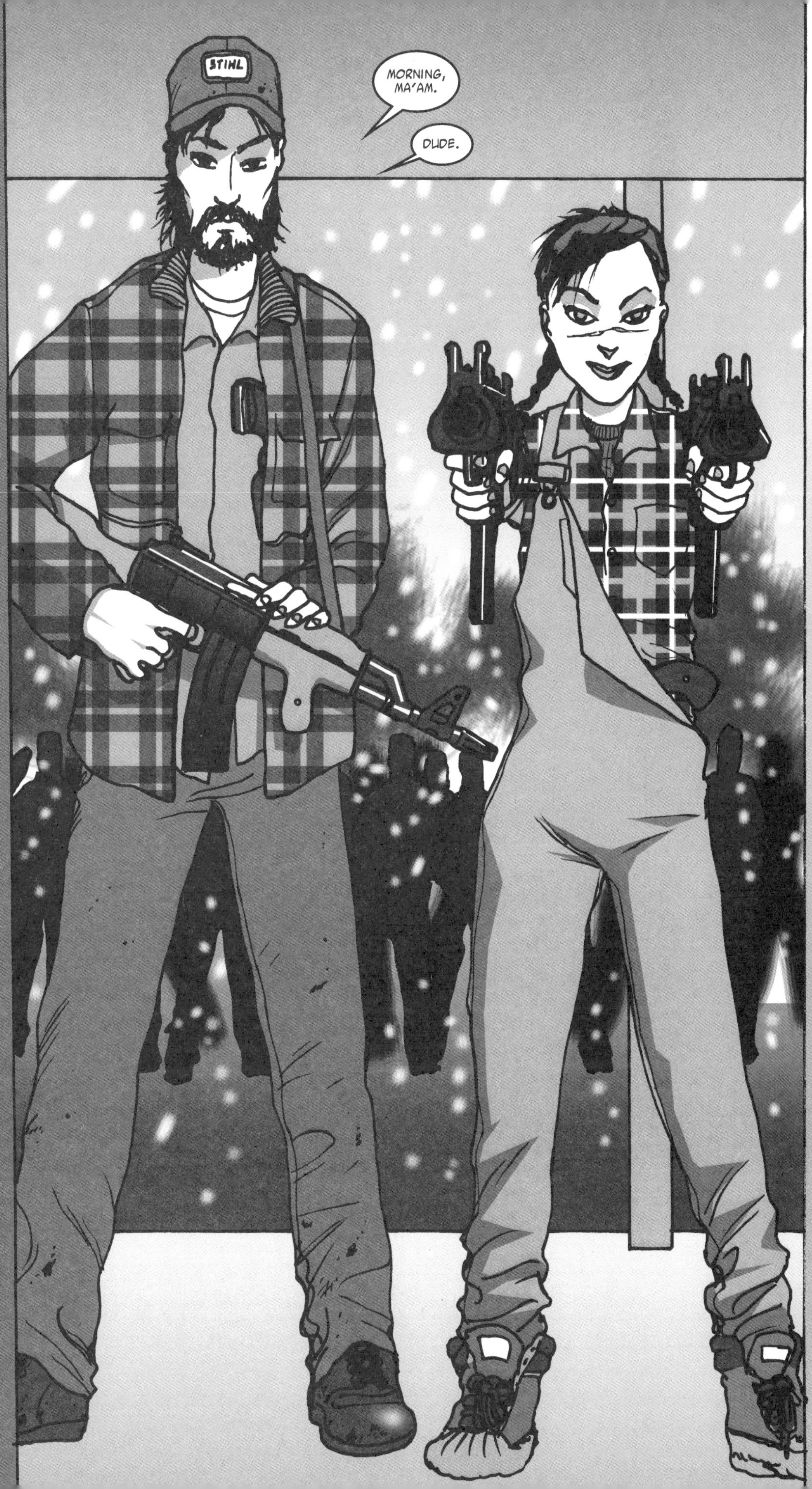
MORNING, MA'AM.
DUDE.
STIHL

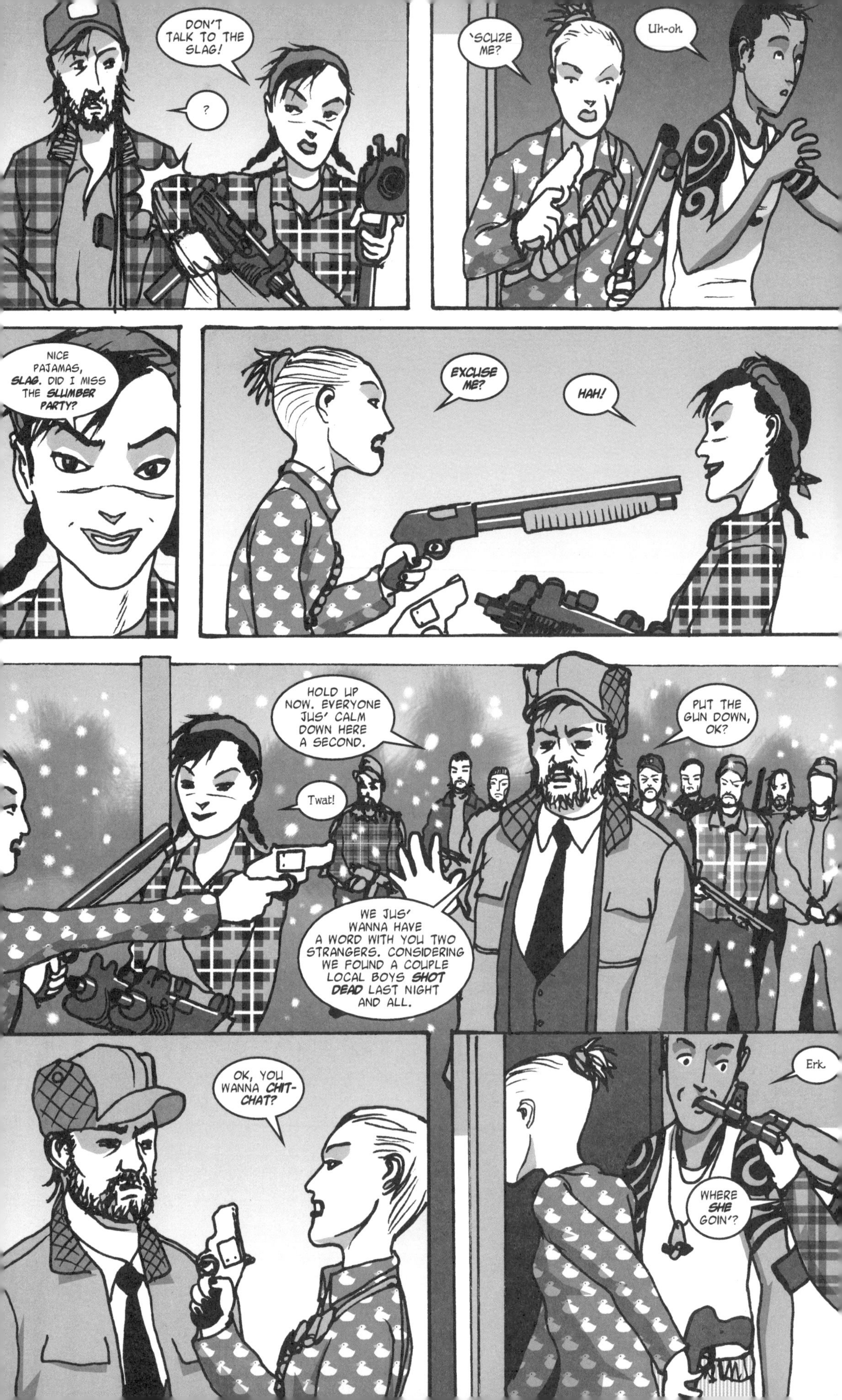

DON'T TALK TO THE SLAG!
?
`SCUZE ME?
Uh-oh.
NICE PAJAMAS, SLAG. DID I MISS THE SLUMBER PARTY?
EXCUSE ME?
HAH!
HOLD UP NOW. EVERYONE JUS' CALM DOWN HERE A SECOND.
Twat!
PUT THE GUN DOWN, OK?
WE JUS' WANNA HAVE A WORD WITH YOU TWO STRANGERS. CONSIDERING WE FOUND A COUPLE LOCAL BOYS SHOT DEAD LAST NIGHT AND ALL.
OK, YOU WANNA CHIT-CHAT?
Erk.
WHERE SHE GOIN'?

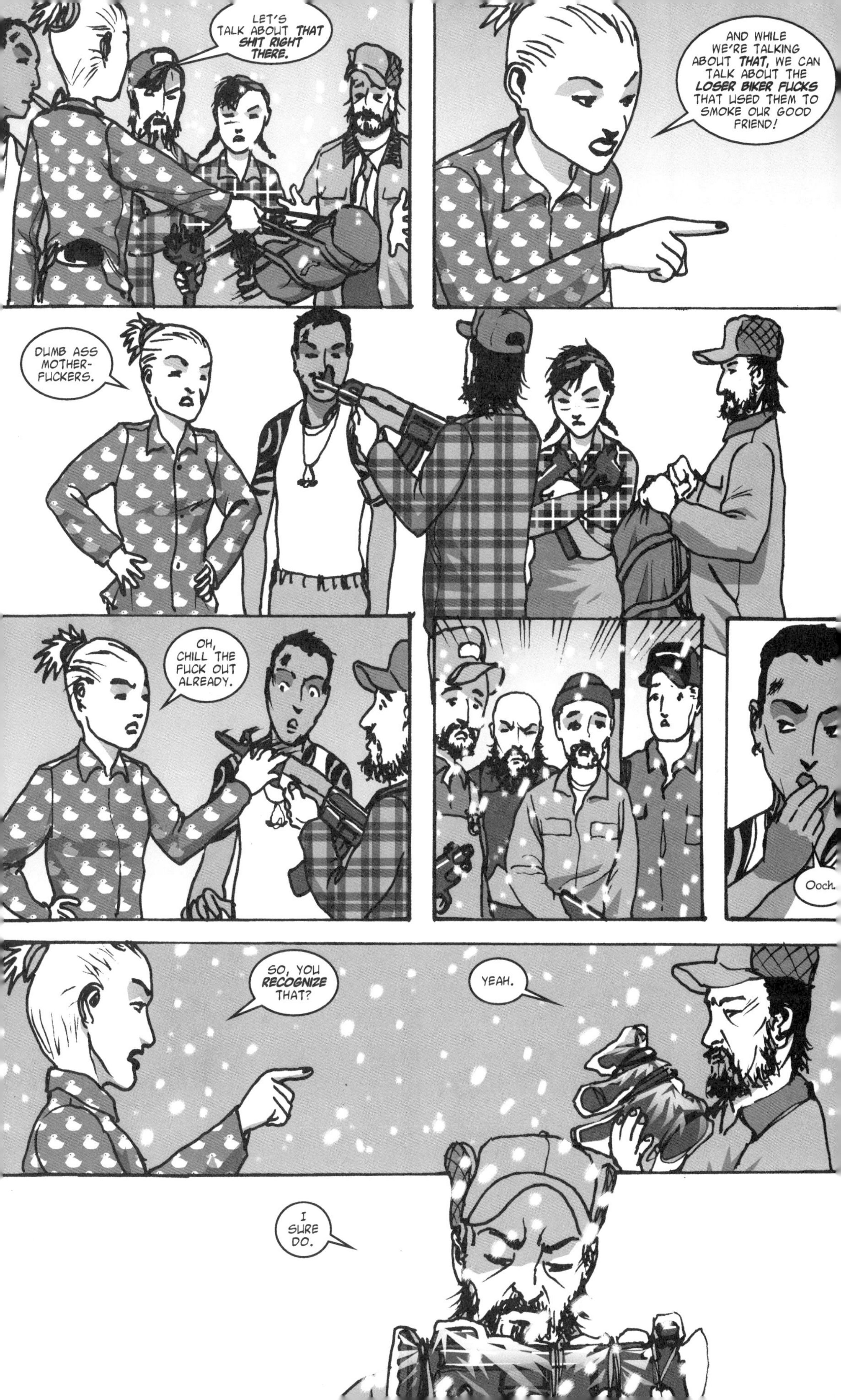
LET'S TALK ABOUT THAT SHIT RIGHT THERE.
AND WHILE WE'RE TALKING ABOUT THAT, WE CAN TALK ABOUT THE LOSER BIKER FUCKS THAT USED THEM TO SMOKE OUR GOOD FRIEND!
DUMB ASS MOTHER-FUCKERS.
OH, CHILL THE FUCK OUT ALREADY.
Ooch.
SO, YOU RECOGNIZE THAT?
YEAH.
I SURE DO.

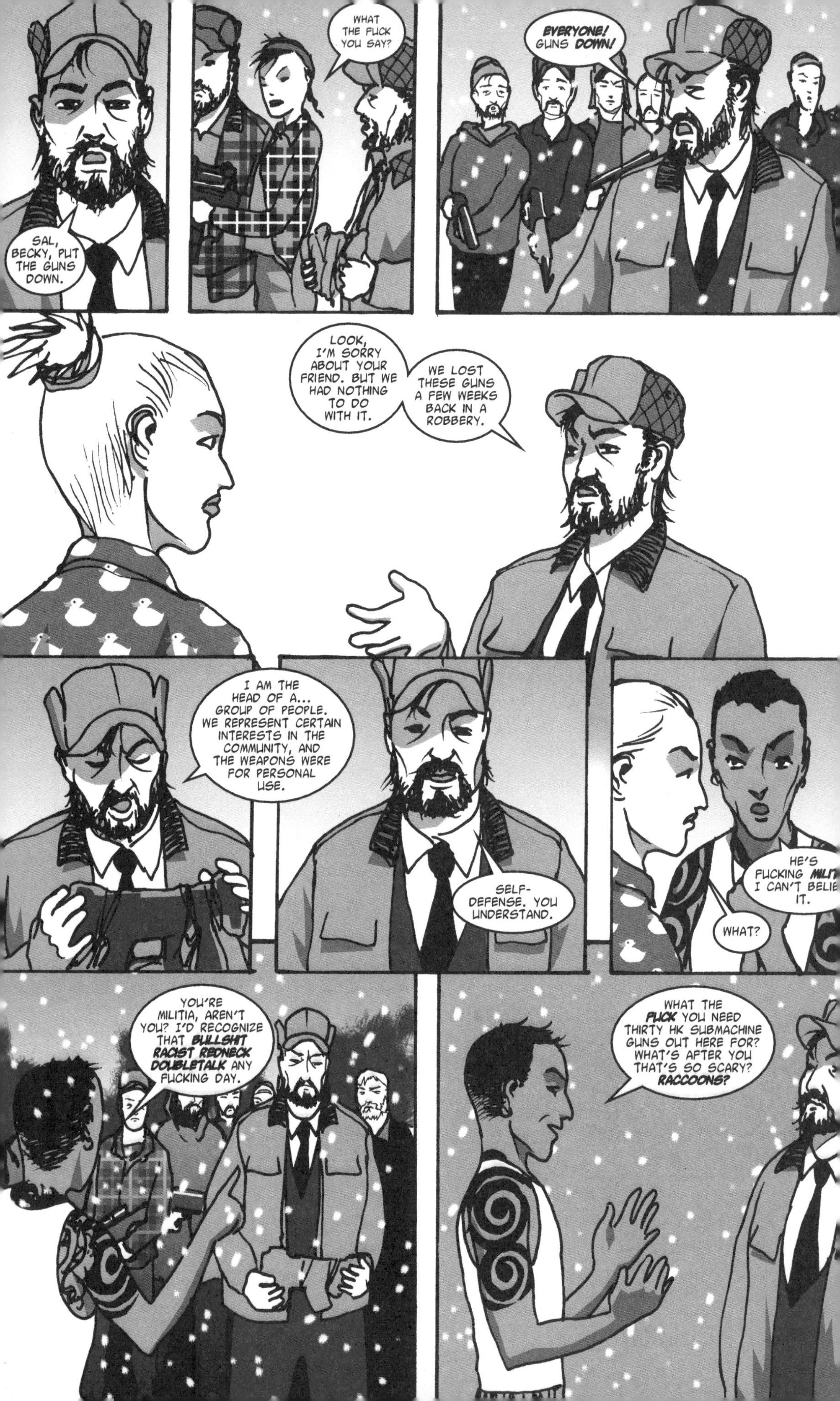
SAL, BECKY, PUT THE GUNS DOWN.
WHAT THE FUCK YOU SAY?
EVERYONE! GUNS DOWN!
LOOK, I'M SORRY ABOUT YOUR FRIEND. BUT WE HAD NOTHING TO DO WITH IT.
WE LOST THESE GUNS A FEW WEEKS BACK IN A ROBBERY.
I AM THE HEAD OF A... GROUP OF PEOPLE. WE REPRESENT CERTAIN INTERESTS IN THE COMMUNITY, AND THE WEAPONS WERE FOR PERSONAL USE.
SELF-DEFENSE. YOU UNDERSTAND.
WHAT?
YOU'RE MILITIA, AREN'T YOU? I'D RECOGNIZE THAT BULLSHIT RACIST REDNECK DOUBLETALK ANY FUCKING DAY.
WHAT THE FUCK YOU NEED THIRTY HK SUBMACHINE GUNS OUT HERE FOR? WHAT'S AFTER YOU THAT'S SO SCARY? RACCOONS?

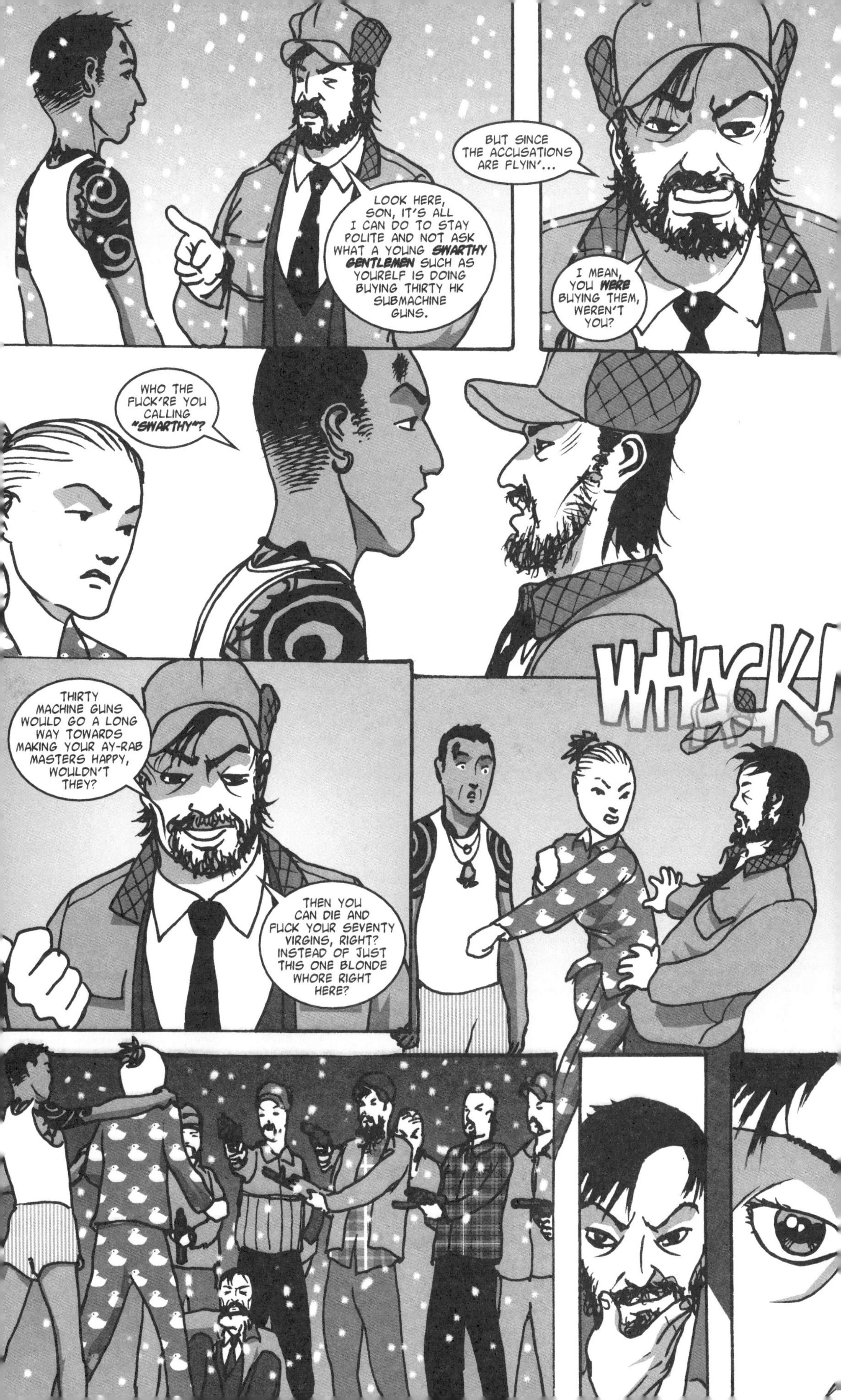

LOOK HERE, SON, IT'S ALL I CAN DO TO STAY POLITE AND NOT ASK WHAT A YOUNG SWARTHY GENTLEMEN SUCH AS YOURELF IS DOING BUYING THIRTY HK SUBMACHINE GUNS.
BUT SINCE THE ACCUSATIONS ARE FLYIN'...
I MEAN, YOU WERE BUYING THEM, WEREN'T YOU?
WHO THE FUCK'RE YOU CALLING "SWARTHY"?
THIRTY MACHINE GUNS WOULD GO A LONG WAY TOWARDS MAKING YOUR AY-RAB MASTERS HAPPY, WOULDN'T THEY?
THEN YOU CAN DIE AND FUCK YOUR SEVENTY VIRGINS, RIGHT? INSTEAD OF JUST THIS ONE BLONDE WHORE RIGHT HERE?
WHACK!

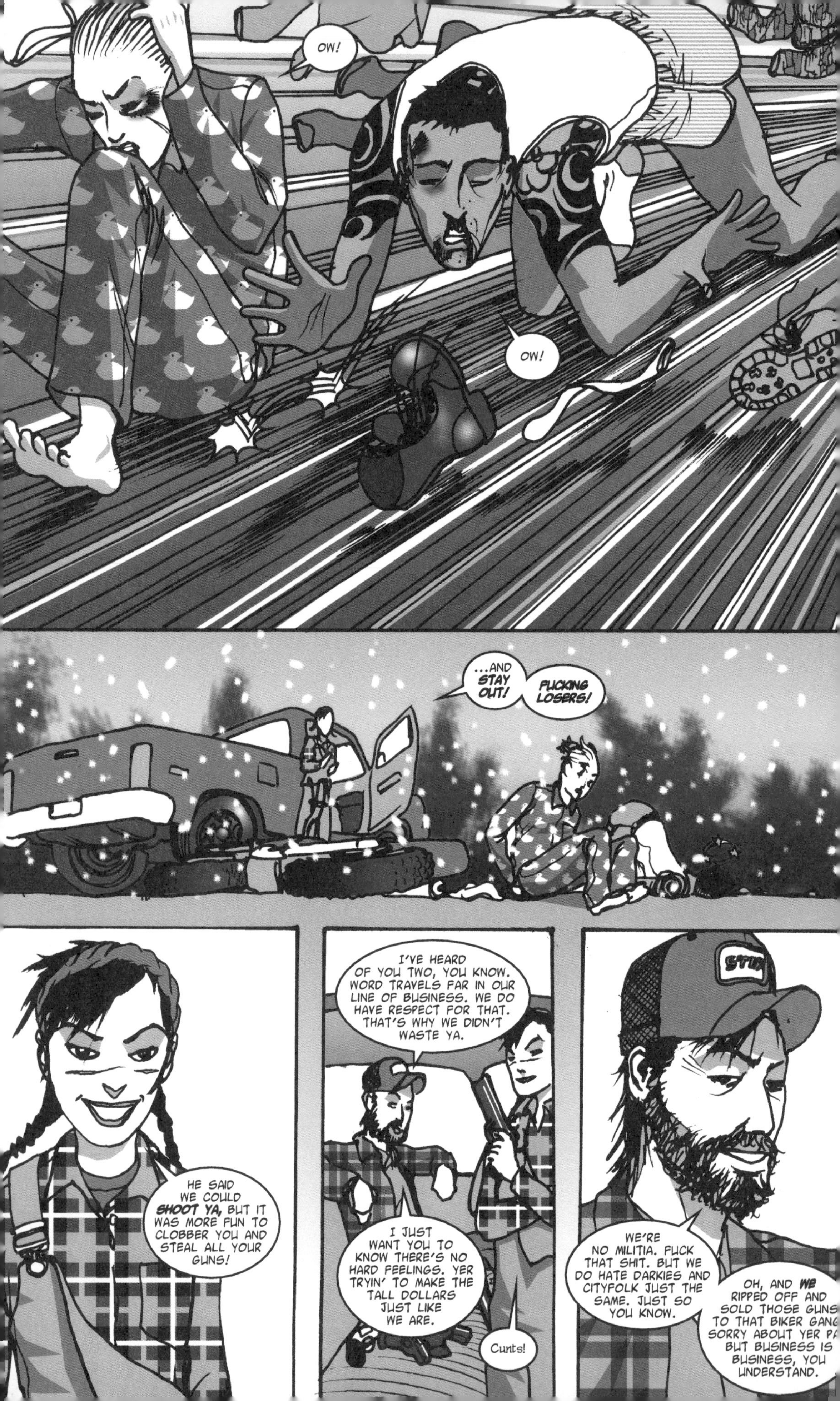
OW!
OW!
...AND STAY OUT!
FUCKING LOSERS!
HE SAID WE COULD SHOOT YA, BUT IT WAS MORE FUN TO CLOBBER YOU AND STEAL ALL YOUR GUNS!
I'VE HEARD OF YOU TWO, YOU KNOW. WORD TRAVELS FAR IN OUR LINE OF BUSINESS. WE DO HAVE RESPECT FOR THAT. THAT'S WHY WE DIDN'T WASTE YA.
I JUST WANT YOU TO KNOW THERE'S NO HARD FEELINGS. YER TRYIN' TO MAKE THE TALL DOLLARS JUST LIKE WE ARE.
Cunts!
WE'RE NO MILITIA. FUCK THAT SHIT. BUT WE DO HATE DARKIES AND CITYFOLK JUST THE SAME. JUST SO YOU KNOW.
OH, AND WE RIPPED OFF AND SOLD THOSE GUNS TO THAT BIKER GANG SORRY ABOUT YER PA BUT BUSINESS IS BUSINESS, YOU UNDERSTAND.

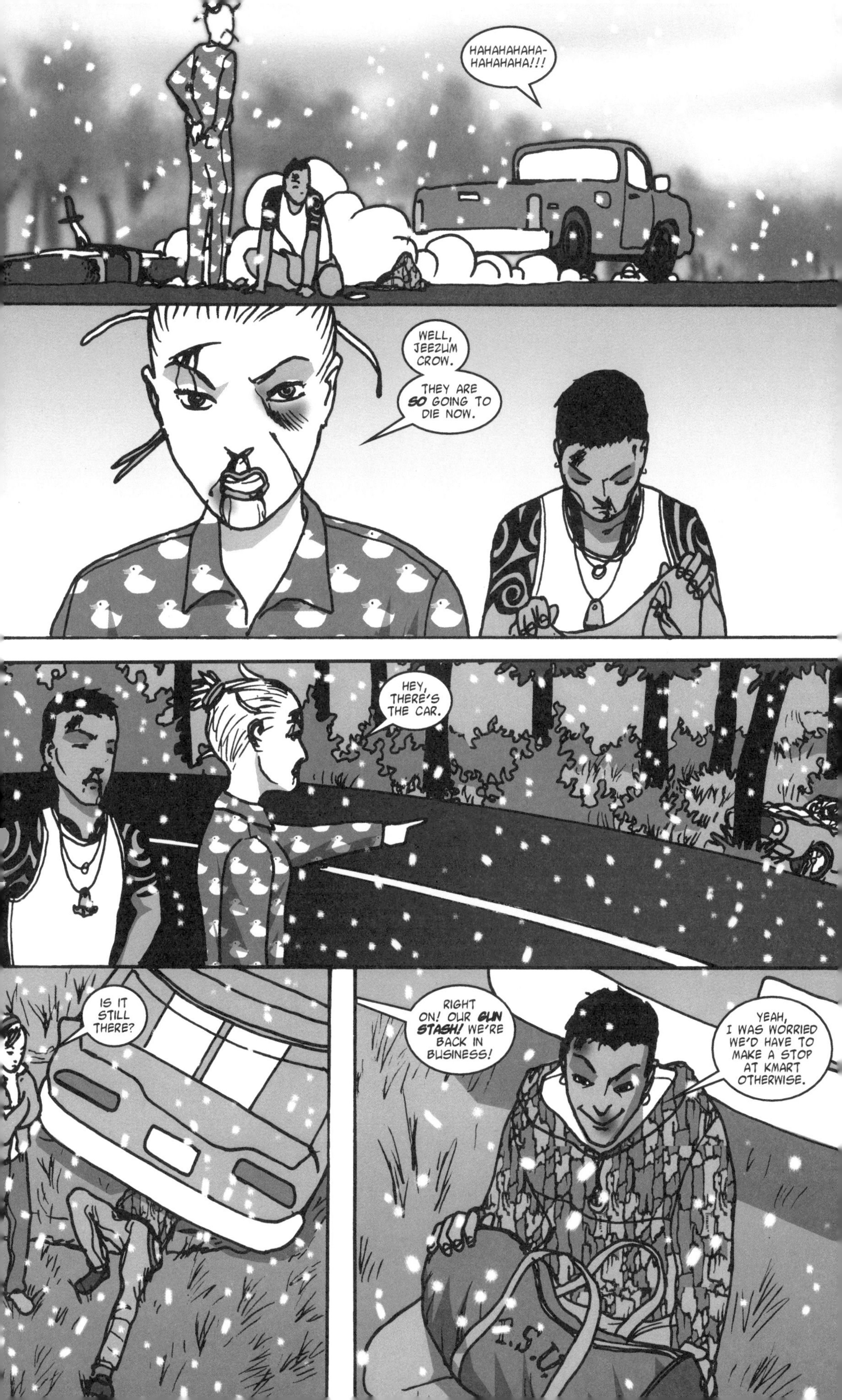
HAHAHAHAHA-HAHAHAHA!!!
WELL, JEEZUM CROW.
THEY ARE SO GOING TO DIE NOW.
HEY, THERE'S THE CAR.
IS IT STILL THERE?
RIGHT ON! OUR GUN STASH! WE'RE BACK IN BUSINESS!
YEAH, I WAS WORRIED WE'D HAVE TO MAKE A STOP AT KMART OTHERWISE.

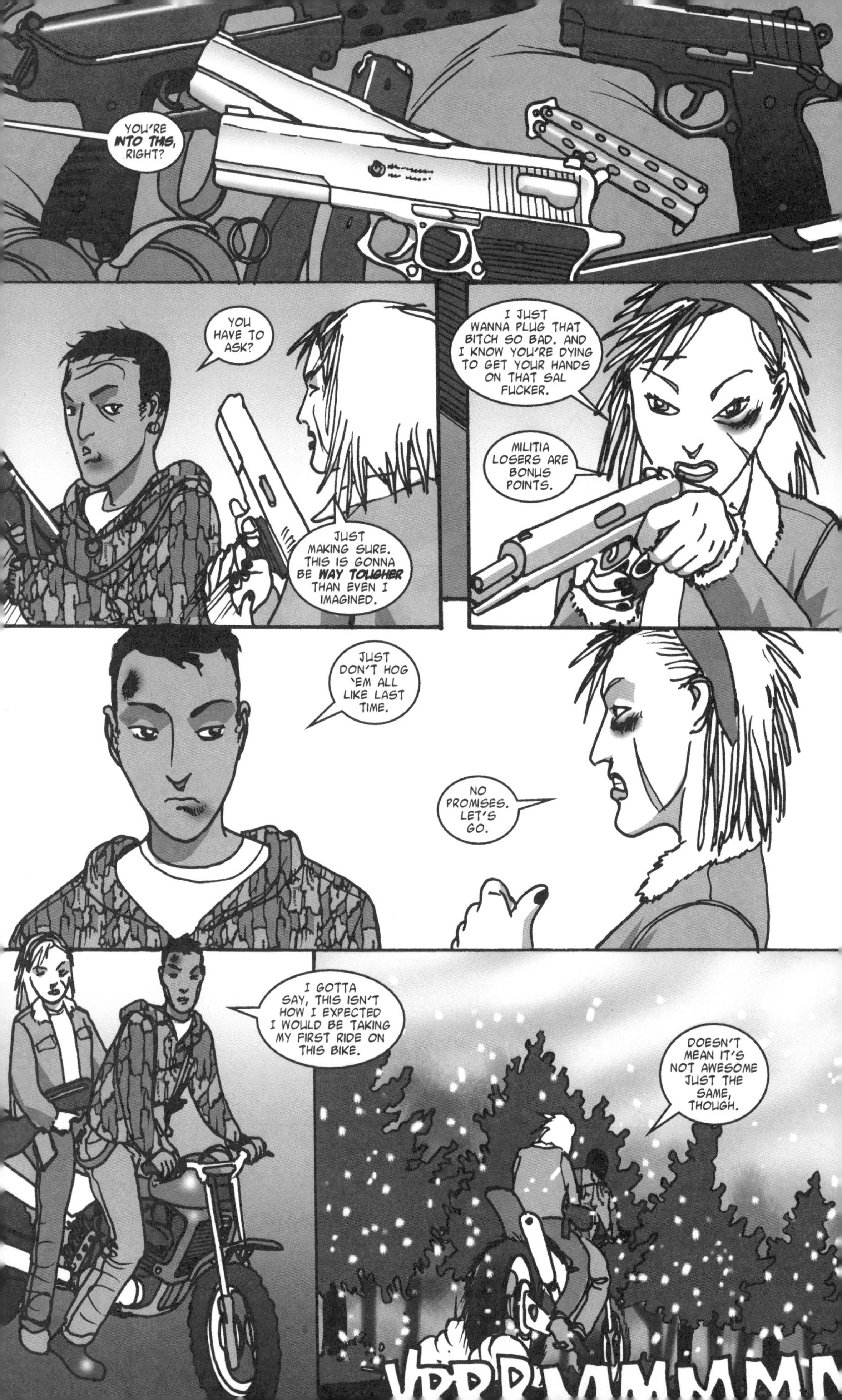
YOU'RE **INTO THIS,** RIGHT?
YOU HAVE TO ASK?
JUST MAKING SURE. THIS IS GONNA BE **WAY TOUGHER** THAN EVEN I IMAGINED.
I JUST WANNA PLUG THAT BITCH SO BAD. AND I KNOW YOU'RE DYING TO GET YOUR HANDS ON THAT SAL FUCKER.
MILITIA LOSERS ARE BONUS POINTS.
JUST DON'T HOG 'EM ALL LIKE LAST TIME.
NO PROMISES. LET'S GO.
I GOTTA SAY, THIS ISN'T HOW I EXPECTED I WOULD BE TAKING MY FIRST RIDE ON THIS BIKE.
DOESN'T MEAN IT'S NOT AWESOME JUST THE SAME, THOUGH.

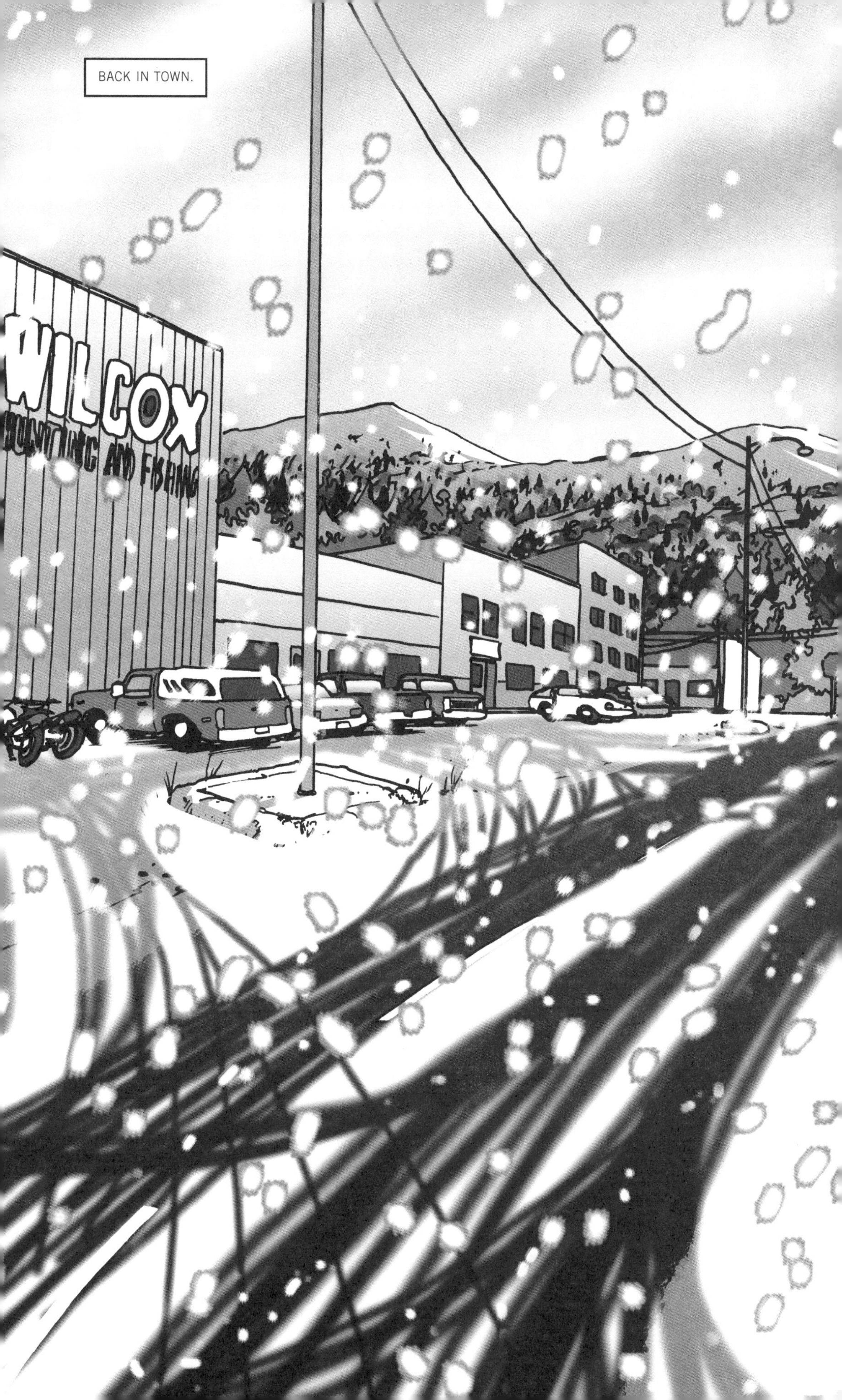
BACK IN TOWN.
WILCOX
HUNTING AND FISHING

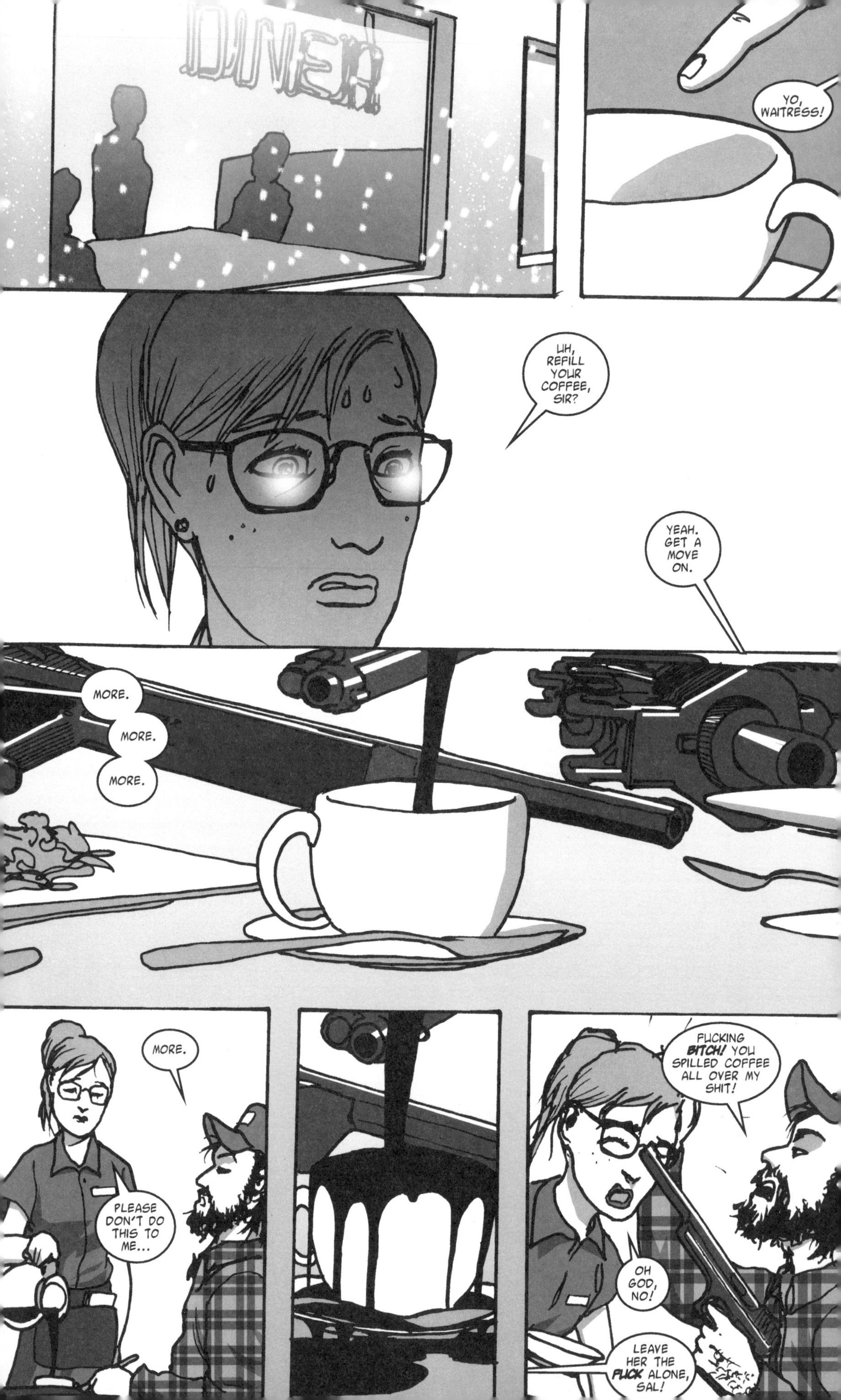
DINER
YO, WAITRESS!
UH, REFILL YOUR COFFEE, SIR?
YEAH. GET A MOVE ON.
MORE.
MORE.
MORE.
MORE.
PLEASE DON'T DO THIS TO ME...
FUCKING BITCH! YOU SPILLED COFFEE ALL OVER MY SHIT!
OH GOD, NO!
LEAVE HER THE FUCK ALONE, SAL!

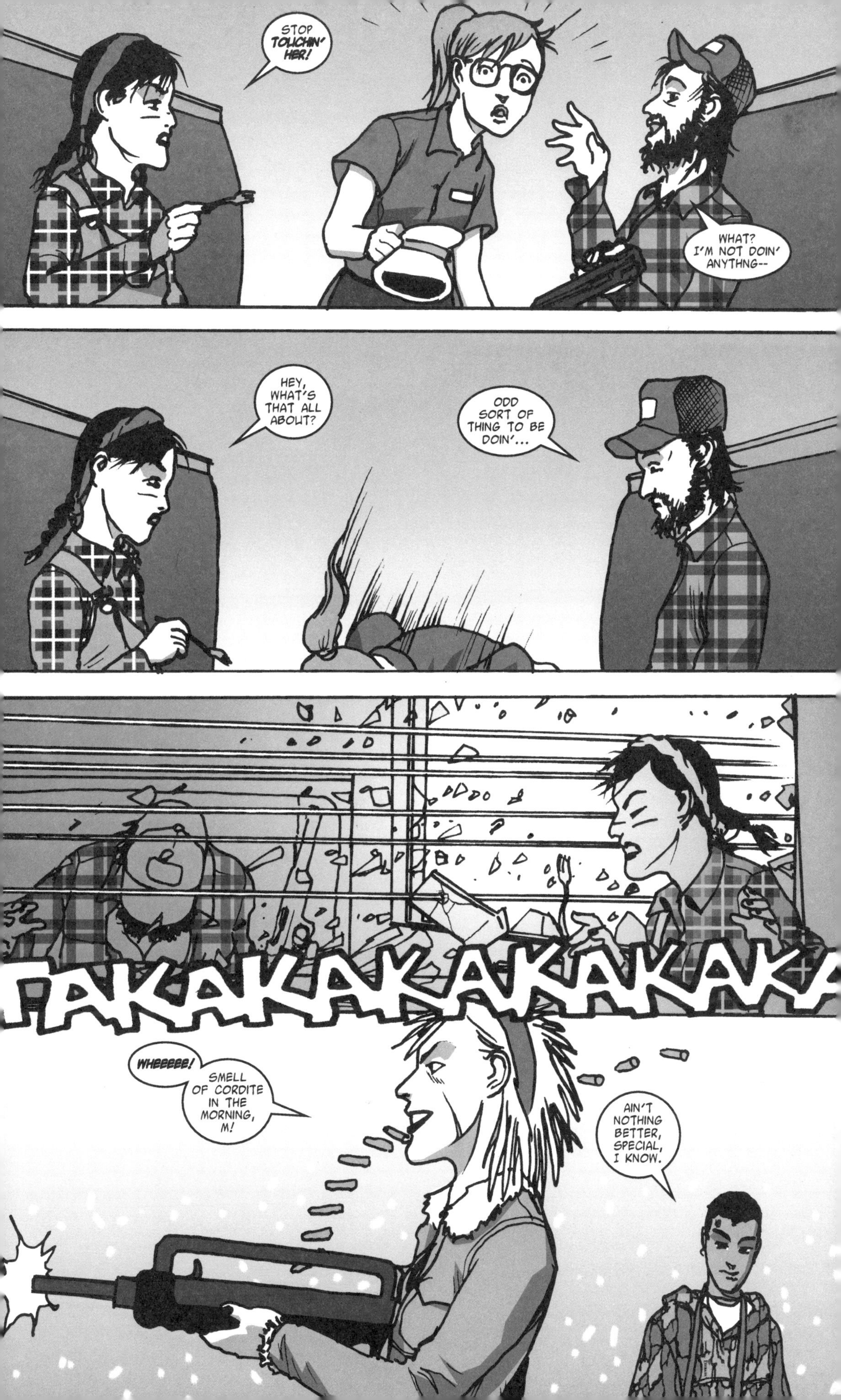
STOP TOUCHIN' HER!
WHAT? I'M NOT DOIN' ANYTHNG--
HEY, WHAT'S THAT ALL ABOUT?
ODD SORT OF THING TO BE DOIN'...
TAKAKAKAKAKAKAKA
WHEEEEEE! SMELL OF CORDITE IN THE MORNING, M!
AIN'T NOTHING BETTER, SPECIAL, I KNOW.

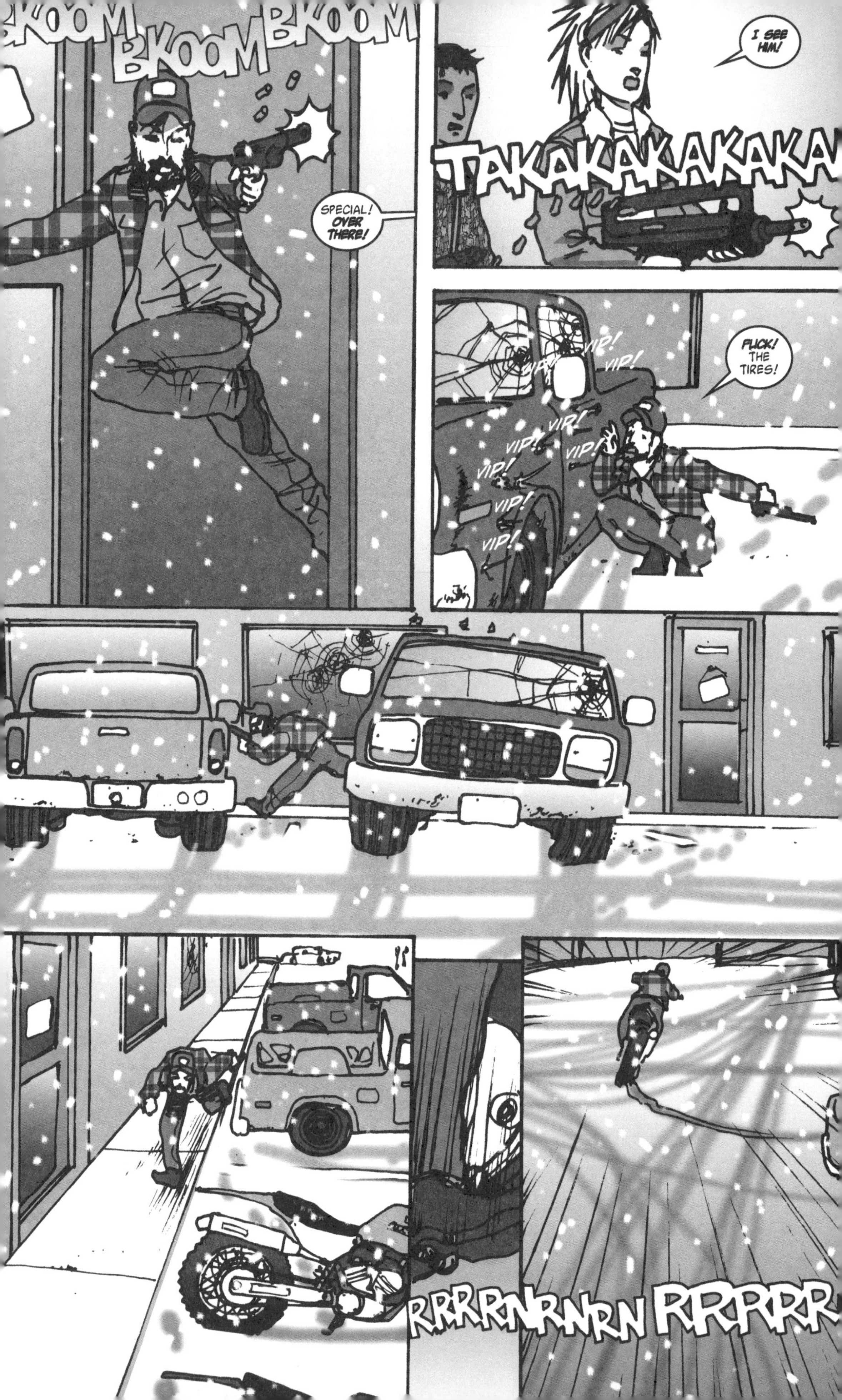
BKOOM BKOOM BKOOM
SPECIAL! OVER THERE!
I SEE HIM!
TAKAKAKAKAKA
VIP! VIP! VIP! VIP! VIP! VIP! VIP! VIP!
FUCK! THE TIRES!
RRRRNRNRN RRRRR

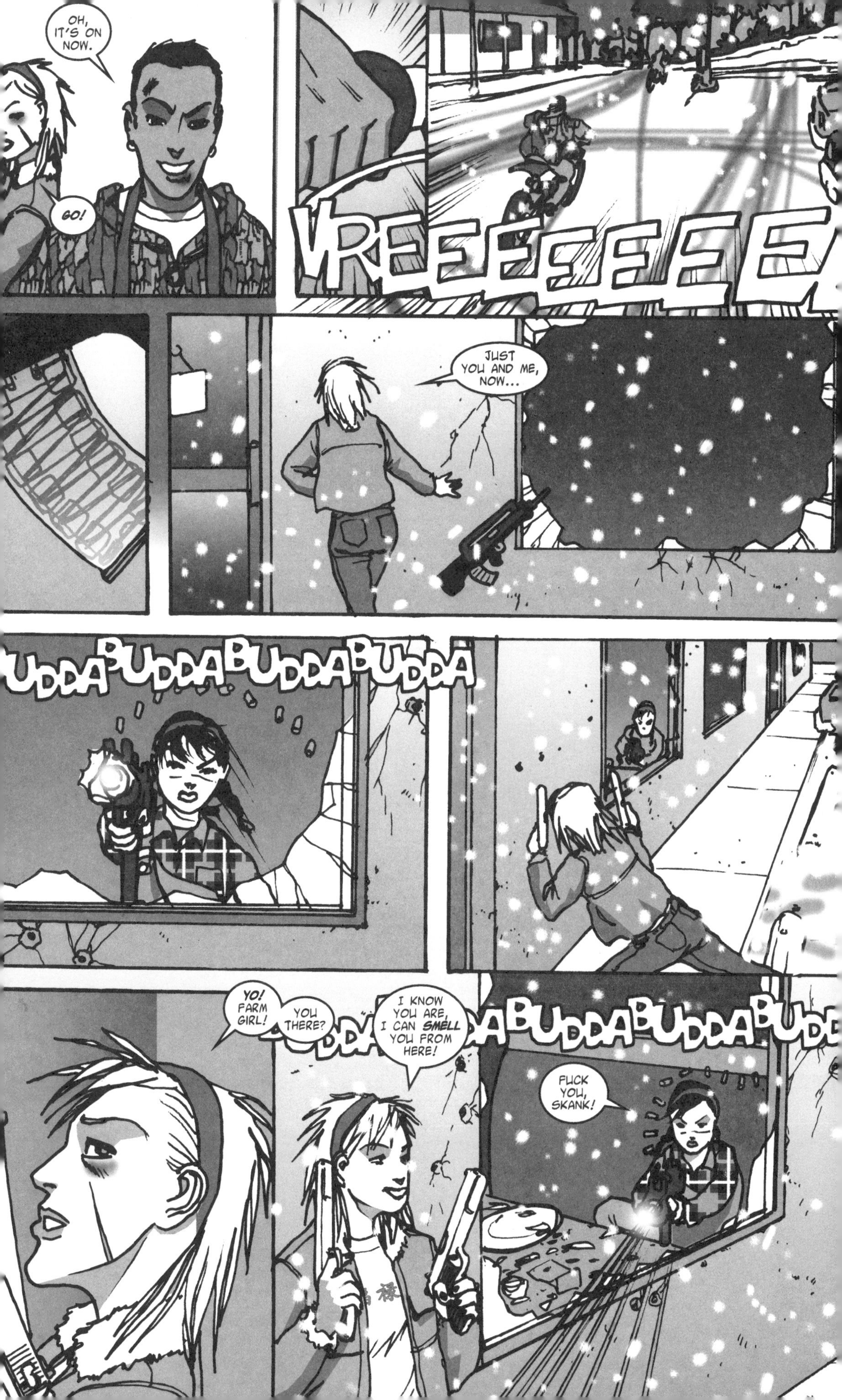

OH, IT'S ON NOW.
GO!
VREEEEEEEE
JUST YOU AND ME, NOW...
BUDDABUDDABUDDABUDDA
YO! FARM GIRL!
YOU THERE?
I KNOW YOU ARE, I CAN SMELL YOU FROM HERE!
BUDDABUDDABUDDABUDD
FUCK YOU, SKANK!

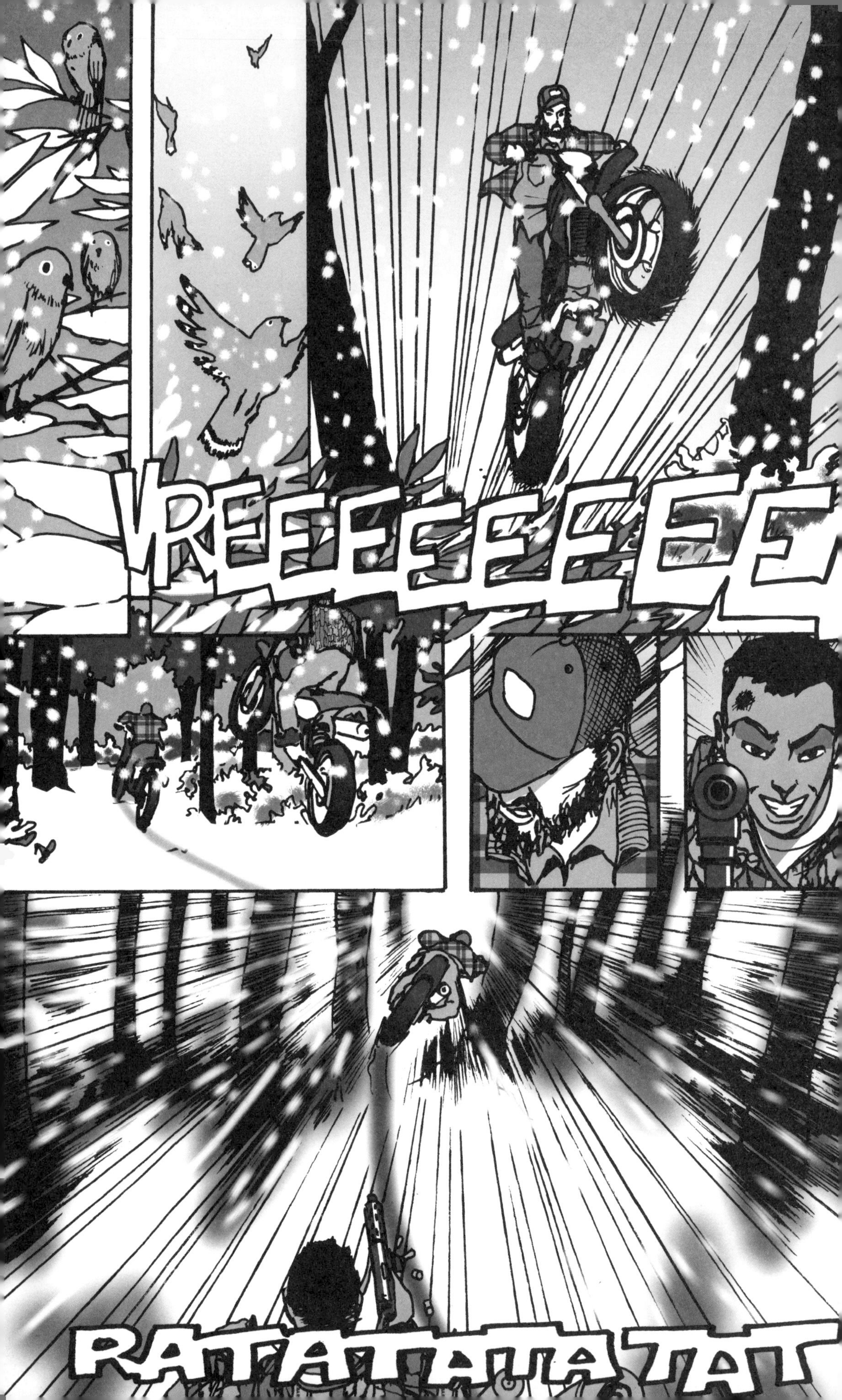

VREEEEEEEEE
RATATATATA TAT

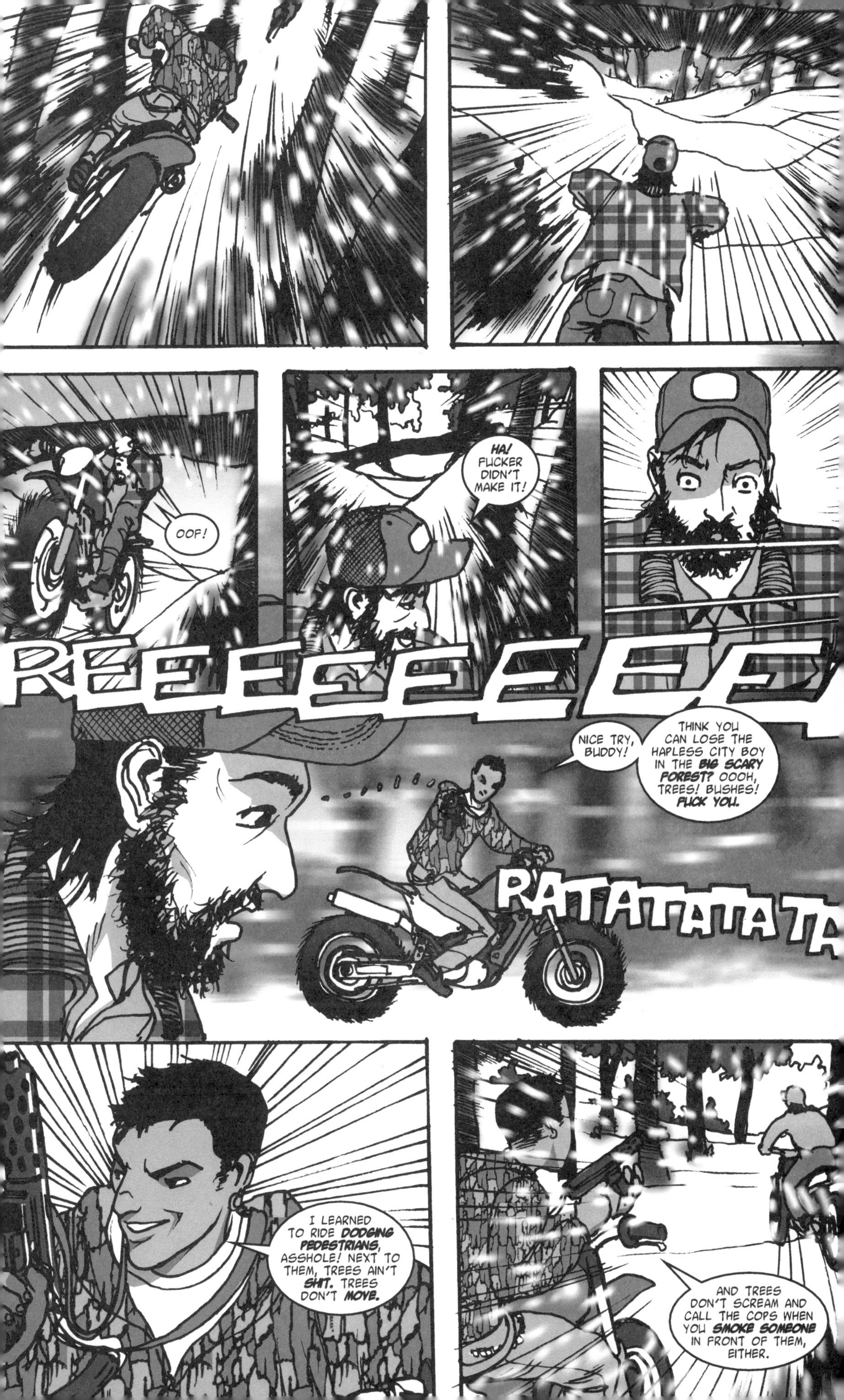
OOF!
HA! FUCKER DIDN'T MAKE IT!
REEEEEEEE
NICE TRY, BUDDY!
THINK YOU CAN LOSE THE HAPLESS CITY BOY IN THE BIG SCARY FOREST? OOOH, TREES! BUSHES! FUCK YOU.
RATATATATA
I LEARNED TO RIDE DODGING PEDESTRIANS, ASSHOLE! NEXT TO THEM, TREES AIN'T SHIT. TREES DON'T MOVE.
AND TREES DON'T SCREAM AND CALL THE COPS WHEN YOU SMOKE SOMEONE IN FRONT OF THEM, EITHER.

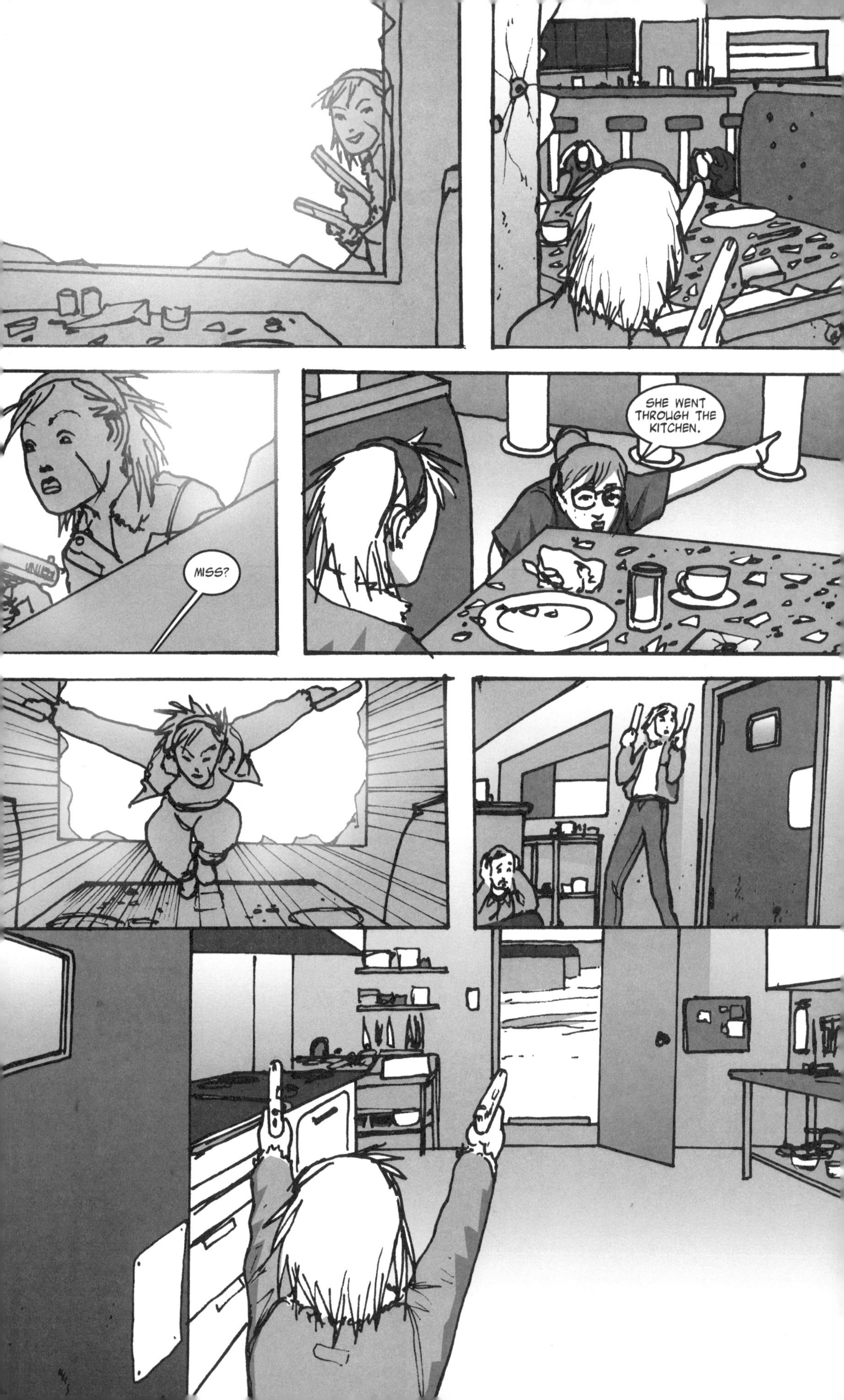
MISS?
SHE WENT THROUGH THE KITCHEN.

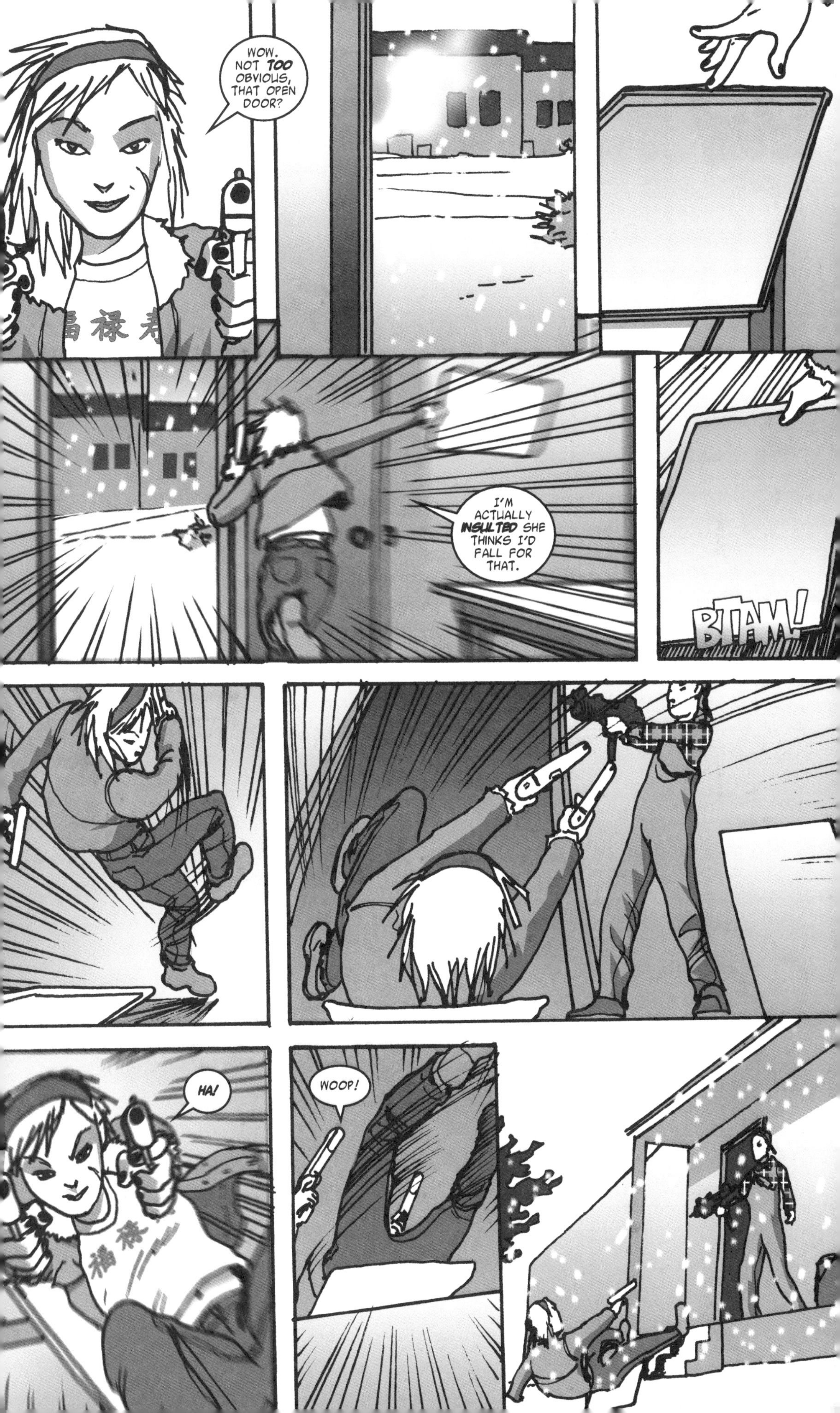
WOW. NOT TOO OBVIOUS, THAT OPEN DOOR?
I'M ACTUALLY INSULTED SHE THINKS I'D FALL FOR THAT.
BLAM!
HA!
WOOP!

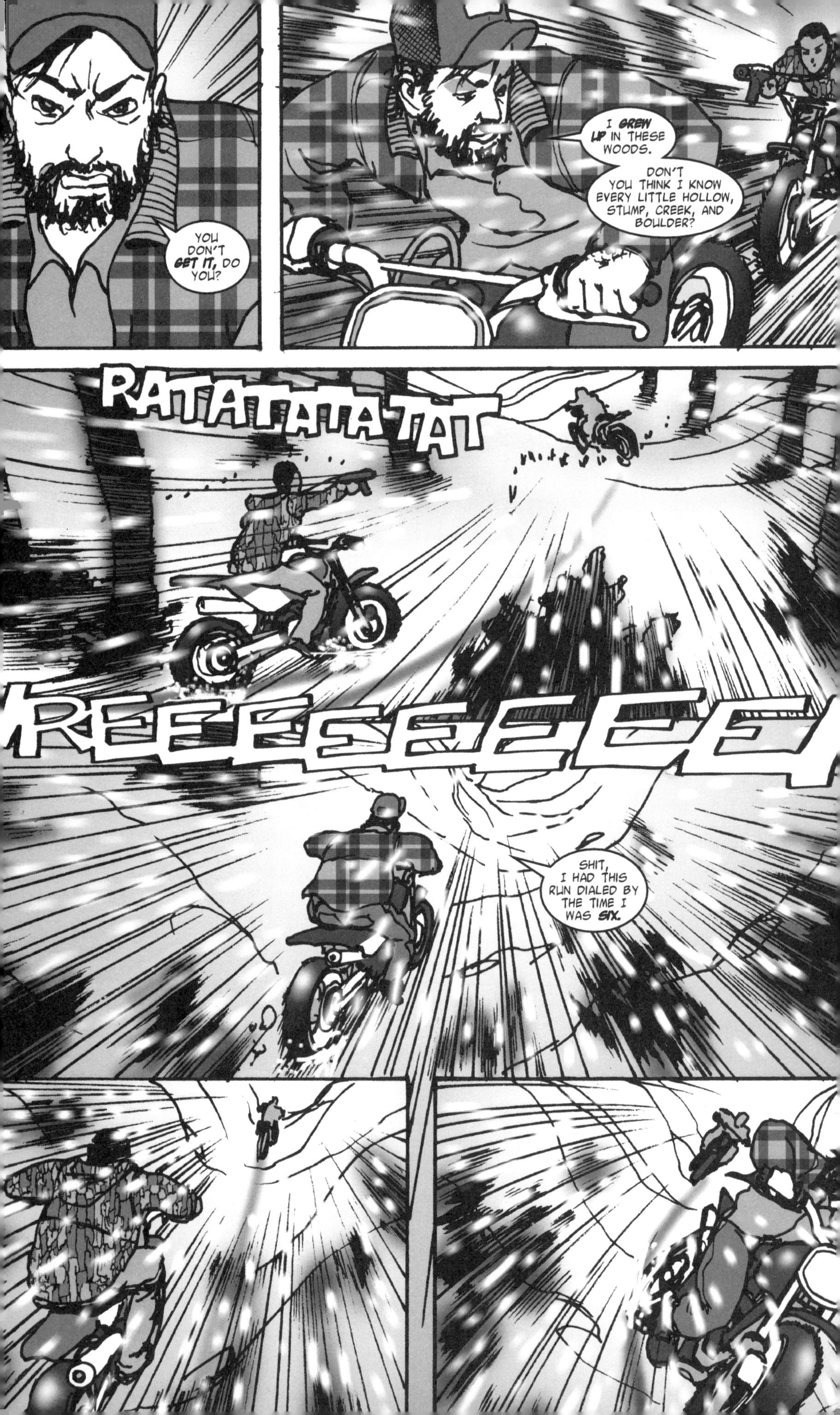
YOU DON'T GET IT, DO YOU?
I GREW UP IN THESE WOODS.
DON'T YOU THINK I KNOW EVERY LITTLE HOLLOW, STUMP, CREEK, AND BOULDER?
RATATATATA TAT
REEESEEEEE
SHIT, I HAD THIS RUN DIALED BY THE TIME I WAS SIX.

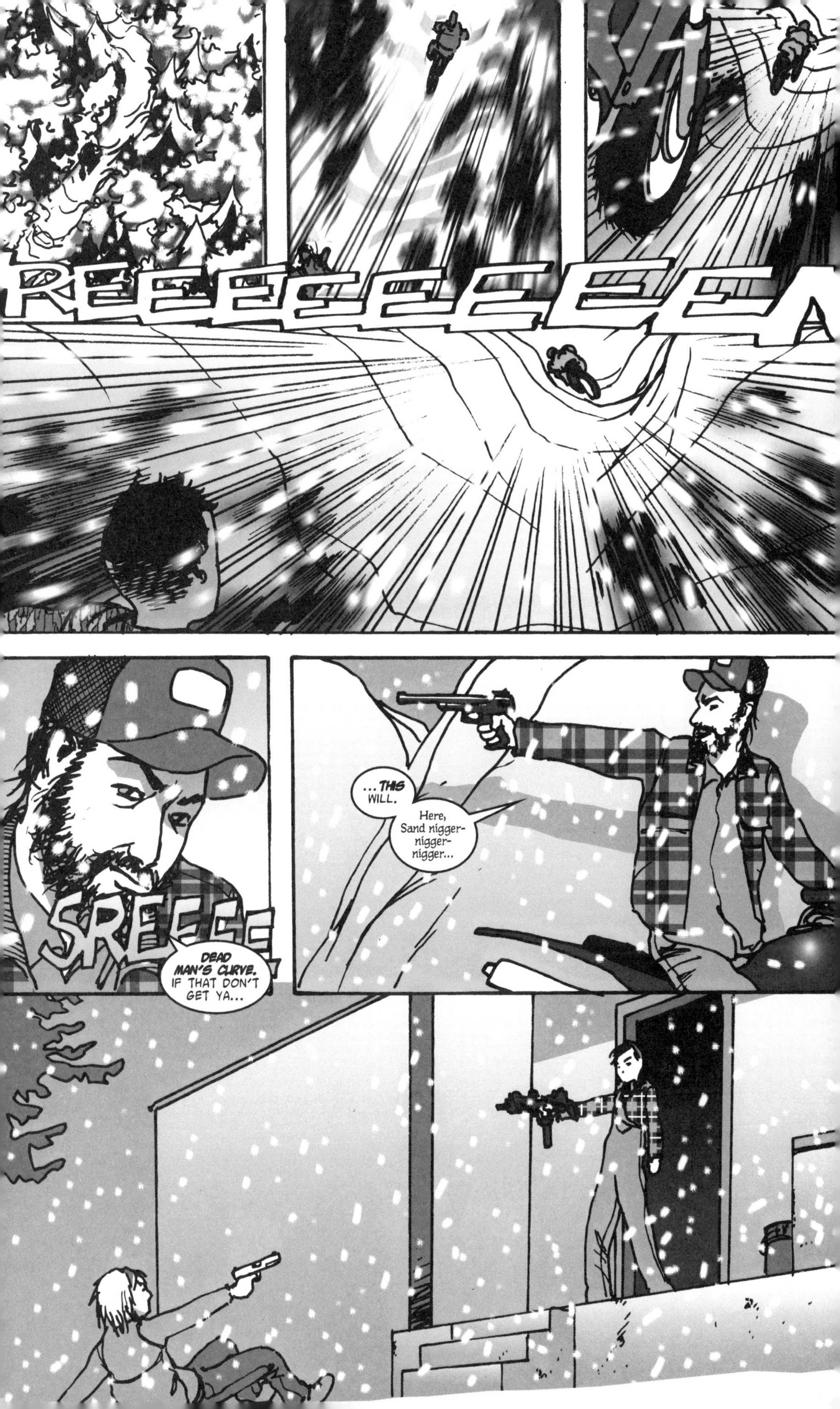

REEEEEEEEEEA
SREEE
DEAD MAN'S CURVE. IF THAT DON'T GET YA...
...THIS WILL.
Here, Sand nigger-nigger-nigger...

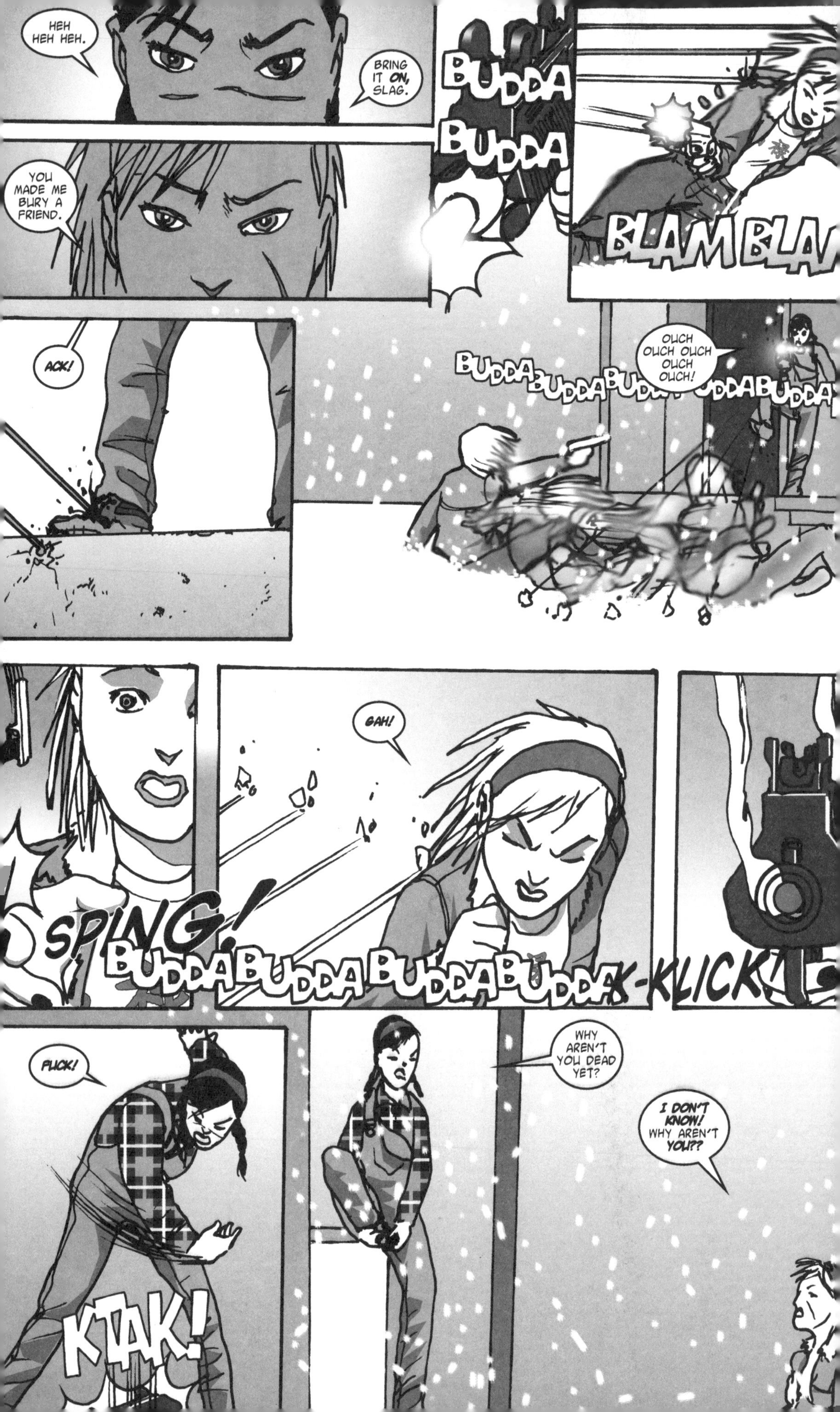

HEH HEH HEH.
BRING IT ON, SLAG.
BUDDA BUDDA
BLAM BLA
YOU MADE ME BURY A FRIEND.
ACK!
OUCH OUCH OUCH OUCH OUCH!
BUDDA BUDDA BUDDA BUDDA BUDDA
GAH!
SPING!
BUDDA BUDDA BUDDA BUDDA
K-KLICK!
FUCK!
KTAK!
WHY AREN'T YOU DEAD YET?
I DON'T KNOW! WHY AREN'T YOU??

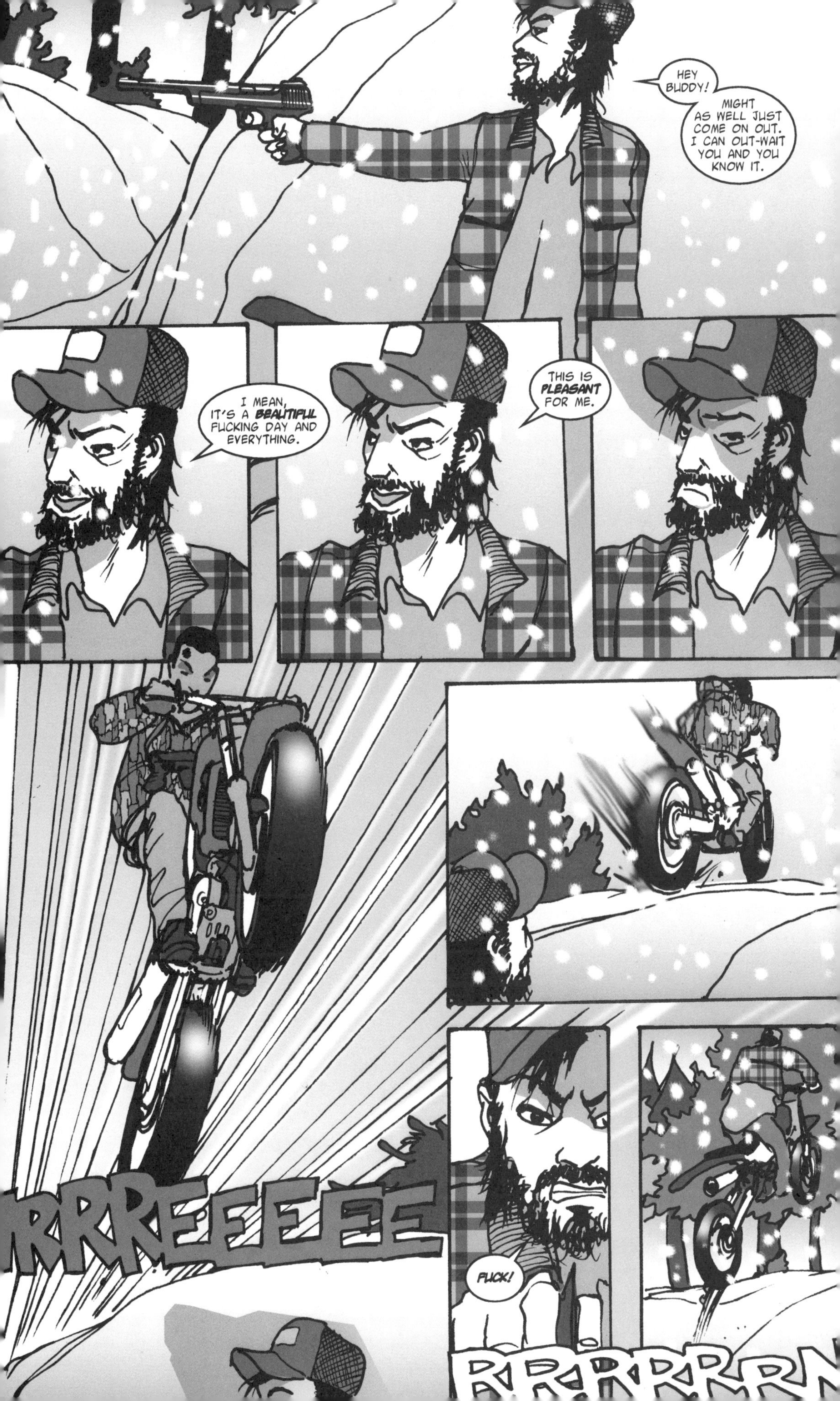

HEY BUDDY!
MIGHT AS WELL JUST COME ON OUT. I CAN OUT-WAIT YOU AND YOU KNOW IT.
I MEAN, IT'S A BEAUTIFUL FUCKING DAY AND EVERYTHING.
THIS IS PLEASANT FOR ME.
RRREEEEEE
FUCK!
RRRRRRRN

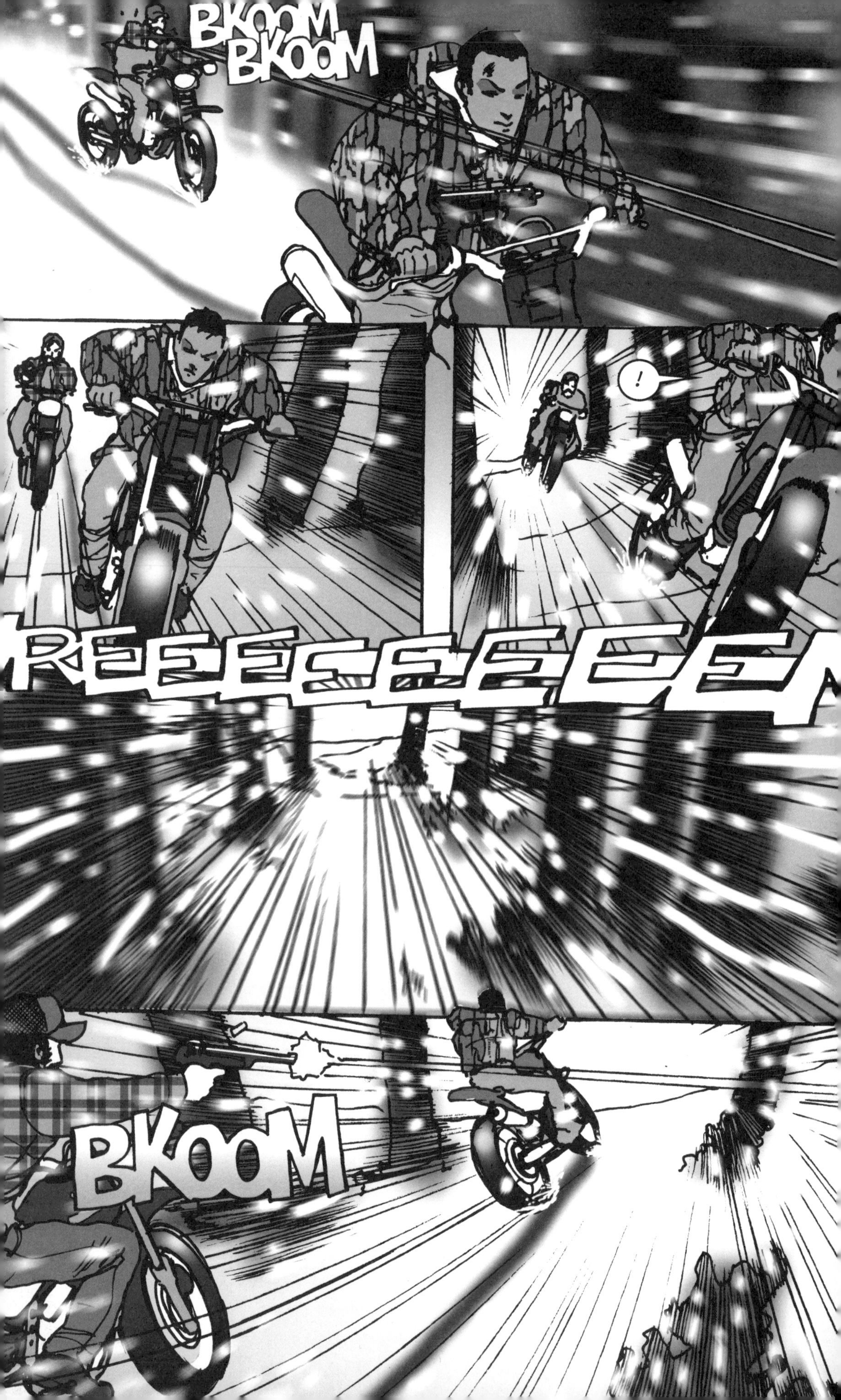
BKOOM
BKOOM
!
REEEEEEEEEEM
BKOOM

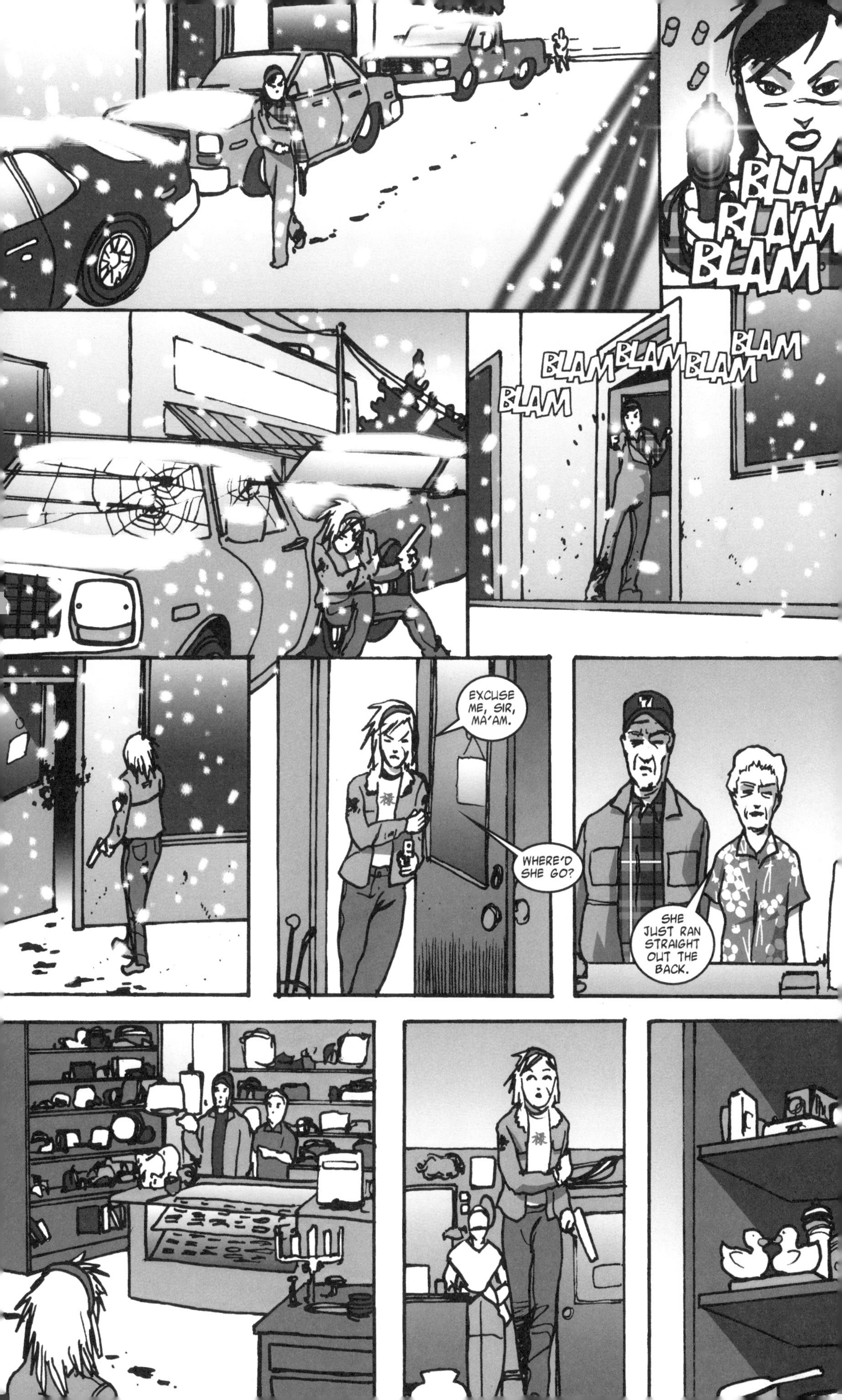
BLAM
BLAM
BLAM
BLAM
BLAM BLAM BLAM
BLAM
EXCUSE ME, SIR, MA'AM.
WHERE'D SHE GO?
SHE JUST RAN STRAIGHT OUT THE BACK.

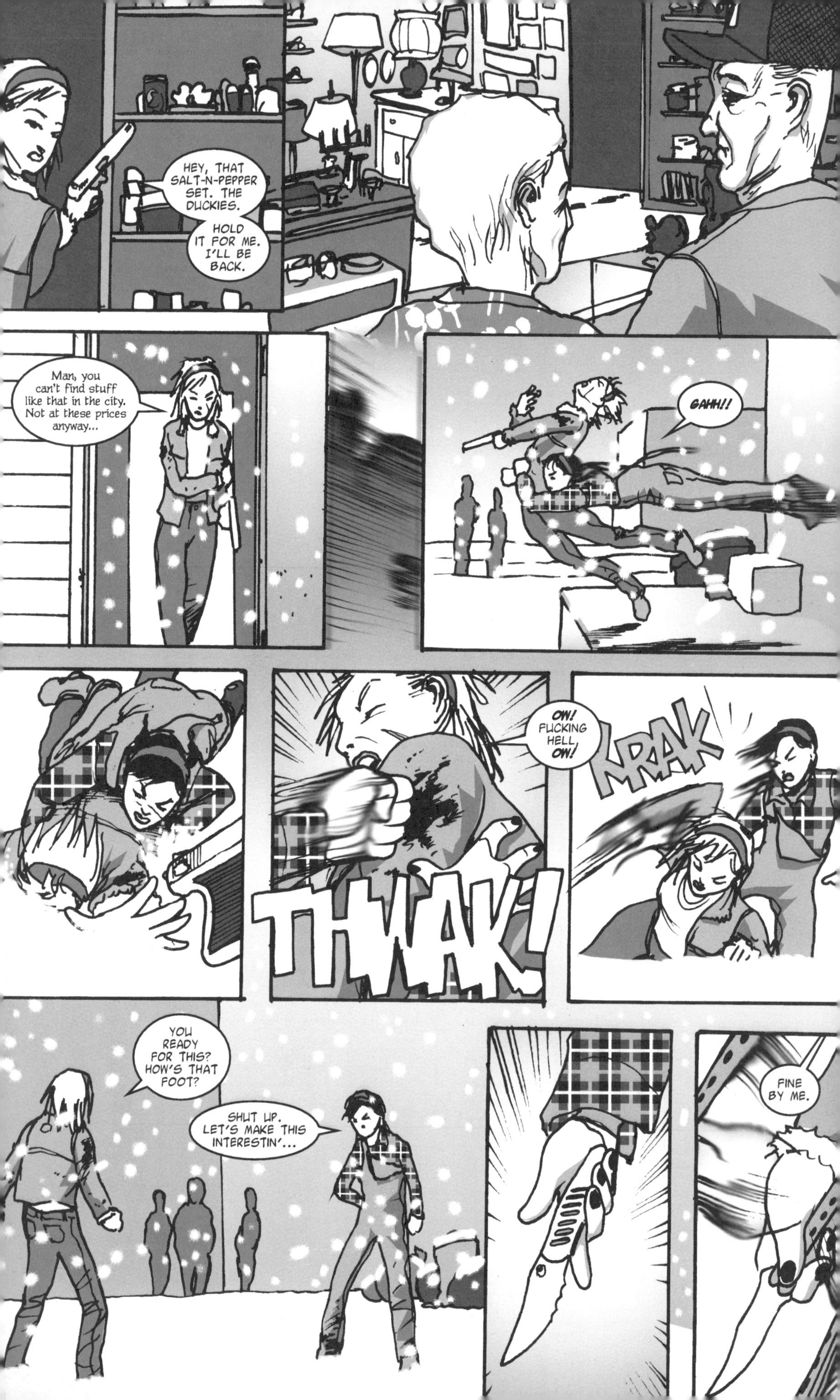
HEY, THAT SALT-N-PEPPER SET. THE DUCKIES.
HOLD IT FOR ME. I'LL BE BACK.
Man, you can't find stuff like that in the city. Not at these prices anyway...
GAHH!!
OW! FUCKING HELL, OW!
THWAK!
KRAK
YOU READY FOR THIS? HOW'S THAT FOOT?
SHUT UP. LET'S MAKE THIS INTERESTIN'...
FINE BY ME.

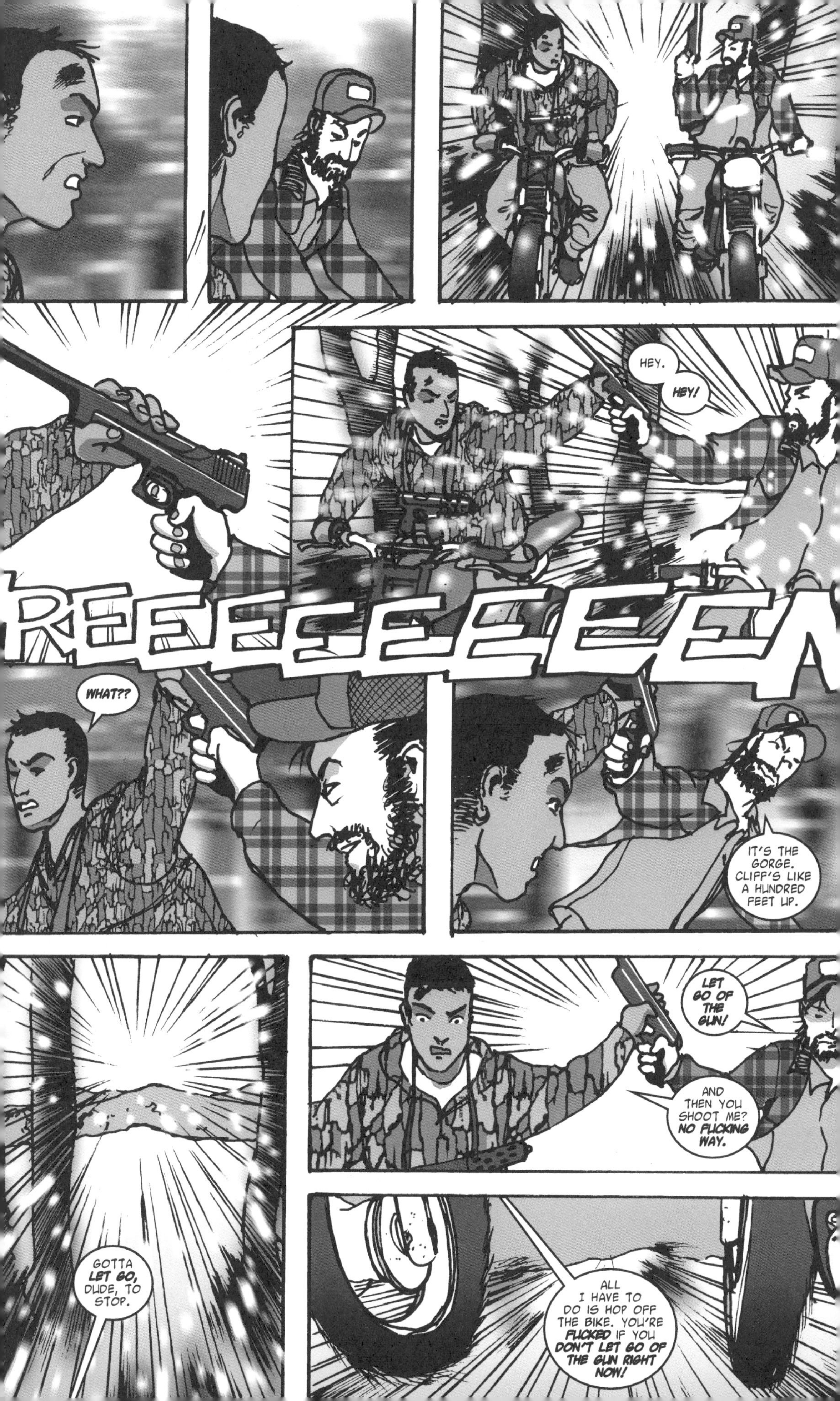
HEY.
HEY!
REEEEEEEEEN
WHAT??
IT'S THE GORGE. CLIFF'S LIKE A HUNDRED FEET UP.
GOTTA LET GO, DUDE, TO STOP.
LET GO OF THE GUN!
AND THEN YOU SHOOT ME? NO FUCKING WAY.
ALL I HAVE TO DO IS HOP OFF THE BIKE. YOU'RE FUCKED IF YOU DON'T LET GO OF THE GUN RIGHT NOW!

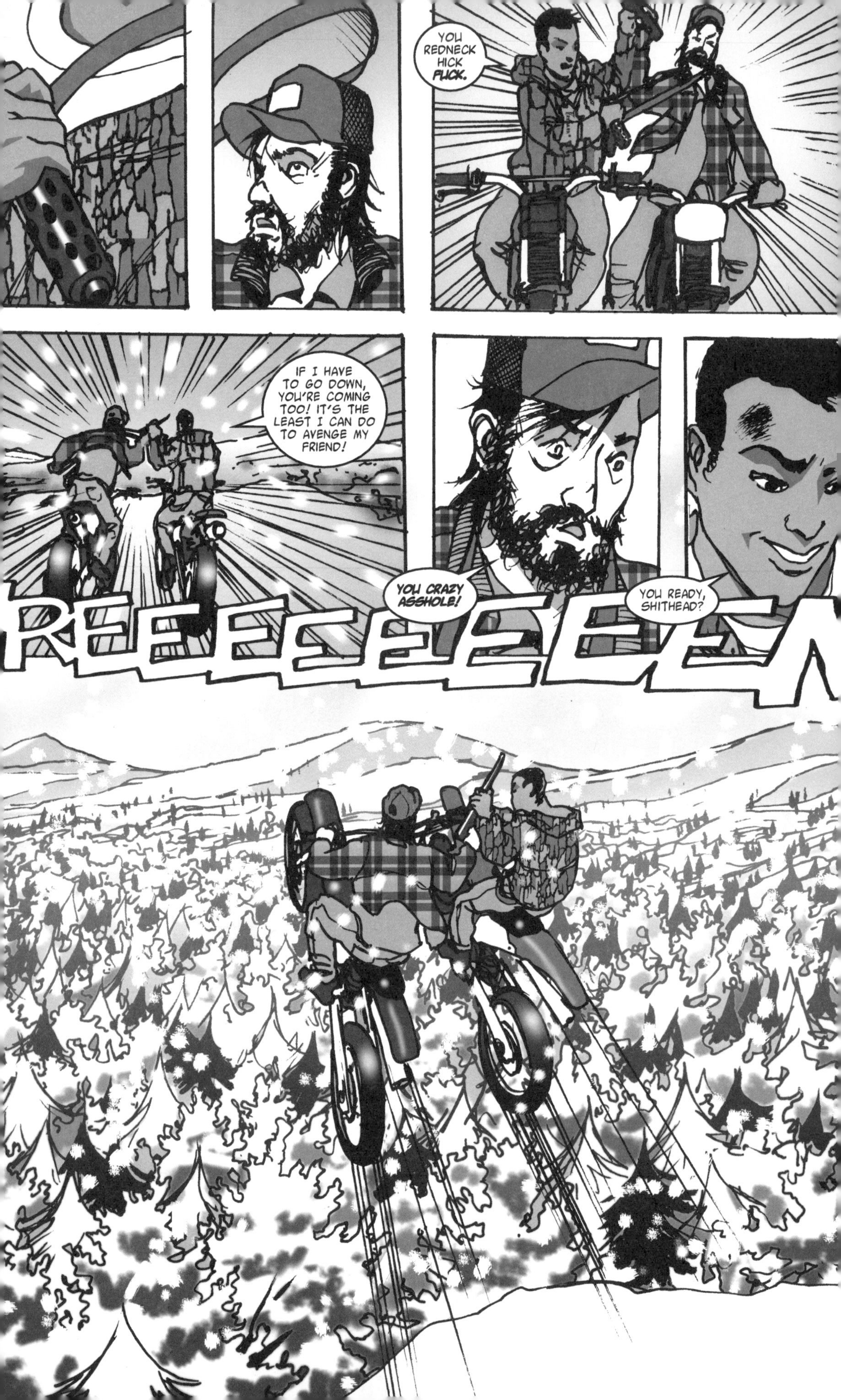

YOU REDNECK HICK FUCK.
IF I HAVE TO GO DOWN, YOU'RE COMING TOO! IT'S THE LEAST I CAN DO TO AVENGE MY FRIEND!
YOU CRAZY ASSHOLE!
YOU READY, SHITHEAD?
REEEEEEEEEN

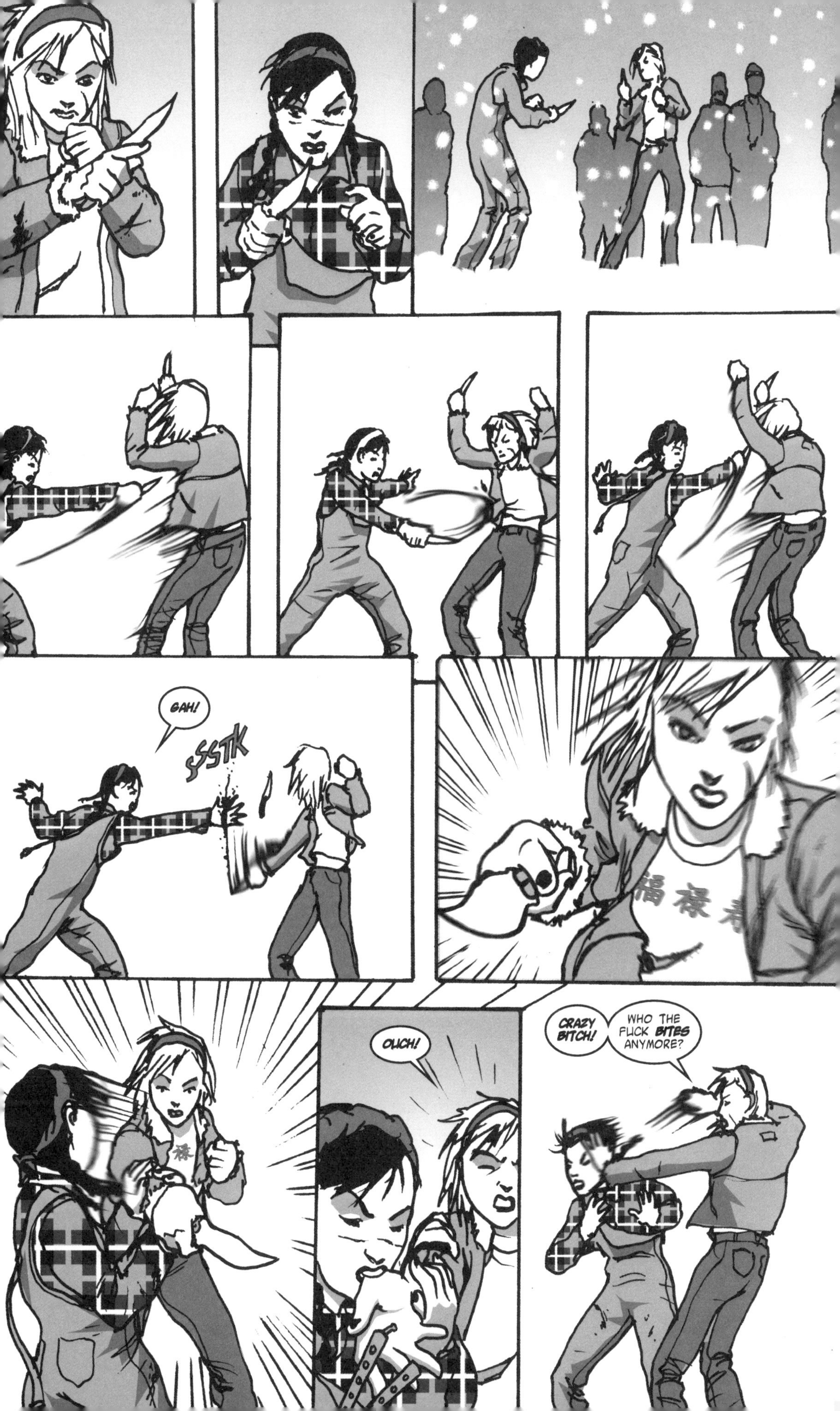
GAH!
SSSTK
OUCH!
CRAZY BITCH!
WHO THE FUCK BITES ANYMORE?

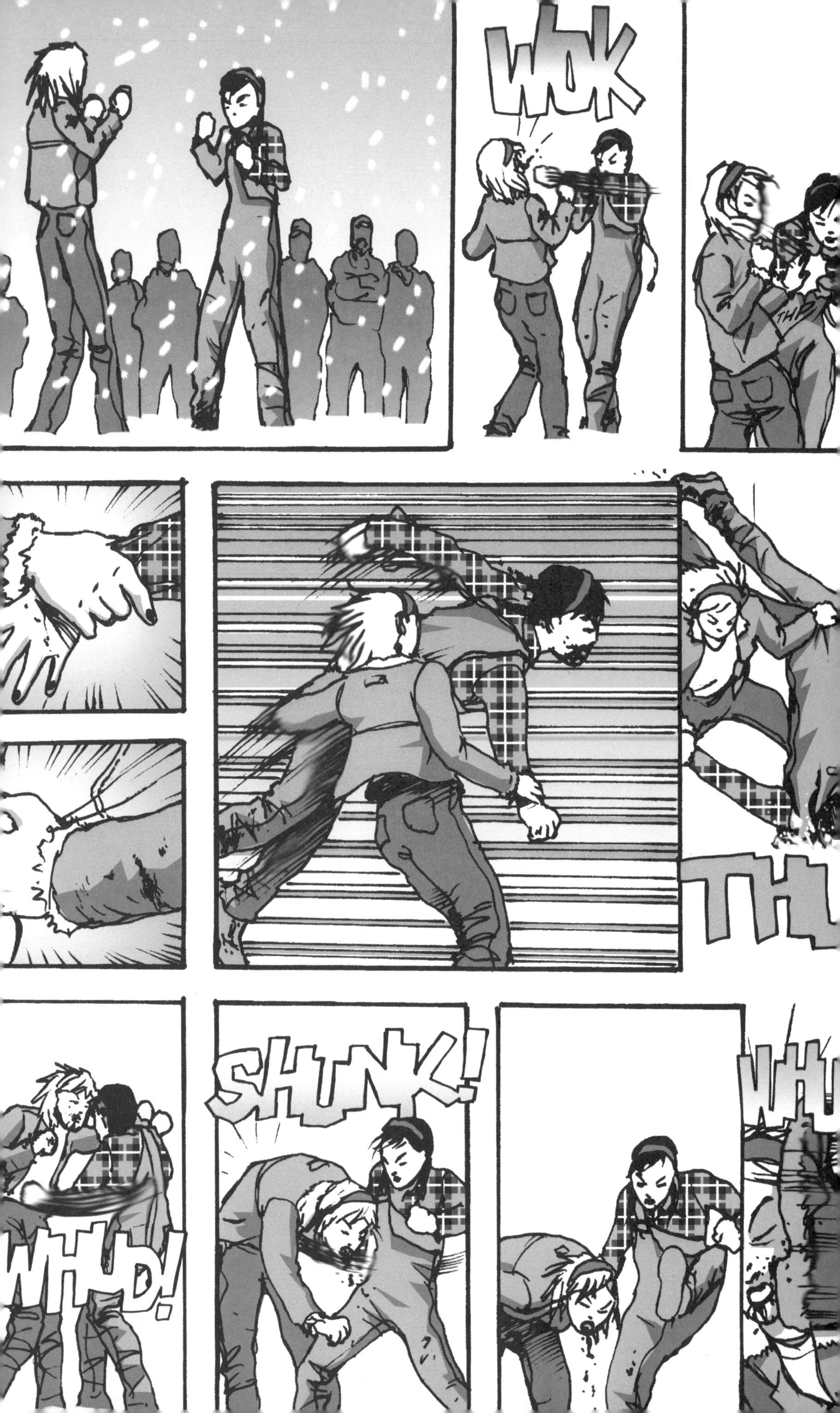
WOK
THP
SHUNK!
WHUD!

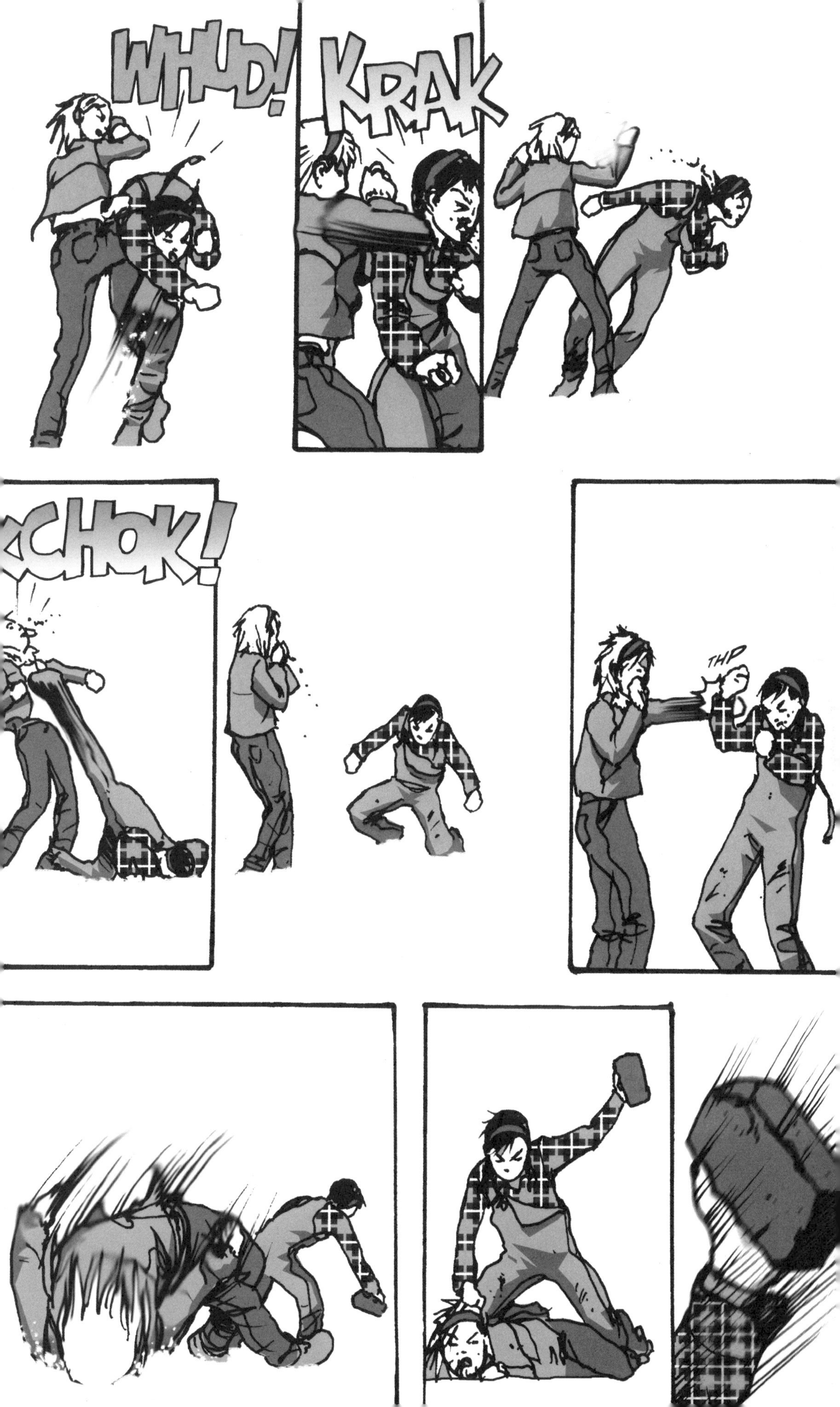
WHUD!
KRAK
CHOK!
THD

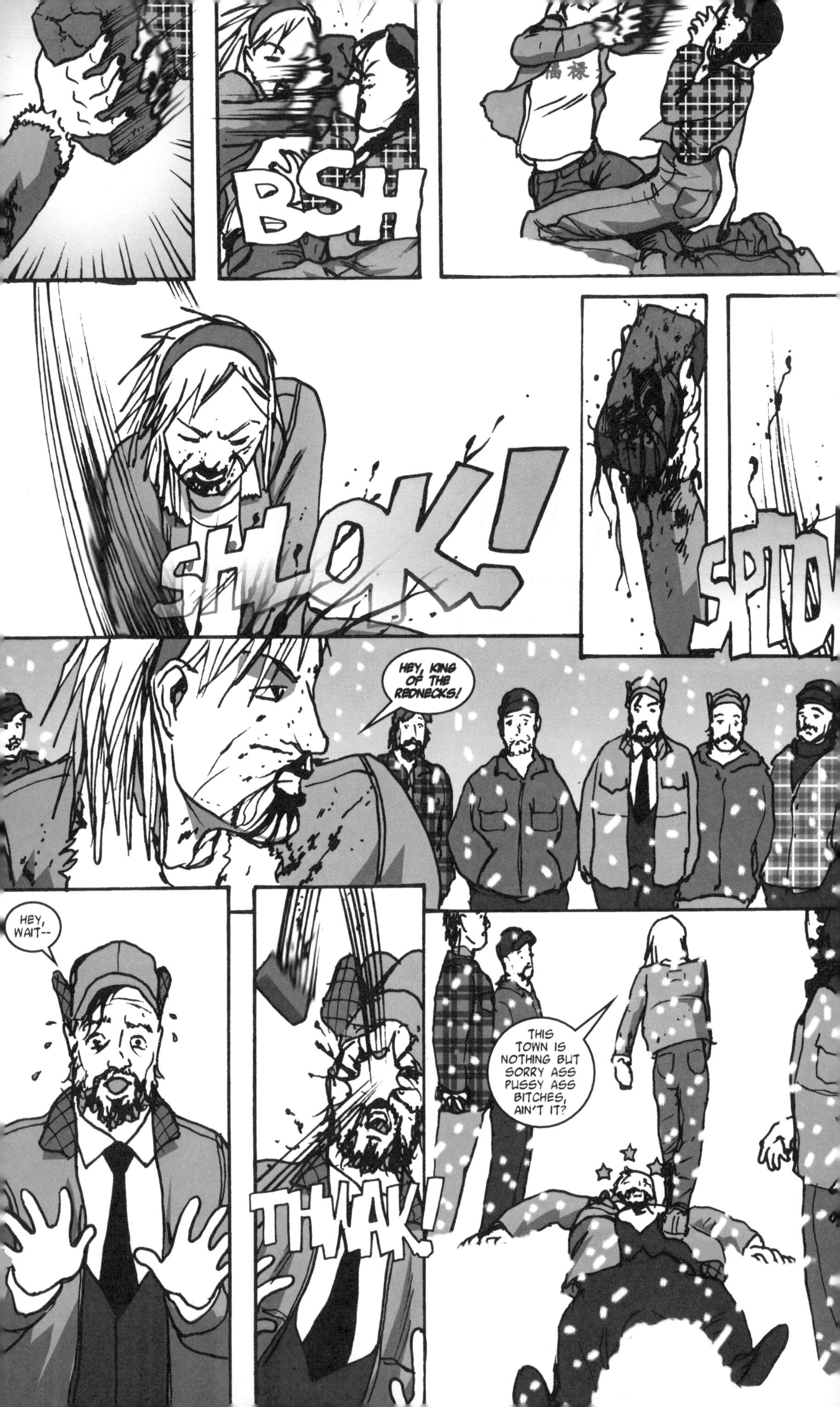
BSH
SHLOK!
SPLOW
HEY, KING OF THE REDNECKS!
HEY, WAIT--
THWAK!
THIS TOWN IS NOTHING BUT SORRY ASS PUSSY ASS BITCHES, AIN'T IT?

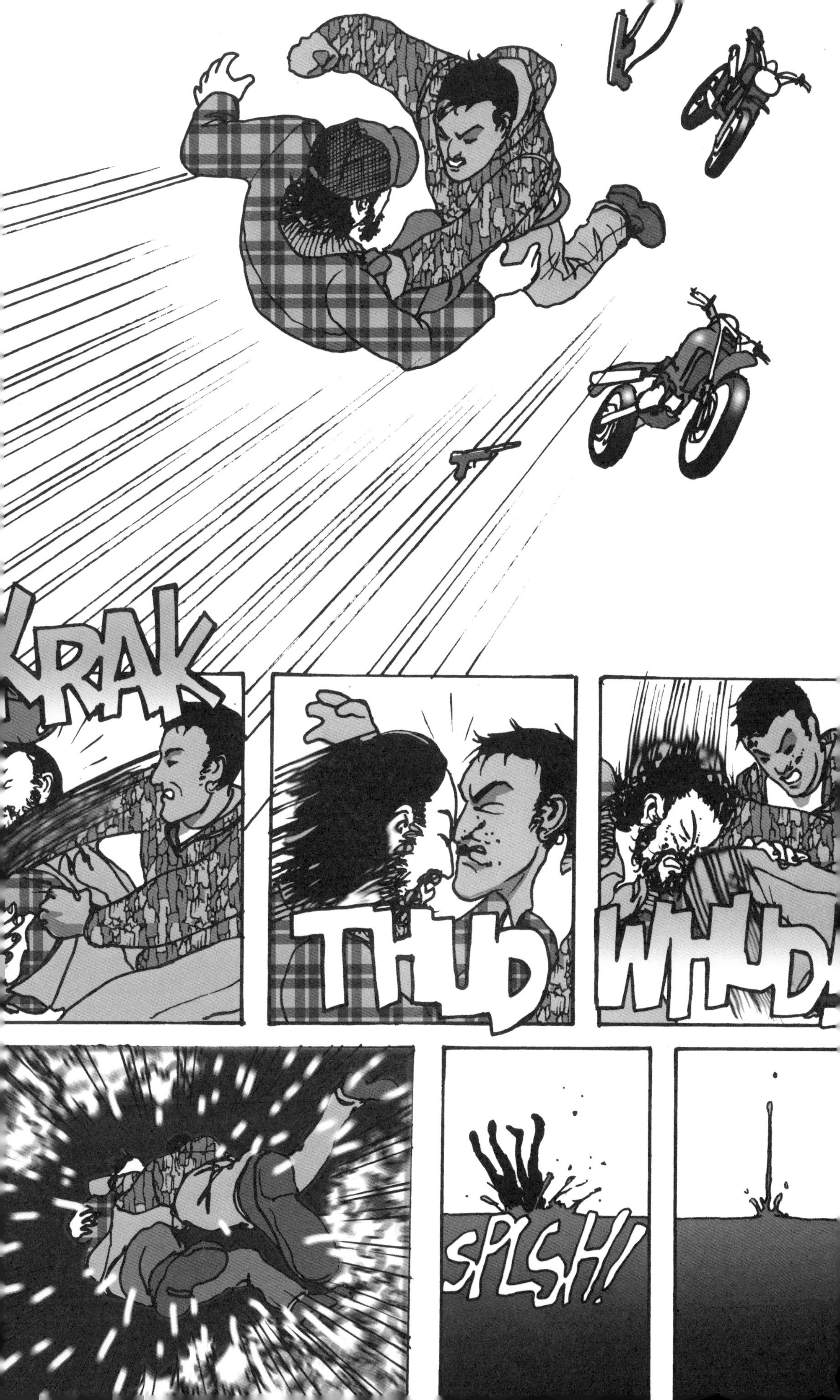
THUD
SPLSH!

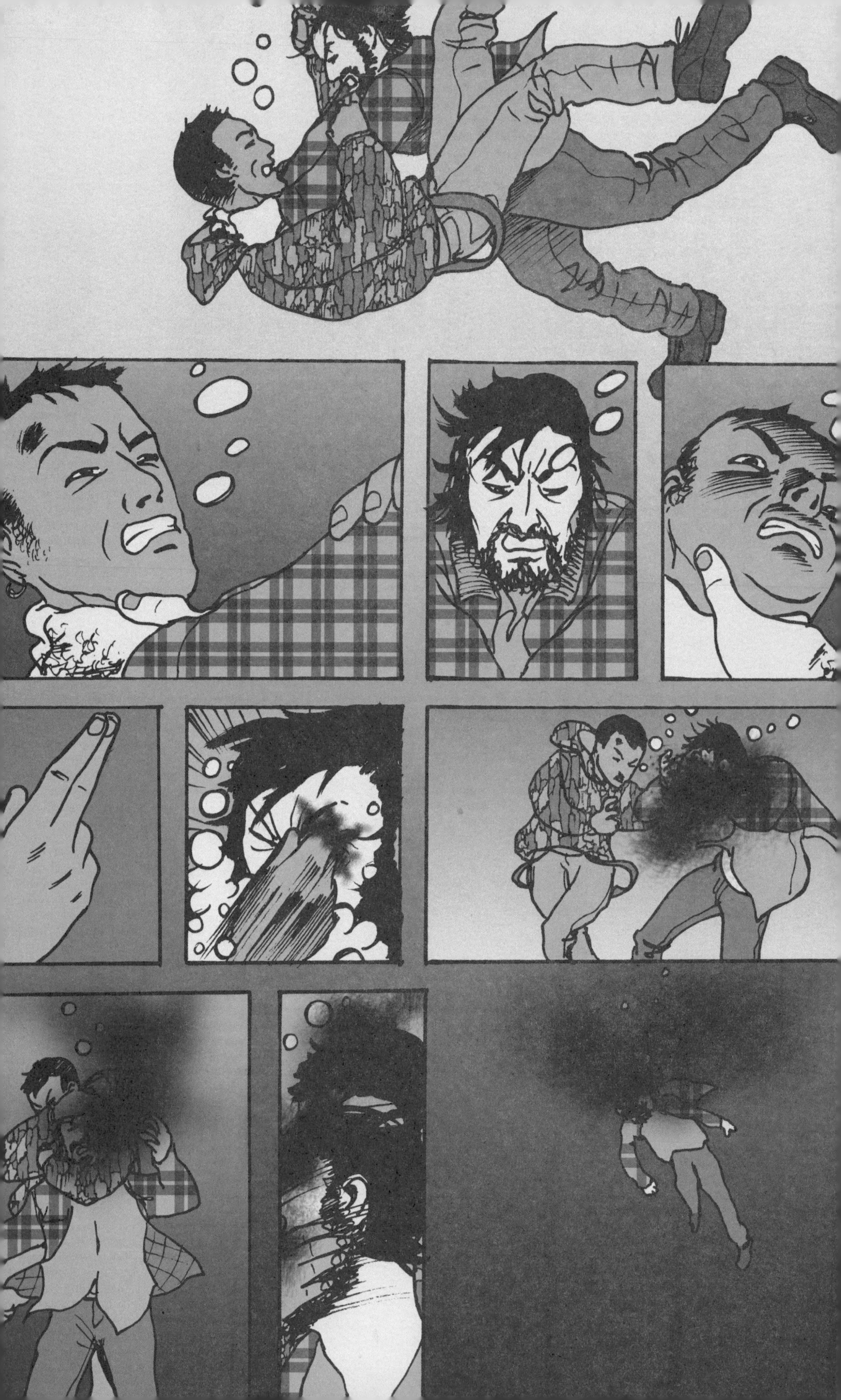

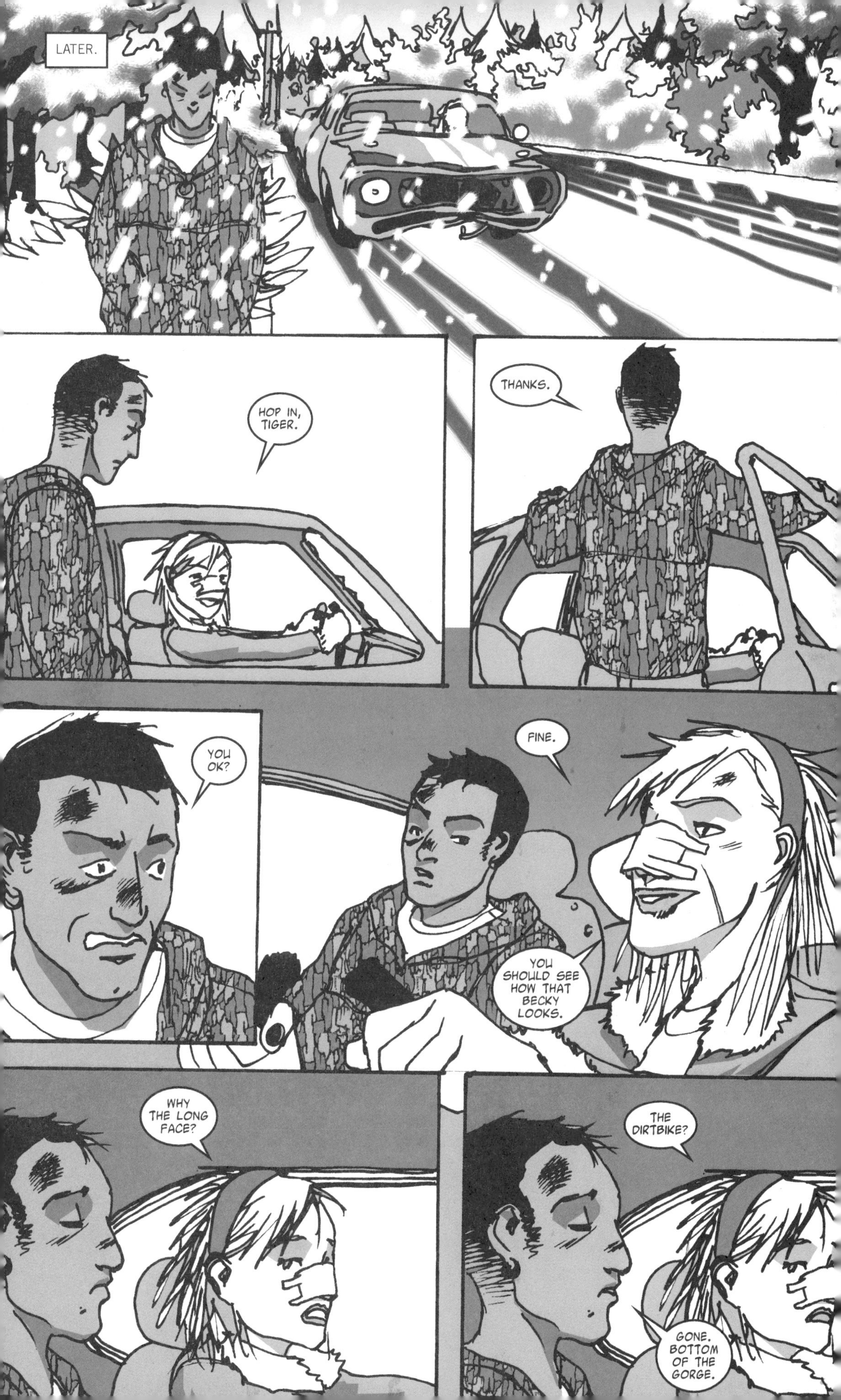
LATER.
HOP IN, TIGER.
THANKS.
YOU OK?
FINE.
YOU SHOULD SEE HOW THAT BECKY LOOKS.
WHY THE LONG FACE?
THE DIRTBIKE?
GONE. BOTTOM OF THE GORGE.

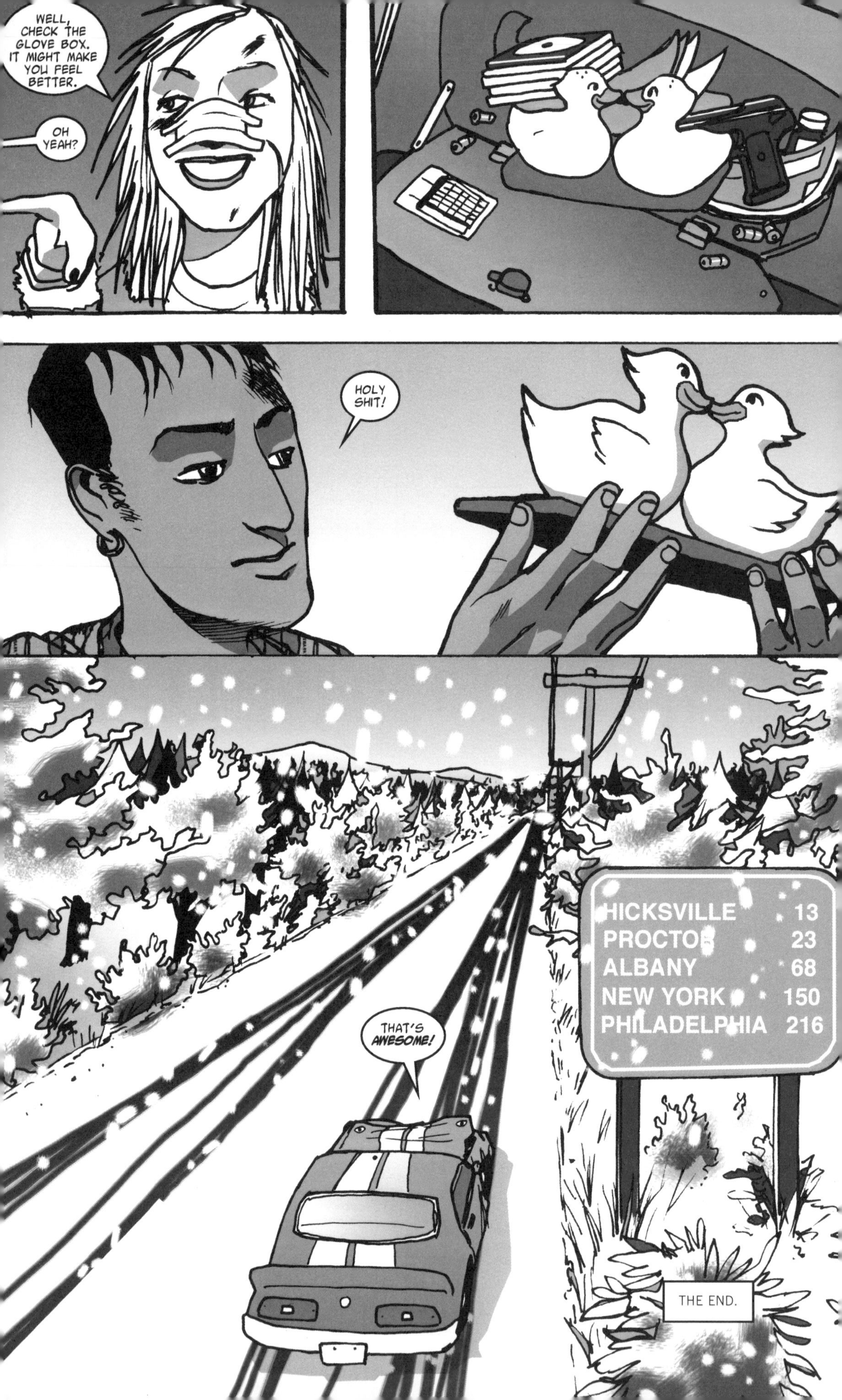
WELL, CHECK THE GLOVE BOX. IT MIGHT MAKE YOU FEEL BETTER.
OH YEAH?
HOLY SHIT!
HICKSVILLE 13
PROCTOR 23
ALBANY 68
NEW YORK 150
PHILADELPHIA 216
THAT'S AWESOME!
THE END.

03

The Couriers
THE BALLAD OF JOHNNY FUNWRECKER

Brian Wood x Rob G x Ryan Yount

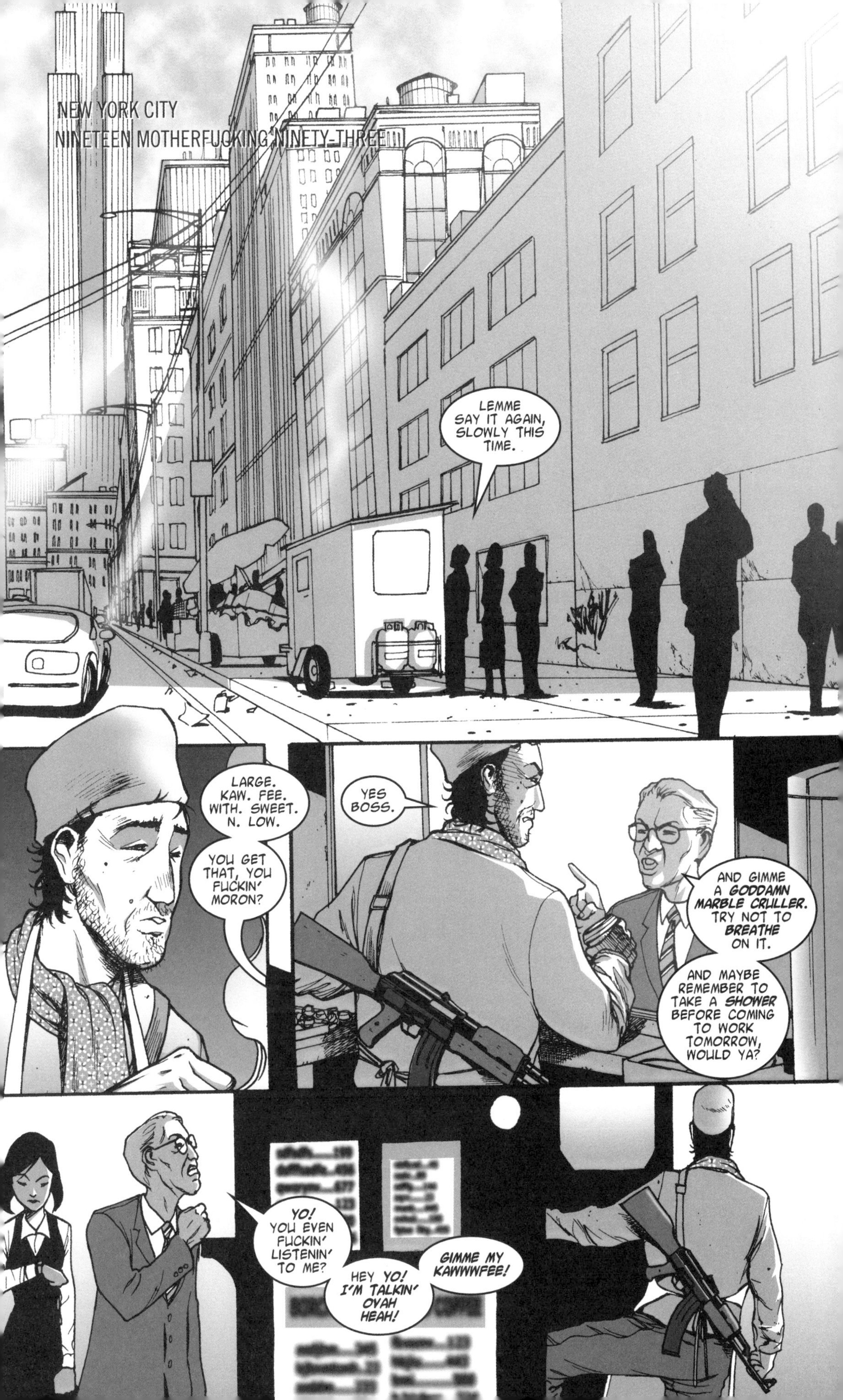
NEW YORK CITY
NINETEEN MOTHERFUCKING NINETY-THREE
LEMME SAY IT AGAIN, SLOWLY THIS TIME.
LARGE. KAW. FEE. WITH. SWEET. N. LOW.
YOU GET THAT, YOU FUCKIN' MORON?
YES BOSS.
AND GIMME A GODDAMN MARBLE CRULLER. TRY NOT TO BREATHE ON IT.
AND MAYBE REMEMBER TO TAKE A SHOWER BEFORE COMING TO WORK TOMORROW, WOULD YA?
YO! YOU EVEN FUCKIN' LISTENIN' TO ME?
HEY YO! I'M TALKIN' OYAH HEAH!
GIMME MY KAWWWFEE!

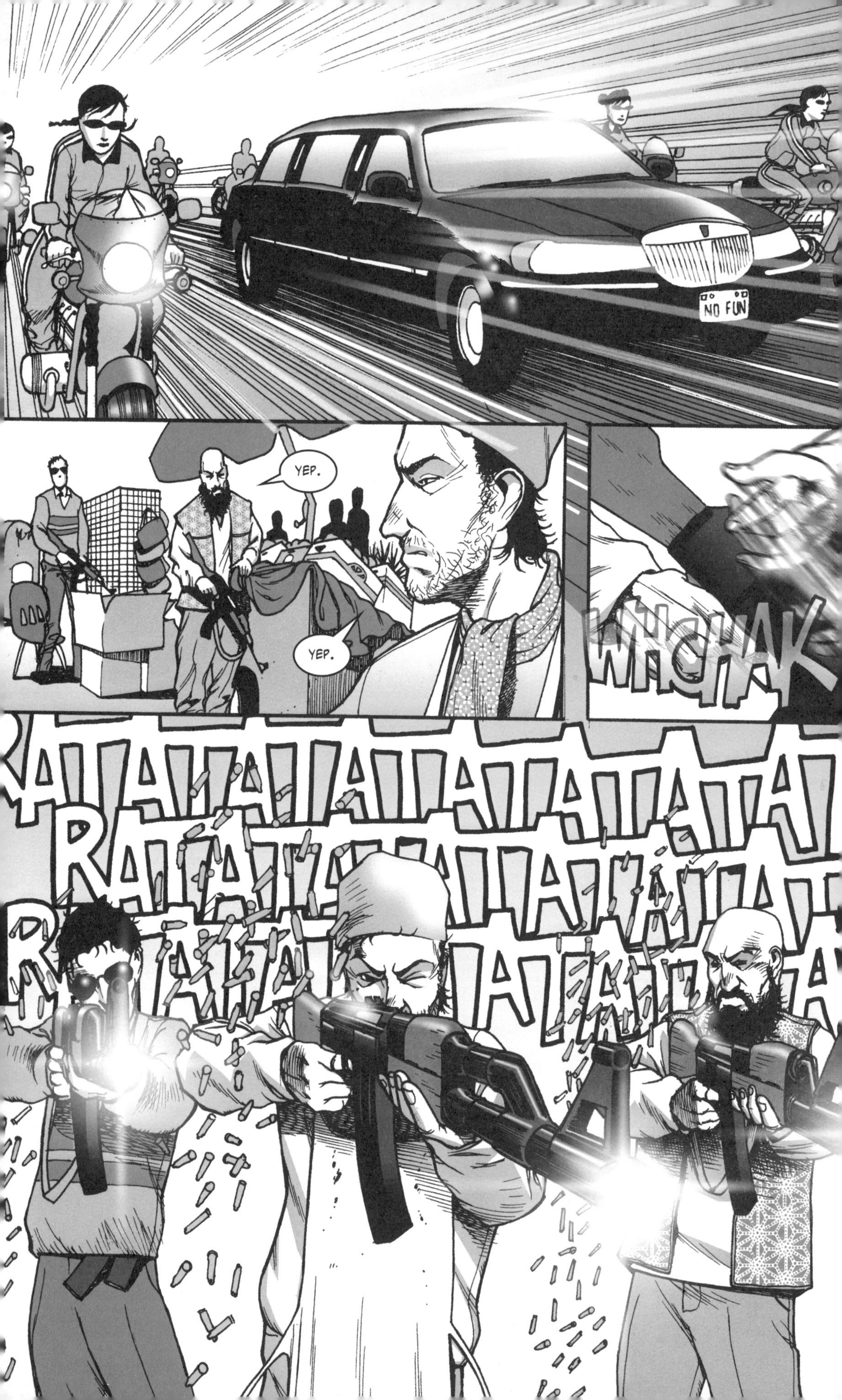
NO FUN
YEP.
YEP.
WHCHAK
RATATATATATATATATA
RATATATATATATATATATAT
RATATATATATATATATATATA

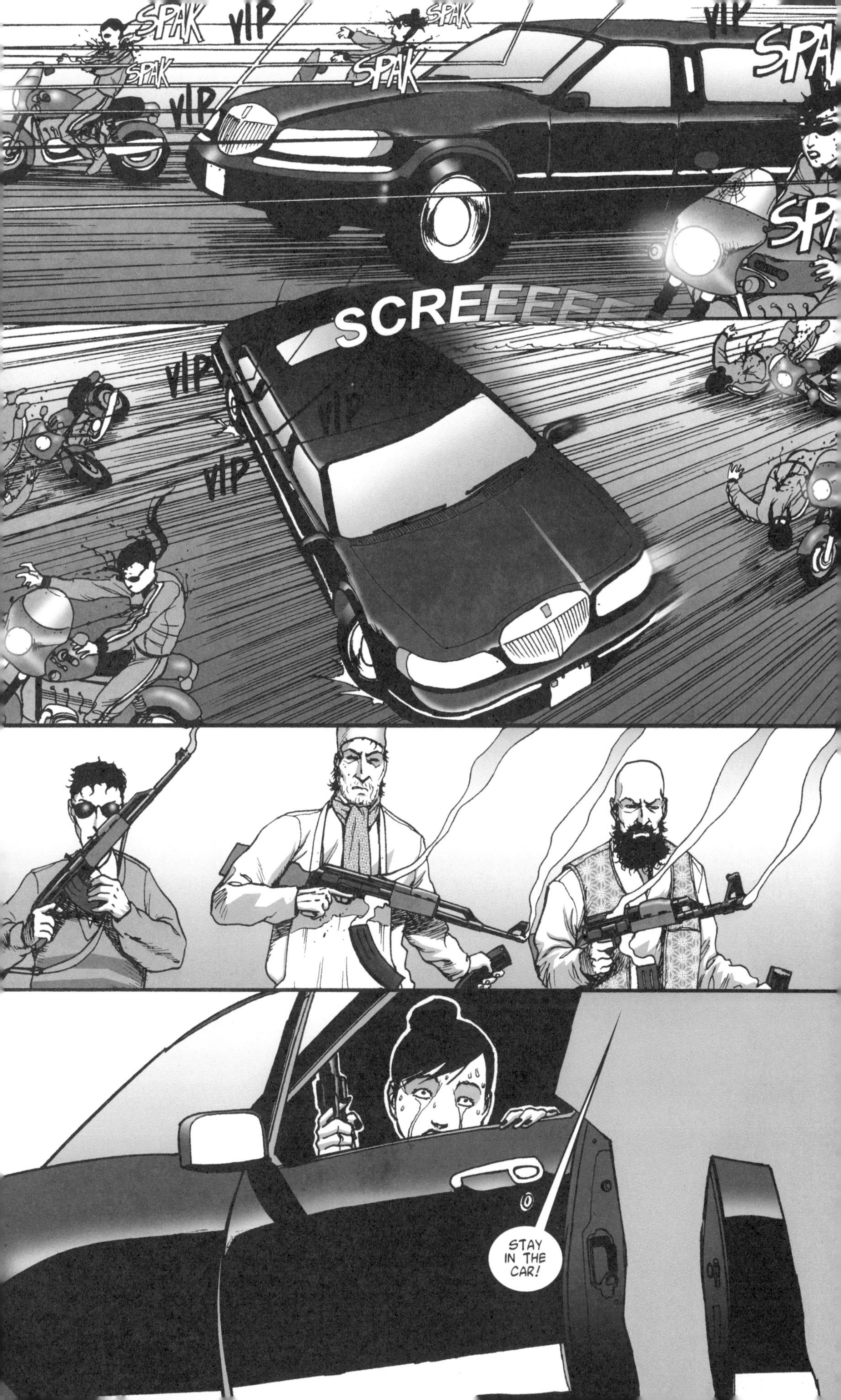

SPAK
VIP
SPAK
SPAK
SPAK
VIP
VIP
SPAK
SCREEEEEE
VIP
VIP
VIP
STAY IN THE CAR!

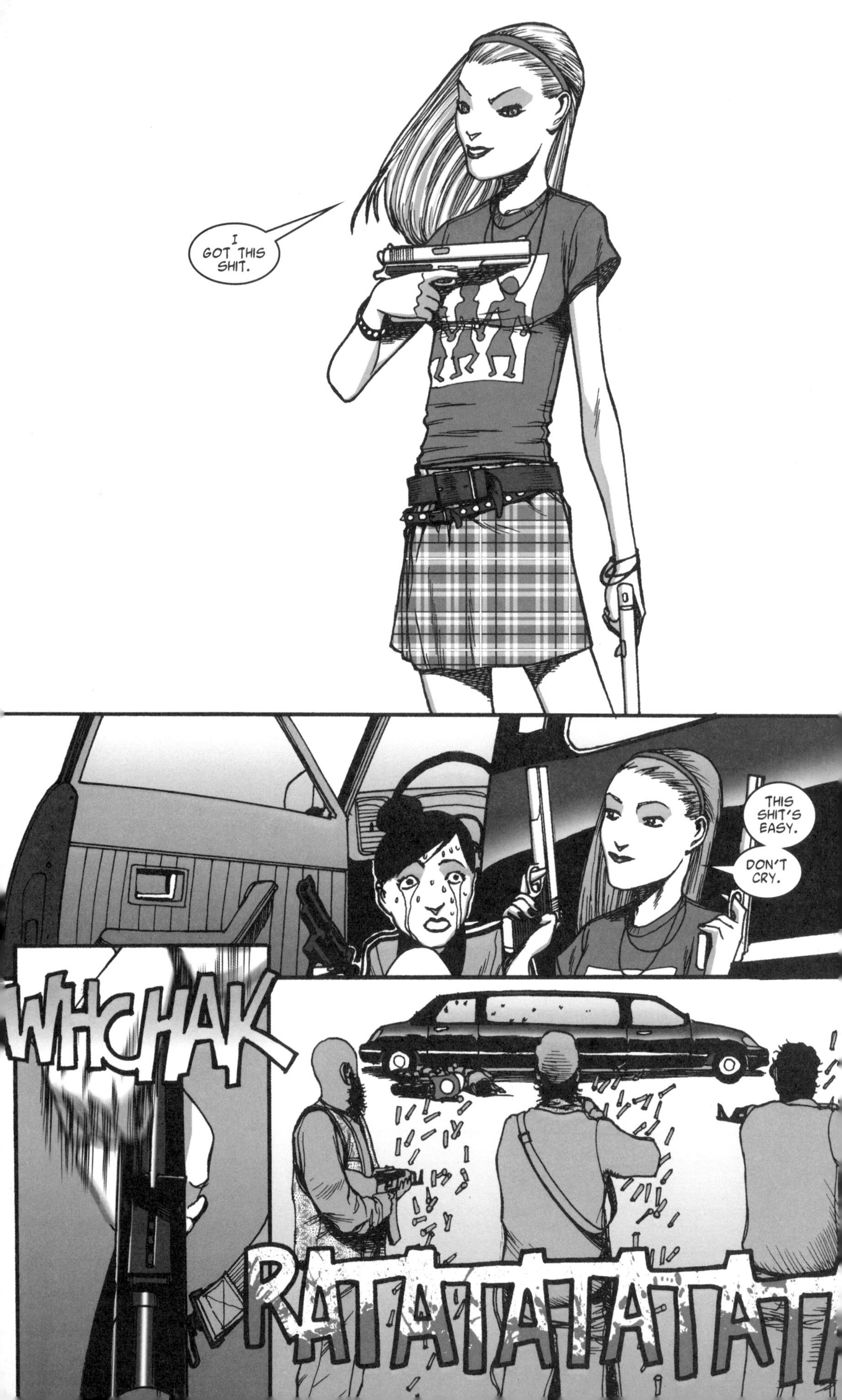
I GOT THIS SHIT.
THIS SHIT'S EASY.
DON'T CRY.
WHCHAK
RATATATATATAT

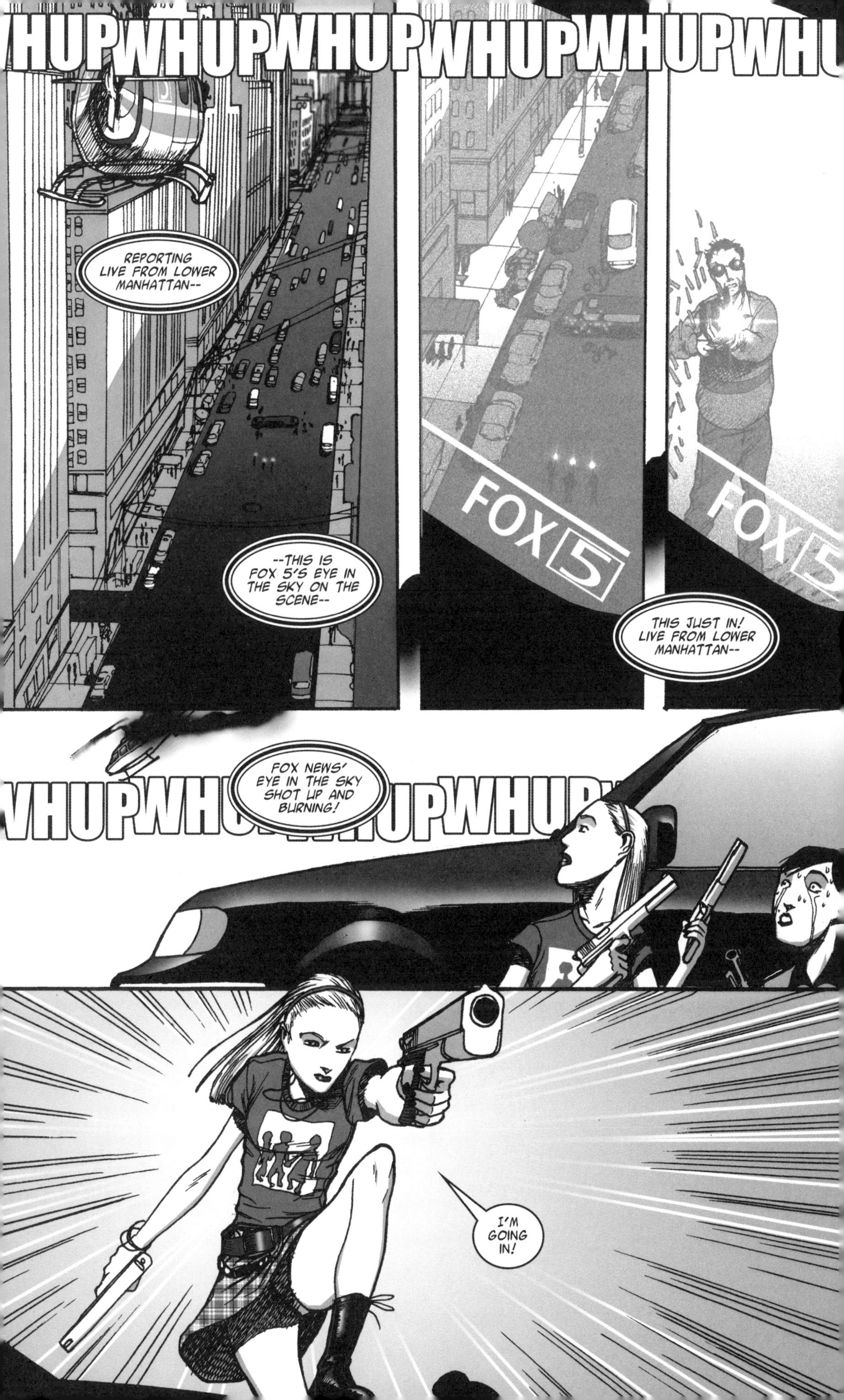
WHUPWHUPWHUPWHUPWHUPWHU
REPORTING LIVE FROM LOWER MANHATTAN--
--THIS IS FOX 5'S EYE IN THE SKY ON THE SCENE--
FOX 5
THIS JUST IN! LIVE FROM LOWER MANHATTAN--
FOX 5
FOX NEWS' EYE IN THE SKY SHOT UP AND BURNING!
VHUPWHUPWHUPWHUP
I'M GOING IN!

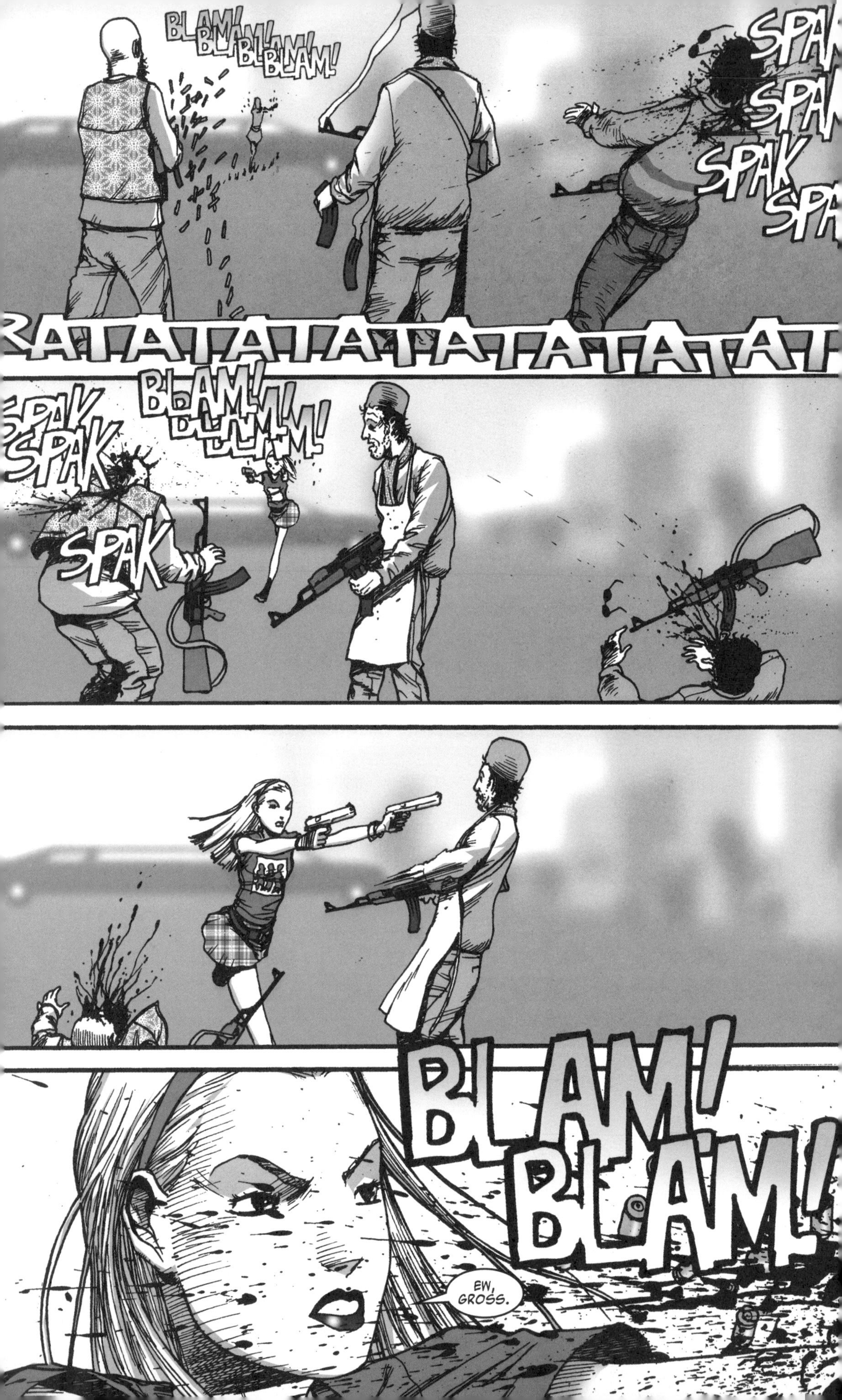
BLAM! BLAM! BLAM! BLAM!
SPAK SPAK SPAK SPAK
RATATATATATATATAT
SPAK SPAK
BLAM! BLAM! BLAM!
SPAK
BLAM! BLAM!
EW, GROSS.

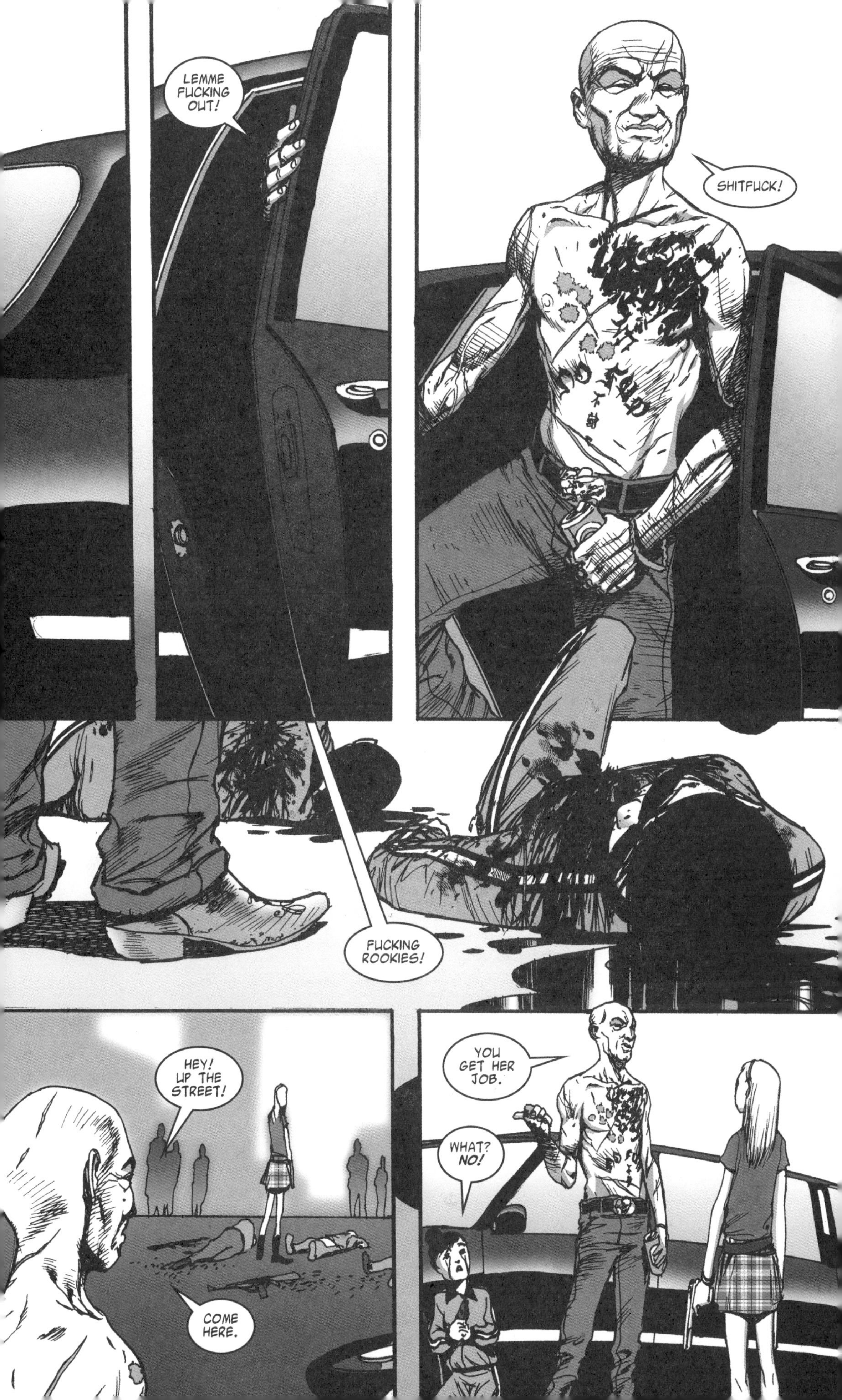
LEMME FUCKING OUT!
SHITFUCK!
FUCKING ROOKIES!
HEY! UP THE STREET!
COME HERE.
YOU GET HER JOB.
WHAT? NO!

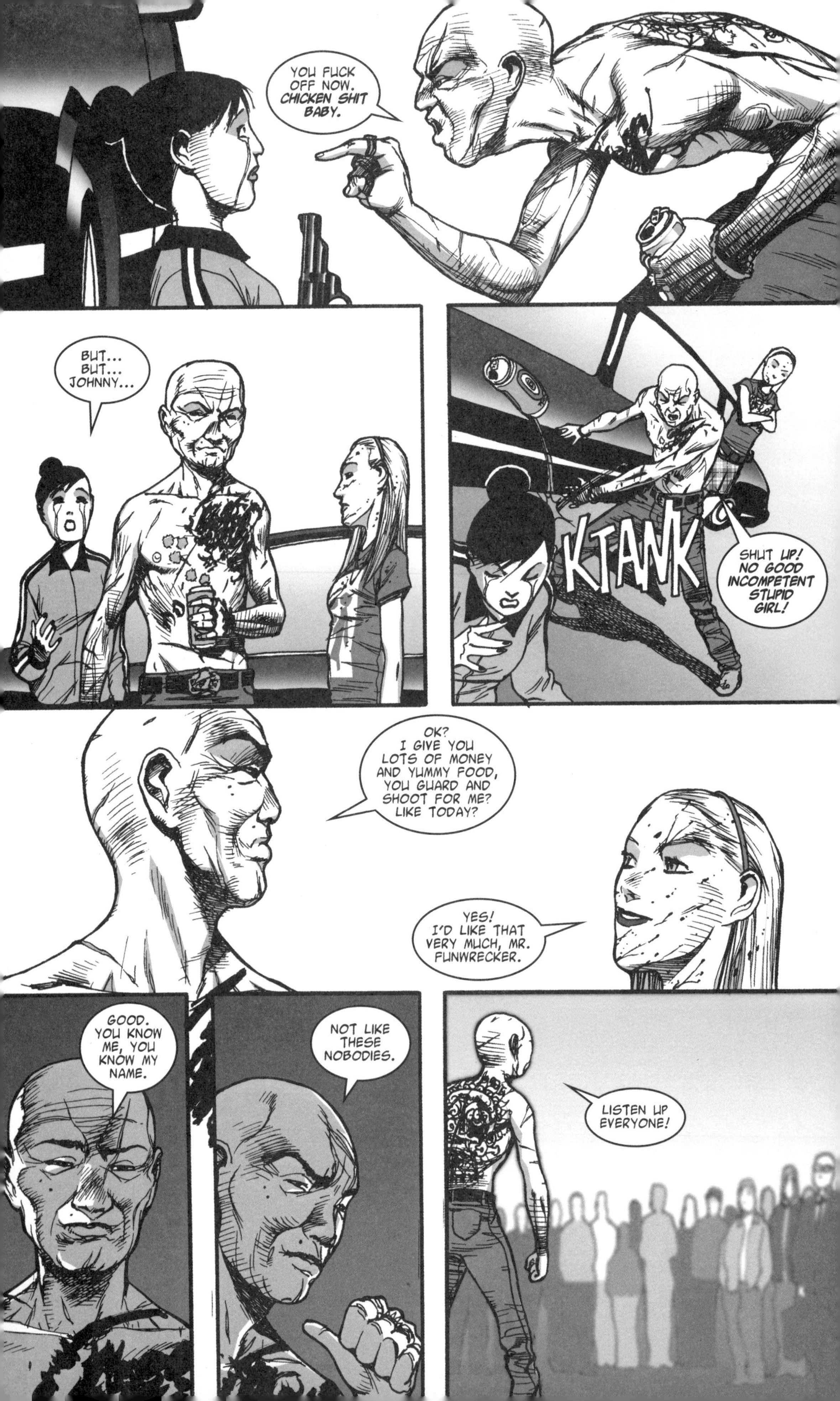

YOU FUCK OFF NOW. CHICKEN SHIT BABY.
BUT... BUT... JOHNNY...
KTANK
SHUT UP! NO GOOD INCOMPETENT STUPID GIRL!
OK? I GIVE YOU LOTS OF MONEY AND YUMMY FOOD, YOU GUARD AND SHOOT FOR ME? LIKE TODAY?
YES! I'D LIKE THAT VERY MUCH, MR. FUNWRECKER.
GOOD. YOU KNOW ME, YOU KNOW MY NAME.
NOT LIKE THESE NOBODIES.
LISTEN UP EVERYONE!

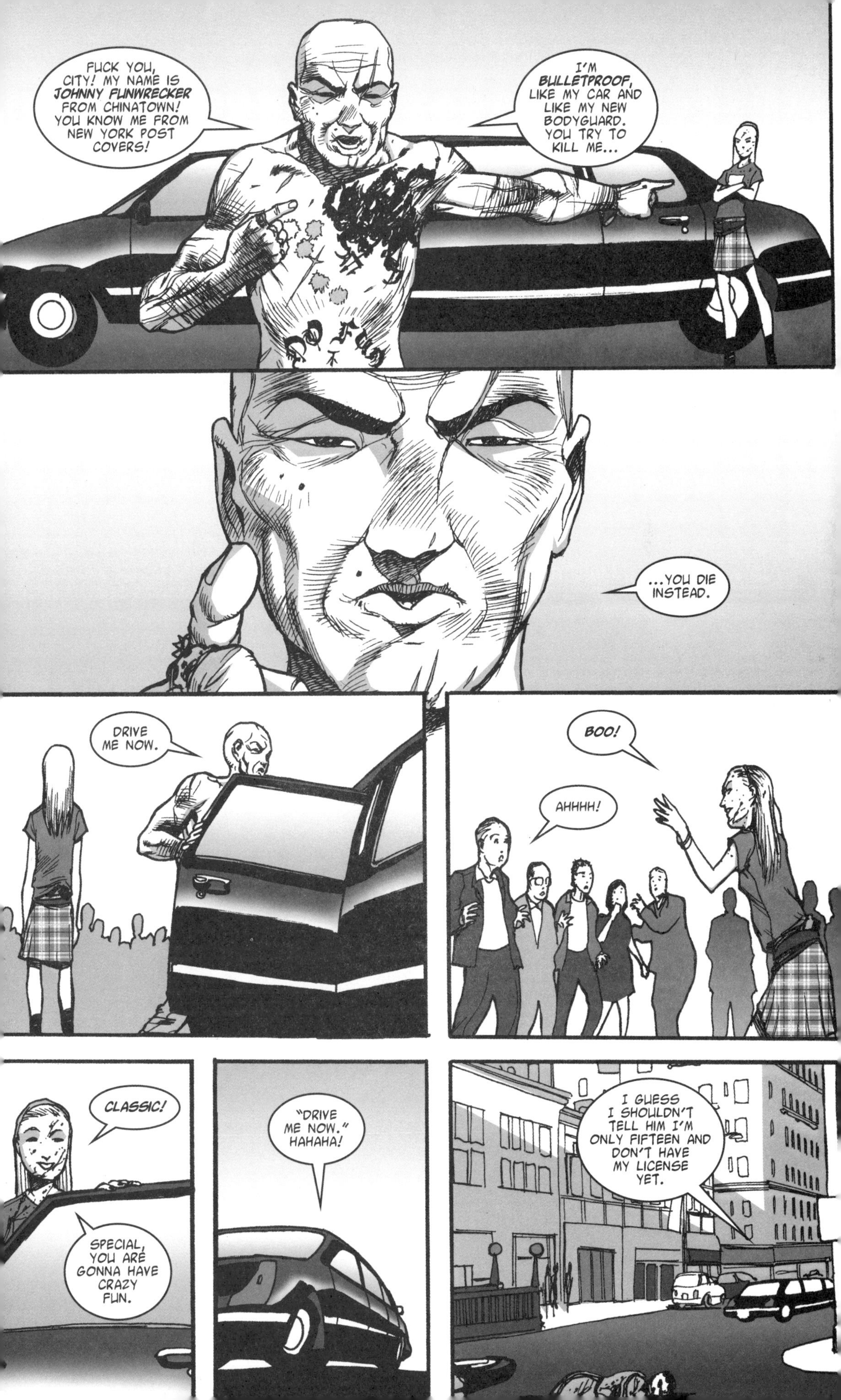
FUCK YOU, CITY! MY NAME IS JOHNNY FUNWRECKER FROM CHINATOWN! YOU KNOW ME FROM NEW YORK POST COVERS!
I'M BULLETPROOF, LIKE MY CAR AND LIKE MY NEW BODYGUARD. YOU TRY TO KILL ME...
...YOU DIE INSTEAD.
DRIVE ME NOW.
BOO!
AHHHH!
CLASSIC!
SPECIAL, YOU ARE GONNA HAVE CRAZY FUN.
"DRIVE ME NOW." HAHAHA!
I GUESS I SHOULDN'T TELL HIM I'M ONLY FIFTEEN AND DON'T HAVE MY LICENSE YET.

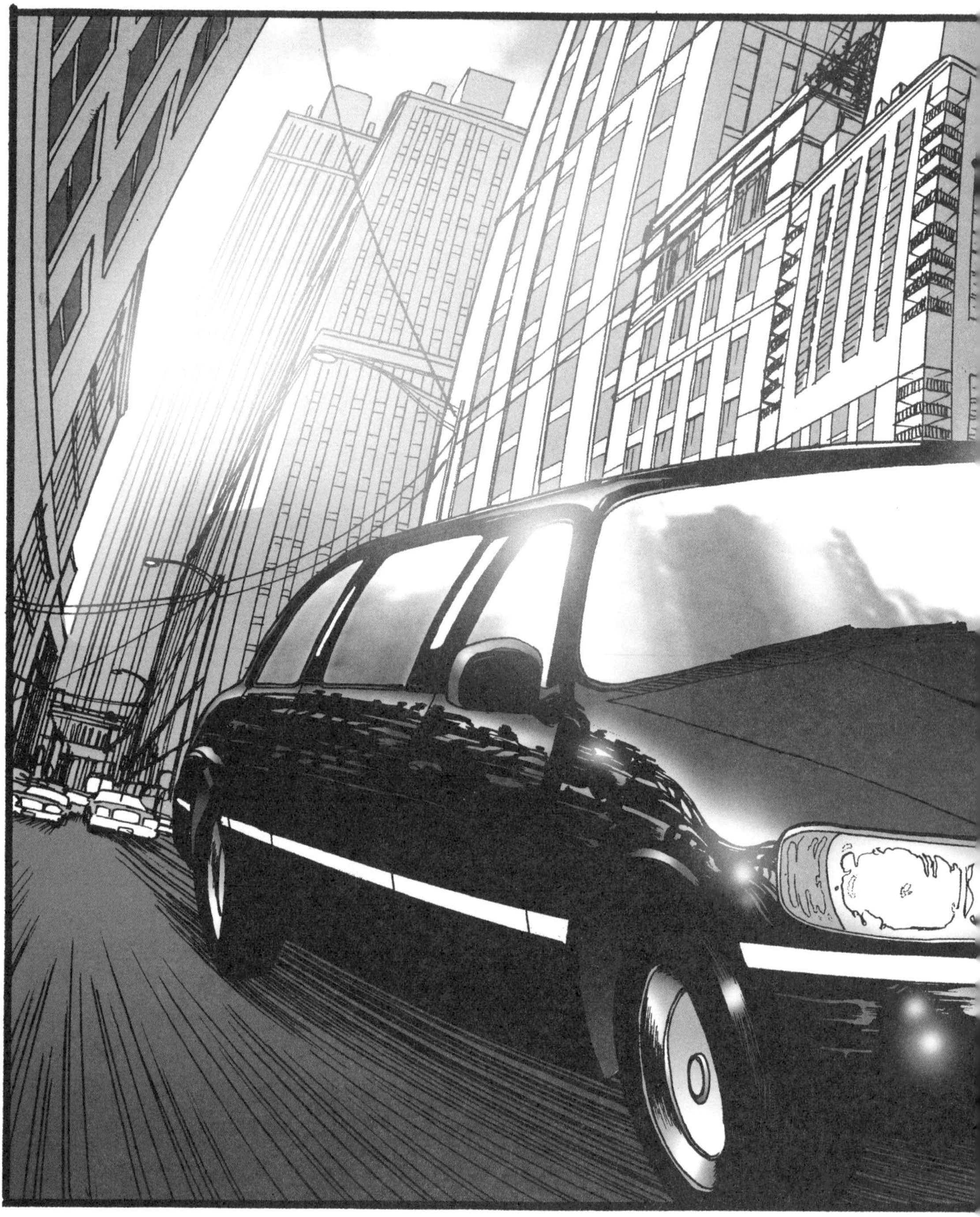

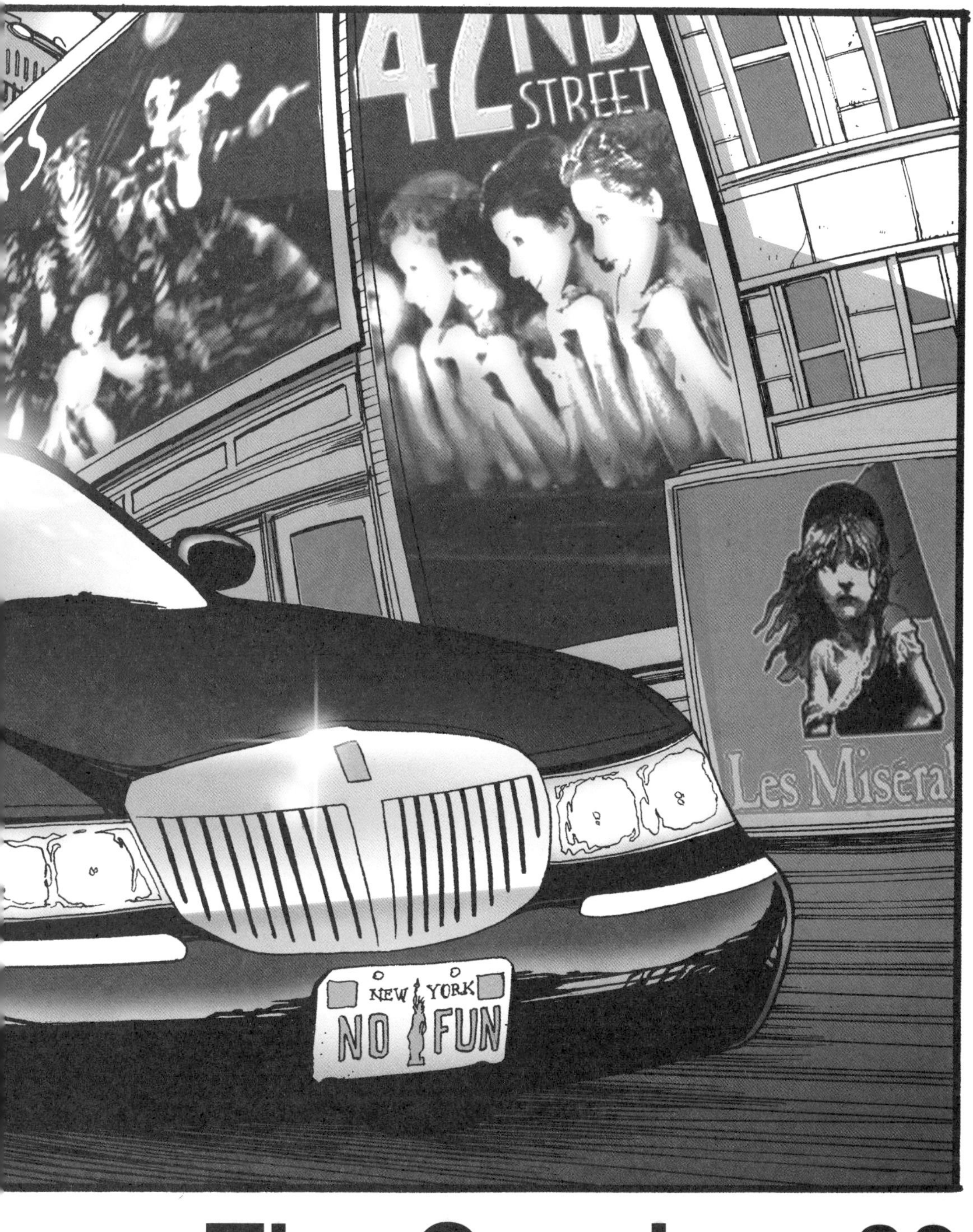
42ND
STREET
NEW YORK
NO FUN
Les Misérab

The Couriers 03

THE BALLAD OF JOHNNY FUNWRECKER

written by BRIAN WOOD
art by ROB G
letters RYAN YOUNT

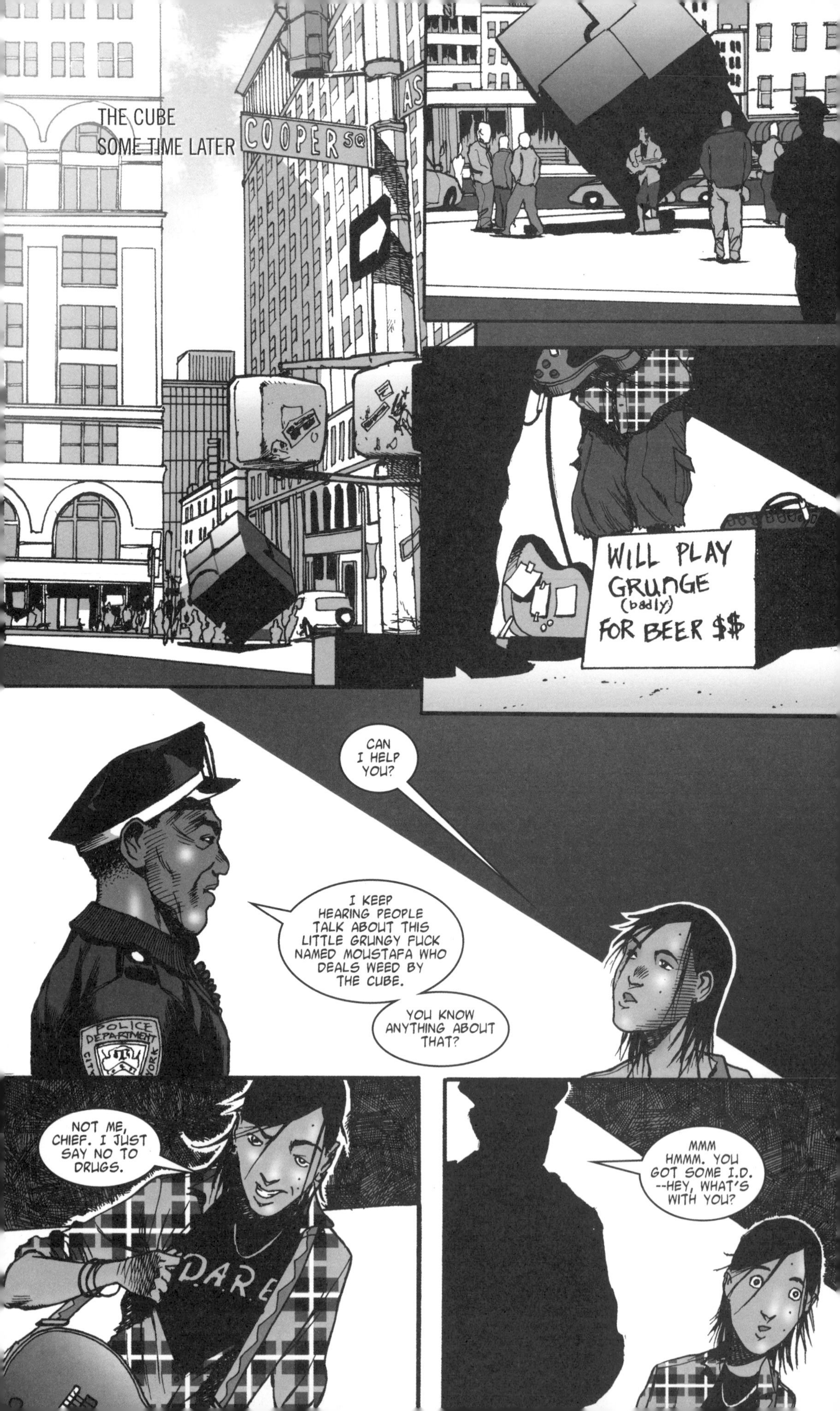

THE CUBE
SOME TIME LATER
COOPER SQ
AS
WILL PLAY GRUNGE (badly) FOR BEER $$
CAN I HELP YOU?
I KEEP HEARING PEOPLE TALK ABOUT THIS LITTLE GRUNGY FUCK NAMED MOUSTAFA WHO DEALS WEED BY THE CUBE.
YOU KNOW ANYTHING ABOUT THAT?
POLICE DEPARTMENT
NOT ME, CHIEF. I JUST SAY NO TO DRUGS.
D.A.R.E
MMM HMMM. YOU GOT SOME I.D. --HEY, WHAT'S WITH YOU?

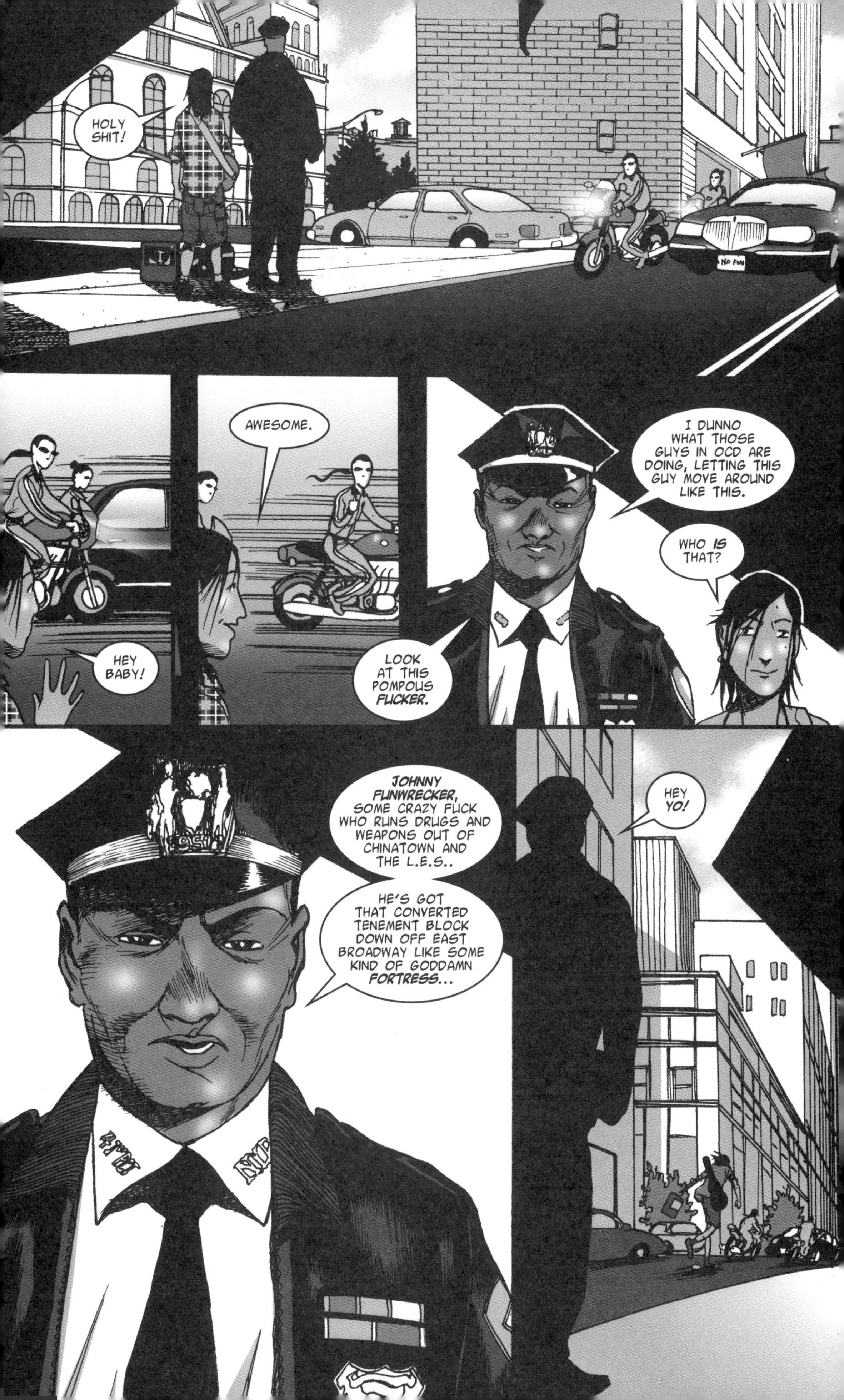
HOLY SHIT!
HEY BABY!
AWESOME.
I DUNNO WHAT THOSE GUYS IN OCD ARE DOING, LETTING THIS GUY MOVE AROUND LIKE THIS.
WHO IS THAT?
LOOK AT THIS POMPOUS FUCKER.
JOHNNY FUNWRECKER, SOME CRAZY FUCK WHO RUNS DRUGS AND WEAPONS OUT OF CHINATOWN AND THE L.E.S..
HE'S GOT THAT CONVERTED TENEMENT BLOCK DOWN OFF EAST BROADWAY LIKE SOME KIND OF GODDAMN FORTRESS...
HEY YO!

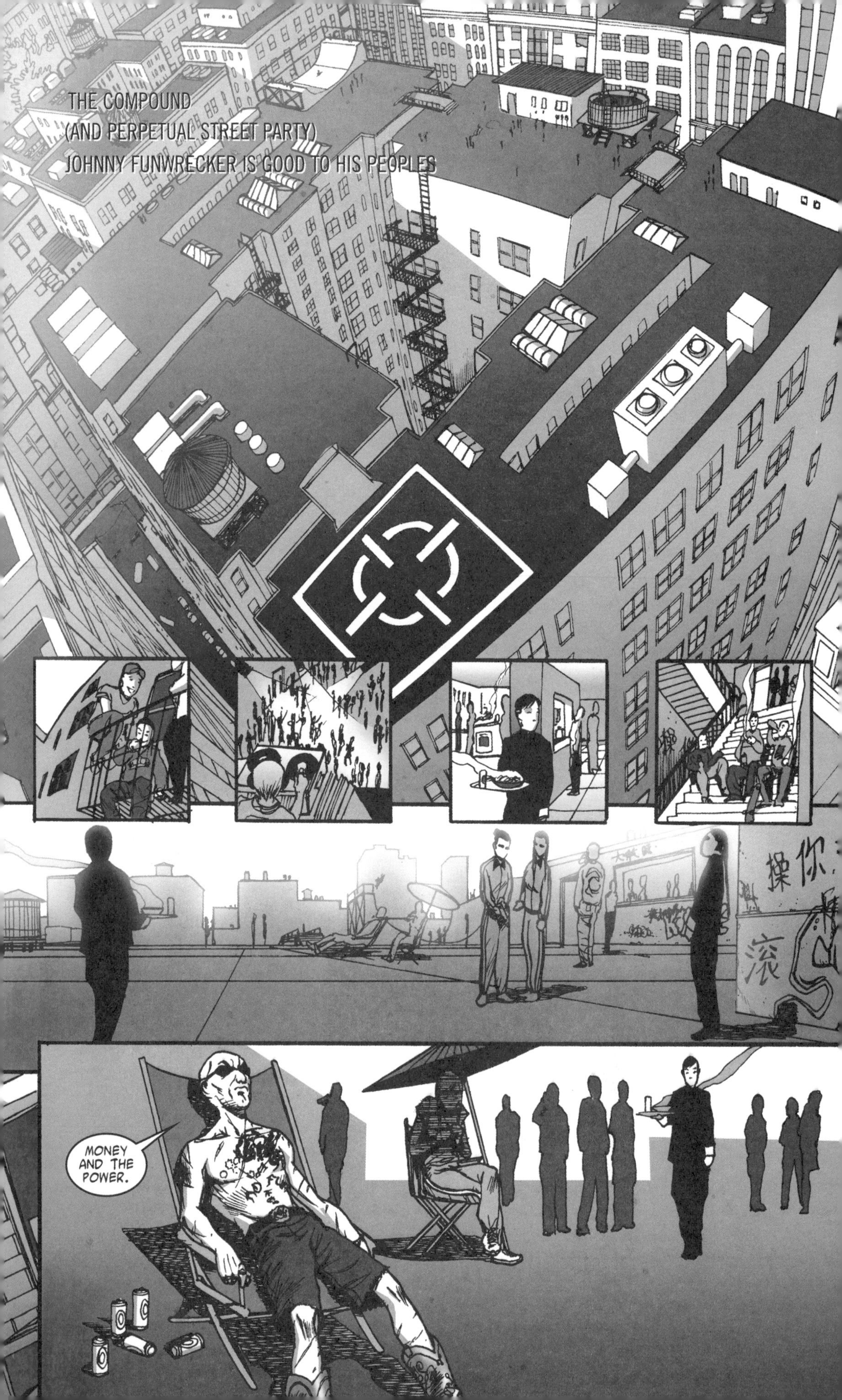
THE COMPOUND
(AND PERPETUAL STREET PARTY)
JOHNNY FUNWRECKER IS GOOD TO HIS PEOPLES
操你
滚
MONEY AND THE POWER.

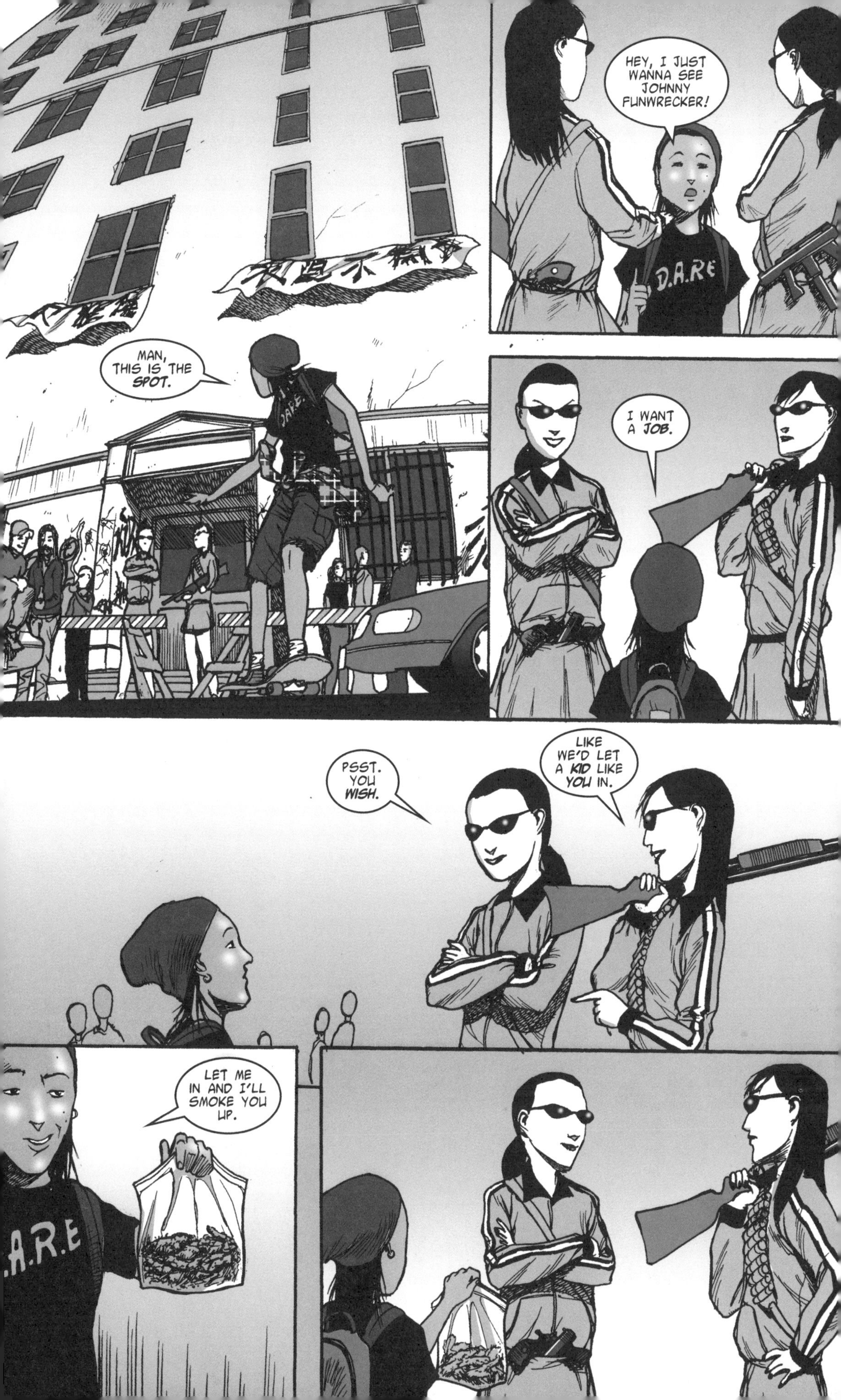
MAN, THIS IS THE SPOT.
HEY, I JUST WANNA SEE JOHNNY FUNWRECKER!
D.A.R.E
I WANT A JOB.
PSST. YOU WISH.
LIKE WE'D LET A KID LIKE YOU IN.
LET ME IN AND I'LL SMOKE YOU UP.

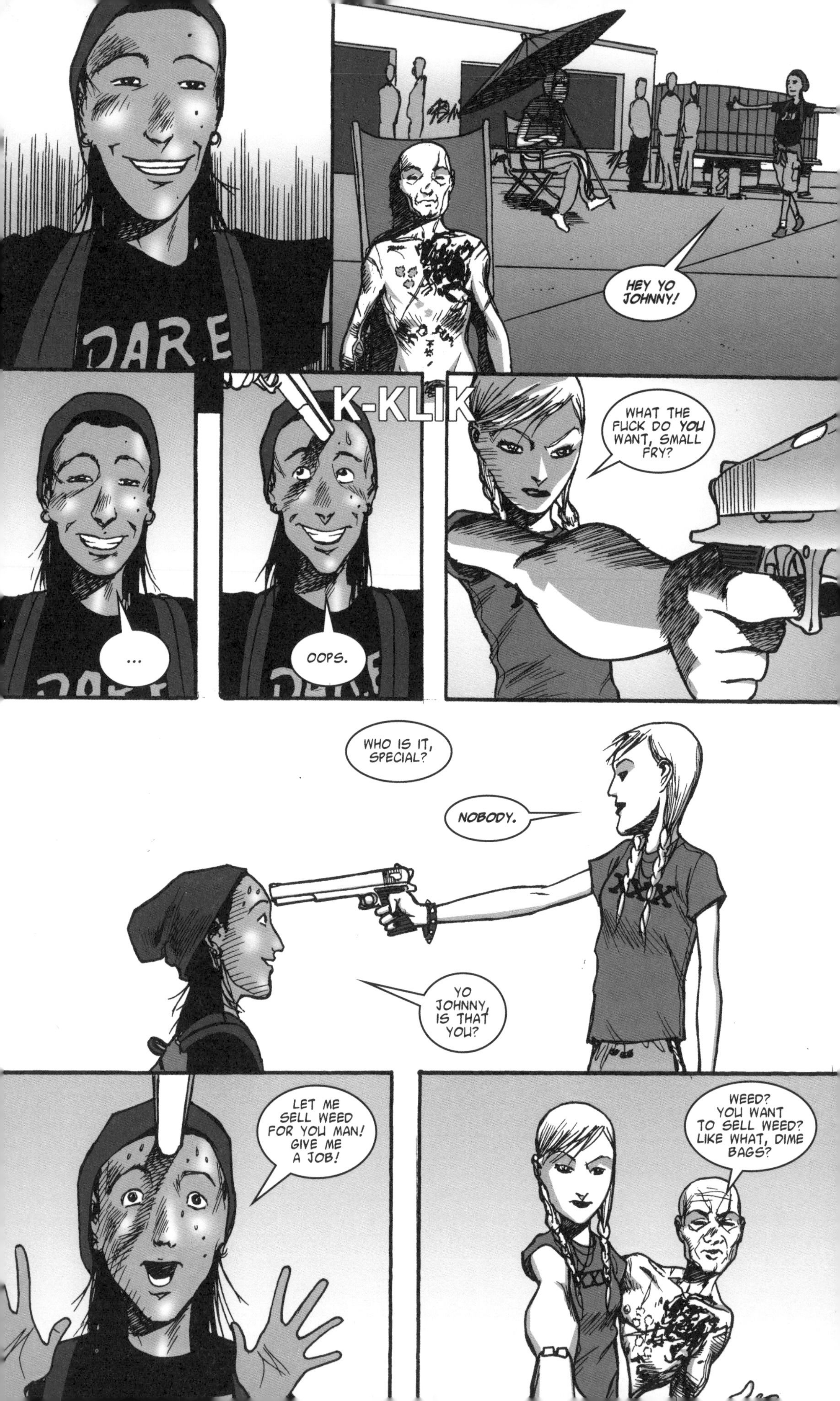

DARE
HEY YO JOHNNY!
...
K-KLIK
OOPS.
WHAT THE FUCK DO YOU WANT, SMALL FRY?
WHO IS IT, SPECIAL?
NOBODY.
YO JOHNNY, IS THAT YOU?
LET ME SELL WEED FOR YOU MAN! GIVE ME A JOB!
WEED? YOU WANT TO SELL WEED? LIKE WHAT, DIME BAGS?

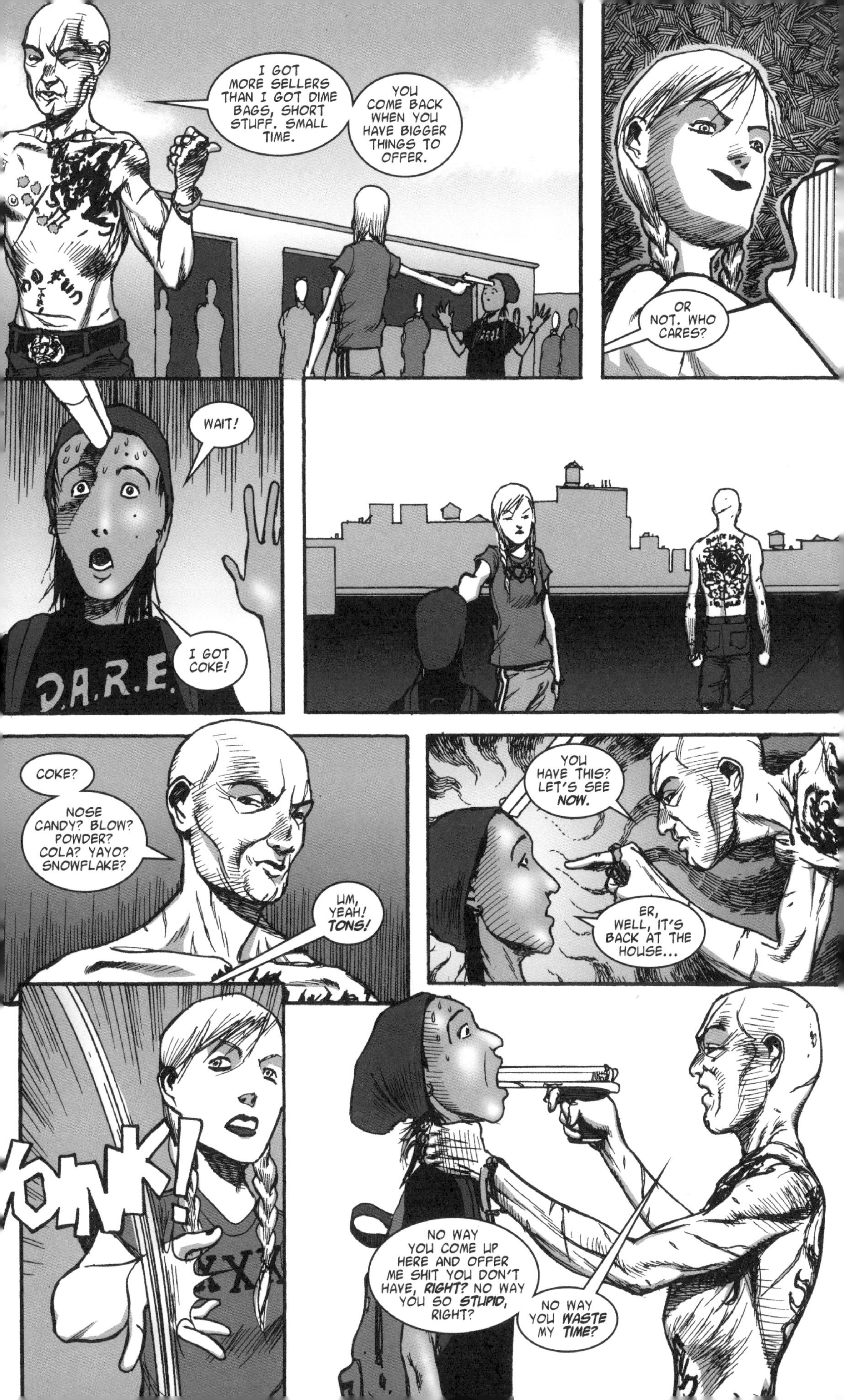
I GOT MORE SELLERS THAN I GOT DIME BAGS, SHORT STUFF. SMALL TIME.
YOU COME BACK WHEN YOU HAVE BIGGER THINGS TO OFFER.
OR NOT. WHO CARES?
WAIT!
I GOT COKE!
D.A.R.E.
COKE?
NOSE CANDY? BLOW? POWDER? COLA? YAYO? SNOWFLAKE?
UM, YEAH! TONS!
YOU HAVE THIS? LET'S SEE NOW.
ER, WELL, IT'S BACK AT THE HOUSE...
NO WAY YOU COME UP HERE AND OFFER ME SHIT YOU DON'T HAVE, RIGHT? NO WAY YOU SO STUPID, RIGHT?
NO WAY YOU WASTE MY TIME?

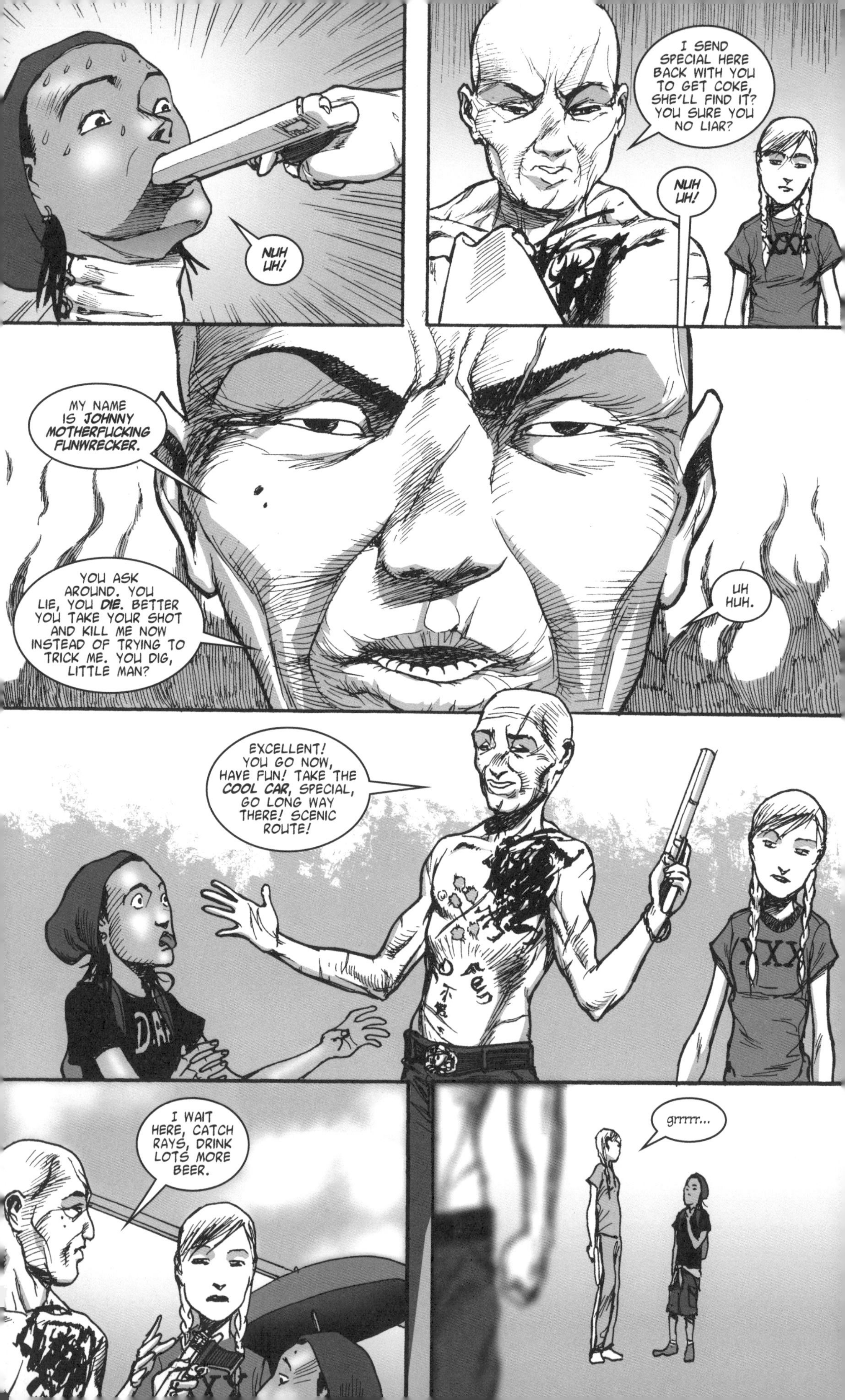
NUH UH!
I SEND SPECIAL HERE BACK WITH YOU TO GET COKE, SHE'LL FIND IT? YOU SURE YOU NO LIAR?
NUH UH!
MY NAME IS JOHNNY MOTHERFUCKING FUNWRECKER.
YOU ASK AROUND. YOU LIE, YOU DIE. BETTER YOU TAKE YOUR SHOT AND KILL ME NOW INSTEAD OF TRYING TO TRICK ME. YOU DIG, LITTLE MAN?
UH HUH.
EXCELLENT! YOU GO NOW, HAVE FUN! TAKE THE COOL CAR, SPECIAL, GO LONG WAY THERE! SCENIC ROUTE!
I WAIT HERE, CATCH RAYS, DRINK LOTS MORE BEER.
grrrrr...

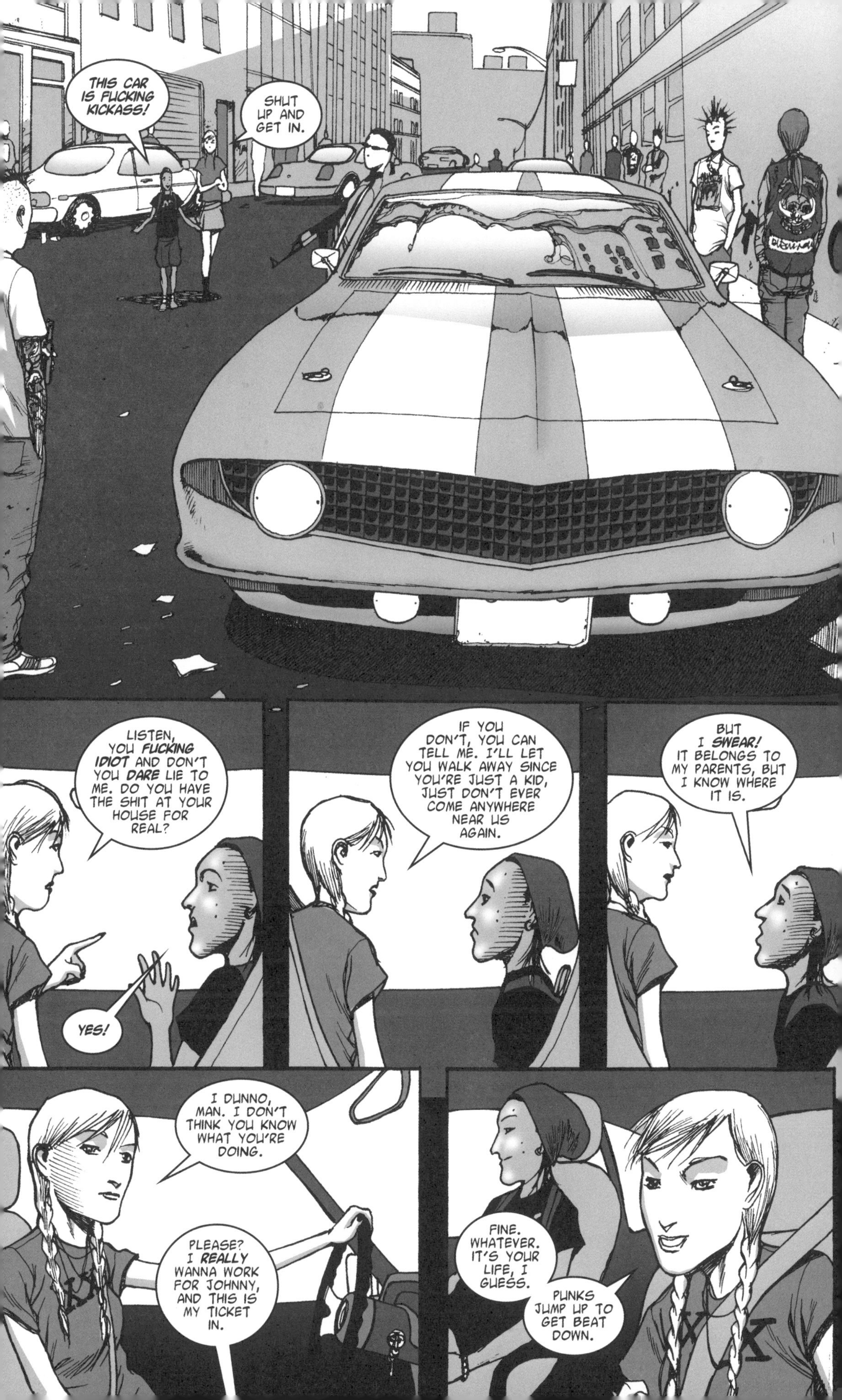

THIS CAR IS FUCKING KICKASS!
SHUT UP AND GET IN.
LISTEN, YOU FUCKING IDIOT AND DON'T YOU DARE LIE TO ME. DO YOU HAVE THE SHIT AT YOUR HOUSE FOR REAL?
YES!
IF YOU DON'T, YOU CAN TELL ME. I'LL LET YOU WALK AWAY SINCE YOU'RE JUST A KID, JUST DON'T EVER COME ANYWHERE NEAR US AGAIN.
BUT I SWEAR! IT BELONGS TO MY PARENTS, BUT I KNOW WHERE IT IS.
I DUNNO, MAN. I DON'T THINK YOU KNOW WHAT YOU'RE DOING.
PLEASE? I REALLY WANNA WORK FOR JOHNNY, AND THIS IS MY TICKET IN.
FINE. WHATEVER. IT'S YOUR LIFE, I GUESS.
PUNKS JUMP UP TO GET BEAT DOWN.

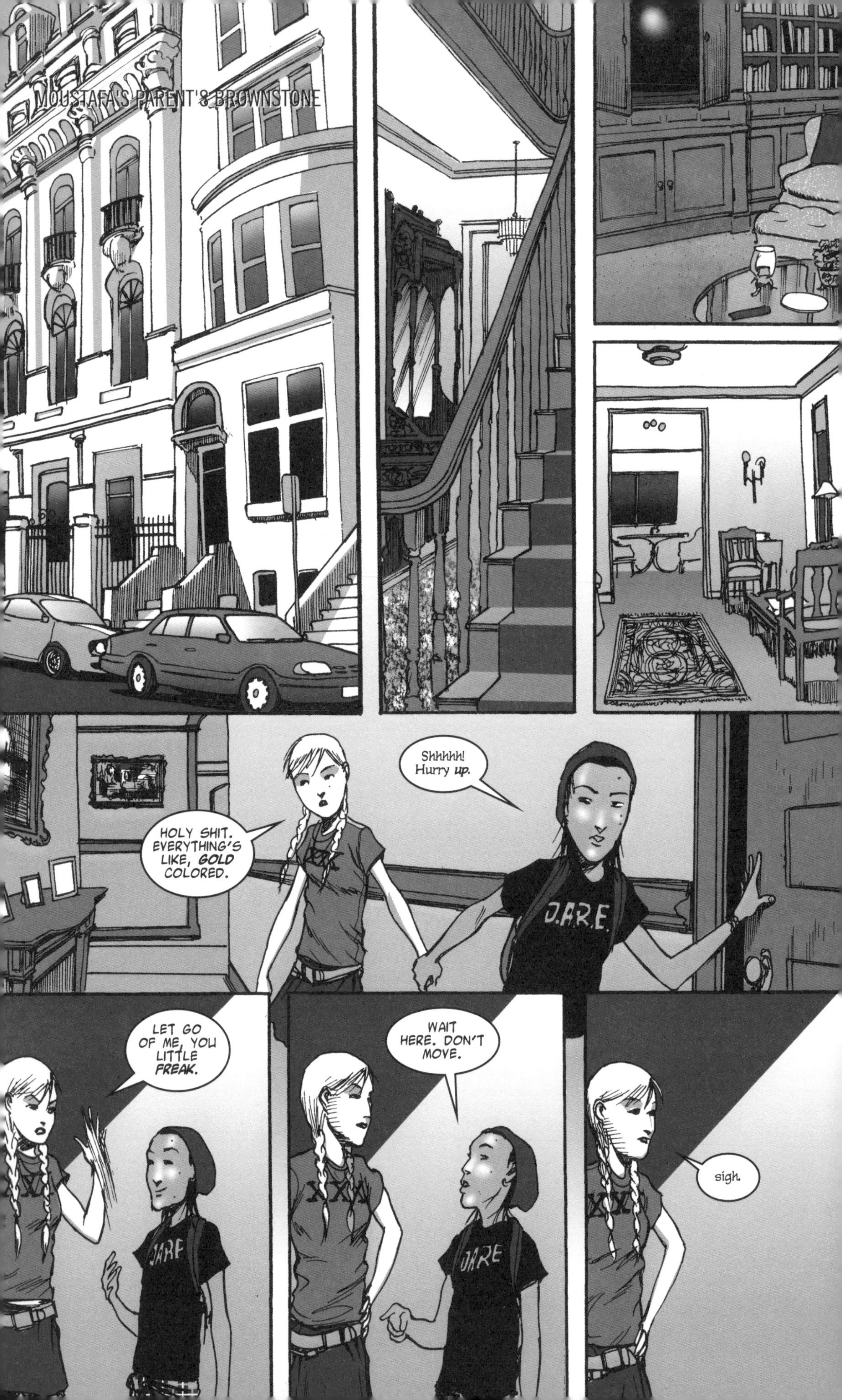
MOUSTAFA'S PARENT'S BROWNSTONE
Shhhhh! Hurry up.
HOLY SHIT. EVERYTHING'S LIKE, GOLD COLORED.
D.A.R.E.
LET GO OF ME, YOU LITTLE FREAK.
WAIT HERE. DON'T MOVE.
sigh.

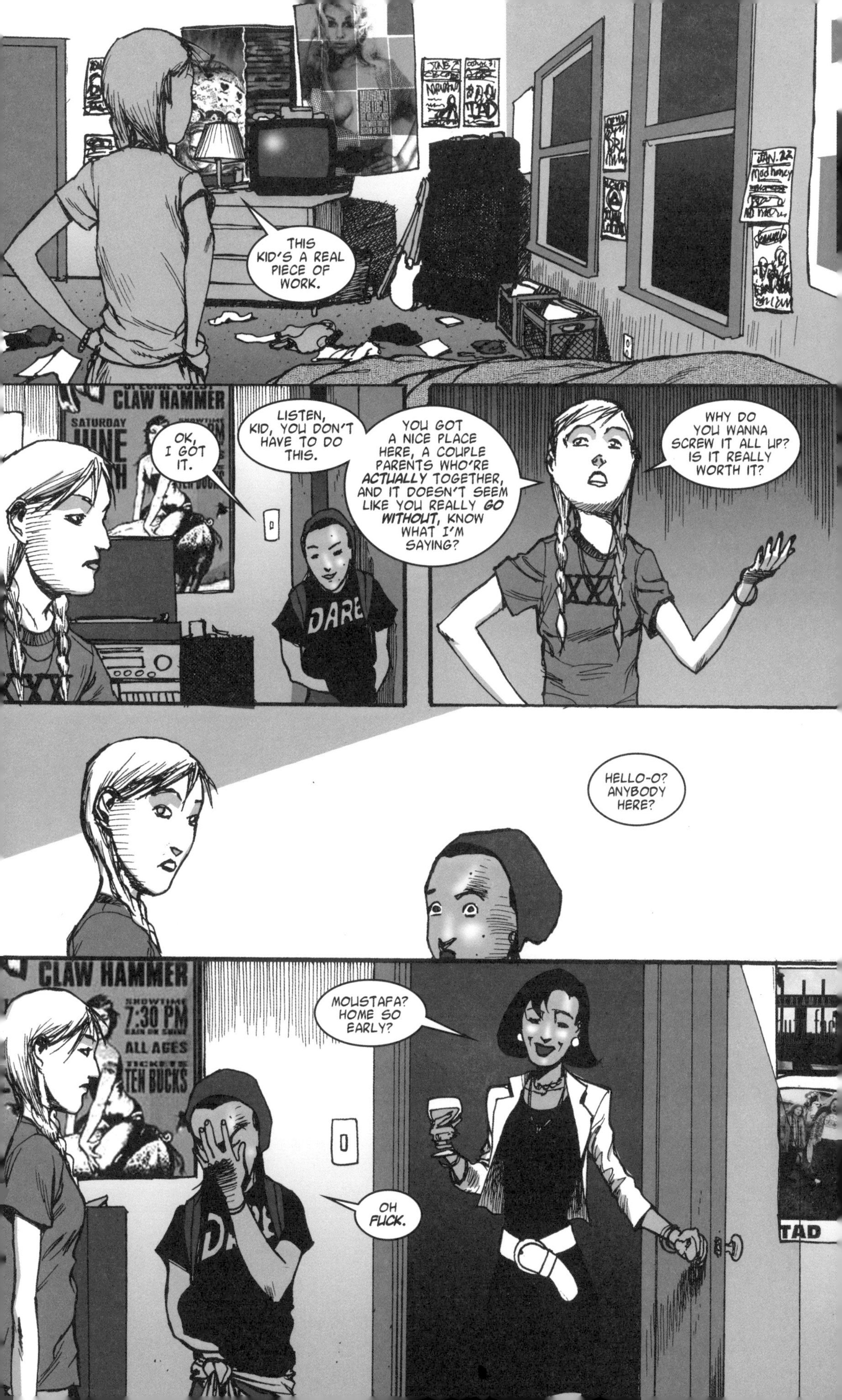

THIS KID'S A REAL PIECE OF WORK.
CLAW HAMMER
OK, I GOT IT.
LISTEN, KID, YOU DON'T HAVE TO DO THIS.
YOU GOT A NICE PLACE HERE, A COUPLE PARENTS WHO'RE ACTUALLY TOGETHER, AND IT DOESN'T SEEM LIKE YOU REALLY GO WITHOUT, KNOW WHAT I'M SAYING?
WHY DO YOU WANNA SCREW IT ALL UP? IS IT REALLY WORTH IT?
HELLO-O? ANYBODY HERE?
CLAW HAMMER
SHOWTIME 7:30 PM
ALL AGES
TEN BUCKS
MOUSTAFA? HOME SO EARLY?
OH FUCK.
TAD

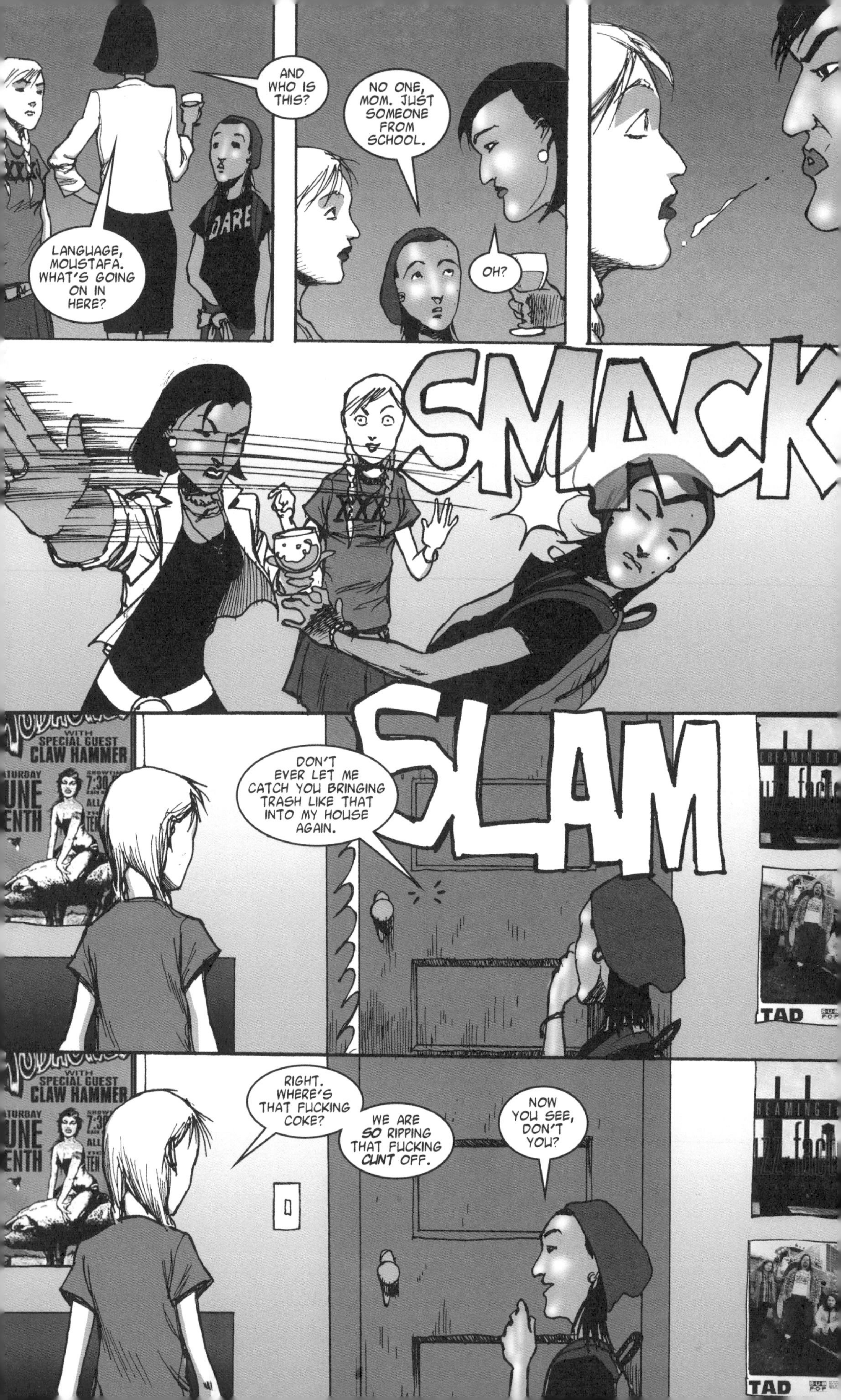
LANGUAGE, MOUSTAFA. WHAT'S GOING ON IN HERE?
AND WHO IS THIS?
NO ONE, MOM. JUST SOMEONE FROM SCHOOL.
OH?
SMACK
SLAM
DON'T EVER LET ME CATCH YOU BRINGING TRASH LIKE THAT INTO MY HOUSE AGAIN.
RIGHT. WHERE'S THAT FUCKING COKE?
WE ARE SO RIPPING THAT FUCKING CUNT OFF.
NOW YOU SEE, DON'T YOU?
WITH SPECIAL GUEST CLAW HAMMER
TAD
SUB POP

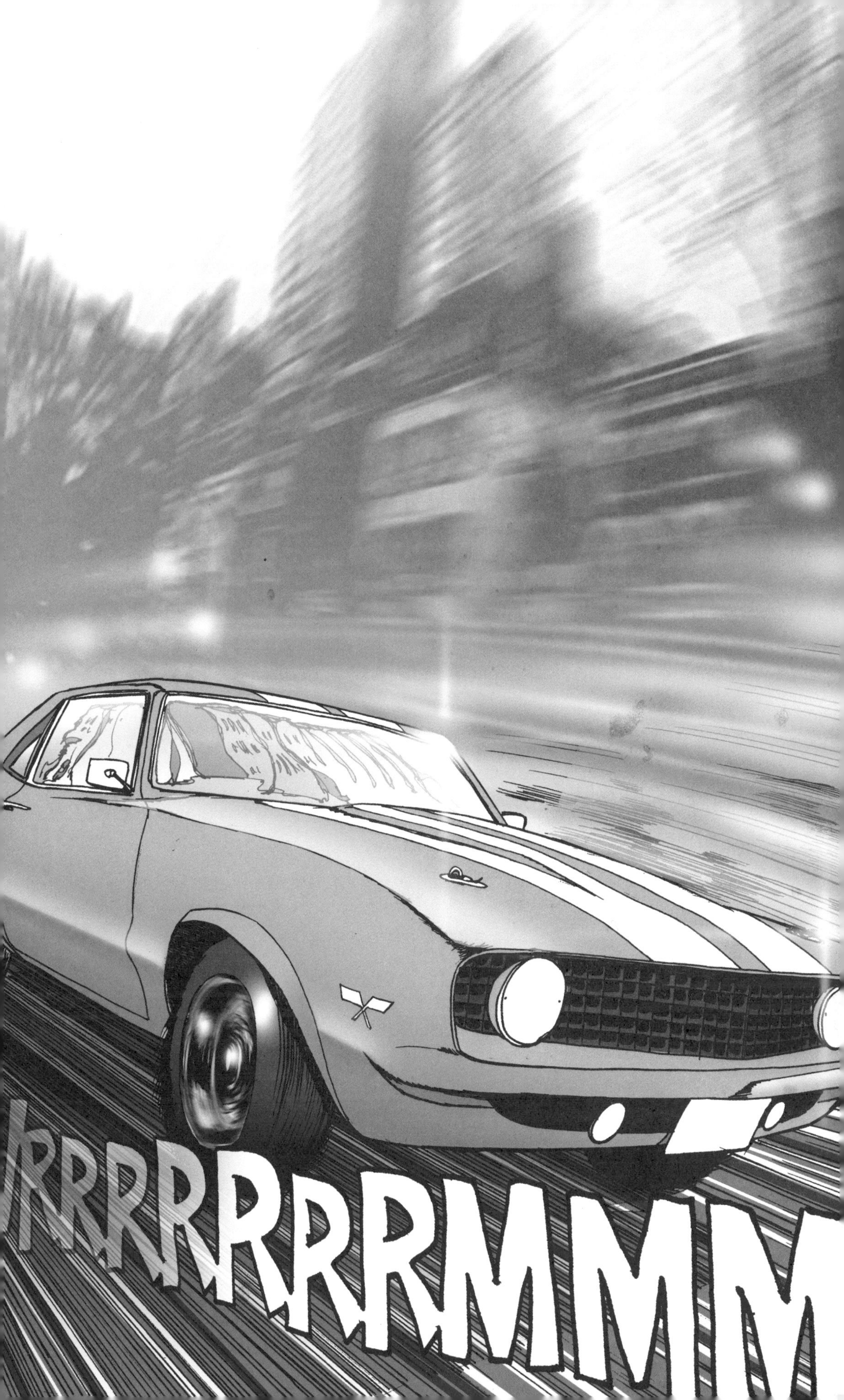
RRRRRRMMM

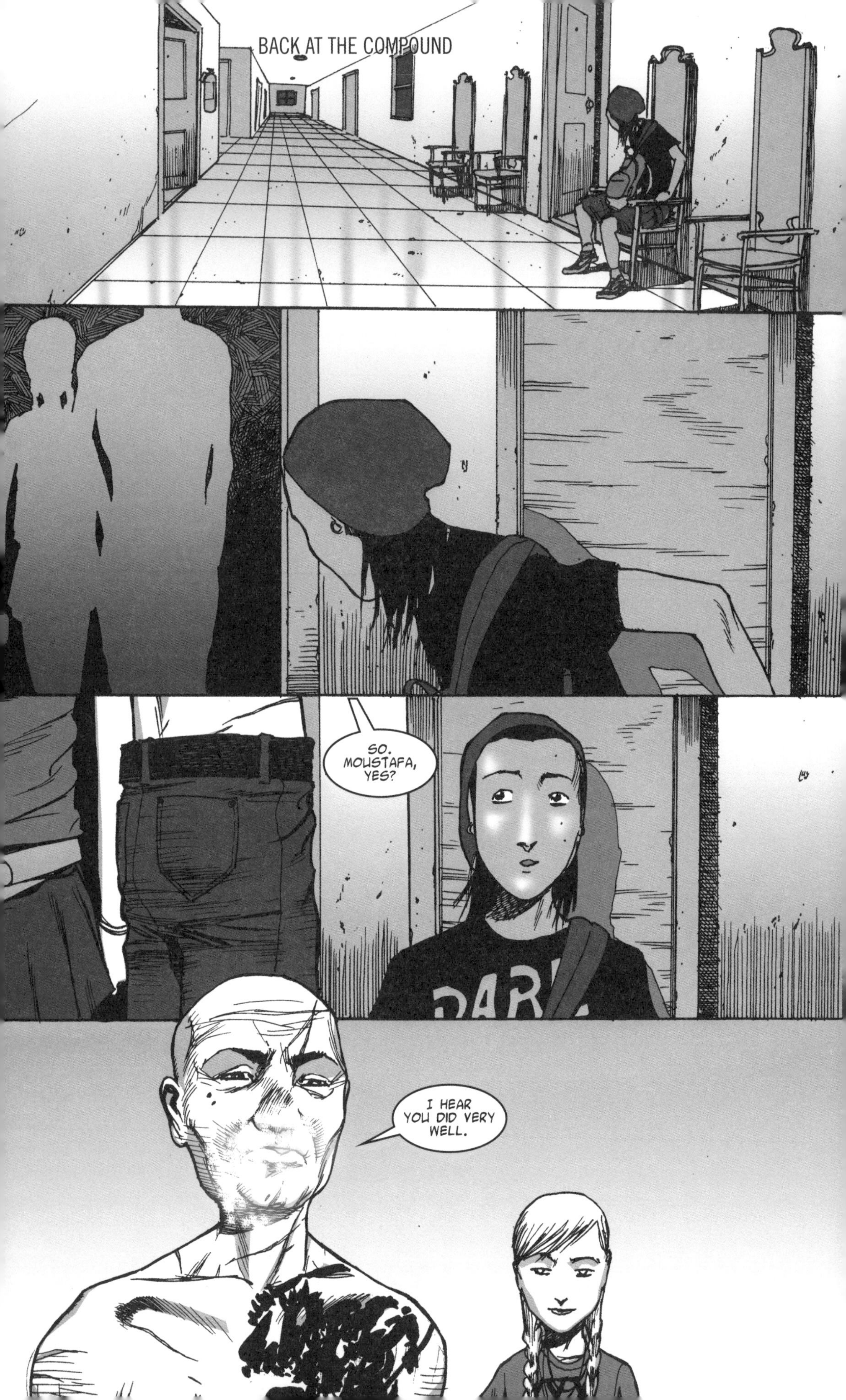
BACK AT THE COMPOUND
SO. MOUSTAFA, YES?
I HEAR YOU DID VERY WELL.

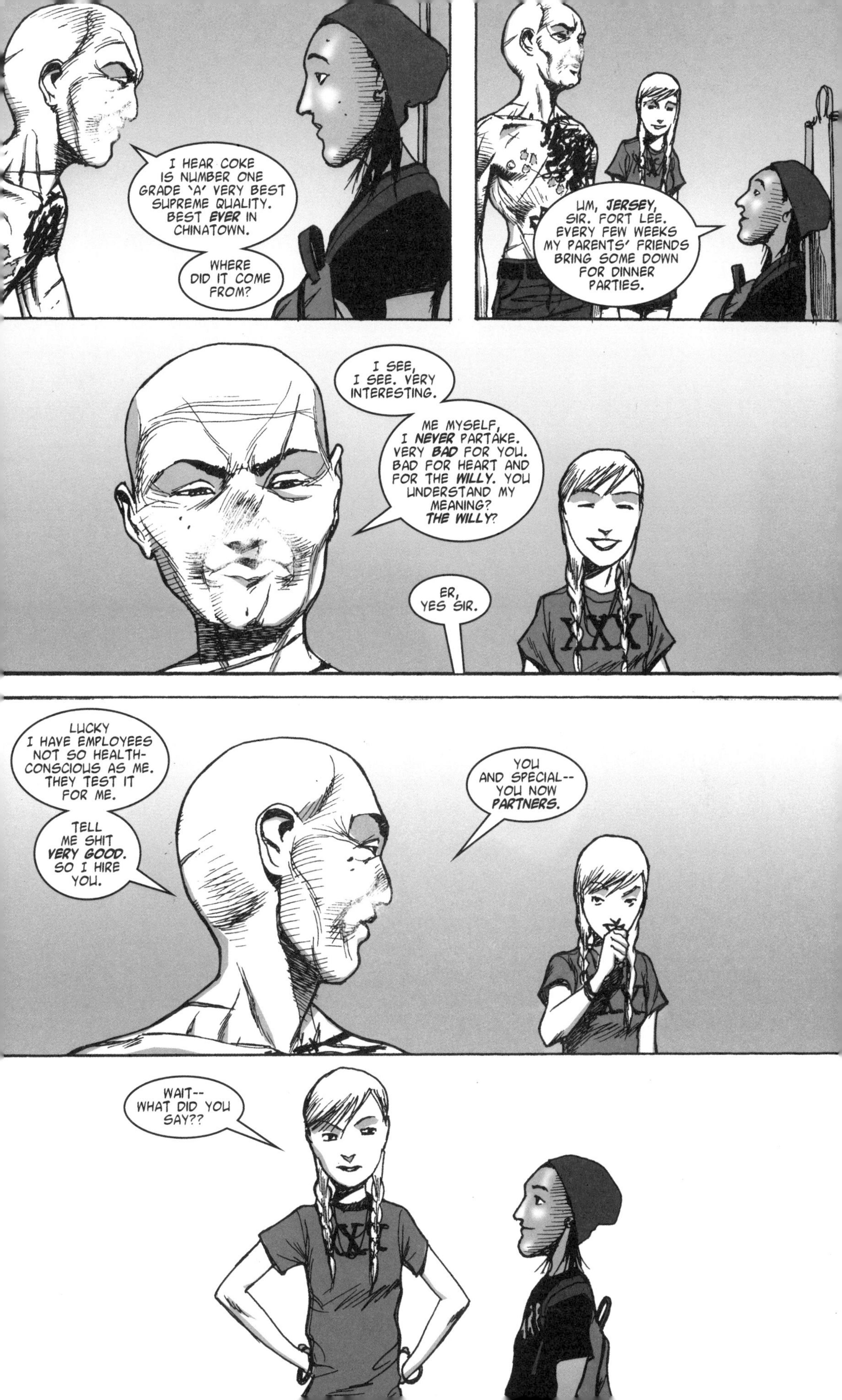
I HEAR COKE IS NUMBER ONE GRADE 'A' VERY BEST SUPREME QUALITY. BEST EVER IN CHINATOWN.
WHERE DID IT COME FROM?
UM, JERSEY, SIR. FORT LEE. EVERY FEW WEEKS MY PARENTS' FRIENDS BRING SOME DOWN FOR DINNER PARTIES.
I SEE, I SEE. VERY INTERESTING.
ME MYSELF, I NEVER PARTAKE. VERY BAD FOR YOU. BAD FOR HEART AND FOR THE WILLY. YOU UNDERSTAND MY MEANING? THE WILLY?
ER, YES SIR.
LUCKY I HAVE EMPLOYEES NOT SO HEALTH-CONSCIOUS AS ME. THEY TEST IT FOR ME.
TELL ME SHIT VERY GOOD. SO I HIRE YOU.
YOU AND SPECIAL-- YOU NOW PARTNERS.
WAIT-- WHAT DID YOU SAY??

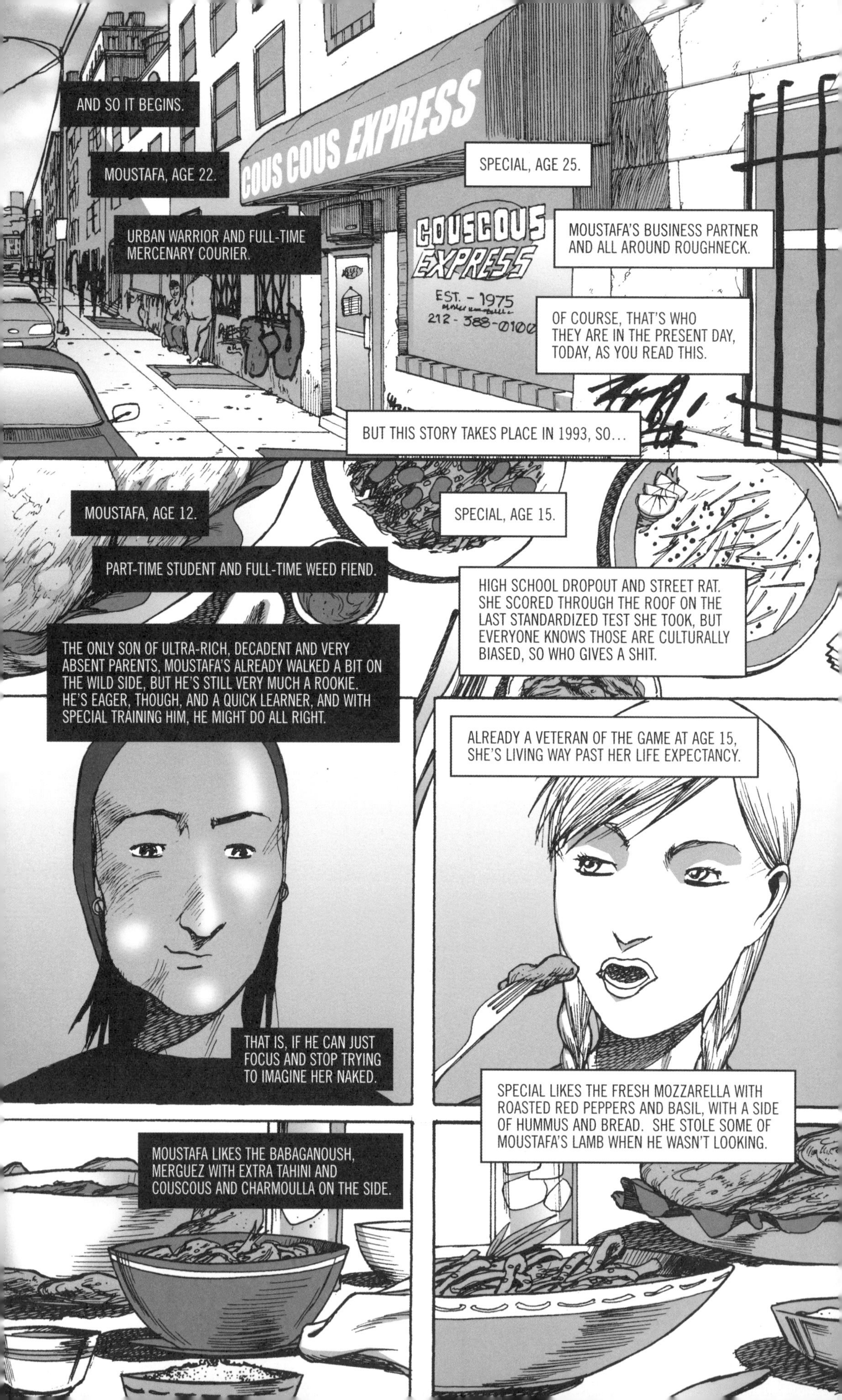
AND SO IT BEGINS.
MOUSTAFA, AGE 22.
URBAN WARRIOR AND FULL-TIME MERCENARY COURIER.
COUS COUS EXPRESS
SPECIAL, AGE 25.
COUSCOUS EXPRESS
EST. - 1975
212-388-0100
MOUSTAFA'S BUSINESS PARTNER AND ALL AROUND ROUGHNECK.
OF COURSE, THAT'S WHO THEY ARE IN THE PRESENT DAY, TODAY, AS YOU READ THIS.
BUT THIS STORY TAKES PLACE IN 1993, SO...
MOUSTAFA, AGE 12.
SPECIAL, AGE 15.
PART-TIME STUDENT AND FULL-TIME WEED FIEND.
HIGH SCHOOL DROPOUT AND STREET RAT. SHE SCORED THROUGH THE ROOF ON THE LAST STANDARDIZED TEST SHE TOOK, BUT EVERYONE KNOWS THOSE ARE CULTURALLY BIASED, SO WHO GIVES A SHIT.
THE ONLY SON OF ULTRA-RICH, DECADENT AND VERY ABSENT PARENTS, MOUSTAFA'S ALREADY WALKED A BIT ON THE WILD SIDE, BUT HE'S STILL VERY MUCH A ROOKIE. HE'S EAGER, THOUGH, AND A QUICK LEARNER, AND WITH SPECIAL TRAINING HIM, HE MIGHT DO ALL RIGHT.
ALREADY A VETERAN OF THE GAME AT AGE 15, SHE'S LIVING WAY PAST HER LIFE EXPECTANCY.
THAT IS, IF HE CAN JUST FOCUS AND STOP TRYING TO IMAGINE HER NAKED.
SPECIAL LIKES THE FRESH MOZZARELLA WITH ROASTED RED PEPPERS AND BASIL, WITH A SIDE OF HUMMUS AND BREAD. SHE STOLE SOME OF MOUSTAFA'S LAMB WHEN HE WASN'T LOOKING.
MOUSTAFA LIKES THE BABAGANOUSH, MERGUEZ WITH EXTRA TAHINI AND COUSCOUS AND CHARMOULLA ON THE SIDE.

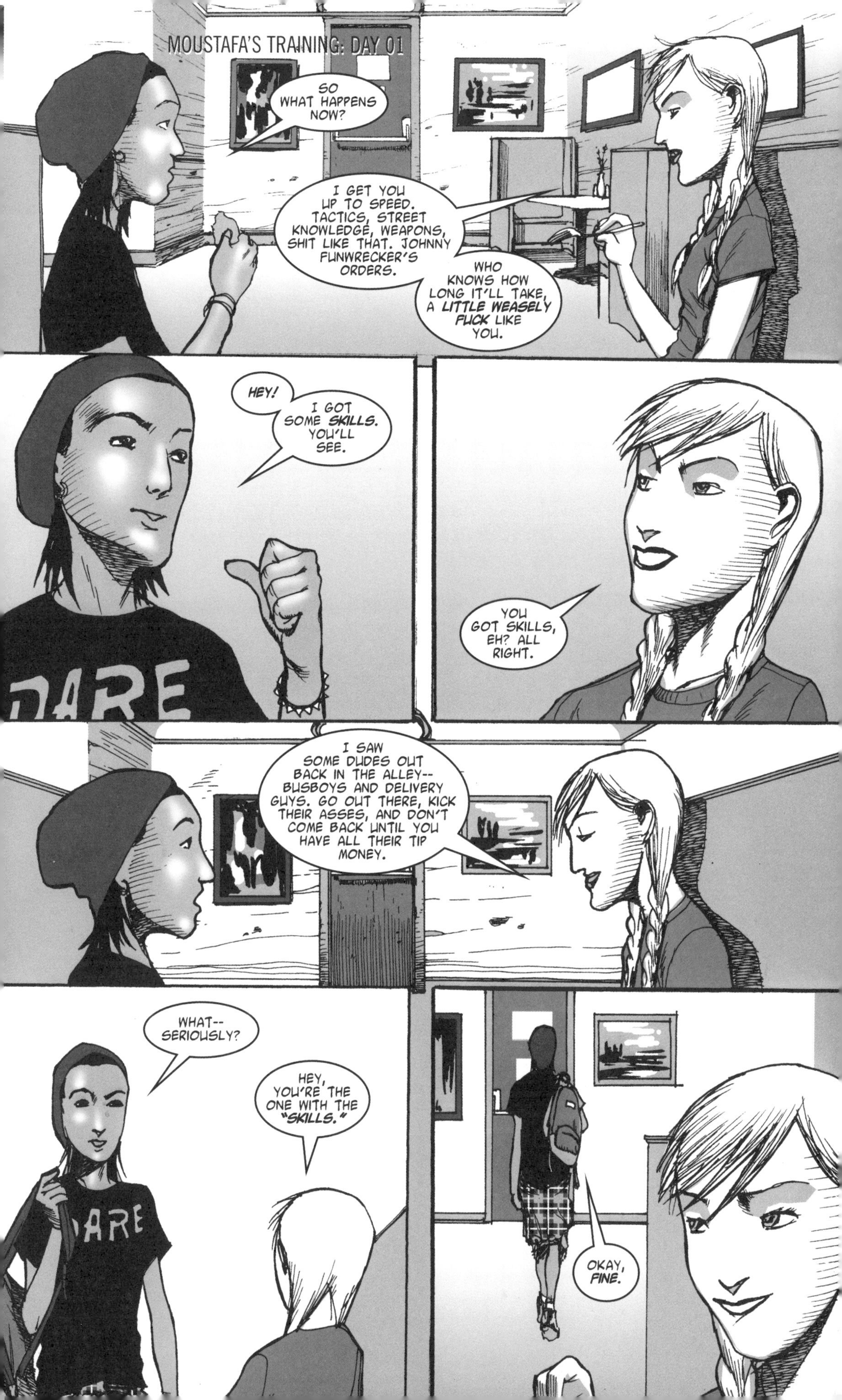
MOUSTAFA'S TRAINING: DAY 01
SO WHAT HAPPENS NOW?
I GET YOU UP TO SPEED. TACTICS, STREET KNOWLEDGE, WEAPONS, SHIT LIKE THAT. JOHNNY FUNWRECKER'S ORDERS.
WHO KNOWS HOW LONG IT'LL TAKE, A LITTLE WEASELY FUCK LIKE YOU.
HEY!
I GOT SOME SKILLS. YOU'LL SEE.
DARE
YOU GOT SKILLS, EH? ALL RIGHT.
I SAW SOME DUDES OUT BACK IN THE ALLEY-- BUSBOYS AND DELIVERY GUYS. GO OUT THERE, KICK THEIR ASSES, AND DON'T COME BACK UNTIL YOU HAVE ALL THEIR TIP MONEY.
WHAT-- SERIOUSLY?
HEY, YOU'RE THE ONE WITH THE "SKILLS."
DARE
OKAY, FINE.

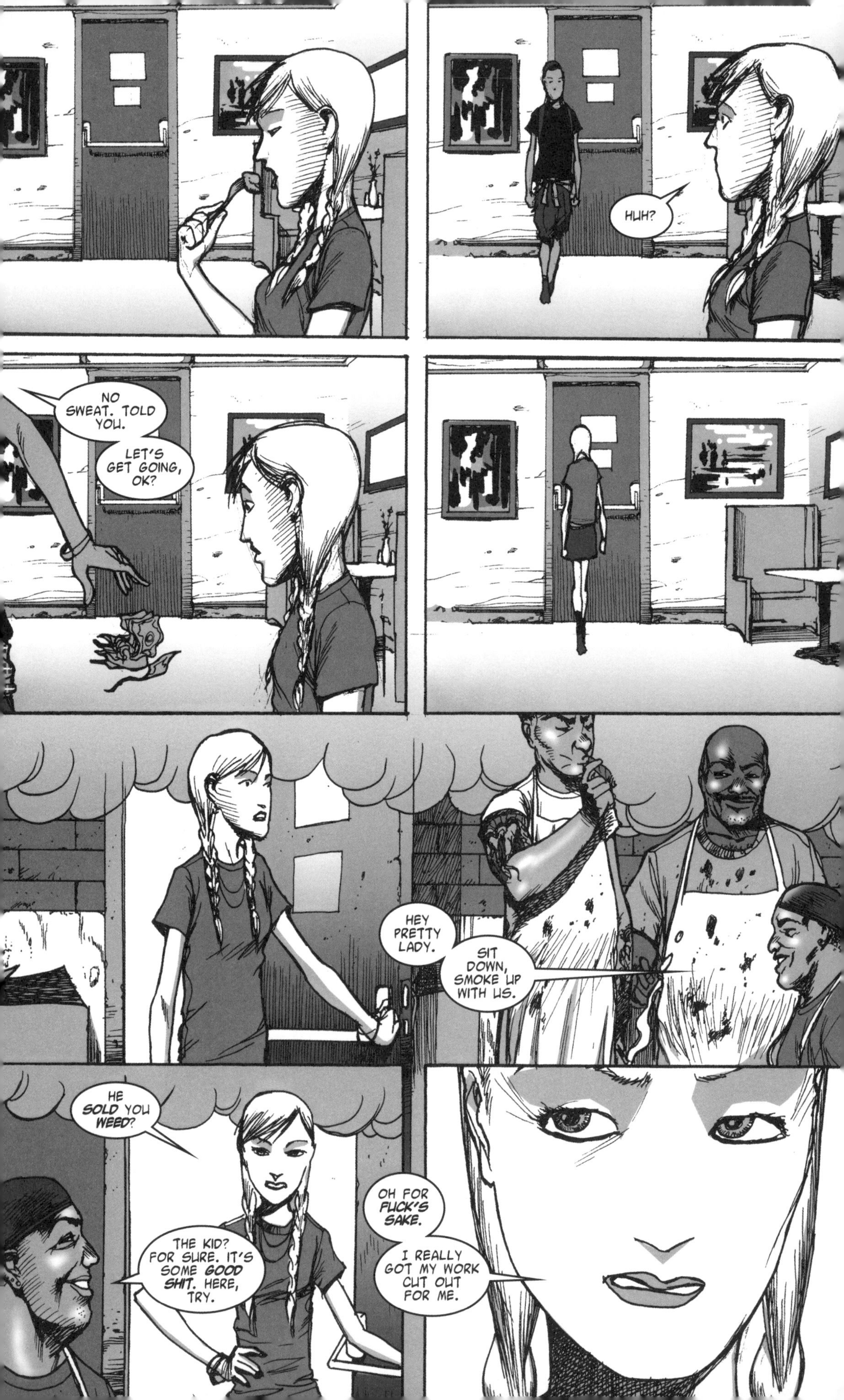
HUH?
NO SWEAT. TOLD YOU.
LET'S GET GOING, OK?
HEY PRETTY LADY.
SIT DOWN, SMOKE UP WITH US.
HE *SOLD* YOU *WEED*?
THE KID? FOR SURE. IT'S SOME *GOOD SHIT*. HERE, TRY.
OH FOR *FUCK'S SAKE*.
I REALLY GOT MY WORK CUT OUT FOR ME.

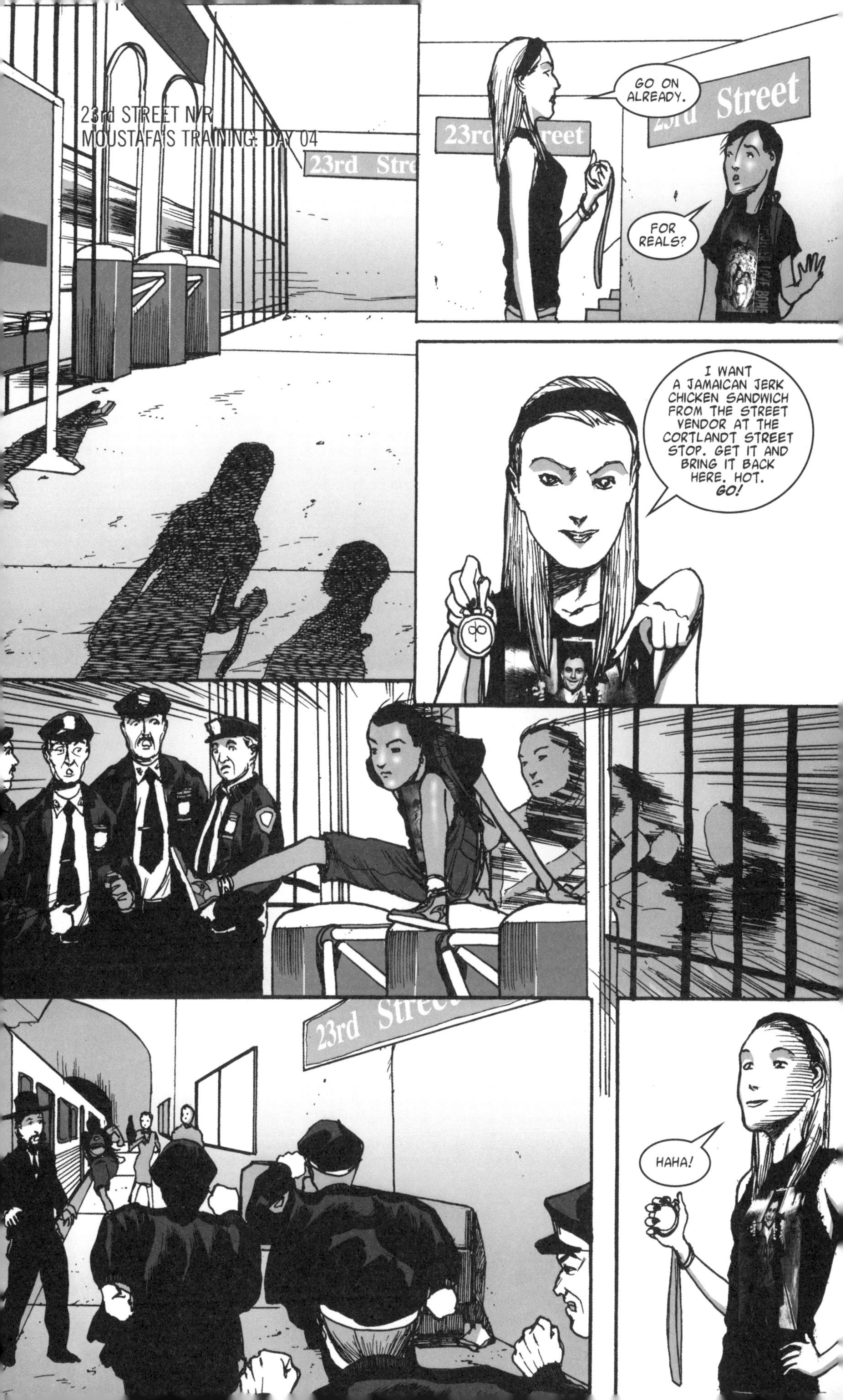
23rd STREET N/R
MOUSTAFA'S TRAINING: DAY 04
23rd Street
GO ON ALREADY.
FOR REALS?
I WANT A JAMAICAN JERK CHICKEN SANDWICH FROM THE STREET VENDOR AT THE CORTLANDT STREET STOP. GET IT AND BRING IT BACK HERE. HOT. GO!
23rd Street
HAHA!

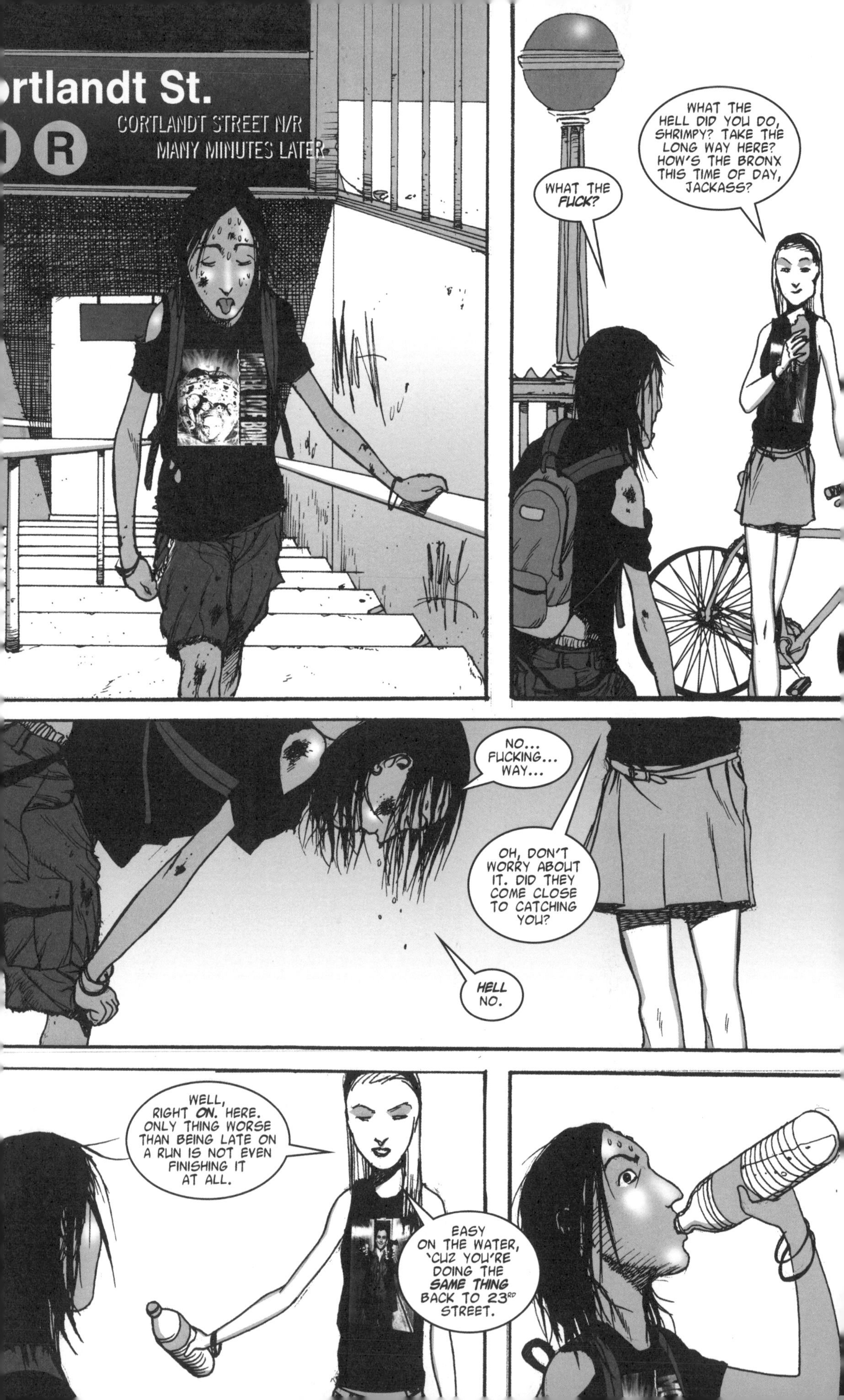

rtlandt St.
R
CORTLANDT STREET N/R
MANY MINUTES LATER
WHAT THE FUCK?
WHAT THE HELL DID YOU DO, SHRIMPY? TAKE THE LONG WAY HERE? HOW'S THE BRONX THIS TIME OF DAY, JACKASS?
NO... FUCKING... WAY...
OH, DON'T WORRY ABOUT IT. DID THEY COME CLOSE TO CATCHING YOU?
HELL NO.
WELL, RIGHT ON. HERE. ONLY THING WORSE THAN BEING LATE ON A RUN IS NOT EVEN FINISHING IT AT ALL.
EASY ON THE WATER, 'CUZ YOU'RE DOING THE SAME THING BACK TO 23RD STREET.

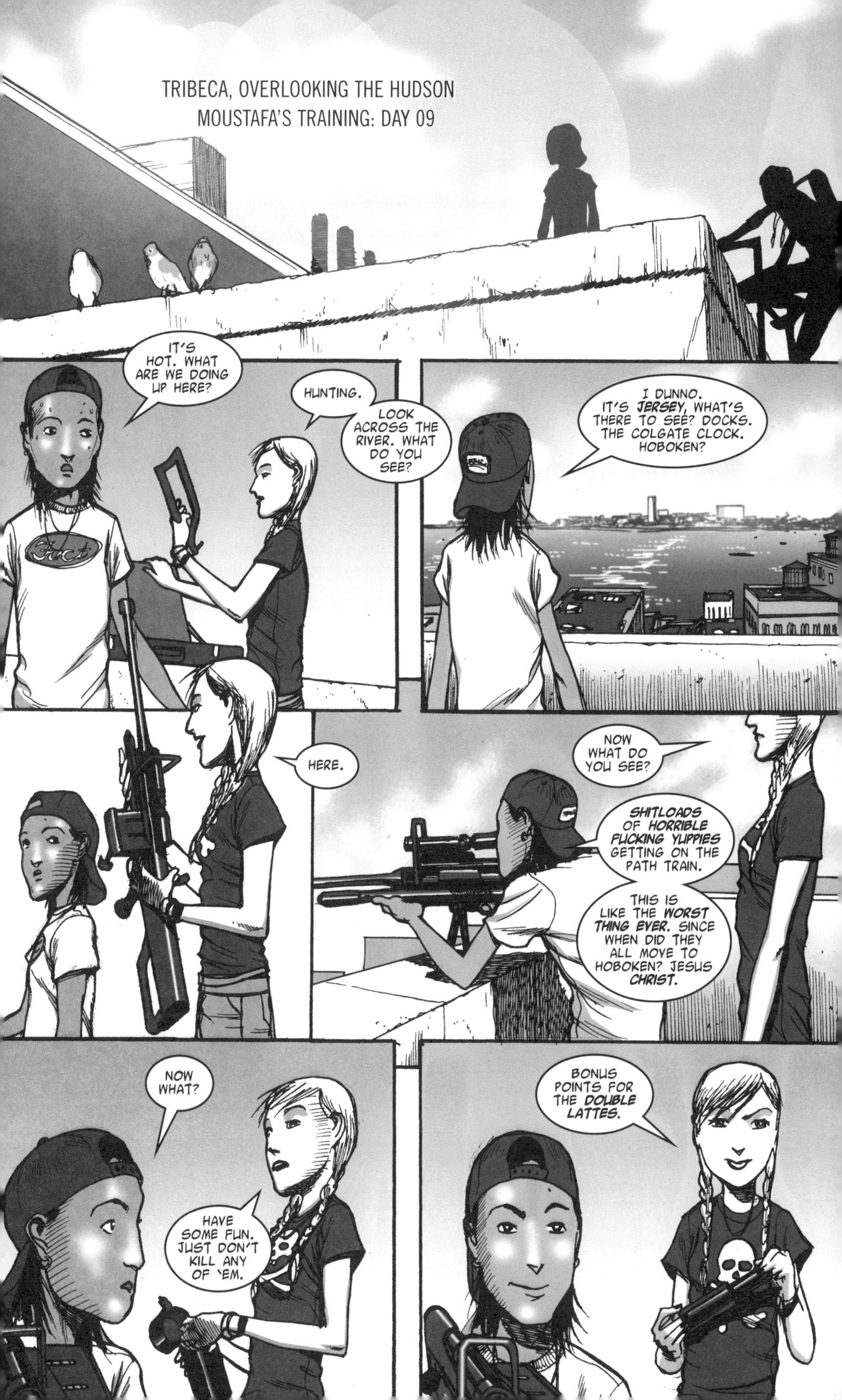
TRIBECA, OVERLOOKING THE HUDSON
MOUSTAFA'S TRAINING: DAY 09
IT'S HOT. WHAT ARE WE DOING UP HERE?
HUNTING.
LOOK ACROSS THE RIVER. WHAT DO YOU SEE?
I DUNNO. IT'S JERSEY, WHAT'S THERE TO SEE? DOCKS. THE COLGATE CLOCK. HOBOKEN?
HERE.
NOW WHAT DO YOU SEE?
SHITLOADS OF HORRIBLE FUCKING YUPPIES GETTING ON THE PATH TRAIN.
THIS IS LIKE THE WORST THING EVER. SINCE WHEN DID THEY ALL MOVE TO HOBOKEN? JESUS CHRIST.
NOW WHAT?
HAVE SOME FUN. JUST DON'T KILL ANY OF 'EM.
BONUS POINTS FOR THE DOUBLE LATTES.

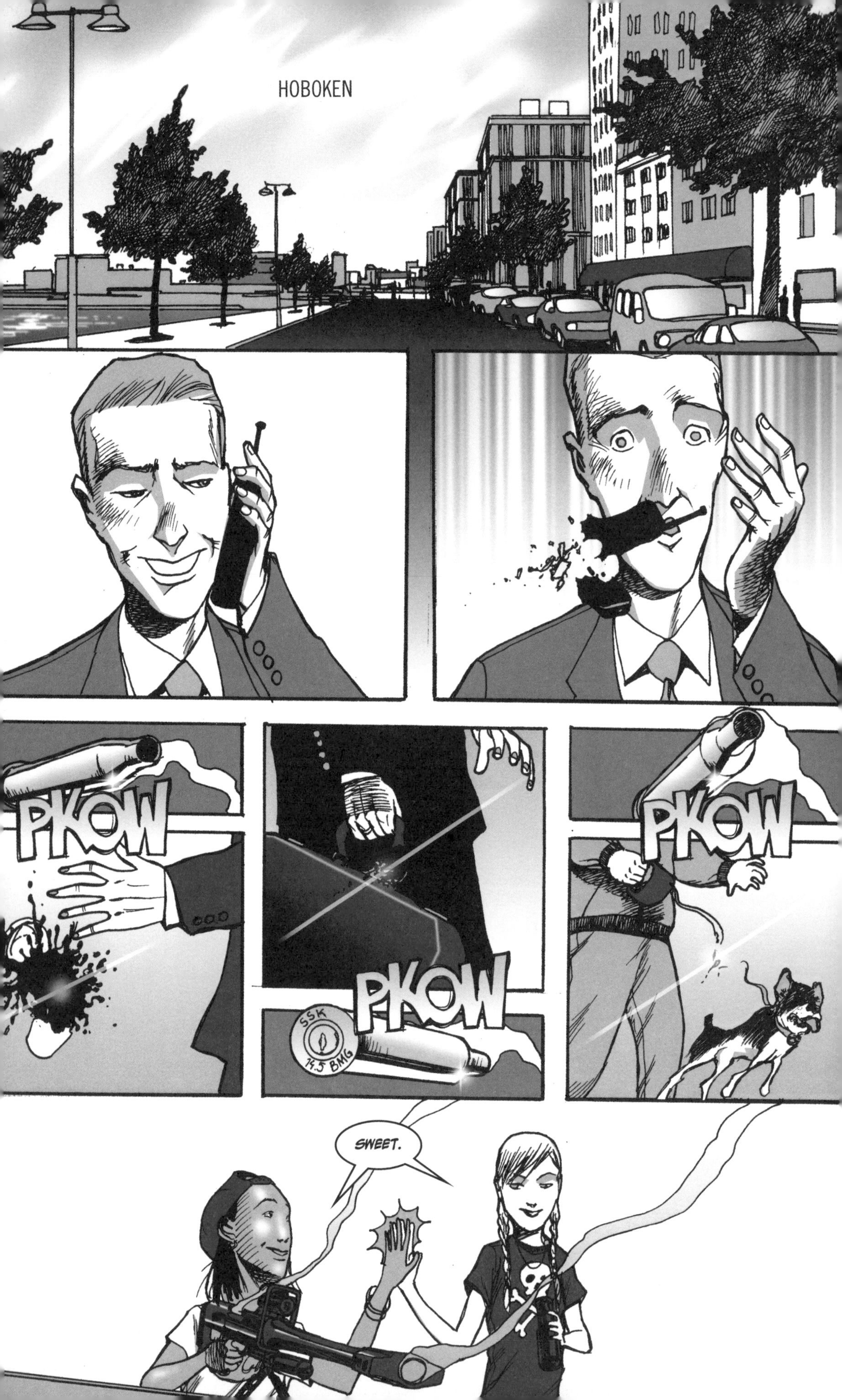
HOBOKEN
PKOW
PKOW
SSK
14.5 BMG
PKOW
SWEET.

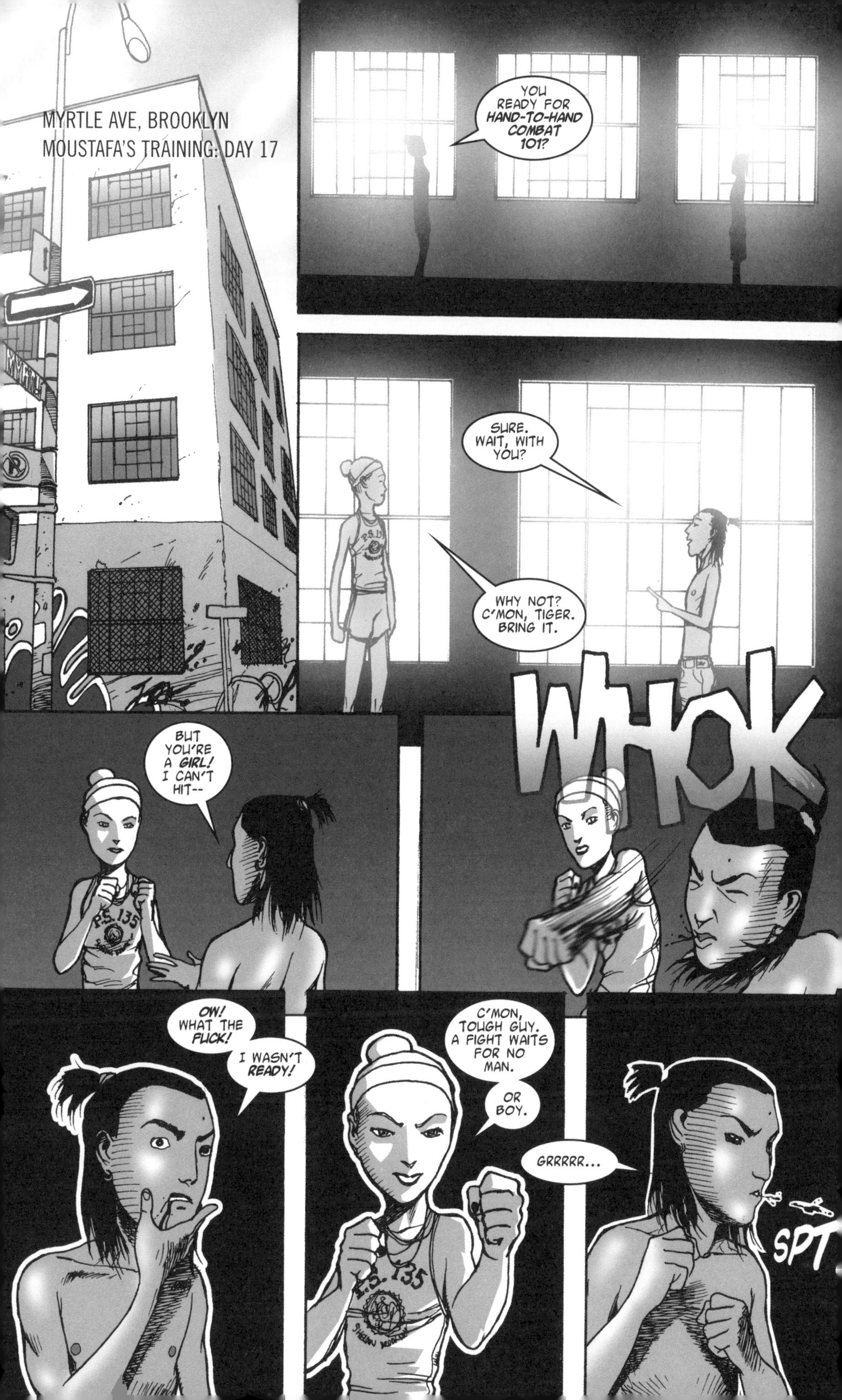
MYRTLE AVE, BROOKLYN
MOUSTAFA'S TRAINING: DAY 17
YOU READY FOR HAND-TO-HAND COMBAT 101?
SURE. WAIT, WITH YOU?
WHY NOT? C'MON, TIGER. BRING IT.
BUT YOU'RE A GIRL! I CAN'T HIT--
WHOK
OW! WHAT THE FUCK!
I WASN'T READY!
C'MON, TOUGH GUY. A FIGHT WAITS FOR NO MAN.
OR BOY.
GRRRRR...
SPT

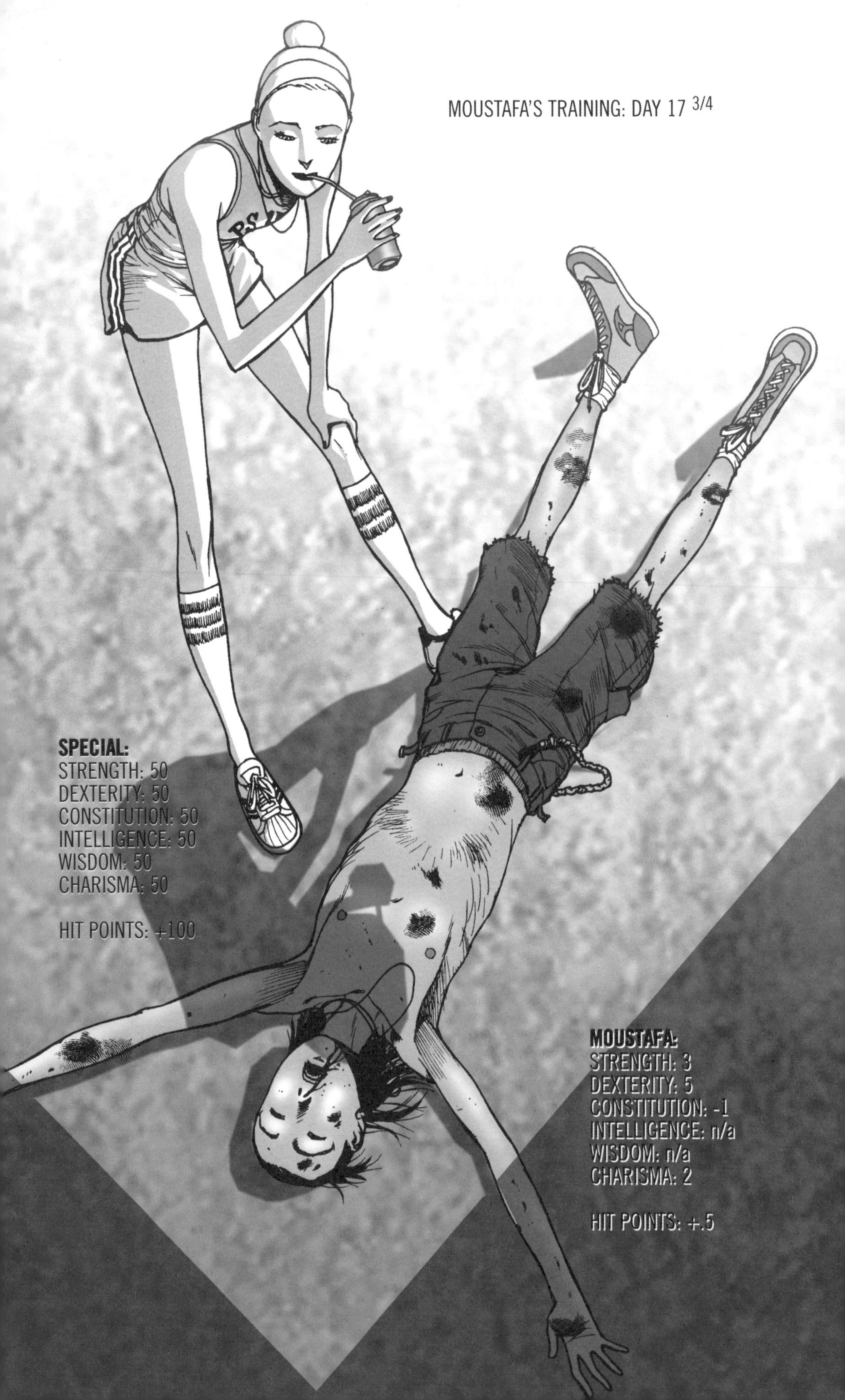
MOUSTAFA'S TRAINING: DAY 17 3/4
SPECIAL:
STRENGTH: 50
DEXTERITY: 50
CONSTITUTION: 50
INTELLIGENCE: 50
WISDOM: 50
CHARISMA: 50
HIT POINTS: +100
MOUSTAFA:
STRENGTH: 3
DEXTERITY: 5
CONSTITUTION: -1
INTELLIGENCE: n/a
WISDOM: n/a
CHARISMA: 2
HIT POINTS: +.5

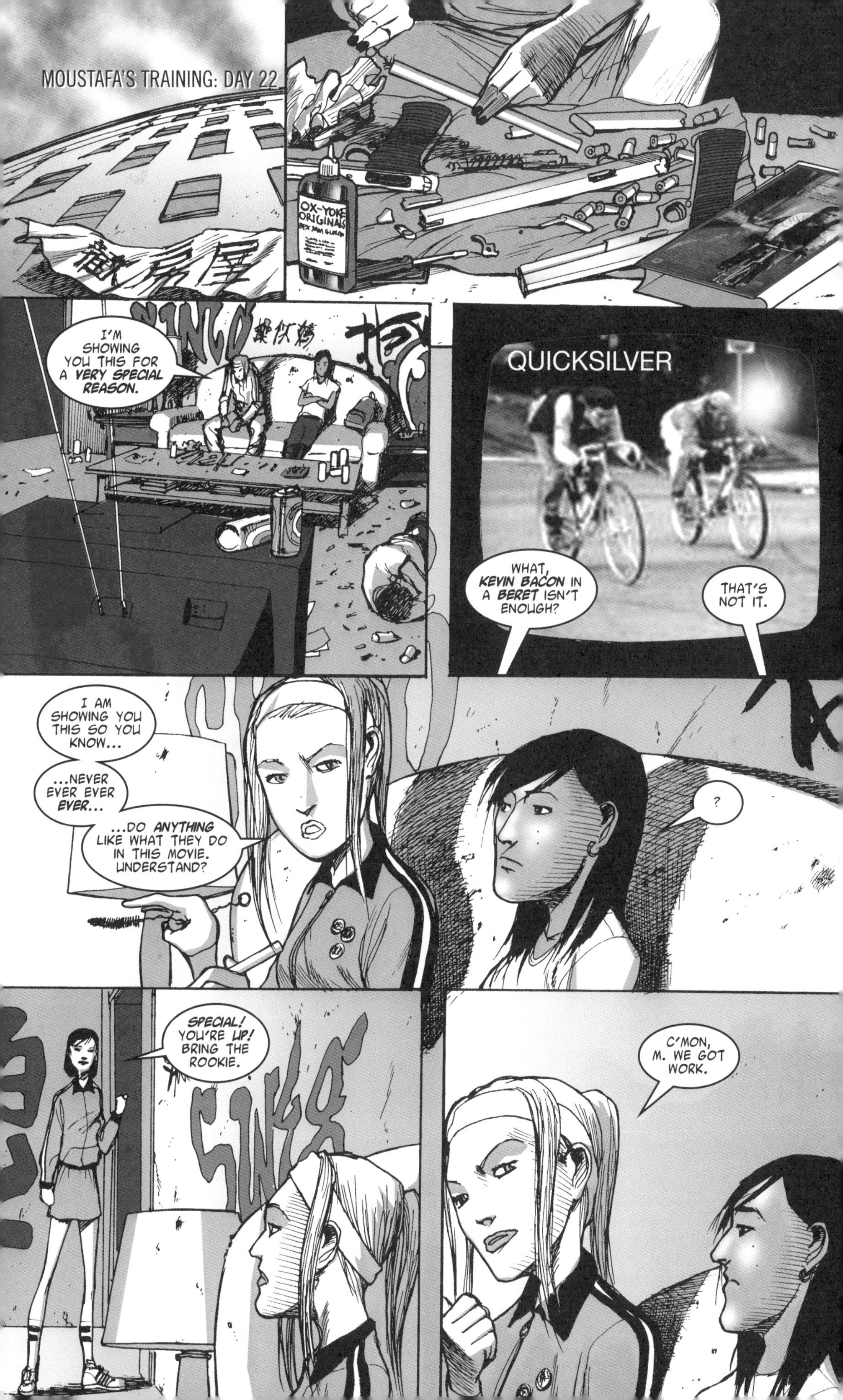
MOUSTAFA'S TRAINING: DAY 22
OX-YOKE ORIGINALS
I'M SHOWING YOU THIS FOR A VERY SPECIAL REASON.
QUICKSILVER
WHAT, KEVIN BACON IN A BERET ISN'T ENOUGH?
THAT'S NOT IT.
I AM SHOWING YOU THIS SO YOU KNOW...
...NEVER EVER EVER EVER...
...DO ANYTHING LIKE WHAT THEY DO IN THIS MOVIE. UNDERSTAND?
?
SPECIAL! YOU'RE UP! BRING THE ROOKIE.
C'MON, M. WE GOT WORK.

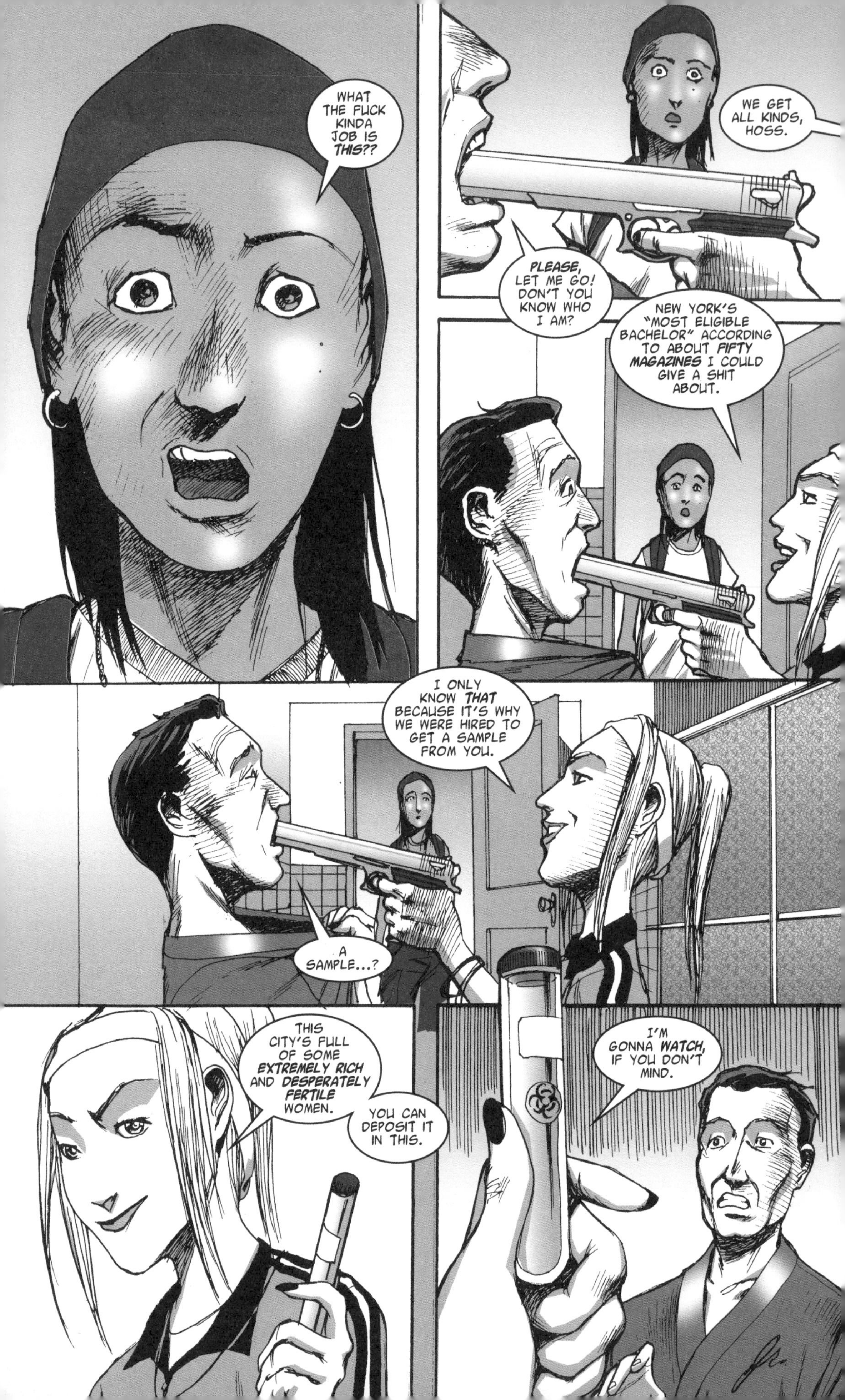
WHAT THE FUCK KINDA JOB IS THIS??
WE GET ALL KINDS, HOSS.
PLEASE, LET ME GO! DON'T YOU KNOW WHO I AM?
NEW YORK'S "MOST ELIGIBLE BACHELOR" ACCORDING TO ABOUT FIFTY MAGAZINES I COULD GIVE A SHIT ABOUT.
I ONLY KNOW THAT BECAUSE IT'S WHY WE WERE HIRED TO GET A SAMPLE FROM YOU.
A SAMPLE...?
THIS CITY'S FULL OF SOME EXTREMELY RICH AND DESPERATELY FERTILE WOMEN.
YOU CAN DEPOSIT IT IN THIS.
I'M GONNA WATCH, IF YOU DON'T MIND.

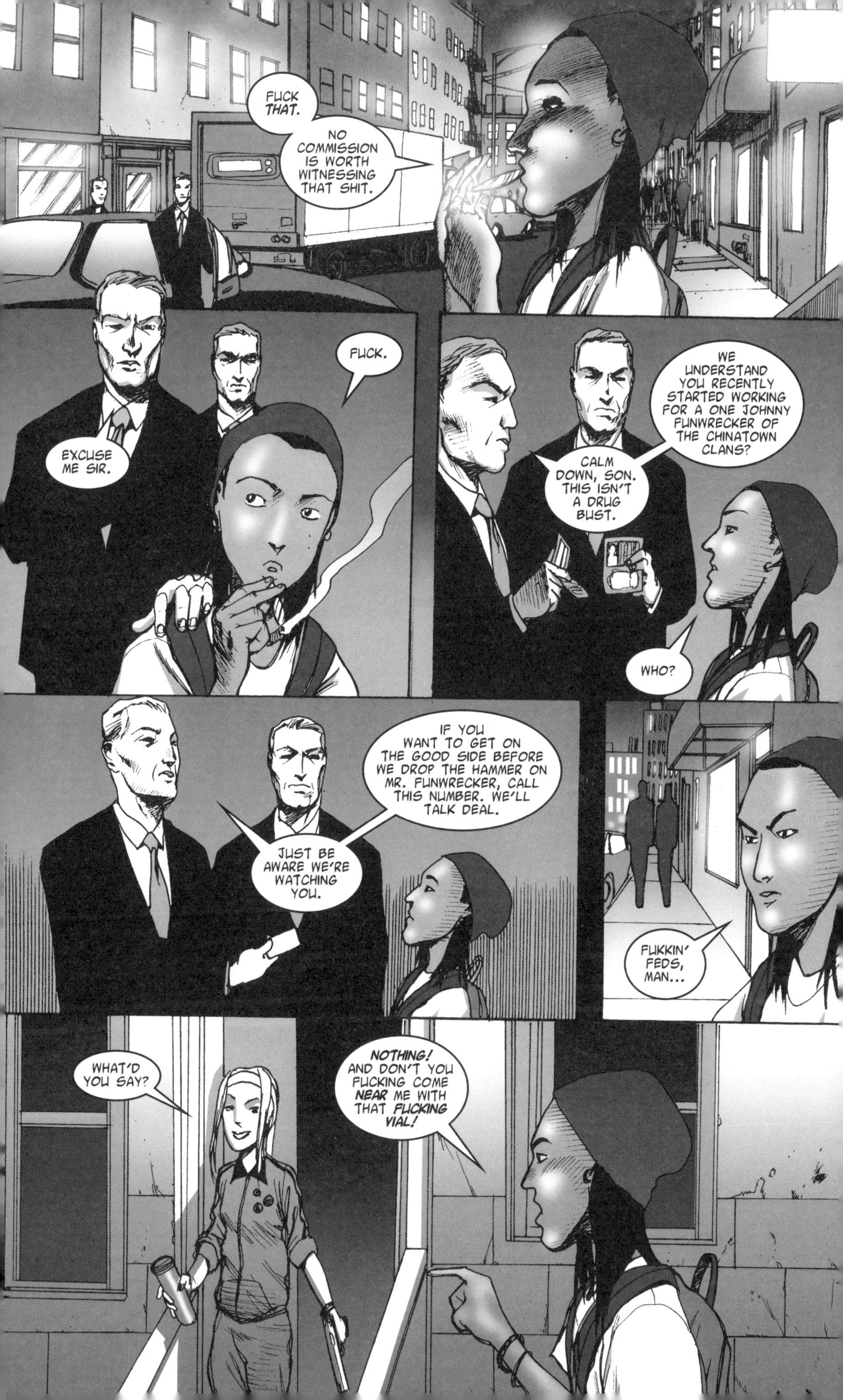
FUCK THAT.
NO COMMISSION IS WORTH WITNESSING THAT SHIT.
EXCUSE ME SIR.
FUCK.
WE UNDERSTAND YOU RECENTLY STARTED WORKING FOR A ONE JOHNNY FUNWRECKER OF THE CHINATOWN CLANS?
CALM DOWN, SON. THIS ISN'T A DRUG BUST.
WHO?
IF YOU WANT TO GET ON THE GOOD SIDE BEFORE WE DROP THE HAMMER ON MR. FUNWRECKER, CALL THIS NUMBER. WE'LL TALK DEAL.
JUST BE AWARE WE'RE WATCHING YOU.
FUKKIN' FEDS, MAN...
WHAT'D YOU SAY?
NOTHING! AND DON'T YOU FUCKING COME NEAR ME WITH THAT FUCKING VIAL!

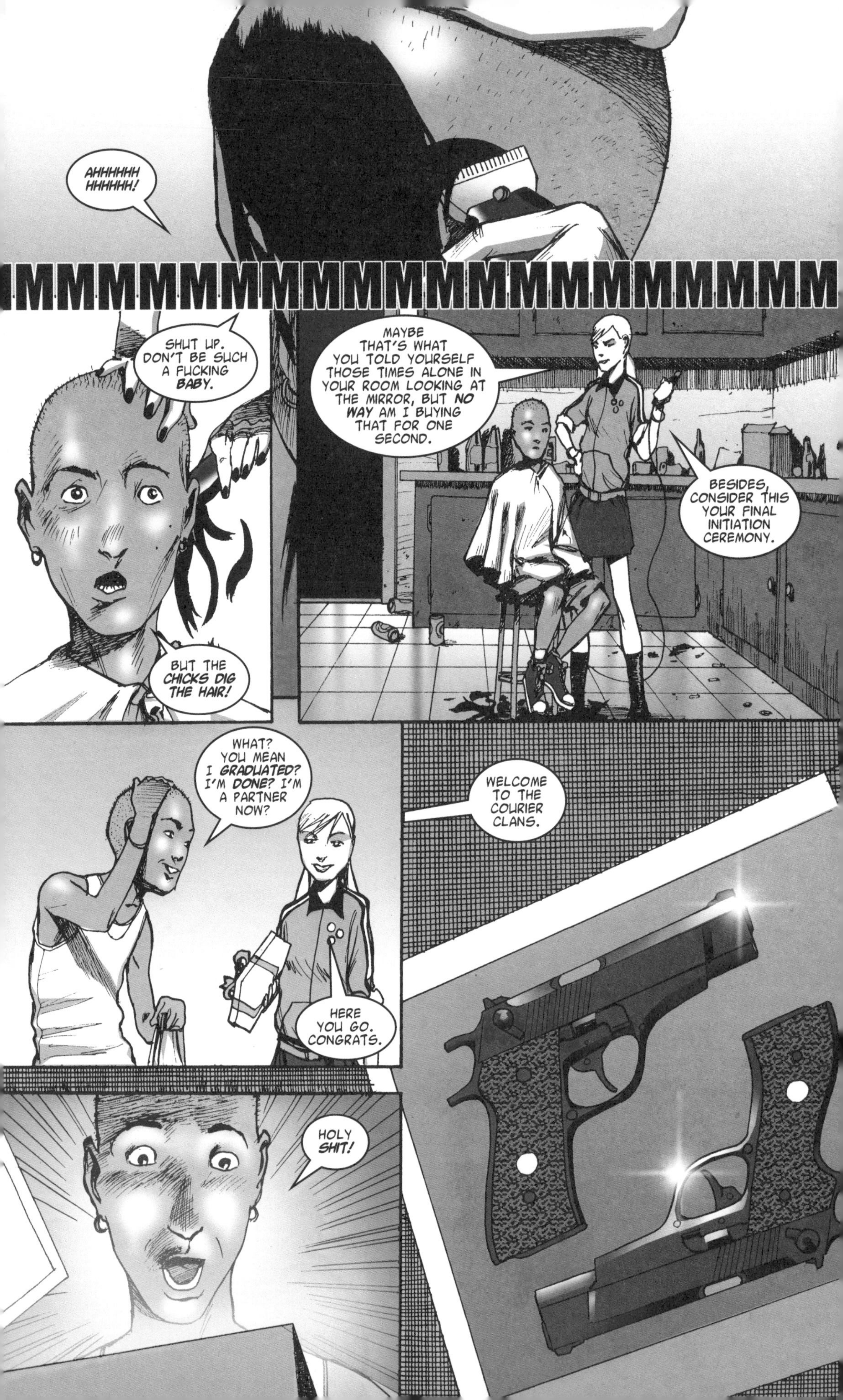

AHHHHHH HHHHHH!
MMMMMMMMMMMMMMMMMMMMMMMMM
SHUT UP. DON'T BE SUCH A FUCKING BABY.
BUT THE CHICKS DIG THE HAIR!
MAYBE THAT'S WHAT YOU TOLD YOURSELF THOSE TIMES ALONE IN YOUR ROOM LOOKING AT THE MIRROR, BUT NO WAY AM I BUYING THAT FOR ONE SECOND.
BESIDES, CONSIDER THIS YOUR FINAL INITIATION CEREMONY.
WHAT? YOU MEAN I GRADUATED? I'M DONE? I'M A PARTNER NOW?
HERE YOU GO. CONGRATS.
WELCOME TO THE COURIER CLANS.
HOLY SHIT!

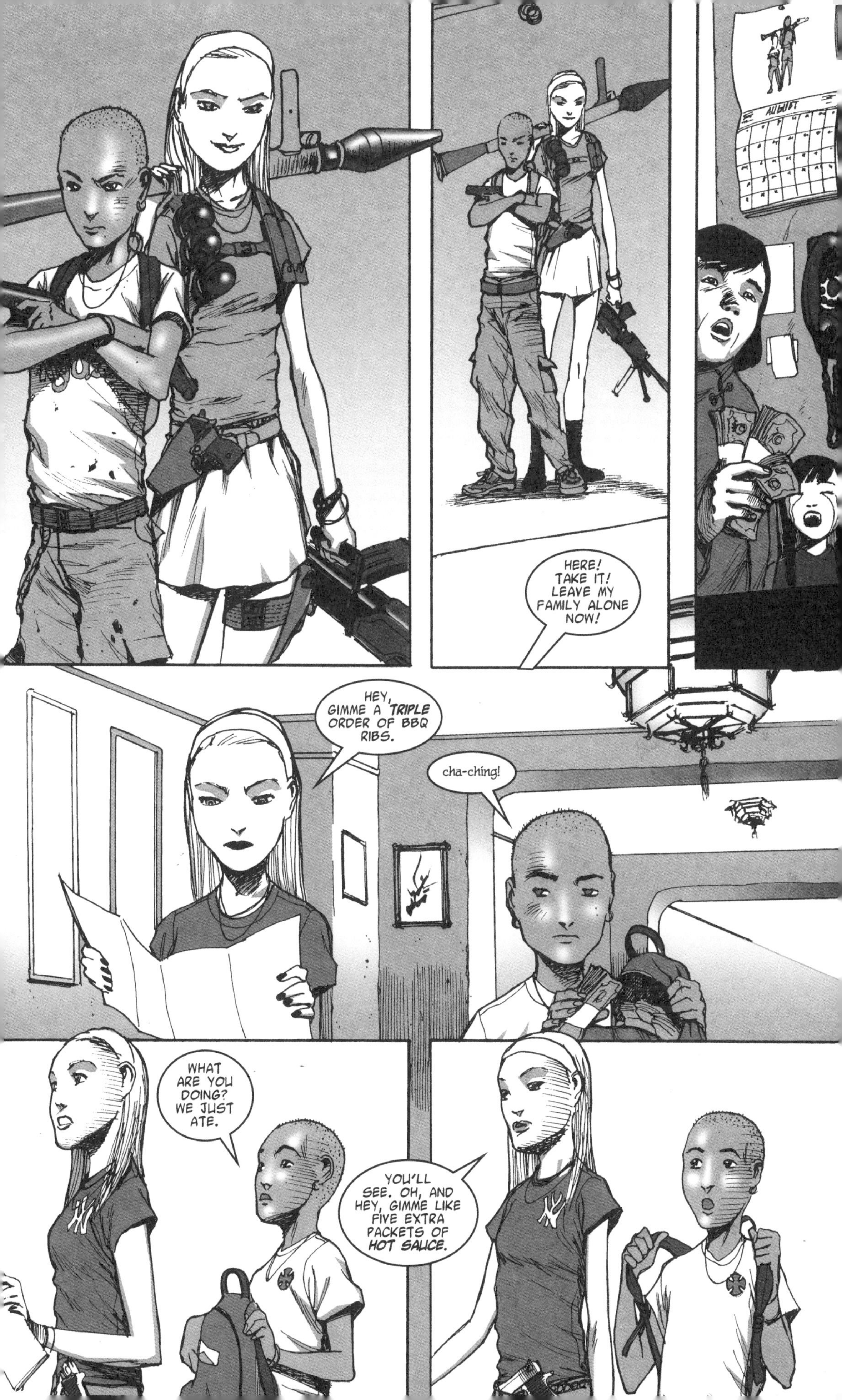
HERE! TAKE IT! LEAVE MY FAMILY ALONE NOW!
HEY, GIMME A TRIPLE ORDER OF BBQ RIBS.
cha-ching!
WHAT ARE YOU DOING? WE JUST ATE.
YOU'LL SEE. OH, AND HEY, GIMME LIKE FIVE EXTRA PACKETS OF HOT SAUCE.

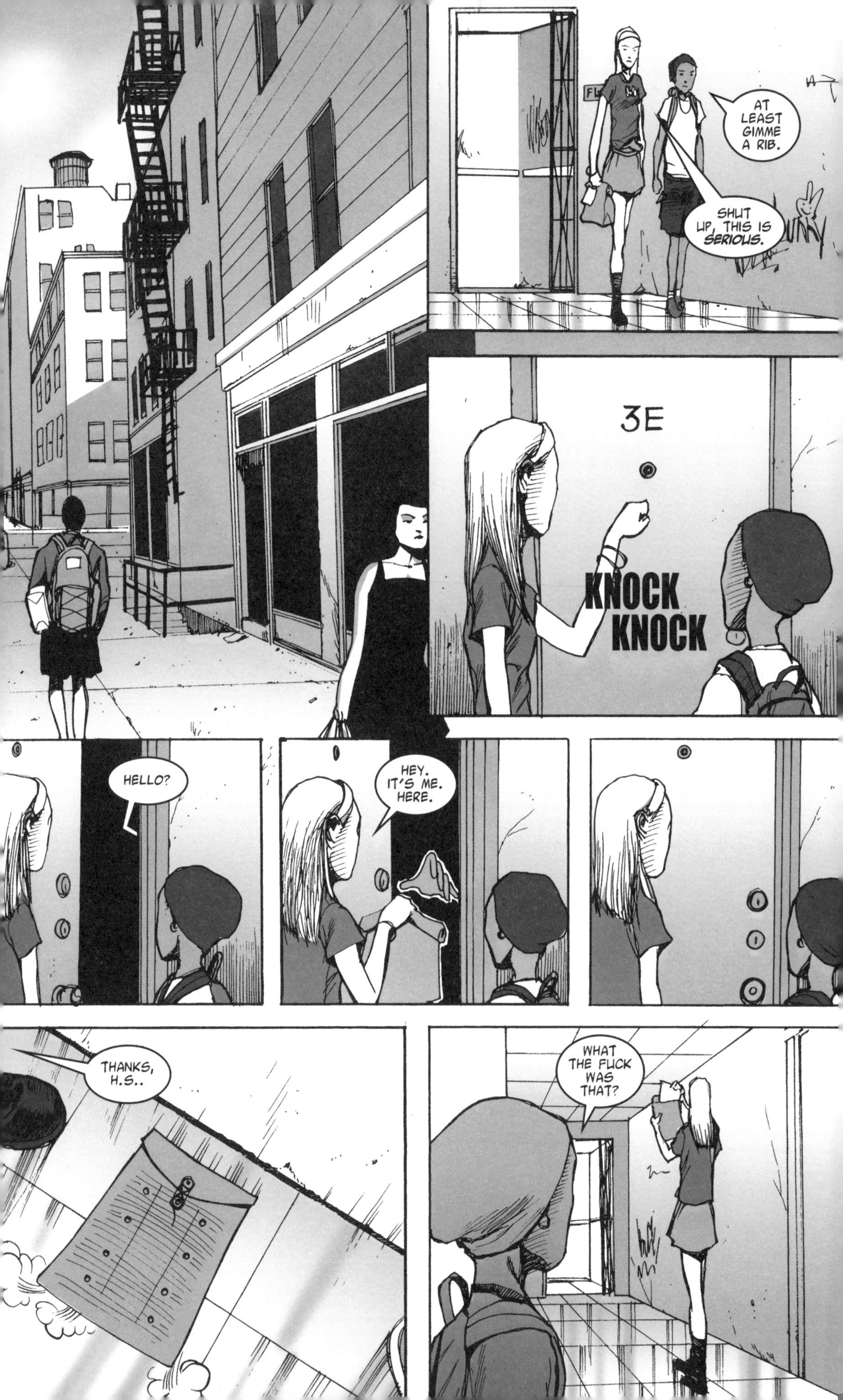
AT LEAST GIMME A RIB.
SHUT UP, THIS IS SERIOUS.
3E
KNOCK KNOCK
HELLO?
HEY. IT'S ME. HERE.
THANKS, H.S..
WHAT THE FUCK WAS THAT?

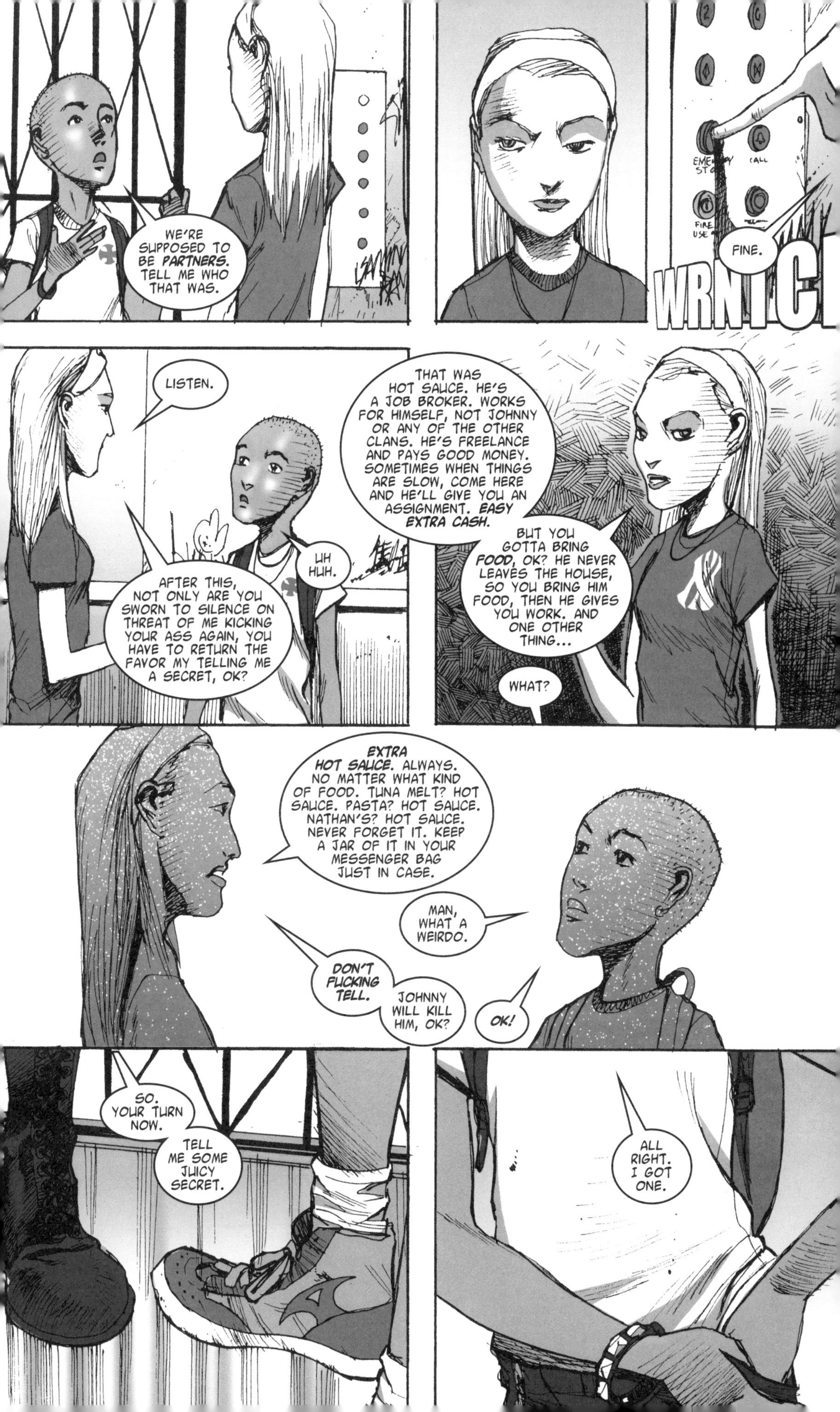
WE'RE SUPPOSED TO BE PARTNERS. TELL ME WHO THAT WAS.
FINE.
WRNTCH
LISTEN.
AFTER THIS, NOT ONLY ARE YOU SWORN TO SILENCE ON THREAT OF ME KICKING YOUR ASS AGAIN, YOU HAVE TO RETURN THE FAVOR MY TELLING ME A SECRET, OK?
UH HUH.
THAT WAS HOT SAUCE. HE'S A JOB BROKER. WORKS FOR HIMSELF, NOT JOHNNY OR ANY OF THE OTHER CLANS. HE'S FREELANCE AND PAYS GOOD MONEY. SOMETIMES WHEN THINGS ARE SLOW, COME HERE AND HE'LL GIVE YOU AN ASSIGNMENT. EASY EXTRA CASH.
BUT YOU GOTTA BRING FOOD, OK? HE NEVER LEAVES THE HOUSE, SO YOU BRING HIM FOOD, THEN HE GIVES YOU WORK. AND ONE OTHER THING...
WHAT?
EXTRA HOT SAUCE. ALWAYS. NO MATTER WHAT KIND OF FOOD. TUNA MELT? HOT SAUCE. PASTA? HOT SAUCE. NATHAN'S? HOT SAUCE. NEVER FORGET IT. KEEP A JAR OF IT IN YOUR MESSENGER BAG JUST IN CASE.
MAN, WHAT A WEIRDO.
DON'T FUCKING TELL.
JOHNNY WILL KILL HIM, OK?
OK!
SO. YOUR TURN NOW.
TELL ME SOME JUICY SECRET.
ALL RIGHT. I GOT ONE.

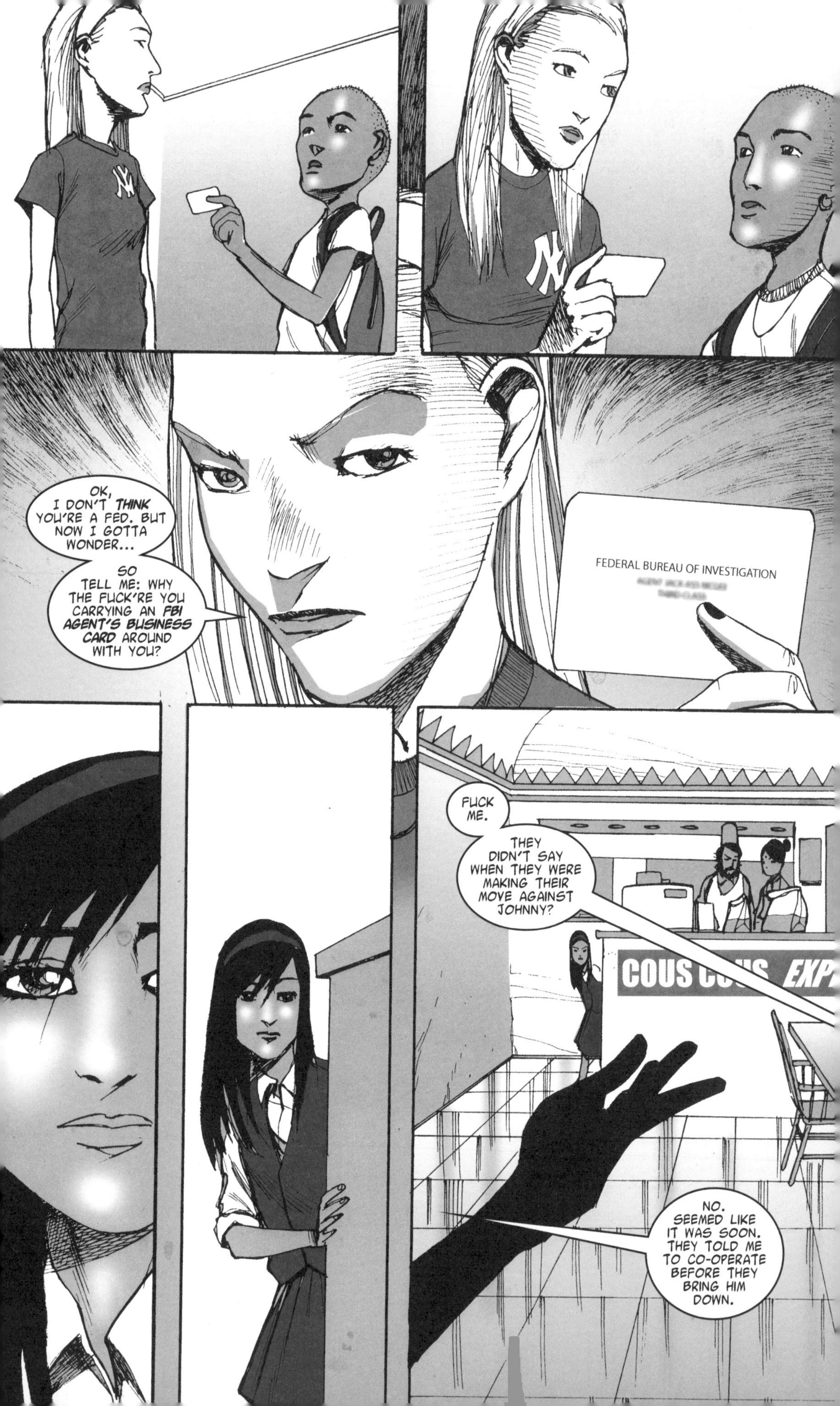

OK, I DON'T **THINK** YOU'RE A FED. BUT NOW I GOTTA WONDER...
SO TELL ME: WHY THE FUCK'RE YOU CARRYING AN ***FBI AGENT'S BUSINESS CARD*** AROUND WITH YOU?
FEDERAL BUREAU OF INVESTIGATION
FUCK ME.
THEY DIDN'T SAY WHEN THEY WERE MAKING THEIR MOVE AGAINST JOHNNY?
COUS
NO. SEEMED LIKE IT WAS SOON. THEY TOLD ME TO CO-OPERATE BEFORE THEY BRING HIM DOWN.

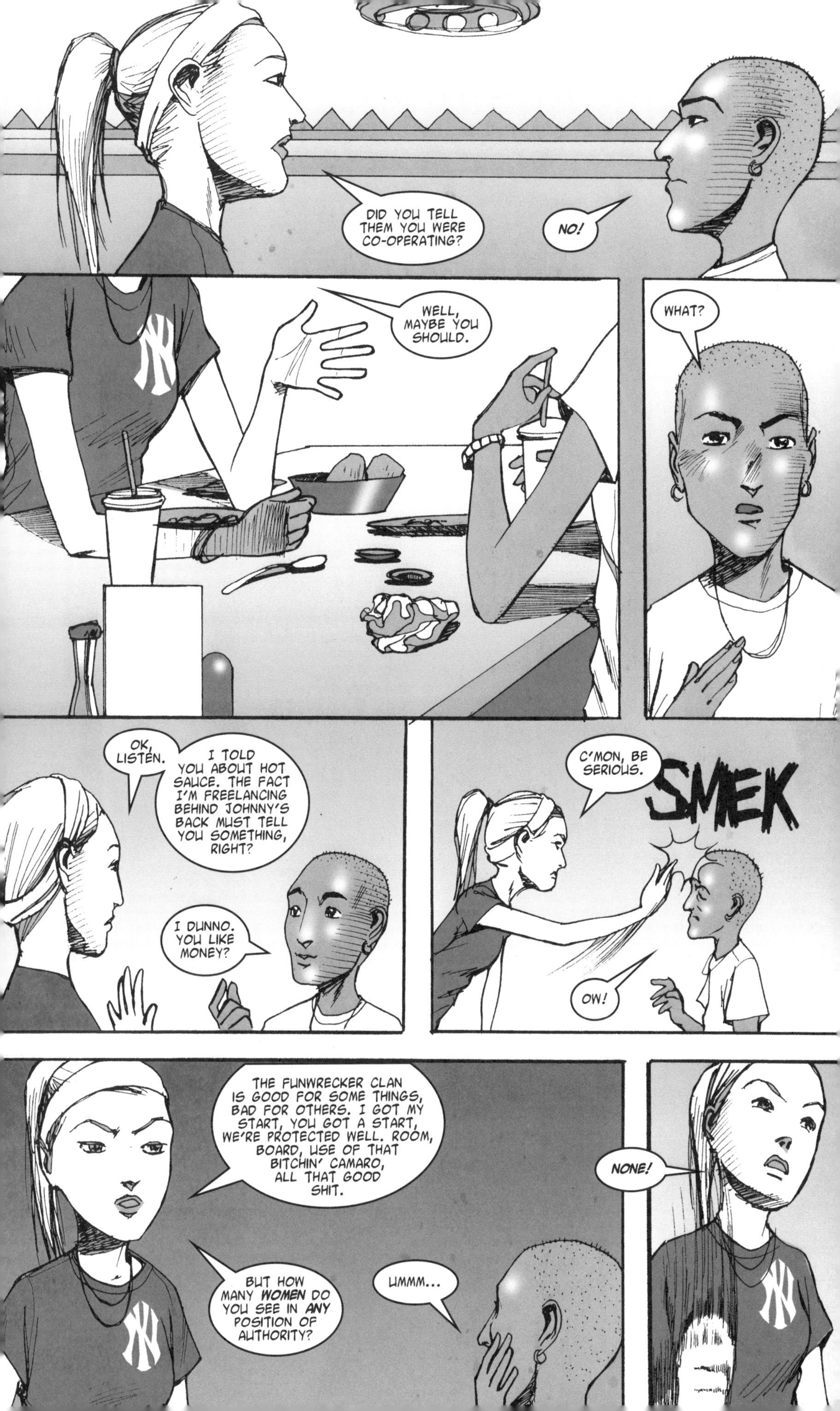
DID YOU TELL THEM YOU WERE CO-OPERATING?
NO!
WELL, MAYBE YOU SHOULD.
WHAT?
OK, LISTEN.
I TOLD YOU ABOUT HOT SAUCE. THE FACT I'M FREELANCING BEHIND JOHNNY'S BACK MUST TELL YOU SOMETHING, RIGHT?
I DUNNO. YOU LIKE MONEY?
C'MON, BE SERIOUS.
SMEK
OW!
THE FUNWRECKER CLAN IS GOOD FOR SOME THINGS, BAD FOR OTHERS. I GOT MY START, YOU GOT A START, WE'RE PROTECTED WELL. ROOM, BOARD, USE OF THAT BITCHIN' CAMARO, ALL THAT GOOD SHIT.
BUT HOW MANY WOMEN DO YOU SEE IN ANY POSITION OF AUTHORITY?
UMMM...
NONE!

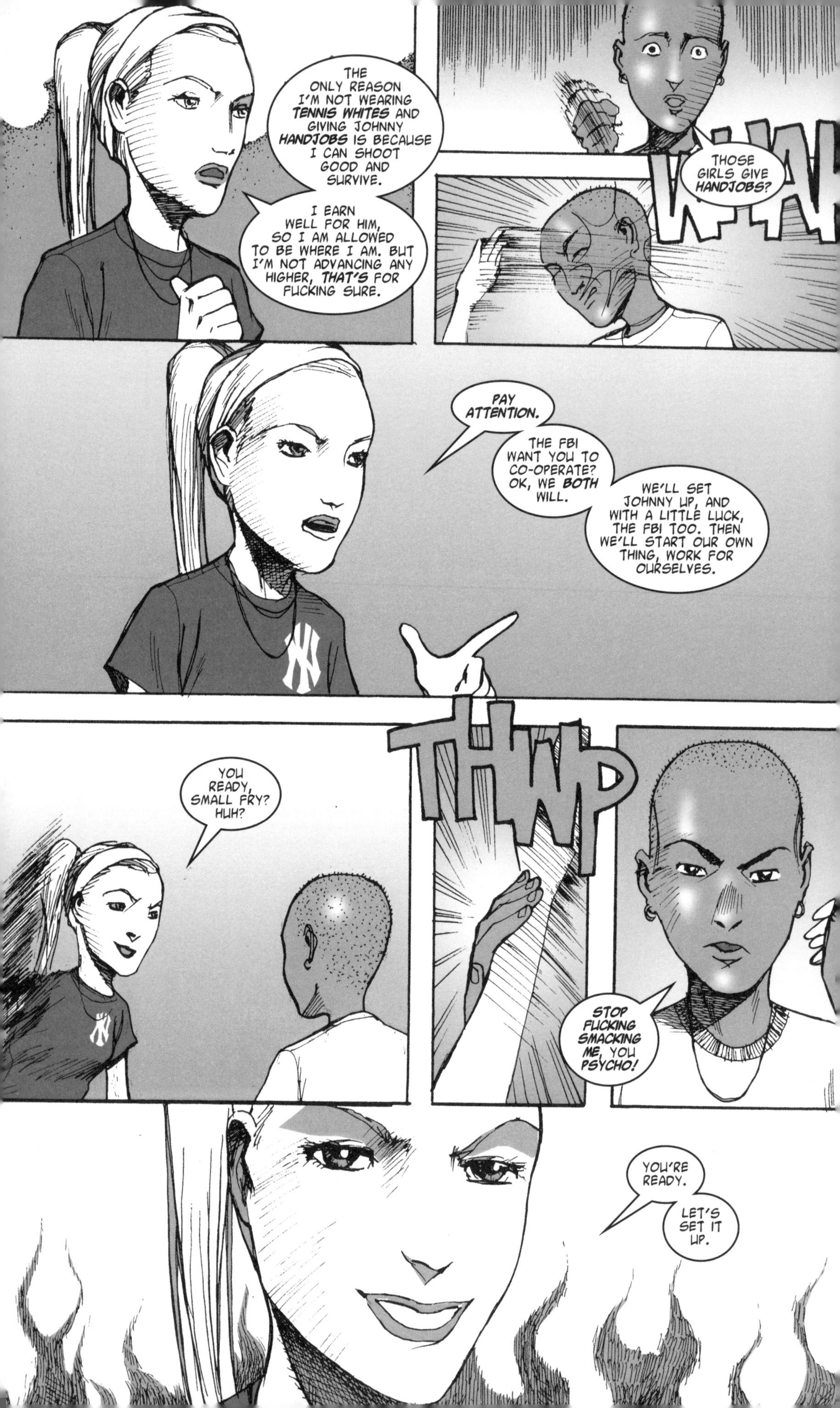

THE ONLY REASON I'M NOT WEARING **TENNIS WHITES** AND GIVING JOHNNY **HANDJOBS** IS BECAUSE I CAN SHOOT GOOD AND SURVIVE.
I EARN WELL FOR HIM, SO I AM ALLOWED TO BE WHERE I AM. BUT I'M NOT ADVANCING ANY HIGHER, **THAT'S** FOR FUCKING SURE.
THOSE GIRLS GIVE **HANDJOBS?**
PAY ATTENTION.
THE FBI WANT YOU TO CO-OPERATE? OK, WE **BOTH** WILL.
WE'LL SET JOHNNY UP, AND WITH A LITTLE LUCK, THE FBI TOO. THEN WE'LL START OUR OWN THING, WORK FOR OURSELVES.
YOU READY, SMALL FRY? HUH?
THWP
STOP FUCKING SMACKING ME, YOU **PSYCHO!**
YOU'RE READY.
LET'S SET IT UP.

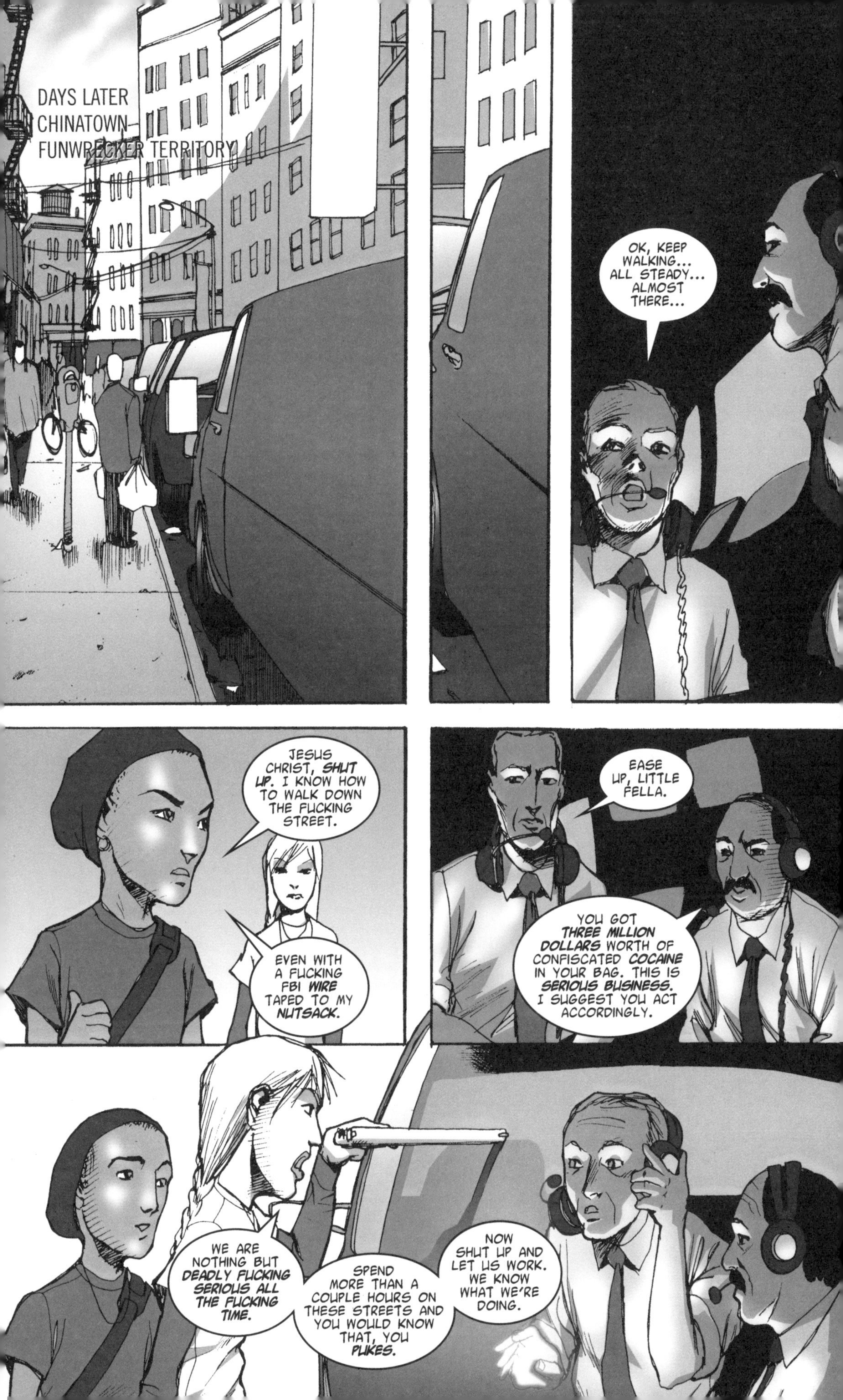
DAYS LATER
CHINATOWN-
FUNWRECKER TERRITORY
OK, KEEP WALKING... ALL STEADY... ALMOST THERE...
JESUS CHRIST, SHUT UP. I KNOW HOW TO WALK DOWN THE FUCKING STREET.
EVEN WITH A FUCKING FBI WIRE TAPED TO MY NUTSACK.
EASE UP, LITTLE FELLA.
YOU GOT THREE MILLION DOLLARS WORTH OF CONFISCATED COCAINE IN YOUR BAG. THIS IS SERIOUS BUSINESS. I SUGGEST YOU ACT ACCORDINGLY.
WE ARE NOTHING BUT DEADLY FUCKING SERIOUS ALL THE FUCKING TIME.
SPEND MORE THAN A COUPLE HOURS ON THESE STREETS AND YOU WOULD KNOW THAT, YOU PUKES.
NOW SHUT UP AND LET US WORK. WE KNOW WHAT WE'RE DOING.

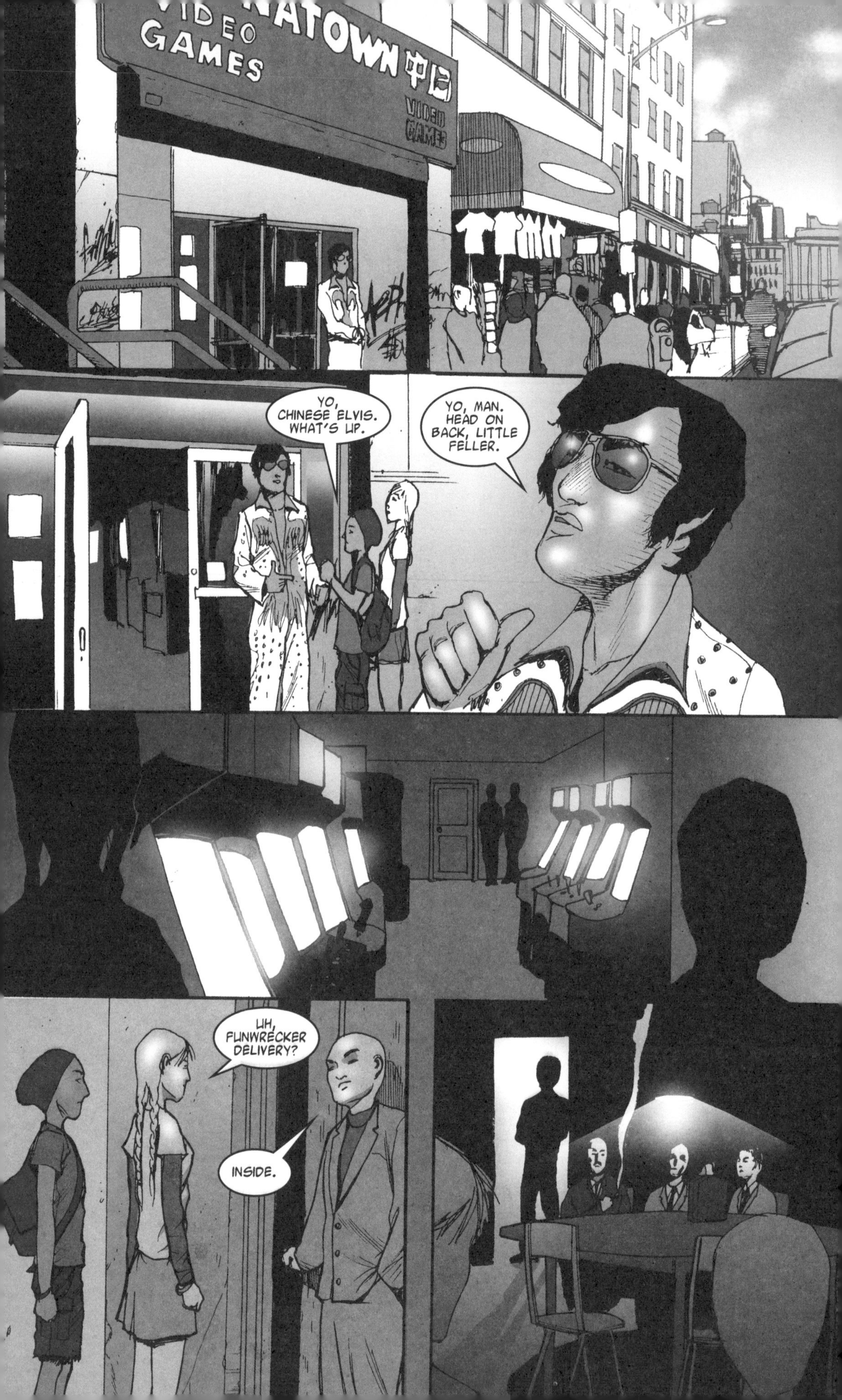
VIDEO
GAMES
NATOWN 中国
VIDEO
GAMES
YO, CHINESE ELVIS. WHAT'S UP.
YO, MAN. HEAD ON BACK, LITTLE FELLER.
UH, FUNWRECKER DELIVERY?
INSIDE.

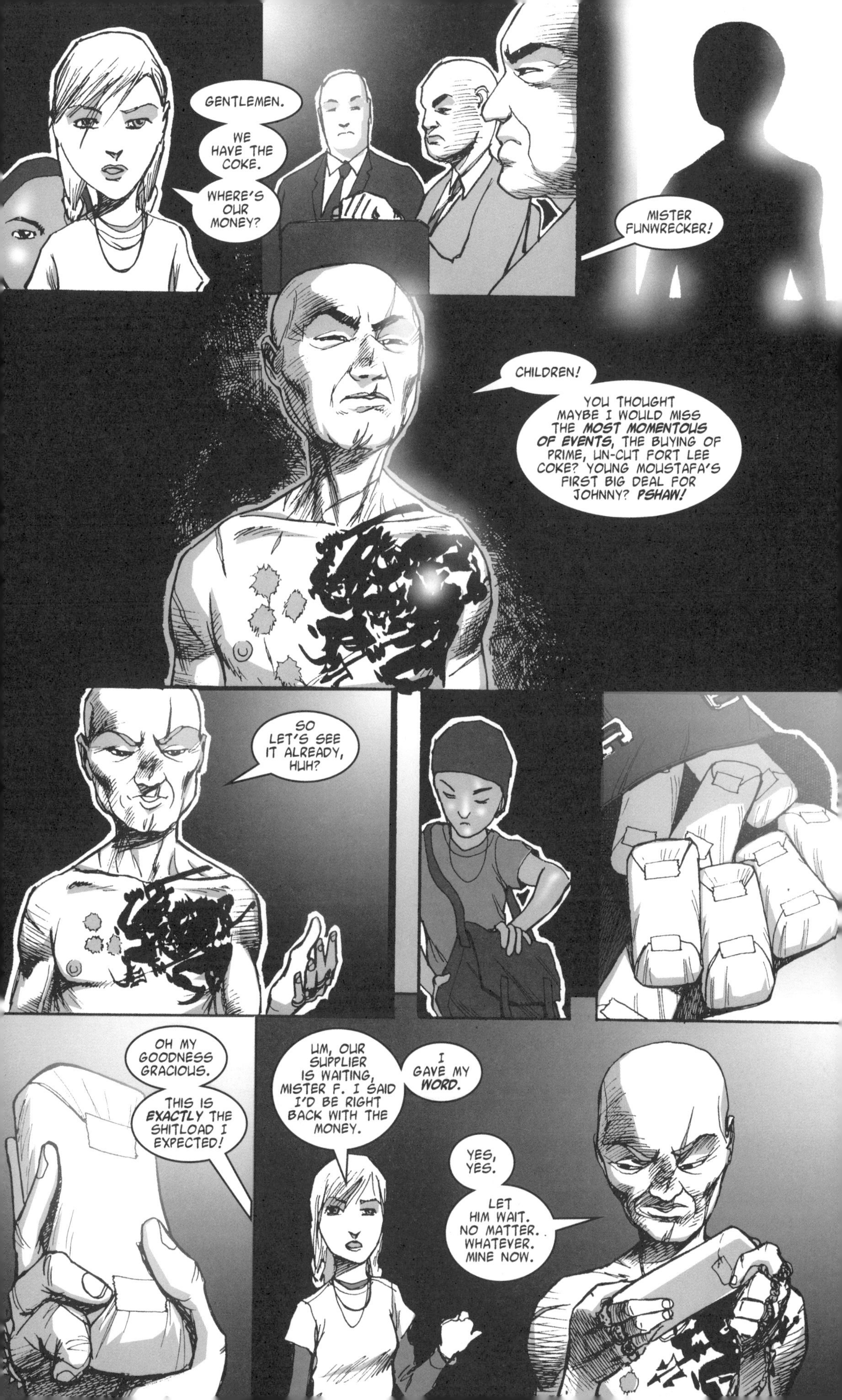
GENTLEMEN.
WE HAVE THE COKE.
WHERE'S OUR MONEY?
MISTER FUNWRECKER!
CHILDREN!
YOU THOUGHT MAYBE I WOULD MISS THE **MOST MOMENTOUS OF EVENTS,** THE BUYING OF PRIME, UN-CUT FORT LEE COKE? YOUNG MOUSTAFA'S FIRST BIG DEAL FOR JOHNNY? **PSHAW!**
SO LET'S SEE IT ALREADY, HUH?
OH MY GOODNESS GRACIOUS.
THIS IS **EXACTLY** THE SHITLOAD I EXPECTED!
UM, OUR SUPPLIER IS WAITING, MISTER F. I SAID I'D BE RIGHT BACK WITH THE MONEY.
I GAVE MY **WORD.**
YES, YES.
LET HIM WAIT. NO MATTER. WHATEVER. MINE NOW.

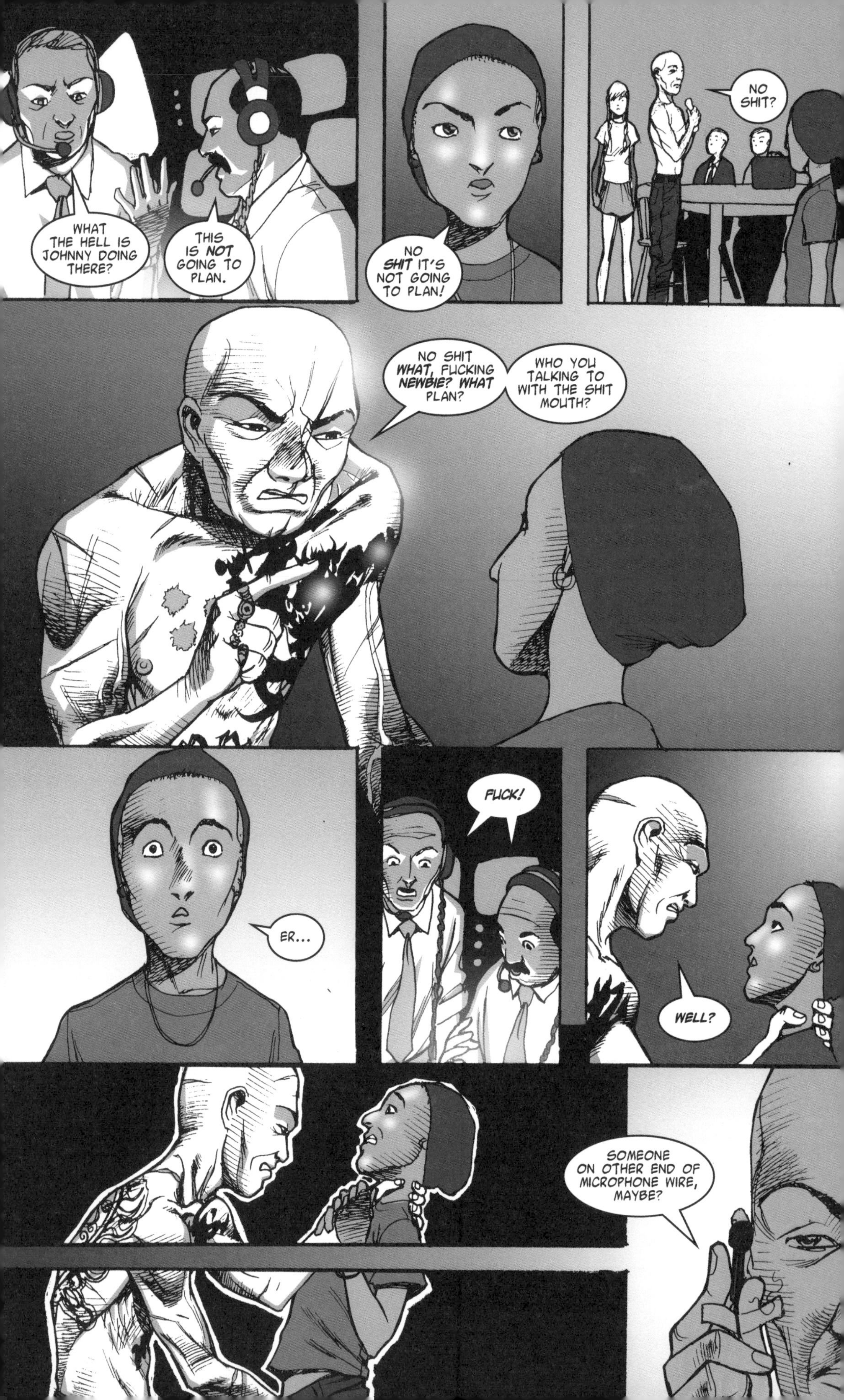
WHAT THE HELL IS JOHNNY DOING THERE?
THIS IS NOT GOING TO PLAN.
NO SHIT IT'S NOT GOING TO PLAN!
NO SHIT?
NO SHIT WHAT, FUCKING NEWBIE? WHAT PLAN?
WHO YOU TALKING TO WITH THE SHIT MOUTH?
ER...
FUCK!
WELL?
SOMEONE ON OTHER END OF MICROPHONE WIRE, MAYBE?

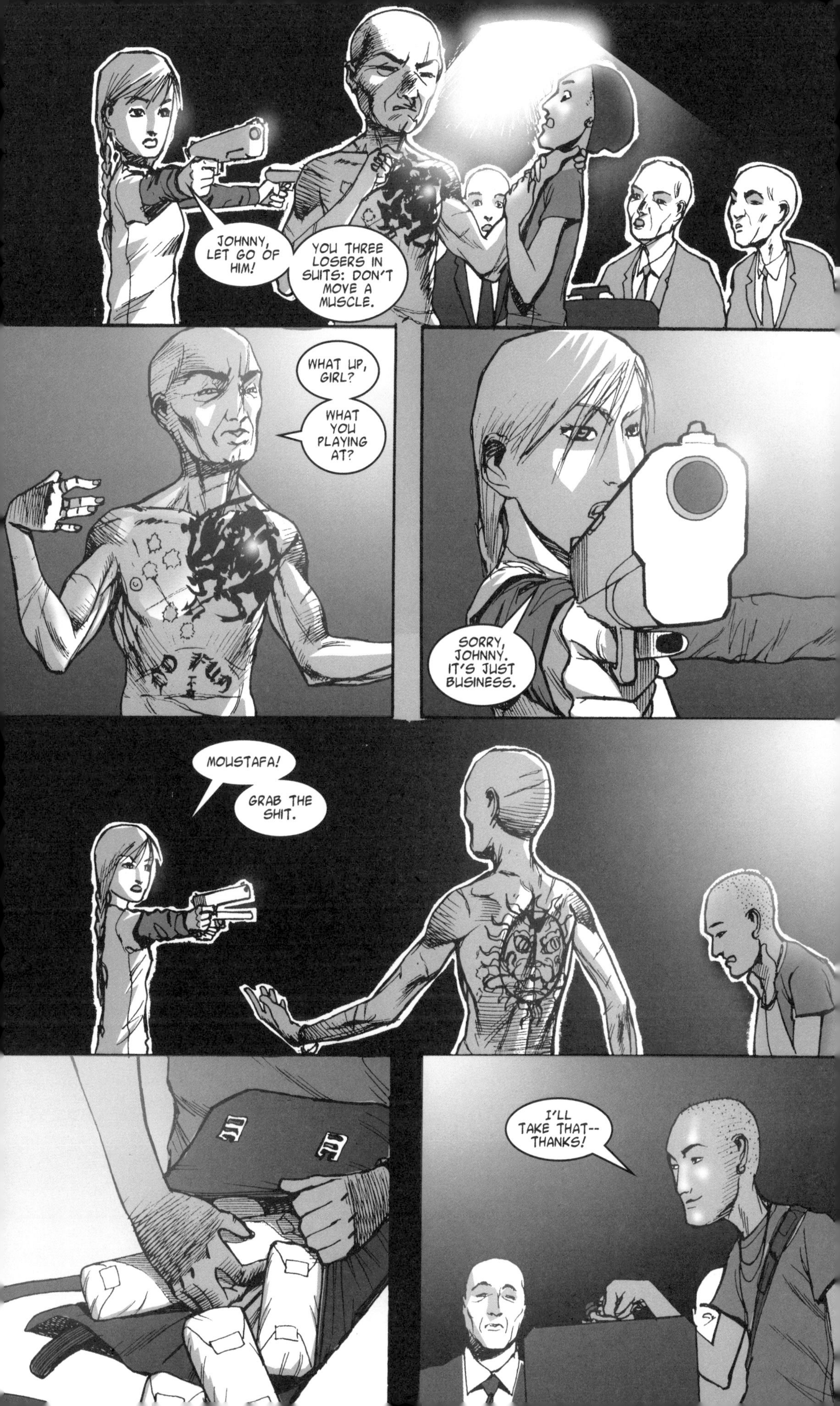
JOHNNY, LET GO OF HIM!
YOU THREE LOSERS IN SUITS: DON'T MOVE A MUSCLE.
WHAT UP, GIRL?
WHAT YOU PLAYING AT?
SORRY, JOHNNY. IT'S JUST BUSINESS.
MOUSTAFA!
GRAB THE SHIT.
I'LL TAKE THAT-- THANKS!

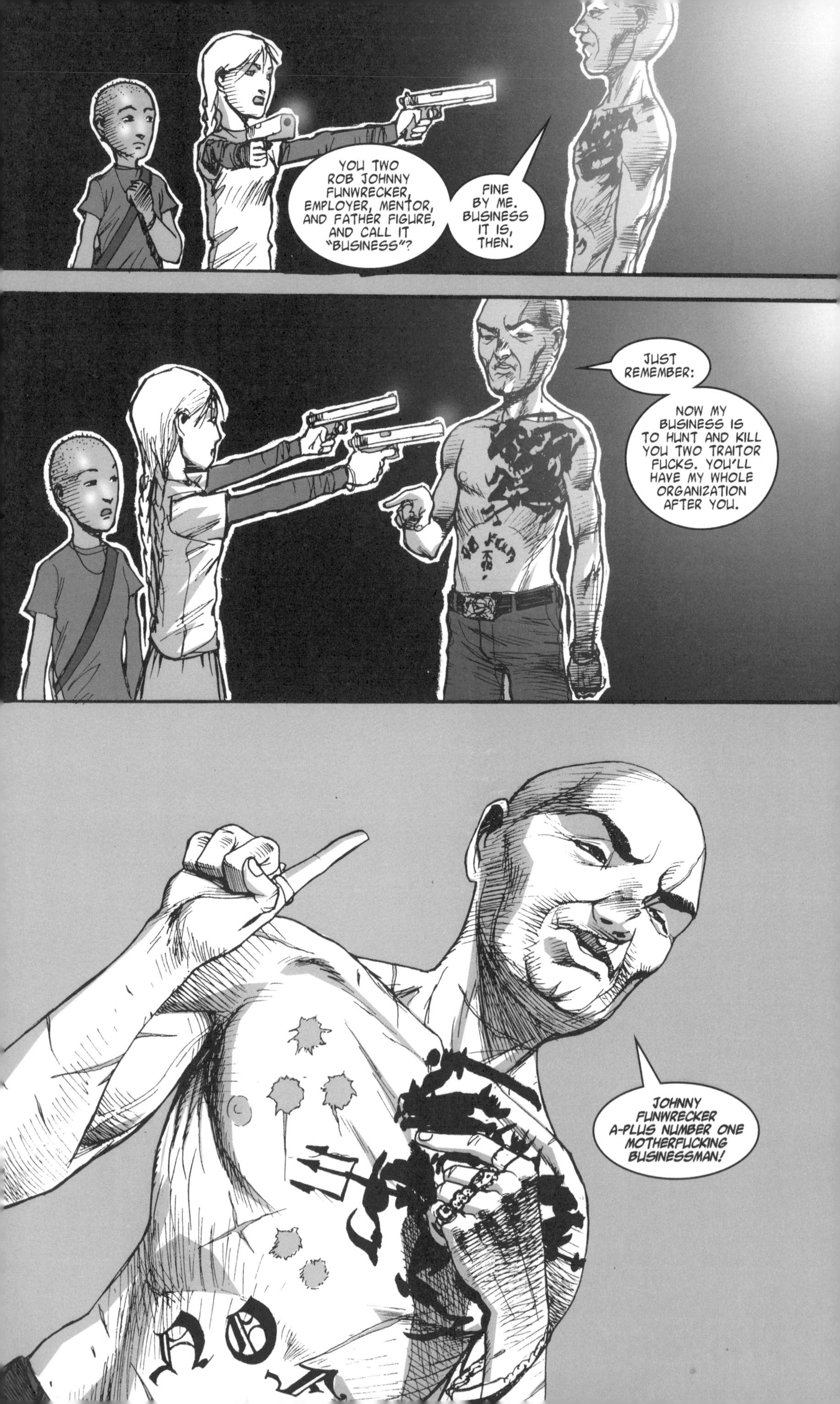
YOU TWO ROB JOHNNY FUNWRECKER, EMPLOYER, MENTOR, AND FATHER FIGURE, AND CALL IT "BUSINESS"?
FINE BY ME. BUSINESS IT IS, THEN.
JUST REMEMBER:
NOW MY BUSINESS IS TO HUNT AND KILL YOU TWO TRAITOR FUCKS. YOU'LL HAVE MY WHOLE ORGANIZATION AFTER YOU.
JOHNNY FUNWRECKER A-PLUS NUMBER ONE MOTHERFUCKING BUSINESSMAN!

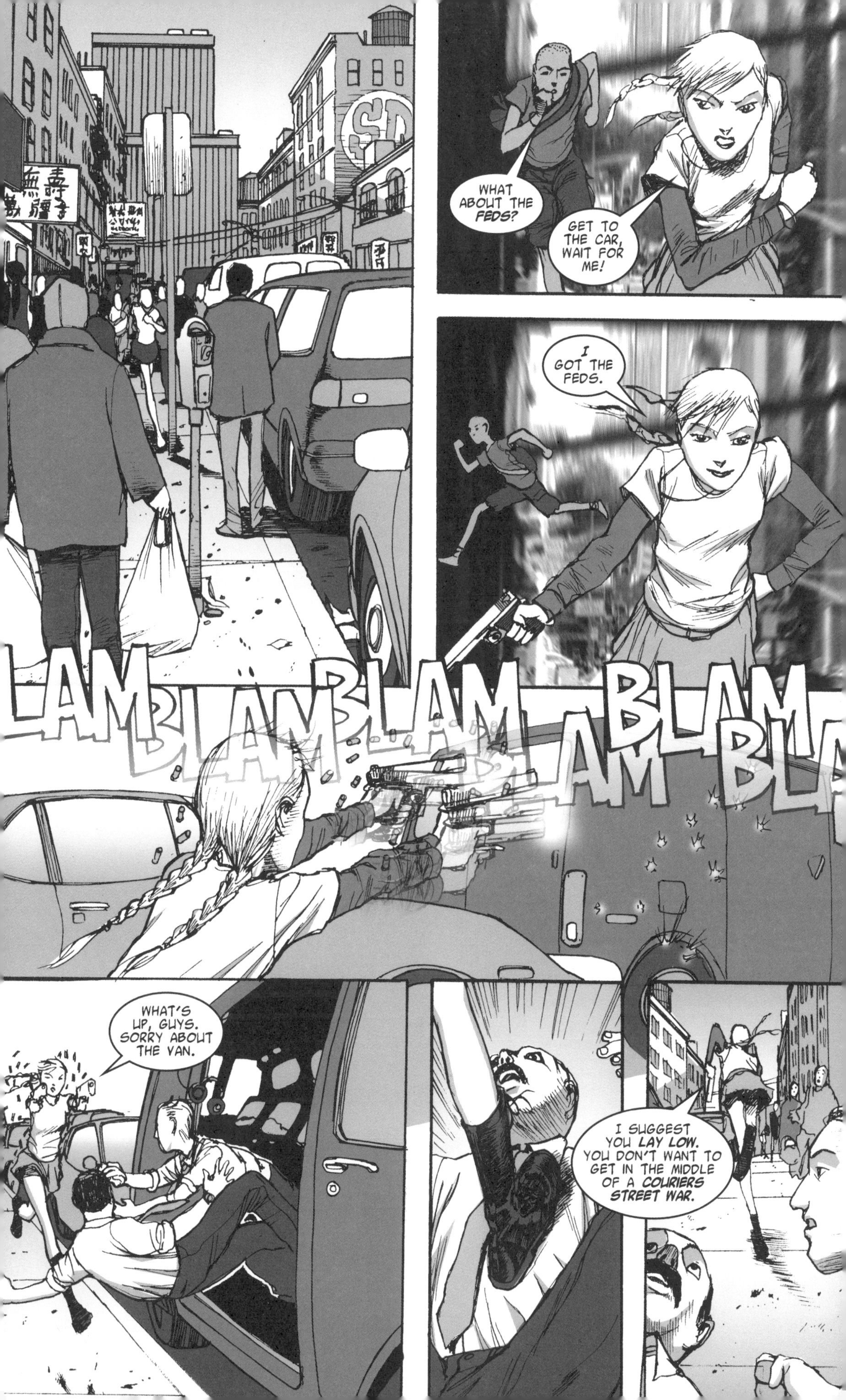
WHAT ABOUT THE FEDS?
GET TO THE CAR, WAIT FOR ME!
I GOT THE FEDS.
BLAM BLAM BLAM BLAM
BLAM BLAM BLAM BLAM
WHAT'S UP, GUYS. SORRY ABOUT THE VAN.
I SUGGEST YOU LAY LOW. YOU DON'T WANT TO GET IN THE MIDDLE OF A COURIERS STREET WAR.

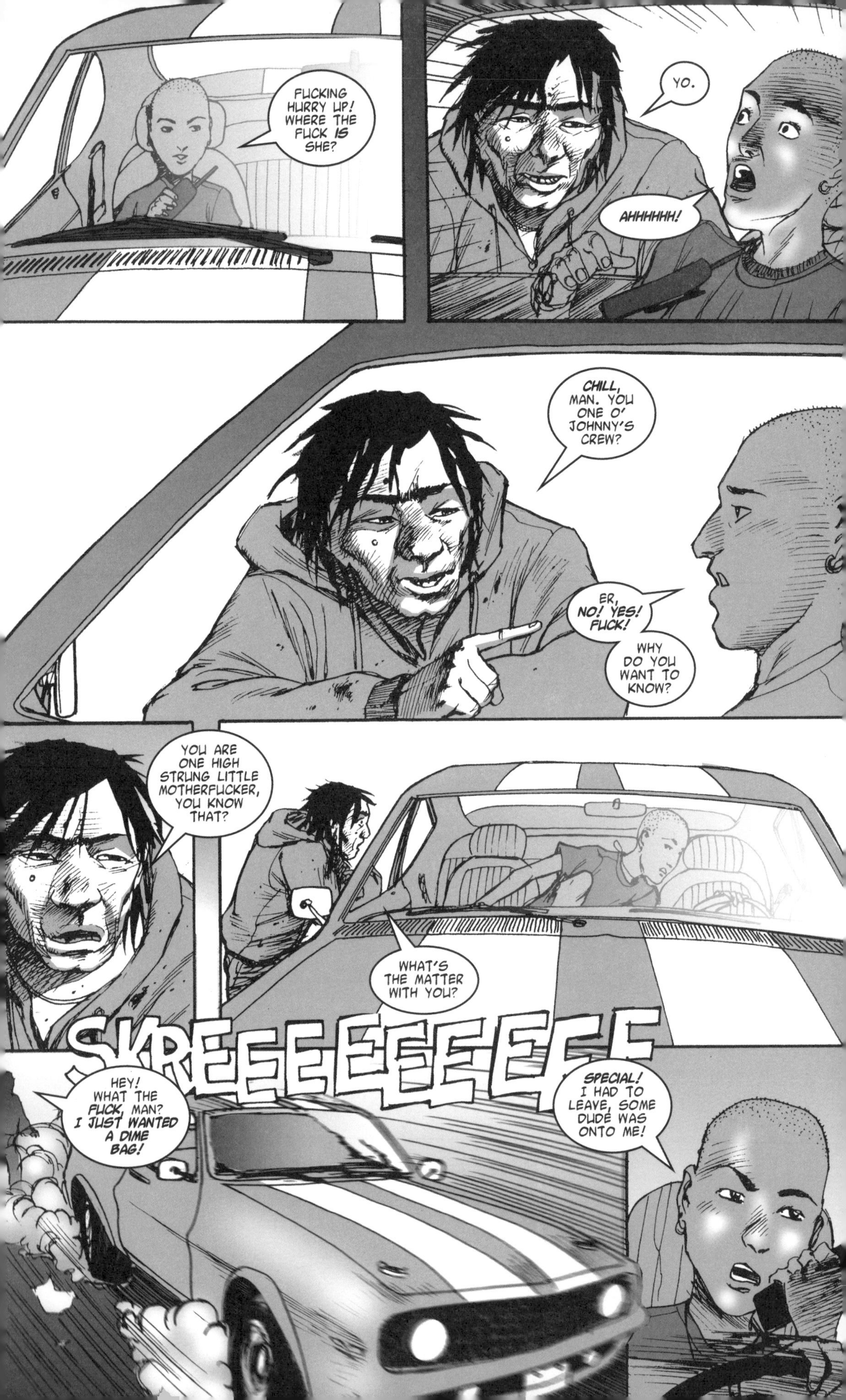
FUCKING HURRY UP! WHERE THE FUCK IS SHE?
YO.
AHHHHHH!
CHILL, MAN. YOU ONE O' JOHNNY'S CREW?
ER, NO! YES! FUCK!
WHY DO YOU WANT TO KNOW?
YOU ARE ONE HIGH STRUNG LITTLE MOTHERFUCKER, YOU KNOW THAT?
WHAT'S THE MATTER WITH YOU?
SKREEEEEEEEEE
HEY! WHAT THE FUCK, MAN? I JUST WANTED A DIME BAG!
SPECIAL! I HAD TO LEAVE, SOME DUDE WAS ONTO ME!

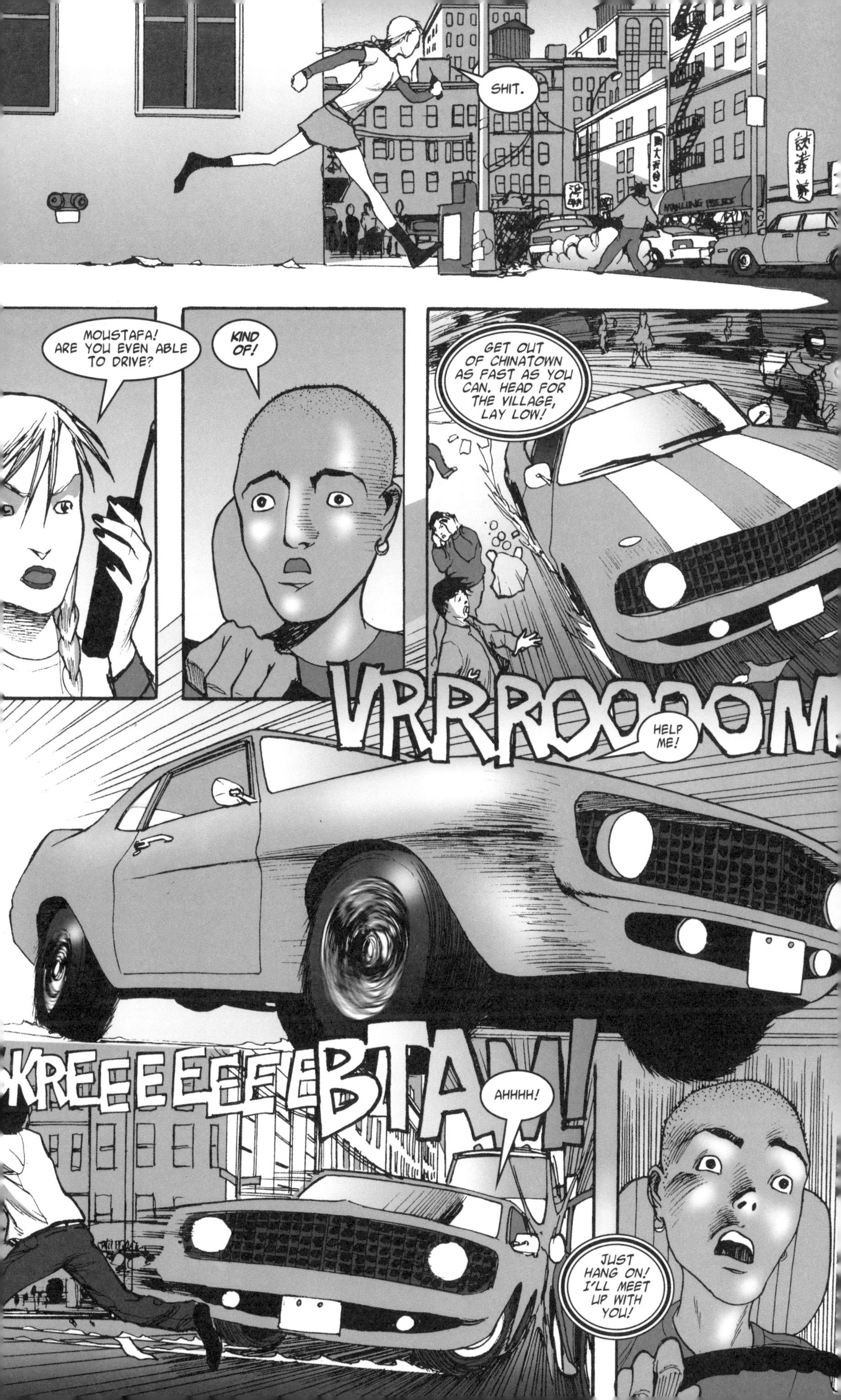
SHIT.
MOUSTAFA! ARE YOU EVEN ABLE TO DRIVE?
KIND OF!
GET OUT OF CHINATOWN AS FAST AS YOU CAN. HEAD FOR THE VILLAGE, LAY LOW!
VRRROOOOOM
HELP ME!
KREEEEEEEBTAM!
AHHHH!
JUST HANG ON! I'LL MEET UP WITH YOU!

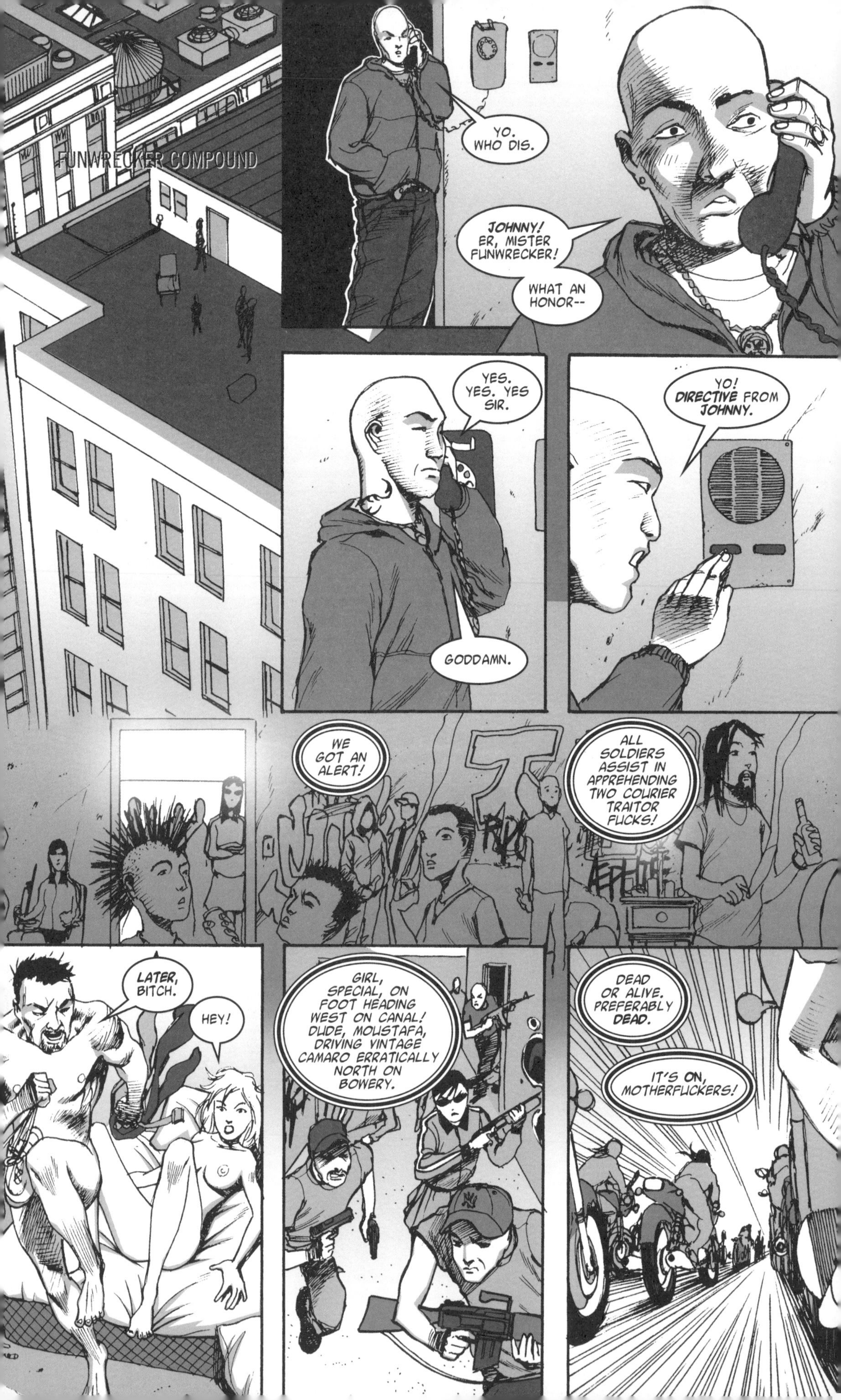
FUNWRECKER COMPOUND
YO. WHO DIS.
JOHNNY! ER, MISTER FUNWRECKER!
WHAT AN HONOR--
YES. YES. YES SIR.
GODDAMN.
YO! DIRECTIVE FROM JOHNNY.
WE GOT AN ALERT!
ALL SOLDIERS ASSIST IN APPREHENDING TWO COURIER TRAITOR FUCKS!
LATER, BITCH.
HEY!
GIRL, SPECIAL, ON FOOT HEADING WEST ON CANAL! DUDE, MOUSTAFA, DRIVING VINTAGE CAMARO ERRATICALLY NORTH ON BOWERY.
DEAD OR ALIVE. PREFERABLY DEAD.
IT'S ON, MOTHERFUCKERS!

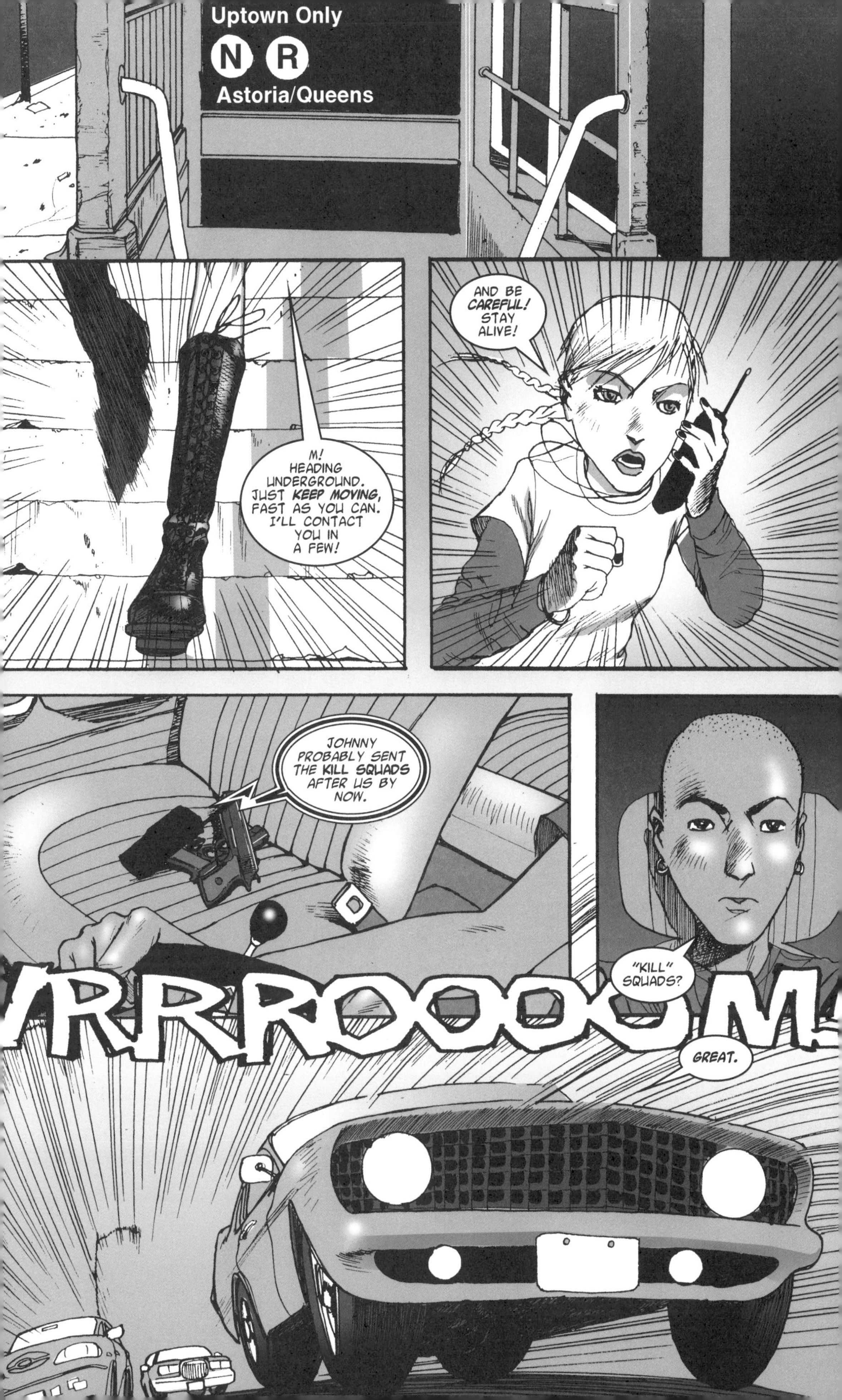
Uptown Only
N R
Astoria/Queens
M! HEADING UNDERGROUND. JUST KEEP MOVING, FAST AS YOU CAN. I'LL CONTACT YOU IN A FEW!
AND BE CAREFUL! STAY ALIVE!
JOHNNY PROBABLY SENT THE KILL SQUADS AFTER US BY NOW.
"KILL" SQUADS?
GREAT.

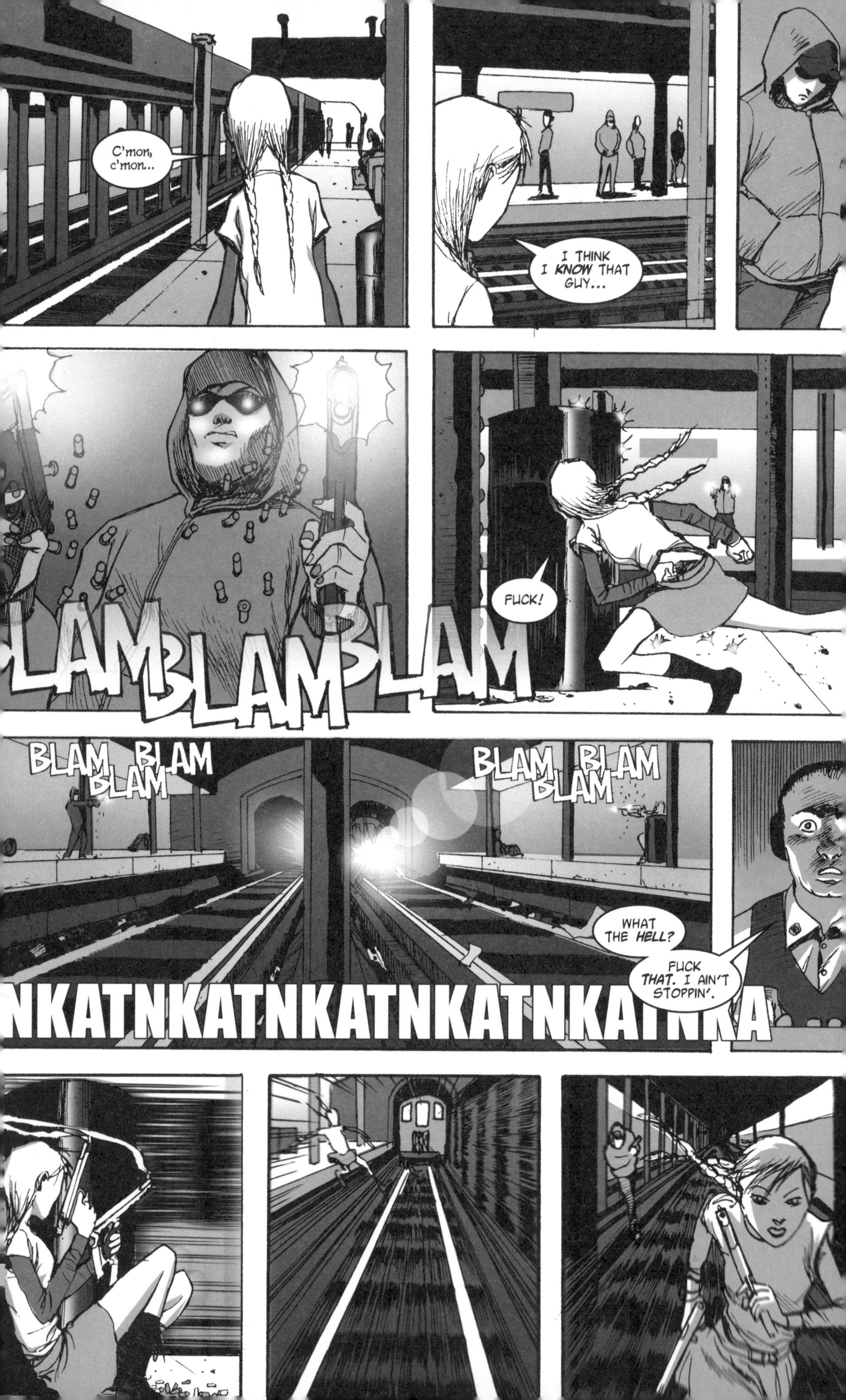
C'mon, c'mon...
I THINK I KNOW THAT GUY...
BLAMBLAMBLAM
FUCK!
BLAM BLAM BLAM
BLAM BLAM BLAM
WHAT THE HELL?
FUCK THAT. I AIN'T STOPPIN'.
NKATNKATNKATNKATNKATNKA

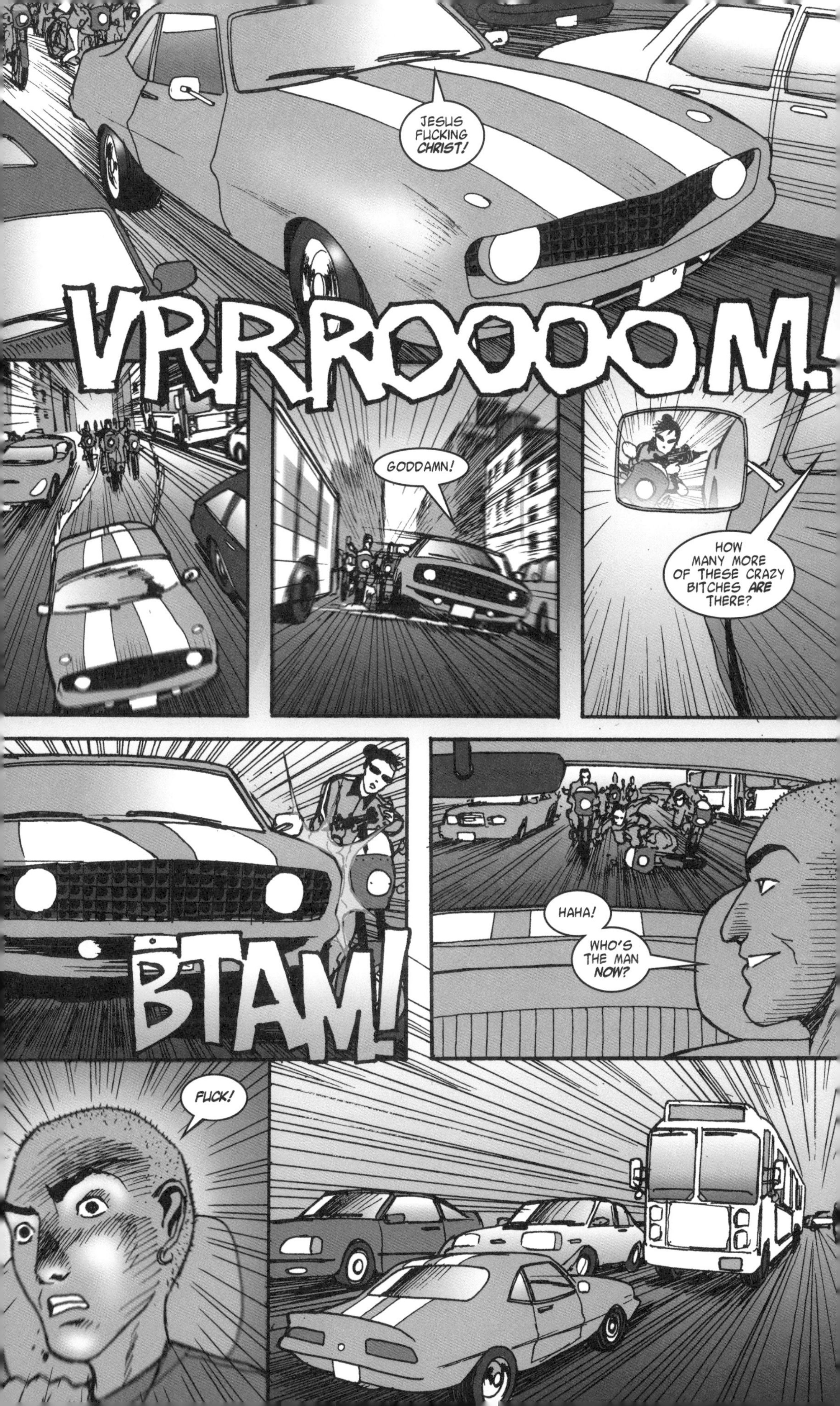

JESUS FUCKING CHRIST!
VRRROOOOM!
GODDAMN!
HOW MANY MORE OF THESE CRAZY BITCHES ARE THERE?
BTAM!
HAHA!
WHO'S THE MAN NOW?
FUCK!

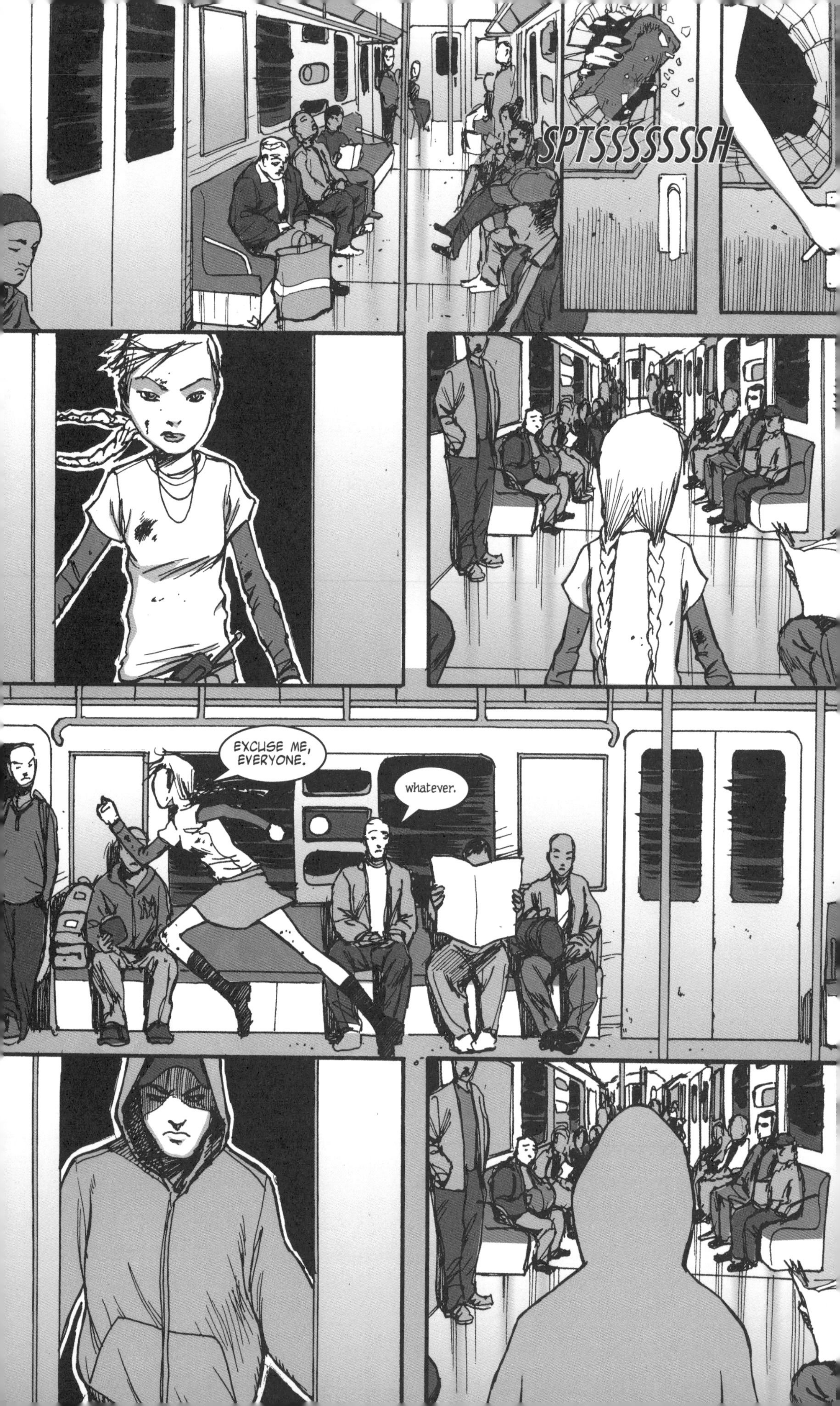
SPTSSSSSSSH
EXCUSE ME, EVERYONE.
whatever.

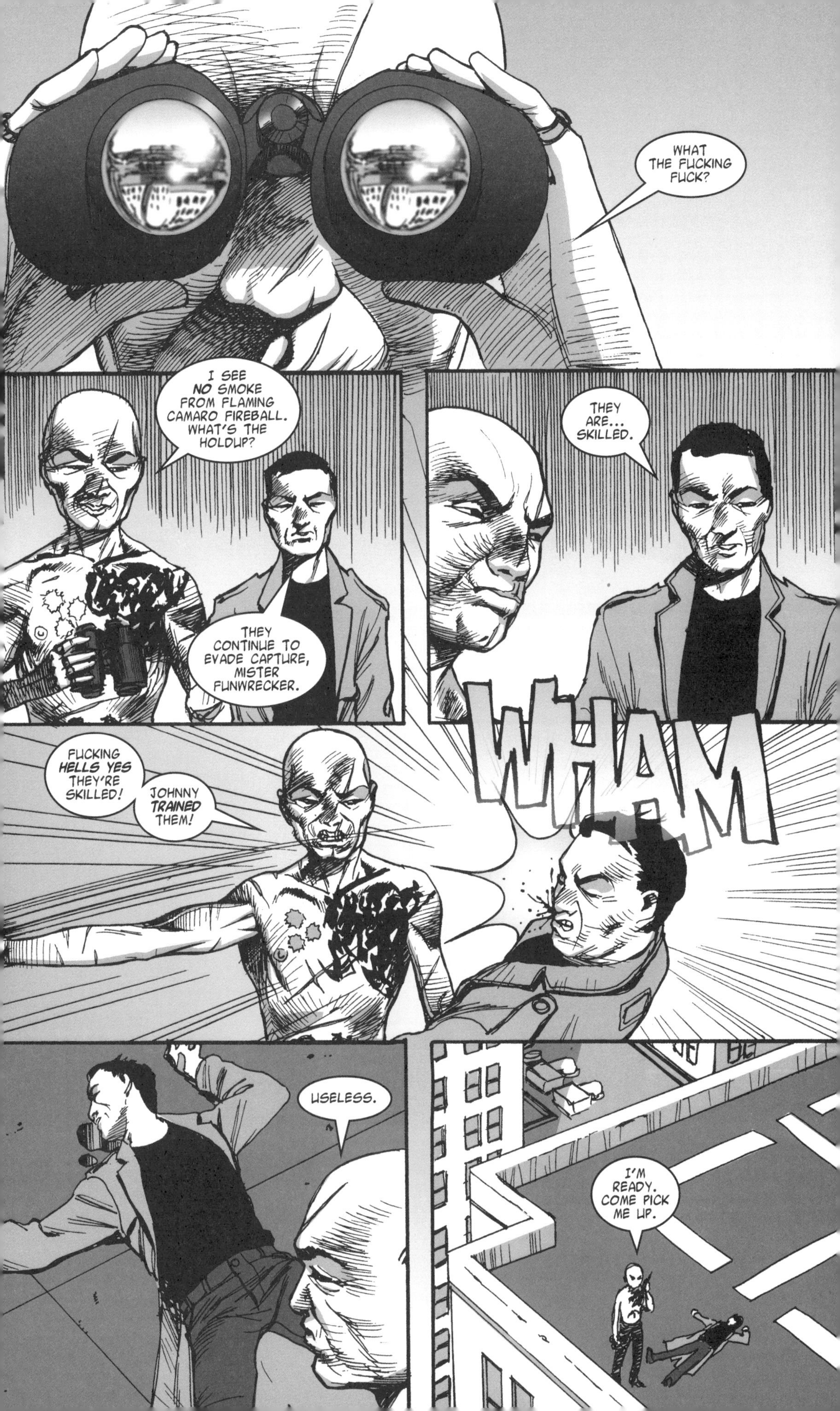
WHAT THE FUCKING FUCK?
I SEE NO SMOKE FROM FLAMING CAMARO FIREBALL. WHAT'S THE HOLDUP?
THEY CONTINUE TO EVADE CAPTURE, MISTER FUNWRECKER.
THEY ARE... SKILLED.
WHAM
FUCKING HELLS YES THEY'RE SKILLED!
JOHNNY TRAINED THEM!
USELESS.
I'M READY. COME PICK ME UP.

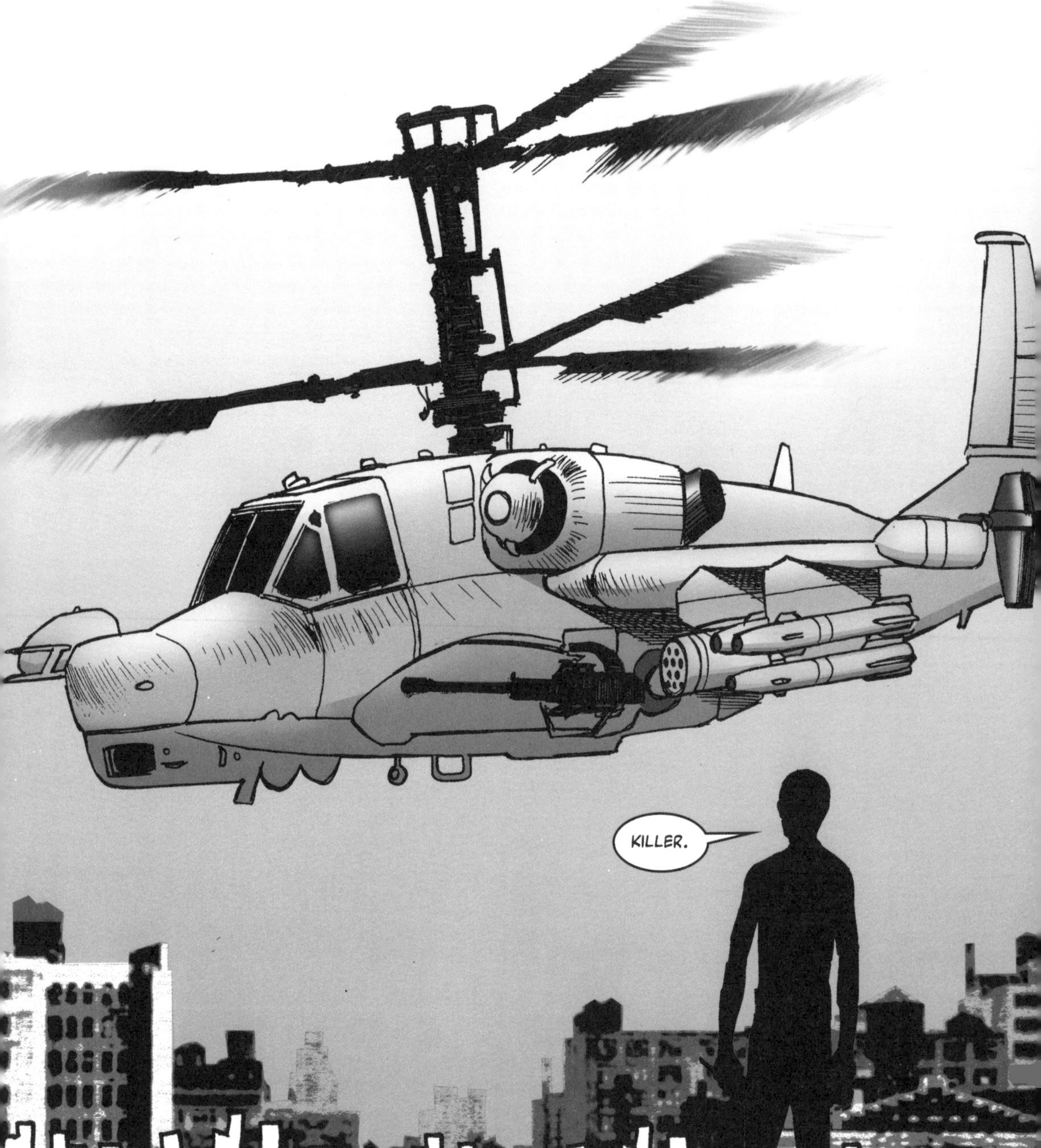
KILLER.
WHUPWHUPWHUPWHUPWHUPW

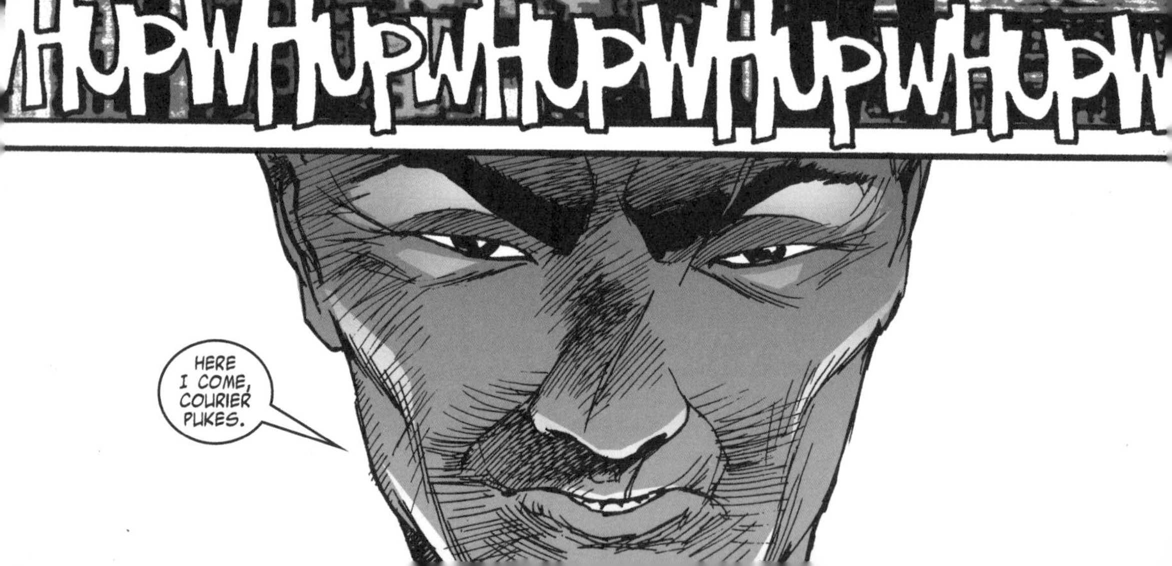
HERE I COME, COURIER PUKES.

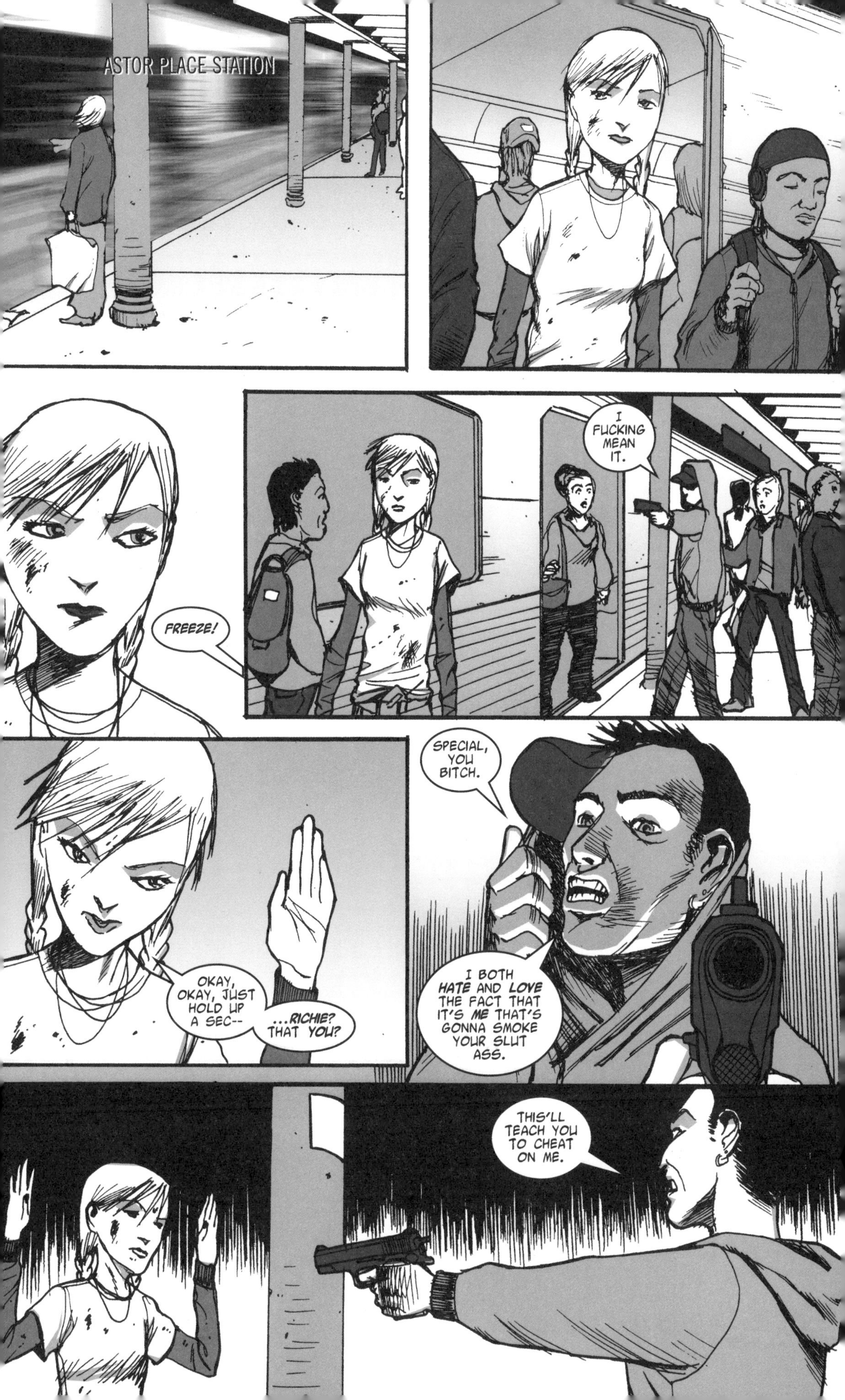
ASTOR PLACE STATION
FREEZE!
I FUCKING MEAN IT.
OKAY, OKAY, JUST HOLD UP A SEC--
...RICHIE? THAT YOU?
SPECIAL, YOU BITCH.
I BOTH HATE AND LOVE THE FACT THAT IT'S ME THAT'S GONNA SMOKE YOUR SLUT ASS.
THIS'LL TEACH YOU TO CHEAT ON ME.

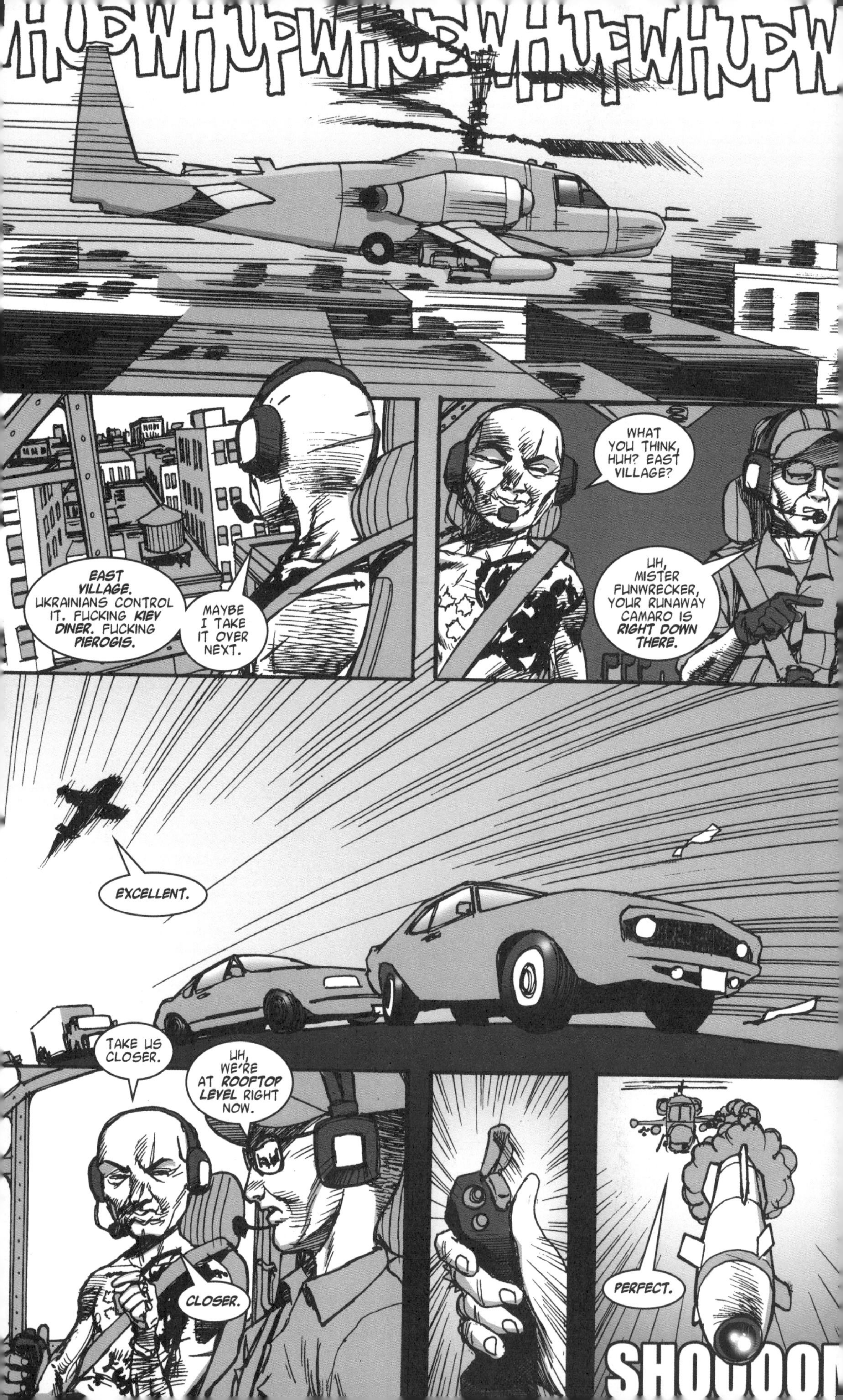

WHUPWHUPWHUPWHUPWHUPW
EAST VILLAGE. UKRAINIANS CONTROL IT. FUCKING KIEV DINER. FUCKING PIEROGIS.
MAYBE I TAKE IT OVER NEXT.
WHAT YOU THINK, HUH? EAST VILLAGE?
UH, MISTER FUNWRECKER, YOUR RUNAWAY CAMARO IS RIGHT DOWN THERE.
EXCELLENT.
TAKE US CLOSER.
UH, WE'RE AT ROOFTOP LEVEL RIGHT NOW.
CLOSER.
PERFECT.
SHOOOOO

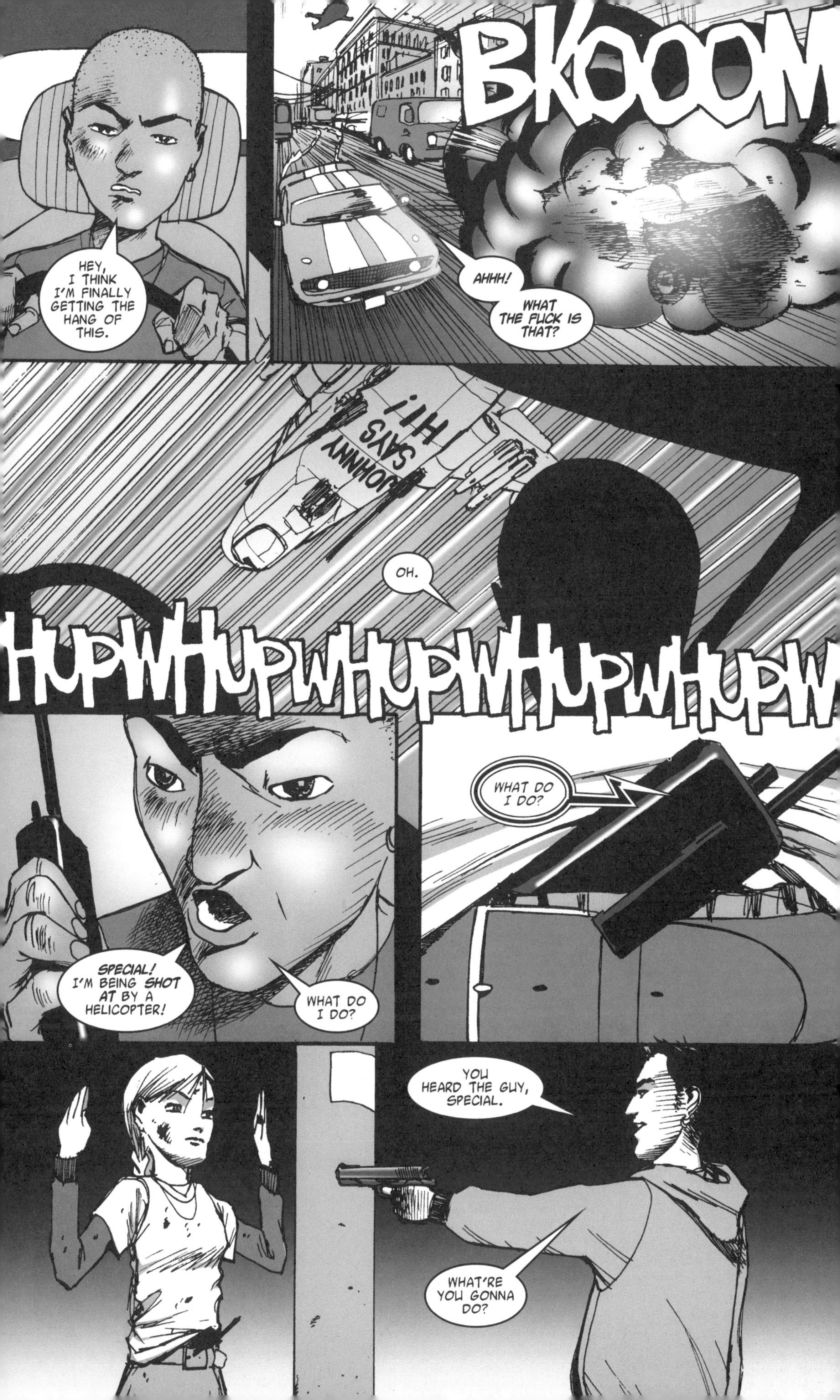
HEY, I THINK I'M FINALLY GETTING THE HANG OF THIS.
BKOOOM
AHHH! WHAT THE FUCK IS THAT?
JOHNNY SAYS HI!
OH.
HUPWHUPWHUPWHUPWHUPW
SPECIAL! I'M BEING SHOT AT BY A HELICOPTER!
WHAT DO I DO?
WHAT DO I DO?
YOU HEARD THE GUY, SPECIAL.
WHAT'RE YOU GONNA DO?

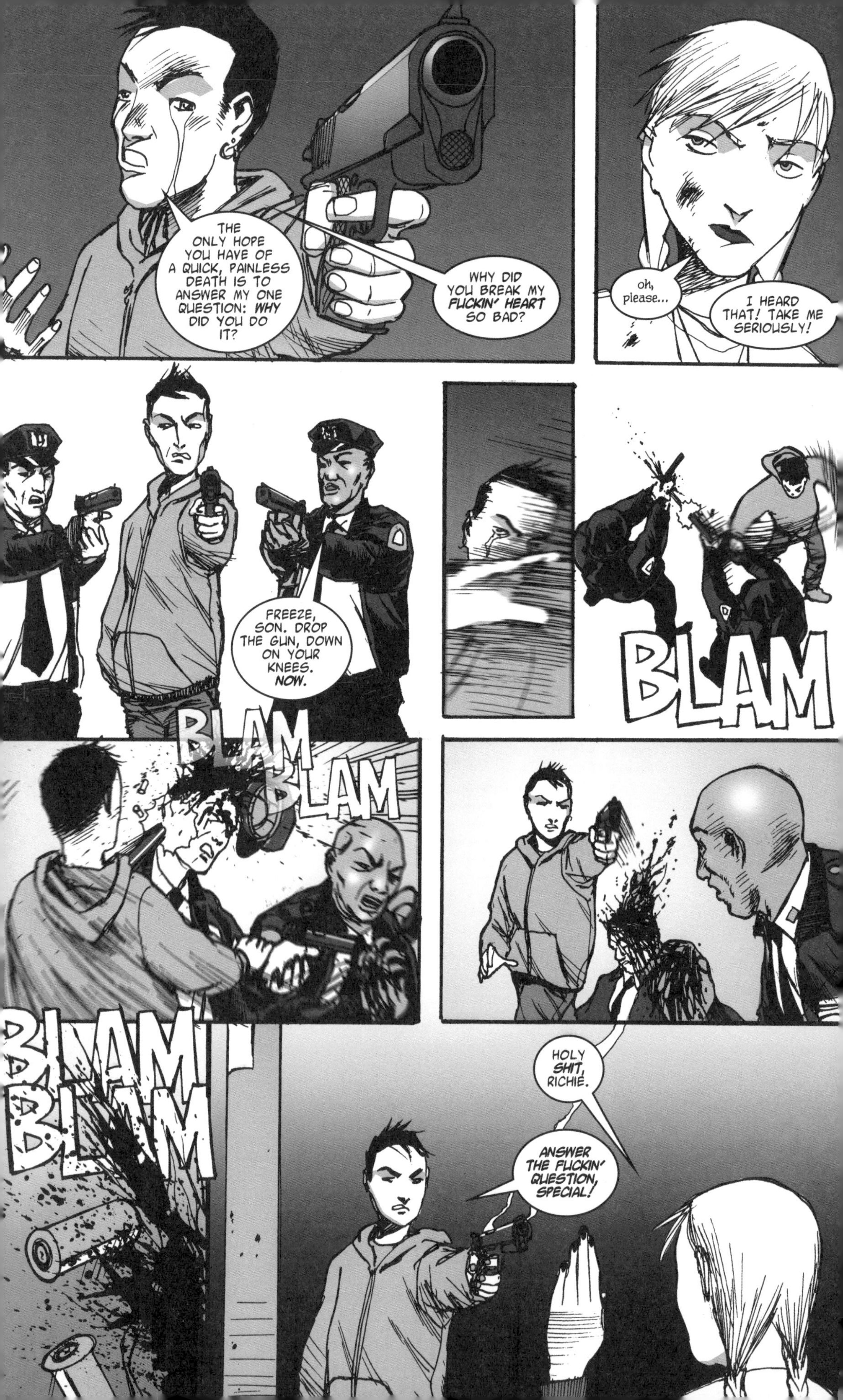
THE ONLY HOPE YOU HAVE OF A QUICK, PAINLESS DEATH IS TO ANSWER MY ONE QUESTION: WHY DID YOU DO IT?
WHY DID YOU BREAK MY FUCKIN' HEART SO BAD?
oh, please...
I HEARD THAT! TAKE ME SERIOUSLY!
FREEZE, SON. DROP THE GUN, DOWN ON YOUR KNEES. NOW.
BLAM
BLAM
BLAM
BLAM
BLAM
HOLY SHIT, RICHIE.
ANSWER THE FUCKIN' QUESTION, SPECIAL!

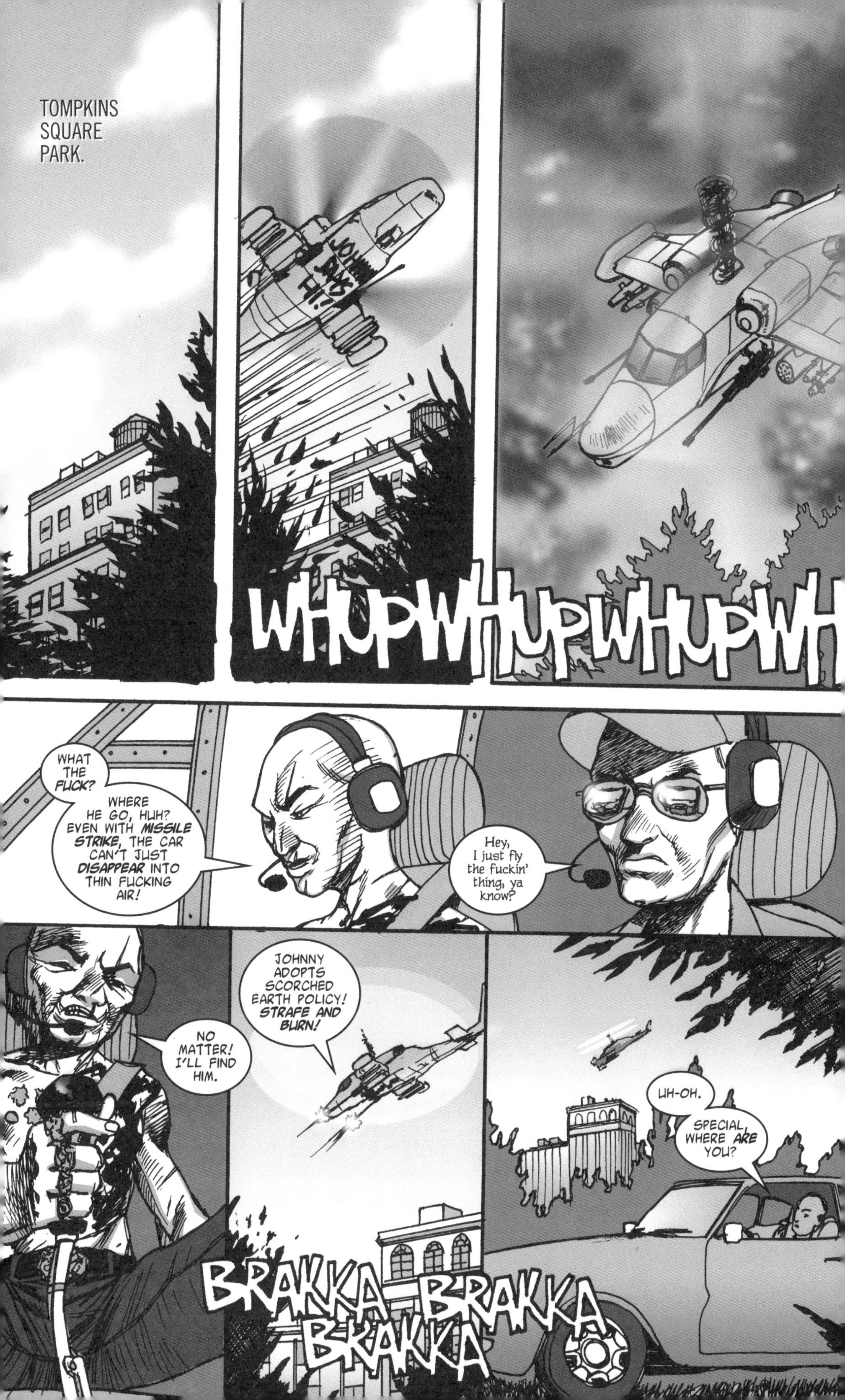
TOMPKINS SQUARE PARK.
WHUPWHUPWHUPWH
WHAT THE *FUCK?*
WHERE HE GO, HUH? EVEN WITH ***MISSILE STRIKE,*** THE CAR CAN'T JUST ***DISAPPEAR*** INTO THIN FUCKING AIR!
Hey, I just fly the fuckin' thing, ya know?
NO MATTER! I'LL FIND HIM.
JOHNNY ADOPTS SCORCHED EARTH POLICY! ***STRAFE AND BURN!***
UH-OH.
SPECIAL, WHERE ***ARE*** YOU?
BRAKKA BRAKKA BRAKKA

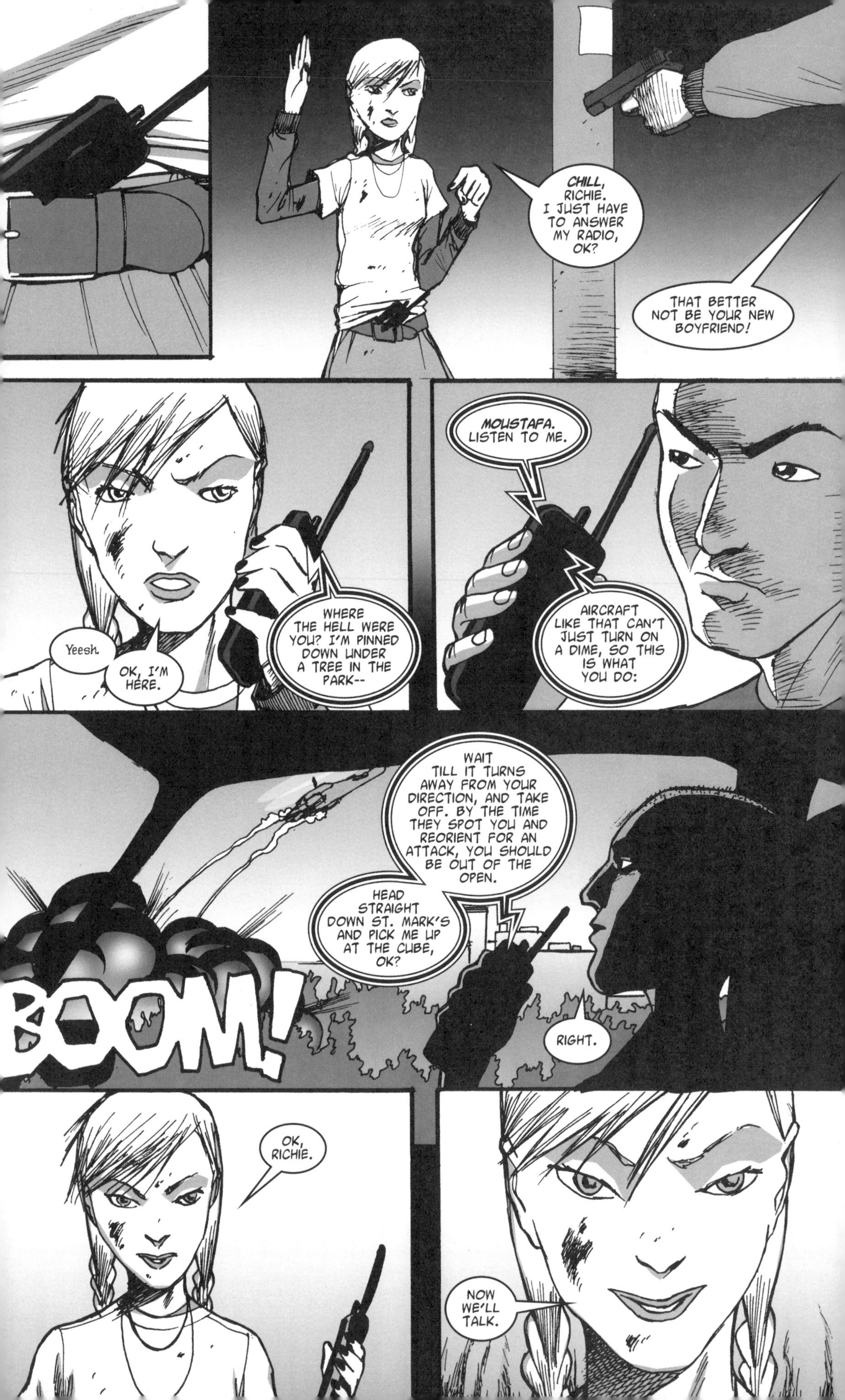

CHILL, RICHIE. I JUST HAVE TO ANSWER MY RADIO, OK?
THAT BETTER NOT BE YOUR NEW BOYFRIEND!
Yeesh.
OK, I'M HERE.
WHERE THE HELL WERE YOU? I'M PINNED DOWN UNDER A TREE IN THE PARK--
MOUSTAFA. LISTEN TO ME.
AIRCRAFT LIKE THAT CAN'T JUST TURN ON A DIME, SO THIS IS WHAT YOU DO:
WAIT TILL IT TURNS AWAY FROM YOUR DIRECTION, AND TAKE OFF. BY THE TIME THEY SPOT YOU AND REORIENT FOR AN ATTACK, YOU SHOULD BE OUT OF THE OPEN.
HEAD STRAIGHT DOWN ST. MARK'S AND PICK ME UP AT THE CUBE, OK?
BOOM!
RIGHT.
OK, RICHIE.
NOW WE'LL TALK.

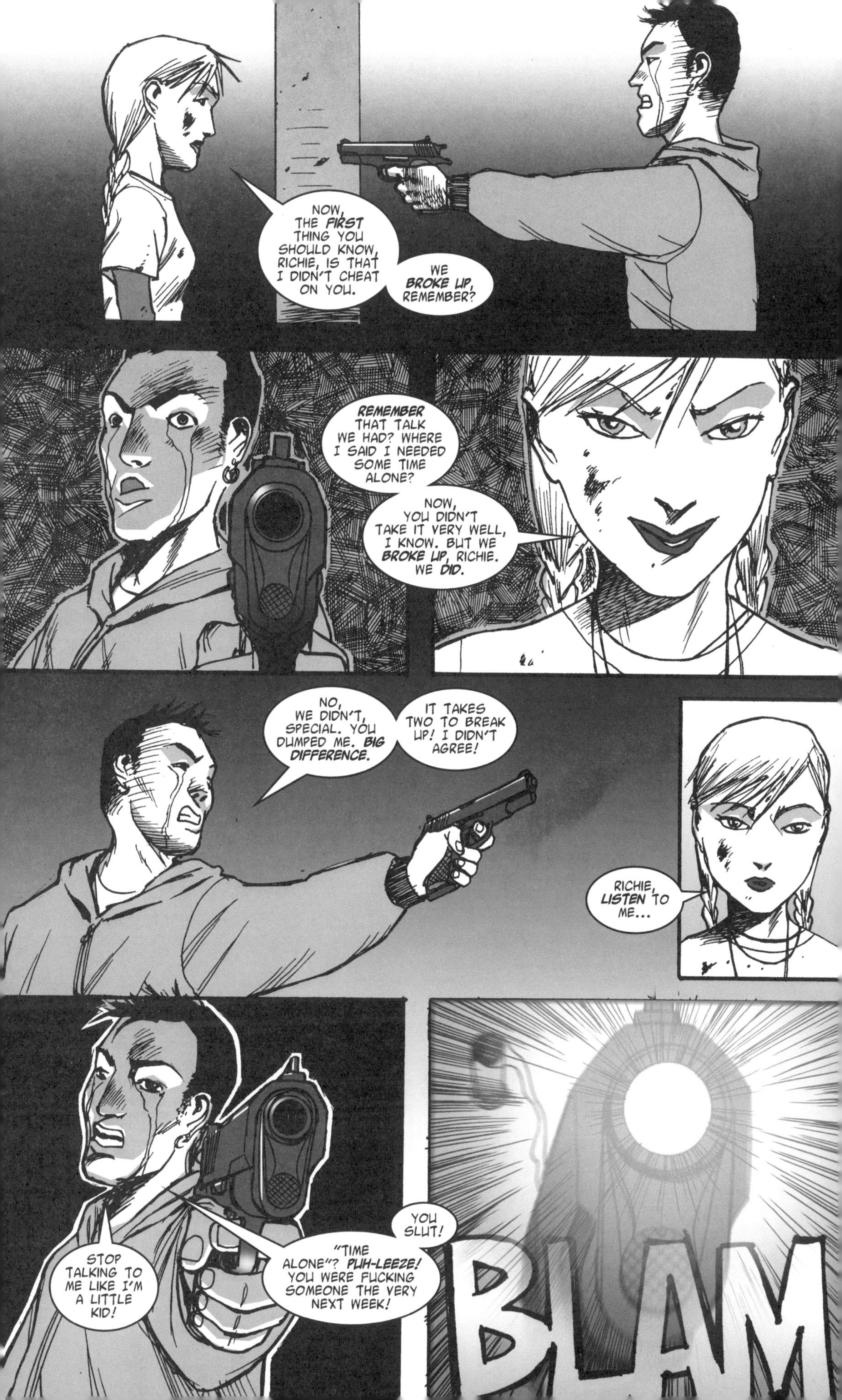
NOW, THE FIRST THING YOU SHOULD KNOW, RICHIE, IS THAT I DIDN'T CHEAT ON YOU.
WE BROKE UP, REMEMBER?
REMEMBER THAT TALK WE HAD? WHERE I SAID I NEEDED SOME TIME ALONE?
NOW, YOU DIDN'T TAKE IT VERY WELL, I KNOW. BUT WE BROKE UP, RICHIE. WE DID.
NO, WE DIDN'T, SPECIAL. YOU DUMPED ME. BIG DIFFERENCE.
IT TAKES TWO TO BREAK UP! I DIDN'T AGREE!
RICHIE, LISTEN TO ME...
STOP TALKING TO ME LIKE I'M A LITTLE KID!
"TIME ALONE"? PUH-LEEZE! YOU WERE FUCKING SOMEONE THE VERY NEXT WEEK!
YOU SLUT!
BLAM

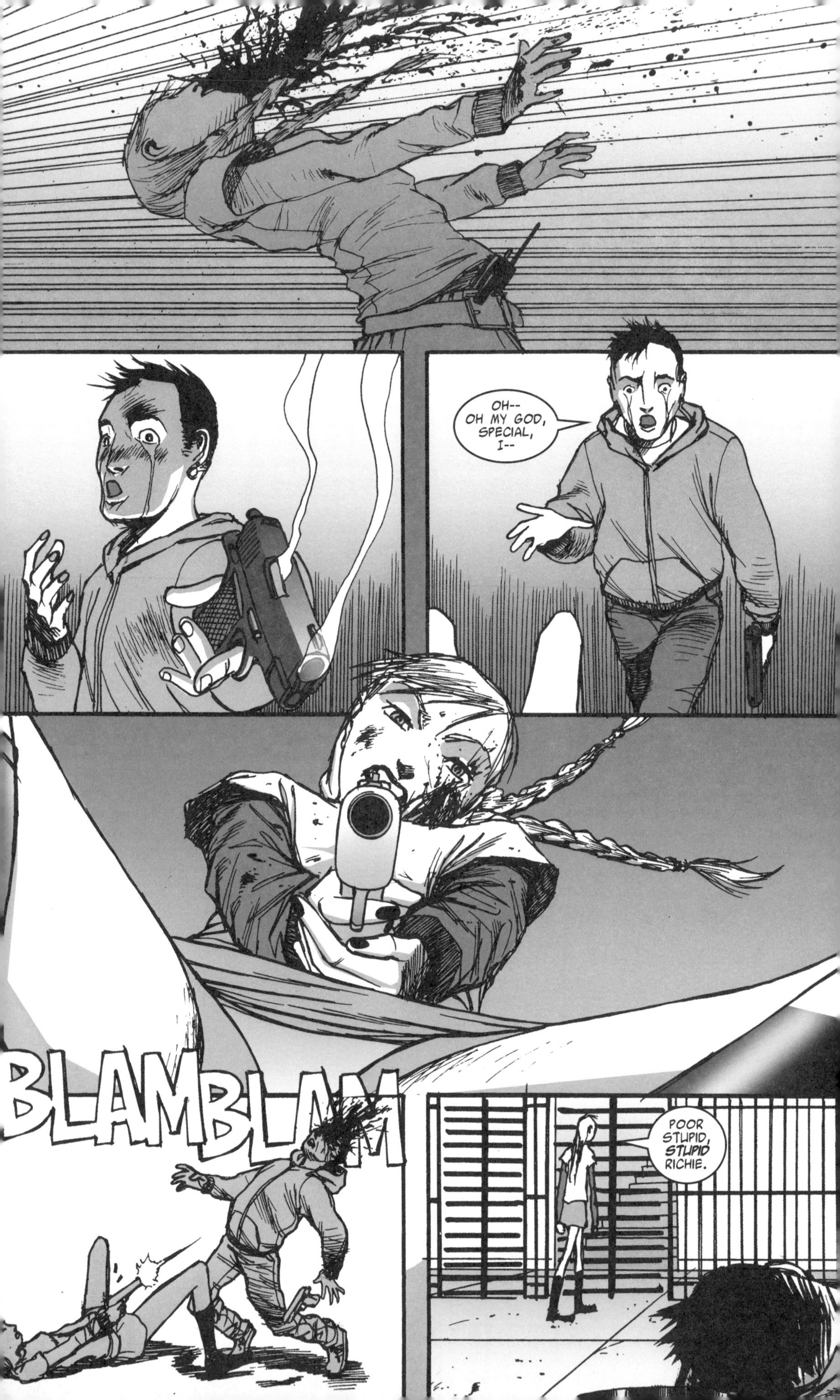

OH-- OH MY GOD, SPECIAL, I--
BLAMBLAM
POOR STUPID, STUPID RICHIE.

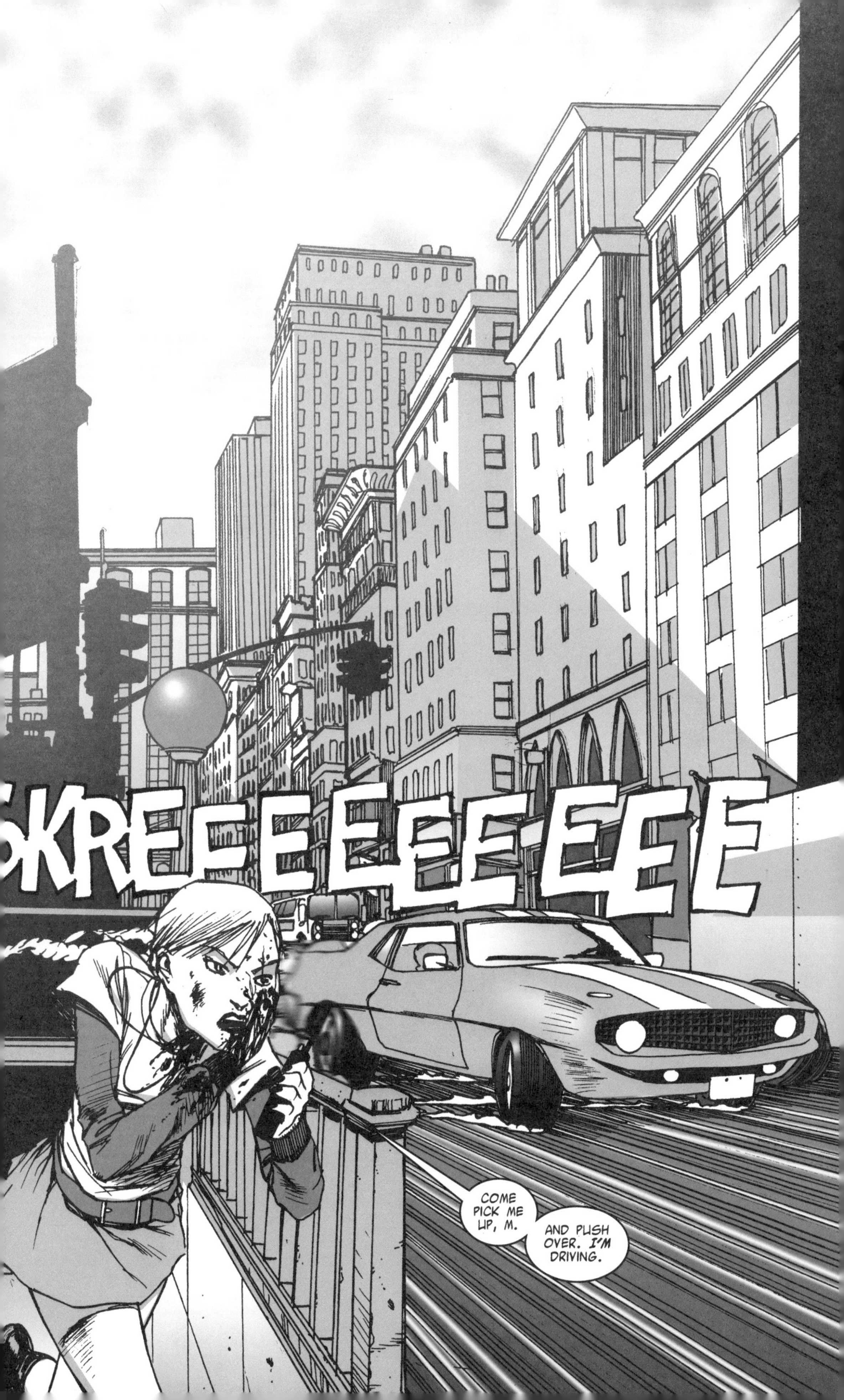
SKREEEEEEEEE
COME PICK ME UP, M.
AND PUSH OVER. I'M DRIVING.

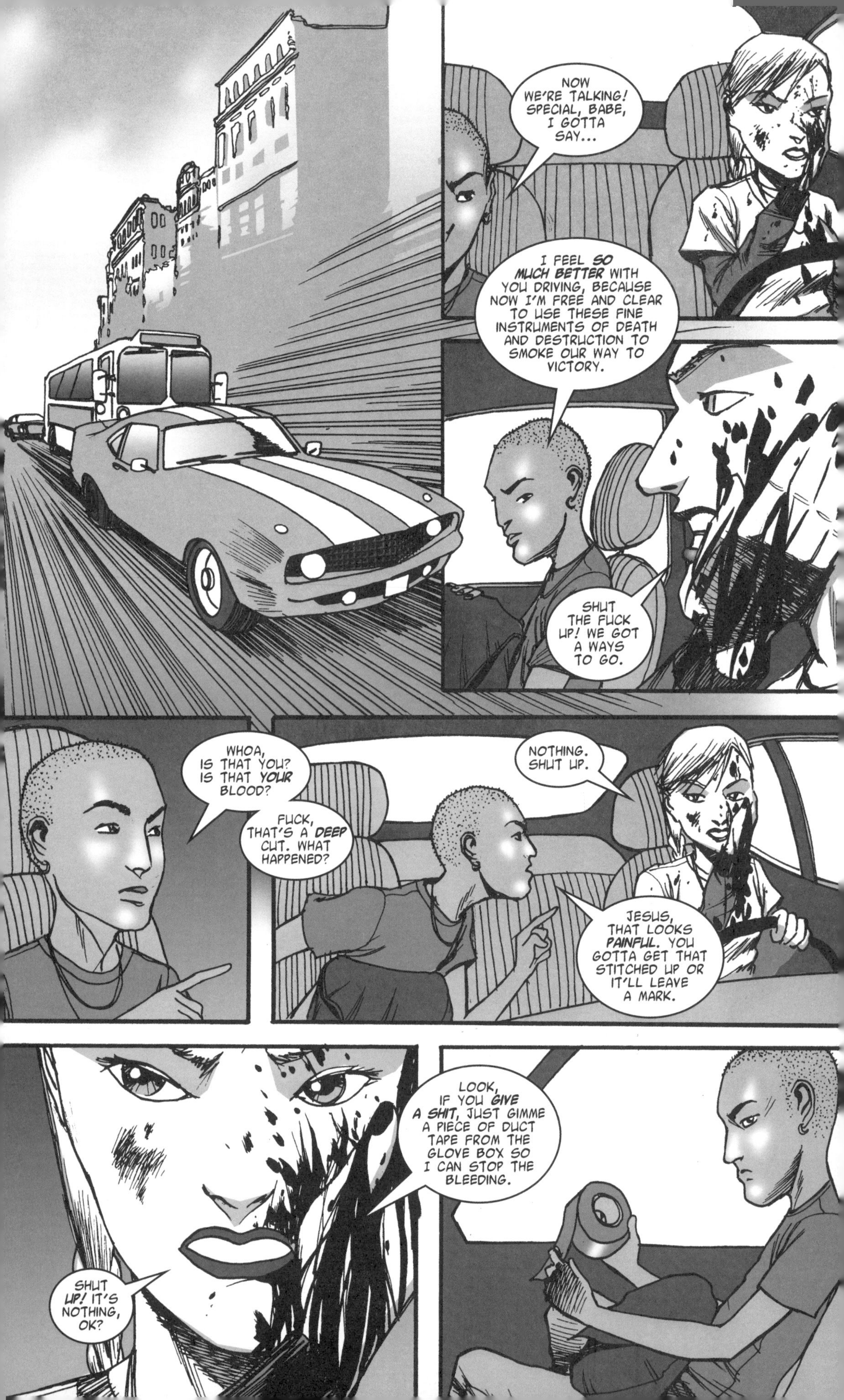
NOW WE'RE TALKING! SPECIAL, BABE, I GOTTA SAY...
I FEEL SO MUCH BETTER WITH YOU DRIVING, BECAUSE NOW I'M FREE AND CLEAR TO USE THESE FINE INSTRUMENTS OF DEATH AND DESTRUCTION TO SMOKE OUR WAY TO VICTORY.
SHUT THE FUCK UP! WE GOT A WAYS TO GO.
WHOA, IS THAT YOU? IS THAT YOUR BLOOD?
FUCK, THAT'S A DEEP CUT. WHAT HAPPENED?
NOTHING. SHUT UP.
JESUS, THAT LOOKS PAINFUL. YOU GOTTA GET THAT STITCHED UP OR IT'LL LEAVE A MARK.
SHUT UP! IT'S NOTHING, OK?
LOOK, IF YOU GIVE A SHIT, JUST GIMME A PIECE OF DUCT TAPE FROM THE GLOVE BOX SO I CAN STOP THE BLEEDING.

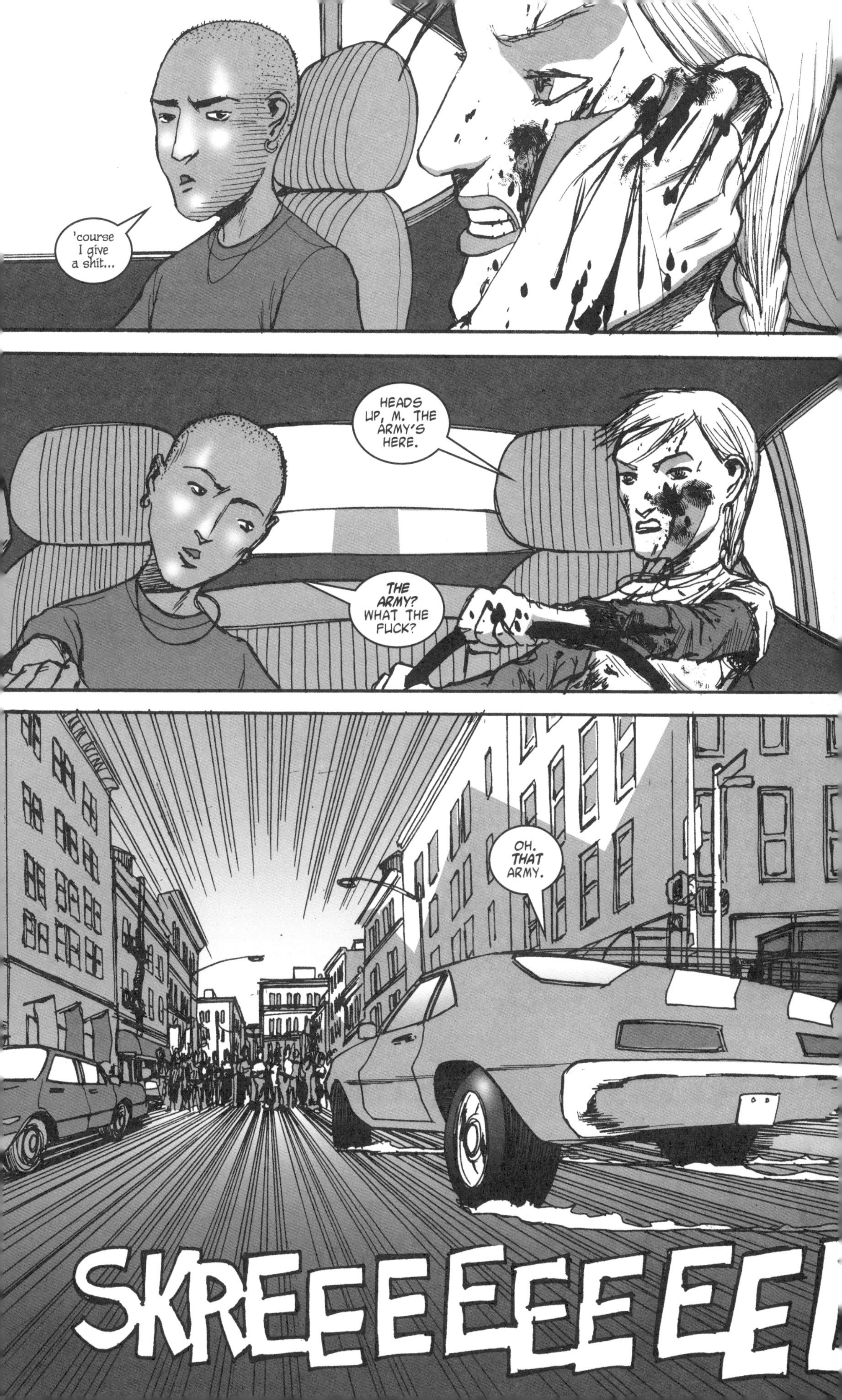
'course I give a shit...
HEADS UP, M. THE ARMY'S HERE.
THE ARMY? WHAT THE FUCK?
OH. THAT ARMY.
SKREEEEEEEEEEL

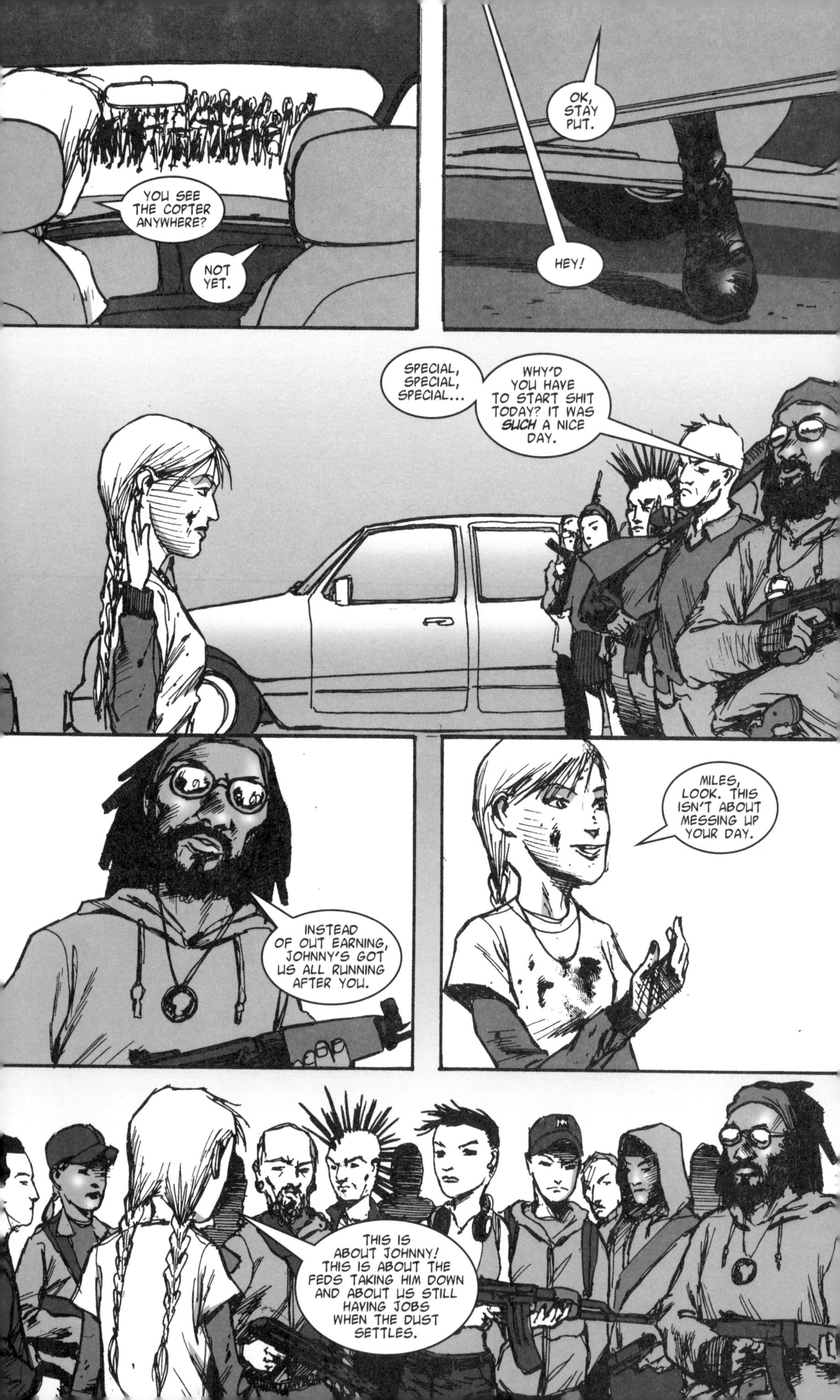
YOU SEE THE COPTER ANYWHERE?
NOT YET.
OK, STAY PUT.
HEY!
SPECIAL, SPECIAL, SPECIAL...
WHY'D YOU HAVE TO START SHIT TODAY? IT WAS SUCH A NICE DAY.
INSTEAD OF OUT EARNING, JOHNNY'S GOT US ALL RUNNING AFTER YOU.
MILES, LOOK. THIS ISN'T ABOUT MESSING UP YOUR DAY.
THIS IS ABOUT JOHNNY! THIS IS ABOUT THE FEDS TAKING HIM DOWN AND ABOUT US STILL HAVING JOBS WHEN THE DUST SETTLES.

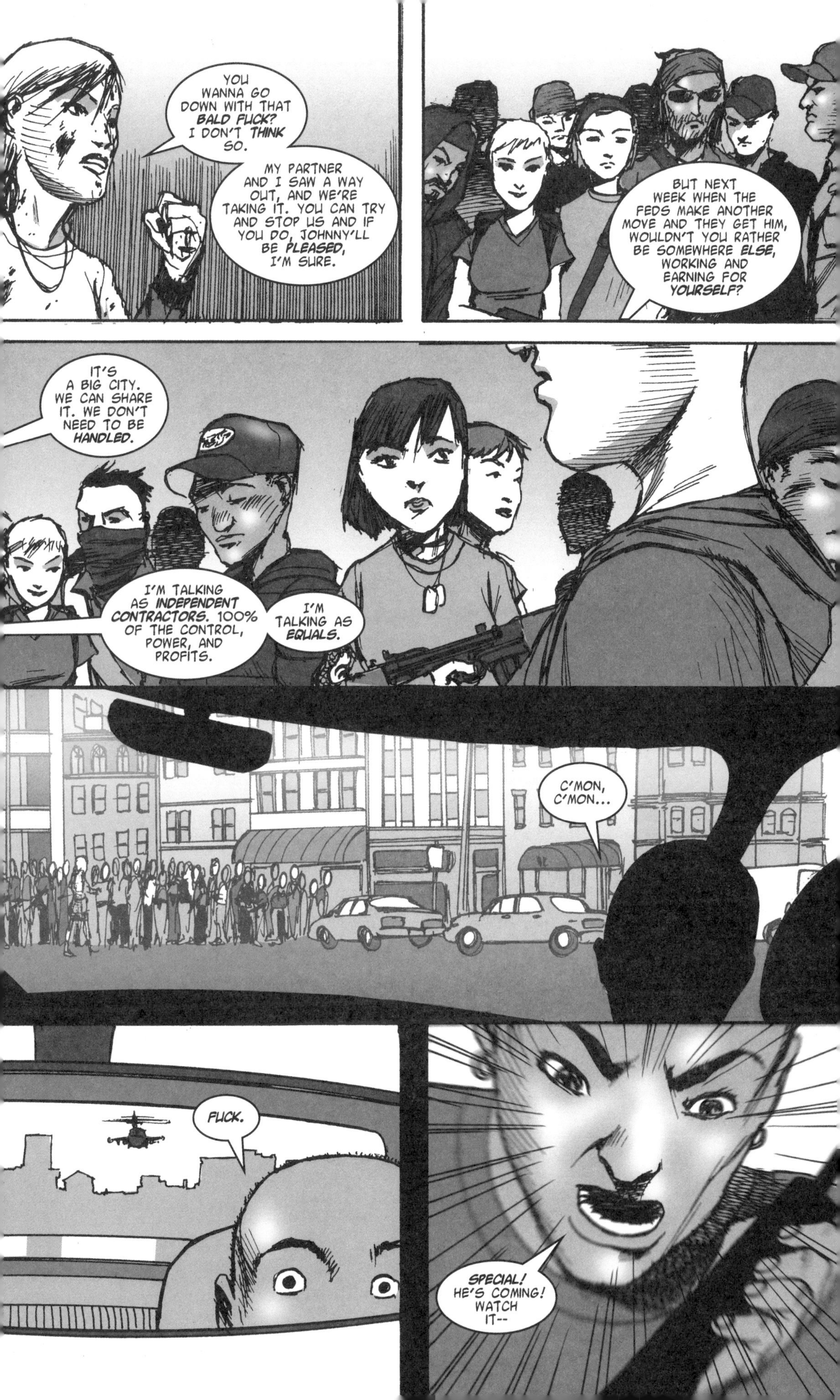

YOU WANNA GO DOWN WITH THAT BALD FUCK? I DON'T THINK SO.
MY PARTNER AND I SAW A WAY OUT, AND WE'RE TAKING IT. YOU CAN TRY AND STOP US AND IF YOU DO, JOHNNY'LL BE PLEASED, I'M SURE.
BUT NEXT WEEK WHEN THE FEDS MAKE ANOTHER MOVE AND THEY GET HIM, WOULDN'T YOU RATHER BE SOMEWHERE ELSE, WORKING AND EARNING FOR YOURSELF?
IT'S A BIG CITY. WE CAN SHARE IT. WE DON'T NEED TO BE HANDLED.
I'M TALKING AS INDEPENDENT CONTRACTORS. 100% OF THE CONTROL, POWER, AND PROFITS.
I'M TALKING AS EQUALS.
C'MON, C'MON...
FUCK.
SPECIAL! HE'S COMING! WATCH IT--

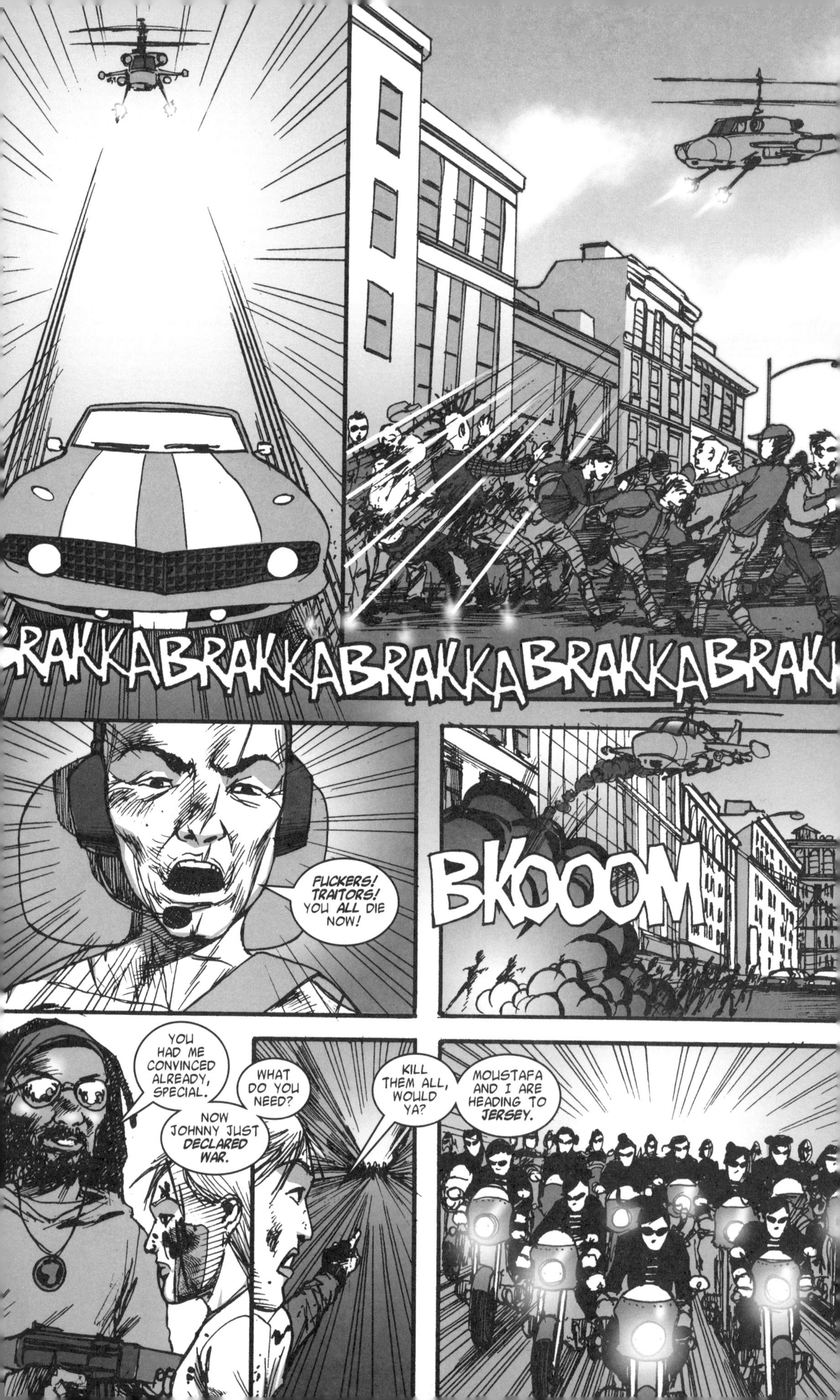
RAKKABRAKKABRAKKABRAKKABRAK
FUCKERS! TRAITORS! YOU ALL DIE NOW!
BKOOOM
YOU HAD ME CONVINCED ALREADY, SPECIAL.
NOW JOHNNY JUST DECLARED WAR.
WHAT DO YOU NEED?
KILL THEM ALL, WOULD YA?
MOUSTAFA AND I ARE HEADING TO JERSEY.

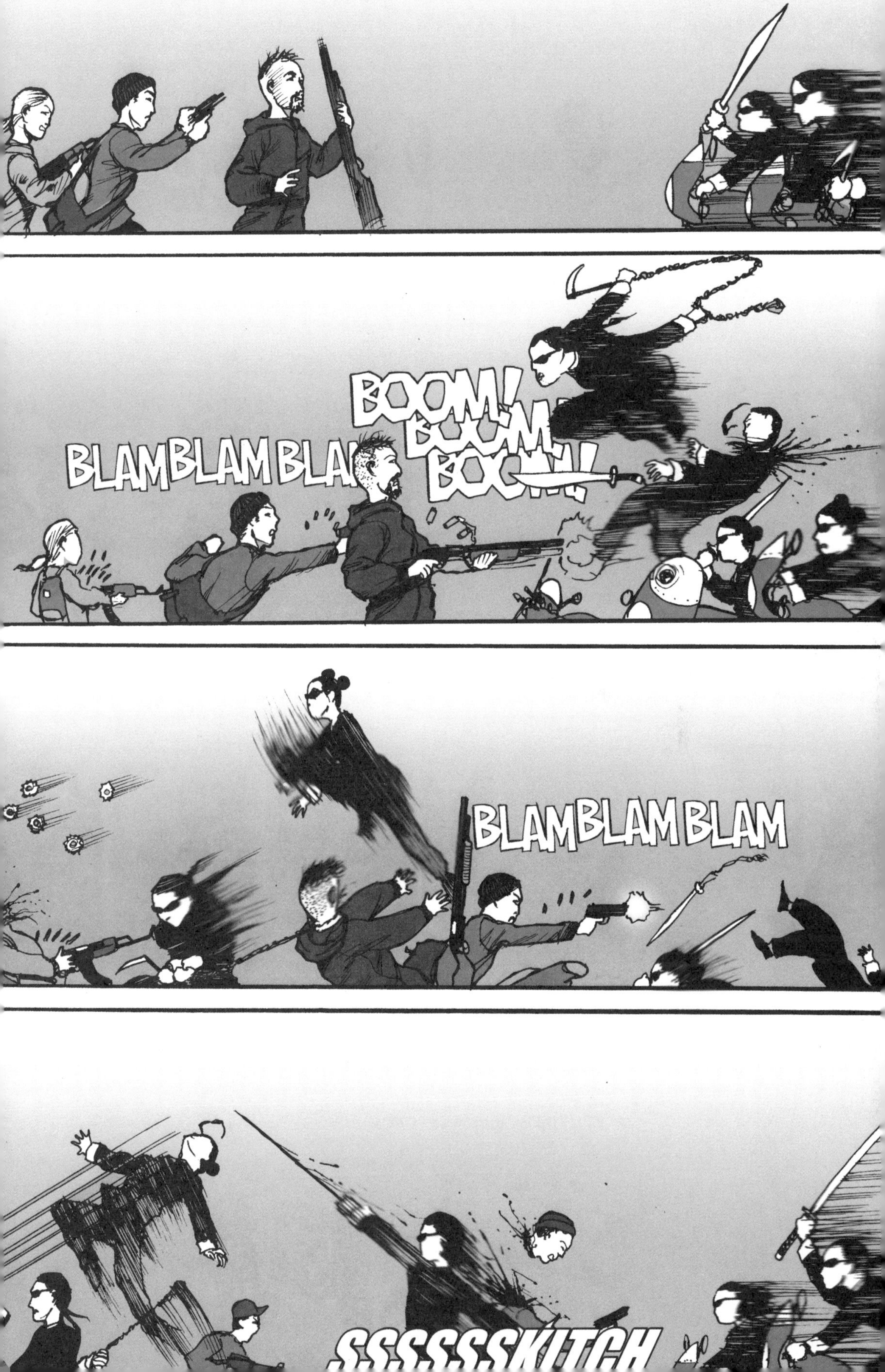

BOOM! BOOM! BOOM!
BLAMBLAM BLAM
BLAMBLAM BLAM
SSSSSSKITCH

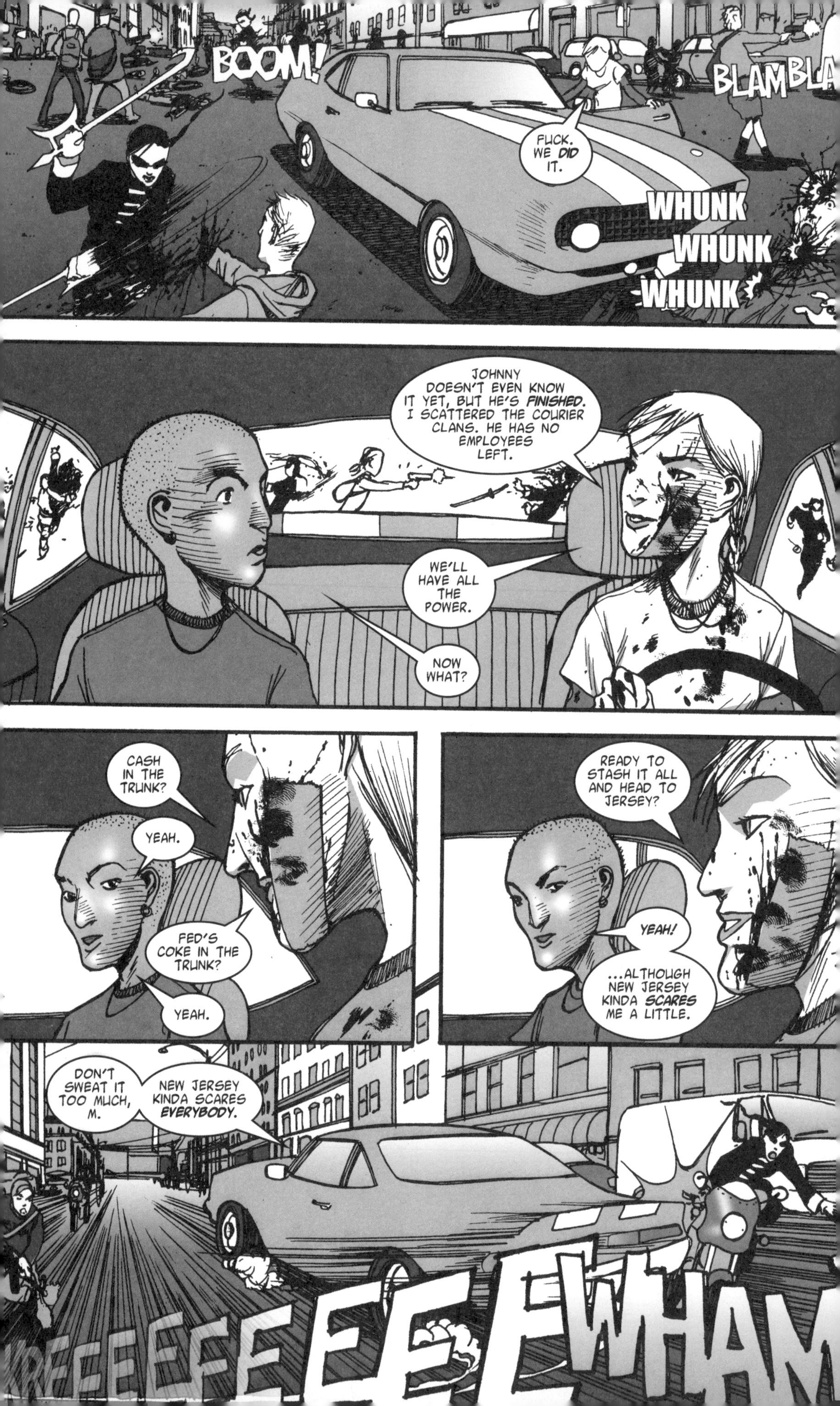
BOOM!
BLAMBLA
FUCK. WE *DID* IT.
WHUNK
WHUNK
WHUNK
JOHNNY DOESN'T EVEN KNOW IT YET, BUT HE'S *FINISHED*. I SCATTERED THE COURIER CLANS. HE HAS NO EMPLOYEES LEFT.
WE'LL HAVE ALL THE POWER.
NOW WHAT?
CASH IN THE TRUNK?
YEAH.
FED'S COKE IN THE TRUNK?
YEAH.
READY TO STASH IT ALL AND HEAD TO JERSEY?
YEAH!
...ALTHOUGH NEW JERSEY KINDA *SCARES* ME A LITTLE.
DON'T SWEAT IT TOO MUCH, M.
NEW JERSEY KINDA SCARES *EVERYBODY*.
REEEEEEEEE
WHAM

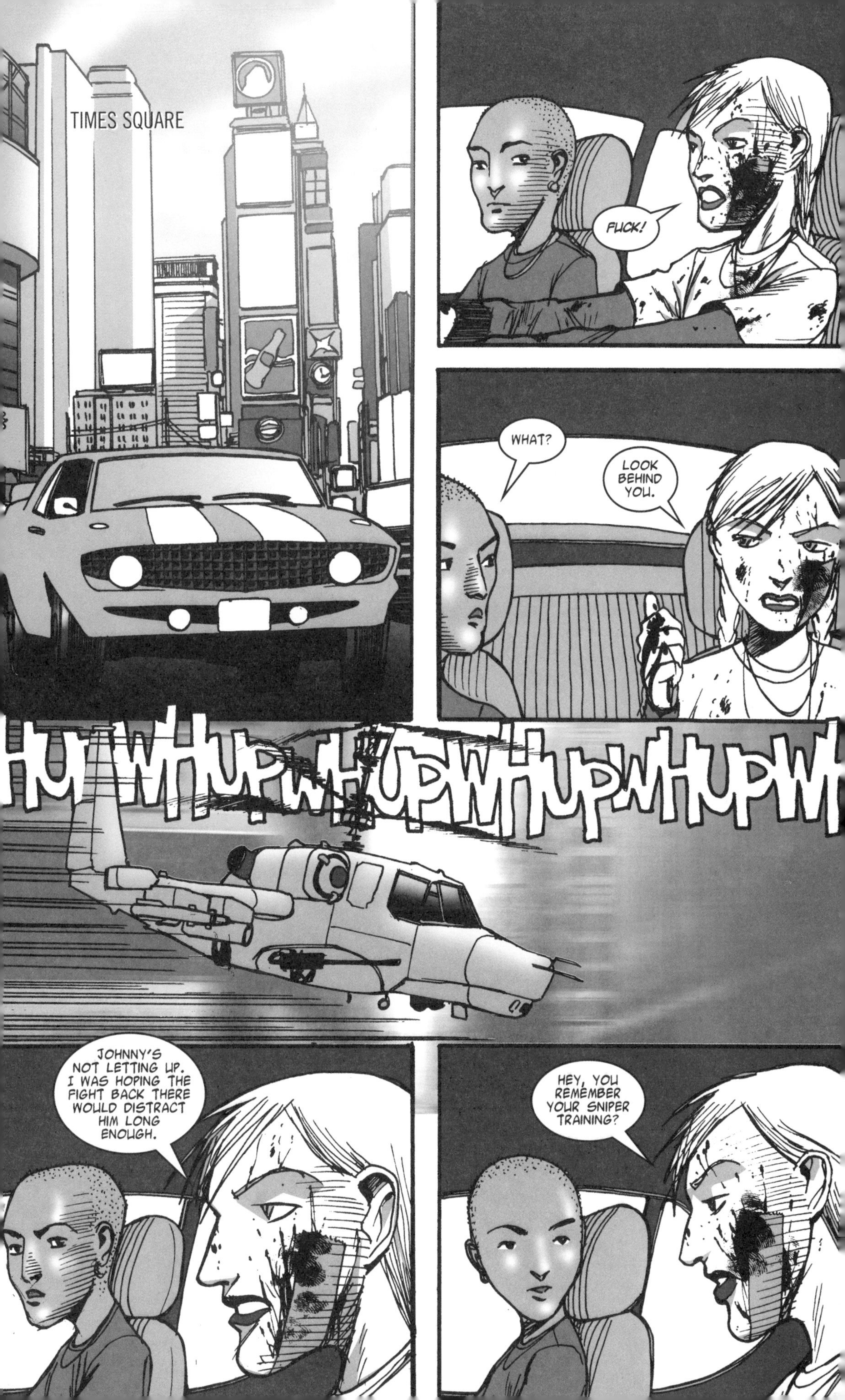
TIMES SQUARE
FUCK!
WHAT?
LOOK BEHIND YOU.
WHUPWHUPWHUPWHUPWHUPWH
JOHNNY'S NOT LETTING UP. I WAS HOPING THE FIGHT BACK THERE WOULD DISTRACT HIM LONG ENOUGH.
HEY, YOU REMEMBER YOUR SNIPER TRAINING?

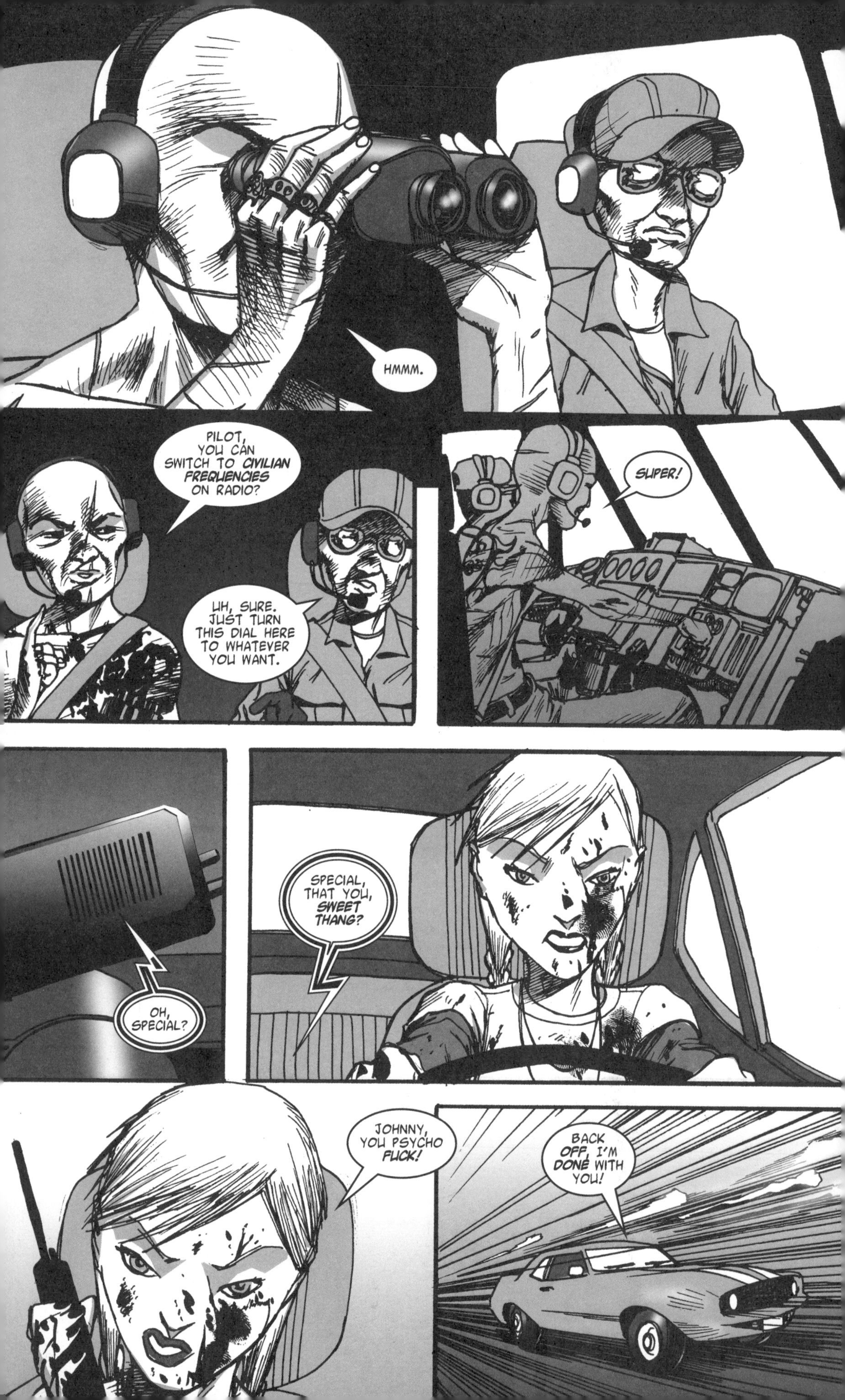
HMMM.
PILOT, YOU CAN SWITCH TO CIVILIAN FREQUENCIES ON RADIO?
UH, SURE. JUST TURN THIS DIAL HERE TO WHATEVER YOU WANT.
SUPER!
OH, SPECIAL?
SPECIAL, THAT YOU, SWEET THANG?
JOHNNY, YOU PSYCHO FUCK!
BACK OFF, I'M DONE WITH YOU!

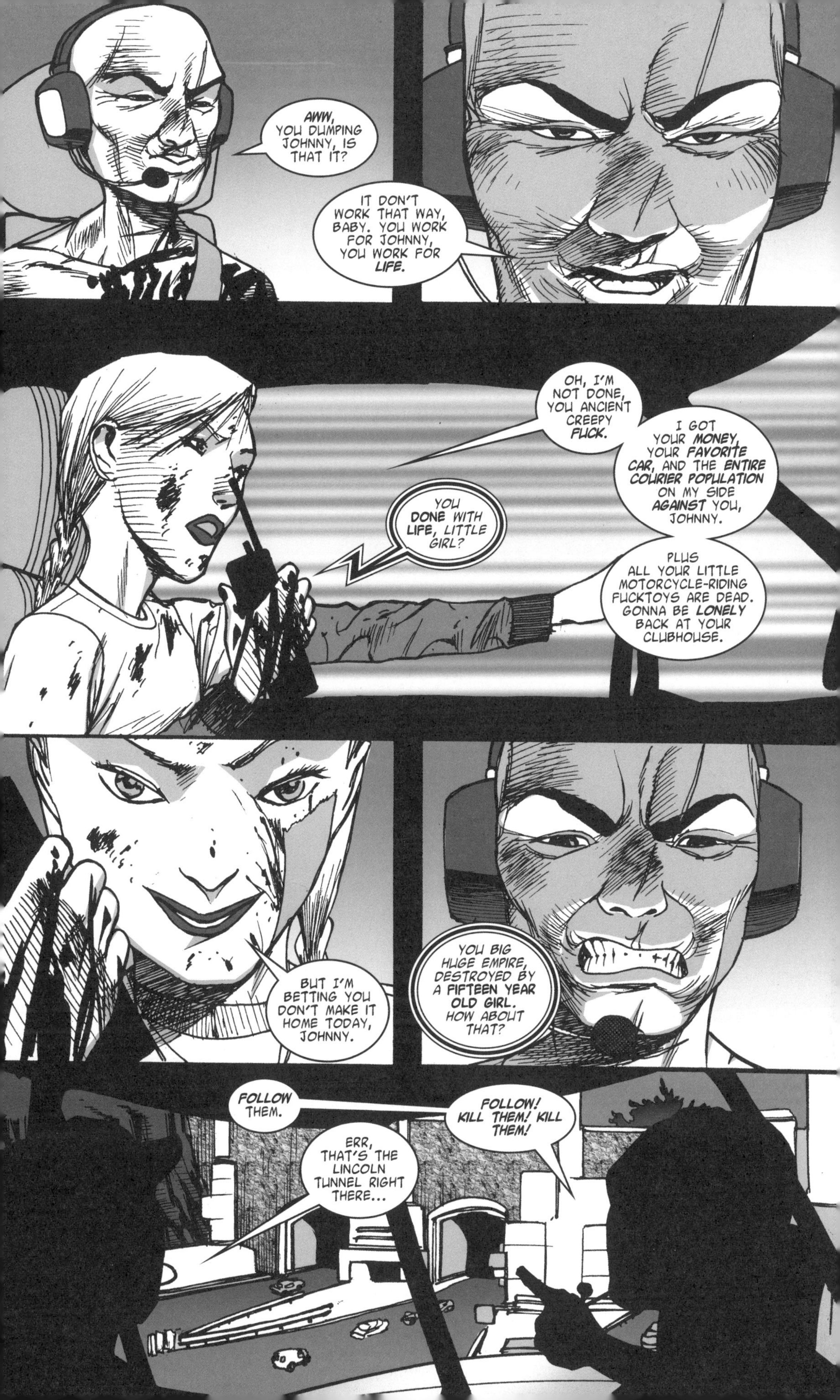
AWW, YOU DUMPING JOHNNY, IS THAT IT?
IT DON'T WORK THAT WAY, BABY. YOU WORK FOR JOHNNY, YOU WORK FOR LIFE.
OH, I'M NOT DONE, YOU ANCIENT CREEPY FUCK.
I GOT YOUR MONEY, YOUR FAVORITE CAR, AND THE ENTIRE COURIER POPULATION ON MY SIDE AGAINST YOU, JOHNNY.
YOU DONE WITH LIFE, LITTLE GIRL?
PLUS ALL YOUR LITTLE MOTORCYCLE-RIDING FUCKTOYS ARE DEAD. GONNA BE LONELY BACK AT YOUR CLUBHOUSE.
BUT I'M BETTING YOU DON'T MAKE IT HOME TODAY, JOHNNY.
YOU BIG HUGE EMPIRE, DESTROYED BY A FIFTEEN YEAR OLD GIRL. HOW ABOUT THAT?
FOLLOW THEM.
FOLLOW! KILL THEM! KILL THEM!
ERR, THAT'S THE LINCOLN TUNNEL RIGHT THERE...

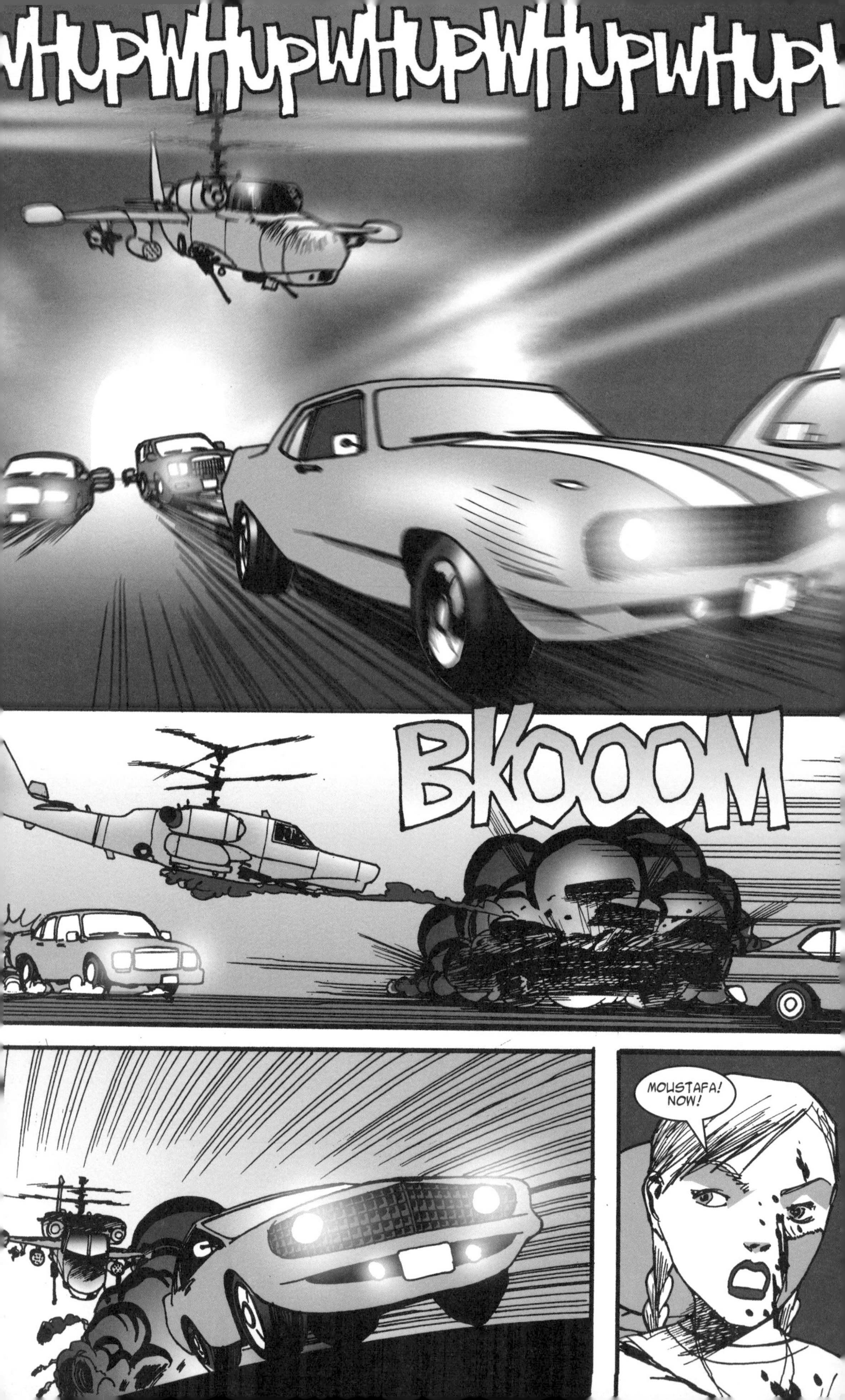
WHUPWHUPWHUPWHUPWHUP
BKOOOM
MOUSTAFA! NOW!

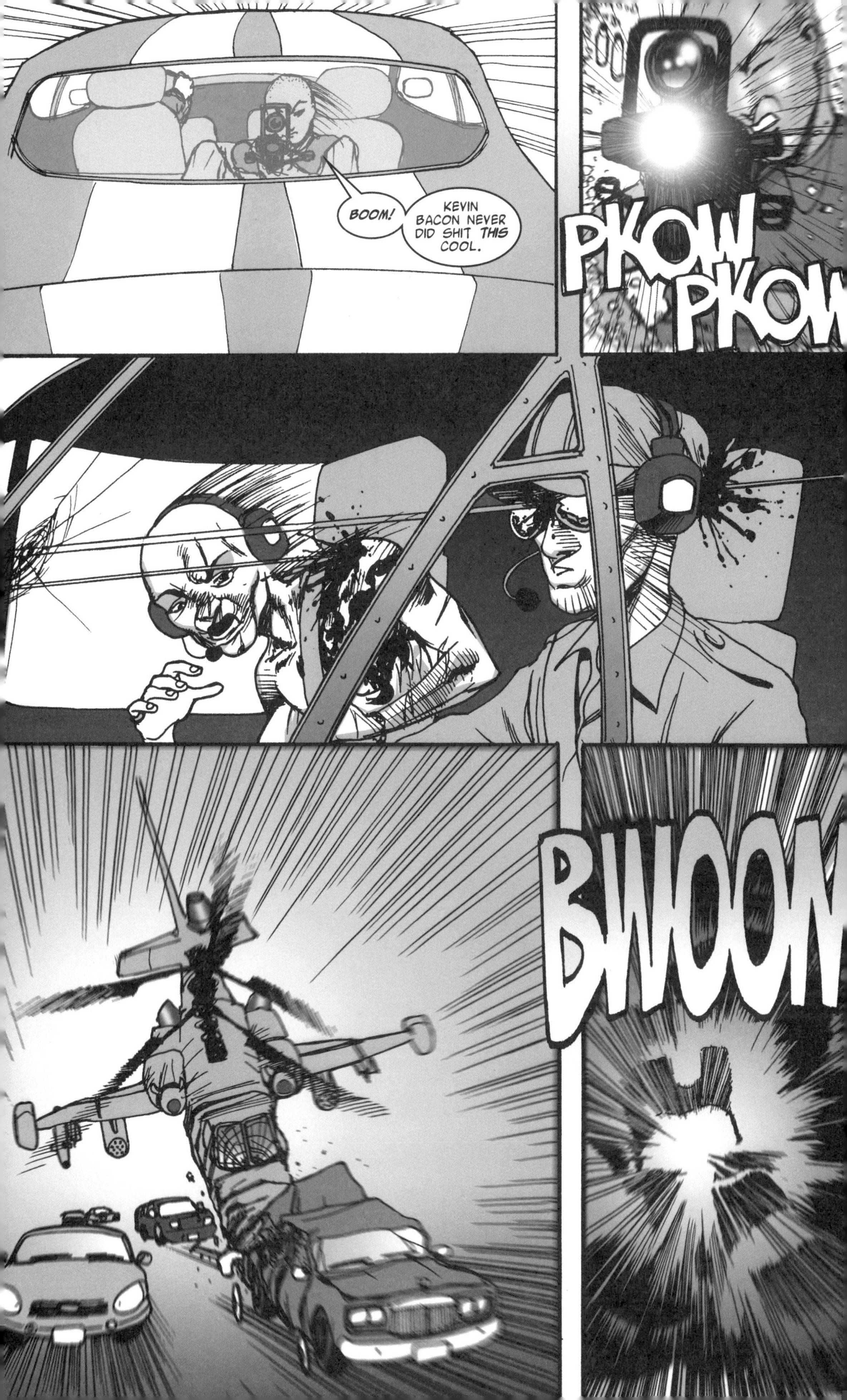
BOOM!
KEVIN BACON NEVER DID SHIT THIS COOL.
PKOW PKOW
BWOOM

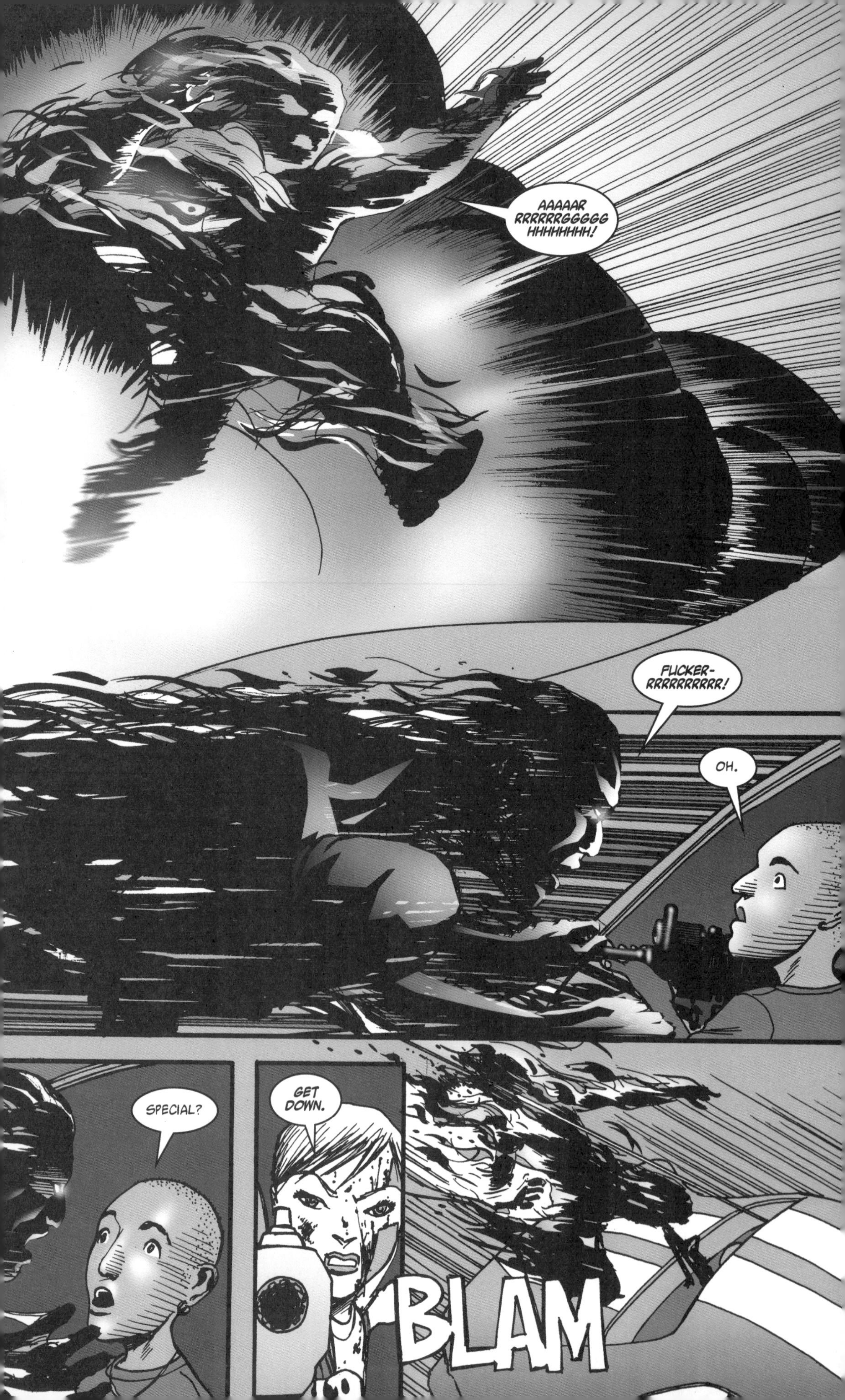
AAAAAR RRRRRRGGGGG HHHHHHHH!
FUCKER-RRRRRRRRRR!
OH.
SPECIAL?
GET DOWN.
BLAM

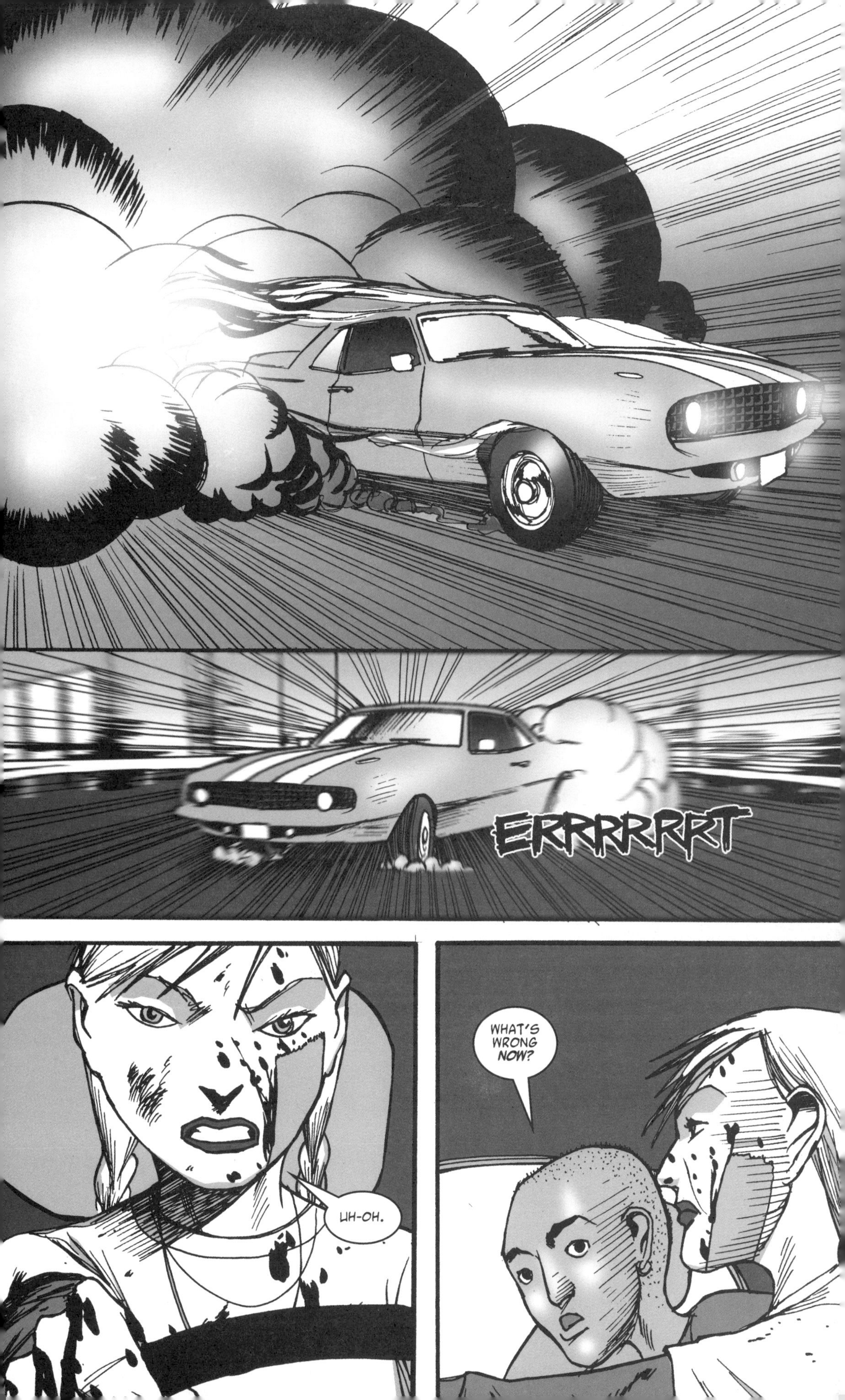
ERRRRRRRT
UH-OH.
WHAT'S WRONG NOW?

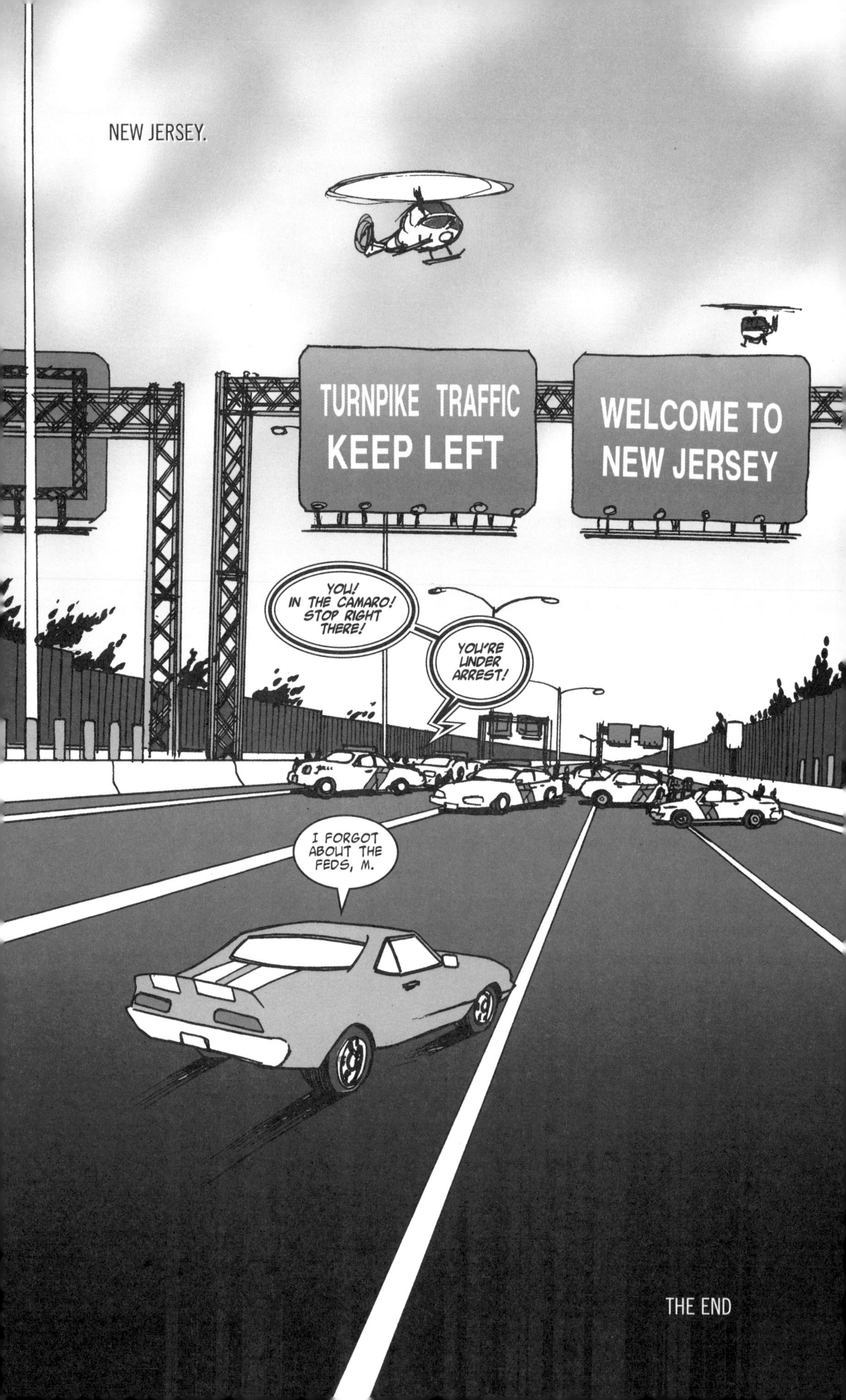
NEW JERSEY.
TURNPIKE TRAFFIC KEEP LEFT
WELCOME TO NEW JERSEY
YOU! IN THE CAMARO! STOP RIGHT THERE!
YOU'RE UNDER ARREST!
I FORGOT ABOUT THE FEDS, M.
THE END

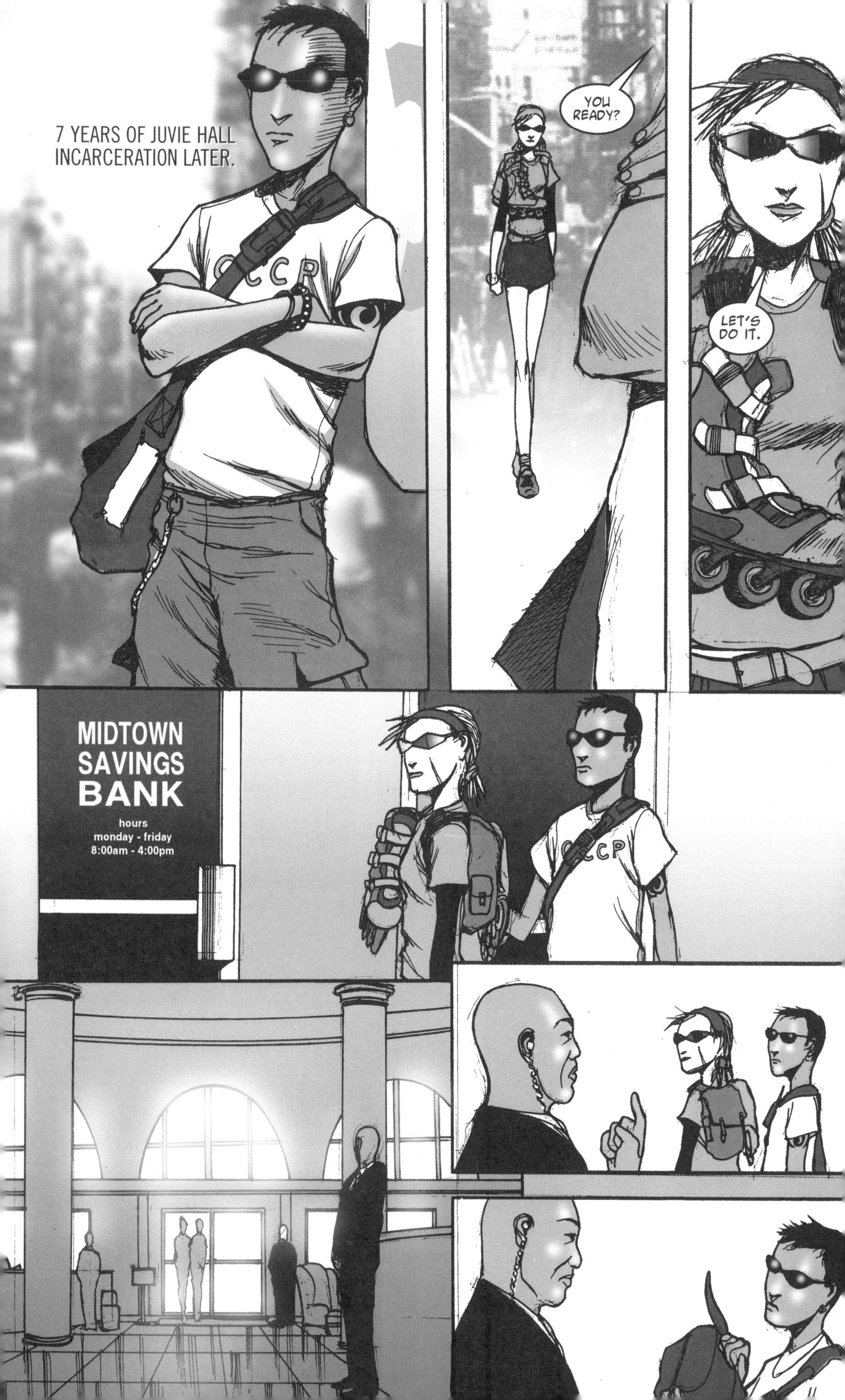
7 YEARS OF JUVIE HALL INCARCERATION LATER.
YOU READY?
LET'S DO IT.
MIDTOWN SAVINGS BANK
hours
monday - friday
8:00am - 4:00pm

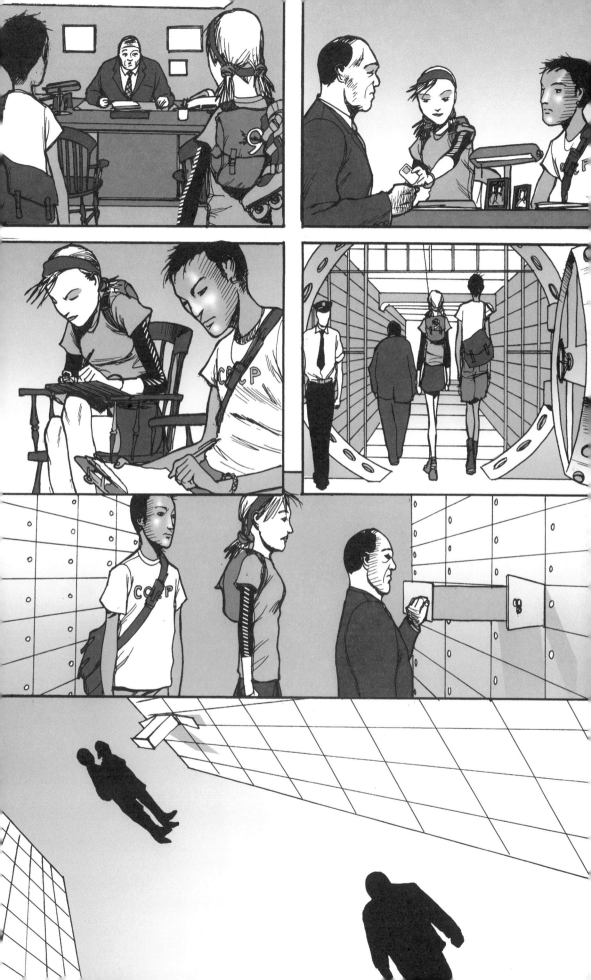

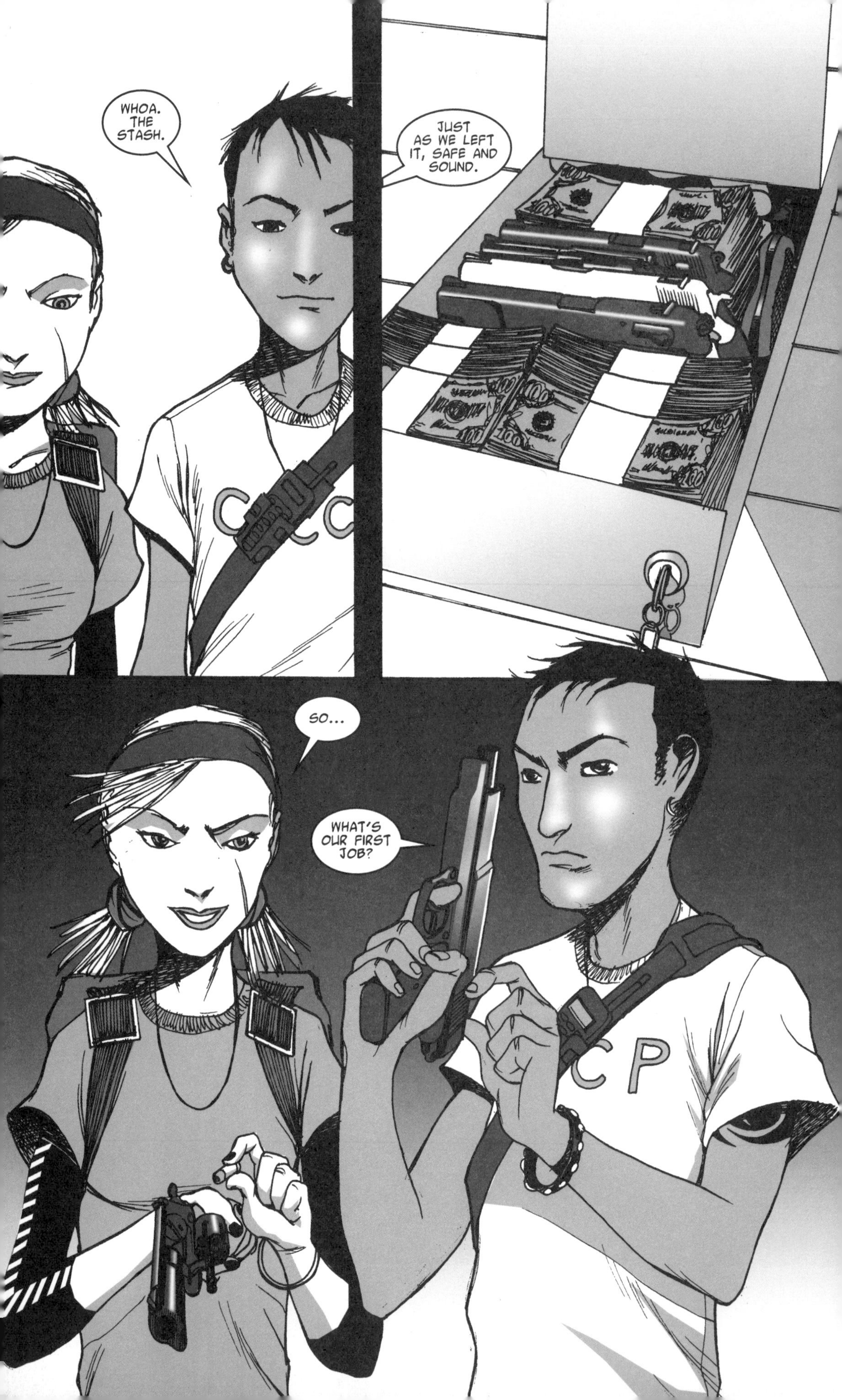
WHOA. THE STASH.
JUST AS WE LEFT IT, SAFE AND SOUND.
SO...
WHAT'S OUR FIRST JOB?

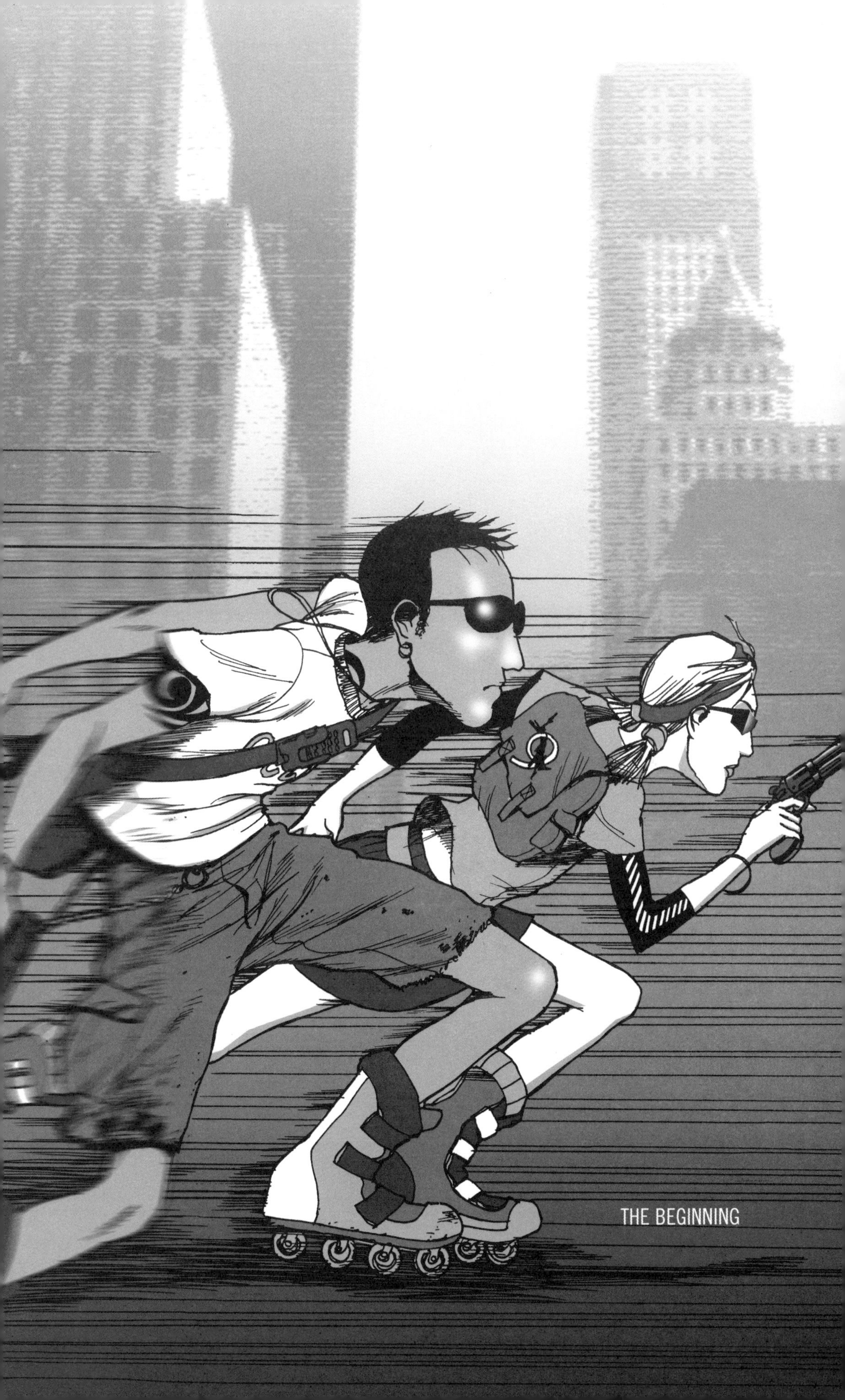
THE BEGINNING

04

Couscous Express

Brian Wood x Brett Weldele x Larry Young

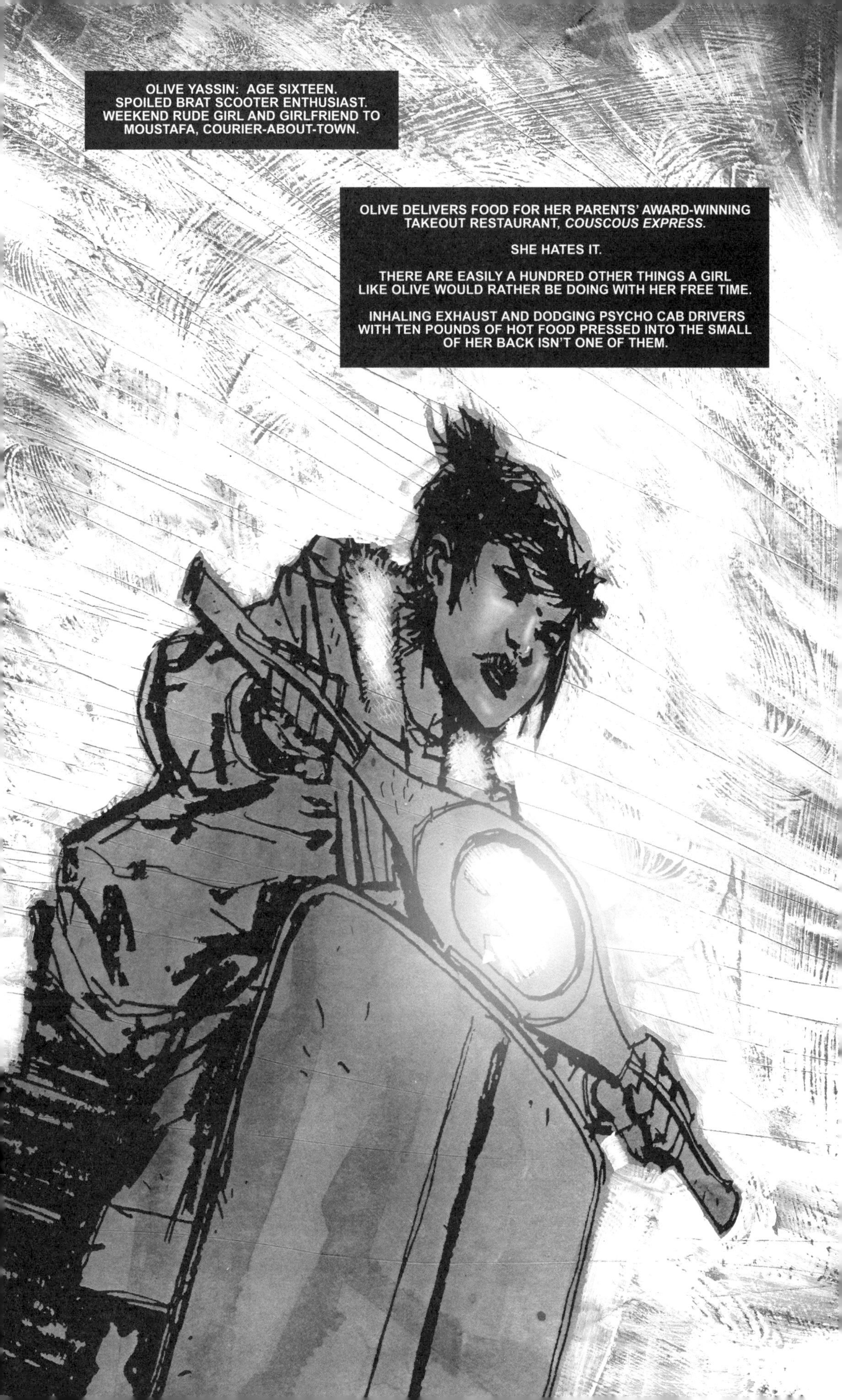
OLIVE YASSIN: AGE SIXTEEN.
SPOILED BRAT SCOOTER ENTHUSIAST.
WEEKEND RUDE GIRL AND GIRLFRIEND TO MOUSTAFA, COURIER-ABOUT-TOWN.
OLIVE DELIVERS FOOD FOR HER PARENTS' AWARD-WINNING TAKEOUT RESTAURANT, *COUSCOUS EXPRESS.*
SHE HATES IT.
THERE ARE EASILY A HUNDRED OTHER THINGS A GIRL LIKE OLIVE WOULD RATHER BE DOING WITH HER FREE TIME.
INHALING EXHAUST AND DODGING PSYCHO CAB DRIVERS WITH TEN POUNDS OF HOT FOOD PRESSED INTO THE SMALL OF HER BACK ISN'T ONE OF THEM.

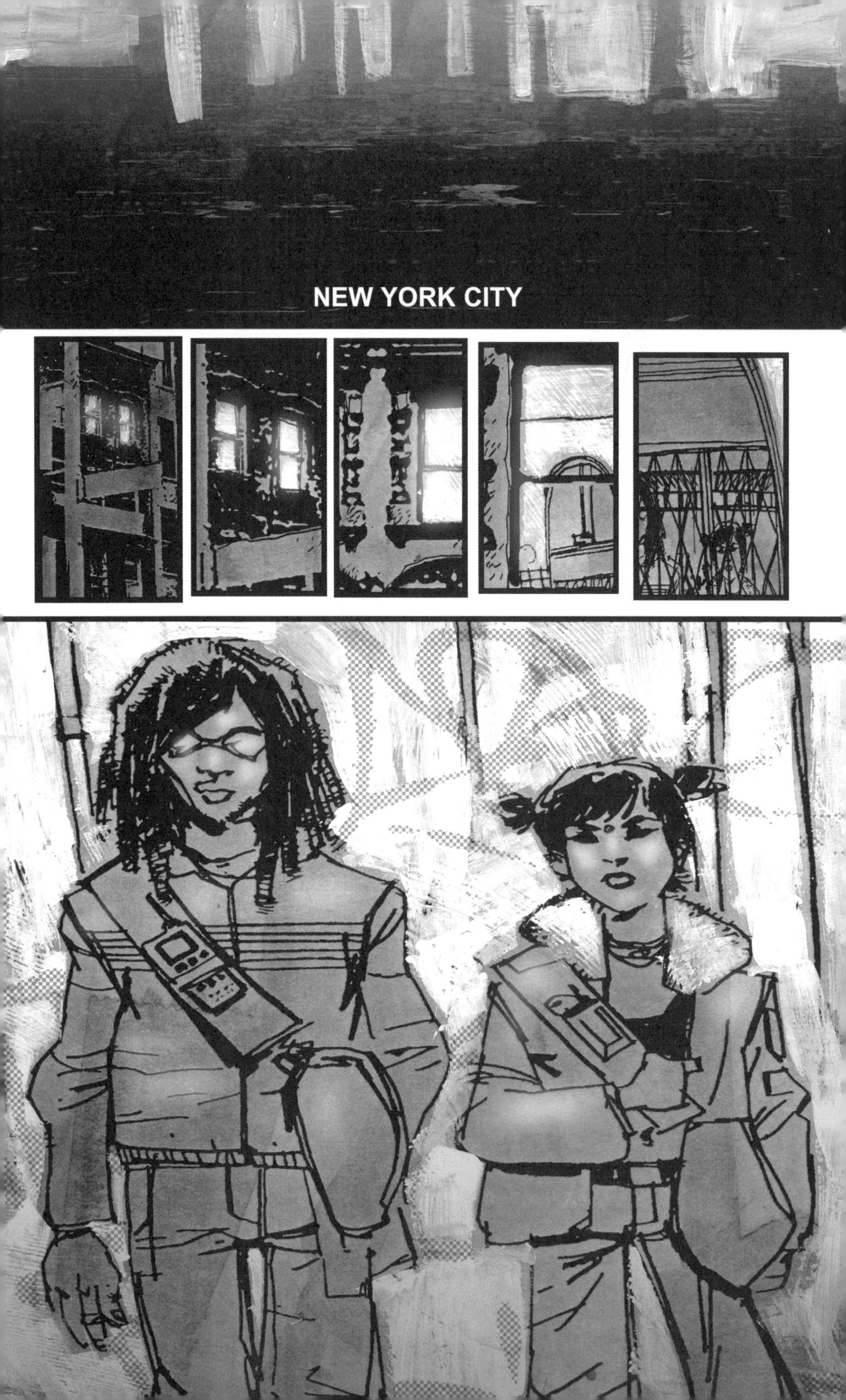
NEW YORK CITY

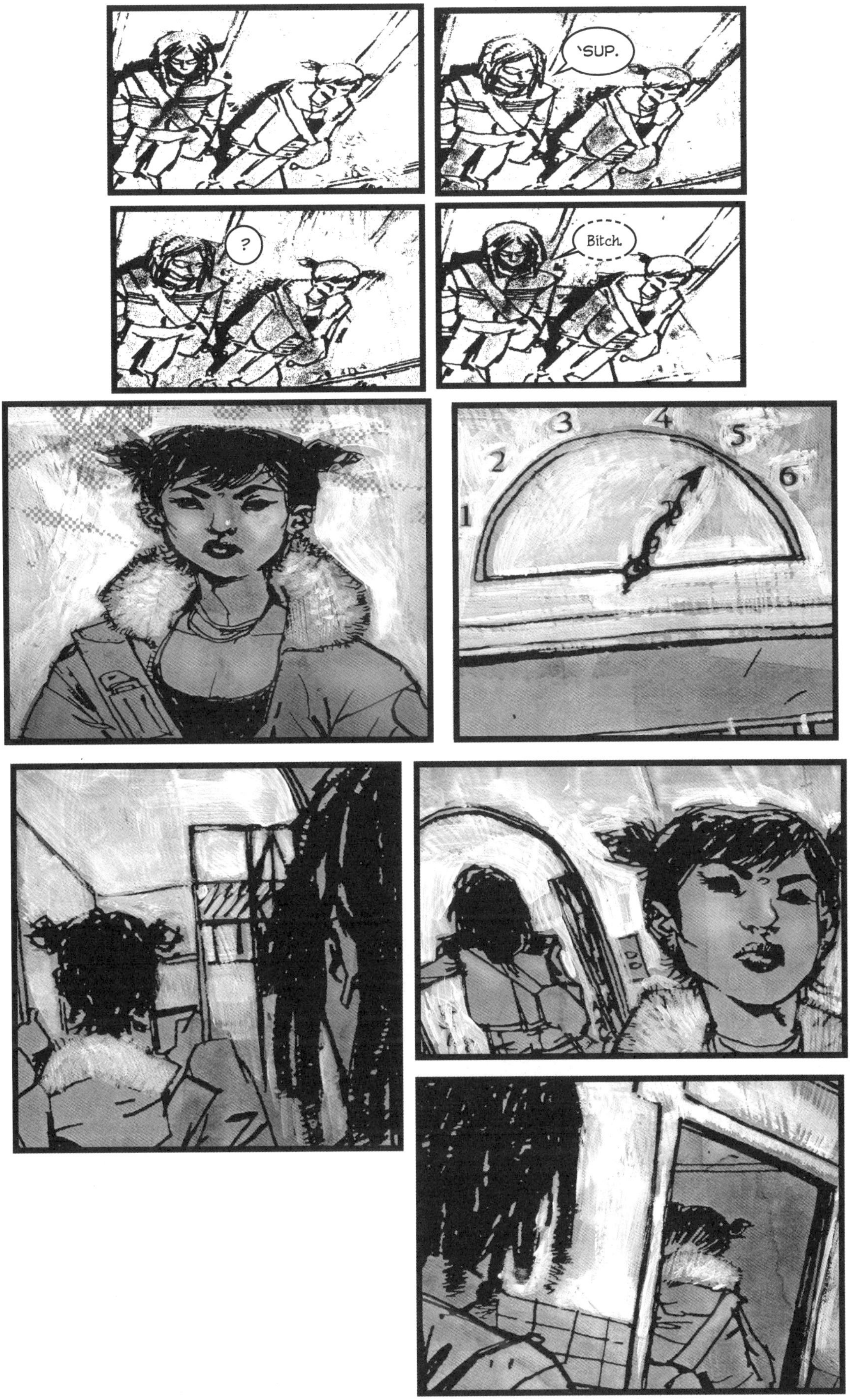
`SUP.
?
Bitch.
1
2
3
4
5
6

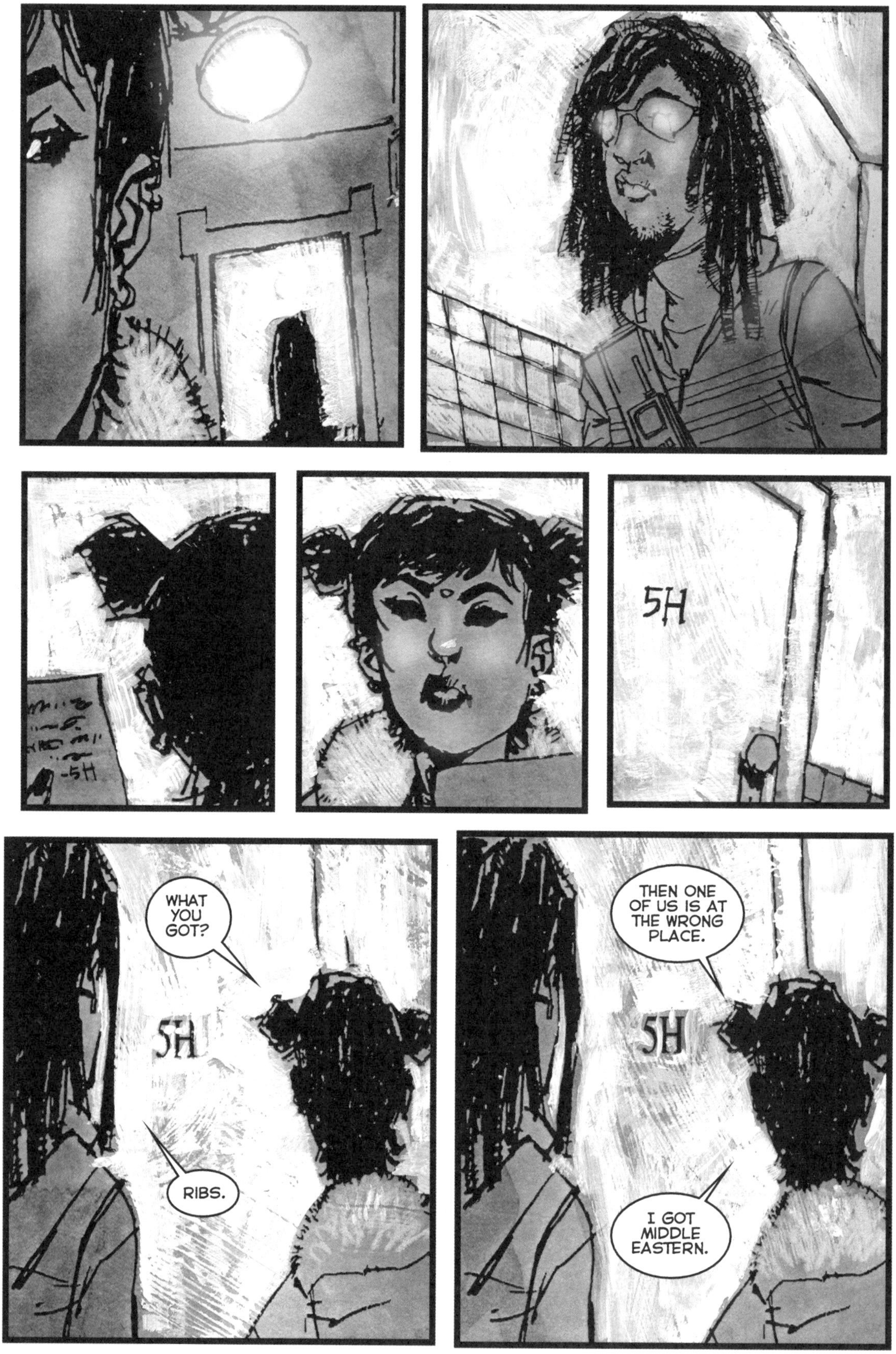
5H
-5H
5H
WHAT YOU GOT?
5H
RIBS.
THEN ONE OF US IS AT THE WRONG PLACE.
5H
I GOT MIDDLE EASTERN.

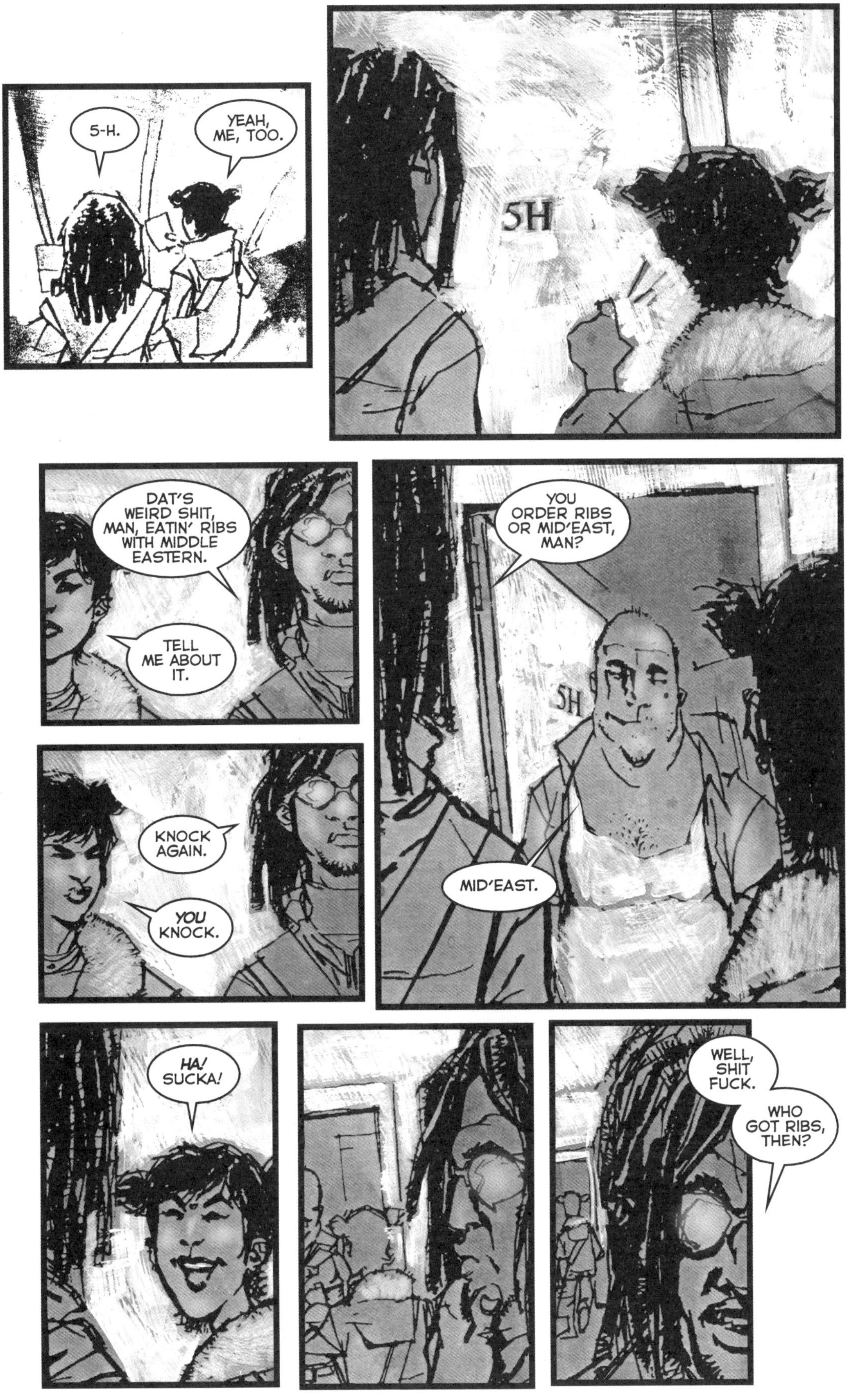
5-H.
YEAH, ME, TOO.
5H
DAT'S WEIRD SHIT, MAN, EATIN' RIBS WITH MIDDLE EASTERN.
TELL ME ABOUT IT.
KNOCK AGAIN.
YOU KNOCK.
YOU ORDER RIBS OR MID'EAST, MAN?
5H
MID'EAST.
HA! SUCKA!
WELL, SHIT FUCK.
WHO GOT RIBS, THEN?

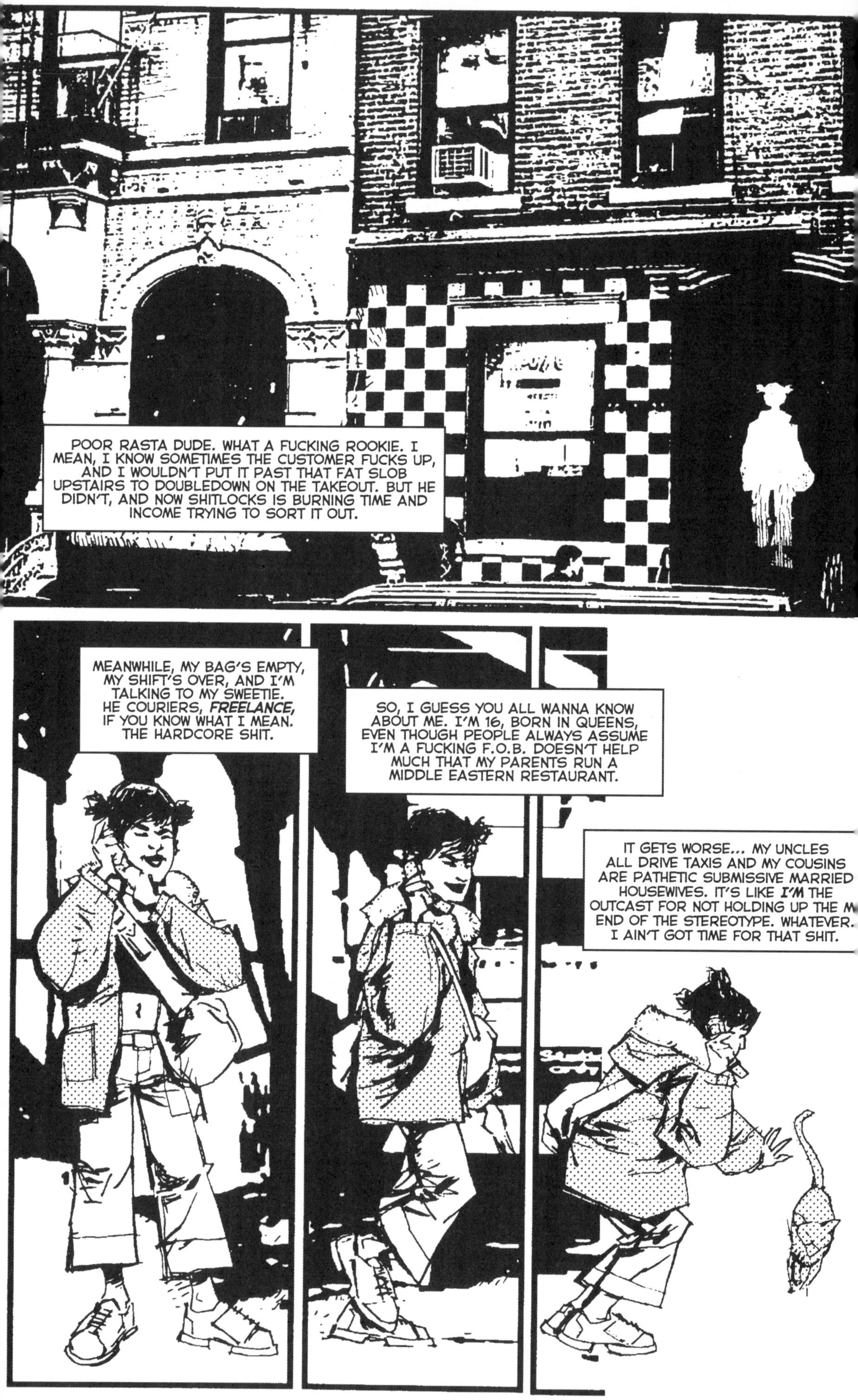
POOR RASTA DUDE. WHAT A FUCKING ROOKIE. I MEAN, I KNOW SOMETIMES THE CUSTOMER FUCKS UP, AND I WOULDN'T PUT IT PAST THAT FAT SLOB UPSTAIRS TO DOUBLEDOWN ON THE TAKEOUT. BUT HE DIDN'T, AND NOW SHITLOCKS IS BURNING TIME AND INCOME TRYING TO SORT IT OUT.
MEANWHILE, MY BAG'S EMPTY, MY SHIFT'S OVER, AND I'M TALKING TO MY SWEETIE. HE COURIERS, ***FREELANCE,*** IF YOU KNOW WHAT I MEAN. THE HARDCORE SHIT.
SO, I GUESS YOU ALL WANNA KNOW ABOUT ME. I'M 16, BORN IN QUEENS, EVEN THOUGH PEOPLE ALWAYS ASSUME I'M A FUCKING F.O.B. DOESN'T HELP MUCH THAT MY PARENTS RUN A MIDDLE EASTERN RESTAURANT.
IT GETS WORSE... MY UNCLES ALL DRIVE TAXIS AND MY COUSINS ARE PATHETIC SUBMISSIVE MARRIED HOUSEWIVES. IT'S LIKE ***I'M*** THE OUTCAST FOR NOT HOLDING UP THE M END OF THE STEREOTYPE. WHATEVER. I AIN'T GOT TIME FOR THAT SHIT.

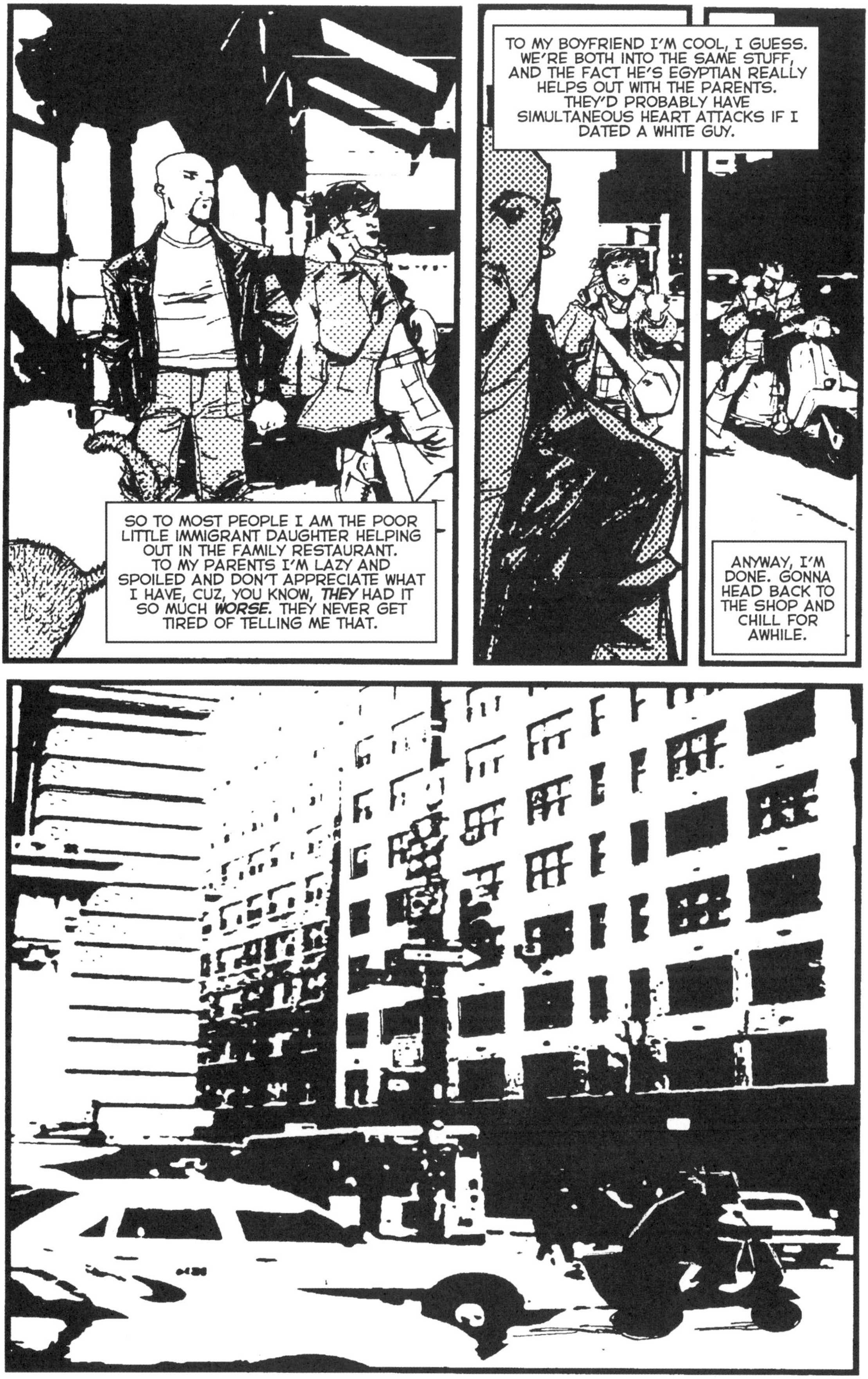
SO TO MOST PEOPLE I AM THE POOR LITTLE IMMIGRANT DAUGHTER HELPING OUT IN THE FAMILY RESTAURANT. TO MY PARENTS I'M LAZY AND SPOILED AND DON'T APPRECIATE WHAT I HAVE, CUZ, YOU KNOW, THEY HAD IT SO MUCH WORSE. THEY NEVER GET TIRED OF TELLING ME THAT.
TO MY BOYFRIEND I'M COOL, I GUESS. WE'RE BOTH INTO THE SAME STUFF, AND THE FACT HE'S EGYPTIAN REALLY HELPS OUT WITH THE PARENTS. THEY'D PROBABLY HAVE SIMULTANEOUS HEART ATTACKS IF I DATED A WHITE GUY.
ANYWAY, I'M DONE. GONNA HEAD BACK TO THE SHOP AND CHILL FOR AWHILE.

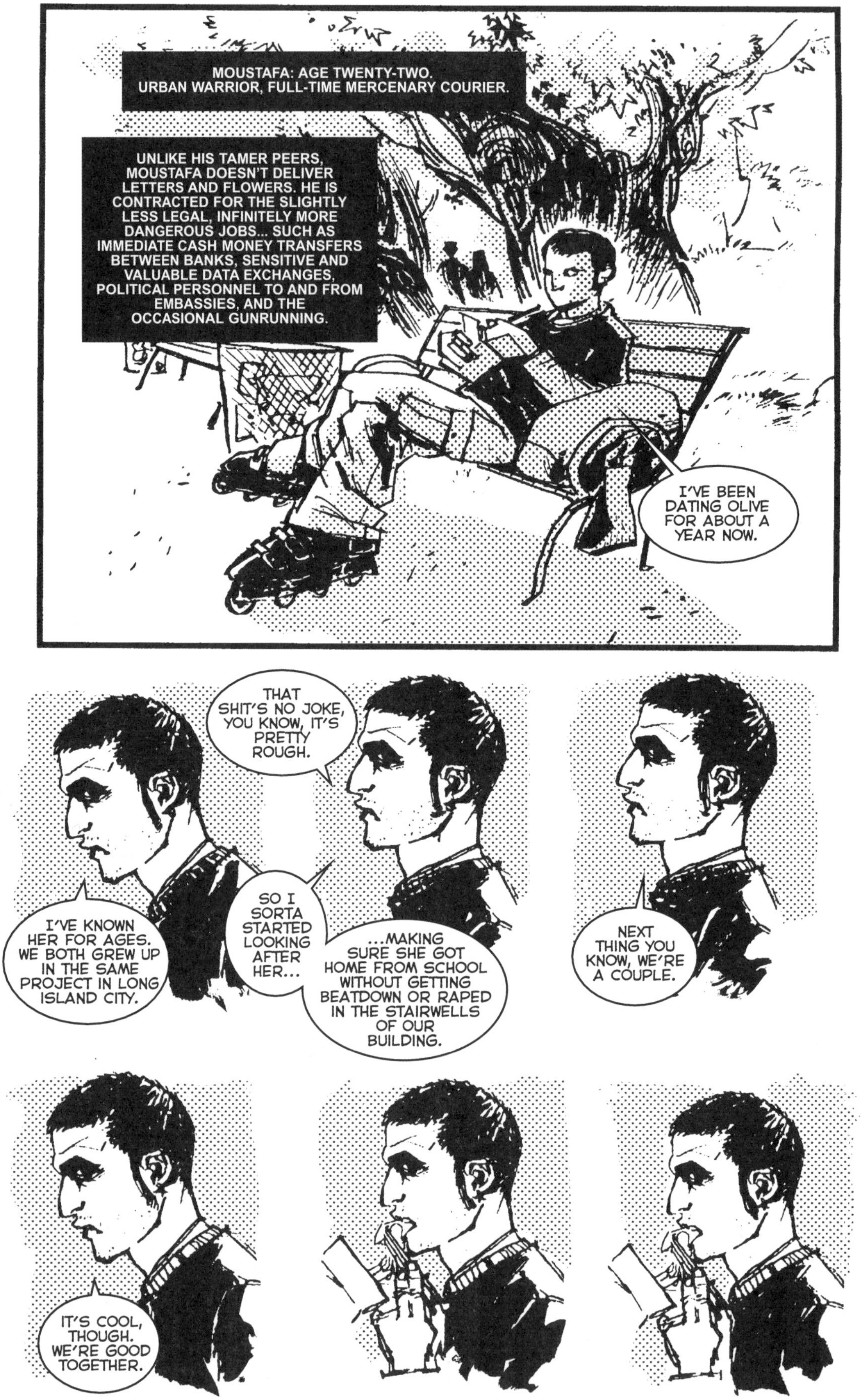
MOUSTAFA: AGE TWENTY-TWO. URBAN WARRIOR, FULL-TIME MERCENARY COURIER.
UNLIKE HIS TAMER PEERS, MOUSTAFA DOESN'T DELIVER LETTERS AND FLOWERS. HE IS CONTRACTED FOR THE SLIGHTLY LESS LEGAL, INFINITELY MORE DANGEROUS JOBS... SUCH AS IMMEDIATE CASH MONEY TRANSFERS BETWEEN BANKS, SENSITIVE AND VALUABLE DATA EXCHANGES, POLITICAL PERSONNEL TO AND FROM EMBASSIES, AND THE OCCASIONAL GUNRUNNING.
I'VE BEEN DATING OLIVE FOR ABOUT A YEAR NOW.
I'VE KNOWN HER FOR AGES. WE BOTH GREW UP IN THE SAME PROJECT IN LONG ISLAND CITY.
THAT SHIT'S NO JOKE, YOU KNOW, IT'S PRETTY ROUGH.
SO I SORTA STARTED LOOKING AFTER HER...
...MAKING SURE SHE GOT HOME FROM SCHOOL WITHOUT GETTING BEATDOWN OR RAPED IN THE STAIRWELLS OF OUR BUILDING.
NEXT THING YOU KNOW, WE'RE A COUPLE.
IT'S COOL, THOUGH. WE'RE GOOD TOGETHER.

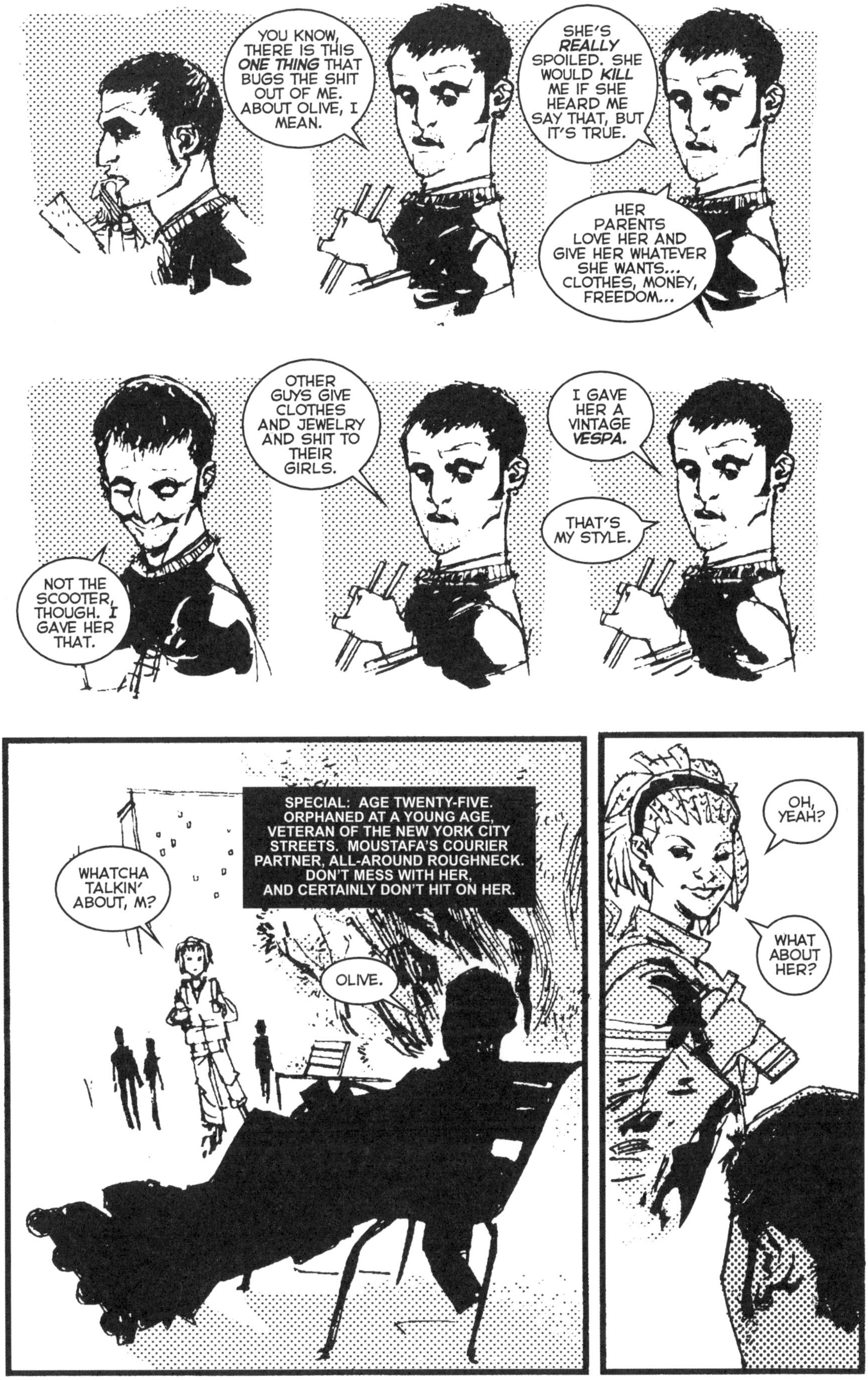
YOU KNOW, THERE IS THIS ONE THING THAT BUGS THE SHIT OUT OF ME. ABOUT OLIVE, I MEAN.
SHE'S REALLY SPOILED. SHE WOULD KILL ME IF SHE HEARD ME SAY THAT, BUT IT'S TRUE.
HER PARENTS LOVE HER AND GIVE HER WHATEVER SHE WANTS... CLOTHES, MONEY, FREEDOM...
NOT THE SCOOTER, THOUGH. I GAVE HER THAT.
OTHER GUYS GIVE CLOTHES AND JEWELRY AND SHIT TO THEIR GIRLS.
I GAVE HER A VINTAGE VESPA.
THAT'S MY STYLE.
SPECIAL: AGE TWENTY-FIVE. ORPHANED AT A YOUNG AGE, VETERAN OF THE NEW YORK CITY STREETS. MOUSTAFA'S COURIER PARTNER, ALL-AROUND ROUGHNECK. DON'T MESS WITH HER, AND CERTAINLY DON'T HIT ON HER.
WHATCHA TALKIN' ABOUT, M?
OLIVE.
OH, YEAH?
WHAT ABOUT HER?

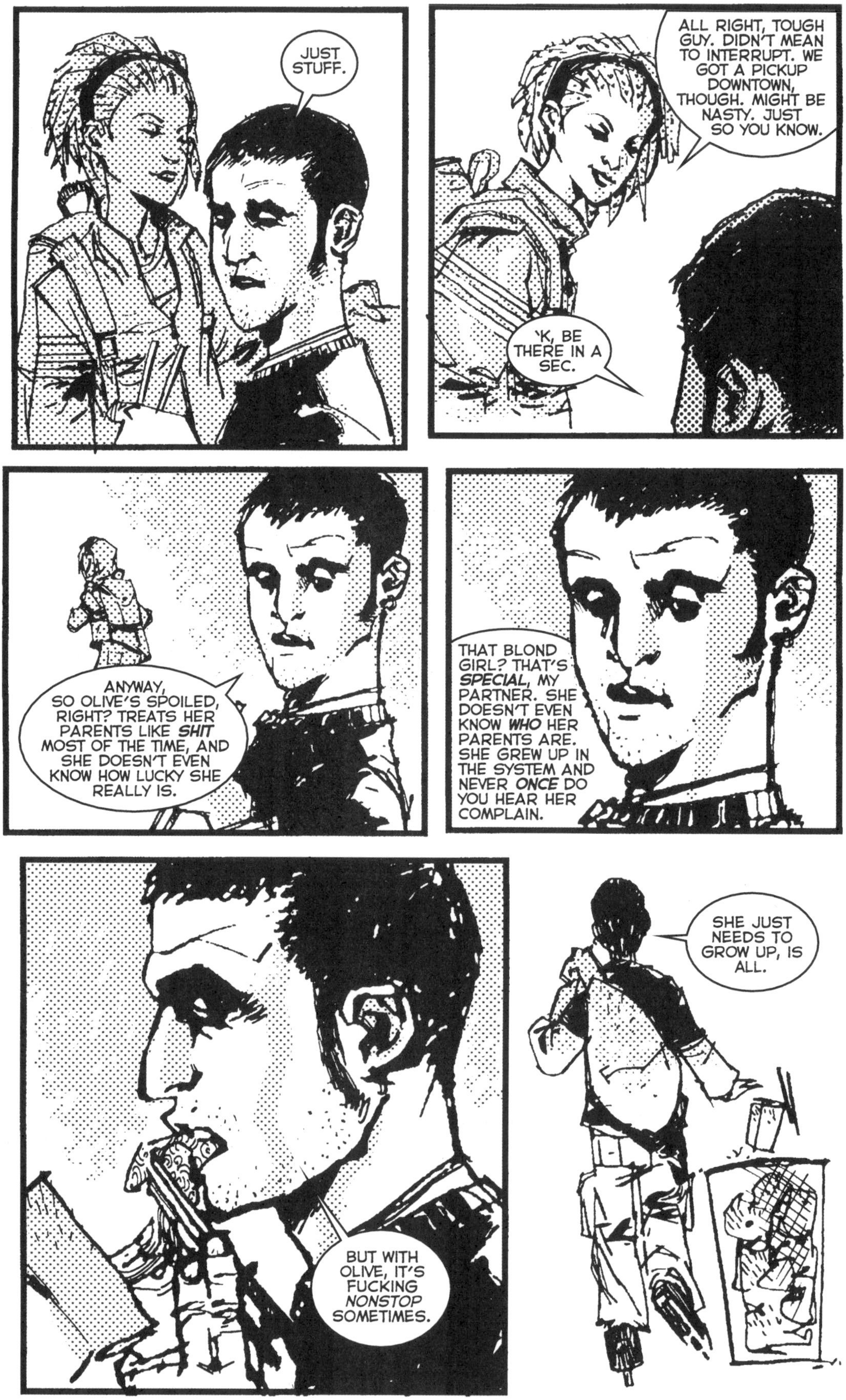
JUST STUFF.
ALL RIGHT, TOUGH GUY. DIDN'T MEAN TO INTERRUPT. WE GOT A PICKUP DOWNTOWN, THOUGH. MIGHT BE NASTY. JUST SO YOU KNOW.
'K, BE THERE IN A SEC.
ANYWAY, SO OLIVE'S SPOILED, RIGHT? TREATS HER PARENTS LIKE *SHIT* MOST OF THE TIME, AND SHE DOESN'T EVEN KNOW HOW LUCKY SHE REALLY IS.
THAT BLOND GIRL? THAT'S *SPECIAL*, MY PARTNER. SHE DOESN'T EVEN KNOW *WHO* HER PARENTS ARE. SHE GREW UP IN THE SYSTEM AND NEVER *ONCE* DO YOU HEAR HER COMPLAIN.
BUT WITH OLIVE, IT'S FUCKING *NONSTOP* SOMETIMES.
SHE JUST NEEDS TO GROW UP, IS ALL.

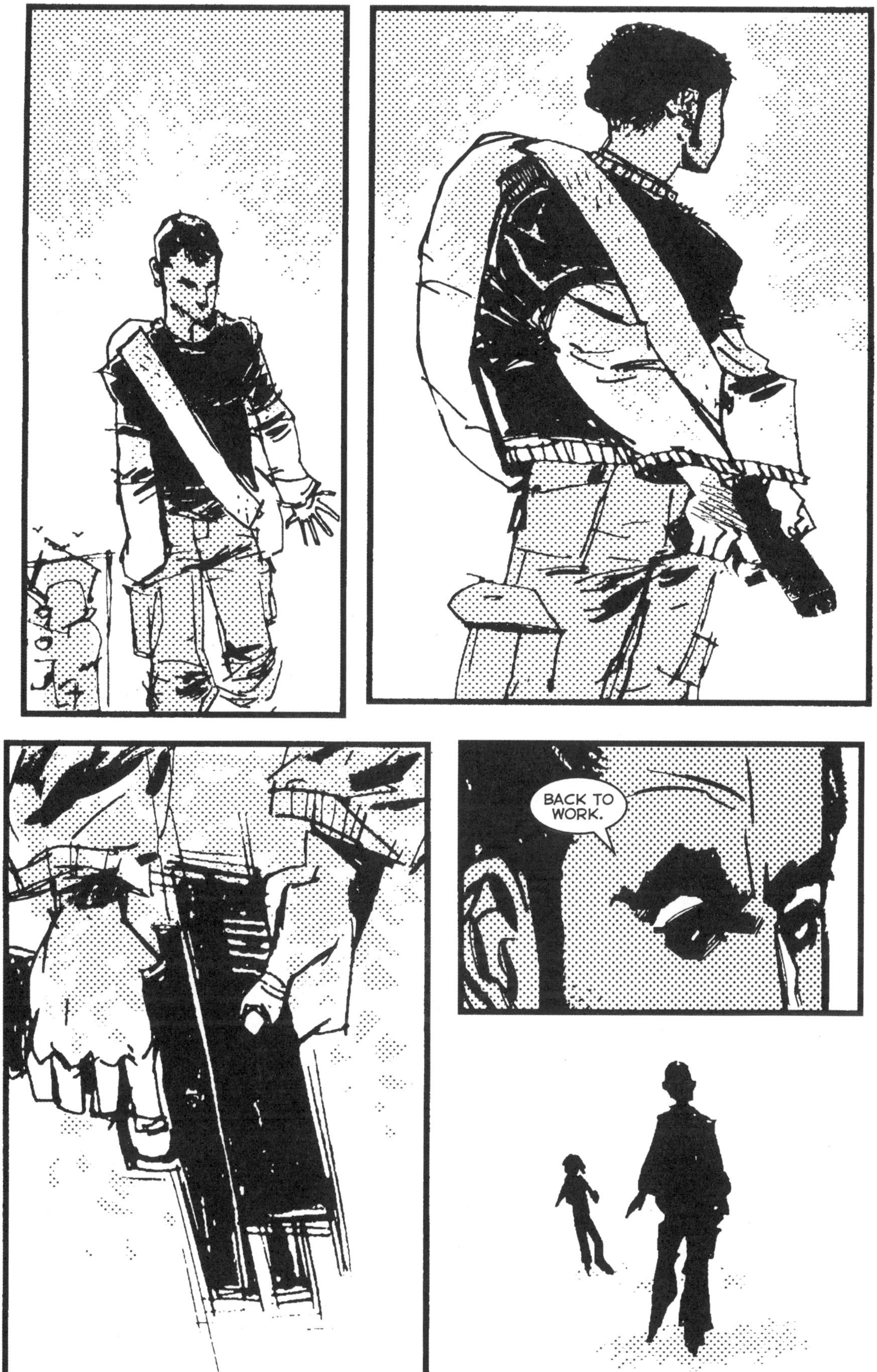
BACK TO WORK.

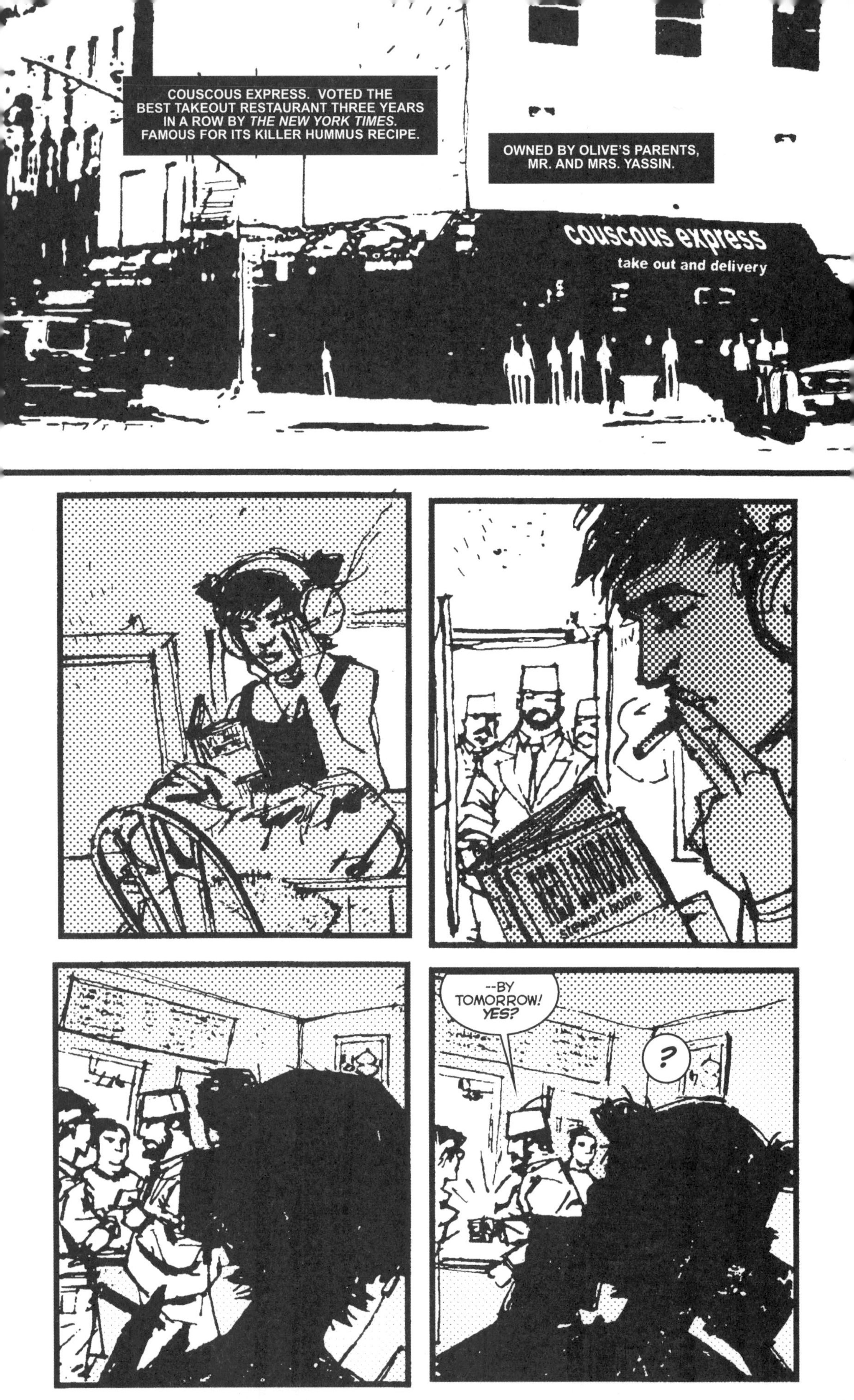
COUSCOUS EXPRESS. VOTED THE BEST TAKEOUT RESTAURANT THREE YEARS IN A ROW BY *THE NEW YORK TIMES*. FAMOUS FOR ITS KILLER HUMMUS RECIPE.
OWNED BY OLIVE'S PARENTS, MR. AND MRS. YASSIN.
couscous express
take out and delivery
stewart home
--BY TOMORROW! *YES?*
?

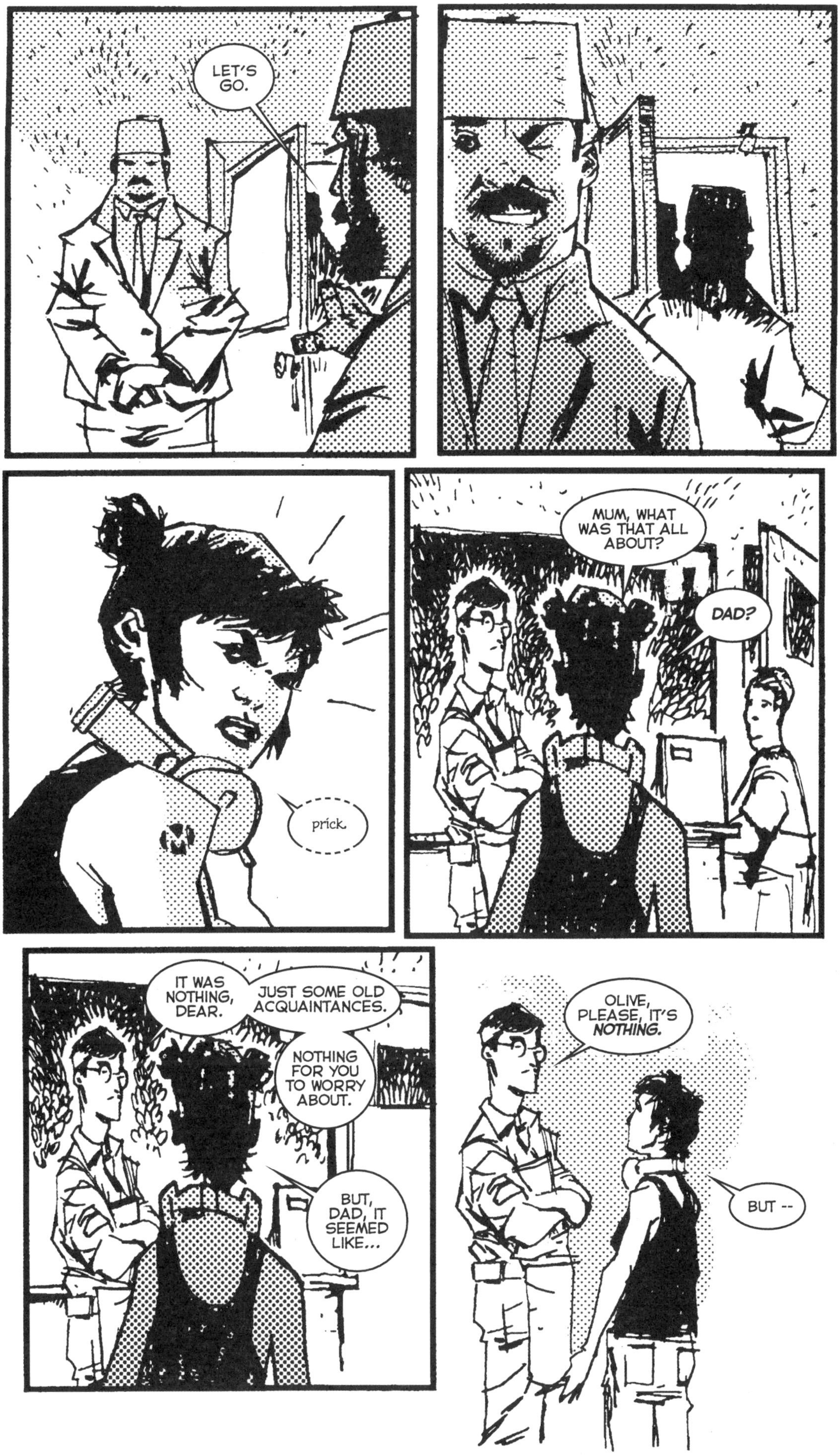
LET'S GO.
MUM, WHAT WAS THAT ALL ABOUT?
DAD?
prick.
IT WAS NOTHING, DEAR.
JUST SOME OLD ACQUAINTANCES.
NOTHING FOR YOU TO WORRY ABOUT.
BUT, DAD, IT SEEMED LIKE...
OLIVE, PLEASE, IT'S *NOTHING.*
BUT --

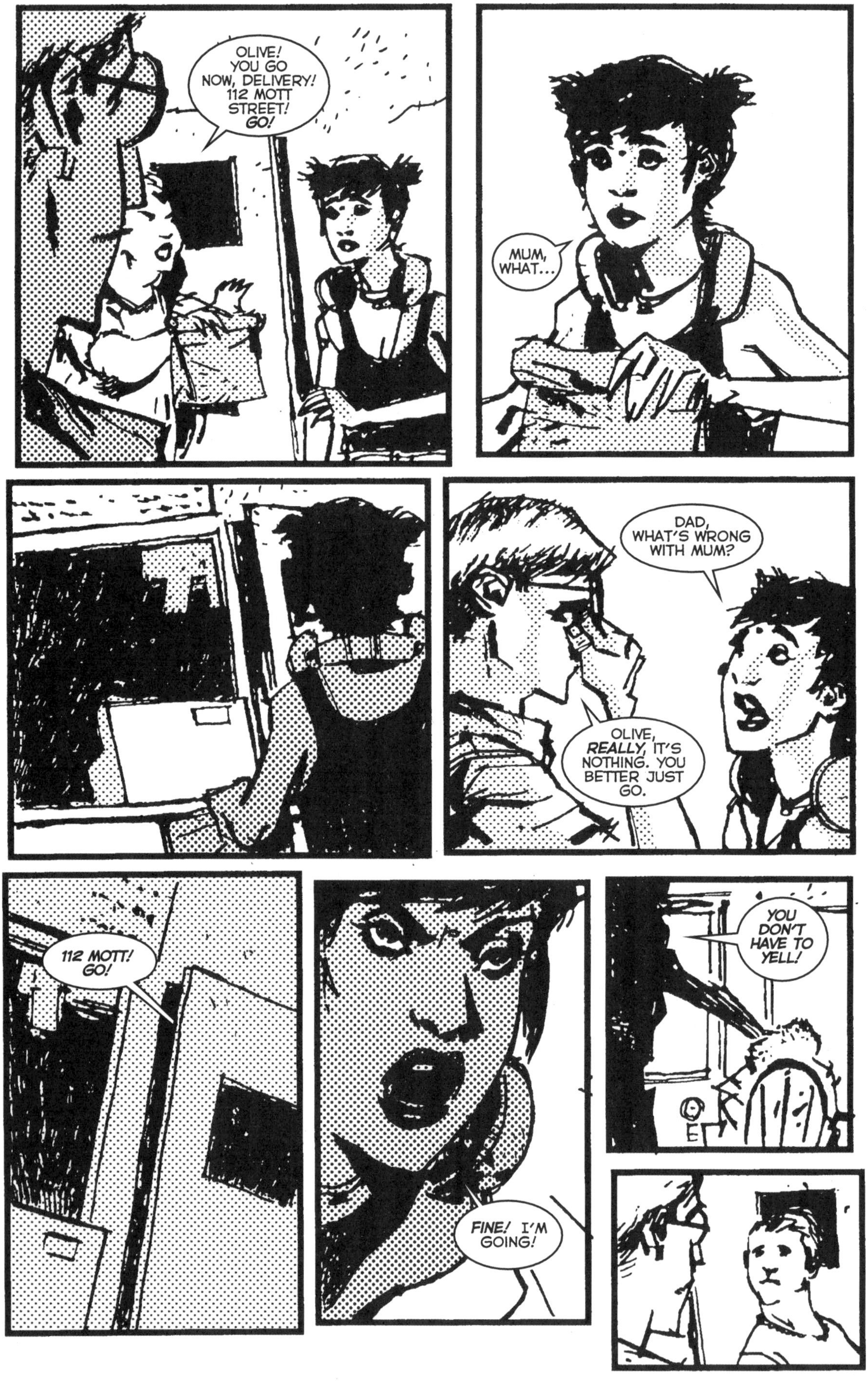
OLIVE! YOU GO NOW, DELIVERY! 112 MOTT STREET! GO!
MUM, WHAT...
DAD, WHAT'S WRONG WITH MUM?
OLIVE, REALLY, IT'S NOTHING. YOU BETTER JUST GO.
112 MOTT! GO!
FINE! I'M GOING!
YOU DON'T HAVE TO YELL!

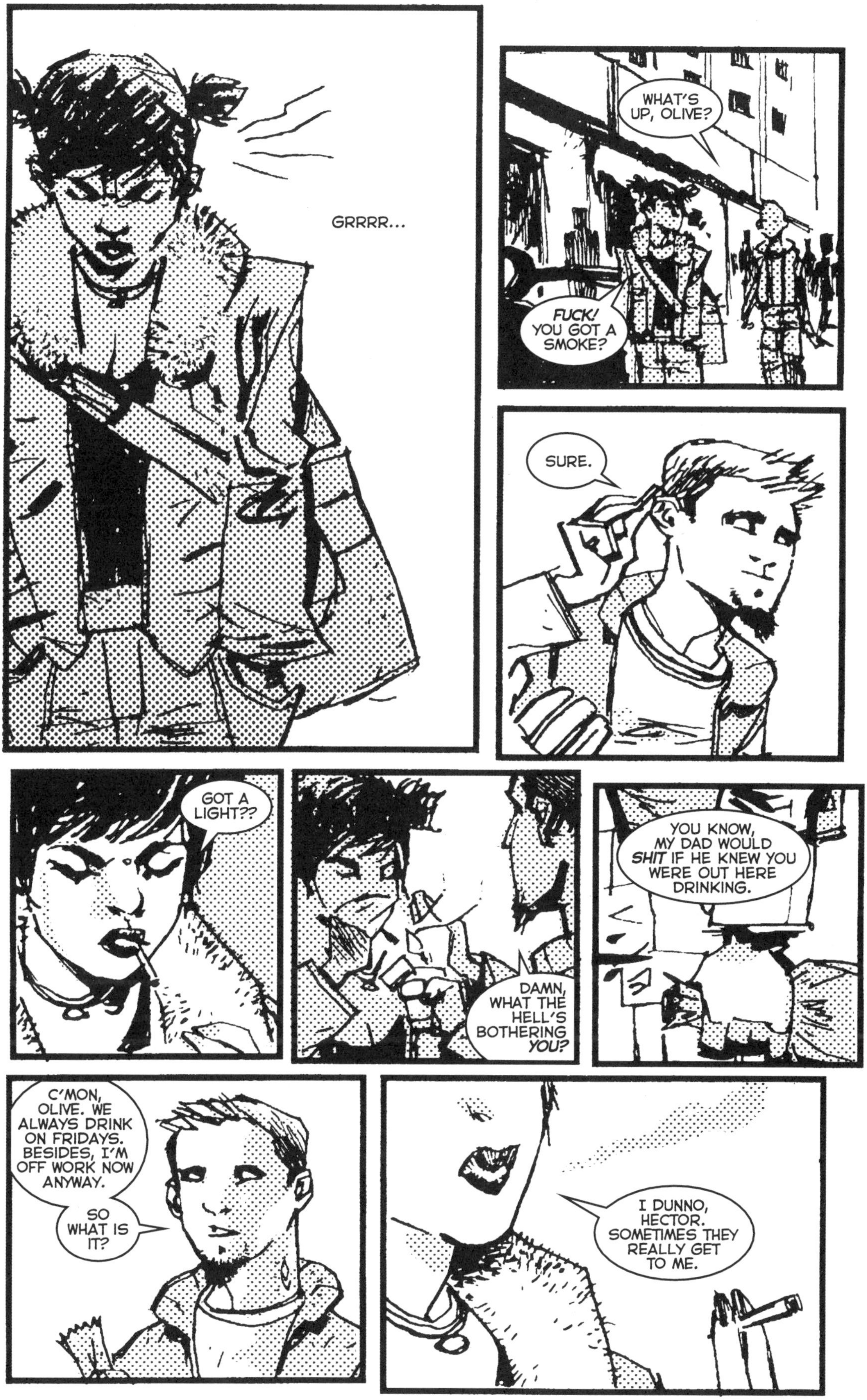
GRRRR...
WHAT'S UP, OLIVE?
FUCK! YOU GOT A SMOKE?
SURE.
GOT A LIGHT??
DAMN, WHAT THE HELL'S BOTHERING *YOU?*
YOU KNOW, MY DAD WOULD *SHIT* IF HE KNEW YOU WERE OUT HERE DRINKING.
C'MON, OLIVE. WE ALWAYS DRINK ON FRIDAYS. BESIDES, I'M OFF WORK NOW ANYWAY.
SO WHAT IS IT?
I DUNNO, HECTOR. SOMETIMES THEY REALLY GET TO ME.

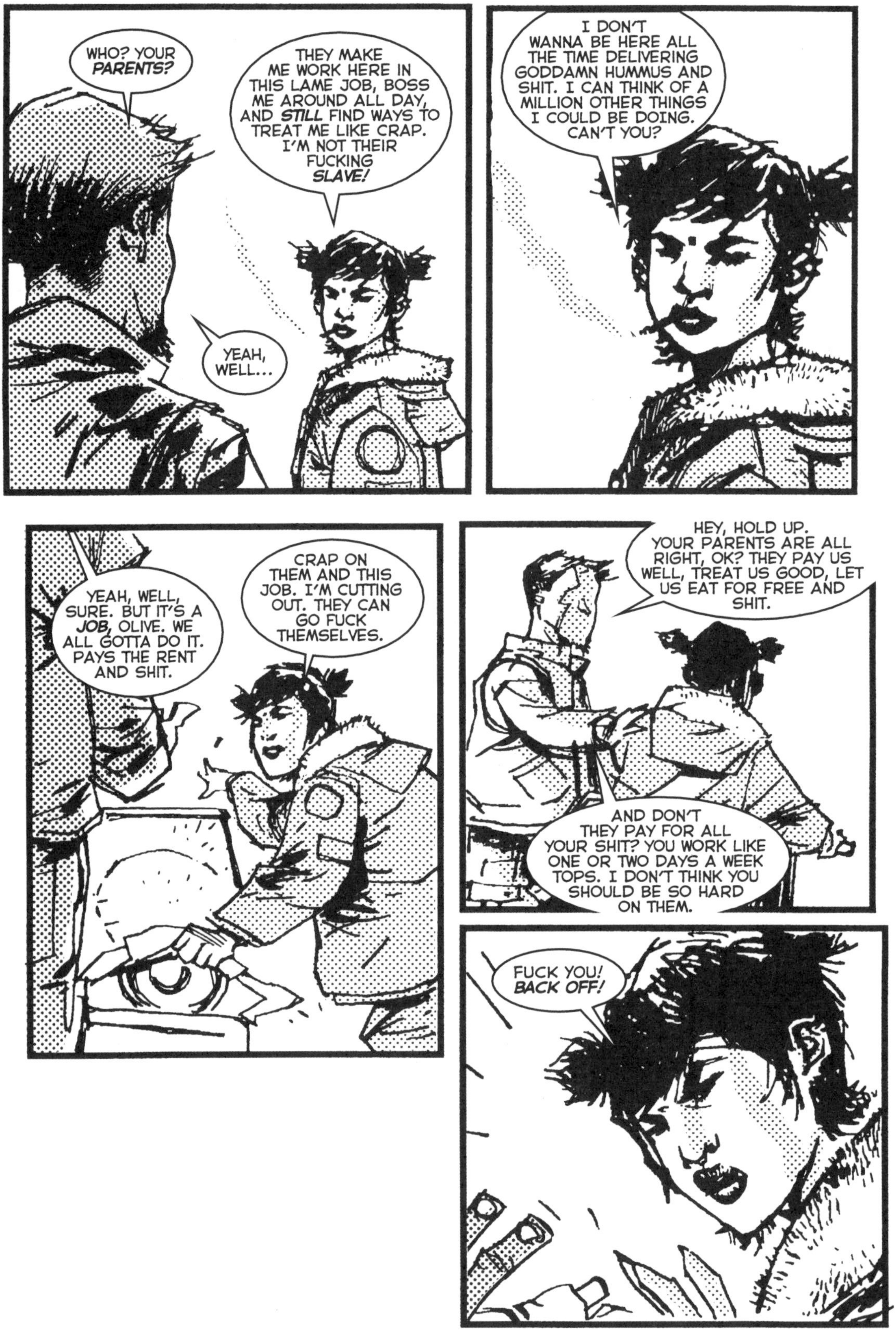
WHO? YOUR PARENTS?
THEY MAKE ME WORK HERE IN THIS LAME JOB, BOSS ME AROUND ALL DAY, AND STILL FIND WAYS TO TREAT ME LIKE CRAP. I'M NOT THEIR FUCKING SLAVE!
YEAH, WELL...
I DON'T WANNA BE HERE ALL THE TIME DELIVERING GODDAMN HUMMUS AND SHIT. I CAN THINK OF A MILLION OTHER THINGS I COULD BE DOING. CAN'T YOU?
YEAH, WELL, SURE. BUT IT'S A JOB, OLIVE. WE ALL GOTTA DO IT. PAYS THE RENT AND SHIT.
CRAP ON THEM AND THIS JOB. I'M CUTTING OUT. THEY CAN GO FUCK THEMSELVES.
HEY, HOLD UP. YOUR PARENTS ARE ALL RIGHT, OK? THEY PAY US WELL, TREAT US GOOD, LET US EAT FOR FREE AND SHIT.
AND DON'T THEY PAY FOR ALL YOUR SHIT? YOU WORK LIKE ONE OR TWO DAYS A WEEK TOPS. I DON'T THINK YOU SHOULD BE SO HARD ON THEM.
FUCK YOU! BACK OFF!

jesus christ.

SHIT, WHAT WAS *THAT* ALL ABOUT?

NOTHING. TYPICAL SPOILED BRAT SHIT. I JUST GET REALLY SICK OF HEARING IT FROM HER.

SHE DON'T KNOW HOW GOOD SHE GOT IT.

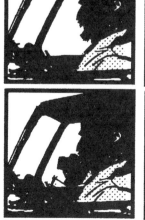

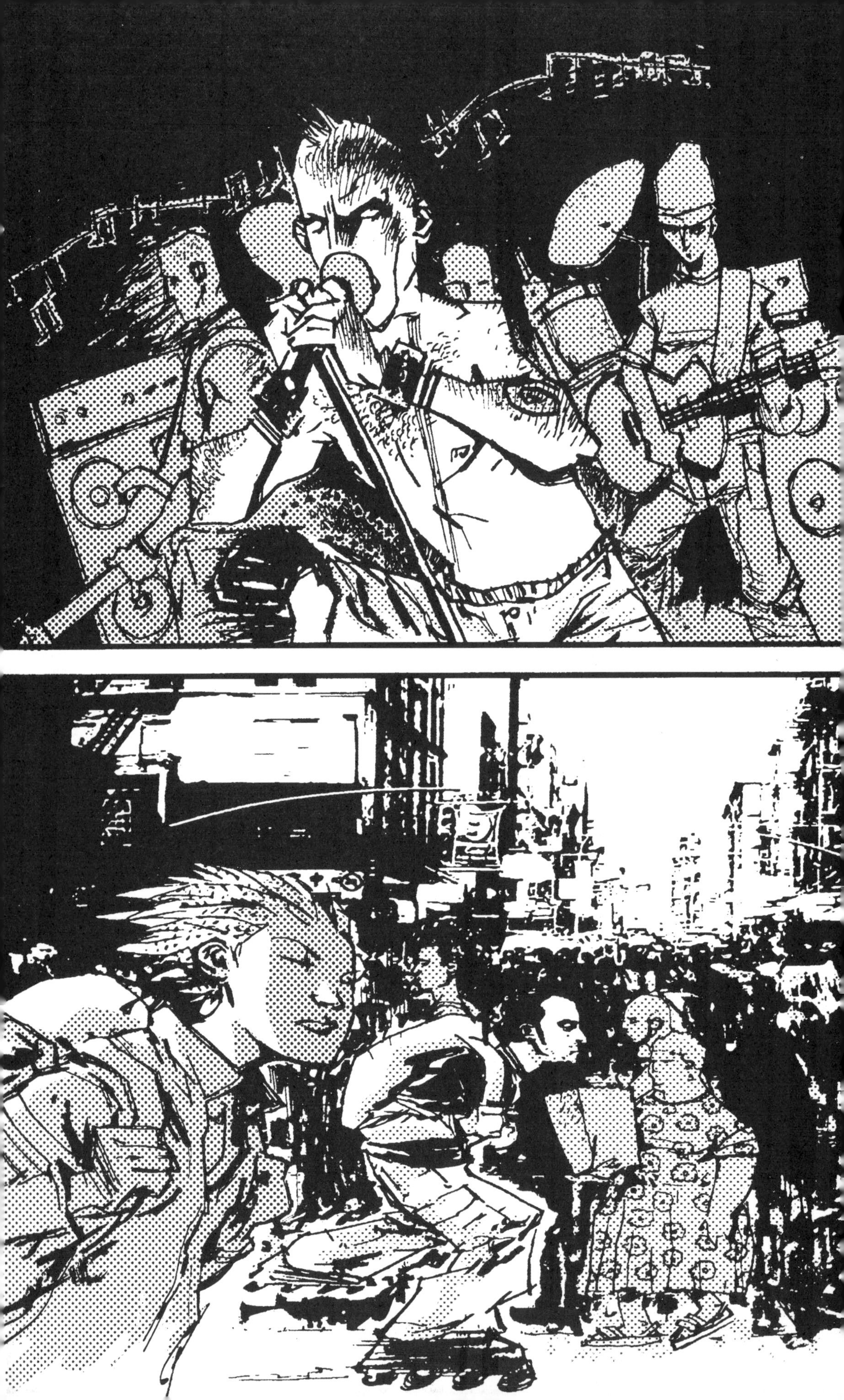

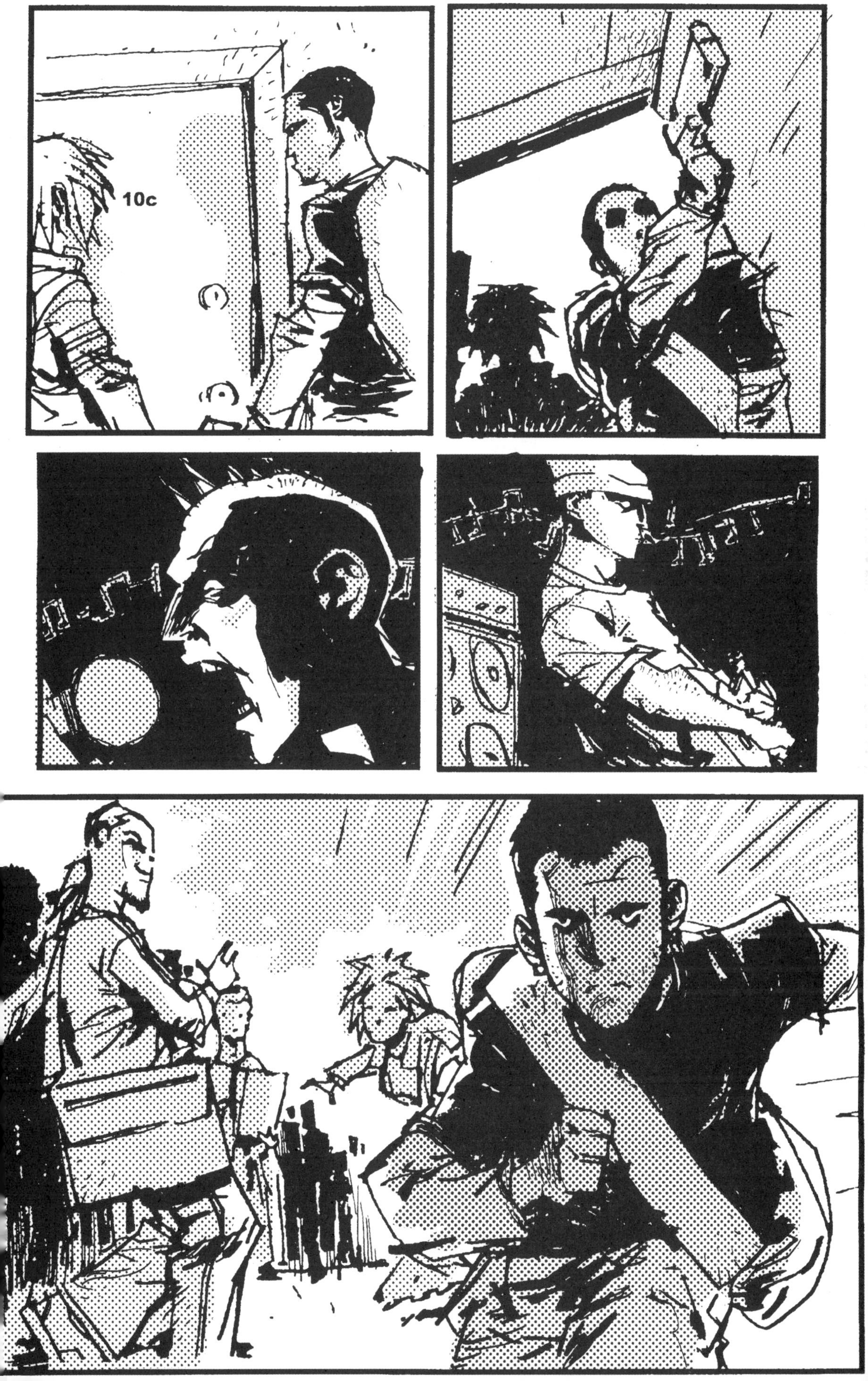
10c

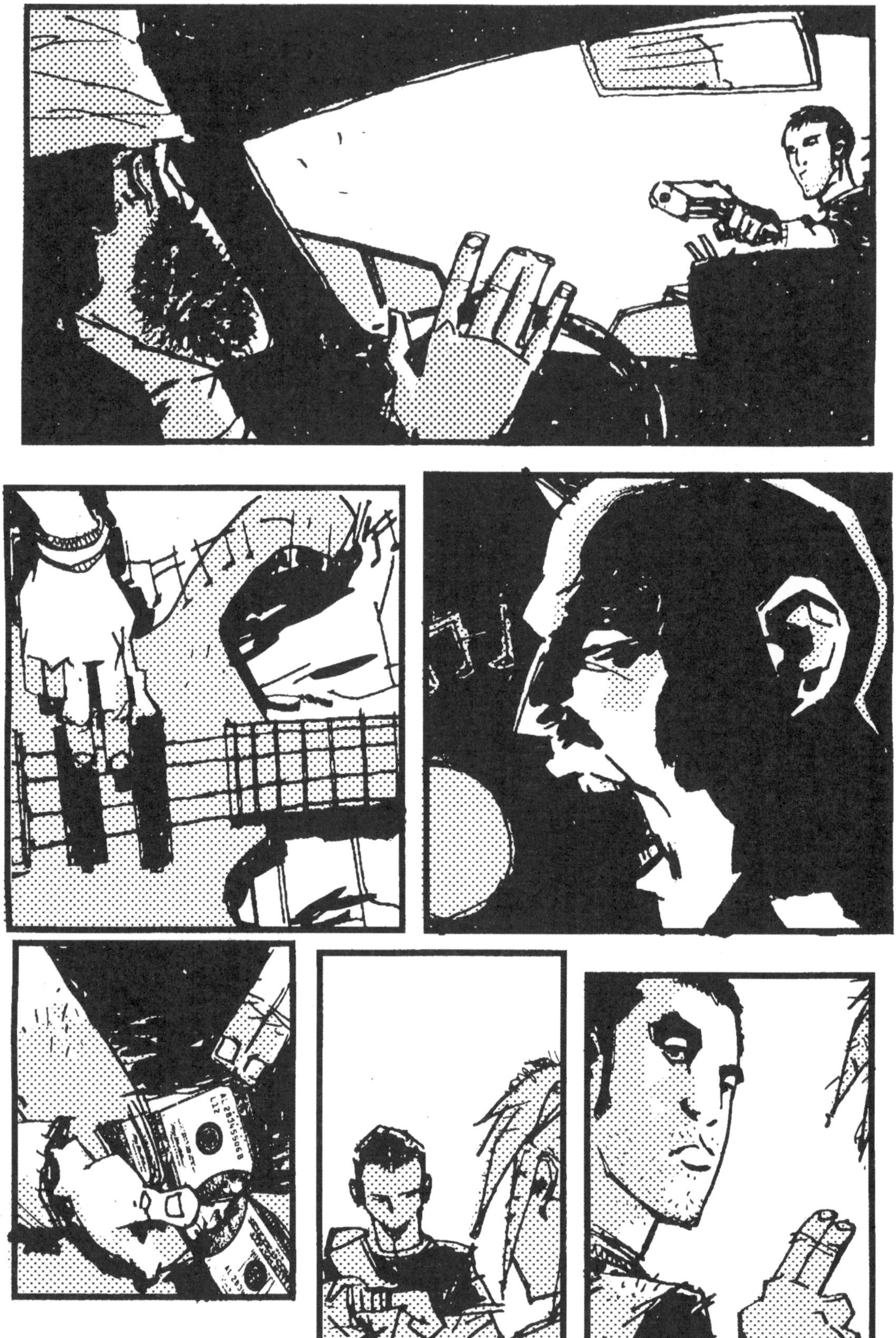

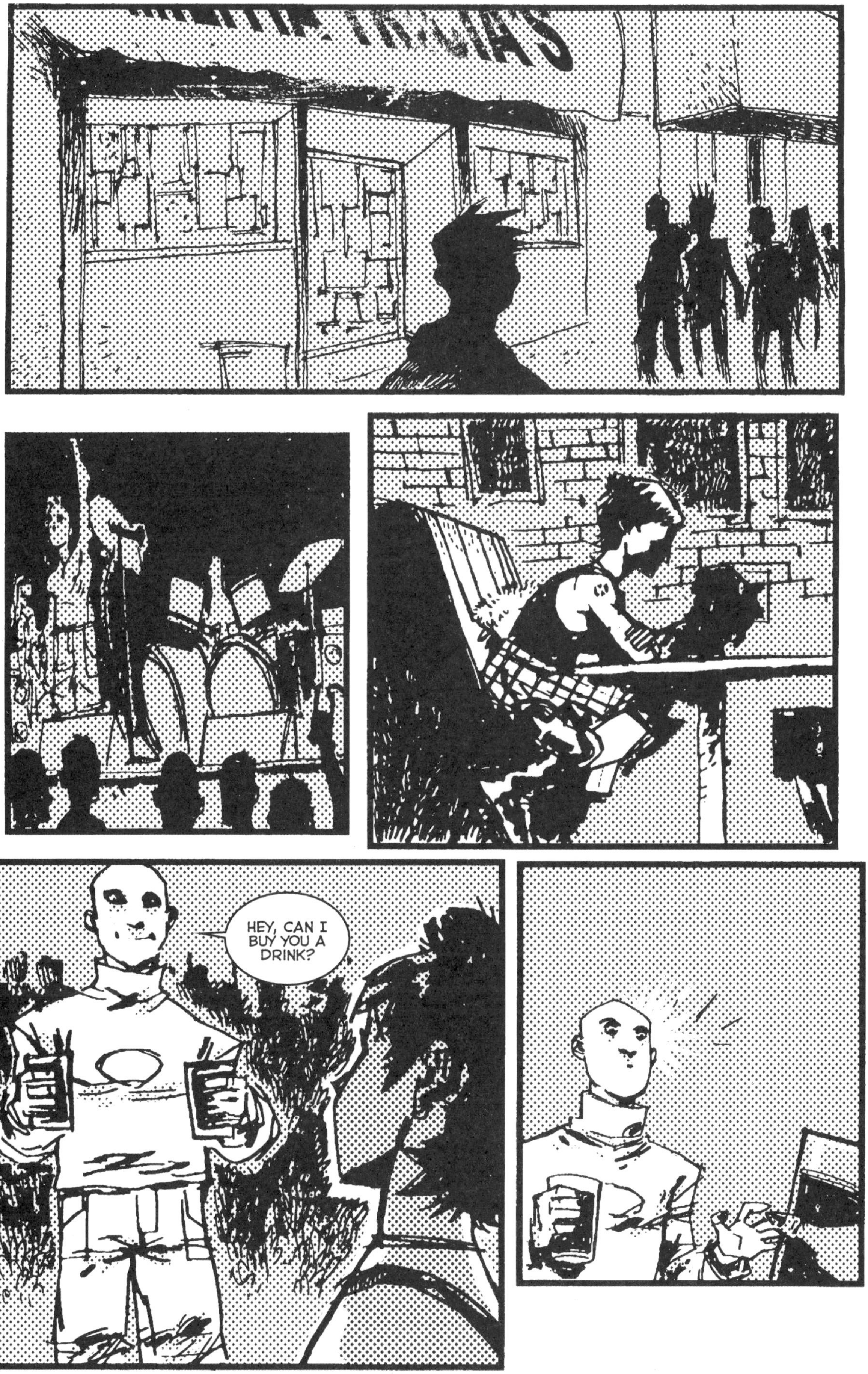
HEY, CAN I BUY YOU A DRINK?

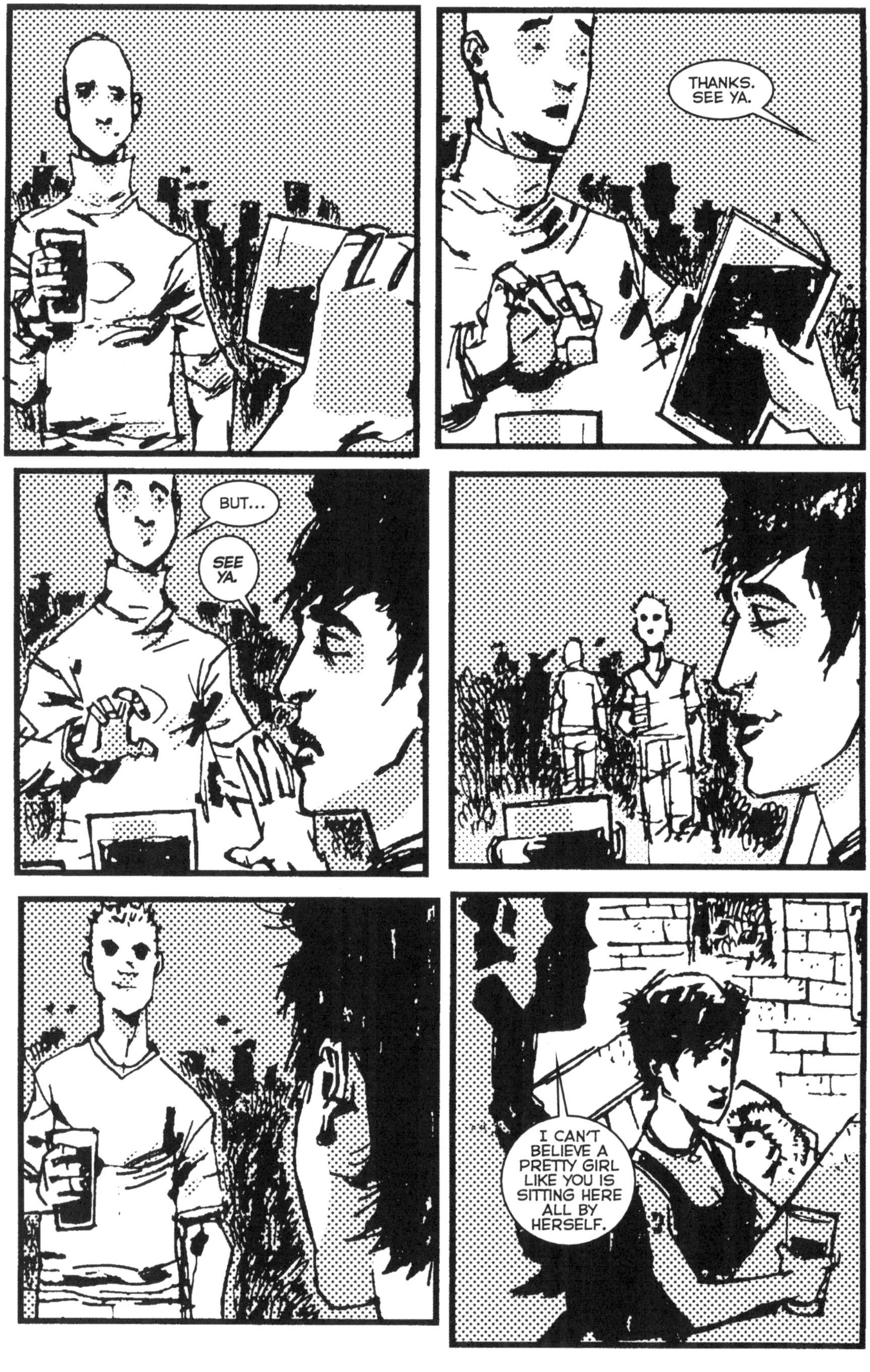
THANKS. SEE YA.
BUT...
SEE YA.
I CAN'T BELIEVE A PRETTY GIRL LIKE YOU IS SITTING HERE ALL BY HERSELF.

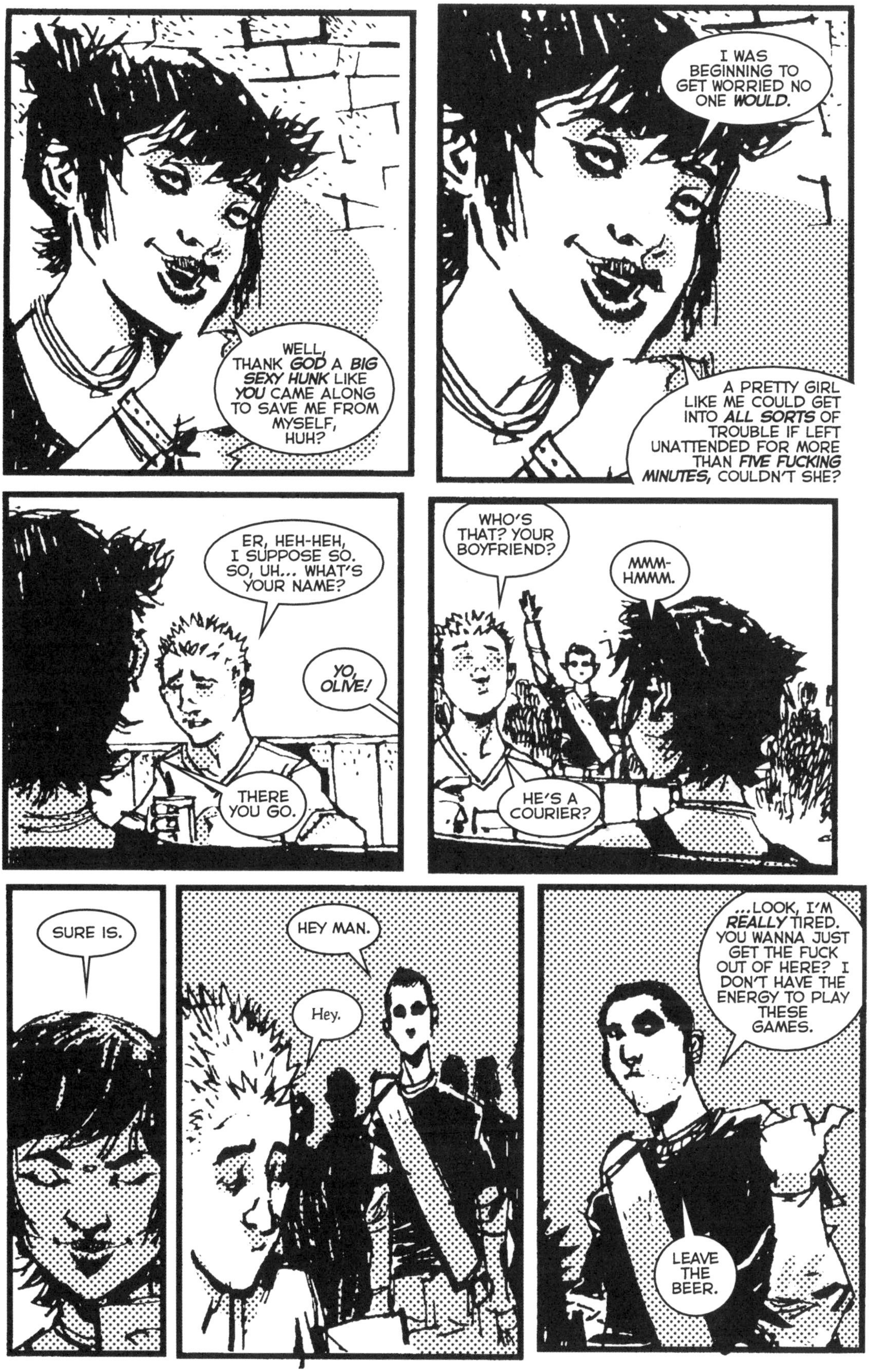
WELL, THANK GOD A BIG SEXY HUNK LIKE YOU CAME ALONG TO SAVE ME FROM MYSELF, HUH?
I WAS BEGINNING TO GET WORRIED NO ONE WOULD.
A PRETTY GIRL LIKE ME COULD GET INTO ALL SORTS OF TROUBLE IF LEFT UNATTENDED FOR MORE THAN FIVE FUCKING MINUTES, COULDN'T SHE?
ER, HEH-HEH, I SUPPOSE SO. SO, UH... WHAT'S YOUR NAME?
YO, OLIVE!
THERE YOU GO.
WHO'S THAT? YOUR BOYFRIEND?
MMM-HMMM.
HE'S A COURIER?
SURE IS.
HEY MAN.
Hey.
...LOOK, I'M REALLY TIRED. YOU WANNA JUST GET THE FUCK OUT OF HERE? I DON'T HAVE THE ENERGY TO PLAY THESE GAMES.
LEAVE THE BEER.

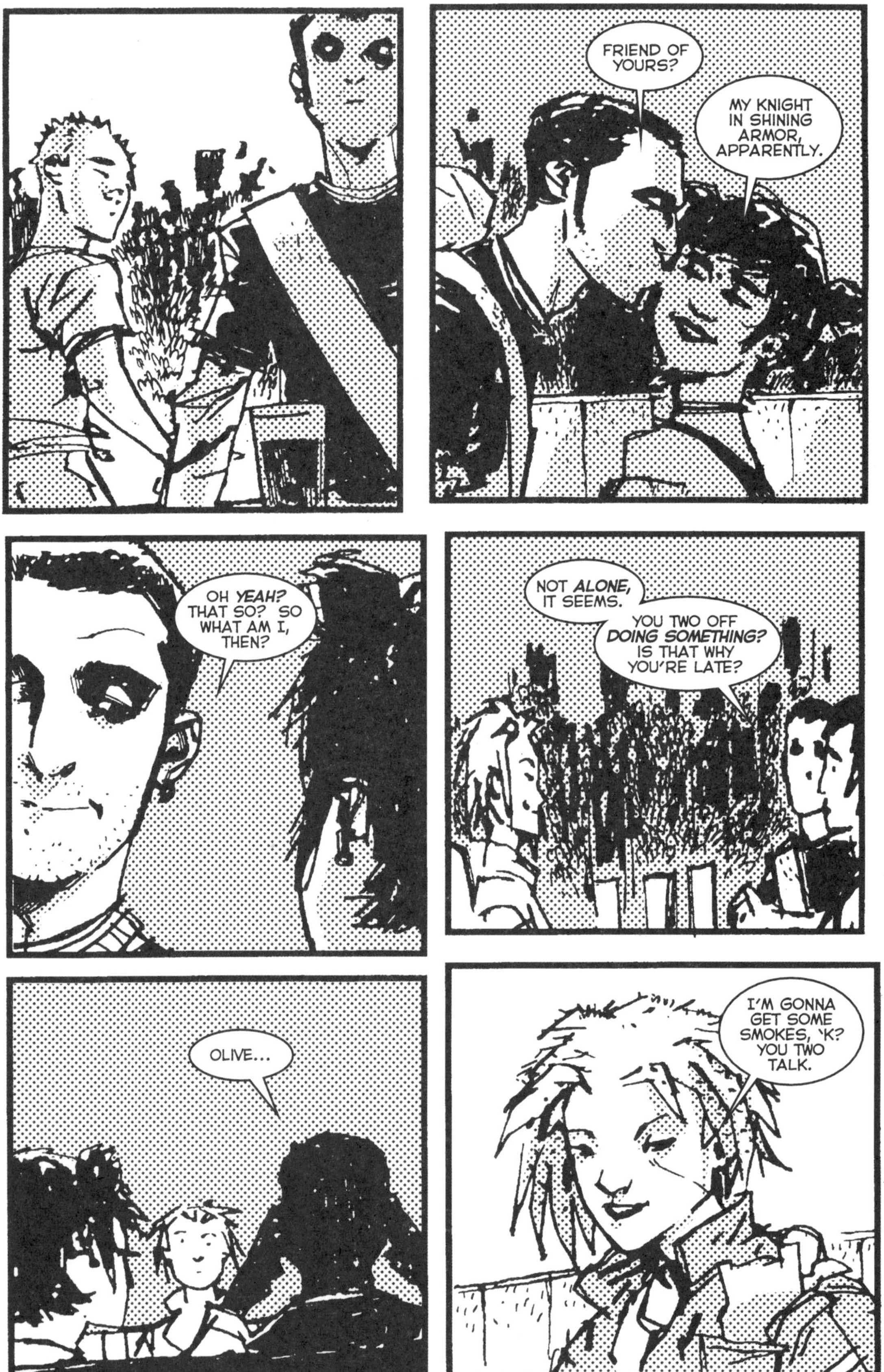
FRIEND OF YOURS?
MY KNIGHT IN SHINING ARMOR, APPARENTLY.
OH *YEAH?* THAT SO? SO WHAT AM I, THEN?
NOT *ALONE,* IT SEEMS.
YOU TWO OFF *DOING SOMETHING?* IS THAT WHY YOU'RE LATE?
OLIVE...
I'M GONNA GET SOME SMOKES, 'K? YOU TWO TALK.

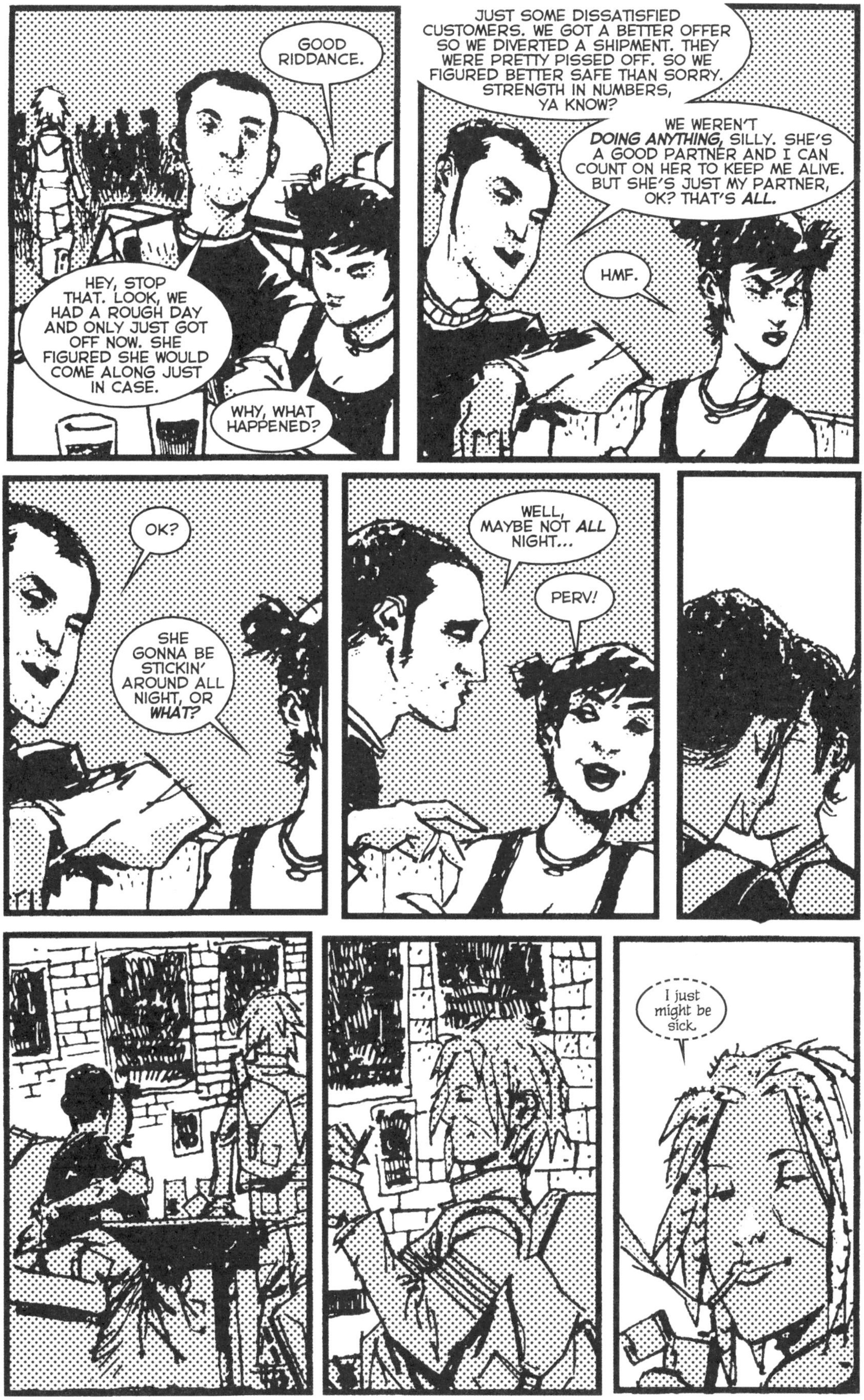
GOOD RIDDANCE.
HEY, STOP THAT. LOOK, WE HAD A ROUGH DAY AND ONLY JUST GOT OFF NOW. SHE FIGURED SHE WOULD COME ALONG JUST IN CASE.
WHY, WHAT HAPPENED?
JUST SOME DISSATISFIED CUSTOMERS. WE GOT A BETTER OFFER SO WE DIVERTED A SHIPMENT. THEY WERE PRETTY PISSED OFF. SO WE FIGURED BETTER SAFE THAN SORRY. STRENGTH IN NUMBERS, YA KNOW?
WE WEREN'T *DOING ANYTHING,* SILLY. SHE'S A GOOD PARTNER AND I CAN COUNT ON HER TO KEEP ME ALIVE. BUT SHE'S JUST MY PARTNER, OK? THAT'S *ALL.*
HMF.
OK?
SHE GONNA BE STICKIN' AROUND ALL NIGHT, OR *WHAT?*
WELL, MAYBE NOT *ALL* NIGHT...
PERV!
I just might be sick.

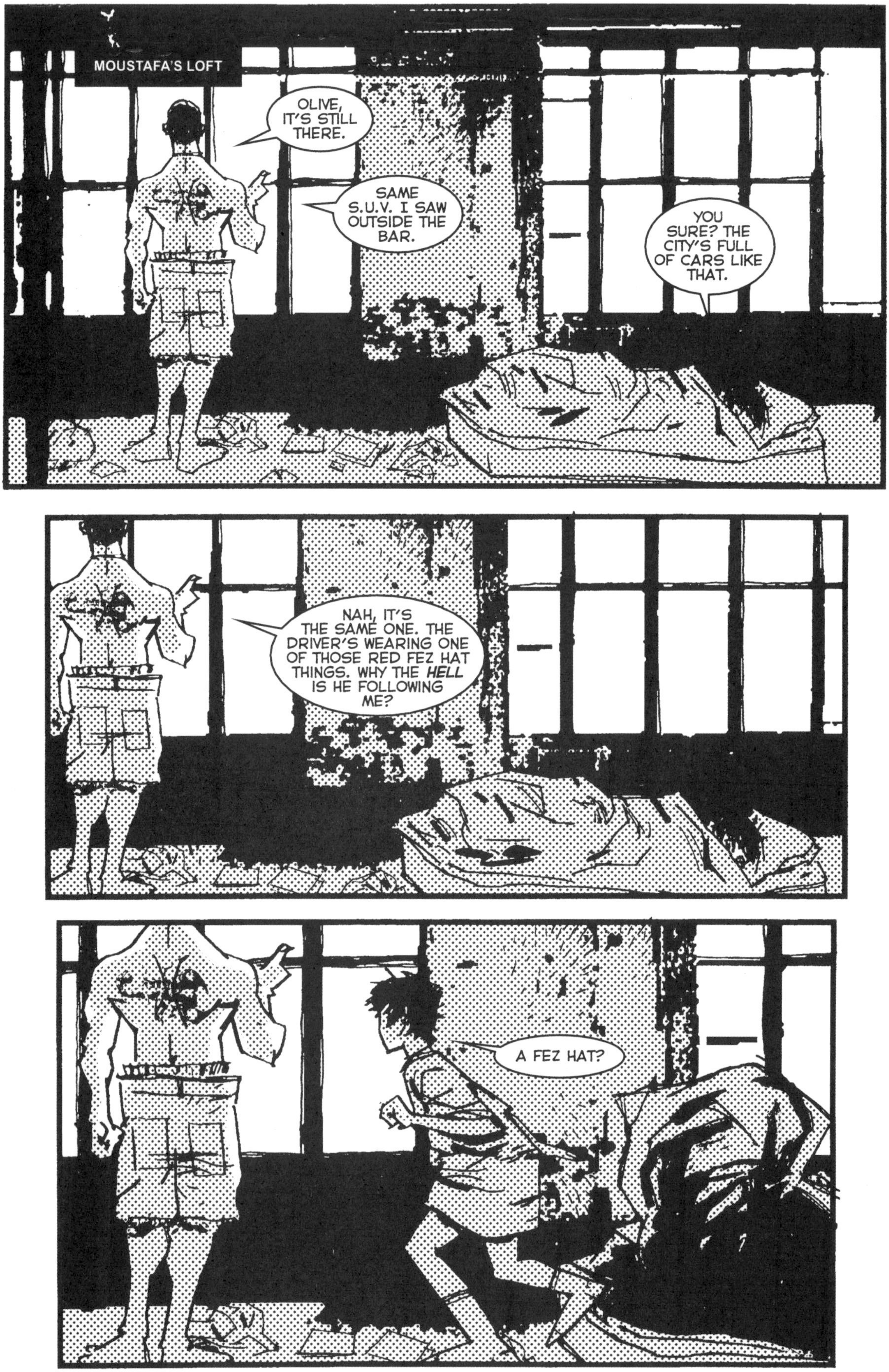
MOUSTAFA'S LOFT
OLIVE, IT'S STILL THERE.
SAME S.U.V. I SAW OUTSIDE THE BAR.
YOU SURE? THE CITY'S FULL OF CARS LIKE THAT.
NAH, IT'S THE SAME ONE. THE DRIVER'S WEARING ONE OF THOSE RED FEZ HAT THINGS. WHY THE *HELL* IS HE FOLLOWING ME?
A FEZ HAT?

SHIT, MAYBE IT'S THOSE GUYS THAT WERE IN THE RESTAURANT TODAY.
WHAT GUYS?
I DUNNO. I COULDN'T TELL WHAT THEY WANTED, BUT THEY SPOOKED MY PARENTS REAL GOOD.
OLIVE, YOU SHOULD *TELL* ME THESE THINGS. JESUS *CHRIST!*
I, UH... I FORGOT ABOUT IT.
BUT THEY *DID* SAY THEY WERE COMING BACK TOMORROW. I DUNNO WHAT FOR.
HMMM.
MAYBE I'LL SWING BY THEN, MAKE SURE THINGS ARE COOL. GET SOME OF YOUR MOM'S KILLER HUMMUS WHILE I'M AT IT. THAT SHIT IS *GOOD!*
COME BACK TO BED, M. IT'S COLD.

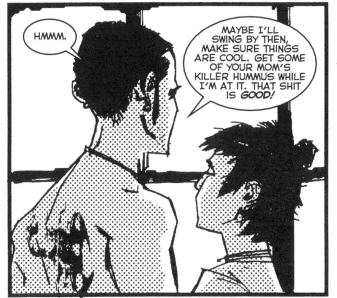

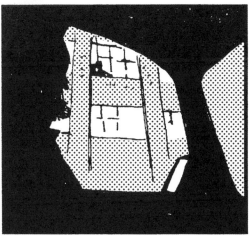

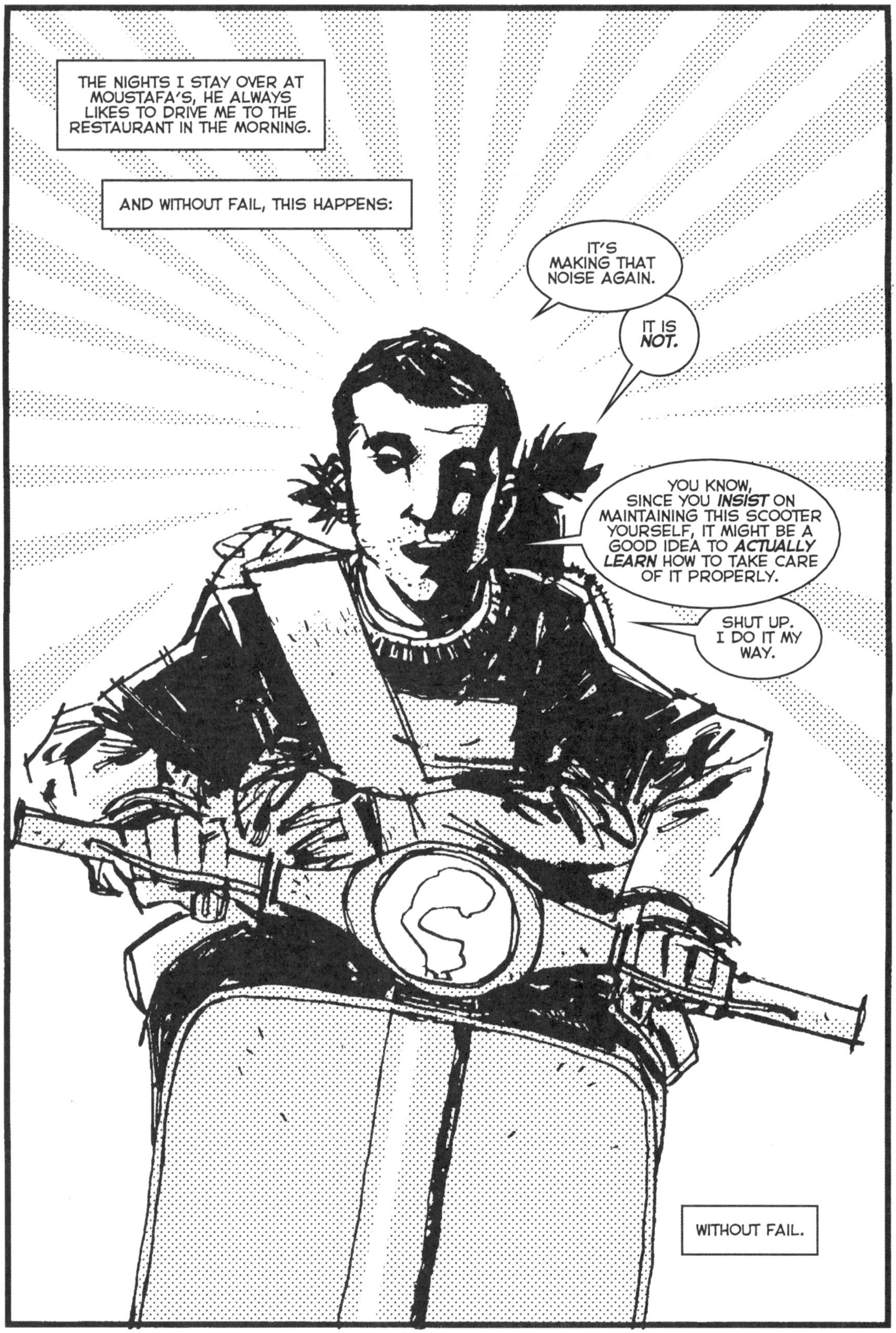
THE NIGHTS I STAY OVER AT MOUSTAFA'S, HE ALWAYS LIKES TO DRIVE ME TO THE RESTAURANT IN THE MORNING.
AND WITHOUT FAIL, THIS HAPPENS:
IT'S MAKING THAT NOISE AGAIN.
IT IS *NOT.*
YOU KNOW, SINCE YOU *INSIST* ON MAINTAINING THIS SCOOTER YOURSELF, IT MIGHT BE A GOOD IDEA TO *ACTUALLY LEARN* HOW TO TAKE CARE OF IT PROPERLY.
SHUT UP. I DO IT MY WAY.
WITHOUT FAIL.

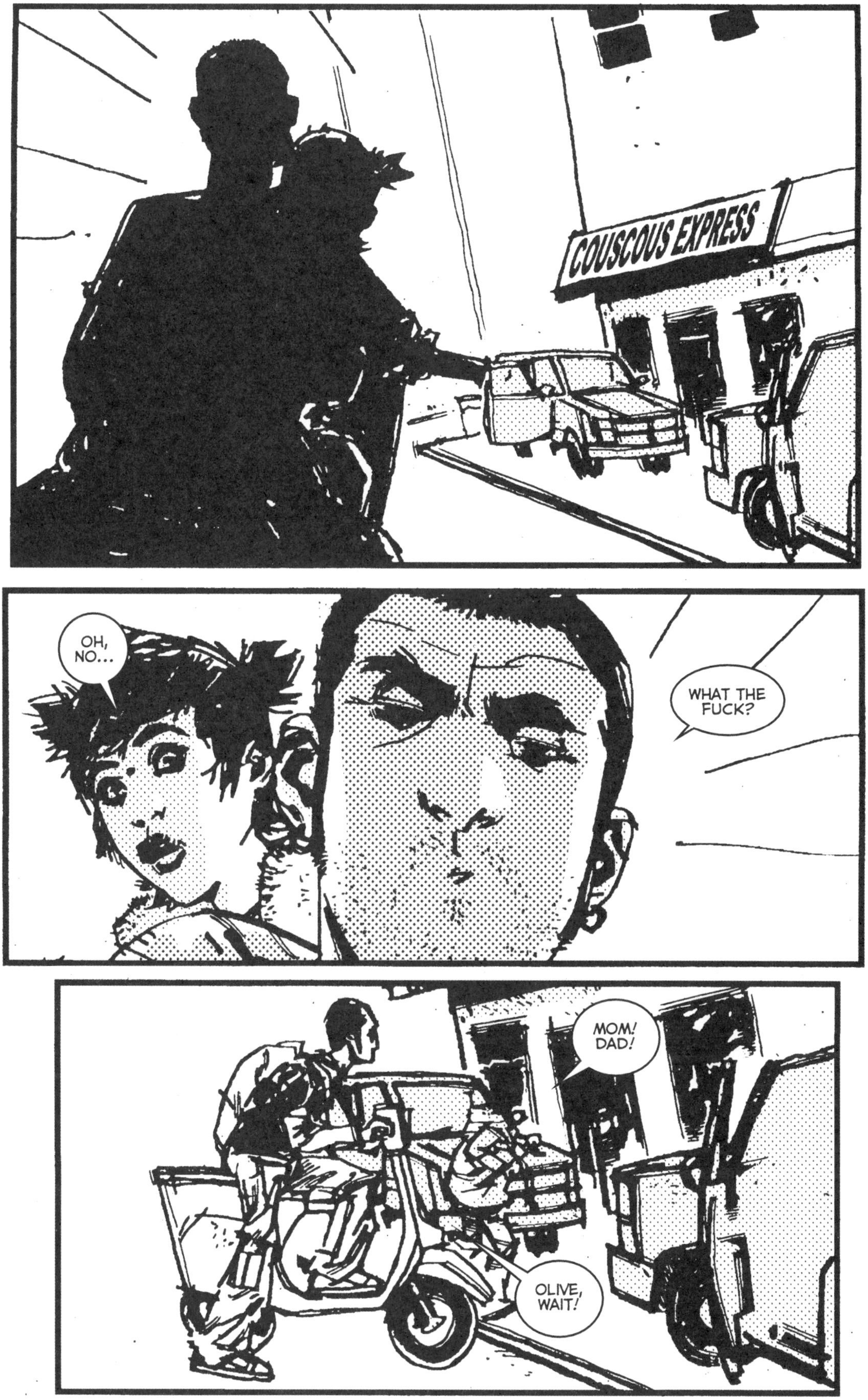
COUSCOUS EXPRESS
OH, NO...
WHAT THE FUCK?
MOM! DAD!
OLIVE, WAIT!

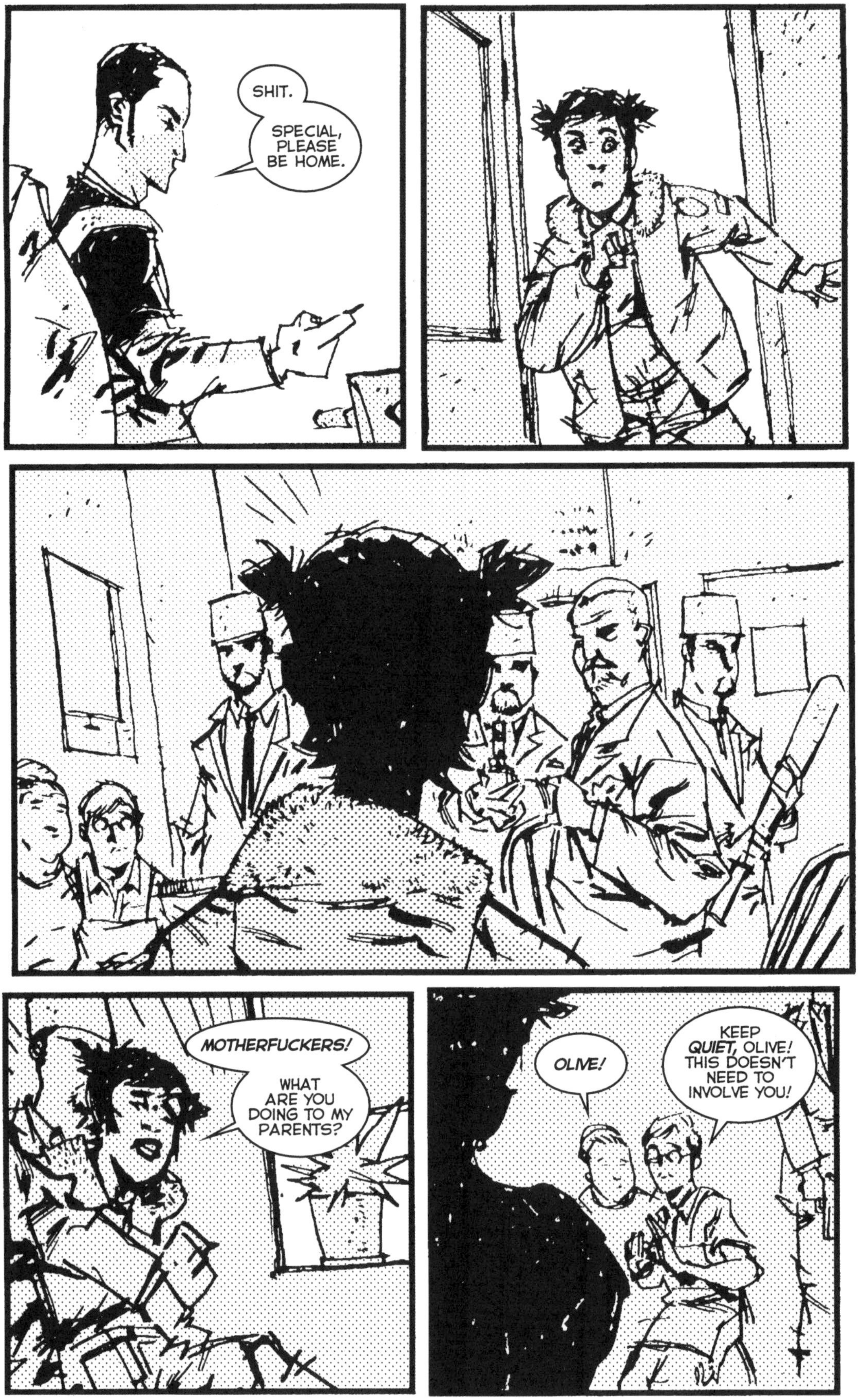
SHIT.
SPECIAL, PLEASE BE HOME.
MOTHERFUCKERS!
WHAT ARE YOU DOING TO MY PARENTS?
OLIVE!
KEEP QUIET, OLIVE! THIS DOESN'T NEED TO INVOLVE YOU!

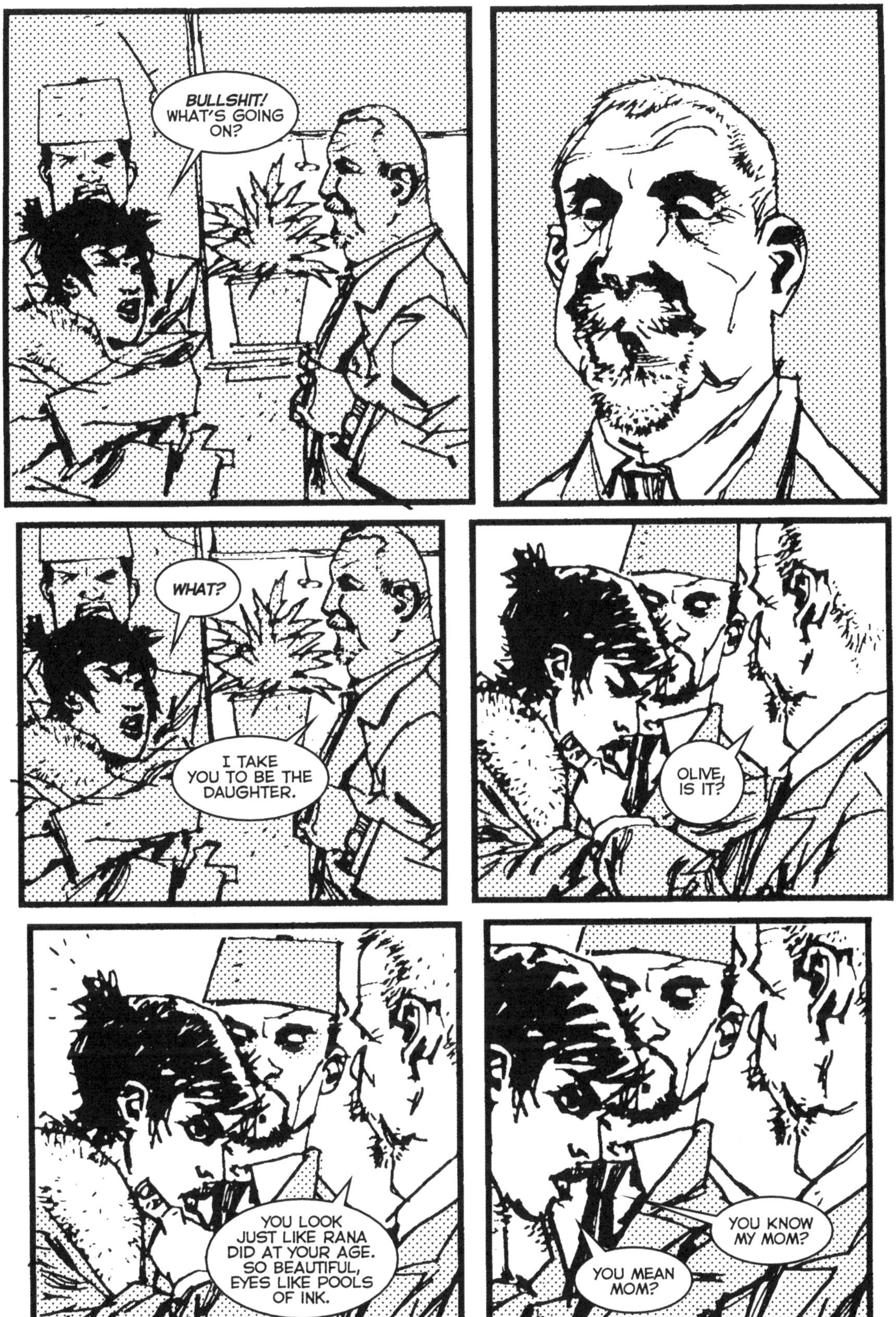
BULLSHIT! WHAT'S GOING ON?
WHAT?
I TAKE YOU TO BE THE DAUGHTER.
OLIVE, IS IT?
YOU LOOK JUST LIKE RANA DID AT YOUR AGE. SO BEAUTIFUL, EYES LIKE POOLS OF INK.
YOU KNOW MY MOM?
YOU MEAN MOM?

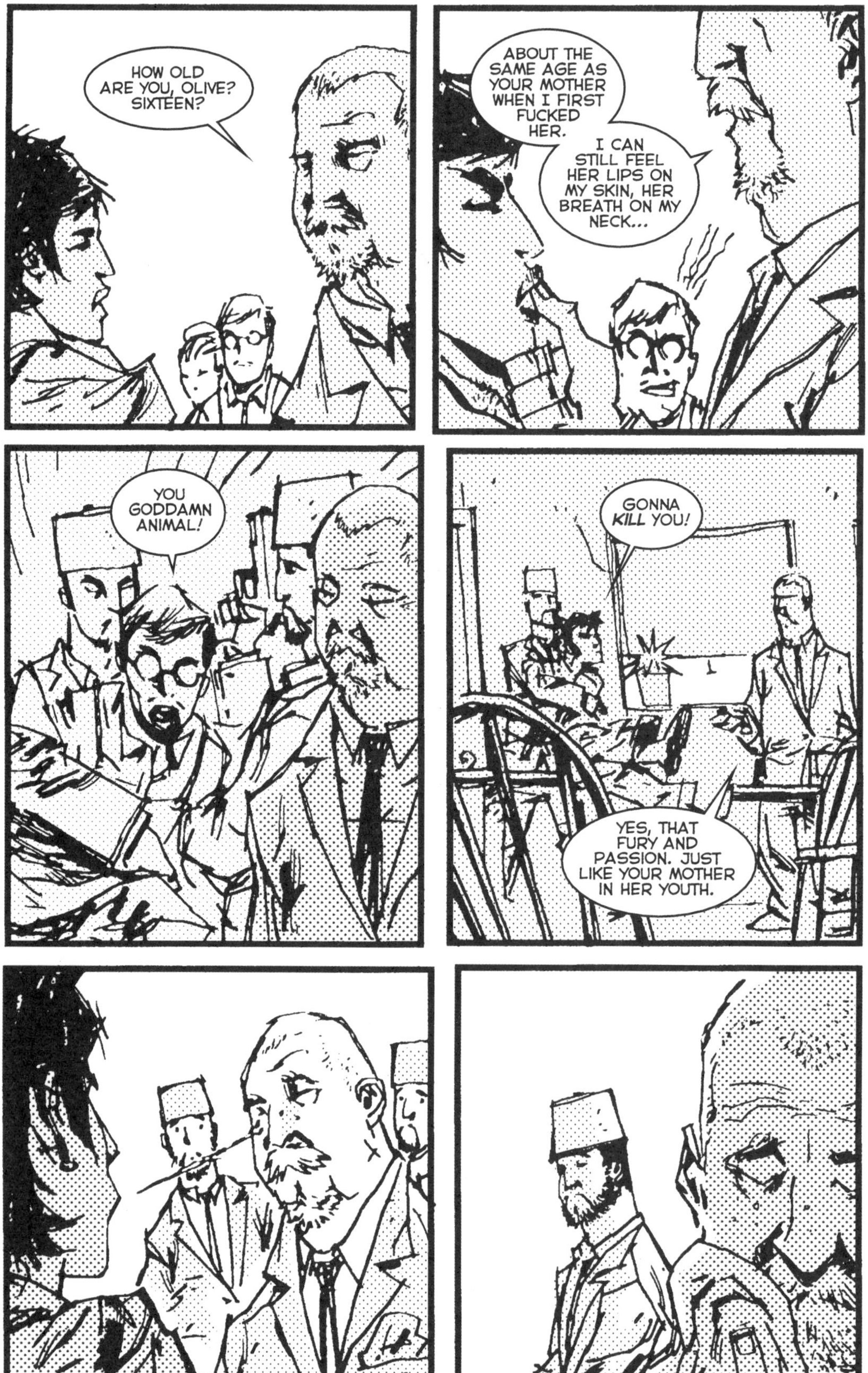
HOW OLD ARE YOU, OLIVE? SIXTEEN?
ABOUT THE SAME AGE AS YOUR MOTHER WHEN I FIRST FUCKED HER.
I CAN STILL FEEL HER LIPS ON MY SKIN, HER BREATH ON MY NECK...
YOU GODDAMN ANIMAL!
GONNA *KILL* YOU!
YES, THAT FURY AND PASSION. JUST LIKE YOUR MOTHER IN HER YOUTH.

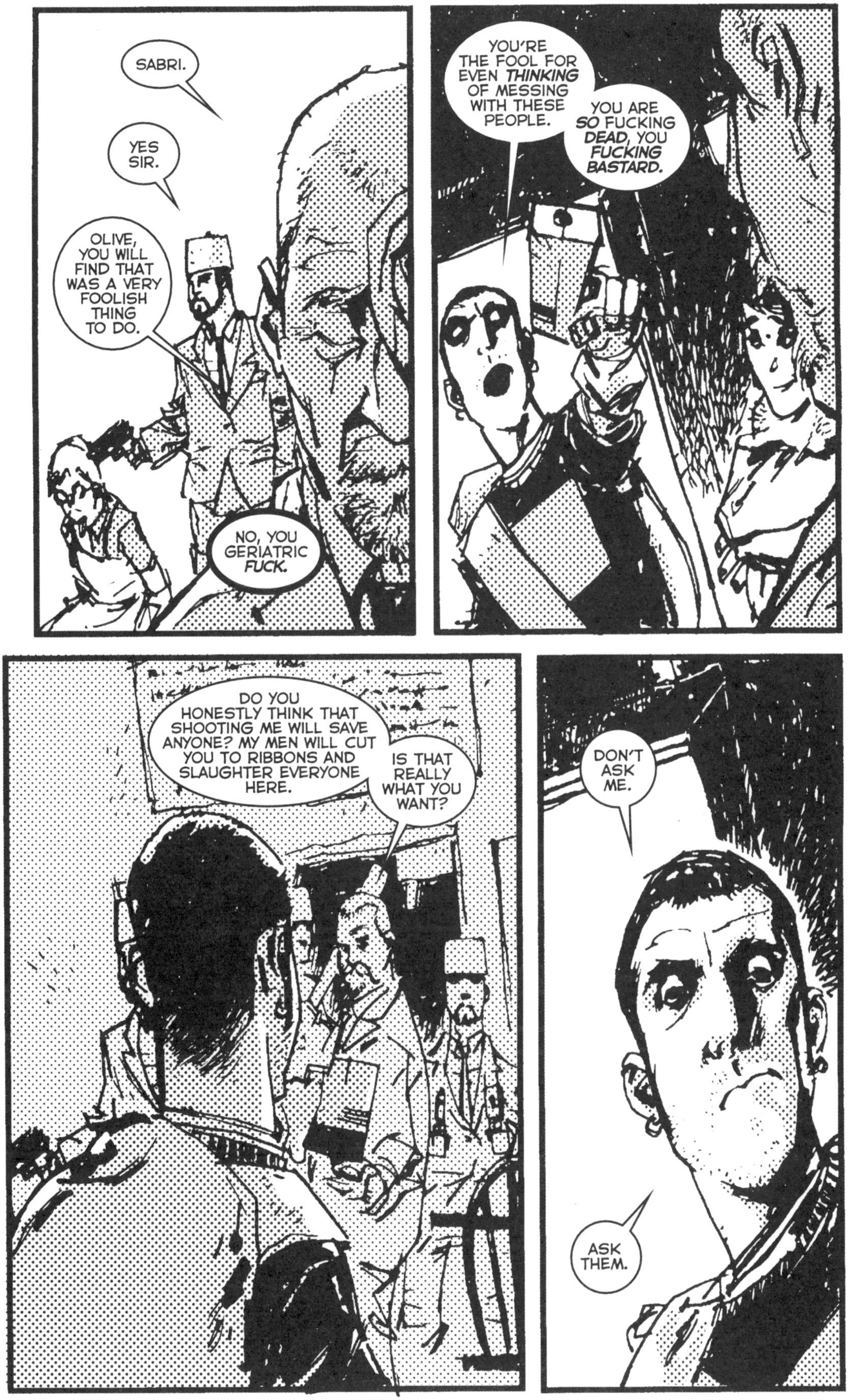
SABRI.
YES SIR.
OLIVE, YOU WILL FIND THAT WAS A VERY FOOLISH THING TO DO.
NO, YOU GERIATRIC *FUCK.*
YOU'RE THE FOOL FOR EVEN *THINKING* OF MESSING WITH THESE PEOPLE.
YOU ARE *SO* FUCKING *DEAD,* YOU *FUCKING BASTARD.*
DO YOU HONESTLY THINK THAT SHOOTING ME WILL SAVE ANYONE? MY MEN WILL CUT YOU TO RIBBONS AND SLAUGHTER EVERYONE HERE.
IS THAT REALLY WHAT YOU WANT?
DON'T ASK ME.
ASK THEM.

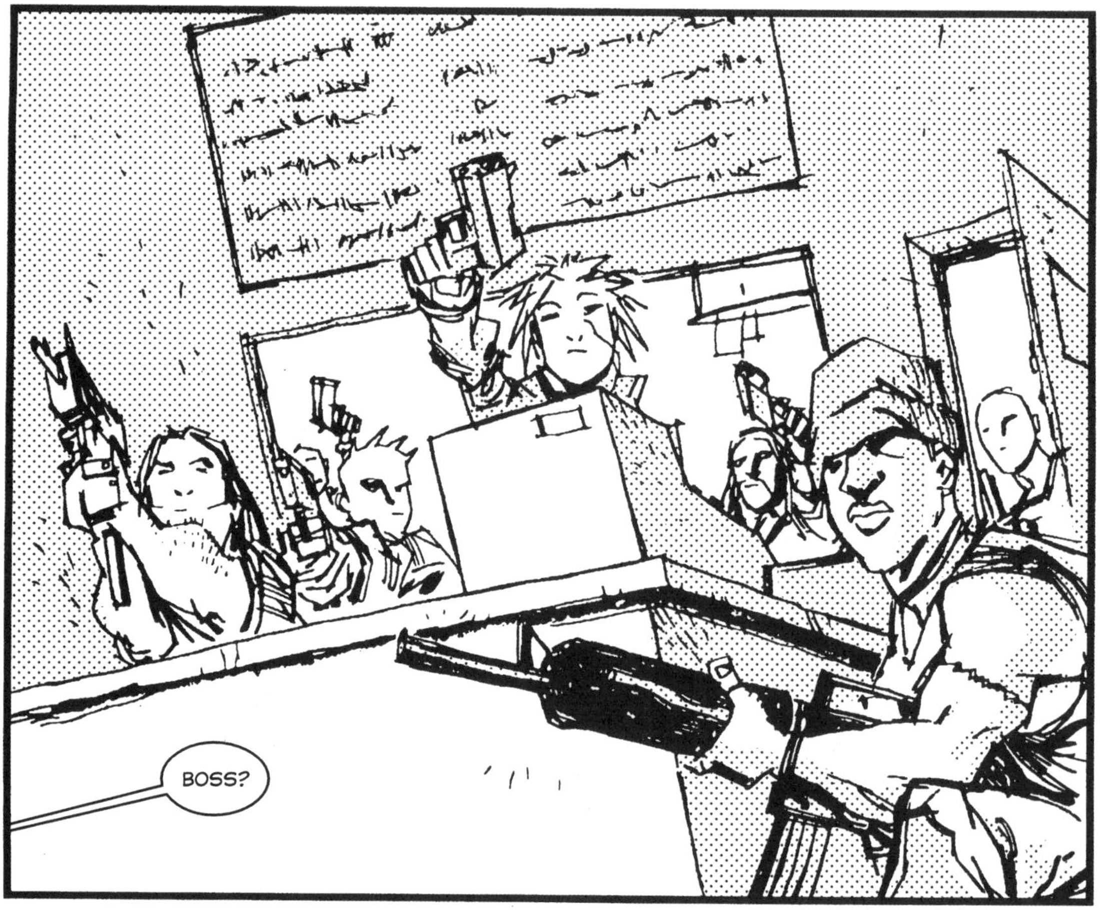
BOSS?

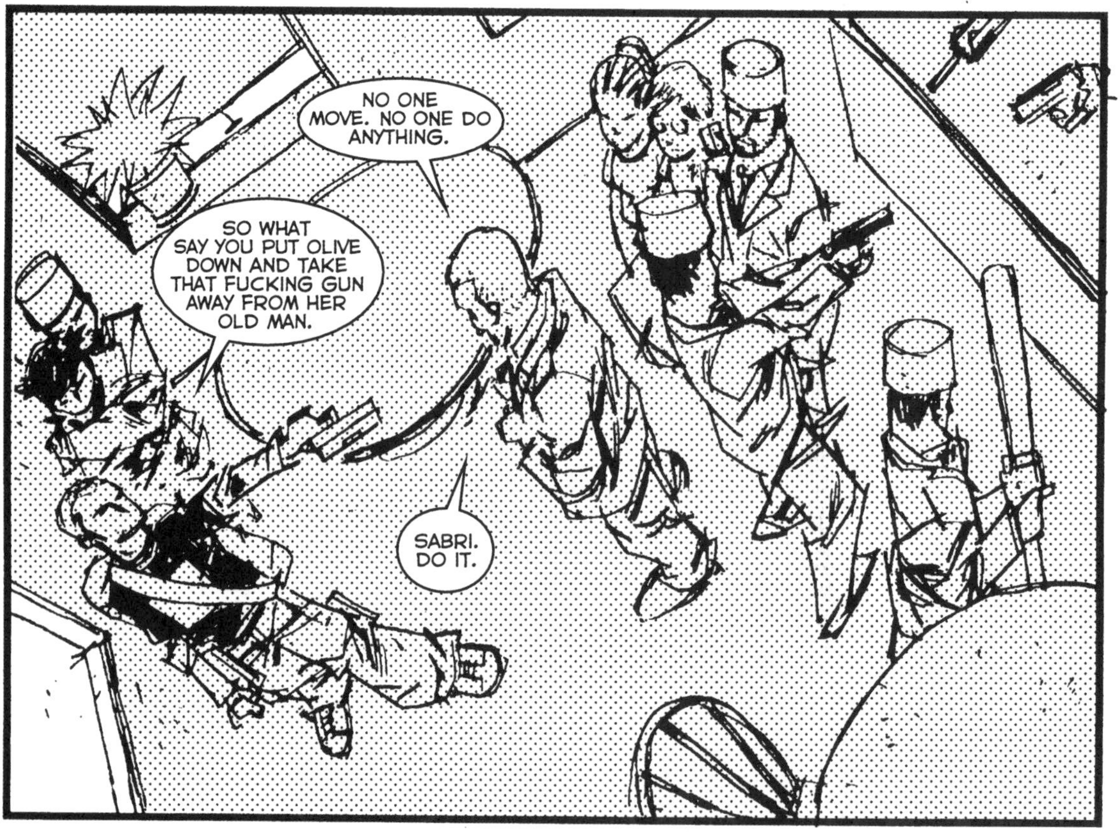
NO ONE MOVE. NO ONE DO ANYTHING.
SO WHAT SAY YOU PUT OLIVE DOWN AND TAKE THAT FUCKING GUN AWAY FROM HER OLD MAN.
SABRI. DO IT.

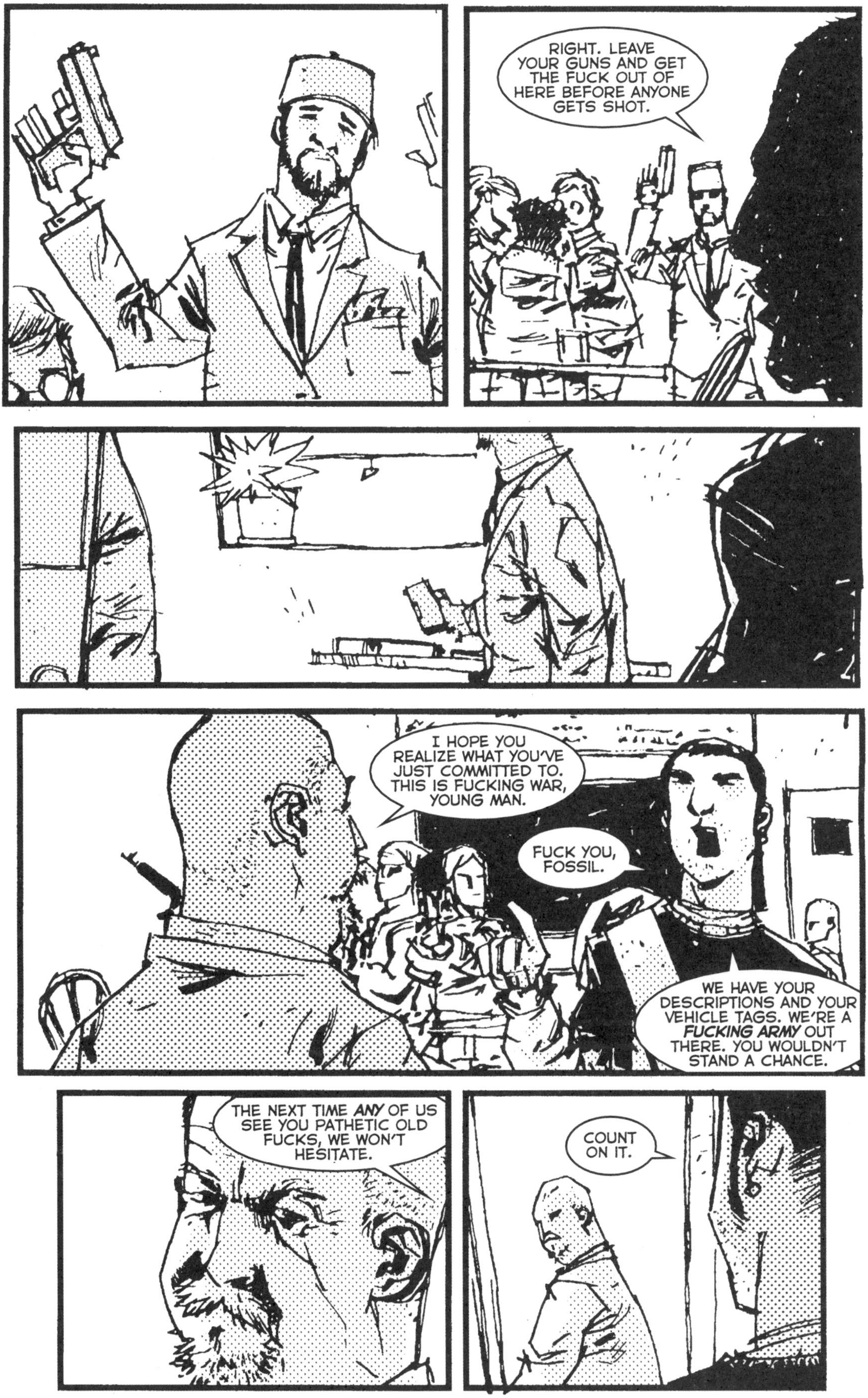
RIGHT. LEAVE YOUR GUNS AND GET THE FUCK OUT OF HERE BEFORE ANYONE GETS SHOT.
I HOPE YOU REALIZE WHAT YOU'VE JUST COMMITTED TO. THIS IS FUCKING WAR, YOUNG MAN.
FUCK YOU, FOSSIL.
WE HAVE YOUR DESCRIPTIONS AND YOUR VEHICLE TAGS. WE'RE A *FUCKING ARMY* OUT THERE. YOU WOULDN'T STAND A CHANCE.
THE NEXT TIME *ANY* OF US SEE YOU PATHETIC OLD FUCKS, WE WON'T HESITATE.
COUNT ON IT.

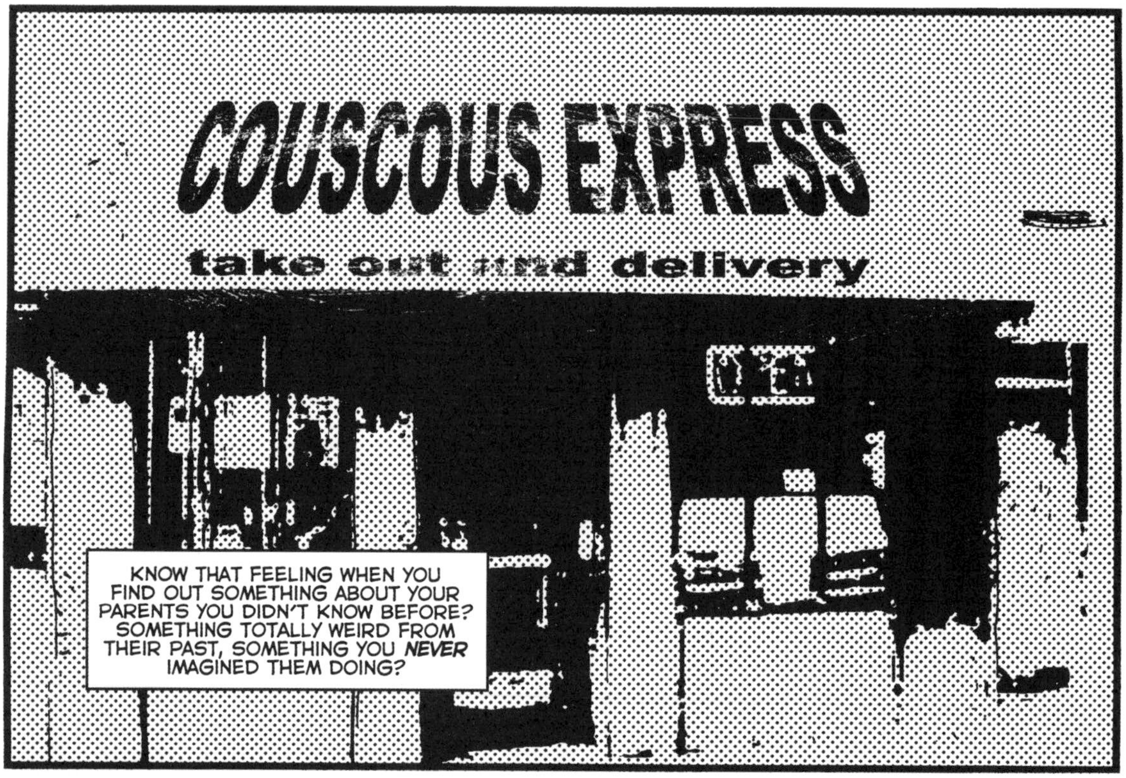
COUSCOUS EXPRESS
take out and delivery
KNOW THAT FEELING WHEN YOU FIND OUT SOMETHING ABOUT YOUR PARENTS YOU DIDN'T KNOW BEFORE? SOMETHING TOTALLY WEIRD FROM THEIR PAST, SOMETHING YOU *NEVER* IMAGINED THEM DOING?

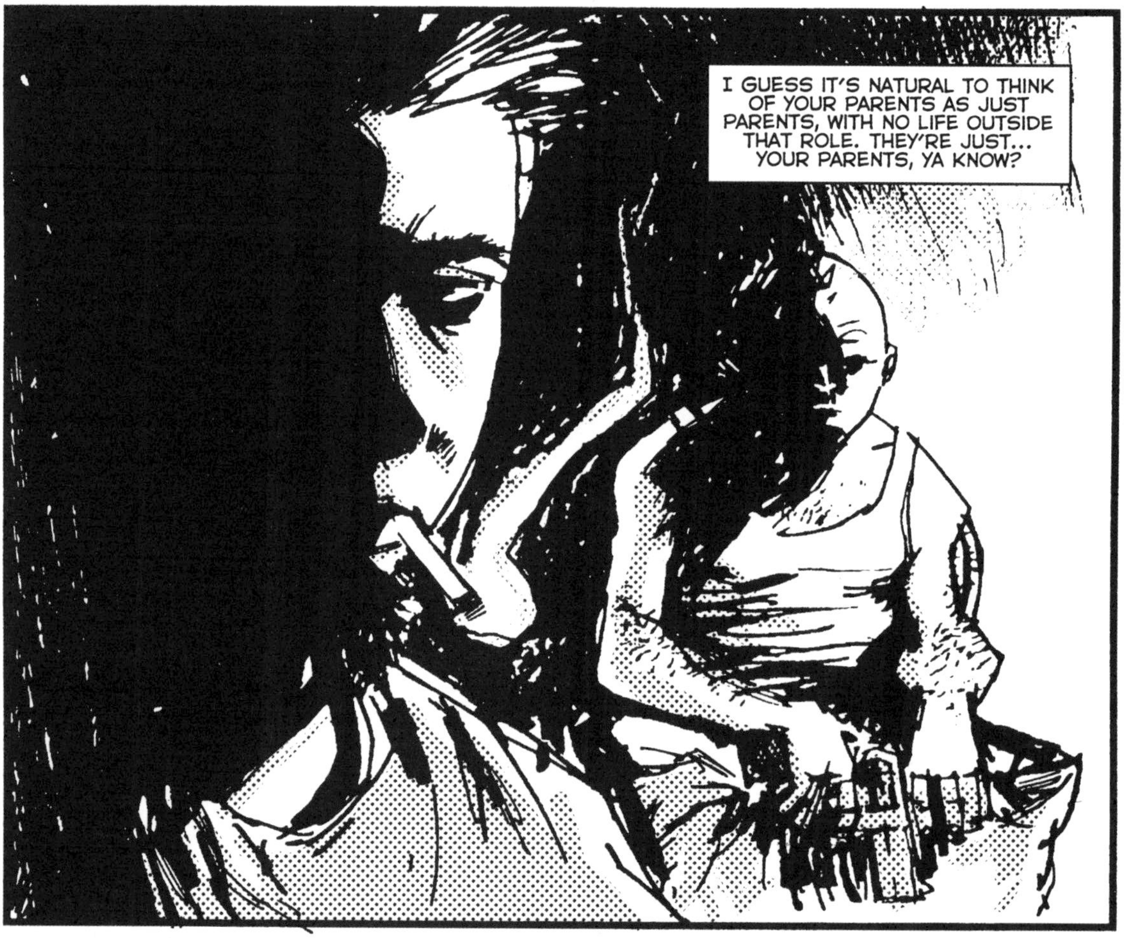
I GUESS IT'S NATURAL TO THINK OF YOUR PARENTS AS JUST PARENTS, WITH NO LIFE OUTSIDE THAT ROLE. THEY'RE JUST... YOUR PARENTS, YA KNOW?

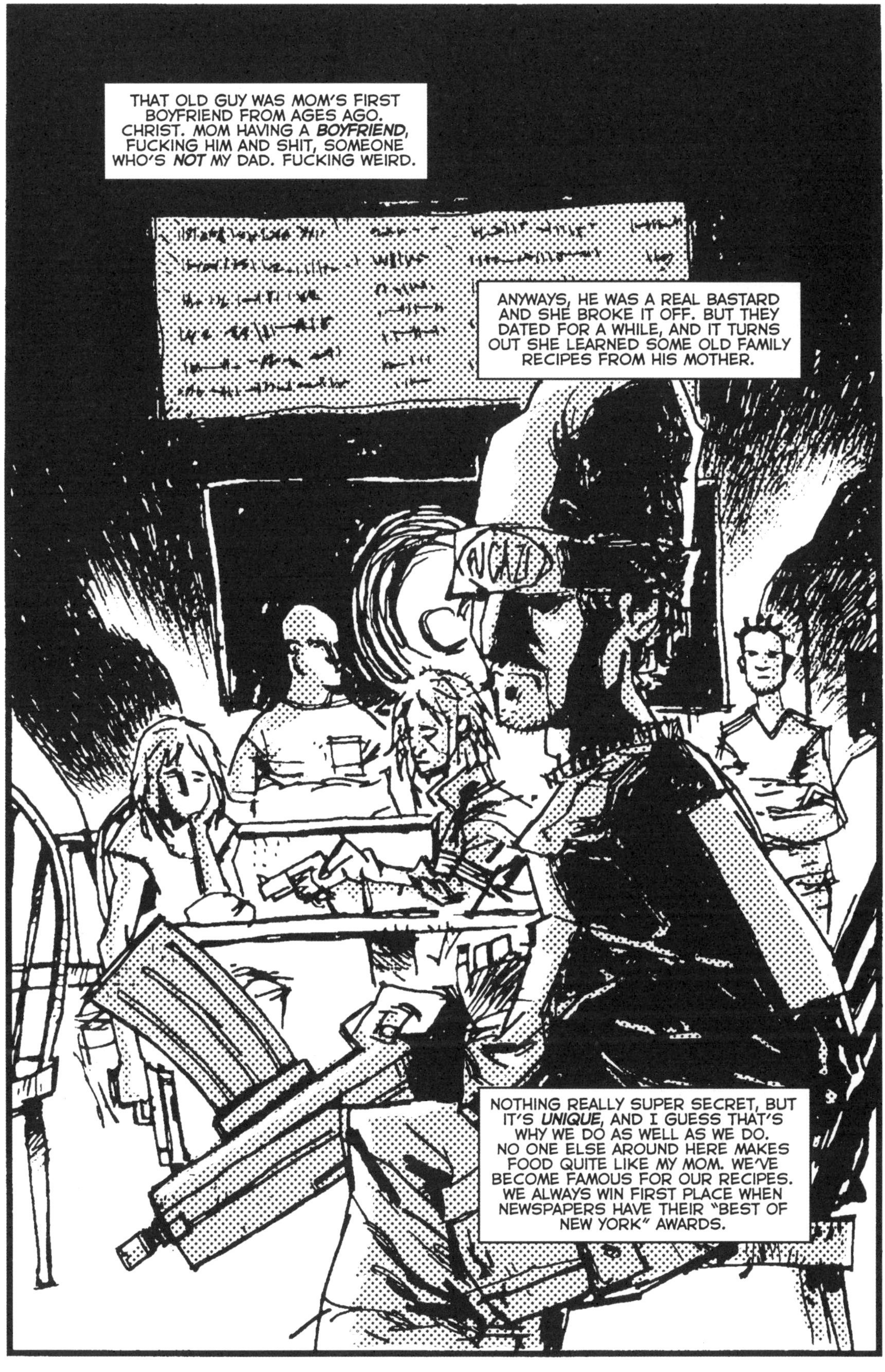
THAT OLD GUY WAS MOM'S FIRST BOYFRIEND FROM AGES AGO. CHRIST. MOM HAVING A ***BOYFRIEND***, FUCKING HIM AND SHIT, SOMEONE WHO'S ***NOT*** MY DAD. FUCKING WEIRD.
ANYWAYS, HE WAS A REAL BASTARD AND SHE BROKE IT OFF. BUT THEY DATED FOR A WHILE, AND IT TURNS OUT SHE LEARNED SOME OLD FAMILY RECIPES FROM HIS MOTHER.
NOTHING REALLY SUPER SECRET, BUT IT'S ***UNIQUE***, AND I GUESS THAT'S WHY WE DO AS WELL AS WE DO. NO ONE ELSE AROUND HERE MAKES FOOD QUITE LIKE MY MOM. WE'VE BECOME FAMOUS FOR OUR RECIPES. WE ALWAYS WIN FIRST PLACE WHEN NEWSPAPERS HAVE THEIR "BEST OF NEW YORK" AWARDS.

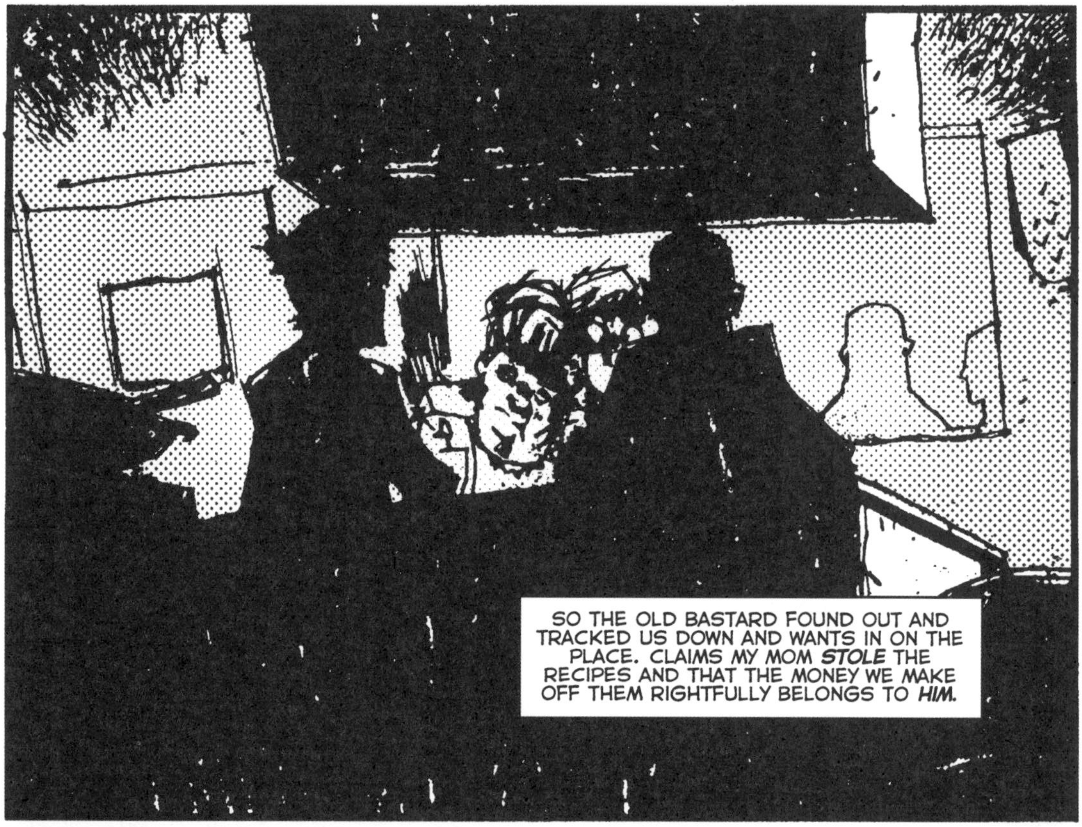
SO THE OLD BASTARD FOUND OUT AND TRACKED US DOWN AND WANTS IN ON THE PLACE. CLAIMS MY MOM *STOLE* THE RECIPES AND THAT THE MONEY WE MAKE OFF THEM RIGHTFULLY BELONGS TO *HIM*.

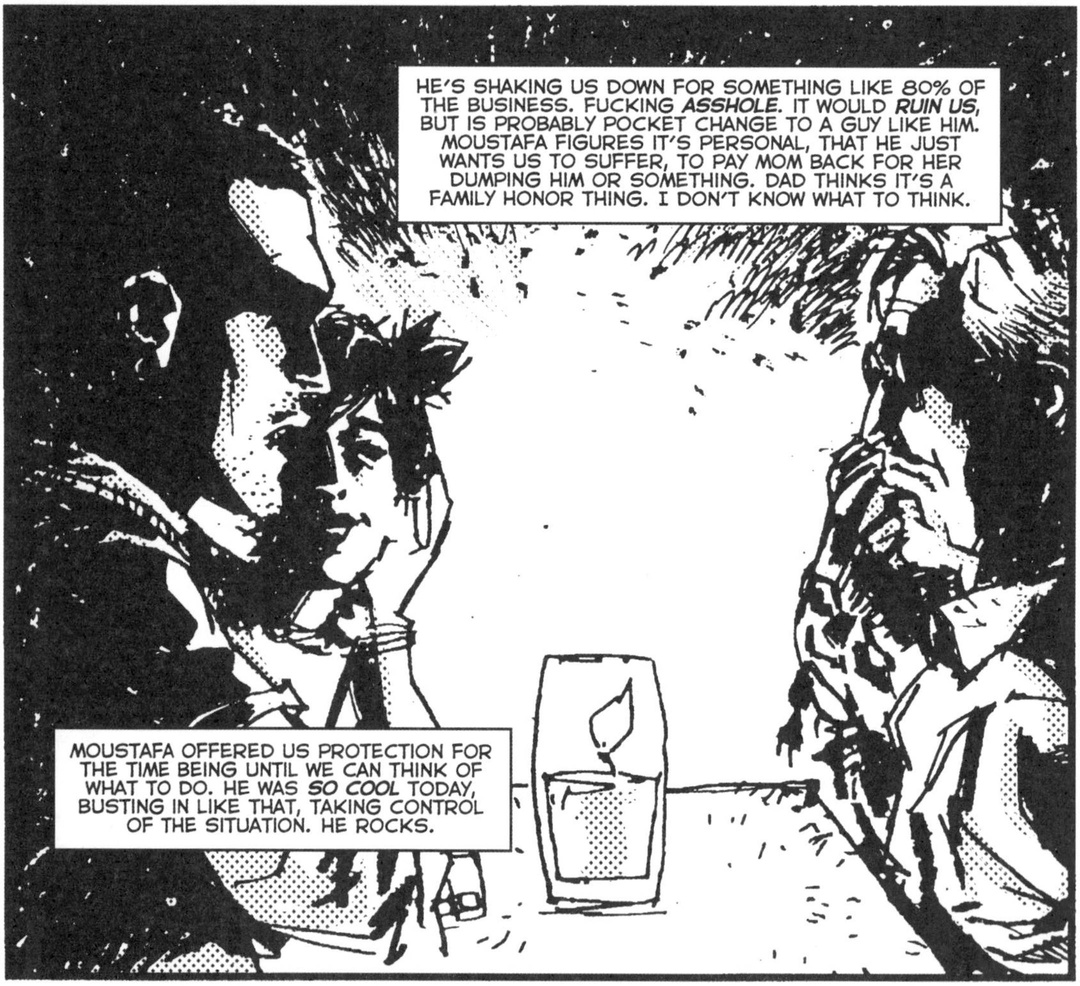
HE'S SHAKING US DOWN FOR SOMETHING LIKE 80% OF THE BUSINESS. FUCKING *ASSHOLE*. IT WOULD *RUIN US*, BUT IS PROBABLY POCKET CHANGE TO A GUY LIKE HIM. MOUSTAFA FIGURES IT'S PERSONAL, THAT HE JUST WANTS US TO SUFFER, TO PAY MOM BACK FOR HER DUMPING HIM OR SOMETHING. DAD THINKS IT'S A FAMILY HONOR THING. I DON'T KNOW WHAT TO THINK.
MOUSTAFA OFFERED US PROTECTION FOR THE TIME BEING UNTIL WE CAN THINK OF WHAT TO DO. HE WAS *SO COOL* TODAY, BUSTING IN LIKE THAT, TAKING CONTROL OF THE SITUATION. HE ROCKS.

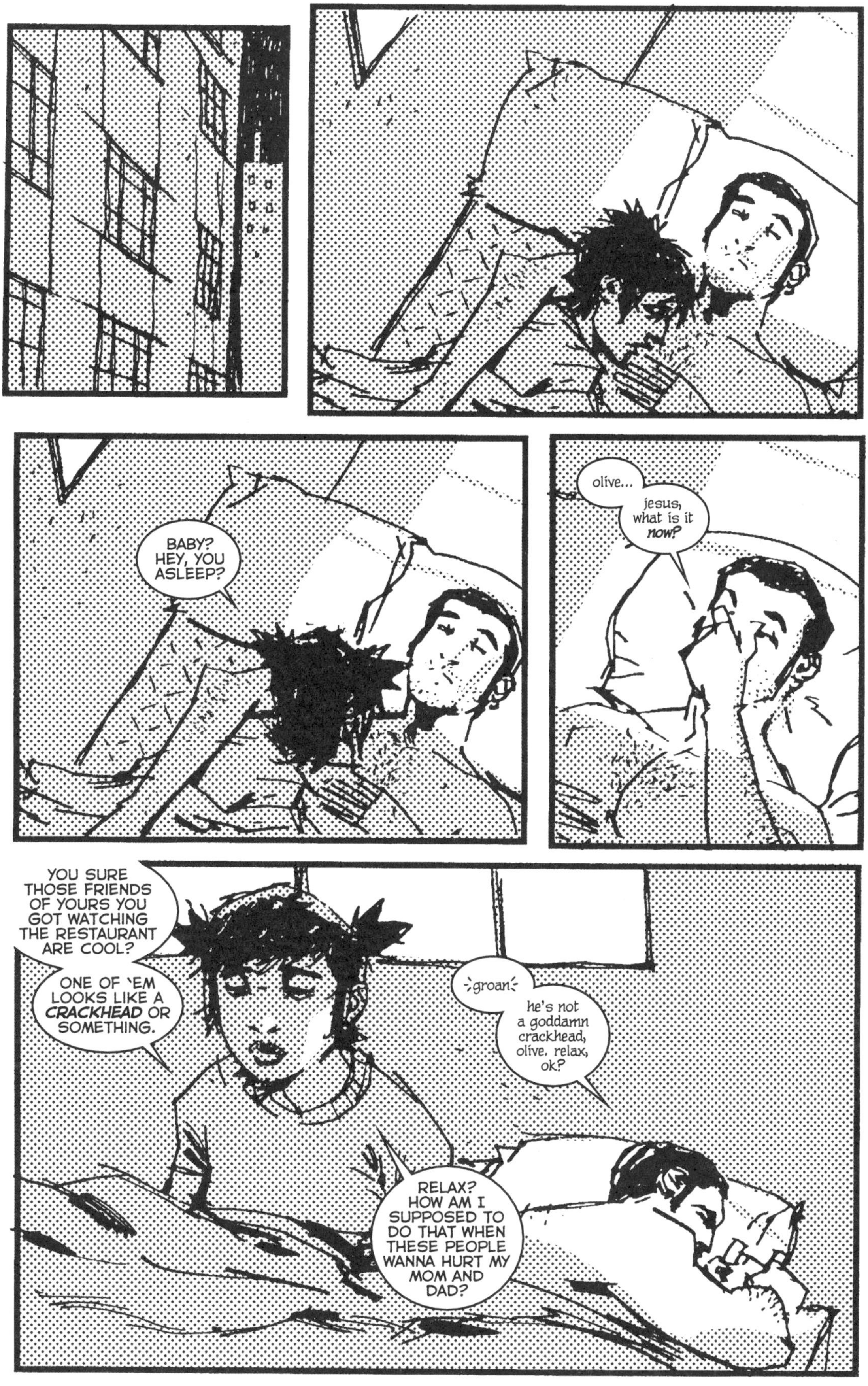

BABY? HEY, YOU ASLEEP?
olive...
jesus, what is it *now?*
YOU SURE THOSE FRIENDS OF YOURS YOU GOT WATCHING THE RESTAURANT ARE COOL?
ONE OF 'EM LOOKS LIKE A *CRACKHEAD* OR SOMETHING.
groan
he's not a goddamn crackhead, olive. relax, ok?
RELAX? HOW AM I SUPPOSED TO DO THAT WHEN THESE PEOPLE WANNA HURT MY MOM AND DAD?

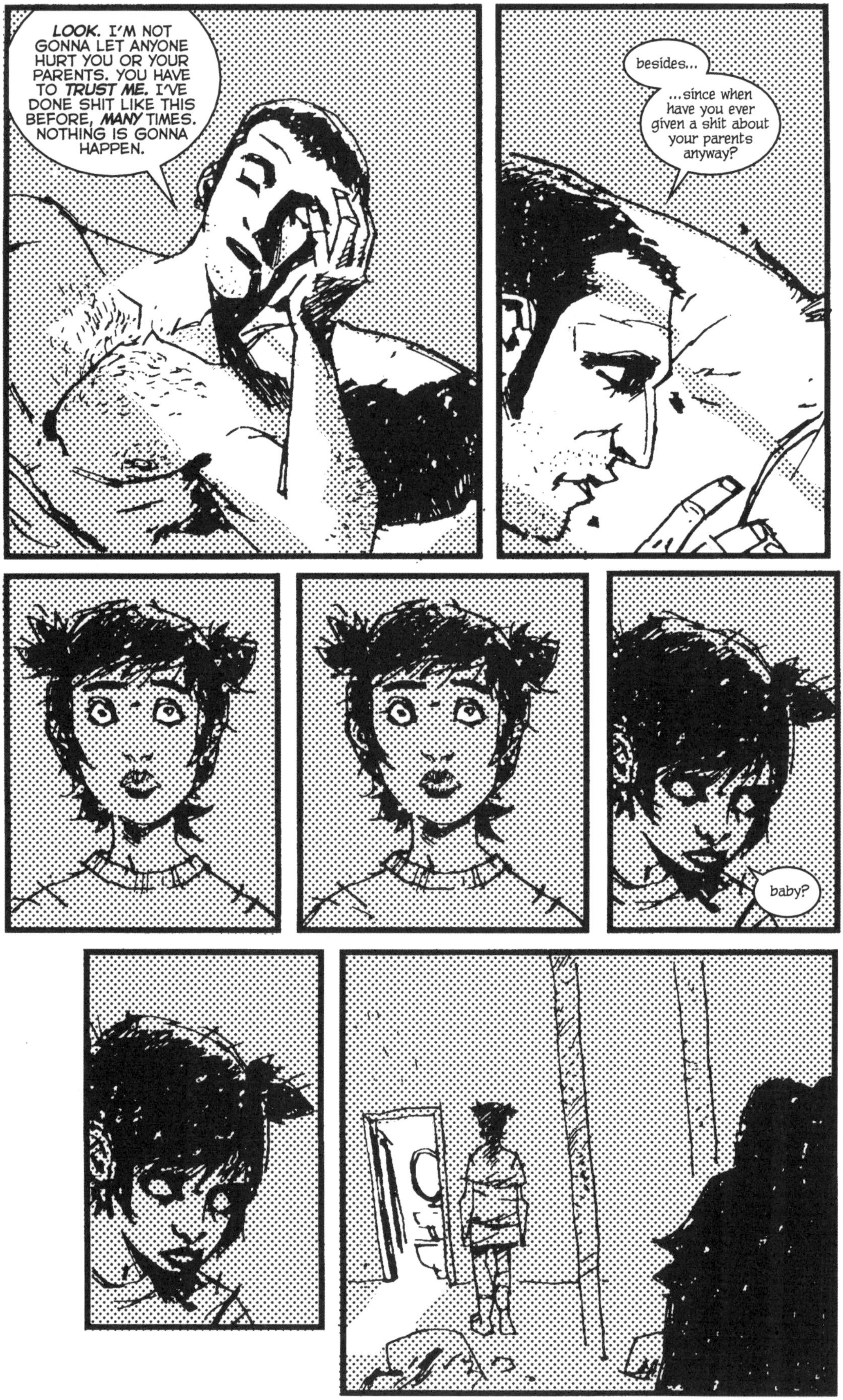
LOOK. I'M NOT GONNA LET ANYONE HURT YOU OR YOUR PARENTS. YOU HAVE TO TRUST ME. I'VE DONE SHIT LIKE THIS BEFORE, MANY TIMES. NOTHING IS GONNA HAPPEN.
besides...
...since when have you ever given a shit about your parents anyway?
baby?

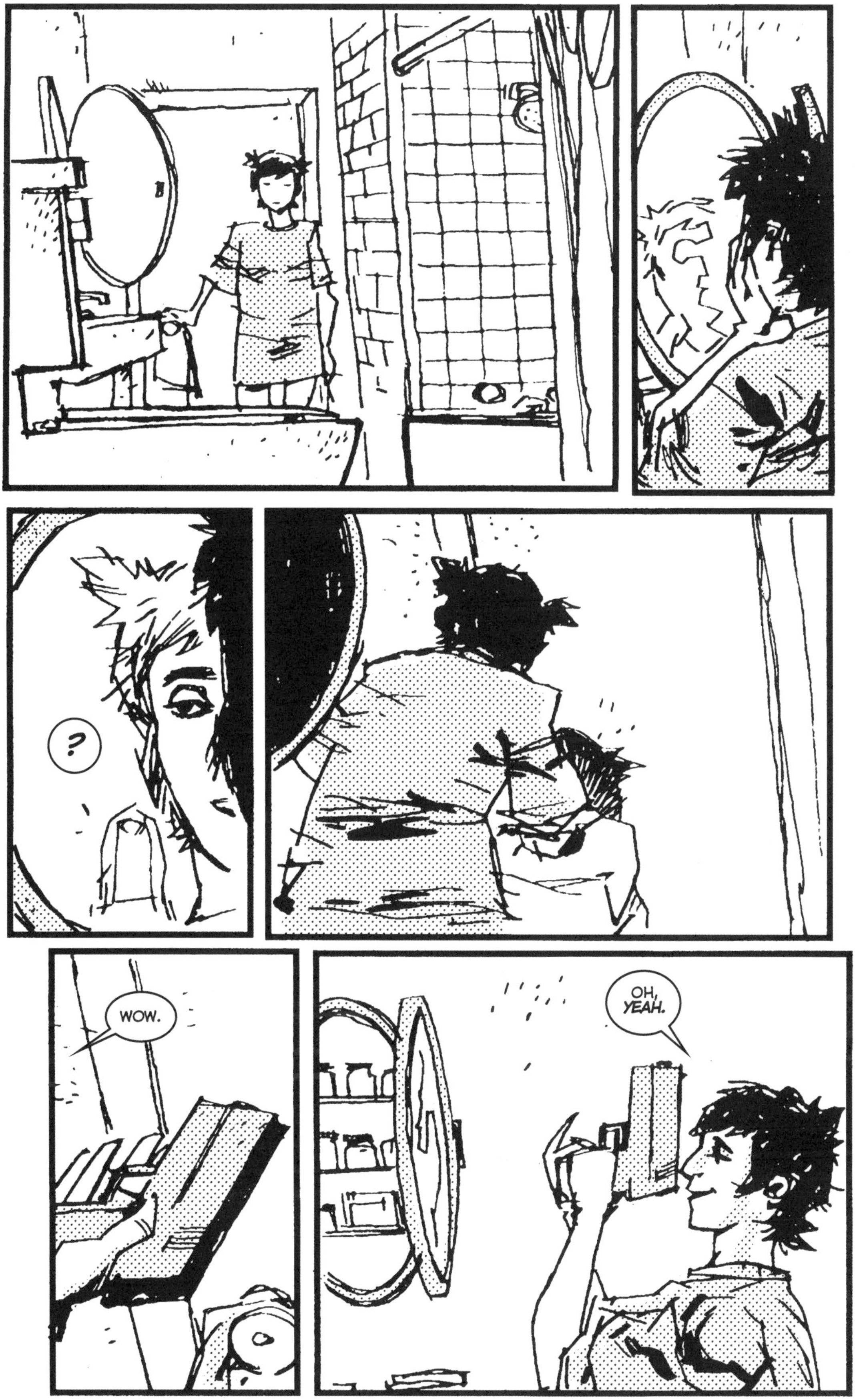
?
WOW.
OH, YEAH.

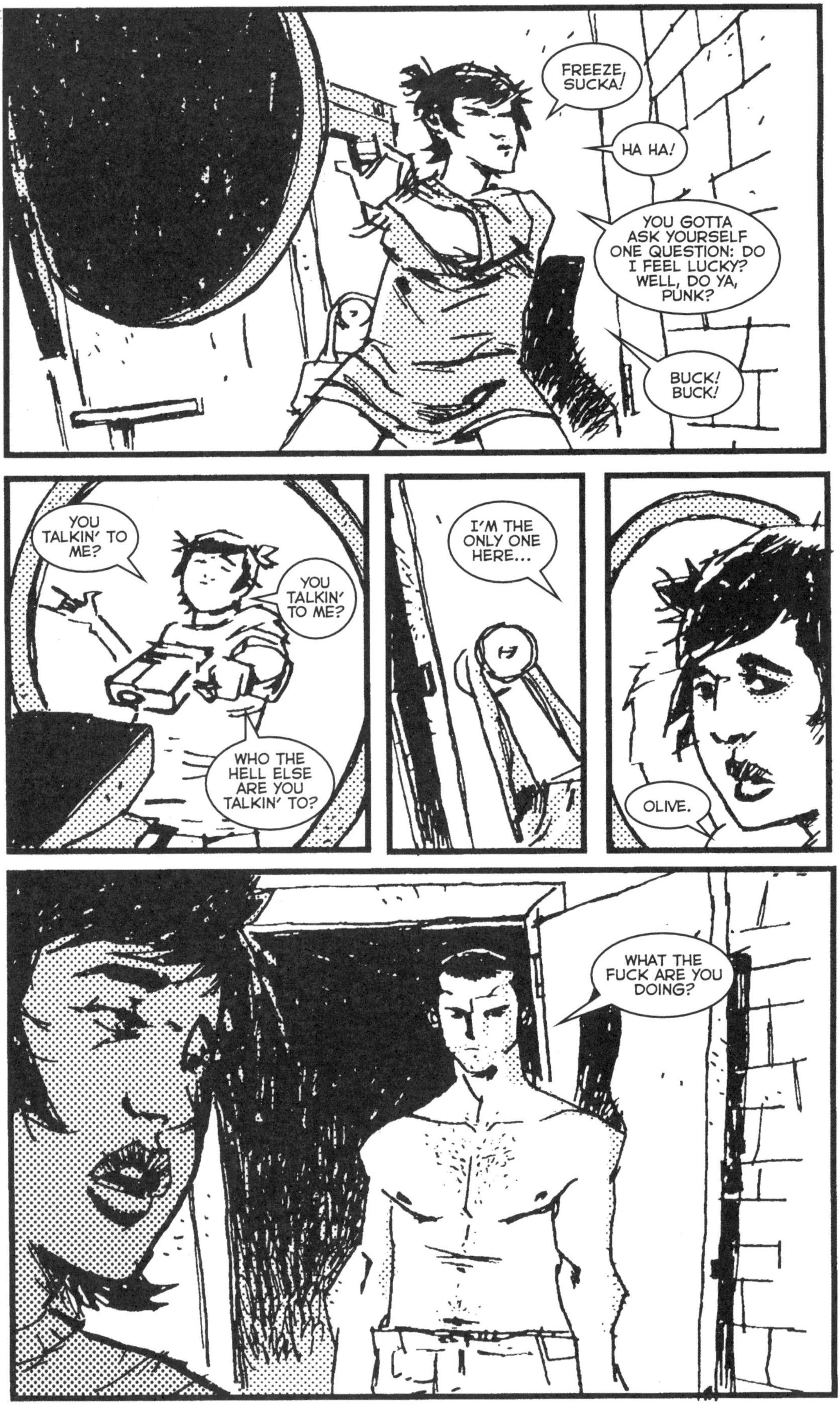
FREEZE, SUCKA!
HA HA!
YOU GOTTA ASK YOURSELF ONE QUESTION: DO I FEEL LUCKY? WELL, DO YA, PUNK?
BUCK! BUCK!
YOU TALKIN' TO ME?
YOU TALKIN' TO ME?
WHO THE HELL ELSE ARE YOU TALKIN' TO?
I'M THE ONLY ONE HERE...
OLIVE.
WHAT THE FUCK ARE YOU DOING?

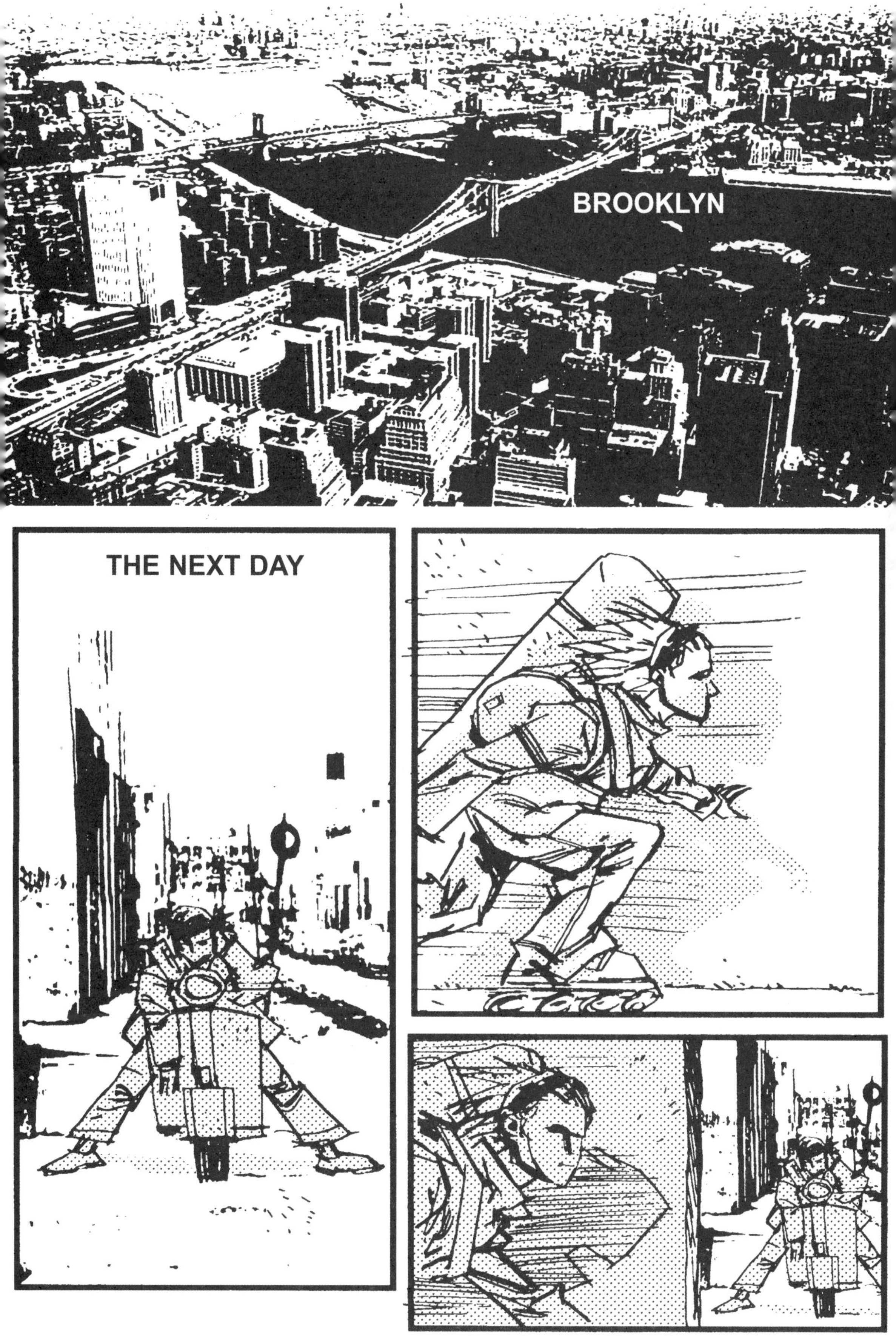
BROOKLYN
THE NEXT DAY

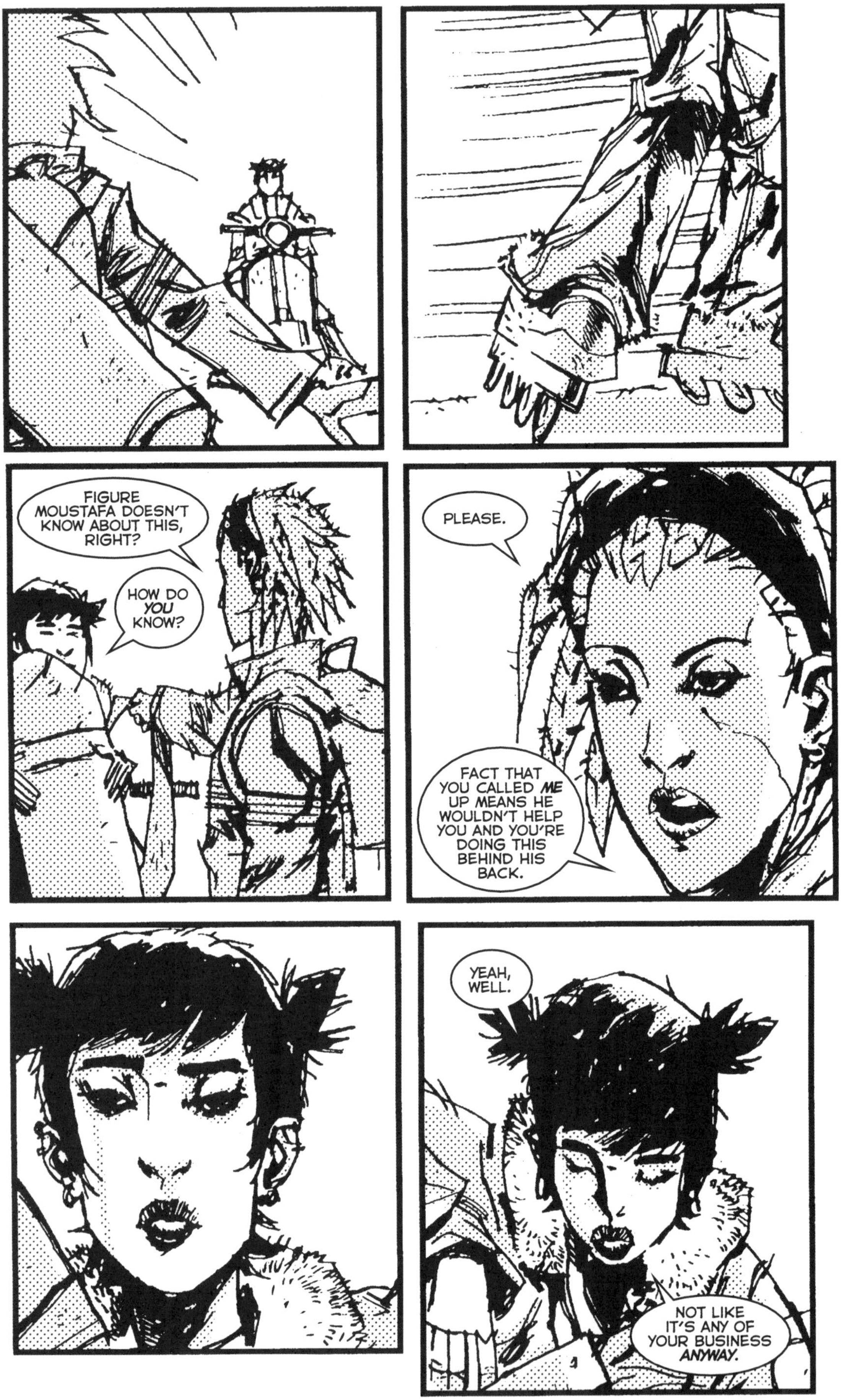
FIGURE MOUSTAFA DOESN'T KNOW ABOUT THIS, RIGHT?
HOW DO *YOU* KNOW?
PLEASE.
FACT THAT YOU CALLED *ME* UP MEANS HE WOULDN'T HELP YOU AND YOU'RE DOING THIS BEHIND HIS BACK.
YEAH, WELL.
NOT LIKE IT'S ANY OF YOUR BUSINESS *ANYWAY.*

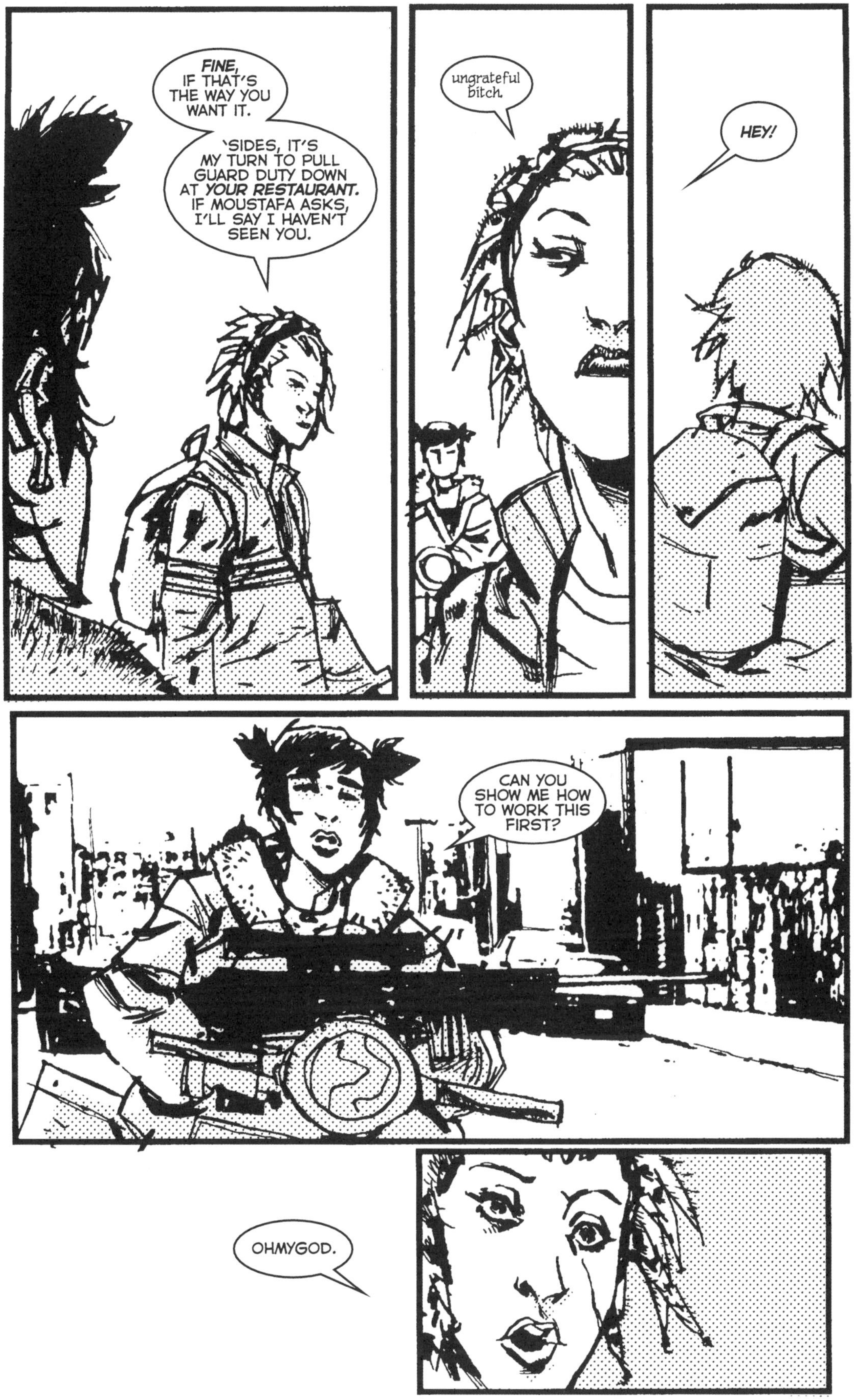
FINE, IF THAT'S THE WAY YOU WANT IT.
'SIDES, IT'S MY TURN TO PULL GUARD DUTY DOWN AT YOUR RESTAURANT. IF MOUSTAFA ASKS, I'LL SAY I HAVEN'T SEEN YOU.
ungrateful bitch.
HEY!
CAN YOU SHOW ME HOW TO WORK THIS FIRST?
OHMYGOD.

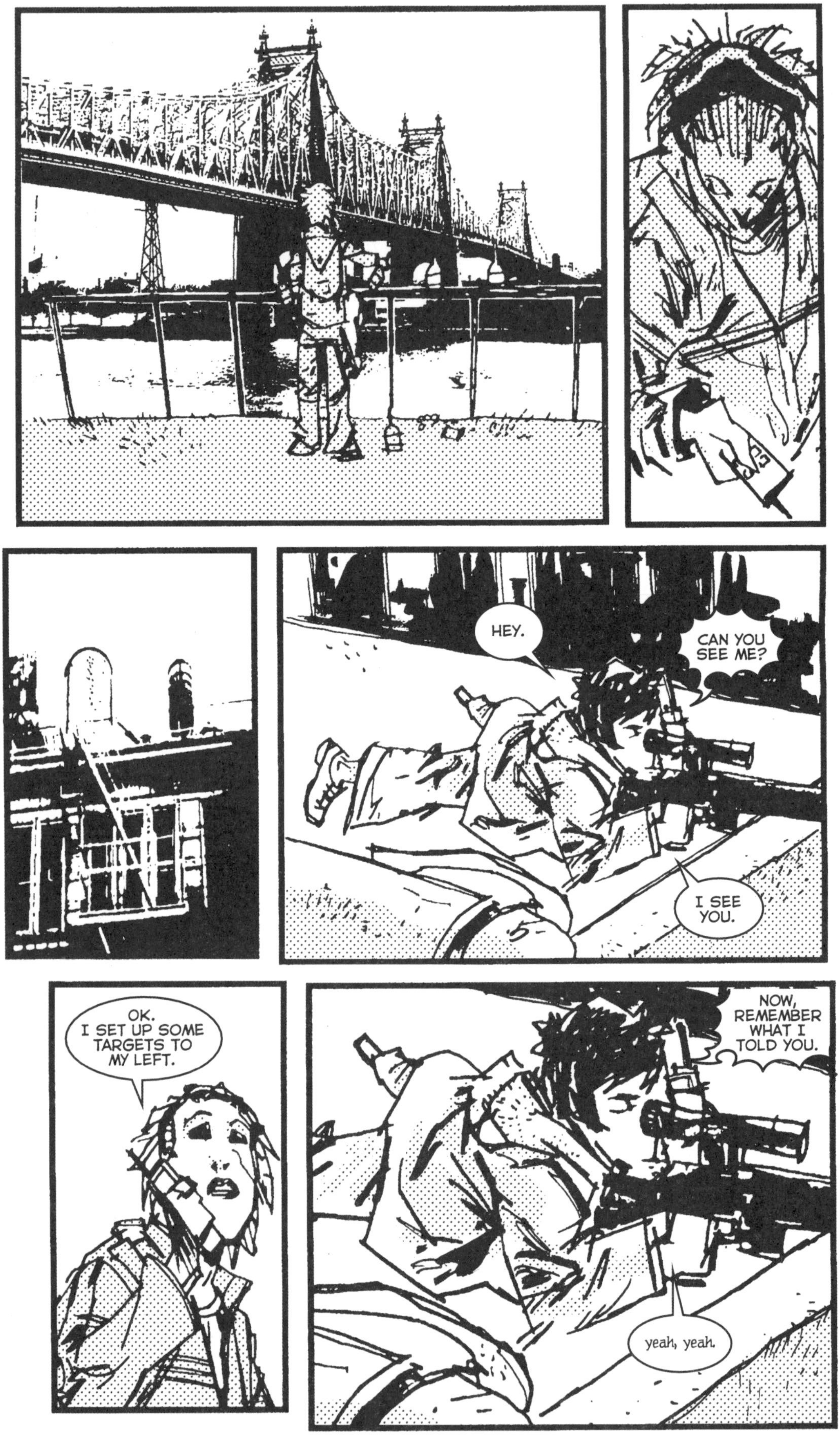
HEY.
CAN YOU SEE ME?
I SEE YOU.
OK. I SET UP SOME TARGETS TO MY LEFT.
NOW, REMEMBER WHAT I TOLD YOU.
yeah, yeah.

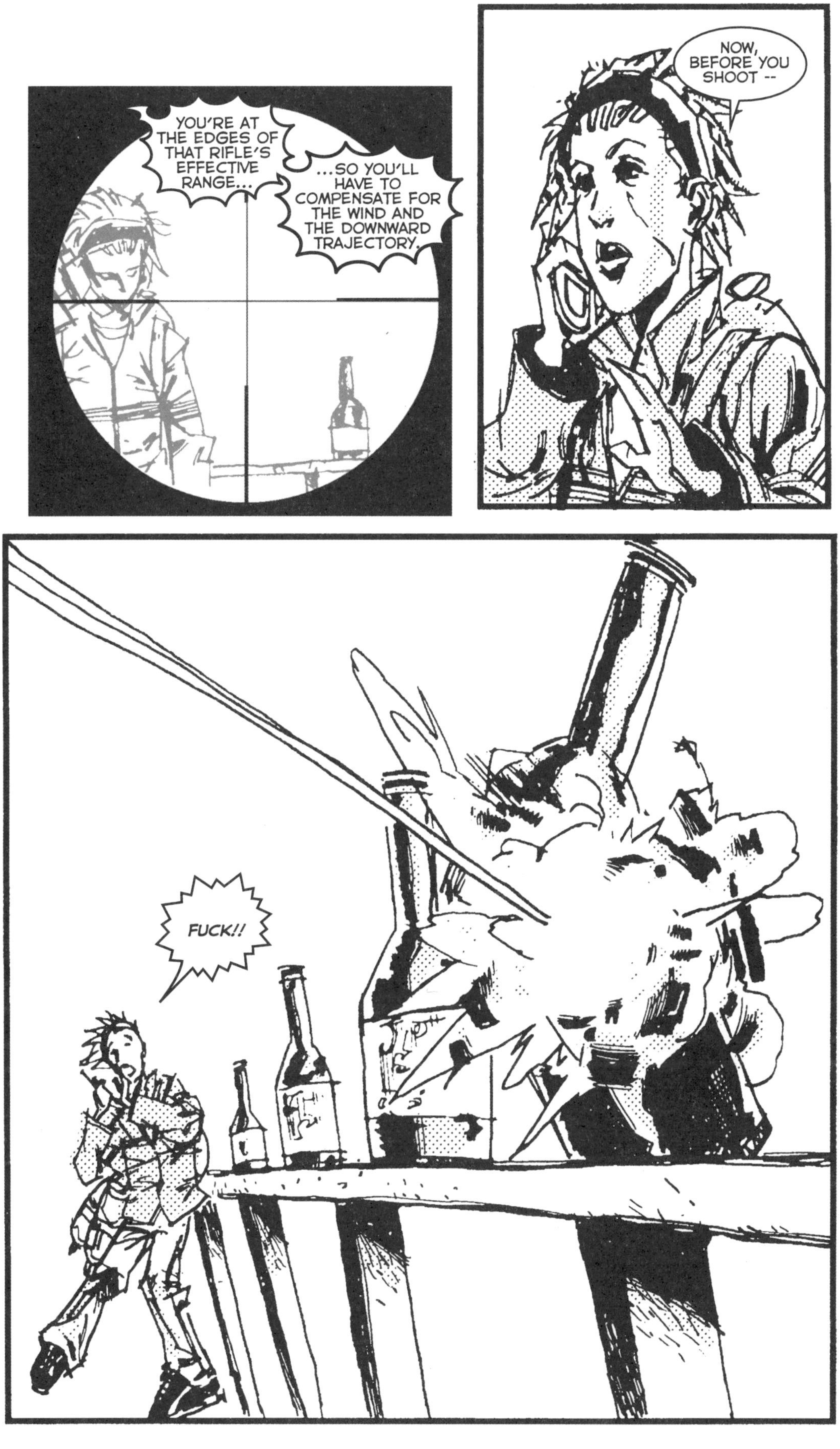
YOU'RE AT THE EDGES OF THAT RIFLE'S EFFECTIVE RANGE...
...SO YOU'LL HAVE TO COMPENSATE FOR THE WIND AND THE DOWNWARD TRAJECTORY.
NOW, BEFORE YOU SHOOT --
FUCK!!

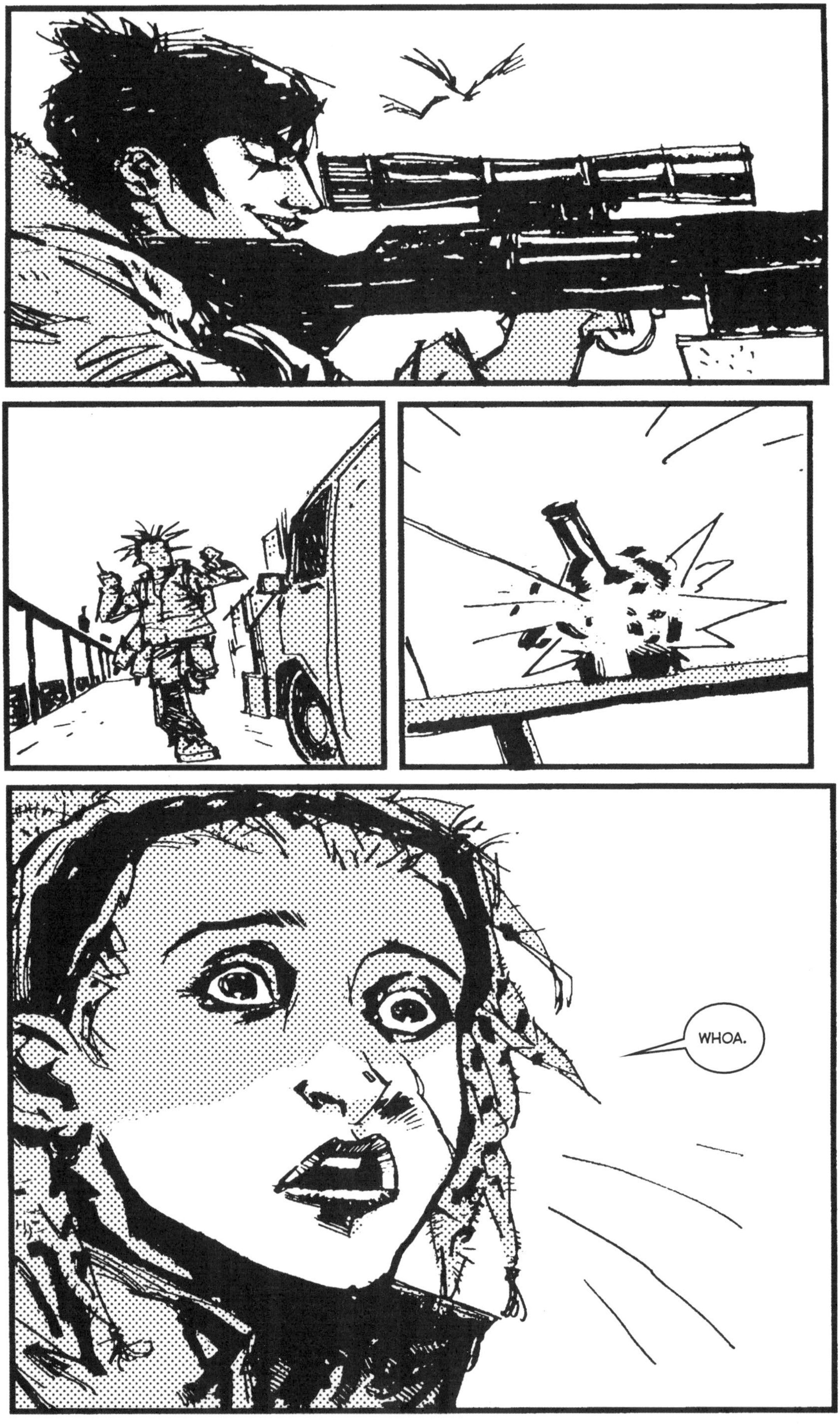
WHOA.

LATER THAT DAY

SPECIAL, THE FUCKING HOTSHOT, TELLING ME WHAT TO DO.

I GOT *CABLE TV.* I KNOW HOW TO *SHOOT.* JESUS.

JUST WATCH.

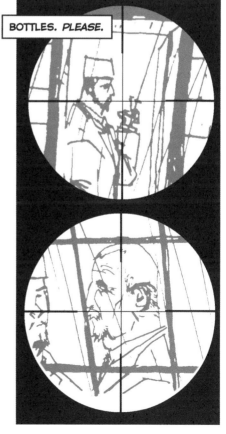

BOTTLES. *PLEASE.*

FUCK!
SCREW THIS.

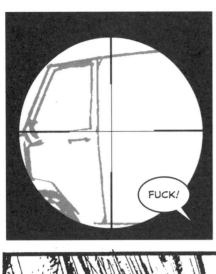

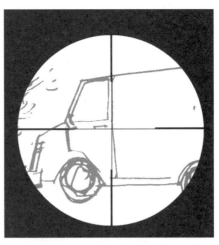

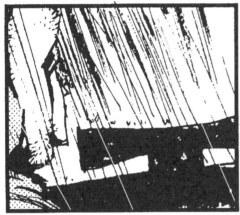

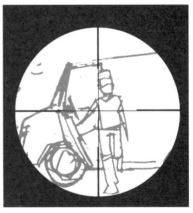

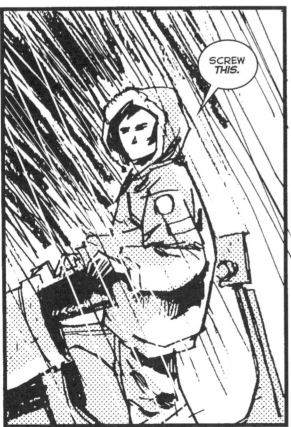

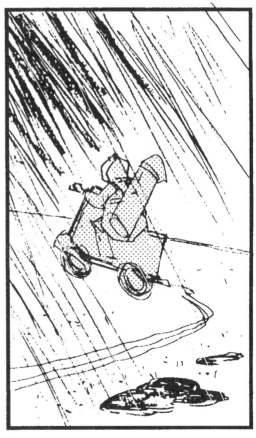

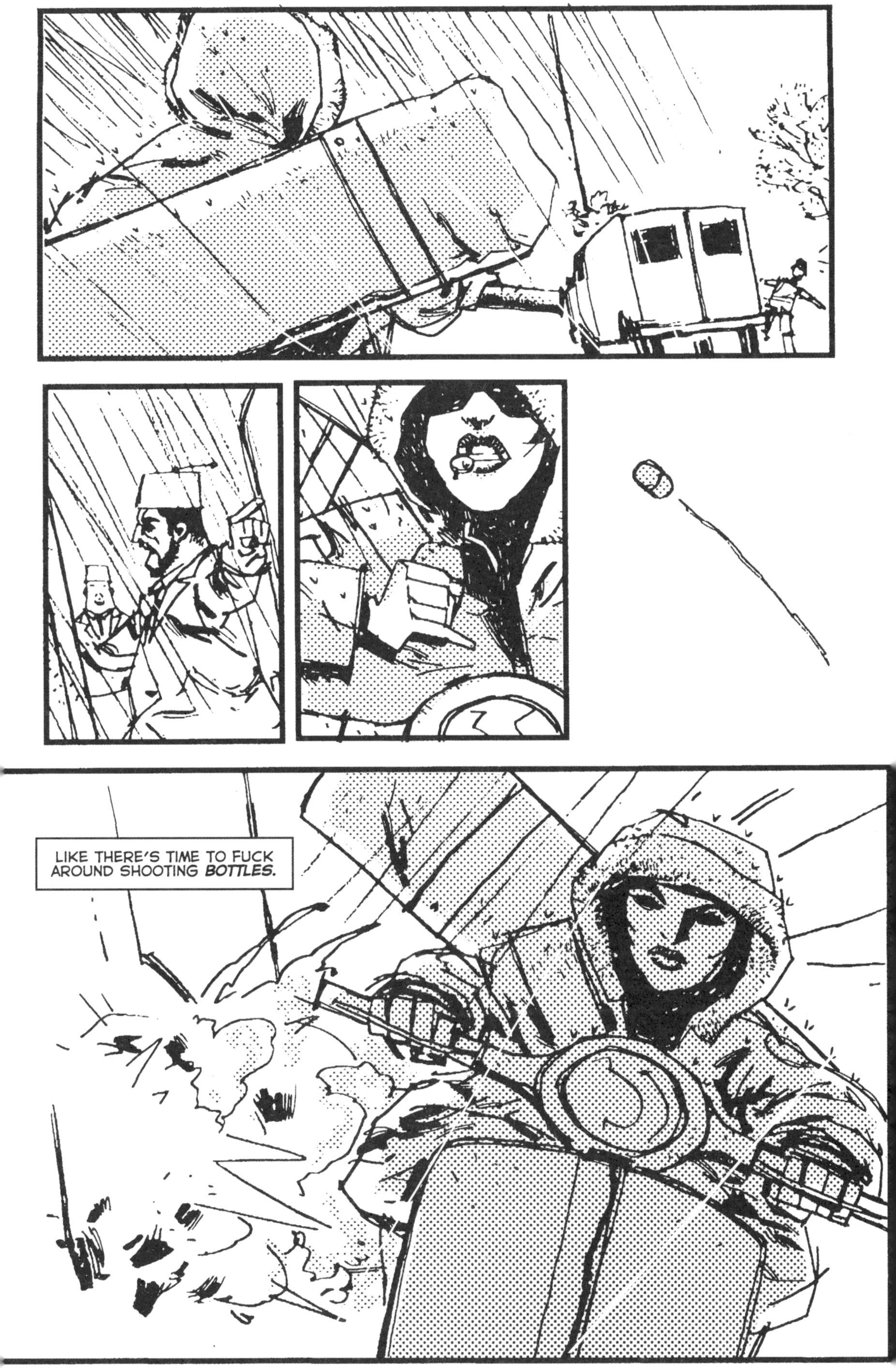
LIKE THERE'S TIME TO FUCK AROUND SHOOTING *BOTTLES*.

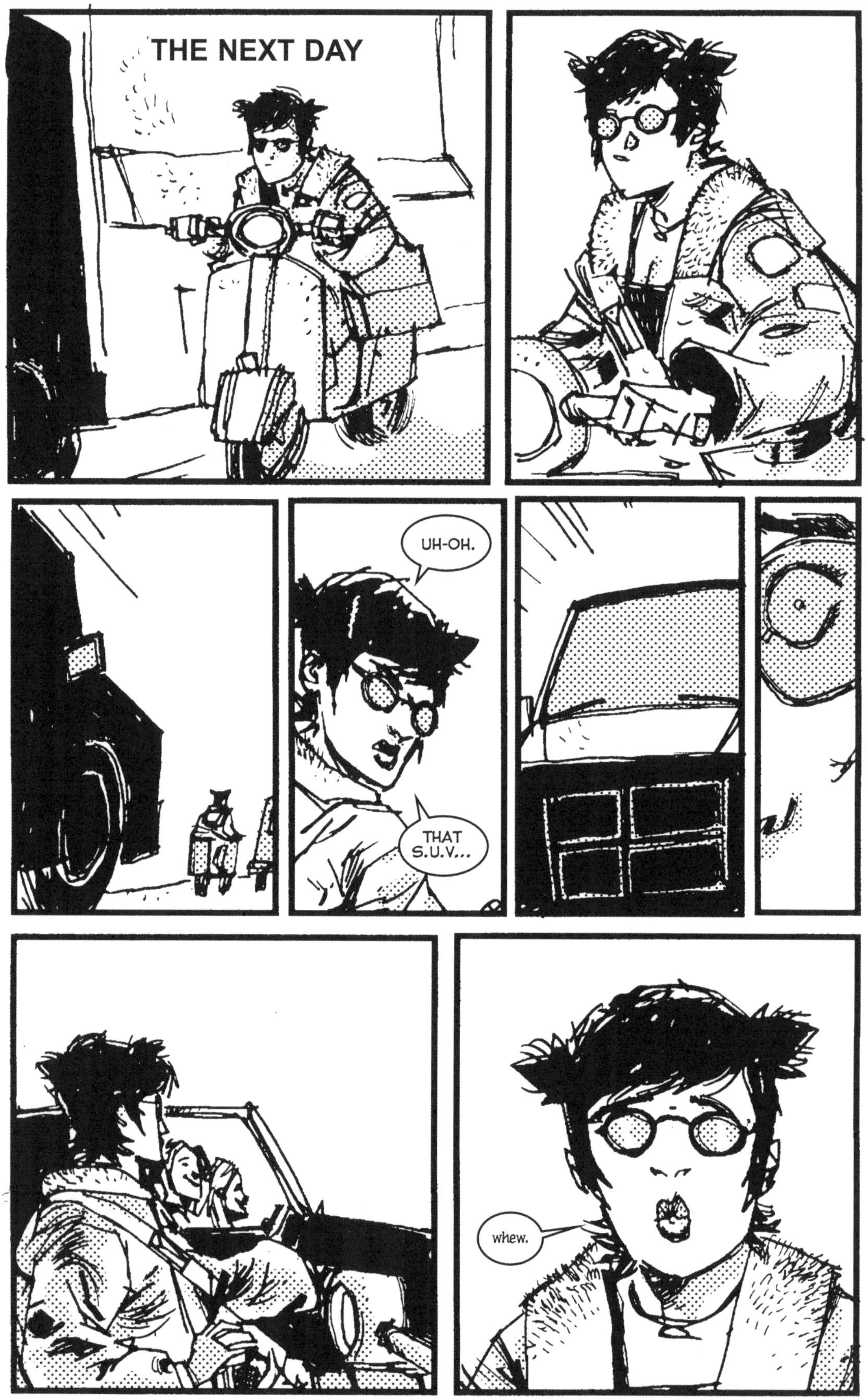
THE NEXT DAY
UH-OH.
THAT S.U.V...
whew.

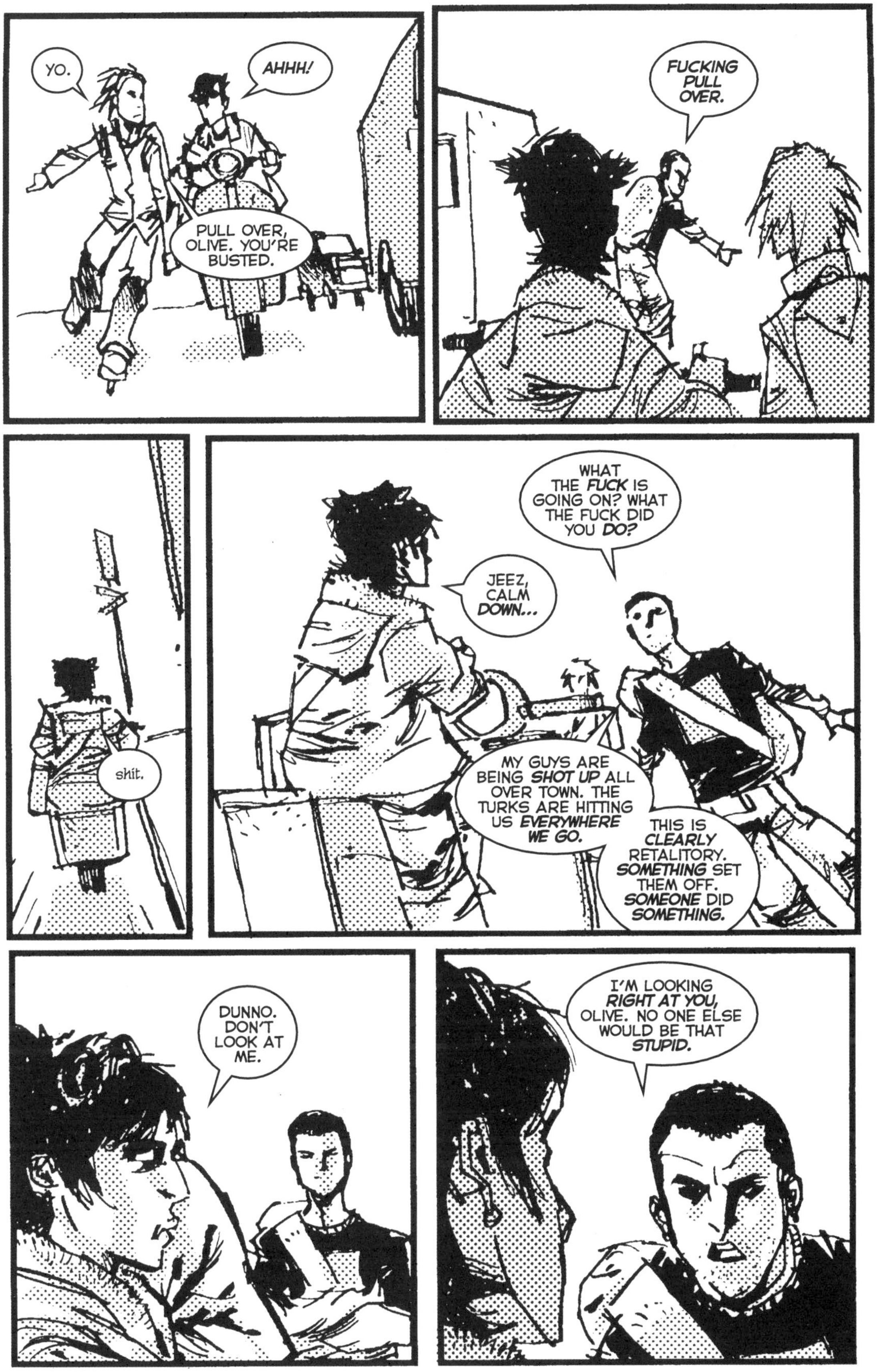
YO.
AHHH!
PULL OVER, OLIVE. YOU'RE BUSTED.
FUCKING PULL OVER.
shit.
WHAT THE FUCK IS GOING ON? WHAT THE FUCK DID YOU DO?
JEEZ, CALM DOWN...
MY GUYS ARE BEING SHOT UP ALL OVER TOWN. THE TURKS ARE HITTING US EVERYWHERE WE GO.
THIS IS CLEARLY RETALITORY. SOMETHING SET THEM OFF. SOMEONE DID SOMETHING.
DUNNO. DON'T LOOK AT ME.
I'M LOOKING RIGHT AT YOU, OLIVE. NO ONE ELSE WOULD BE THAT STUPID.

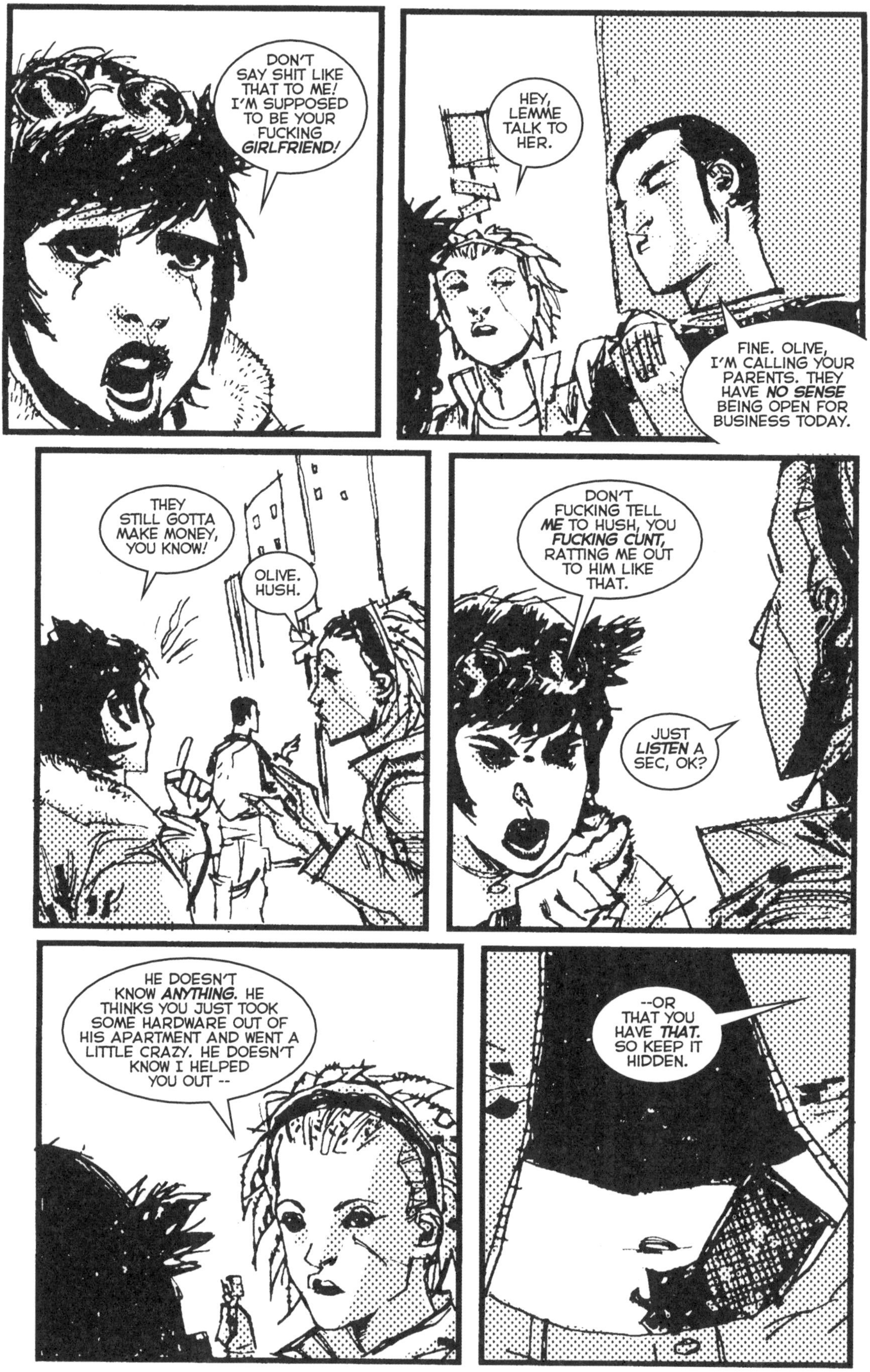
DON'T SAY SHIT LIKE THAT TO ME! I'M SUPPOSED TO BE YOUR FUCKING GIRLFRIEND!
HEY, LEMME TALK TO HER.
FINE. OLIVE, I'M CALLING YOUR PARENTS. THEY HAVE NO SENSE BEING OPEN FOR BUSINESS TODAY.
THEY STILL GOTTA MAKE MONEY, YOU KNOW!
OLIVE. HUSH.
DON'T FUCKING TELL ME TO HUSH, YOU FUCKING CUNT, RATTING ME OUT TO HIM LIKE THAT.
JUST LISTEN A SEC, OK?
HE DOESN'T KNOW ANYTHING. HE THINKS YOU JUST TOOK SOME HARDWARE OUT OF HIS APARTMENT AND WENT A LITTLE CRAZY. HE DOESN'T KNOW I HELPED YOU OUT --
--OR THAT YOU HAVE THAT. SO KEEP IT HIDDEN.

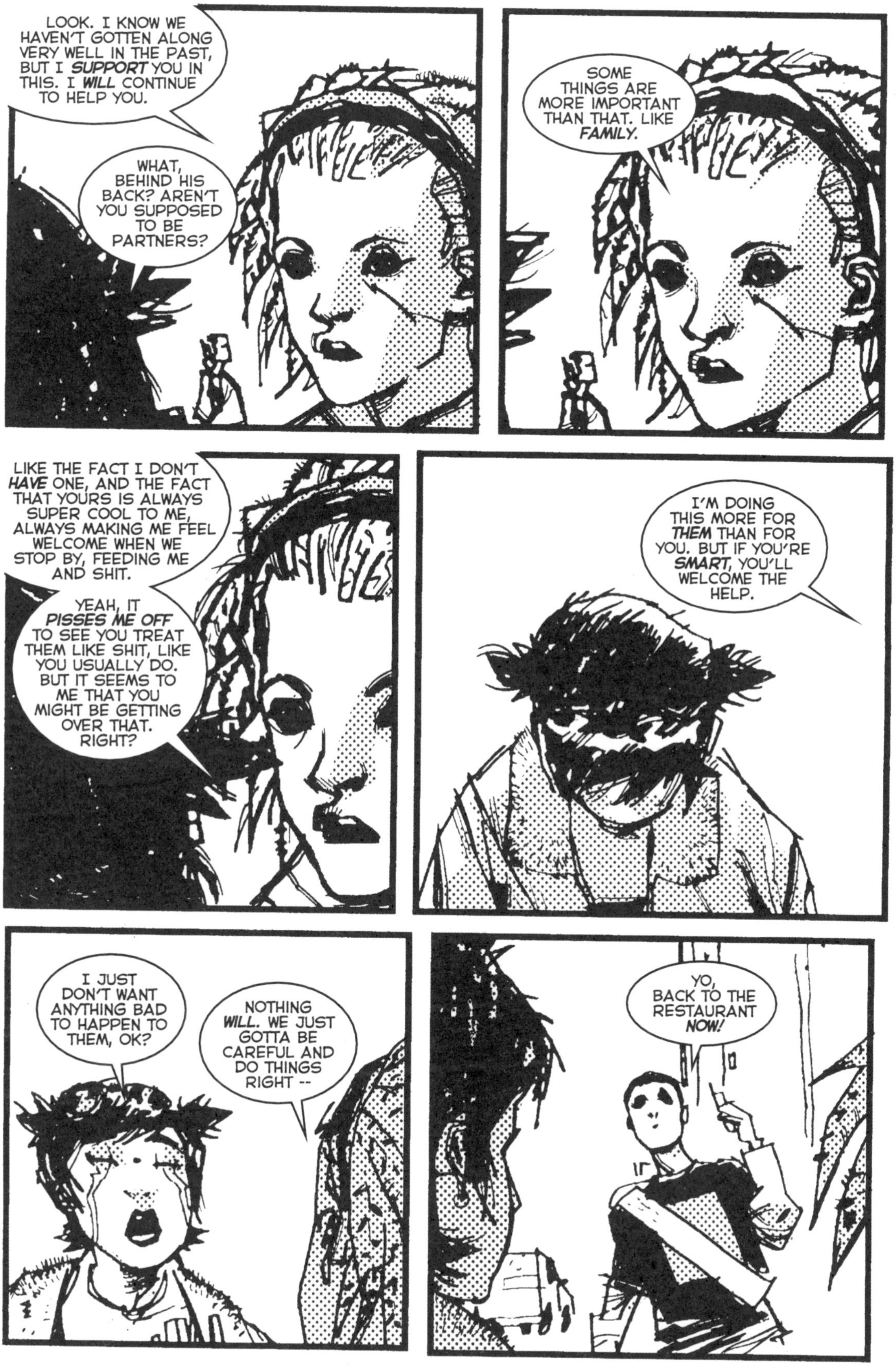
LOOK. I KNOW WE HAVEN'T GOTTEN ALONG VERY WELL IN THE PAST, BUT I SUPPORT YOU IN THIS. I WILL CONTINUE TO HELP YOU.
WHAT, BEHIND HIS BACK? AREN'T YOU SUPPOSED TO BE PARTNERS?
SOME THINGS ARE MORE IMPORTANT THAN THAT. LIKE FAMILY.
LIKE THE FACT I DON'T HAVE ONE, AND THE FACT THAT YOURS IS ALWAYS SUPER COOL TO ME, ALWAYS MAKING ME FEEL WELCOME WHEN WE STOP BY, FEEDING ME AND SHIT.
YEAH, IT PISSES ME OFF TO SEE YOU TREAT THEM LIKE SHIT, LIKE YOU USUALLY DO. BUT IT SEEMS TO ME THAT YOU MIGHT BE GETTING OVER THAT. RIGHT?
I'M DOING THIS MORE FOR THEM THAN FOR YOU. BUT IF YOU'RE SMART, YOU'LL WELCOME THE HELP.
I JUST DON'T WANT ANYTHING BAD TO HAPPEN TO THEM, OK?
NOTHING WILL. WE JUST GOTTA BE CAREFUL AND DO THINGS RIGHT --
YO, BACK TO THE RESTAURANT NOW!

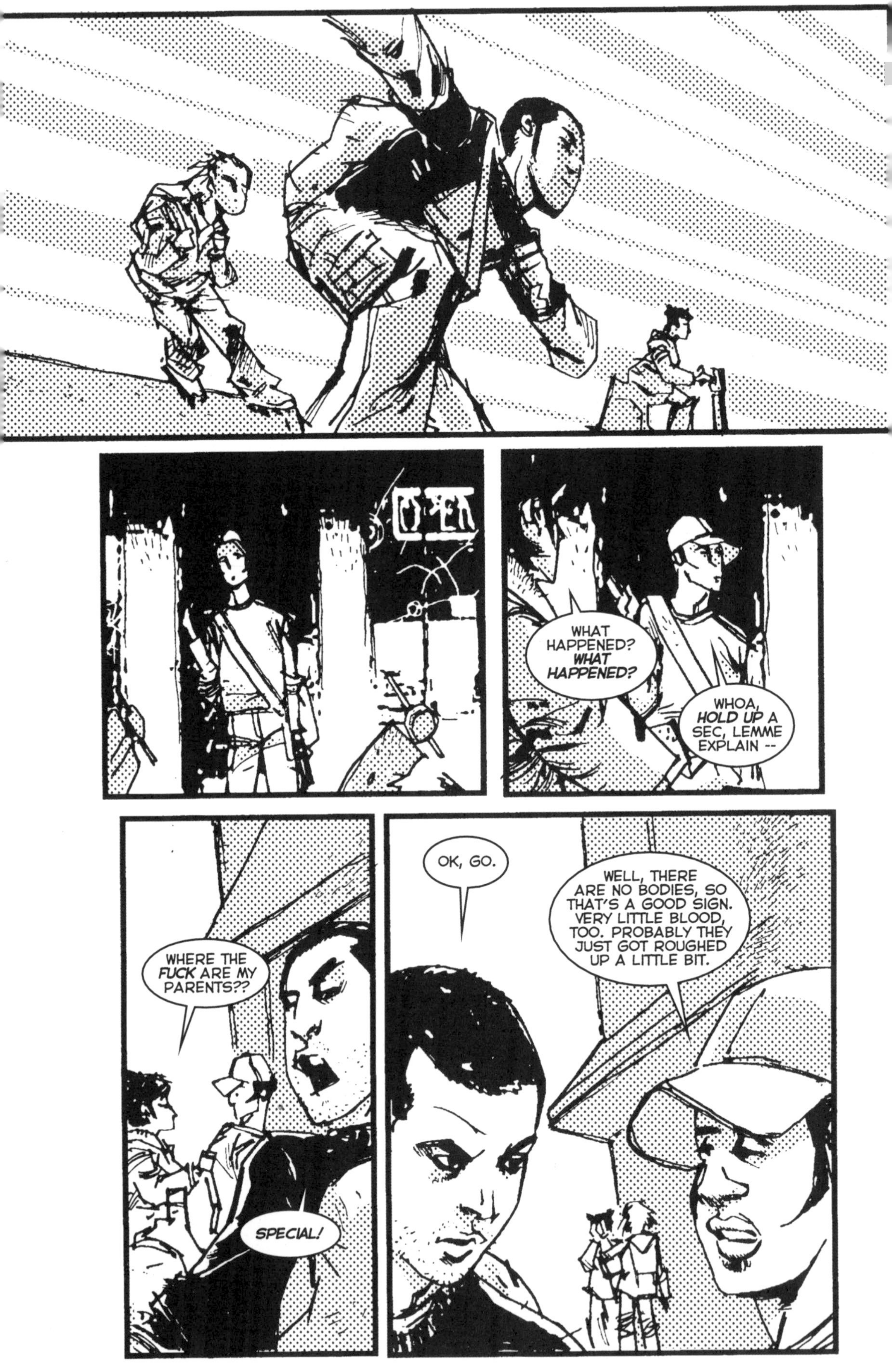
WHAT HAPPENED? WHAT HAPPENED?
WHOA, HOLD UP A SEC, LEMME EXPLAIN --
WHERE THE FUCK ARE MY PARENTS??
SPECIAL!
OK, GO.
WELL, THERE ARE NO BODIES, SO THAT'S A GOOD SIGN. VERY LITTLE BLOOD, TOO. PROBABLY THEY JUST GOT ROUGHED UP A LITTLE BIT.

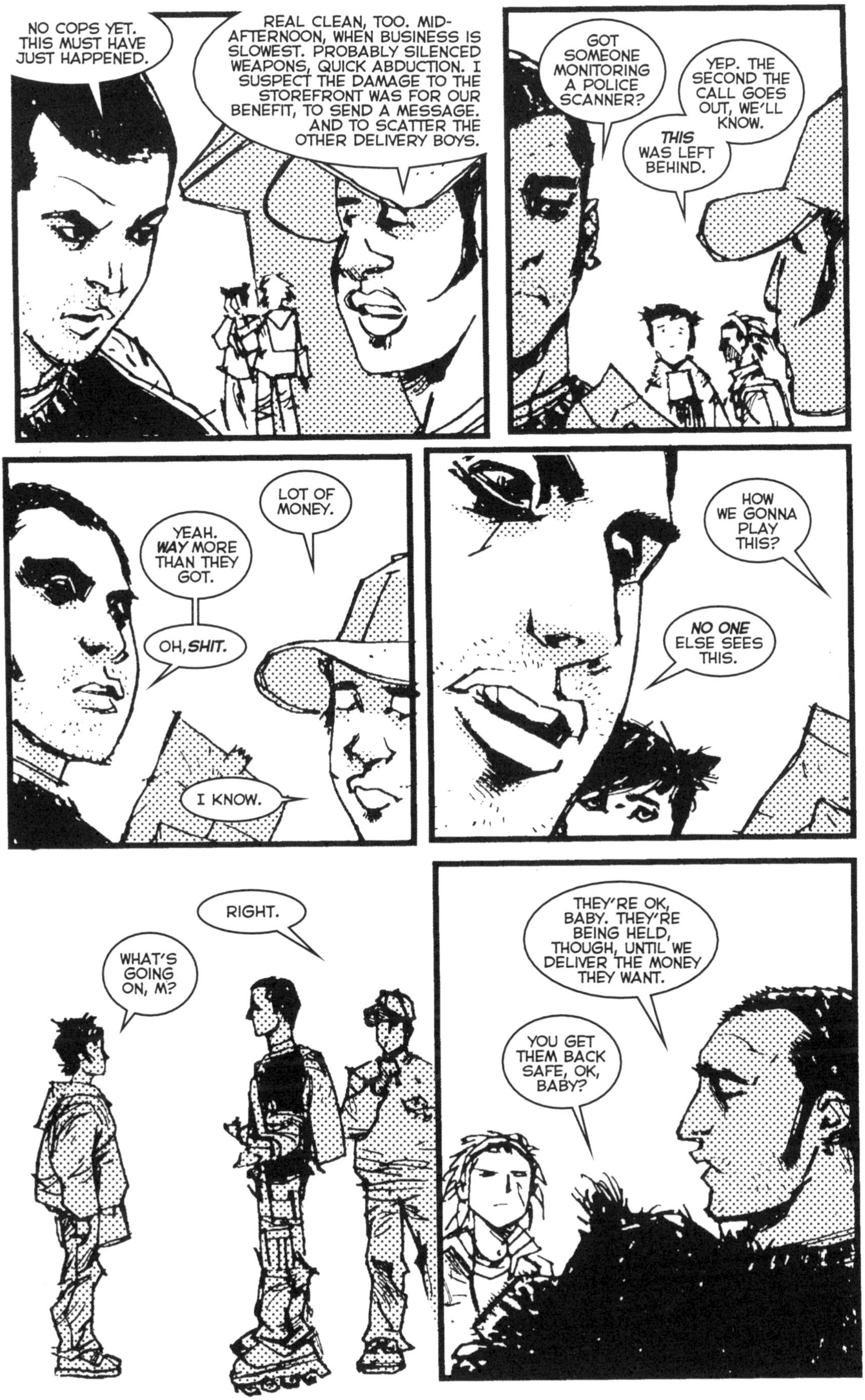
NO COPS YET. THIS MUST HAVE JUST HAPPENED.
REAL CLEAN, TOO. MID-AFTERNOON, WHEN BUSINESS IS SLOWEST. PROBABLY SILENCED WEAPONS, QUICK ABDUCTION. I SUSPECT THE DAMAGE TO THE STOREFRONT WAS FOR OUR BENEFIT, TO SEND A MESSAGE. AND TO SCATTER THE OTHER DELIVERY BOYS.
GOT SOMEONE MONITORING A POLICE SCANNER?
YEP. THE SECOND THE CALL GOES OUT, WE'LL KNOW.
THIS WAS LEFT BEHIND.
LOT OF MONEY.
YEAH. WAY MORE THAN THEY GOT.
OH, SHIT.
I KNOW.
HOW WE GONNA PLAY THIS?
NO ONE ELSE SEES THIS.
RIGHT.
WHAT'S GOING ON, M?
THEY'RE OK, BABY. THEY'RE BEING HELD, THOUGH, UNTIL WE DELIVER THE MONEY THEY WANT.
YOU GET THEM BACK SAFE, OK, BABY?

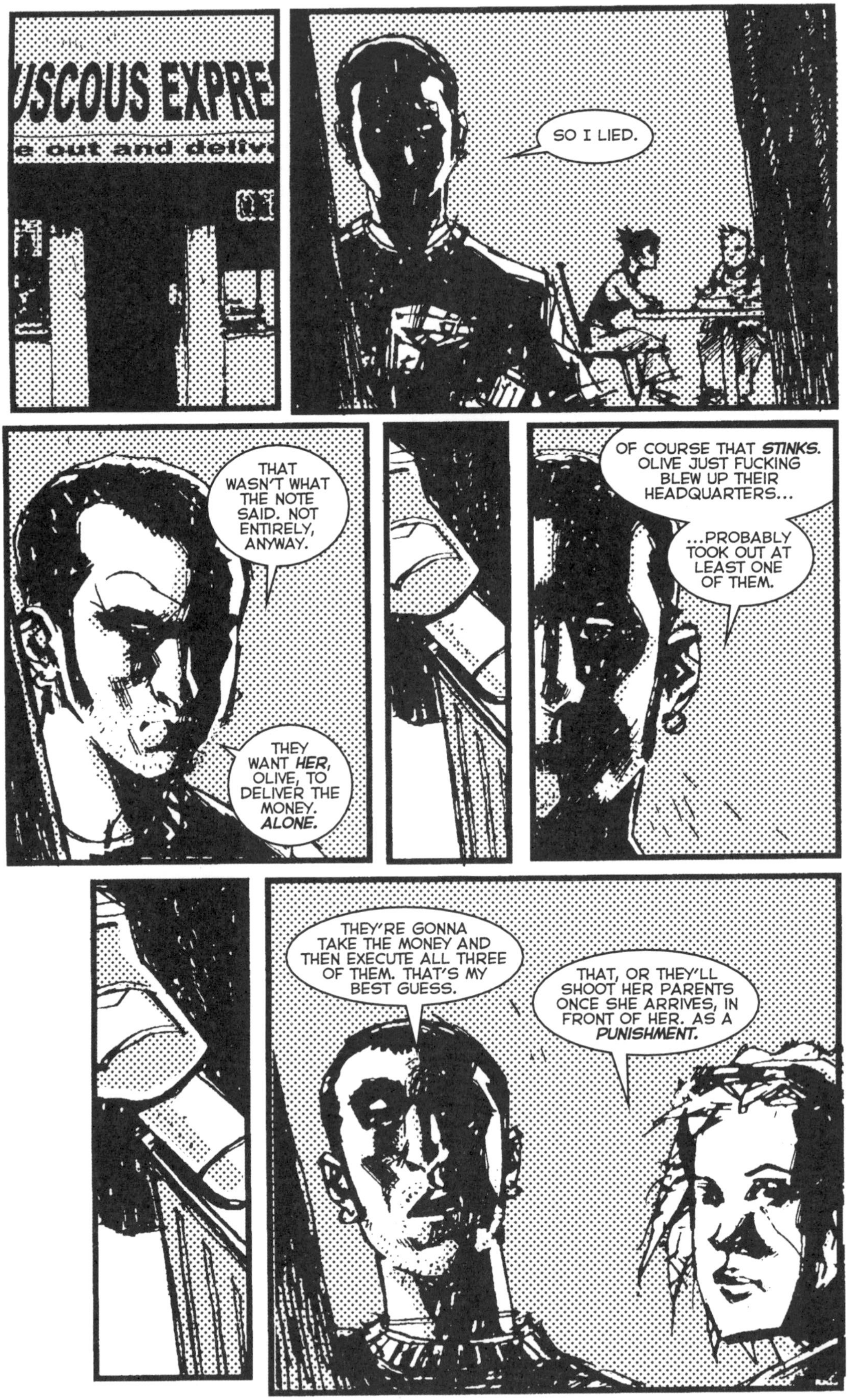
USCOUS EXPRE
e out and deliv
SO I LIED.
THAT WASN'T WHAT THE NOTE SAID. NOT ENTIRELY, ANYWAY.
THEY WANT HER, OLIVE, TO DELIVER THE MONEY. ALONE.
OF COURSE THAT STINKS. OLIVE JUST FUCKING BLEW UP THEIR HEADQUARTERS...
...PROBABLY TOOK OUT AT LEAST ONE OF THEM.
THEY'RE GONNA TAKE THE MONEY AND THEN EXECUTE ALL THREE OF THEM. THAT'S MY BEST GUESS.
THAT, OR THEY'LL SHOOT HER PARENTS ONCE SHE ARRIVES, IN FRONT OF HER. AS A PUNISHMENT.

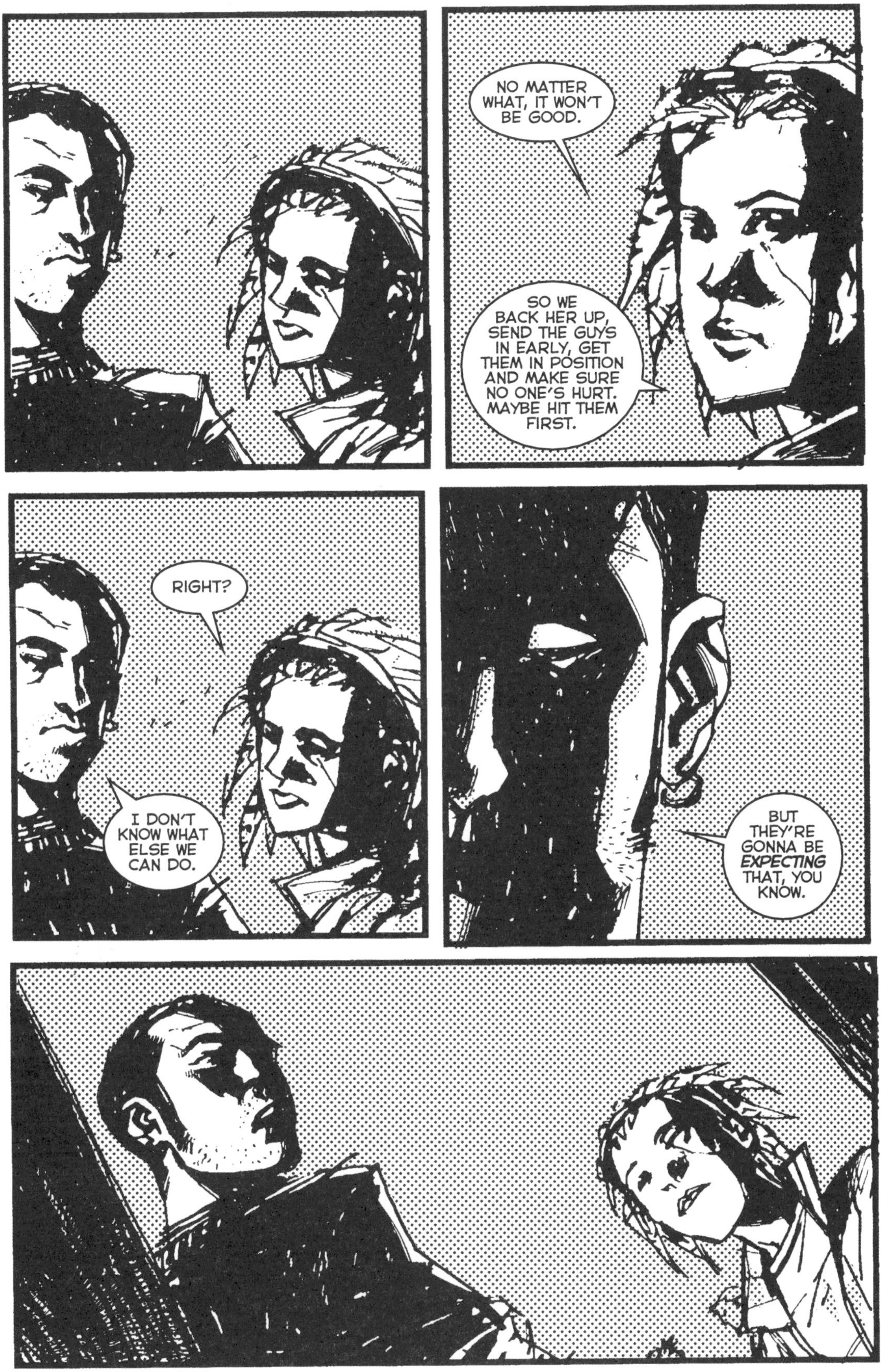
NO MATTER WHAT, IT WON'T BE GOOD.
SO WE BACK HER UP, SEND THE GUYS IN EARLY, GET THEM IN POSITION AND MAKE SURE NO ONE'S HURT. MAYBE HIT THEM FIRST.
RIGHT?
I DON'T KNOW WHAT ELSE WE CAN DO.
BUT THEY'RE GONNA BE *EXPECTING* THAT, YOU KNOW.

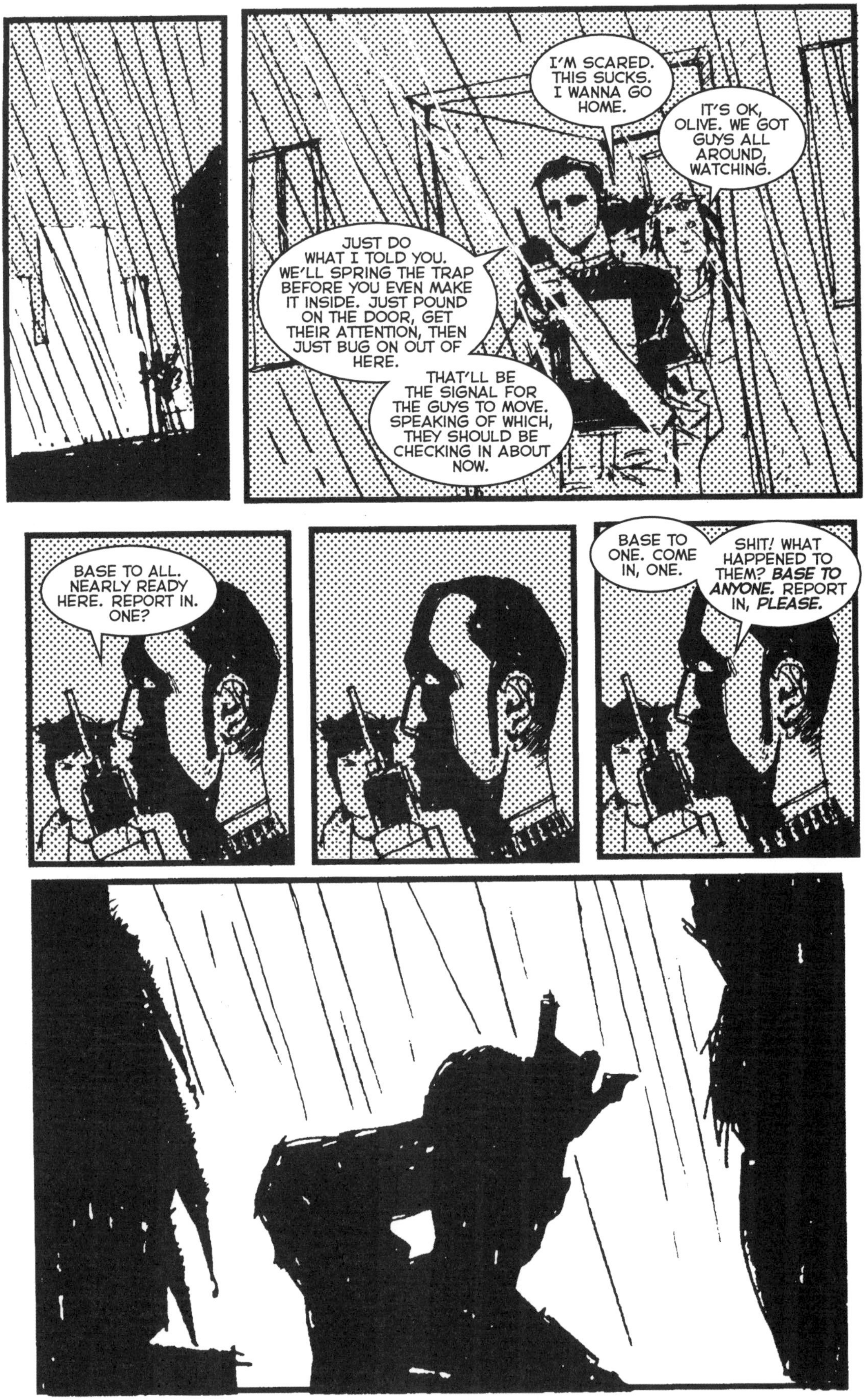
I'M SCARED. THIS SUCKS. I WANNA GO HOME.
IT'S OK, OLIVE. WE GOT GUYS ALL AROUND, WATCHING.
JUST DO WHAT I TOLD YOU. WE'LL SPRING THE TRAP BEFORE YOU EVEN MAKE IT INSIDE. JUST POUND ON THE DOOR, GET THEIR ATTENTION, THEN JUST BUG ON OUT OF HERE.
THAT'LL BE THE SIGNAL FOR THE GUYS TO MOVE. SPEAKING OF WHICH, THEY SHOULD BE CHECKING IN ABOUT NOW.
BASE TO ALL. NEARLY READY HERE. REPORT IN. ONE?
BASE TO ONE. COME IN, ONE.
SHIT! WHAT HAPPENED TO THEM? ***BASE TO ANYONE.*** REPORT IN, ***PLEASE.***

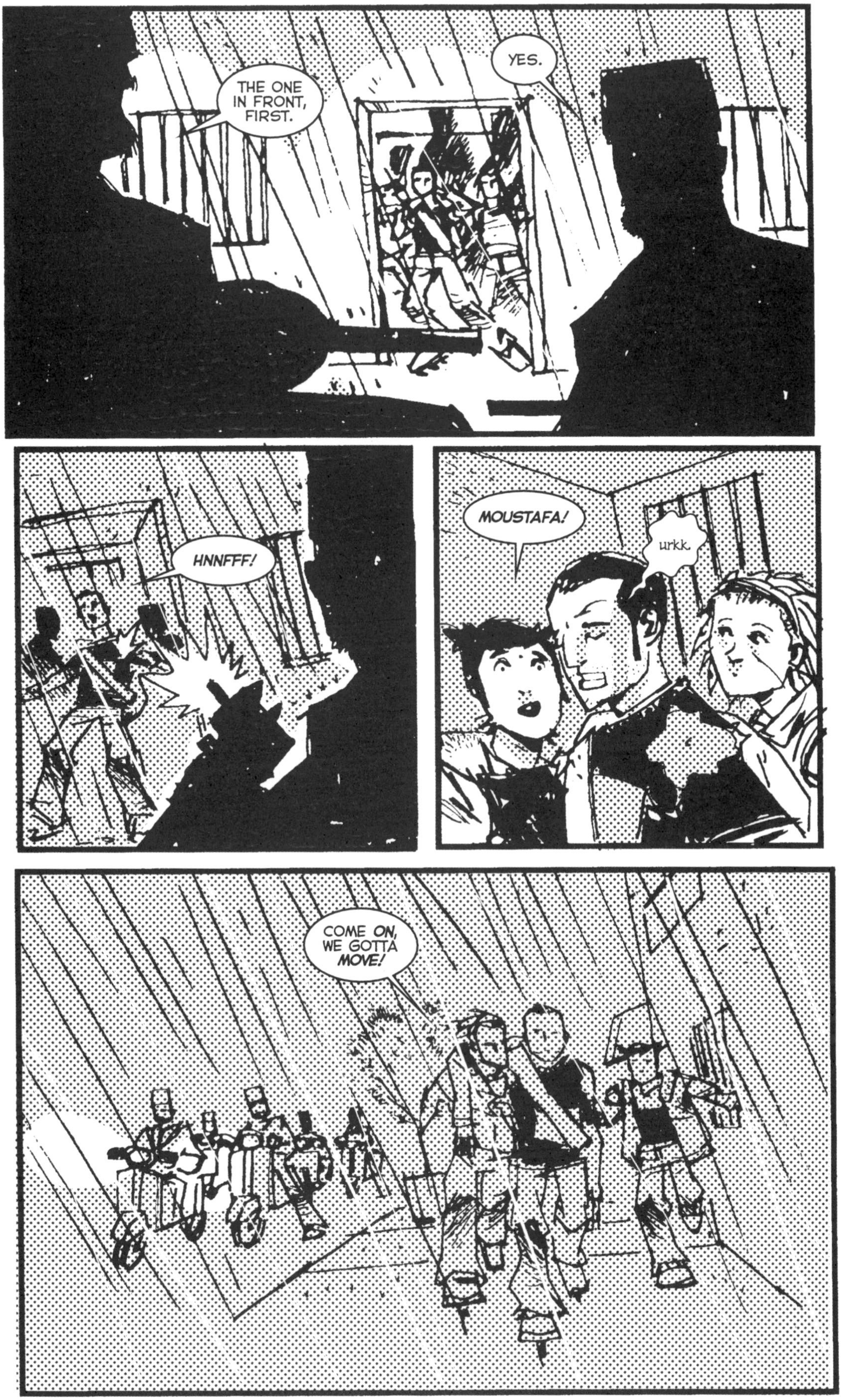
THE ONE IN FRONT, FIRST.
YES.
HNNFFF!
MOUSTAFA!
urkk.
COME ON, WE GOTTA MOVE!

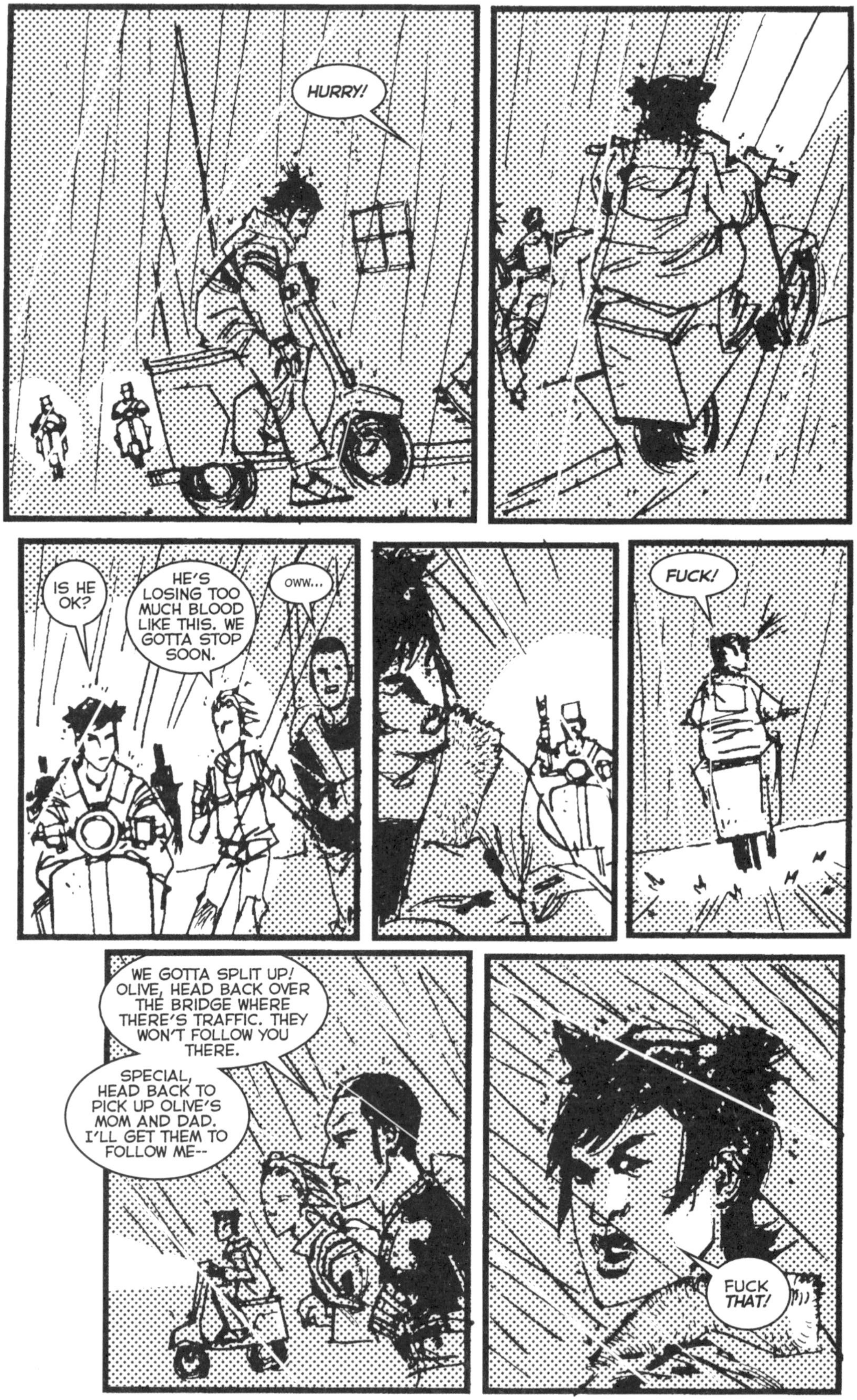
HURRY!
IS HE OK?
HE'S LOSING TOO MUCH BLOOD LIKE THIS. WE GOTTA STOP SOON.
OWW...
FUCK!
WE GOTTA SPLIT UP! OLIVE, HEAD BACK OVER THE BRIDGE WHERE THERE'S TRAFFIC. THEY WON'T FOLLOW YOU THERE.
SPECIAL, HEAD BACK TO PICK UP OLIVE'S MOM AND DAD. I'LL GET THEM TO FOLLOW ME--
FUCK THAT!

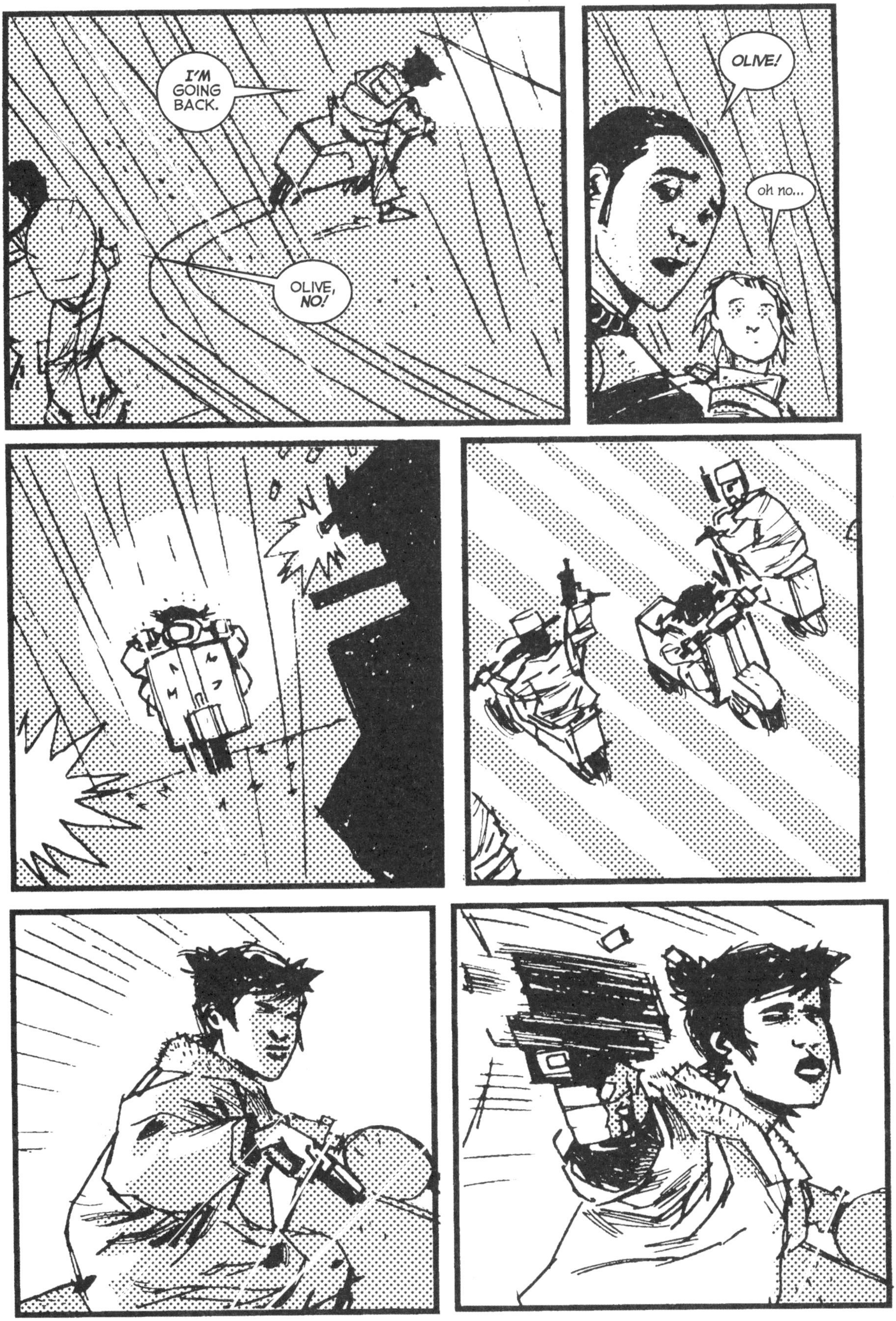
I'M GOING BACK.
OLIVE, NO!
OLIVE!
oh no...

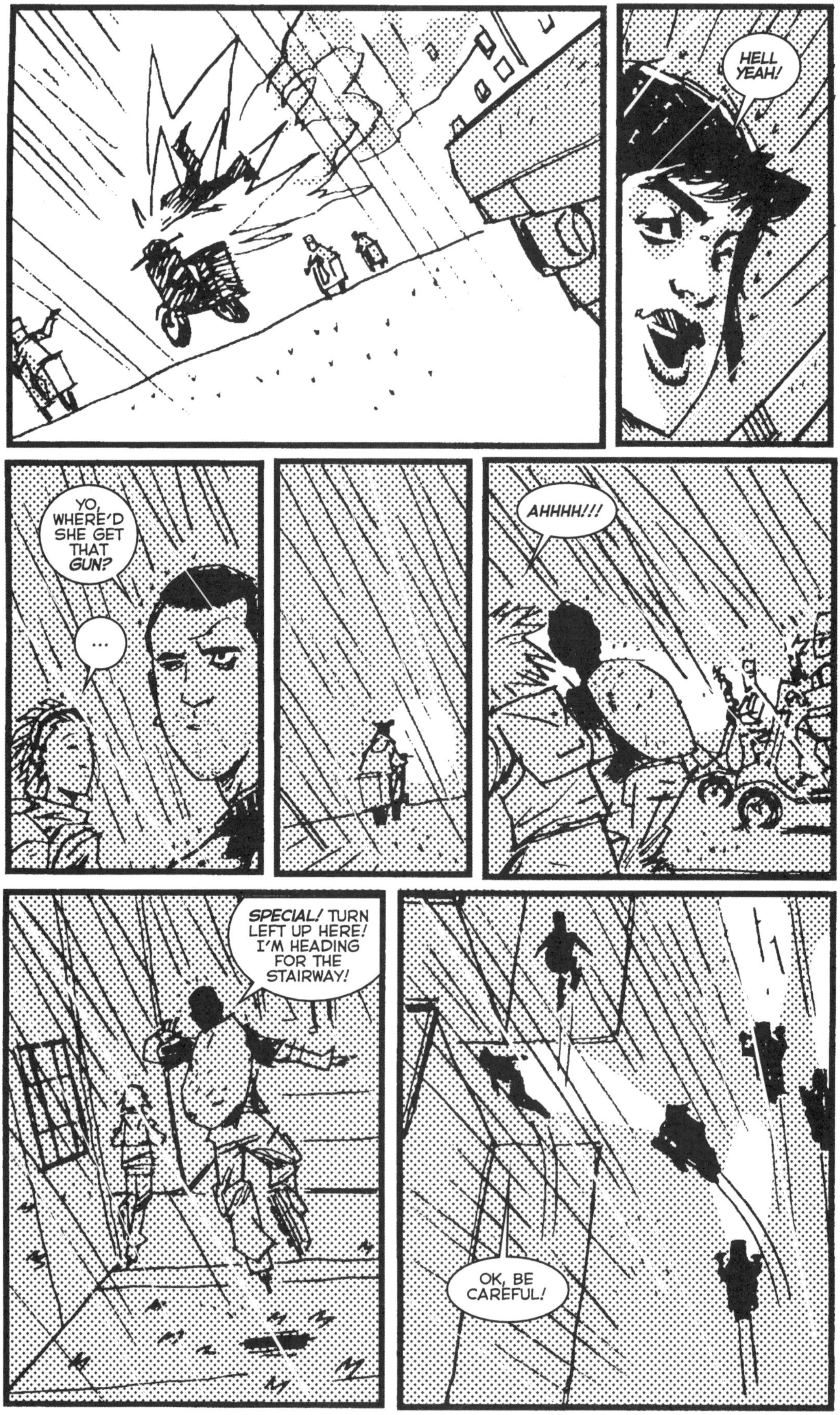
HELL YEAH!
YO, WHERE'D SHE GET THAT *GUN?*
...
AHHHH!!!
SPECIAL! TURN LEFT UP HERE! I'M HEADING FOR THE STAIRWAY!
OK, BE CAREFUL!

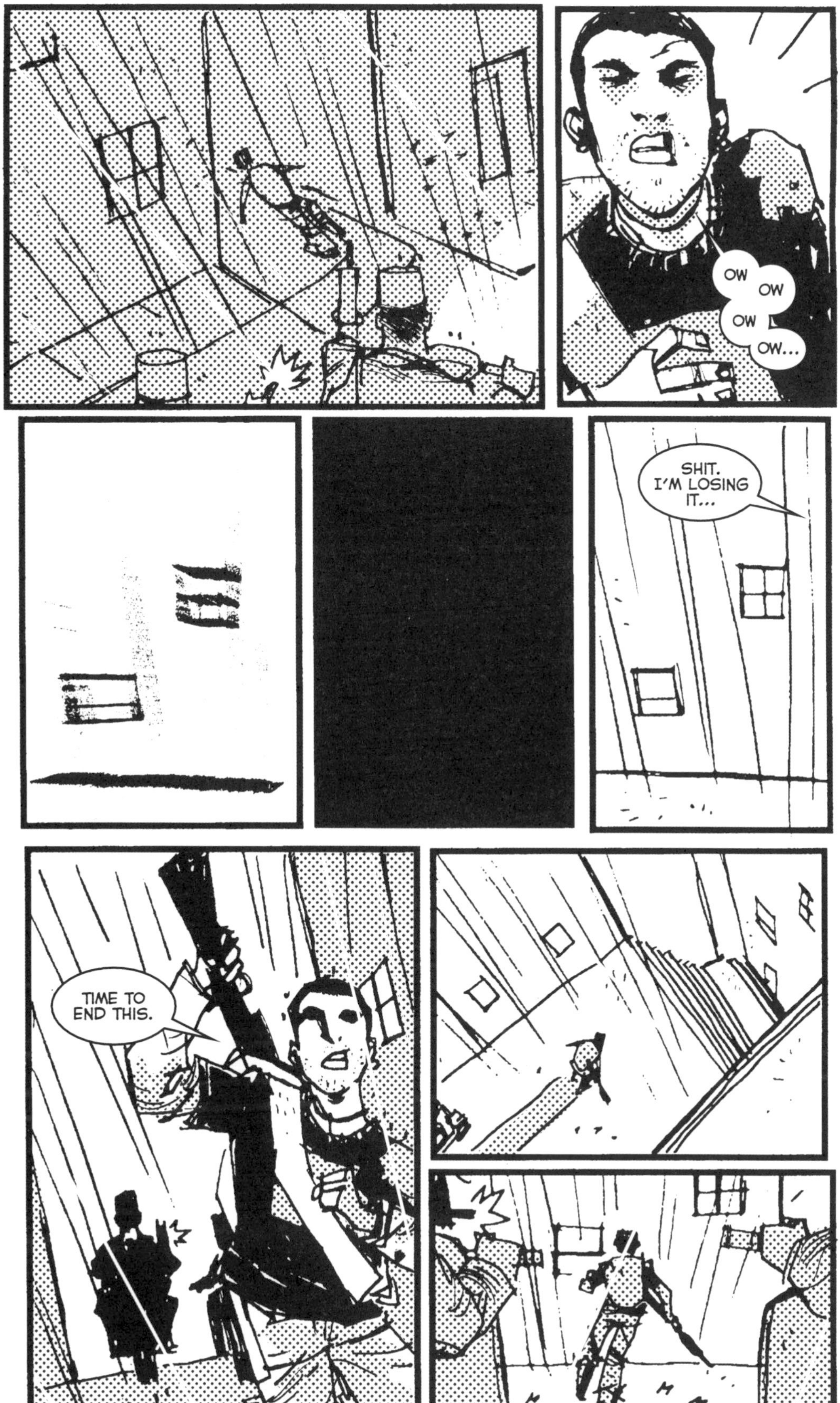

OW OW OW OW...
SHIT. I'M LOSING IT...
TIME TO END THIS.

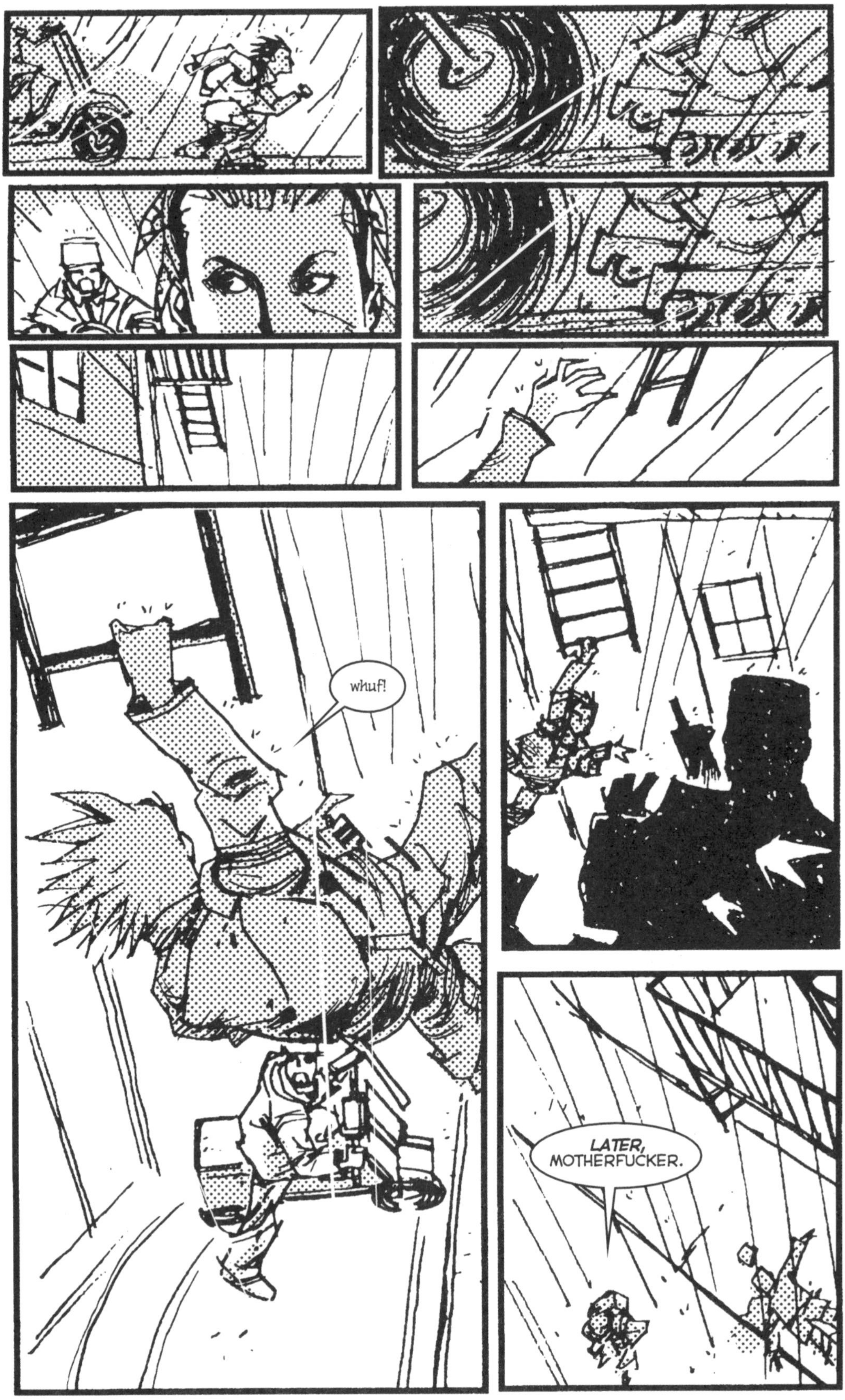
whuf!
LATER, MOTHERFUCKER.

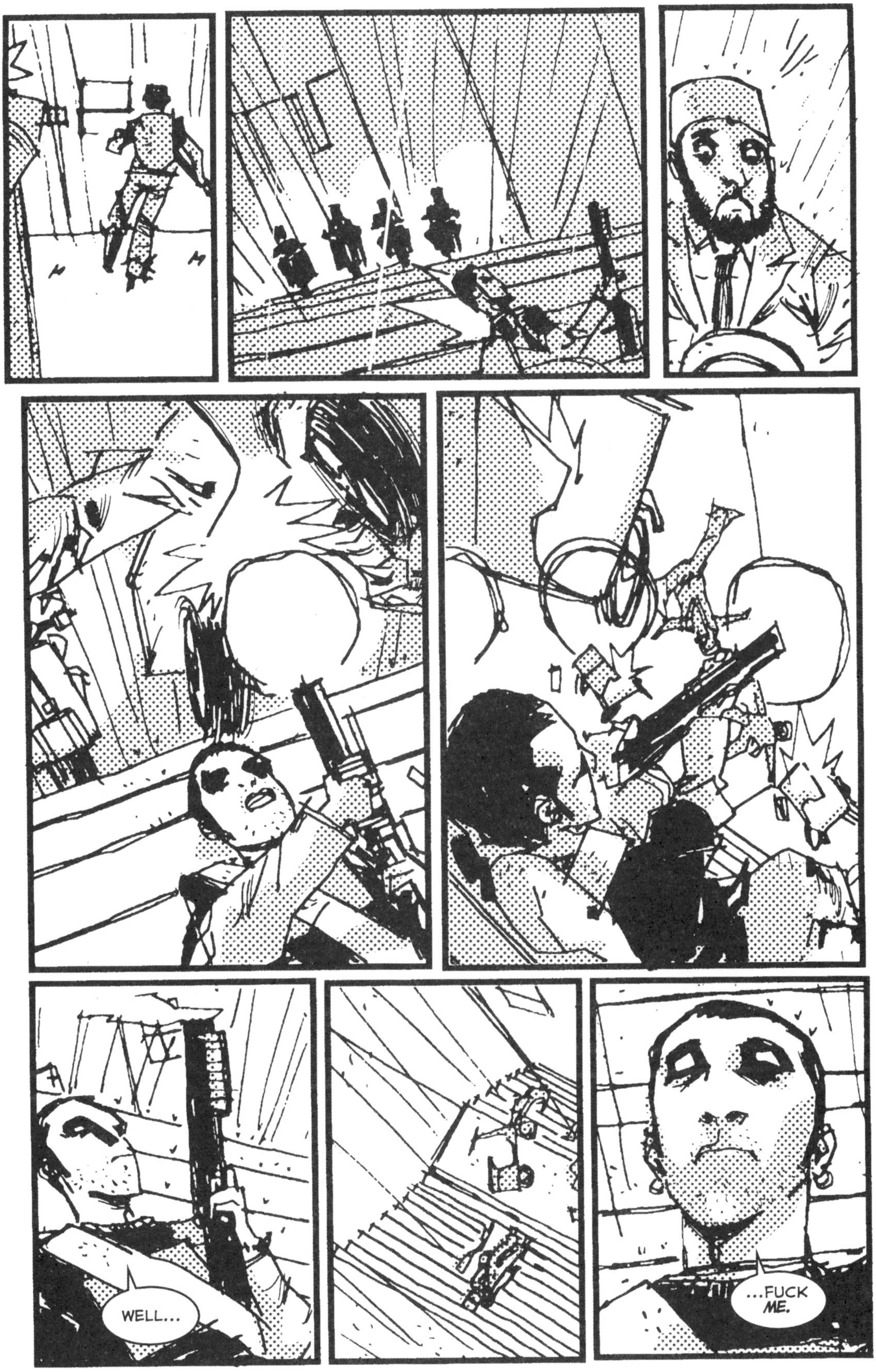
WELL...
...FUCK ME.

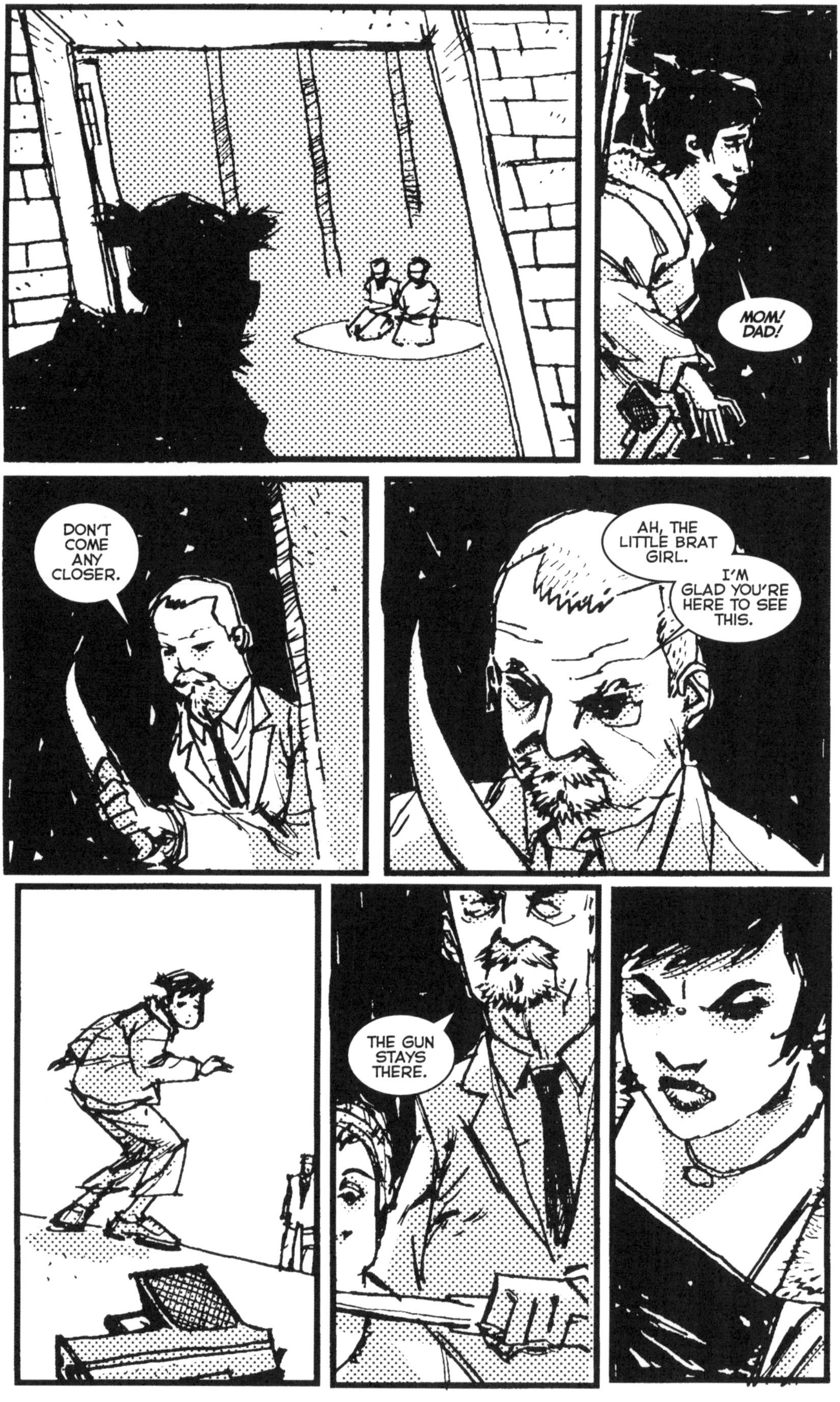
MOM! DAD!
DON'T COME ANY CLOSER.
AH, THE LITTLE BRAT GIRL.
I'M GLAD YOU'RE HERE TO SEE THIS.
THE GUN STAYS THERE.

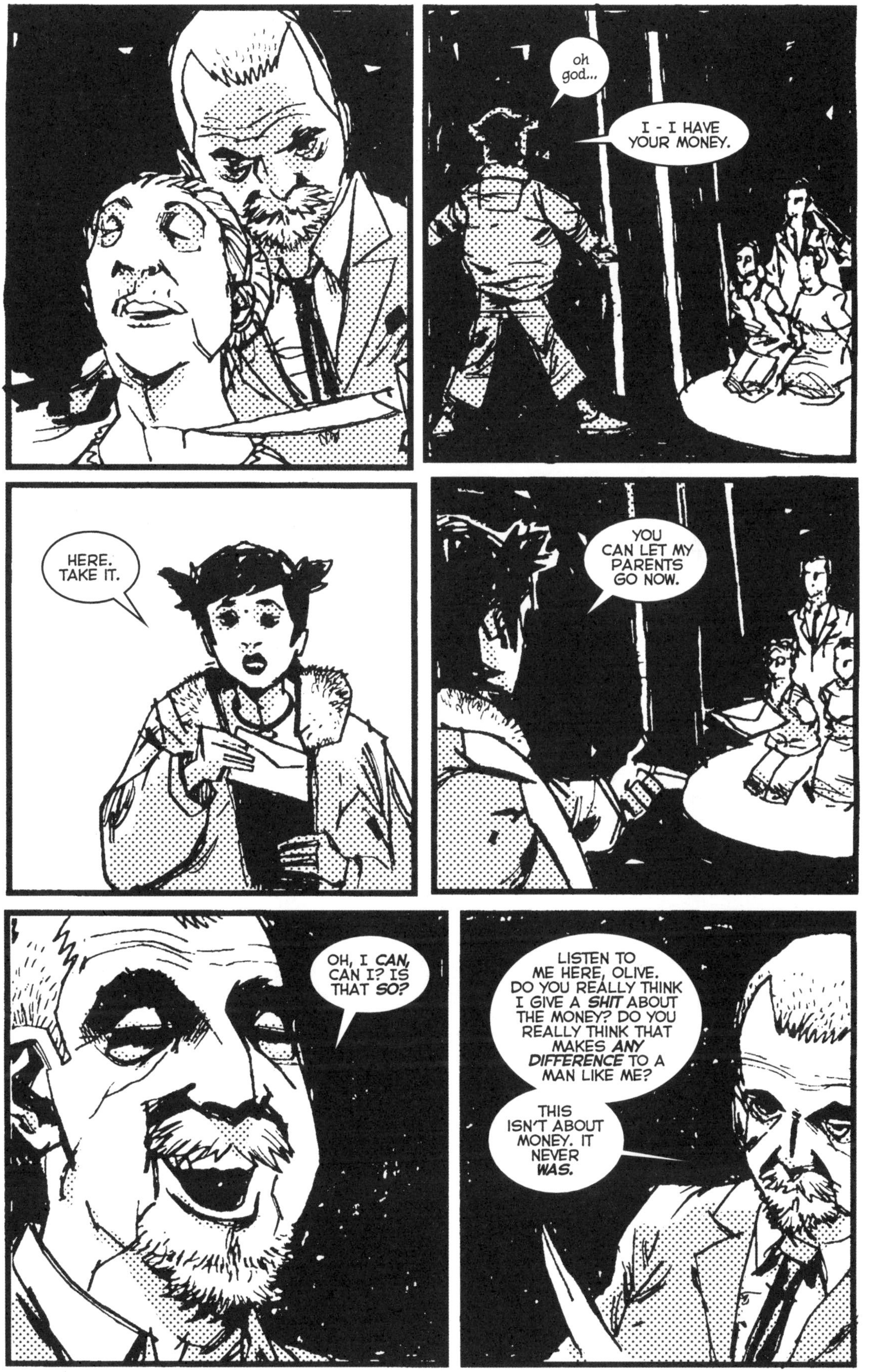
oh god...
I - I HAVE YOUR MONEY.
HERE. TAKE IT.
YOU CAN LET MY PARENTS GO NOW.
OH, I *CAN,* CAN I? IS THAT *SO?*
LISTEN TO ME HERE, OLIVE. DO YOU REALLY THINK I GIVE A *SHIT* ABOUT THE MONEY? DO YOU REALLY THINK THAT MAKES *ANY DIFFERENCE* TO A MAN LIKE ME?
THIS ISN'T ABOUT MONEY. IT NEVER *WAS.*

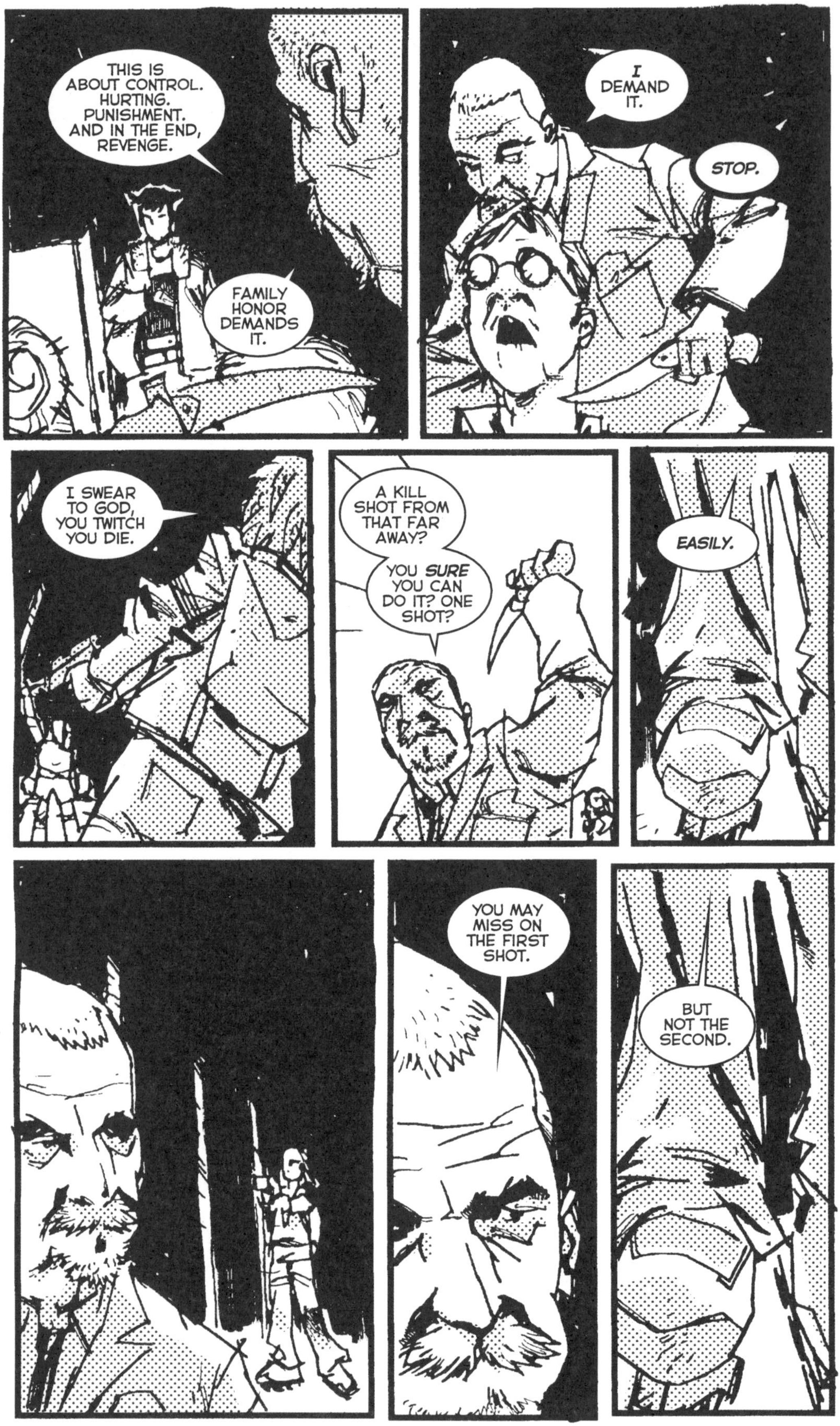

THIS IS ABOUT CONTROL. HURTING. PUNISHMENT. AND IN THE END, REVENGE.
FAMILY HONOR DEMANDS IT.
I DEMAND IT.
STOP.
I SWEAR TO GOD, YOU TWITCH YOU DIE.
A KILL SHOT FROM THAT FAR AWAY?
YOU SURE YOU CAN DO IT? ONE SHOT?
EASILY.
YOU MAY MISS ON THE FIRST SHOT.
BUT NOT THE SECOND.

I WOULD HAVE ALREADY CUT HER THROAT, PROBABLY.
NO!
ONLY IF I MISS THE FIRST SHOT.
SPECIAL, BE CAREFUL!
OLIVE, HUSH. LET ME CONCENTRATE.
AT ANY RATE, YOU GET CLOSER WITH EACH STEP. I MUST ACT SOON.
I LITERALLY HAVE NO CHOICE IN THE MATTER.
SO WE SHALL SEE, EH? WHO'S SKILL IS GREATER?

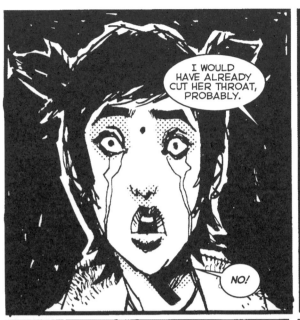

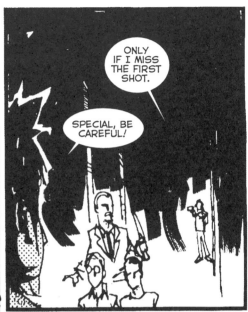

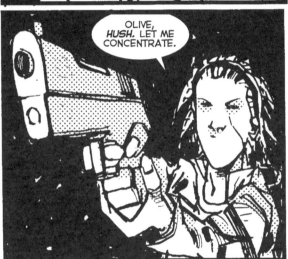

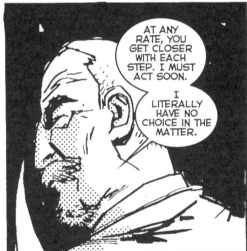

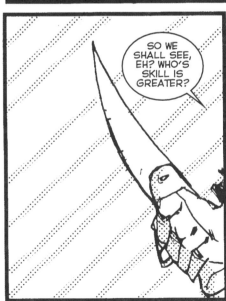

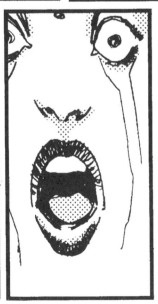

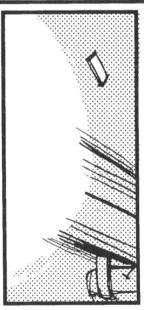

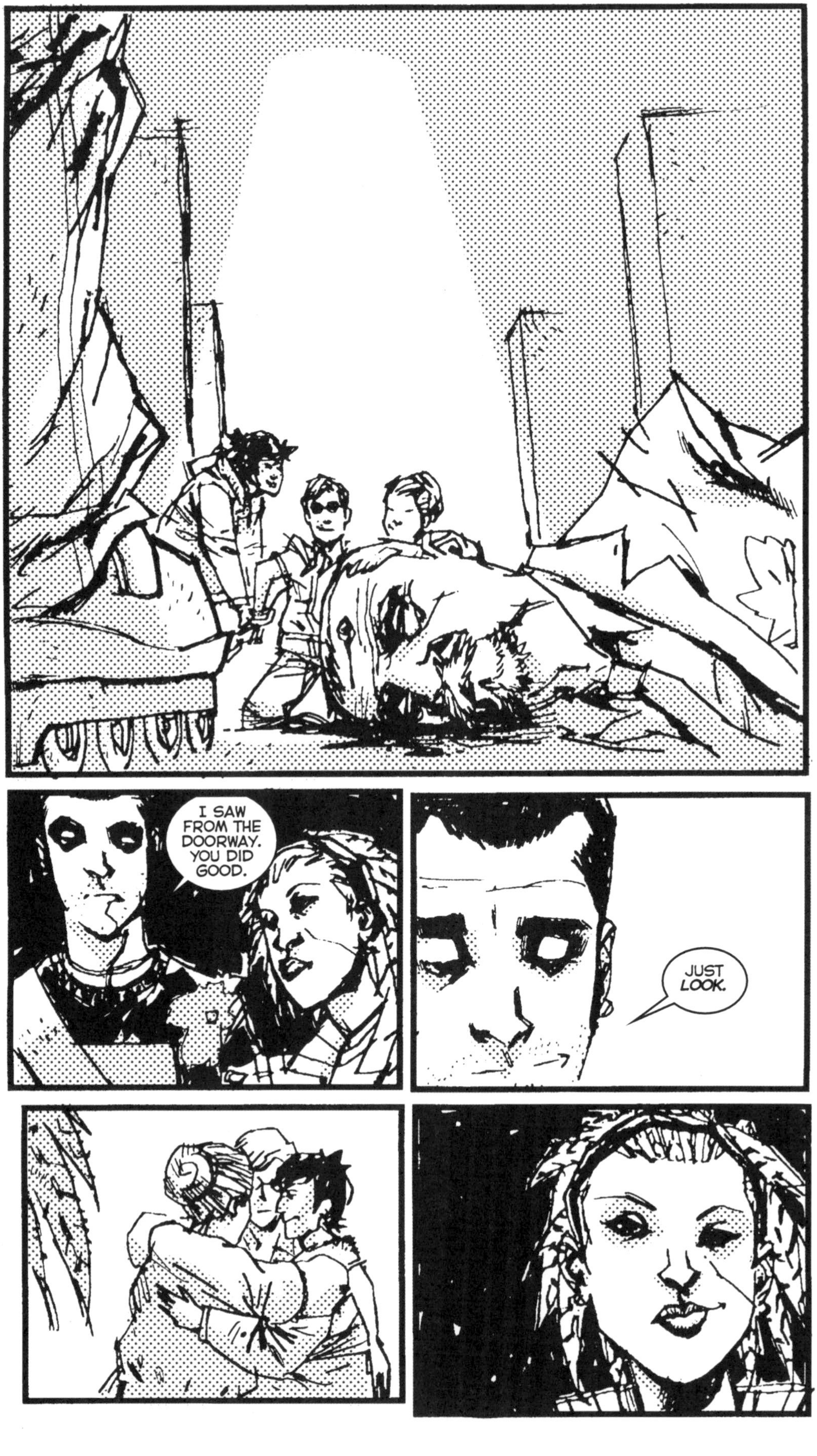
I SAW FROM THE DOORWAY. YOU DID GOOD.
JUST *LOOK.*

SO THAT'S IT, THEN.

THE TURKISH SCOOTER MAFIA BACKED OFF ONCE THEY HEARD THE BOSS WAS DEAD. HIS STUPID VENDETTA WASN'T WORTH IT, THEY FIGURED. SUITS US JUST FINE. ENOUGH PEOPLE HAD DIED ALREADY.

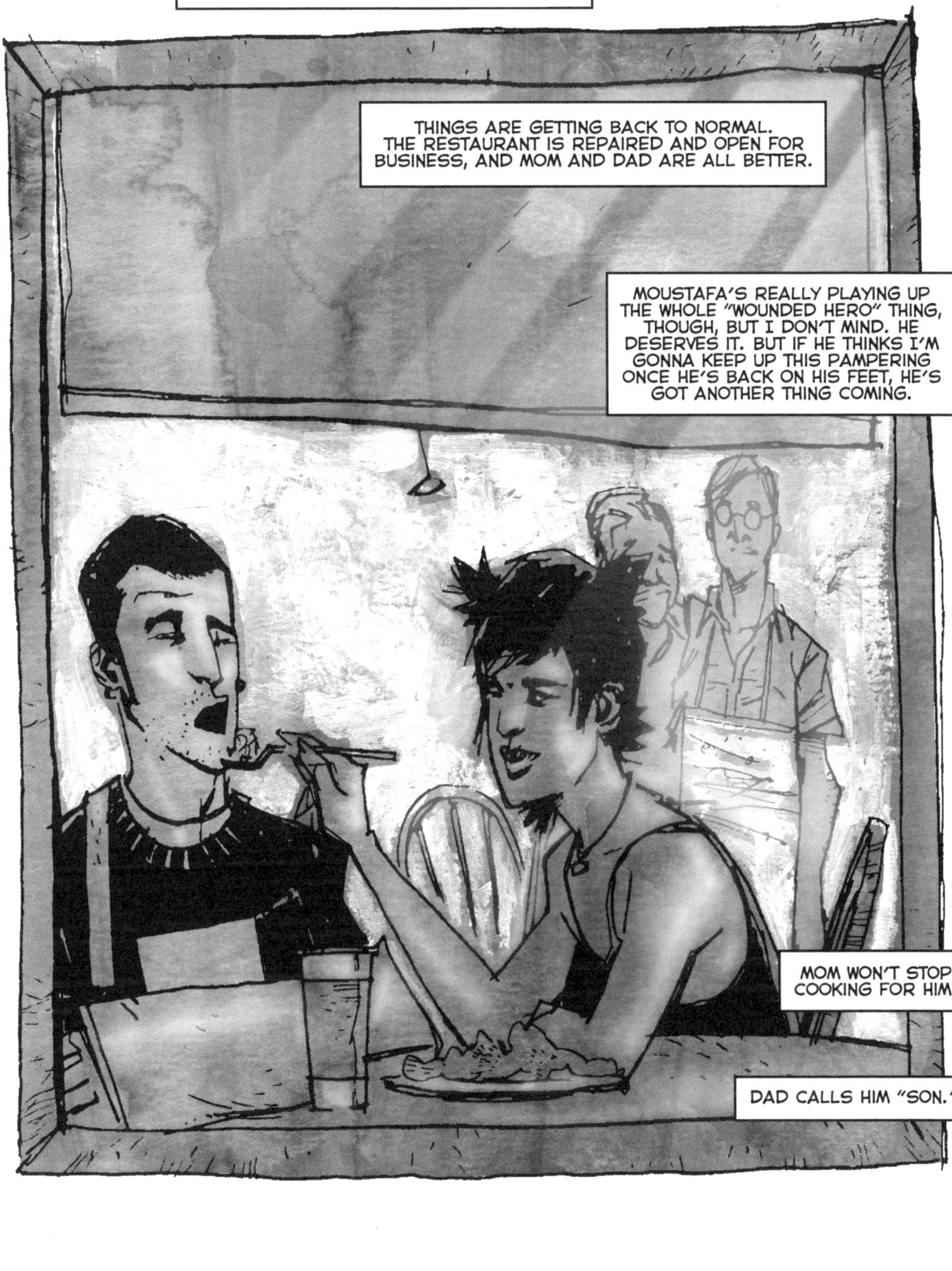
THINGS ARE GETTING BACK TO NORMAL. THE RESTAURANT IS REPAIRED AND OPEN FOR BUSINESS, AND MOM AND DAD ARE ALL BETTER.
MOUSTAFA'S REALLY PLAYING UP THE WHOLE "WOUNDED HERO" THING, THOUGH, BUT I DON'T MIND. HE DESERVES IT. BUT IF HE THINKS I'M GONNA KEEP UP THIS PAMPERING ONCE HE'S BACK ON HIS FEET, HE'S GOT ANOTHER THING COMING.
MOM WON'T STOP COOKING FOR HIM.
DAD CALLS HIM "SON."

SPECIAL JUST HANGS BACK AND LOOKS EMBARRASSED AT ALL THEIR THANKS AND PRAISE. SHE DOESN'T QUITE KNOW HOW TO TAKE IT. SHE'S HAPPY TO HAVE HELPED, THOUGH.

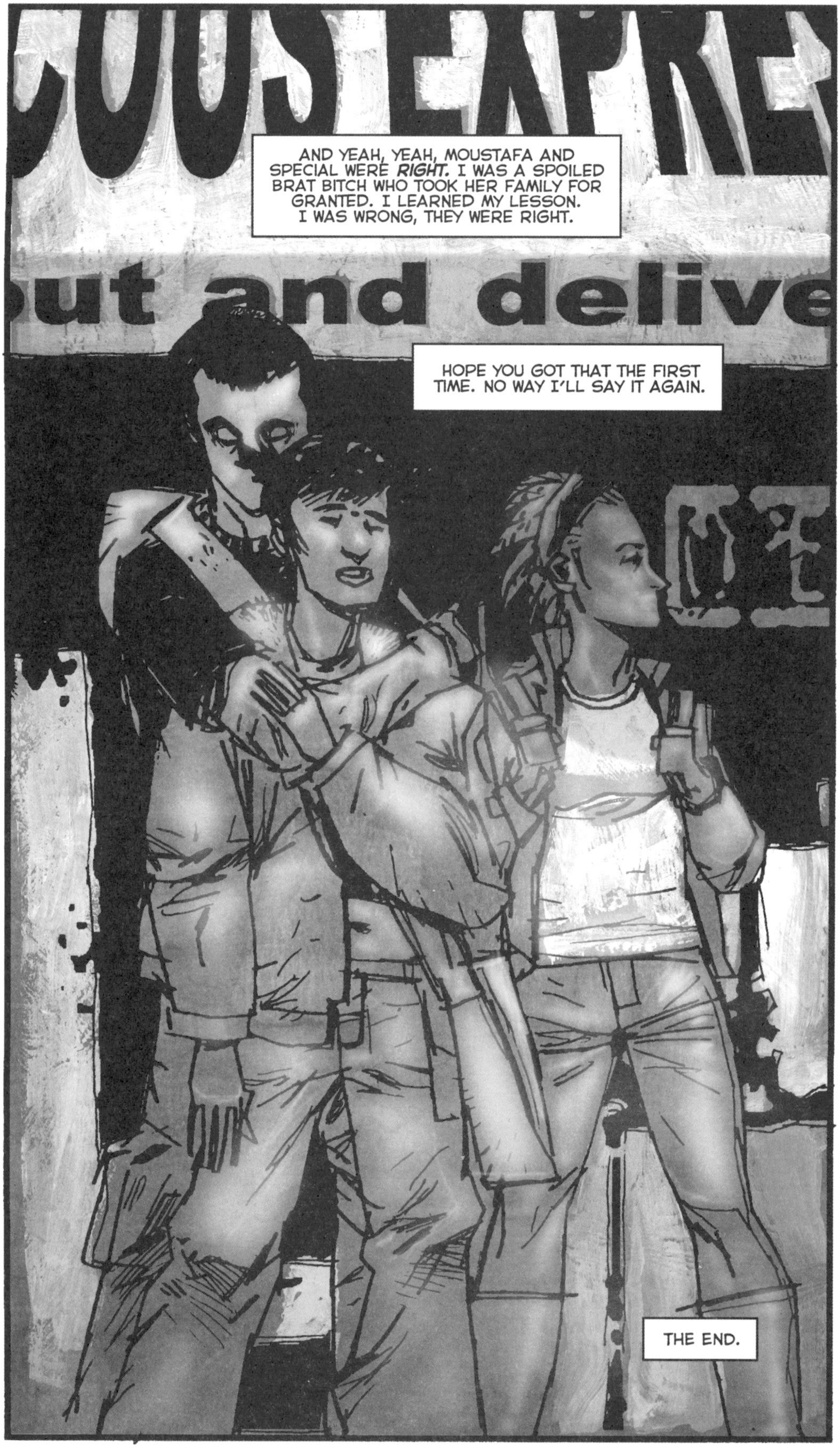

COUS EXPRE
out and delive
AND YEAH, YEAH, MOUSTAFA AND SPECIAL WERE *RIGHT.* I WAS A SPOILED BRAT BITCH WHO TOOK HER FAMILY FOR GRANTED. I LEARNED MY LESSON. I WAS WRONG, THEY WERE RIGHT.
HOPE YOU GOT THAT THE FIRST TIME. NO WAY I'LL SAY IT AGAIN.
THE END.

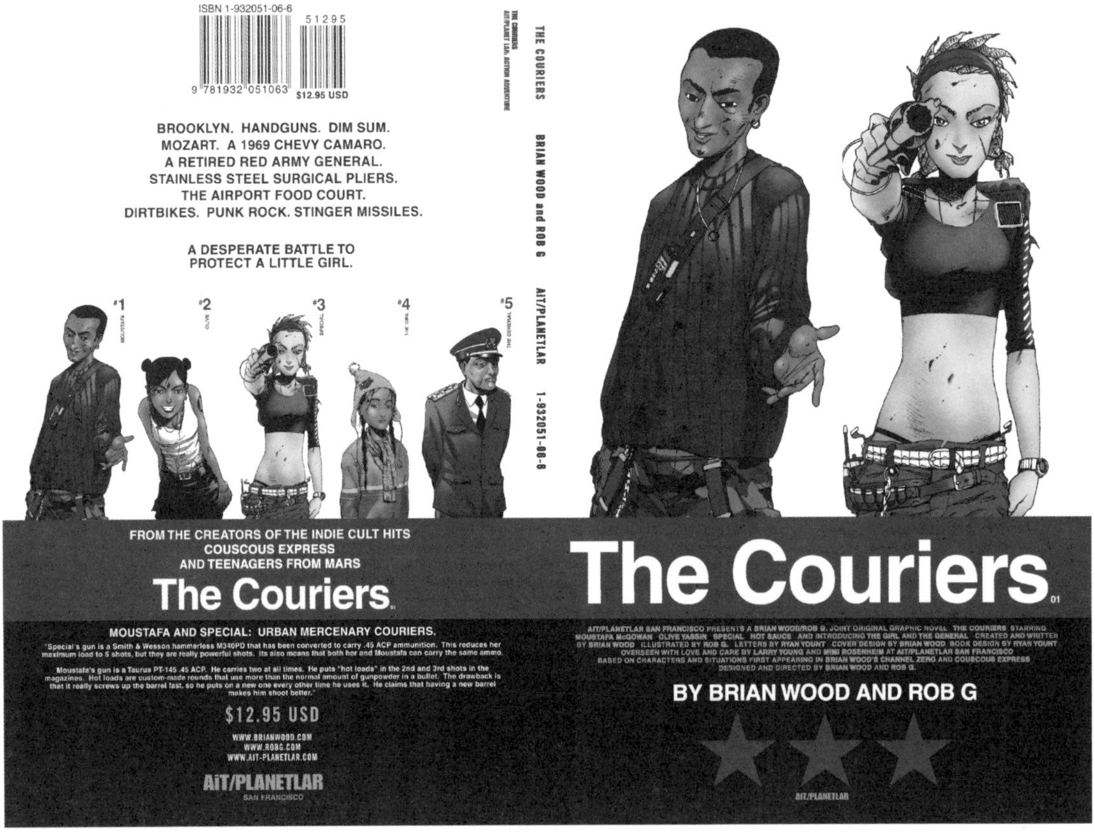
ISBN 1-932051-06-6
$12.95 USD
BROOKLYN. HANDGUNS. DIM SUM.
MOZART. A 1969 CHEVY CAMARO.
A RETIRED RED ARMY GENERAL.
STAINLESS STEEL SURGICAL PLIERS.
THE AIRPORT FOOD COURT.
DIRTBIKES. PUNK ROCK. STINGER MISSILES.
A DESPERATE BATTLE TO
PROTECT A LITTLE GIRL.
#1
#2
#3
#4
#5
THE COURIERS BRIAN WOOD and ROB G AIT/PLANETLAR 1-932051-06-6
FROM THE CREATORS OF THE INDIE CULT HITS
COUSCOUS EXPRESS
AND TEENAGERS FROM MARS
The Couriers
MOUSTAFA AND SPECIAL: URBAN MERCENARY COURIERS.
"Special's gun is a Smith & Wesson hammerless M340PD that has been converted to carry .45 ACP ammunition. This reduces her maximum load to 5 shots, but they are really powerful shots. Its also means that both her and Moustafa can carry the same ammo.
Moustafa's gun is a Taurus PT-145 .45 ACP. He carries two at all times. He puts "hot loads" in the 2nd and 3rd shots in the magazines. Hot loads are custom-made rounds that use more than the normal amount of gunpowder in a bullet. The drawback is that it really screws up the barrel fast, so he puts on a new one every other time he uses it. He claims that having a new barrel makes him shoot better."
$12.95 USD
WWW.BRIANWOOD.COM
WWW.ROBG.COM
WWW.AIT-PLANETLAR.COM
AiT/PLANETLAR
SAN FRANCISCO
The Couriers 01
AIT/PLANETLAR SAN FRANCISCO PRESENTS A BRIAN WOOD/ROB G. JOINT ORIGINAL GRAPHIC NOVEL THE COURIERS STARRING MOUSTAFA McGOWAN OLIVE YASSIN SPECIAL HOT SAUCE AND INTRODUCING THE GIRL AND THE GENERAL CREATED AND WRITTEN BY BRIAN WOOD ILLUSTRATED BY ROB G. LETTERS BY RYAN YOUNT COVER DESIGN BY BRIAN WOOD BOOK DESIGN BY RYAN YOUNT OVERSEEN WITH LOVE AND CARE BY LARRY YOUNG AND MIMI ROSENHEIM AT AIT/PLANETLAR SAN FRANCISCO BASED ON CHARACTERS AND SITUATIONS FIRST APPEARING IN BRIAN WOOD'S CHANNEL ZERO AND COUSCOUS EXPRESS DESIGNED AND DIRECTED BY BRIAN WOOD AND ROB G.
BY BRIAN WOOD AND ROB G
AIT/PLANETLAR

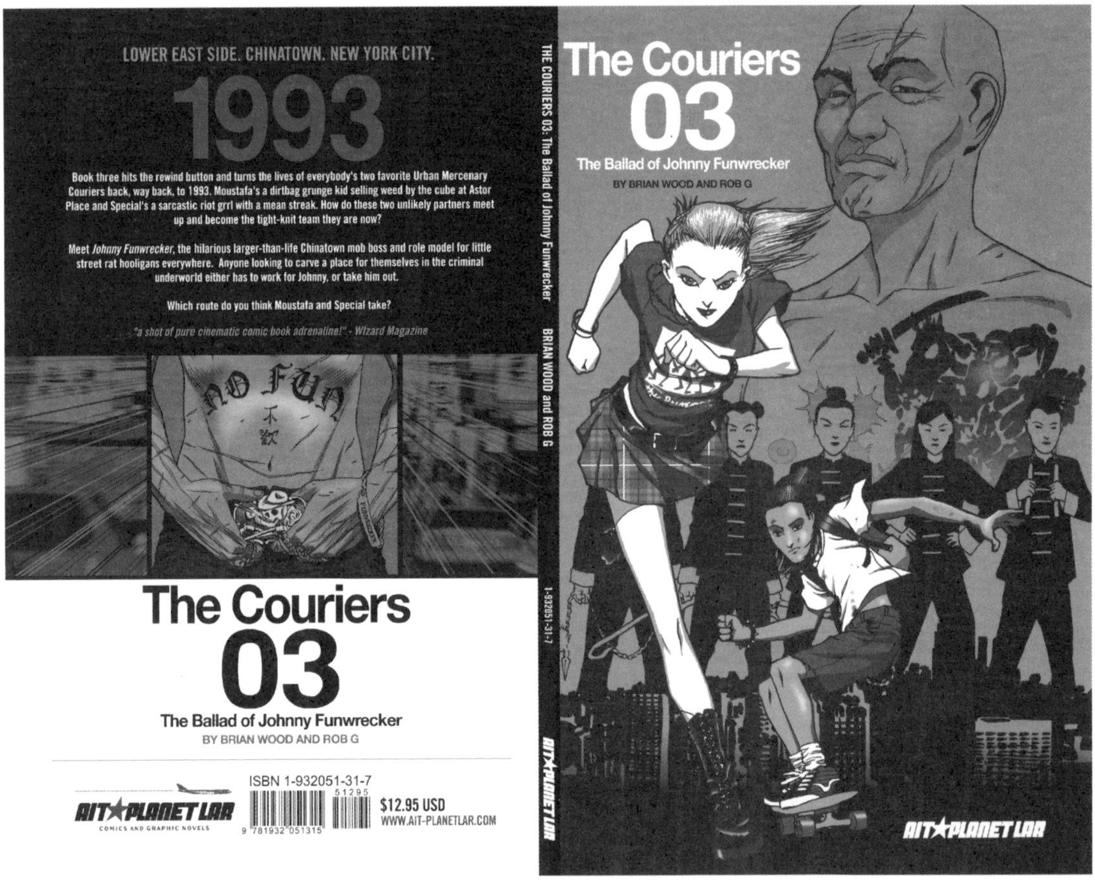
LOWER EAST SIDE. CHINATOWN. NEW YORK CITY.
1993
Book three hits the rewind button and turns the lives of everybody's two favorite Urban Mercenary Couriers back, way back, to 1993. Moustafa's a dirtbag grunge kid selling weed by the cube at Astor Place and Special's a sarcastic riot grrl with a mean streak. How do these two unlikely partners meet up and become the tight-knit team they are now?
Meet Johnny Funwrecker, the hilarious larger-than-life Chinatown mob boss and role model for little street rat hooligans everywhere. Anyone looking to carve a place for themselves in the criminal underworld either has to work for Johnny, or take him out.
Which route do you think Moustafa and Special take?
"a shot of pure cinematic comic book adrenaline!" - Wizard Magazine
NO FUN
The Couriers
03
The Ballad of Johnny Funwrecker
BY BRIAN WOOD AND ROB G
ISBN 1-932051-31-7
$12.95 USD
WWW.AIT-PLANETLAR.COM
AIT★PLANET LAR
COMICS AND GRAPHIC NOVELS
THE COURIERS 03: The Ballad of Johnny Funwrecker BRIAN WOOD and ROB G 1-932051-31-7
The Couriers
03
The Ballad of Johnny Funwrecker
BY BRIAN WOOD AND ROB G
AIT★PLANET LAR

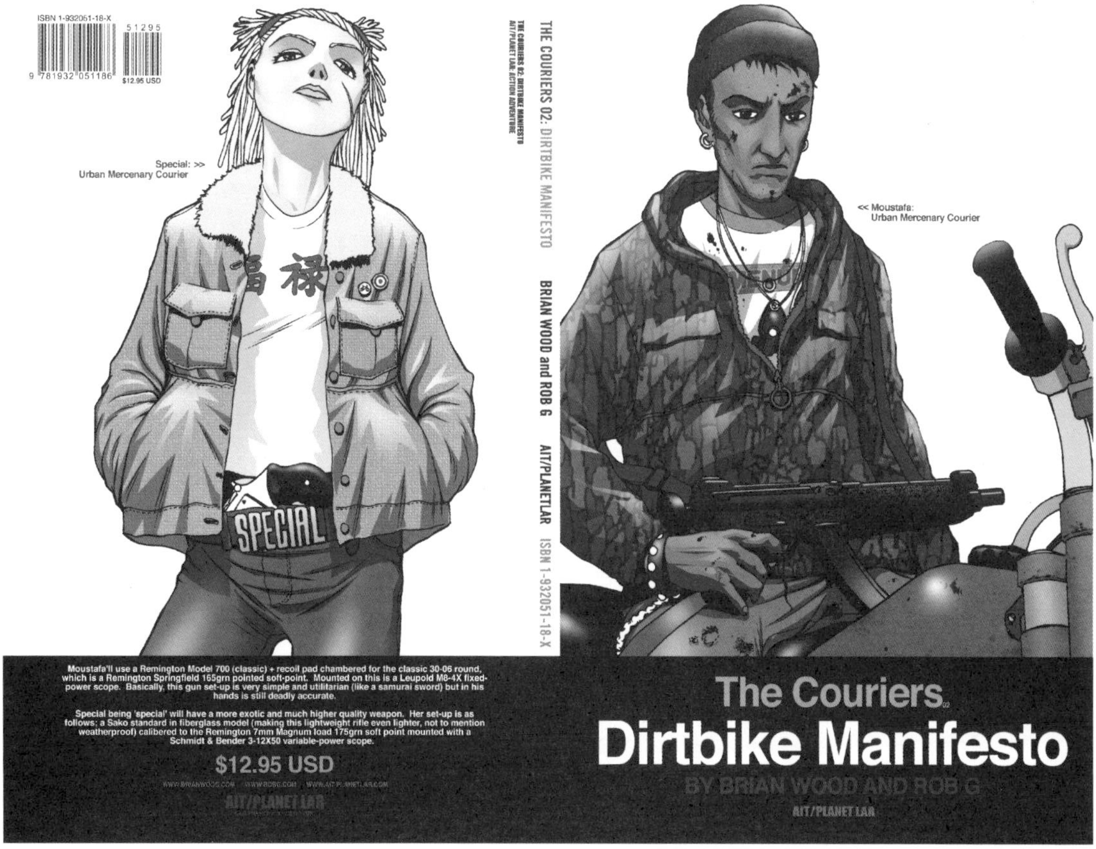
ISBN 1-932051-18-X
$12.95 USD
Special: >>
Urban Mercenary Courier
THE COURIERS 02: DIRTBIKE MANIFESTO
BRIAN WOOD and ROB G
AIT/PLANETLAR
ISBN 1-932051-18-X
<< Moustafa:
Urban Mercenary Courier
SPECIAL
Moustafa'll use a Remington Model 700 (classic) + recoil pad chambered for the classic 30-06 round, which is a Remington Springfield 165grn pointed soft-point. Mounted on this is a Leupold M8-4X fixed-power scope. Basically, this gun set-up is very simple and utilitarian (like a samurai sword) but in his hands is still deadly accurate.
Special being 'special' will have a more exotic and much higher quality weapon. Her set-up is as follows: a Sako standard in fiberglass model (making this lightweight rifle even lighter, not to mention weatherproof) calibered to the Remington 7mm Magnum load 175grn soft point mounted with a Schmidt & Bender 3-12X50 variable-power scope.
$12.95 USD
The Couriers 02
Dirtbike Manifesto
BY BRIAN WOOD AND ROB G
AIT/PLANET LAR

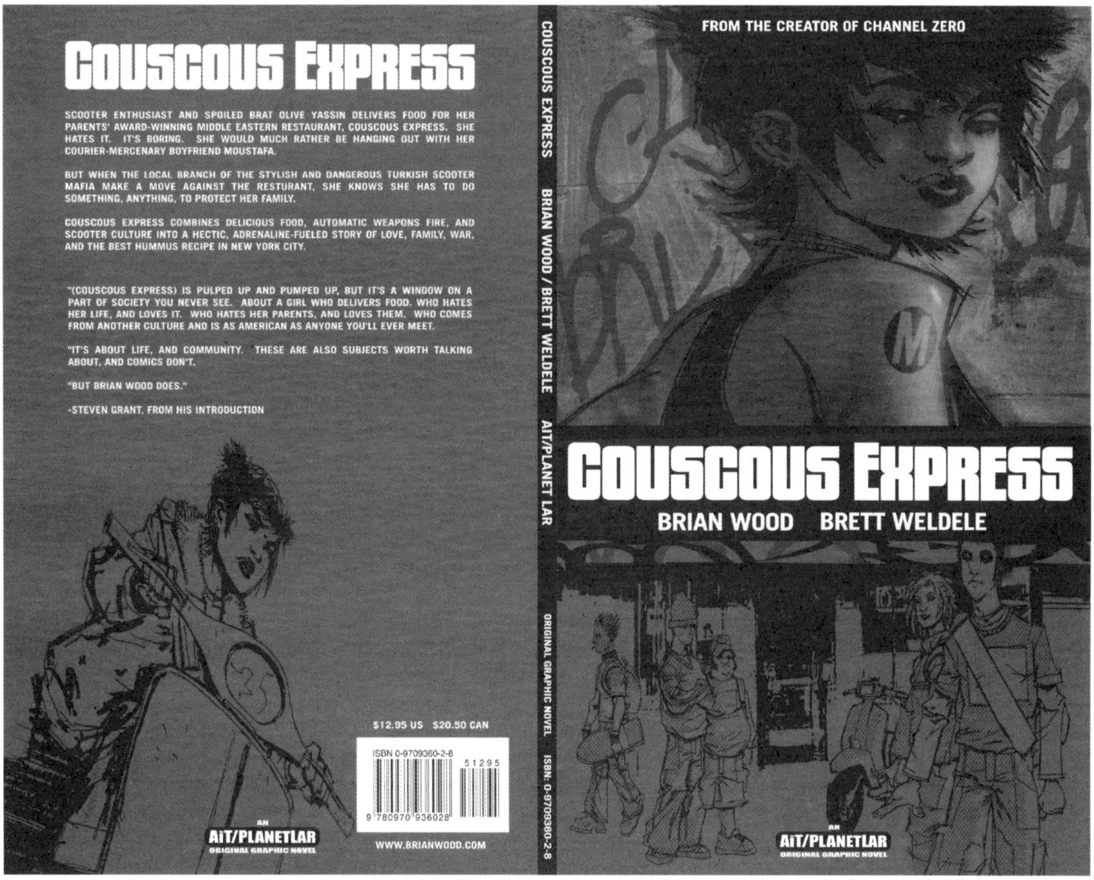
COUSCOUS EXPRESS
SCOOTER ENTHUSIAST AND SPOILED BRAT OLIVE YASSIN DELIVERS FOOD FOR HER PARENTS' AWARD-WINNING MIDDLE EASTERN RESTAURANT, COUSCOUS EXPRESS. SHE HATES IT. IT'S BORING. SHE WOULD MUCH RATHER BE HANGING OUT WITH HER COURIER-MERCENARY BOYFRIEND MOUSTAFA.
BUT WHEN THE LOCAL BRANCH OF THE STYLISH AND DANGEROUS TURKISH SCOOTER MAFIA MAKE A MOVE AGAINST THE RESTURANT, SHE KNOWS SHE HAS TO DO SOMETHING, ANYTHING, TO PROTECT HER FAMILY.
COUSCOUS EXPRESS COMBINES DELICIOUS FOOD, AUTOMATIC WEAPONS FIRE, AND SCOOTER CULTURE INTO A HECTIC, ADRENALINE-FUELED STORY OF LOVE, FAMILY, WAR, AND THE BEST HUMMUS RECIPE IN NEW YORK CITY.
"(COUSCOUS EXPRESS) IS PULPED UP AND PUMPED UP, BUT IT'S A WINDOW ON A PART OF SOCIETY YOU NEVER SEE. ABOUT A GIRL WHO DELIVERS FOOD. WHO HATES HER LIFE, AND LOVES IT. WHO HATES HER PARENTS, AND LOVES THEM. WHO COMES FROM ANOTHER CULTURE AND IS AS AMERICAN AS ANYONE YOU'LL EVER MEET.
"IT'S ABOUT LIFE, AND COMMUNITY. THESE ARE ALSO SUBJECTS WORTH TALKING ABOUT, AND COMICS DON'T.
"BUT BRIAN WOOD DOES."
-STEVEN GRANT, FROM HIS INTRODUCTION
$12.95 US $20.50 CAN
ISBN 0-9709360-2-8
AN AIT/PLANETLAR ORIGINAL GRAPHIC NOVEL
WWW.BRIANWOOD.COM
COUSCOUS EXPRESS
BRIAN WOOD / BRETT WELDELE
AIT/PLANET LAR
ORIGINAL GRAPHIC NOVEL
ISBN: 0-9709360-2-8
FROM THE CREATOR OF CHANNEL ZERO
COUSCOUS EXPRESS
BRIAN WOOD BRETT WELDELE
AN AIT/PLANETLAR ORIGINAL GRAPHIC NOVEL

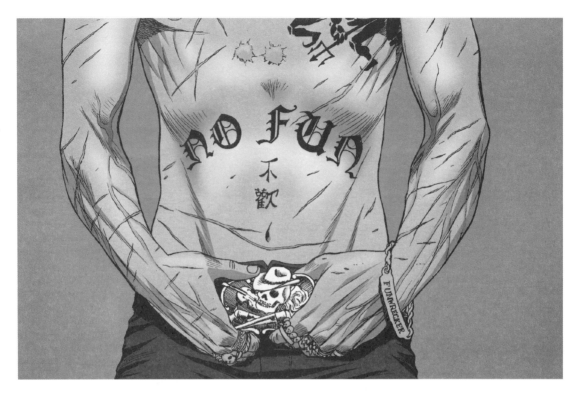

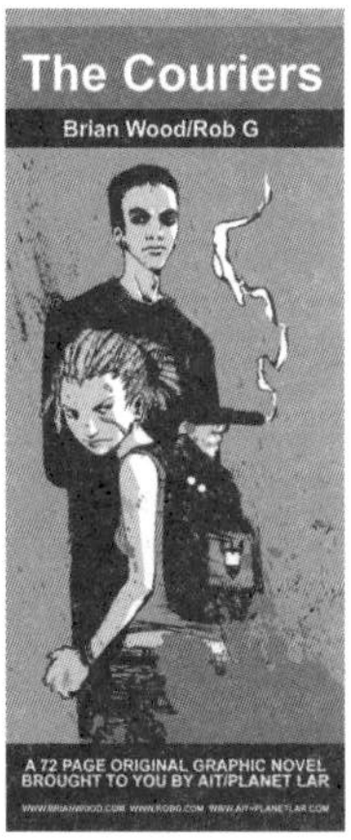
The Couriers
Brian Wood/Rob G
A 72 PAGE ORIGINAL GRAPHIC NOVEL
BROUGHT TO YOU BY AIT/PLANET LAR

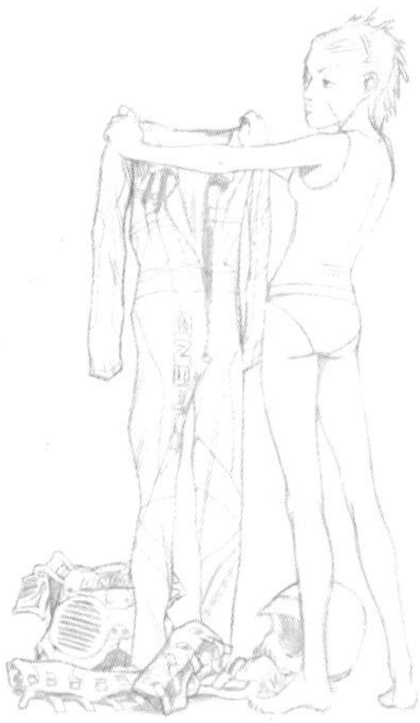

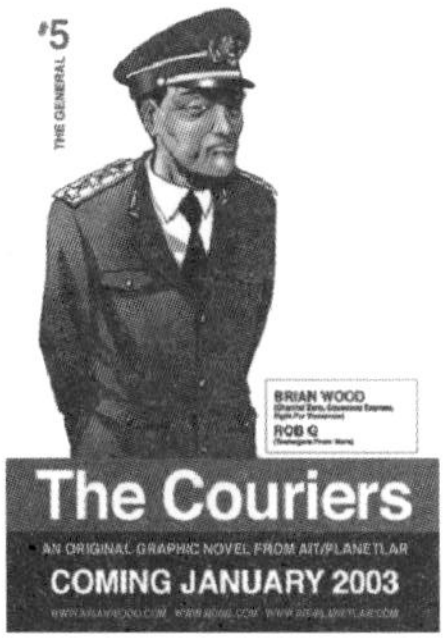
#5
THE GENERAL
BRIAN WOOD
ROB G
The Couriers
AN ORIGINAL GRAPHIC NOVEL FROM AIT/PLANETLAR
COMING JANUARY 2003

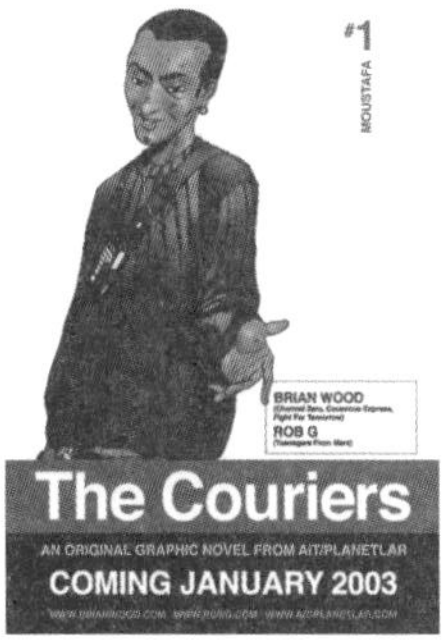
#1
MOUSTAFA
BRIAN WOOD
ROB G
The Couriers
AN ORIGINAL GRAPHIC NOVEL FROM AIT/PLANETLAR
COMING JANUARY 2003

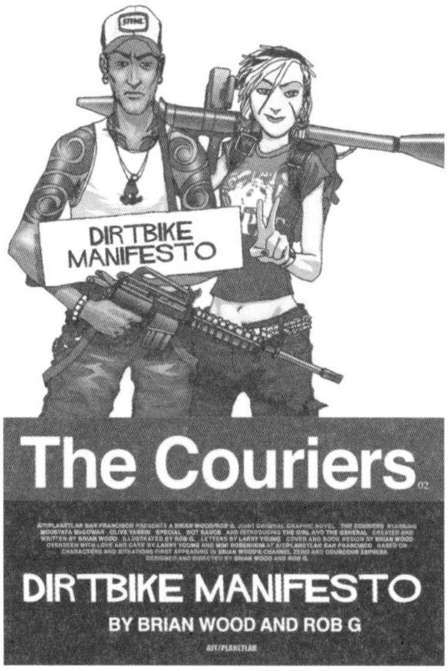
DIRTBIKE
MANIFESTO
The Couriers 02
DIRTBIKE MANIFESTO
BY BRIAN WOOD AND ROB G
AIT/PLANETLAR

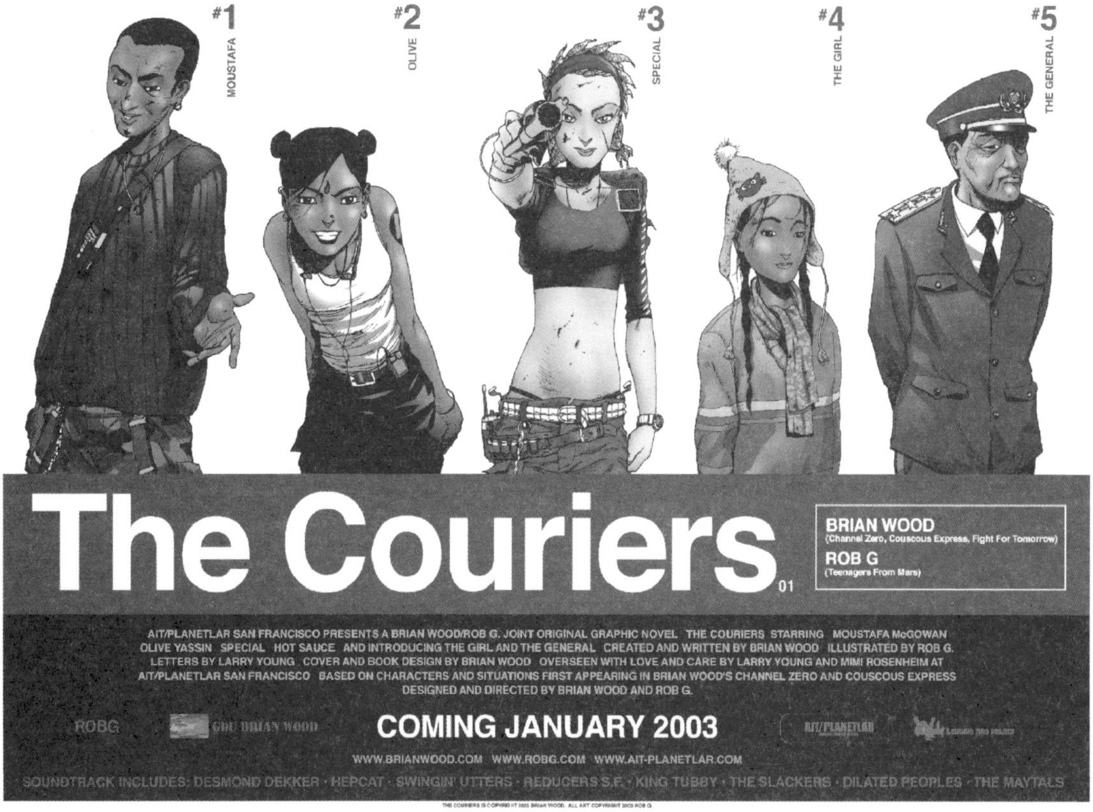
#1
MOUSTAFA
#2
OLIVE
#3
SPECIAL
#4
THE GIRL
#5
THE GENERAL
The Couriers 01
BRIAN WOOD
(Channel Zero, Couscous Express, Fight For Tomorrow)
ROB G
(Teenagers From Mars)
AIT/PLANETLAR SAN FRANCISCO PRESENTS A BRIAN WOOD/ROB G. JOINT ORIGINAL GRAPHIC NOVEL THE COURIERS STARRING MOUSTAFA McGOWAN OLIVE YASSIN SPECIAL HOT SAUCE AND INTRODUCING THE GIRL AND THE GENERAL CREATED AND WRITTEN BY BRIAN WOOD ILLUSTRATED BY ROB G. LETTERS BY LARRY YOUNG COVER AND BOOK DESIGN BY BRIAN WOOD OVERSEEN WITH LOVE AND CARE BY LARRY YOUNG AND MIMI ROSENHEIM AT AIT/PLANETLAR SAN FRANCISCO BASED ON CHARACTERS AND SITUATIONS FIRST APPEARING IN BRIAN WOOD'S CHANNEL ZERO AND COUSCOUS EXPRESS
DESIGNED AND DIRECTED BY BRIAN WOOD AND ROB G.
ROBG
COMING JANUARY 2003
AIT/PLANETLAR
WWW.BRIANWOOD.COM WWW.ROBG.COM WWW.AIT-PLANETLAR.COM
SOUNDTRACK INCLUDES: DESMOND DEKKER · HEPCAT · SWINGIN' UTTERS · REDUCERS S.F. · KING TUBBY · THE SLACKERS · DILATED PEOPLES · THE MAYTALS

The Crew

01. Brian Wood

Brian Wood started making comics in 1997 and has never looked back. Best known for his series' *DMZ, Northlanders, Demo,* and *The Massive,* he's violated the worlds of The *X-Men, Conan The Barbarian, Lord Of The Rings,* and *Star Wars.* A one-time designer for Rockstar Games and a two-time t-shirt entrepreneur, Brian lives in Brooklyn with his wife and kids.

02. Rob G

Rob G is a sequential artist most known for the influential *Teenagers From Mars,* and has made his mark on the world of *Detective Comics* and *Humanoids.* He's a survivor of both a house fire and the east coast small press comics world. Now cooking for fun and profit in Portland, Oregon, he lives with his wife and daughter.

03. Brett Weldele

Eisner-nominated painter Brett Weldele's work has covered a wide range of genres including crime, science fiction and superheroes. Projects have included the bestselling graphic novel for Top Shelf, *The Surrogates,* adapted into a major motion picture from Touchstone Films starring Bruce Willis, and its follow-up, *The Surrogates: Flesh and Bone.* Recent releases *The Light, Spontaneous,* and *Pariah* continue to showcase Weldele's love of atmosphere. Weldele lives in Oregon and spends his free time making experimental music on a Mac.

collection + cover designer JARED K. FLETCHER ★

Made in Brooklyn.

This book was designed using the font HELEVTICA. Developed in 1957 by Max Miedinger with Eduard Hoffmann at the Haas'sche Schriftgiesserei (Haas type foundry) of Münchenstein, Switzerland.

brianwood.com
giganticgraphicnovels.com
brettweldele.com
imagecomics.com

IMAGE COMICS INC.

ROBERT KIRKMAN chief operating officer
ERIK LARSEN chief financial officer
TODD McFARLANE president
MARC SILVERSTRI chief executive officer
JIM VALENTINO vice-president

ERIC STEPHENSON publisher
TODD MARTINEZ sales & licensing coordinator
JENNIFER de GUZMAN pr & marketing director
BRANWYN BIGGLESTONE accounts manager
EMILY MILLER administrative assistant
JAMIE PARRENO marketing assistant
SARAH deLAINE events coordinator
KEVIN YUEN digital rights coordinator
JONATHAN CHAN production manager
DREW GILL art director
MONICA GARCIA production artist
VINCENT KUKUA production artist
JANA COOK production artist

THE COURIERS COMPLETE COLLECTION

First Printing. November 2012. Published by Image Comics, Inc.
Office of publication: 2134 Allston Way, Second Floor, Berkeley, California 94704.

Printed in South Korea.

ISBN 978-1-60706-641-5

image